Soviet and Post-Soviet Politics and Society (SPPS)

ISSN 1614-3515

Founded in 2004 and refereed since 2007, SPPS makes available affordable English-, German-, and Russian-language studies on the history of the countries of the former Soviet bloc from the late Tsarist period to today. It publishes between 5 and 20 volumes per year and focuses on issues in transitions to and from democracy such as economic crisis, identity formation, civil society development, and constitutional reform in CEE and the NIS. SPPS also aims to highlight so far understudied themes in East European studies such as right-wing radicalism, religious life, higher education, or human rights protection. The authors and titles of all previously published volumes are listed at the end of this book. For a full description of the series and reviews of its books, see www.ibidem-verlag.de/red/spps.

Editorial correspondence & manuscripts should be sent to: Dr. Andreas Umland, Department of Political Science, Kyiv-Mohyla Academy, vul. Voloska 8/5, UA-04070 Kyiv, UKRAINE; andreas.umland@cantab.net

Business correspondence & review copy requests should be sent to: *ibidem* Press, Leuschnerstr. 40, 30457 Hannover, Germany; tel.: +49 511 2622200; fax: +49 511 2622201; spps@ibidem.eu.

Authors, reviewers, referees, and editors for (as well as all other persons sympathetic to) SPPS are invited to join its networks at www.facebook.com/group.php?gid=52638198614
www.linkedin.com/groups?about=&gid=103012
www.xing.com/net/spps-ibidem-verlag/

Recent Volumes

254   *Winfried Schneider-Deters*
Ukraine's Fateful Years 2013–2019
Vol. I: The Popular Uprising in Winter 2013/2014
ISBN 978-3-8382-1725-3

255   *Winfried Schneider-Deters*
Ukraine's Fateful Years 2013–2019
Vol. II: The Annexation of Crimea and the War in Donbas
ISBN 978-3-8382-1726-0

256   *Robert M. Cutler*
Soviet and Post-Soviet Russian Foreign Policies II
East-West Relations in Europe and the Political Economy of the Communist Bloc, 1971–1991
With a foreword by Roger E. Kanet
ISBN 978-3-8382-1727-7

257   *Robert M. Cutler*
Soviet and Post-Soviet Russian Foreign Policies III
East-West Relations in Europe and Eurasia in the Post-Cold War Transition, 1991–2001
With a foreword by Roger E. Kanet
ISBN 978-3-8382-1728-4

258   *Pawel Kowal, Iwona Reichardt, Kateryna Pryshchepa (Eds.)*
Three Revolutions: Mobilization and Change in Contemporary Ukraine III
Archival Records and Historical Sources on the 1990 Revolution on Granite
ISBN 978-3-8382-1376-7

259   *Mykhailo Minakov (Ed.)*
Philosophy Unchained
Developments in Post-Soviet Philosophical Thought
With a foreword by Christopher Donohue
ISBN 978-3-8382-1768-0

260   *David Dalton*
The Ukrainian Oligarchy After the Euromaidan
How Ukraine's Political Economy Regime Survived the Crisis
With a foreword by Andrew Wilson
ISBN 978-3-8382-1740-6

261   *Andreas Heinemann-Grüder (Ed.)*
Who Are the Fighters?
Irregular Armed Groups in the Russian-Ukrainian War in 2014–2015
ISBN 978-3-8382-1777-2

262   *Taras Kuzio (Ed.)*
Russian Disinformation and Western Scholarship
Bias and Prejudice in Journalistic, Expert, and Academic Analyses of East European and Eurasian Affairs
ISBN 978-3-8382-1685-0

Darius Furmonavicius

LITHUANIA TRANSFORMS THE WEST

Lithuania's Liberation from Soviet Occupation and the
Enlargement of NATO (1988–2022)

With a foreword by Vytautas Landsbergis

with all the best wishes,

Darius

29 Oct, 2024

dfurmonavicius@gmail.com

+44-7843-373131

ibidem
Verlag

Bibliografische Information der Deutschen Nationalbibliothek

Die Deutsche Nationalbibliothek verzeichnet diese Publikation in der Deutschen Nationalbibliografie; detaillierte bibliografische Daten sind im Internet über http://dnb.d-nb.de abrufbar.

Bibliographic information published by the Deutsche Nationalbibliothek

Die Deutsche Nationalbibliothek lists this publication in the Deutsche Nationalbibliografie; detailed bibliographic data are available in the Internet at http://dnb.d-nb.de.

Cover picture: President Vytautas Landsbergis (standing next to the sign of Lithuania) and Foreign Minister Algirdas Saudargas (on his right) during the meeting of the General Assembly of the United Nations in New York. Lithuania joins the UN, September 17, 1991.

Sitting: on the left of Pres. Vytautas Landsbergis—Emanuelis Zingeris, MP, Chairman of the Foreign Relations Committee of the Lithuanian Parliament.

Standing: on the right of Foreign Minister Algirdas Saudargas—Anicetas Simutis, independent Lithuania's Consul in New York.

We thank the National Museum of Lithuania, Vilnius, for the kind permission.

ISBN-13: 978-3-8382-1779-6

© *ibidem*-Verlag, Hannover • Stuttgart 2024

Alle Rechte vorbehalten

Printed in the EU

To my wife Ruta,
my daughter Ieva,
my grandchildren
Sofia,
Joshua,
Noah,
and everyone else in my family

Contents

Abbreviations 9

Brief Chronology 11

Foreword by *Vytautas Landsbergis* 17

1. State Reborn 19

2. Lithuania's European Roots 37

3. Lithuanian Resistance and the Determination to Remain in
    Europe 67

4. Winning the West 121

5. The Parliamentary Road to Freedom 153

6. Sąjūdis' Peaceful Revolution 177

7. Legality or Brutality: The Road Towards Negotiations 225

8. Lithuania's Success in the Helsinki Process 263

9. Lithuania's Integration into NATO: Adding Value to the
    Alliance 299

10. European Enlargement and the Königsberg Question:
    Stalin's Legacy Within an Enlarged Europe 335

11. Concluding Remarks 367

Selected Bibliography 381

Illustrations 411

Index 447

Abbreviations

APN	Soviet News Agency (Agentura pechatij i novosti)
BAFL	Baltic American Freedom League
BALTBAT	The Joint Baltic Battalion
BALTNET	The Baltic Regional Air Surveillance Network
BALTRON	The Baltic Joint Marine Corps
BBC	British Broadcasting Corporation
c	Crowned
CIA	Central Intelligence Agency
CNN	Cable News Network
CSBMs	Confidence and security building measures
CSCE	Conference for Security & Cooperation in Europe
EC	European Community
ELTA	Independent Lithuania's News Agency
EU	European Union
FDR	Franklin D. Roosevelt
FO	Foreign Office
GDP	Gross Domestic Product
GRU	Soviet military intelligence (Glavnoje Razvetovatelnoje Upravlenije)
IFOR	The Implementation Force
JBANC	The Joint Baltic American National Committee
KGB	Soviet intelligence (Komitet Gosudarstvenoj Bezopasnosti)
LAF	The Lithuanian Activists Front
LITPOLBAT	The Joint Lithuanian and Polish Peacekeeping Battalion
MA	Master of Arts
MP	Member of Parliament
NATO	The North Atlantic Treaty Organisation
NATO PfP	NATO Program for Partnership and Peace
NKVD	Soviet security forces
OMON	Soviet special forces
OSCE	Organization for Security and Cooperation in Europe

PhD	Doctoral dissertation
POTUS	President of the United States
PRO	Public Record Office
RFE	Radio Free Europe
RSFSR	Russian Soviet Federal Socialist Republic
SFOR	Stabilization Force
SSR	Soviet Socialist Republic
TASS	Soviet information agency
TV	Television
UK	The United Kingdom
UN	The United Nations
UNPROFOR	The United Nations Protection Force
USSR	The Union of Soviet Socialist Republics
VOA	The Voice of America
WEU	Western European Union

Brief Chronology

1009	The earliest documentary mention of Lithuania in the annals of the German Benedictine abbey at Quedlinburg in Thuringia
1248	Lithuania, independent state, created under Grand Duke Mindaugas in 1248
1236	Lithuania was defended against the German Knights of the Sword in Saulės (Sun) battle near Šiauliai
July 6, 1253	Great Duke Mindaugas is crowned as the first King of Lithuania
1316 - 1341	Reign of Gediminas, Vilnius, Lithuania's capital was founded by Grand Duke Gediminas
1345 - 1377	Reign of Algirdas
1363	Grand Duke Algirdas won the decisive Battle of the Blue Waters at the Black Sea against the Golden Horde Reign of Kęstutis Reign of Vytautas, the Great
July 15, 1410	The battle of Žalgiris (Grunwald, Tannenberg)
Sept. 8, 1430	Coronation day of Vytautas, the Great
Oct. 27, 1430	Death of Vytautas, the Great Reign of Casimir
1492 - 1494	War with the Muscovites
1500 - 1503	War with the Muscovites Reign of Sigisimund the Elder War with the Muscovites
1521	Lithuania defeats the Teutonic Order War with the Muscovites Reign of Sigisimund Augustus
1569 - 1795	The Union of Lublin (analogous of the European Union) between Lithuania and Poland
1573	The First Statute

1579	The establishment of Vilnius University, the first university in the Baltic region, by Jesuits
1629	War with Sweden
1655	War with Sweden
	Russian occupation of Lithuania
1772	The first partition of the Grand Duchy of Lithuania
1793	The second partition of the Grand Duchy of Lithuania
1797	The third partition of the Grand Duchy of Lithuania; Lithuania, Poland and the union between them were removed from political map Russian occupation of Lithuania
1794 – 1795	Lithuanian rebellion against the Russian (Tsarist) regime
1812	Lithuanian rebellion against the Russian (Tsarist) regime
1831	Lithuanian rebellion against the Russian (Tsarist) regime
1863 - 1864	Lithuanian rebellion against the Russian (Tsarist) regime
1904	Ban on the Lithuanian press was lifted
1905	Lithuanian rebellion against the Russian (Tsarist) regime
Nov. 1914	Committee to Assist the Victims of the War was founded in Vilnius
Dec. 11, 1917	Convention of the National Council in Vilnius
Feb. 16, 1918	the National Council proclaimed the independent Lithuanian state based on democratic political structures
Nov. 11, 1918	The first cabinet took office under Prime Minister Augustinas Valdemaras

Nov. 23, 1918	Lithuanian Army was founded
April 4, 1919	Antanas Smetona elected as the first President of Lithuania
1918-1920	Three liberation wars against Bolsheviks in the East, Bermondists (remnants of Tsarist army) in the North and Poland in the South
1920 - 1939	Poland's seizure of Vilnius, Lithuania's capital
July 12, 1920	Peace Treaty was signed in Moscow between the Republic of Lithuania and Soviet Russia
May 15, 1920	The first session of Seimas, Parliament of the Republic of Lithuania
Aug. 1, 1922	Constitution adopted
Dec. 17, 1926	Military coup
Sept. 28, 1926	Non-aggression and neutrality treaty with the Soviet Union was signed
May 1, 1934	Lithuania joined the Baltic Entente
Mar. 26, 1935	The first Nazi activists trial in Europe
Mar. 20, 1939	German ultimatum, requiring the cession of the territory of Klaipėda to the German Reich
Aug. 23, 1939	The Soviet Union and Nazi Germany signed "mutual non-aggression pact," and the first secret protocol (the Molotov-Ribbentrop pact)
Sept. 17, 1939	Soviet troops occupied Vilnius region
Sept. 28, 1939	The second protocol of the secret Molotov-Ribbentrop pact was signed under which the majority of Lithuania's territory was transferred from the German influence zone into the Soviet zone of interests
Oct. 3, 1939	Soviet ultimatum to Lithuania
Jun. 14-15, 1940	Soviet army occupied Lithuania
Jul. 11-12, 1940	Mass arrests to Soviet concentration camps

Jul. 23, 1940	The United States announced the Stimson Doctrine of non-recognition of Soviet annexation of the Baltic States
Oct. 15, 1940	President Franklin D. Roosevelt met with the delegation of the American Lithuanian Council, confirming the US policy of non-recognition of the incorporation of the Baltic States into the Soviet Union
Jan. 10, 1941	The third secret protocol of the Stalin – Hitler (Molotov – Ribbentrop) pact between the Soviet Union and Germany was signed in Moscow
1941 - 1944	German (Nazi) occupation of Lithuania
Jun. 22-29, 1941	The uprising against the Russian (Soviet) regime in occupied Lithuania
1944 - 1990	Russian (Soviet) occupation of Lithuania
1944 - 1965	Partisan war in Lithuania
Dec. 1947	Partisan Juozas Lukša Daumantas broke through the Iron Curtain (border between occupied Lithuania and Poland)
March 1948	Partisan Juozas Lukša Daumantas reached Stockholm
1951	Partisan Juozas Lukša Daumantas was parachuted back into Lithuania with CIA help and he perished
	dissident activities
Mar. 19, 1972	First issue of the Chronicle of the Catholic Church of Lithuania was published
Aug. 23, 1987	Gathering near the monument for Adomas Mickevičius in Vilnius, organised by the Lithuanian Freedom League
Aug. 23, 1988	Vingis park rally organised by Sąjūdis
Oct. 22-23, 1988	Lithuanian liberation movement Sąjūdis held founding congress

Aug. 23, 1989	The Baltic Way, the largest demonstration, when people of Lithuania, Latvia, and Estonia linked their hands along the highway running from Vilnius, through Riga to Tallinn
Dec. 24, 1989	The Soviet Congress of People's Deputies acknowledged that the Soviet take-over of the Baltic States had been illegal
Mar. 11, 1990	Declaration of Independence
Jan. 13, 1991	Failure of communist coup d'étate in Lithuania
Feb. 11, 1991	Iceland passed a resolution stating that its recognition of the Republic of Lithuania of 1922 remained valid
Sept. 6, 1991	Soviet Union recognized the Republic of Lithuania
Sept. 17, 1991	Lithuania joined the UN
Sept. 8, 1992	The agreement about the withdrawal of the Russian troops was signed between the Lithuanian and the Russian governments
Aug. 31, 1993	Russian army was withdrawn from Lithuania
Nov. 22-23, 2002	President George W. Bush visited Lithuania
Mar. 29, 2004	Lithuania joined NATO
May 1, 2004	Lithuania joined the EU
Oct. 17, 2006	Her Majesty the Queen Elizabeth II visited Lithuania
2009	Lithuania commemorated the millennium since the first written mentioning of its name
Feb. 16, 2018	Lithuania commemorated the centenary anniversary of the Declaration of Independence
March 11, 2021	Lithuania commemorated the 30th anniversary of the Declaration of Independence on March 11, 1990
Jan. 25, 2023	Vilnius celebrated the 700th anniversary

July 11-12, 2023   NATO Heads of states and Government summit in Vilnius

July 9-11, 2024   NATO's summit in Washington, DC. The 75th anniversary of NATO

Foreword
Königsberg's Status Needs to be Restored

While Putin's terrorist regime tugs at maps and pulls apart borders, it's worth taking a look at one of the first cases of Soviet-Russian occupation. The annexation of the Königsberg region (a part of East Prussia now known as Kaliningrad) took place after the 1940 annexation of Lithuania and its re-occupation in 1944-1945.

When Joseph Stalin made the unilateral decision to annex Königsberg - a part of the former territory of Germany - neither the Soviet Union, nor its former larger counterpart, the Russian Soviet Socialist Republic, acquired any legal rights to that European land or its inhabitants. (This is reminiscent of the recent "annexation" of Donetsk or Mariupol in occupied Ukraine.)

The then Soviet action also did not receive any direct international recognition or legal confirmation. There was no accord. In fact, the timid West remained silent.

In addition, genocidal extermination and the forced resettlement of local people – the indigenous communities – has never been legally evaluated. Königsberg was handed over to hostile and lawless murderers and colonists. Moscow erased historical documentation. It changed all geographical names, thus destroying ethnic and linguistic evidence that native people had ever lived in the region.

A so-called end of war

Usually, wars end with some sort of peace treaty. But there was none in this case – just a provision confirming that it would be in future. The Potsdam Declaration was signed, which laid out the future boundaries of defeated and conquered Germany. The declaration stated that the Königsberg territory would be administered by the Soviet Union "pending a Peace Treaty," at which time all issues would be addressed.

However, to this day, a Peace Treaty (agreed to be concluded by Stalin himself in writing) has not addressed the Königsberg region. Temporary administration of the territory was granted to a now non-existent entity, the USSR, and continues to the present day. Who in fact administers the Königsberg region?

At the time of the Potsdam Conference, the Soviet Union included a number of occupied countries, including Ukraine and Belarus. However, they do not administer this region, so the agreement has been violated. Russia announced that it had inherited the rights of the Soviet Union after the state created by Stalin ceased to exist in 1991. So, post-Soviet Russia has potentially "inherited" the right to temporarily administer the former region of Königsberg, a temporary administration which continues to this day. So much for "post-war legality"! The question is apparently closed. Or is it?

The United Nations General Assembly could prepare and approve a newer provision declaring that the previous 1945 provision was never withdrawn and is therefore still valid, despite current Russia not being equivalent to the former USSR. This could be followed by encouragement to organize a delayed post-war peace conference, which would at least define issues related to this territory.

This would allow Europe to move forward in a more legally correct and stable manner that is based on international law, a legality which Russia has never addressed.

Dr Darius Furmonavicius' important monograph *Lithuania Transforms the West* opens up fundamental historical research into the issues highlighted above, deserving further research work and wider international debate.

President Vytautas Landsbergis

Vilnius, December 24, 2022

1. State Reborn

Lithuania is not a small state in Europe. It is roughly twice as large as Belgium, and by territory, Denmark and or the Netherlands are smaller than Lithuania by a factor of a third.[1] With a population of more than three million people, Lithuania, though it may not be immediately apparent, is situated at the geographical center of the European continent. Its history, although not well understood among western Europeans, is a long one. During the last millennium Lithuania has sometimes played a crucial strategic role in the protection, and therefore the shaping, of European civilization. The goal of the present work is to clarify the role played by Lithuania in the momentous changes in the political life of the continent and in the global shift of power in the closing years of the twentieth century. This will be done by analyzing security developments in Lithuania between 1988 and 2020, a period marked by the liberation and integration of the country into NATO and the EU.

It is important to note that Lithuania continued to exist as a legal entity in international law, albeit in a tenuous form, because of its continuing diplomatic presence in international relations which continued, despite the occupation of its homeland, until Lithuania declared its independence once again on March 11, 1990. This work will focus upon how this liberation was achieved, and how the country's consequent search for integration into the European and transatlantic security framework has influenced both its own security development and European security. One of the most important factors in the process of Lithuania's liberation from

---

1   Lithuania (65,300 sq. km or 25,212 sq mi) is larger than Latvia (24,938 sq mi), Croatia (21,851 sq mi), Slovakia (18,933 sq mi), Estonia (17,462 sq mi), Denmark (16,640 sq mi), Netherlands (16,034 sq mi), Switzerland (15,940 sq mi), Belgium (11,787 sq mi), Albania (11,082 sq mi), Macedonia (9,928 sq mi), Israel (8,367 sq mi), Slovenia (7,827 sq mi), Kuwait (6,880 sq mi), Cyprus (3,572 sq mi), Luxembourg (999 sq mi), Andorra (179 sq mi), San Marino (23.6 sq mi), Monaco (0.76 sq mi), Malta (122 sq mi), Liechtenstein (62 sq mi), Vatican City State (44 ha or 109 ac). It is a bit smaller than Georgia (27,086 sq mi), Ireland (27,133 sq mi), Czech Republic (30,450 sq mi), Austria (32,383 sq mi), Portugal (35,580 sq mi), Hungary (35,919 sq mi) or Iceland (39,741 sq mi). It is roughly twice as small as Greece (50,949 sq mi).

Soviet occupation was its rather fragile, but nevertheless significant continuity of statehood, which gave a basis in international law for this resumed international recognition, and for the country's consequent determination to define its future path as lying within the western framework of security. Despite fifty years of occupation, the country continued to exist in international relations, its presence being embodied in the embassies and consulates of independent Lithuania, which continued their work in the United States, the United Kingdom, Canada, the Holy See, France, Italy, Switzerland, and other Western states.

It is also important to affirm the fact that Lithuania played a key role in the collapse of the Soviet Empire. The key events in this process took place in January 1991, when peaceful Lithuanian demonstrations defended democracy against Soviet tanks, in the interests not only of Lithuania, but also of Europe as a whole. As Richard Krickus has pointed out, "historians may one day conclude that the final chapter in the collapse of the Soviet order began on October 22, 1988, when the Lithuanian national movement *Sąjūdis* held a two-day-long founding congress."[2] However, some researchers have failed to understand the wider importance of these events, probably because they did not have the opportunity to use Lithuanian primary sources.[3] Indeed, some western writers on the "collapse of communism" do not even mention *Sąjūdis* or Lithuania, though this oversight is not universal: Alfred Erich Senn, discussing Lithuania as effectively being the Achilles heel of the former Soviet Union, observes that "the general theories offered by western writers on the development of national revolt in the Soviet Union are too vague to be useful. [...] Western analyses, moreover, contradict each other."[4]

---

2   Richard J. Krickus, *Showdown. The Lithuanian Rebellion and the Breakup of the Soviet Empire* (Washington: Brassey's, 1997), p. 62.

3   Examples of this oversight will be found e.g., in Geoffrey A. Hosking, Jonathan Aves, and Peter Duncan, *The Road to Post-Communism. Independent political Movements in the Soviet Union, 1985 – 1991* (London: Pinter, 1992).

4   See e.g., Wisla Suraska, *How the Soviet Union Disappeared* (Durham: Duke University Press, 1998). Quoted from Alfred E. Senn, *Gorbachev's Failure in Lithuania* (New York: St. Martin's Press, 1995), p. xii.

The implication of Lithuania's integration into the European and transatlantic security framework, which followed her achievement of independence, was particularly important for the Russian withdrawal from its territory. Accomplished on August 31, 1993, this was, perhaps, the most successful case of CSCE multilateral diplomacy in Europe. Lithuania's own actions were crucial to its achievement, as the Soviet army in Lithuania had come under the legal jurisdiction of Russia, only after that country had accepted responsibility for the army of the Soviet Union in Lithuania, because of a bilateral agreement between the two states. Under that agreement, made on September 8, 1992, the Russian government also accepted the commitment to withdraw troops from Lithuania. Constant pressure both from the West and the Balts themselves had been necessary to avert Russia's attempts to retain military bases in the Baltic States. It finally withdrew its army from Lithuania on August 31, 1993, and from Latvia and Estonia a year later. Western authors have often neglected Lithuania's proactive role in this process. Indeed, Anatol Lieven has claimed somewhat astonishingly that the Russian army left the Baltic States because the "Russian military commanders themselves [so] decided at a conference in St. Petersburg in the autumn of 1992"![5]

Some authors have emphasized the "Gorbachev factor" as having been the key to the peaceful solution of the "Baltic crisis" during 1988-91, while others have interpreted Baltic security developments as a continuation of the superpower game.[6] It is suggested that neither of these interpretations provides an adequate explanation for the course of events as they do not give recognition to the contribution of the political culture of the Baltic States and their people or their cooperation, or the firm leadership of Lithuania, nor of the coherent pressure which came from the West.[7] The policy of

---

5   Anatol Lieven, "The Baltic iceberg dead ahead: NATO beware," *The World Today* 52, no. 7 (July 1996): 176.

6   See e.g., memoirs of the former American Ambassador in Moscow, Jack Matlock, *The End of the Soviet Empire* (London: Macmillan, 1995), or Kristian Gerner & Stefan Hedlund, *The Baltic States and the End of the Soviet Empire* (London: Routledge, 1993).

7   Darius Furmonavičius, "Northern European Security Community," *Lithuanian Papers* 10 (1996): 64-65.

non-recognition of the incorporation of Lithuania into the Soviet Union which had been adopted at the onset of the Cold War by the leading western nations and the Helsinki process finally became the major international tools that facilitated change in the Soviet Empire, and permitted the peaceful liberation of the Lithuanians and other Balts from the communist regime. The process took nearly half a century, and while there were considerable other forces at play, a careful appraisal of the course of events will make it clear that this liberation was itself the catalyst of the many other changes which brought that Soviet system to its timely termination.

The methodology of this study is historical, and most sources are primary ones. Among these are extensive references to the contemporary Lithuanian press, and a series of personal interviews with Lithuanian politicians, who played key roles at crucial times in the two decades under consideration, the integrity and reputation of interviewees being the most important criteria for their selection, and for the justification of their testimonies. The diplomatic correspondence between Lithuania and the Soviet Union, which was made publicly available in 1991 to demonstrate Lithuania's search for negotiation, reveals the attempts by the Soviet authorities to avoid those negotiations and was used extensively in the preparation of this study. The biggest value of the study is that it unveils the process of liberation of Lithuania from the Soviet regime using primary Lithuanian sources, which have hitherto been wholly unavailable in English.

This research also greatly benefited from access to the private papers of Secretary James A. Baker III, deposited at the Seeley G. Mudd manuscript library of Princeton University, which clarified American pressure on the Soviets regarding peaceful process, and the author is grateful to Secretary Baker for his permission to examine those papers, including memos, letters to the Soviets, agendas, and the minutes of meetings with the President.

However, the author did not have access to the closed archives of the Kremlin, except for those secret Moscow documents that were reported in the press or were declassified for the collection of documents of the Communist Party of the Soviet state at the

Hoover Institution Archives in Stanford University. The study could not approach in detail the discussions regarding Lithuania which were internal to the Kremlin. However, it does attempt objectively to unveil Moscow's response to Lithuania as it was reported in the Lithuanian press, and how it is understood by Lithuanian and American decision makers.[8]

---

8   Parts of this research have been presented in papers at international conferences: "The Königsberg question in European security," AABS conference, George Washington University, Washington, D.C., June 15-17, 2006; "The questions of the Königsberg region and the Japanese Northern territories in comparative perspective," ECSA-Canada biannual conference, University of Vancouver, British Columbia, May 19-20, 2006; "The Sajudis of Lithuania, Baltic Peaceful Revolutions and the Collapse of the Soviet Union," ISA convention, San Diego, March 22-25, 2006; "The Koenigsberg region: the territorial claim by the EU or an amber revolution?" BISA conference, University of St. Andrew's, December 19-21, 2005; "The Koenigsberg/Kaliningrad issue: Stalin's legacy within an enlarged Europe," ISA convention, Honolulu, Hawaii, March 1-5, 2005; "The Koenigsberg question: Stalin's legacy within an enlarged Europe," ECSA-World conference, Brussels, November 2004; "The Baltic Dimension of European enlargement: the Koenigsberg/Kaliningrad/Karaliaučius question," ECSA-DK conference, Odense, Denmark, September 24-25, 2004; "The Koenigsberg/Kaliningrad/Karaliaučius Question: Stalin's Legacy within an Enlarged Europe," 19th AABS conference, Toronto, June 8-9, 2004; "The European Enlargement: the Koenigsberg/Kaliningrad Issue," ECSA-Canada biannual conference, Montreal, May 27-29, 2004; "The European Enlargement: the Koenigsberg Question Requires Solution," Midwest Political Science Association Annual National Conference, Chicago, April 15-18, 2004; "The EU Enlargement to the Baltic States: Koenigsberg Issue Has to Be Resolved," ISA International Convention, Montreal, March 17-19, 2004; "European enlargement: Koenigsberg problem is still not resolved," ECPR Conference, Marburg, Germany, September 18-21, 2003; "The anomaly of Kaliningrad: Settlement of Sovereignty for KLEIN LITAUEN will End the Second World War," the IPSA World Congress, Durban, South Africa, June 29-July 4, 2003; "The EU Enlargement to the Baltic States: Koenigsberg Issue Is Still Not Resolved," the CEEISA/ISA International Convention, Central European University, Budapest, June 26-28, 2003; "The EU Enlargement to the Baltic States: The Problem of Königsberg Region," EUSA 8th International Conference, Nashville, Tennessee, USA, March 27-29, 2003; "Königsberg/Karaliaučius/Kaliningrad region: Settlement of Sovereignty will End Second World War," the 6th ECSA-World Conference, Brussels, December 4-5, 2002; "NATO Enlargement to the Baltic States," the 18th AABS conference, John Hopkins University, Baltimore, June 6-8, 2002; "The enlargement of the EU to the Baltic States: Königsberg issue is still not resolved," the 5th Biennial Conference of the ECSA– Canada, Toronto, May 31 – June 1, 2002; "Lithuania rejoins the West," the 17th AABS conference, Georgetown University,

The restoration of state independence

When Soviet forces annexed Estonia, Latvia, and Lithuania in June 1940, as early as July 23, 1940, the U.S. Department of State had already announced that it would apply the Stimson Doctrine to the USSR, as it had applied to armed expansion by Japan, Italy, and Germany.[9] "Not only did the United States not recognize Soviet annexation of the Baltic republics, but it also froze Baltic assets (ships, gold, and other properties) in the USA to prevent the USSR from taking them. Most countries followed the American lead. Except for Sweden, no European country outside Moscow's sphere officially recognized Soviet rule over the Baltic. The Soviet Congress of People's Deputies acknowledged on December 24, 1989, that the Soviet take-over of the Baltic States had been illegal. This admission

---

Washington D.C., June 14-17, 2000; "Lithuania rejoins Europe," the 3rd International Conference on Baltic Studies in Europe, Stockholm, June 16-20, 1999; "Lithuania rejoins Europe after Soviet occupation," the 16th AABS conference "The Baltic States in International Perspective," Bloomington, University of Indiana, June 19-21, 1998; "Lietuva sugrįžta į Europą" (*Lithuania Rejoins Europe*), the Xth World Lithuanian Symposium in Arts & Sciences, Chicago, May 18-20, 1997 (invited paper) as well as a chapter in the book: Anthony Packer and Darius Furmonavičius, "Brief history of Lithuania" in Vytautas Landsbergis, *Lithuania independent again* (Cardiff: University of Wales Press, 2000); academic papers "Lithuania at the turn of the new millennium" and "Northern European Security Community" in the *Lithuanian Papers* (2002 and 1996, Australia), articles "Lithuania" in the *Encyclopaedia Britannica Year in Review* books (since 2000), and more than 60 articles in the press.

9   See Basic Declaration. Šimutis, *Lithuanian American Council*, p. 481. Secretary of State Henry L. Stimson (President Hoover's administration) made one last effort to apply the moral suasion concept that had dominated Republican foreign policy in the 1920s by sending notes to both China and Japan on January 7, 1932, announcing what has come to be known as the Stimson Doctrine, a policy of nonrecognition of any territorial changes brought about in violation of Kellogg Pact, i.e., Japan's conquest of Manchuria in China.
See also e.g.: http://courses.knox.edu/hist285schneid/stimsondoctrine.html. During the presentation speech in 1936 Nobel Prize winner Christian Lous Lange, Secretary General of Inter-Parliamentary Union, Brussels, defined the Stimson Doctrine, as the refusal to recognize any territorial expansion or change boundary unless effected by peaceful means. Similar policy of nonrecognition of the incorporation of Lithuania and the other Baltic States into the USSR was applied by the United States since 1940 until their liberation in 1990s, but there were gaps in policy application. See Robert A.Vitas, *The United States and Lithuania: The Stimson Doctrine of Nonrecognition* (Chicago: The Lithuanian Research & Studies Centre, 1990).

ripped all legitimacy from Soviet rule in the Baltic. The United States never closed the Baltic legations in Washington. They were still functioning when the Baltic republics regained full independence in 1991. Washington's refusal to recognize that might makes right helped bring down the Soviet empire."[10] It was one of the major factors in the restoration of an independent Lithuanian state.

These observations give context to the questions of how and why Lithuania became the leader of the liberation process in the Baltic States, and the related question of why Lithuania's peaceful strategy was so successful. However, it is also suggested here that the answers to these questions reflected dispositions, whose formulation was deeply embedded in Lithuanian history, as the traditions of statehood were such that the country would inevitably resist any occupier and would sooner or later liberate itself from foreign oppression. Indeed, the national being, traditions, and historical memory of the Lithuanians were such that one might have to say the country was predestined to resist any kind of Russian imperialism and to counter the insults of occupation by working to reclaim the nation's independence in Europe. Although Russia has occupied Lithuania on four occasions (1655-60, 1795-1914, 1940-41 and 1944-1990), each time its troops were forced to leave the country. Each succeeding generation of Lithuanians has rebelled against this oppressor, despite policies of terror and russification. Indeed, Lithuanian reaction against Russian attempts to control her destiny is almost instinctive. The years 1794-5, 1812, 1831, 1863-4, 1905, 1918-20, 1941, 1944-1956, 1987-1990 were all marked by rebellions, and Lithuania's latest and peaceful liberation from Soviet Russia was based on a political culture of resistance, which was essentially

---

10   Walter C. Clemens, *Dynamics of International Relations. Conflict and Mutual Gain in an Era of Global Interdependence* (Oxford: Rowman & Littlefield Publishers, 1998), p. 448. Nazi Germany in a secret Soviet-Nazi pact authorized the Soviet take-over of the Baltic States but Western Germany never recognized the incorporation of the Baltic States into the Soviet Union, as similarly the United States, Britain and Sweden did not confirm its recognition, even though she transferred Lithuania's gold stored in Stockholm to the Soviet Union. See Dainius Žalimas, *Lietuvos Respublikos Nepriklausomybės Atkūrimas. Pagrindiniai Klausimai Pagal Tarptautinę Teisę* (Vilnius: Rosma, 1997), pp. 110-111.

the continuation of the underground activity of the dissidents and rebels of former times.

The three Baltic States continued their independent existence during the subsequent fifty years of occupation. This remained a key factor in the international relations of the Baltic States which confirmed their continuity as states internationally distinct from the Soviet Union and enabled them to reclaim their independence in the fullness of time when the opportunity occurred. Pre-war Lithuania's embassies continued their work in Washington D.C. and London, Paris and Rome, Bern, and the Vatican as well as in other capitals of Western states throughout this time. This policy of non-recognition of incorporation into the Soviet Union therefore created the background for Lithuania's liberation from the Soviet occupation in the late 1980s and the beginning of the 1990s.

This study does not attempt to create any generalized model of the restoration of independence to an annexed state, but it offers some explanatory patterns, related to broader issues which are widely debated in the discussion of this question in international relations, namely the role of the leadership; the specific influence of political culture; the role of international institutions; and the impact of the legal position of the state in international affairs. The case of Lithuania's liberation provides a clear illustration of the importance and interplay of all these issues. The firm leadership of President Vytautas Landsbergis played a key role in *Sąjūdis'* peaceful revolution as well as in the changing Lithuanian political culture, which was based on increased popular participation, and an accompanying diminution of fear of Soviet repressions and persecutions. Lithuania's success in ridding herself of over half a century of occupation was, however, unthinkable without the continuing existence of the country in the web of international relations. The work of her diplomats, the Lithuanian émigré organizations, and of the press in Western countries, kept the case of freedom alive by a constant lobbying of the political elite and the public to support the legitimate goal of the restoration of their country's independence. That activity resulted in an important international factor which assisted the integration of Lithuania into the European and transatlantic security framework, and which was completed with the country's joining the North Atlantic Treaty Organization (NATO) and the European Union (EU) in 2004.

The continuity of the Lithuanian statehood

It is important to emphasize that the background to Lithuania's continuity as a state and the legal basis of her restored freedom is the significant result of the U.S. policy of non-recognition of the incorporation of Lithuania into the Soviet Union, which we have already noted. President Franklin D. Roosevelt confirmed this policy on October 15, 1940, in response to the efforts of the American Lithuanian Council and the visit of its delegation headed by Leonardas Šimutis, a former MP of Lithuania.[11] Another basis for the legal continuity of the state lay in President Antanas Smetona's authorisation, before the outbreak of the Second World War, of the transfer of a greater part of the gold reserves held by the Lithuanian Government to the Bank of England and the Federal Reserve, in order to assure the continued existence of Lithuania's diplomacy in the West in the event of an occupation of the homeland. Originally, the Independence Fund and the opening of its accounts in the United States and other western countries was proposed by Lithuanian Ambassadors Bronius Balutis (London), Petras Klimas (Paris) and Stasys Lozoraitis (Rome) in their memorandum to Foreign Minister Juozas Urbšys written during their meeting in Paris on October 29

---

11   Leonardas Šimutis, *Lithuanian American Council. 30 Year Struggle for the Liberation of Lithuania. 1940 – 1970* (Chicago: Draugas, 1971), p. 24. The delegation of the American Lithuanian Council presented the memorandum to President Franklin D. Roosevelt. It received the following response by the President: "The address mentioned that Lithuania had lost its independence. That is a mistake. The independence of Lithuania is not lost but only put temporary aside. The time will come when Lithuania will be free again. This may happen sooner than you may expect. It was a mistake on behalf of one of the speakers to say that Lithuania is a small country. In Latin America there are states even smaller than Lithuania, but they live a free and happy life. Even the smallest nation has the same right to enjoy independence as the largest one." See Franklin D. Roosevelt, Memorandums and Statements. Šimutis, *Lithuanian American Council*, p. 458.

– November 2, 1939.[12] Although these transactions were only partially implemented because of the speed of events, the subsequent struggle for freedom on the diplomatic front was made possible on the basis of this initial facility.

A further element in Lithuania's claim to continuity as a state was implicit in the resistance against both Soviet communism and German national socialism. Although it has been fashionable to regard them as polar opposites, the imperialistic intentions of these powers were similar indeed, and both were equal enemies of Lithuania.[13] Little is known today about this resistance, either in political circles or among the general public of Western Europe, which became active once again after Lithuania became a victim of the secret pact between Soviet Russia and Nazi Germany, being occupied by the Soviet Union in 1940.[14] It was, however, the basis of Lithuania's successful rebellion a year later, initiating desperate Soviet withdrawal from the country at the time. That revolt, which took place in 1941, was seen as the first crack in the structure of the Soviet Union, and it was well remembered by those who participated in it. Between June 22 and 29, 1941 more than 100,000 people took part directly in the rebellion, approximately three percent of the population. More than 4,000 people died.[15] Still, it had much wider appeal and symbolic importance. Nevertheless, an independent Provisional Government existed for six weeks, and though it was dismissed by the Nazi regime, it was a significant expression of the national resolve. When Soviet rule was resumed in 1944, the nation rebelled once again. That struggle became the longest partisan war in European history, a fact that gainsays communist claims that Lithuania had entered the Soviet Union freely.

---

12   Trijų Pasiuntinių 1939 m. lapkričio 2 d. Memorandumas Užsienio Reikalų Ministeriui. The Memorandum of the Three Representatives to Foreign Minister of November 2, 1939. Petras Klimas collection, Diary excerpts, 1910-1939. Hoover Institution Archives, Stanford University.
13   Adolfas Damušis, *Lithuania against Soviet and Nazi aggression* (Chicago: The American Foundation for Lithuanian Research, 1998), p. 107.
14   See e.g., Damušis, *Lithuania against Soviet and Nazi aggression.*
15   Damušis, *Lithuania against Soviet and Nazi aggression.*

It must be remarked that this guerrilla war continued Lithuania's long traditions of resistance.[16] But while the partisan response reflected the determination of the Lithuanian people to defend their homeland, the manner of its suppression demonstrated the threat posed by the Soviet system to humanity as a whole, providing clear evidence that bolshevism was "ready to destroy Western civilization, culture and Christianity."[17] A deep academic study of the partisan war period was first made available in the West by Dr. Kęstutis Girnius in 1987 but the author did not have access to Soviet archival material. After Lithuanian independence was achieved, the full scale of the crimes of the occupying power has been effectively presented in visual form for the visitor to Lithuania in the Museum opened since independence by the Government in the former KGB headquarters building on Gediminas street in Vilnius, where it is supported by an array of documentation which could be presented to an international tribunal on the communist crimes of the occupying power.[18]

The last Lithuanian partisans died or melted into the community in 1965. At its peak their effort involved about one percent of the total Lithuanian population, though they enjoyed broad popular support. They struggled against the odds. Misiūnas and Taagepera estimate the average life span of the partisans engaged in action was approximately two years, due to the high level of casualties.[19] Over the nine years of intense partisan activity between 1944 and 1953 about 100,000 people were directly involved in partisan fighting in Lithuania and the estimated figure of their mortality is about 50,000. In addition, more than 300,000 families were

---

16 Kęstutis Girnius, *Partizanų kovos Lietuvoje* (Chicago: Į Laisvę Fondas, 1987), p. 405.

17 Lietuvos Respublikos katalikų laiškas Šv. Tėvui Pijui XII Vatikane (Letter of the Lithuanian Catholics to Holy Fr. Pijus XII in Vatican), in Juozas Daumantas, *Partizanai*. (Vilnius: Vaga, 1990), p. 420.

18 Girnius, *Partizanų kovos*. See also *Antikomunistinis Kongresas ir Tarptautinio Vilniaus Visuomeninio Tribunolo Procesas "Komunizmo nusikaltimų įvertinimas 2000"* (Vilnius: Ramona, 2002). See also: http://www.genocid.lt/Muziejus/eng/muzeum.htm.

19 Romualdas Misiunas and Rein Taagepera. *The Baltic States. Years of Dependence, 1940 – 1990* (London: Hurst & Company, 1993), p. 86.

deported from Lithuania to Siberia during the Stalinist terror of the 1940s to strip away the substantial support the movement enjoyed in the countryside (see Table 3 in the Appendices). The official Soviet response was severely repressive, yet even after the partisan movement was destroyed, opposition to the Soviet system continued to find expression in the covert and dissident defense of national, religious, and human rights.

The later development of this national resistance re-emerged in the late 1960s and the 1970s, when, as Vytautas Vardys has observed, three types of dissident movement were formed: first, in defence of the rights of the Catholic Church and other believers; second, to advocate national rights and self-determination; and, third, for the advancement of human rights and the monitoring of their violation by the Soviet regime.[20] Four major phases of Lithuania's resistance can be discerned through a retrospective analysis: first, the revolt of 1941; second, the Partisan War between 1944 and 1953; third, the underground dissident activity of the period between 1953 and 1987; and, fourth, the overt and peaceful work of the *Sąjūdis* movement between 1987 and 1990. The level of support earned by the activists in each of these phases clearly indicates that the nation never accepted the Soviet regime. Their effect was cumulative, and, in the end, the forces of history were to move in such a way that the deep resentment of the nation was to become apparent to the wider world once again.

Liberation

Lithuania was peacefully liberated from Soviet occupation because of the *Sąjūdis* movement in the years between 1988 and 1990. This reawakening, which led to the restoration of an independent state, was possible, however, only because international circumstances provided a supportive background. There was, in addition, a

---

20   See Vytautas S. Vardys, *The Catholic Church: Dissent and Nationality in Soviet Lithuania* (New York: Columbia University Press, 1978), pp. 128-136; Vytautas S. Vardys, "Lithuania's Catholic Movement Reappraised," *Survey* 25 (1980); Vytautas S. Vardys, "Human Rights Issues in Estonia, Latvia, and Lithuania," *Journal of Baltic Studies* 18, no. 3 (Fall, 1981); Vytautas S. Vardys, "Pogrindžio rezistencija Lietuvoje," *Ateitis* 4 (1982).

growing public awareness of the illegality of the Molotov-Ribben-trop pact, under which Lithuania was incorporated into the Soviet Union. This recognition was to play a significant part in the general shift of attitude. Furthermore, *Sąjūdis'* claims were underwritten by growing public and international awareness of the implications of the long-standing policy of non-recognition of the incorporation of the Baltic States into the Soviet Union by the major Western states. This fact encouraged public political activity in Lithuania in re-sponse to Gorbachev's announcement of *perestroika* and *glasnost* al-lowed its leaders an opportunity to test how far the Soviet system was willing to change. It then provided them with the opportunity to test the nation's resolve, and to reassert the national being.[21]

Sąjūdis was Lithuania's liberation movement and it set the symbolic goal of a free and independent European country from the very beginning. At its first Congress in 1988, the representatives proclaimed that Lithuania "had chosen the parliamentary, peaceful way to restoration of their independence."[22] In this way a "parlia-mentary way of liberation" from Soviet occupation, which involved holding and winning the first free elections to the Supreme Soviet of both the Soviet Union and of occupied Lithuania, was advocated from the start. Against the background of the country's recent his-tory, this was a major assertion of national feeling in the face of for-midable odds, and it was successful.

While the major eventual domestic outcome of the *Sąjūdis* movement was the achievement of this previously stated goal of national independence, its unexpected international consequence was nothing less than the collapse of the Soviet Union. Interna-tional recognition of the Baltic achievement has been remarkably limited and grudging. While Walter Clemens's observation that "the sources of Soviet collapse intertwined, but Baltic independ-ence movements were as weighty as any factors in subverting the USSR," provided a good measure of the general estimation of the

---

21   Anthony Packer, "Editor's preface" in Vytautas Landsbergis, *Lithuania inde-pendent again* (Cardiff: University of Wales Press, 2000), p. X.

22   See e.g., Romas Batūra, *Baltijos kelias - kelias į laisvę. 1989.08.23. Dešimtmetį minint* (Vilnius: Lietuvos Sąjūdis, 1999), p. 14.

historical importance of what these nations achieved at this stage of European history.[23] However, it can be argued that the stand taken by the Lithuanian people was the critical accelerating factor in this shift, and indeed that the fateful events which took place in the Lithuanian capital between March 11, 1990, when Lithuania declared its independence, and the night of January 13, 1991, when the communist coup d'état sponsored by the Kremlin failed in Lithuania, made the final collapse of that Soviet communist system inevitable.

We shall need to document the failure of the communist coup d'état in Lithuania and examine the enormous difficulties which the state faced after the Declaration of Independence, including international pressure to suspend the Declaration for an indefinite period, as well as appraise the Soviet economic blockade and the attempted military coup d'état, the August Putsch, in the Kremlin and its spillover in Lithuania, if we are to underpin the arguments for this viewpoint. However, as we begin to do this, it is important to note that the period of crucial activity was dominated by the obscurantist tactics of the Soviet propaganda machine. The destabilising tactics used in Czechoslovakia in 1968 and in the other states of the Soviet Empire at similar critical junctures were repeated in Lithuania and the other Baltic States in 1990-1991. But it was the non-violent response to this aggression which became a major factor in the final victory of the Lithuanians against Soviet terror, and this response and the firmness of the Lithuanian leadership, notably the personality of *Sąjūdis'* leader, Professor Vytautas Landsbergis, were crucially important factors in enabling Lithuania to be peacefully liberated from Soviet occupation. We have also to give credit to President George H. W. Bush and Secretary James A. Baker III, who encouraged the Soviets not to use military force and who had threatened to freeze all economic relations with the Soviets after the special KGB forces stormed the Lithuanian TV Tower in Vilnius in January 1991 and Gorbachev attempted to install a communist

---

23   Walter C. Clemens, "Who or What killed the Soviet Union? How three Davids undermined Goliath," *Nationalism & Ethnic Politics* 3, no. 1 (January 1997): 136, 138 – 139.

regime in the country once again. The stories which were told to the outside world at the time however were controlled to a considerable degree by a wholly unsympathetic Soviet media operation, and even now the Lithuanian perspective on those events continues to be obscured by the influence which was understandably dominant during that period.[24]

Lithuanian, European, and transatlantic security

The reclamation of independence by the Lithuanian state is an achievement which continues to bring great pride to the people of the country. However, the experience of Soviet rule left Lithuania with significant economic, political, and social deficits, which have affected the country's international position *vis à vis* the rest of the world. Some of these injustices have been formally repaired, e.g., when the country was accepted as a member of the United Nations, the Conference on Security and Co-operation in Europe, and the Council of Europe. More recently, along with other Central European countries Lithuania has also joined NATO and the EU, the major European security organizations. These are vital issues, and, in view of the country's history, there has been little which has been of greater importance than this objective of securing a firm place within the European and transatlantic security institutions. Indeed, assuring national security on these terms has been tantamount, in Lithuania's eyes, to reclaiming her full historical inheritance in the Western European family of nations.

Lithuania's participation in the European and transatlantic security framework to date has already profoundly influenced security developments in Lithuania and has indeed affected Europe as a whole. Lithuania plays an important regional role in the promotion of democracy in the neighborhood: Byelorussia, Ukraine, the Kaliningrad region - and it is a positive example for Georgia,

---

24 Probably the greatest achievement of Landsbergis was "to cast the question of Lithuania's independence as a moral issue, which therefore was not negotiable, and then to persuade so many people to accept that view." quote in Alfred E. Senn, *Gorbachev's Failure in Lithuania* (New York: St. Martin's Press, 1995), p. 155.

Armenia, and Azerbaijan, as well as other states formerly occupied by the Soviet Empire. However, the questions: "What is the impact of Lithuania on the European and transatlantic security framework?" and "How does Lithuania's participation influence European and transatlantic security as a whole?" are the main questions to be faced later in this work. If we reflect on recent history, it will be evident that the Helsinki process was vital to Lithuania's security development from the start. Indeed, the CSCE helped to pave the way for the peaceful revolutions that eventually overtook the Soviet Empire by demanding that the Soviet Union take *glasnost* and *perestroika* seriously. Eventually that process also provided the mechanism for the Soviet (Russian) army's withdrawal from Lithuania and other Baltic States. The evidence for this is the fact that Boris Yeltsin's decision to withdraw Russian troops from Lithuania was made in Helsinki. The Helsinki Second Summit in 1992 provided the international opportunity for its realization. Yet, as we examine its documentation, it is interesting to observe that Russia did not so much demonstrate a willingness to comply with the norms and ethics of international behavior in signing the eventual withdrawal agreement, as it used the occasion to indicate its reluctance to be excluded from the continuing process of European security development. In this light Yeltsin had no other choice than to bow before the friendly pressure of the international community or "miss a chance for photo opportunities."[25]

To outline the evolution of the current security position of Lithuania, being a full member of NATO, inevitably raises questions as to how the country has achieved this status. The Vilnius process, or the speaking in one voice of ten candidate states, seeking NATO membership, was initiated by Lithuania. The Baltic American communities lobbied actively for a positive outcome to the enlargement of the Atlantic Alliance. The importance of Lithuania's invitation to join NATO in the second wave of the organization's enlargement in 2002 reflected the fact that NATO countries had decided to anchor the newly liberated democracies to the West. Without participation at this level, it could be assumed that the

---

25   See *The Baltic Independent*, July 17 - 23, 1992, p. 7.

country had been relegated to a 'second tier' in national status within the European family of nations, remaining therefore in a 'grey area of insecurity' or within a 'cordon sanitaire' surrounding Russia. This fate has now been overcome and the enlargement of NATO has contributed greatly to European stability and security. To have excluded Lithuania and the other Baltic States would have suggested a return to the position determined by the Molotov-Ribbentrop pact, the division of Europe into the zones of Russian and Western spheres of influence, with the effective destabilization of Europe as a result. The North Atlantic Alliance implemented a historic opportunity to increase European security and stability in the Baltic Sea region by its acceptance of the Baltic States into membership, and Lithuania was one of the best-prepared candidate countries of the region. This work argues that for Lithuania and for Europe as a whole, as well as for all the transatlantic Alliance, this was an opportunity which was not to be missed. This study also argues that the significant threats to the region and to Europe as well as to all Alliance, including the United States, coupled with Russian expansionist energy policies and continuous occupation of the Königsberg (Kaliningrad) area by Russian military and security troops, cannot be longer ignored. Therefore, this monograph claims that increasingly active American involvement in Europe's defense is crucially important for European and transatlantic security and stability and it is within the long-term interests of the United States both.

2. Lithuania's European Roots

It is always necessary to comprehend the history of a nation before it is possible to understand its people's response to crisis. This is particularly true of Lithuania, which has an exceptional awareness of its long history and the contribution it has made to the development of Europe. Ernest J. Harrison, formerly British Vice Consul in Kaunas and Vilnius, wrote that "Lithuania is not a 'new state' of Europe either politically or culturally" in 1944, after the second Soviet occupation of the Baltic states, adding that "she is as old as most of the other European nations, and possesses a striking history replete with dramatic vicissitudes." These comments recall the fact that Lithuania emerged as a Christian kingdom in Europe over seven centuries ago, and significantly earlier than Columbus' discovery of America. Her territorial enlargement began as a defense against the Teutonic Order. Later, over several centuries, Lithuania built an empire, which stretched from the Baltic to the Black Seas, and which was notable for its religious, cultural and linguistic tolerance. This greater Lithuanian state is particularly remembered for having held the German drive to the east in check for over five centuries, and for preserving Europe against the simultaneous attacks of the Tartar Golden Horde and the Muscovite Slavs. The nation's conversion to Christianity strengthened the state, and defined its future cultural disposition as western, in clear distinction from the Eastern Orthodoxy of the embryonic Russian state. Within a few generations of this conversion, and notably from the fifteenth century onward, Lithuania's cultural formation clearly identified the nation indivisibly as a part of western European civilization.

Lithuania's distant battle to protect Europe from the invasion of the Tartars has shaped the country's character. Harrison pointed out that the martial prowess of the Lithuanians kept the West from the thralldom which had been imposed upon Russia, and that this defensive action was therefore of considerable importance to the history of European civilization. In 1363 the Grand Duke Algirdas won the decisive 'Battle of the Blue Waters', at a site close to the Black Sea, and more than a thousand miles to the southeast of the

Lithuanian capital Vilnius. As a result, the lands of Kiev and Podol passed to the Lithuanians. Six centuries later, these Ukrainian lands again took a new direction under Lithuania's influence, this time in their declaration of independence from the Soviet Union. These are interesting parallels, as Lithuania's role in the transformation of European political development between 1988 and 1991 was again crucial. The peaceful demonstrations which defended democracy against the Soviet tanks at this time contributed greatly to the liberation of Lithuania, and eventually removed a problem for Europe because the Soviet Union ceased to exist because of the events which followed. At the Vilnius conference on the reintegration of Lithuania into the West in 1998, Vytautas Landsbergis, then President of Lithuania's Parliament, and the leader of Sąjūdis' peaceful revolution in 1988-1990, pointed out the significance of what had happened, saying "we have contributed to your security, we are saying to the West, and you were able to save billions, hundreds of billions" of dollars.

A deeper knowledge of Lithuanian history might have encouraged Gorbachev to steer a different course rather than harden his resolve to keep Lithuania within the Soviet orbit in 1990-1991. He would then have realized that the statehood traditions and historical memory of the Lithuanians were such that Lithuania was bound to continue its attempt to restore its independence. Russia had occupied Lithuania on four previous occasions in the 17th, 18th, 19th, and 20th centuries, but was forced to leave the country each time. Despite the policy of russification, and its associated terror, each succeeding generations of Lithuanians had rebelled in the years 1794-5; 1812; 1831; 1863-4; 1905; 1918-20; 1941; and 1944-1956. It was the memory of these revolts, and the recollection of other struggles and victories, which shaped the nation's unyielding wish for independence at the end of the 1980s. Alfredas Bumblauskas, a contemporary Lithuanian historian, has observed that the most important pillar of the historical consciousness which underlay these Lithuanian rebellions was the memory of the battle of Tannenberg (Žalgiris, in Lithuanian; Grünwald in German) in 1410, when the Grand Duke of Lithuania Vytautas Magnus in alliance with his cousin Jogaila, the Lithuanian King of Poland, won a truly decisive battle against the German Teutonic Order, thereby consolidating Lithuania's domination of the region between the Baltic and the Black Sea for centuries. Under modern conditions, however, Lithuanians were not fighting to create a new empire but were rather promoting democracy and freedom for themselves and their neighbors. It was simply that they knew that history confirmed their place in the world as an independent nation which deserved the dignity of self-determination and respect, as well as the right of existing as an independent democratic European state. The Lithuanians also wish to open this road to freedom for their neighbors.

Early history and the first state

It will be useful at this point to examine the origins of the Lithuanian people and their determination at various stages in their history to resist absorption, whether from German, Russian, or Polish expansionism. Their origins have long been debated, but one thing is clear: that Lithuanians do not belong to the Slavic or German ethnic groups. The European discovery of the classical Indian language of Sanskrit during the eighteenth century, led to the finding of obvious similarities between Lithuanian and Sanskrit. Marija Gimbutas, noting the particularly archaic character of Lithuanian and the related Old Prussian languages as well as archeological evidence, has suggested that the ancient common forefathers of the Baltic and the Indian peoples must have lived in the Eurasian steppes over 4,000 years ago, and that archaic language forms survived in Lithuania because the Lithuanians lived "a secluded life in forests, removed from major routes of many subsequent migrations." This reconstruction is one that still needs to receive widespread acceptance.

Current archaeological research indicates that Baltic people during the Early and Middle Bronze Age inhabited a vast area stretching from the rivers Oder and Vistula, as far as the Ural Mountains in central Russia. The nature of settlement in these territories was scattered and it is interesting to note that even during recorded history the Lithuanian army of the mediaeval period often found isolated settlements, islands of Lithuanian language and culture, preserved from earlier centuries amid the much more brutal and powerful Slavic world and deep into the territories of what is now Russia.

While the memory of the more ancient history of Lithuania is often left to the speculative reconstruction of archaeologists, its long extension reflects a significant strain in the national character, not least because the musical and folklore traditions of the nation reflect continuity from former ages. Importantly, the historical record also shows a continuity of those ancient traditions. The earliest documentary mention of Lithuania dates from 1009, in the annals of the German Benedictine abbey at Quedlinburg in Thuringia and tells of the Crusade conducted by the Teutonic and Livonian Orders, in which Christian knights used techniques originating in the crusades against the Arabs, to force the pagan Baltic peoples to accept Christianity. While most of the other Baltic nations lost control of their territories, or disappeared because of assimilation and conquest, the Lithuanians managed to create their own independent state, under Grand Duke Mindaugas in 1248. These events mark the starting point of the statehood identity, which was to become a driving force in Lithuanian historical determination. King Mindaugas was the real founder of the Lithuanian state and the first ruler formally to introduce Christianity into Lithuania. His success in gathering the Lithuanian lands together into a single united kingdom, and defending them against the German Knights of the Sword, was based on a significant battle near Šiauliai in 1236, where he succeeded in destroying a whole army. He then expanded the Lithuanian lands eastward into the territories of what later became Byelorussia, Ukraine, and Russia.

It was King Mindaugas who consolidated the first Lithuanian state and began its eastern expansion. Its conversion to Christianity was a singular act of realpolitik, which brought papal recognition and permission to be crowned King of Lithuania, an event that took place on July 6, 1253. This date is now commemorated as a national holiday in Lithuania. By this act Mindaugas was acknowledged as a Christian monarch and crowned according to the customary law of Europe. It was a legal recognition from which the later claims to state independence ultimately derived their authority, even though the vicissitudes of history deprived the nation of an autonomous existence at several stages.

Two other famous Lithuanian dukes, Vytenis and Gediminas, greatly strengthened the Lithuanian state. Gediminas (c.1316-1341) and his successors finally established Lithuania as a great power in Eastern Europe. The founder of a dynasty that ruled Lithuania and Poland until 1572, Gediminas, like Mindaugas, focused his foreign policy on protecting Lithuania from the Teutonic Order in the west and enlarging the territory of the state in the east. Preferring diplomacy to war in pursuing Lithuania's foreign policy goals, and through a series of diplomatic marriages arranged for each of his seven sons, he managed to enlarge Lithuania peacefully by acquiring the lands of Vitebsk and other west Russian principalities. Regarded as the true founder of Vilnius, the capital and cultural center of Lithuania, he is also remembered for his attempts to Europeanize the country by inviting free citizens, doctors, monks, nuns, and merchants, and guaranteeing them the rights they enjoyed in the West. Gediminas' tolerant attitudes toward religion brought growing Western European influence into the Grand Duchy as he consciously expanded political and commercial ties with the West, stimulating urban life and trade, and developing the country's administration and army.

His son Algirdas (c.1345-1377) and his brother Kęstutis (c.1381-1382) continued their father's policy. They supported each other against dangerous attacks from the Teutonic Order. Algirdas was mainly concerned with Lithuania's Eastern policy, while Kęstutis defended vulnerable Lithuanian territory in the West, dedicating his entire life to the defense of his country.

Lithuania: A Great Medieval Power

Grand Duke Vytautas Didysis, Vytautas Magnus (c.1392-1430), was medieval Lithuania's most important ruler. It is likely that Algirdas' son Jogaila, who became King of Poland, was himself responsible for the murder of the Grand Duke Kęstutis, father of Vytautas

Magnus, in 1382. He also ensured that Vytautas was imprisoned following the death of his father, a move that allowed him to usurp the Grand Duchy. However, Vytautas escaped and took refuge with the Teutonic Order with whose support he waged a long campaign against his cousin Jogaila to gain the throne of the Grand Duchy for himself. After 1383, when Vytautas was baptized, he was reconciled with Jogaila in 1392 and turned against the Teutonic Order which lost the ideological motivation for its aggression against Lithuania when the country accepted Christianity in 1387 once again. In the 1390s, Vytautas undertook the Grand Duchy's expansion to the east, having married his daughter Sophia to the Grand Prince of Moscow, Vasili I. Vytautas resisted, but failed to subdue the Golden Horde, when his army suffered a crushing defeat at their hands in 1399 at the Battle of Vorksala. Eleven years later his greatest victory was won against the Teutonic Knights at the Žalgirio, Grünwald, battle on July 15, 1410. This led to the establishment of a border with Prussia, which remained secure for the next five centuries.

During the reign of Vytautas, Lithuania became the largest European state of the fifteenth century. The Grand Duchy was ruled independently from Poland during his lifetime, and Vytautas had hoped to be crowned King, though the Poles opposed this. They even robbed the representatives carrying the documents and the crown, sent by the Holy Roman Emperor Sigismund (c.1433-1437) for his coronation and they did not allow the envoys to enter Poland on their way to Lithuania, so the scheduled ceremony in Vilnius on September 8, 1430, could not take place.

After Vytautas' death on October 27 the same year, the influence of Polish culture and language among the powerful noble families in Lithuania increased greatly. Within two decades of his death the tensions between Lithuania and Poland came to a head over the election of the thirteen-year-old Duke Casimir to the Grand Ducal title by the Lithuanian nobles in 1440. The dispute was protracted but was eventually resolved in 1447 when the Poles accepted that the Grand Duke of Lithuania should also become elected as King of Poland. Acceptance of the arrangement by the Lithuanians involved new guarantees for their territorial integrity and political autonomy. Yet, while the deal had every appearance of consolidating Lithuania's position, the continuation of the dynastic link with Poland was ultimately to the country's disadvantage because of the weakening of statehood and polonisation of the nobility. Its consequences led to the beginning of a dynastic dominance of Central Europe that continued into the sixteenth century, but Casimir was probably the last Lithuanian-speaking Grand Duke of Lithuania.

When Casimir died in 1492, he had reigned for fifty-two years. His son Alexander was elected Grand Duke of Lithuania and later Sigismund, also known as Sigismund the Elder, succeeded in October 1506. Sigismund the Elder (1467-1548) was also crowned King of Poland the same year. Russia then emerged as the major security threat for Lithuania and the reign of Alexander and Sigismund the Elder was marked by four major wars with the Muscovites in 1492-1494, 1500-1503, 1507-1508, and in 1512-1522, when Lithuania lost its eastern lands of Smolensk. His major success was the decisive defeat of the Teutonic Order in 1521. This victory set the scene for the secularization of the Order's lands, when its Grand Master converted to Protestantism, a move that led to the emergence of the Duchy of Prussia. His marriage to Bona Sforza (1494-1557), a daughter of the Duke of Milan, in 1518 helped the arrival of the new Renaissance culture in Lithuania, a development which continued on his succession.

Renaissance Lithuania

The mediaeval period from the founding of the state to the Renaissance has left modern Lithuania with a historical memory of a great nation, which dealt with contemporary affairs as a major power. The Renaissance period that began during the reigns of Grand Dukes Sigismund and Sigismund Augustus, saw Lithuania's intellectual, merchant, and social culture being decisively drawn into the patterns characteristic of western European culture and civilization. Sigismund Augustus (c.1544-1572) was the last ruler of the Jogailan dynasty to have been born in Grand Duke Gediminas' Palace in Vilnius, and his marriage to Elizabeth of Habsburg, daughter

of the future Holy Roman Emperor Ferdinand I, reflected an openness to broader western influences. He stimulated trade and man-
ufacturing, and guided taste by his patronage and sponsorship of
Renaissance architecture in the construction of the Lower Castle in
the center of Vilnius. He also encouraged agricultural reform, but
faced prolonged war against Ivan the Terrible, the ruler of Mos-
covy. Though the contested territories were brought back under
Lithuanian rule, his childlessness led to the creation of the Commonwealth of the Grand Duchy of Lithuania and the Kingdom of
Poland which was achieved through the Union of Lublin in 1569. It
was a move that confirmed Lithuania's independence in administrative, military, judicial, and foreign affairs within the joint state,
but it led to an accelerated polonisation of the Lithuanian nobility,
a process which was seriously to weaken the state and one which
embroiled the country in subsequent disastrous consequences.

The Union of Lublin declared the establishment of the Commonwealth of Poland and Lithuania, as "one inseparable body." It
foresaw the establishment of a Senate in Warsaw, the standardiza-
tion of coinage, and a common foreign policy, but prevented Poles
from owning real estate in Lithuania. Moreover, the Grand Duchy
retained a separate army, treasury, and coat of arms. However,
Lithuania lost over a third of its territory and rapid cultural polonisation followed. This Lithuanian-Polish Commonwealth survived
until 1795, but Lithuanians later perceived it as having led to a
weakening of their nation and as a tragedy, as its inception caused
Lithuania's political and military decline under the provisions that
were implemented. Increasing privileges for the nobility were demanded from the monarchy, a demand which was politically irre-
sistible because of an elective principle, and which saw the rulers
being chosen from among the Royal families of other European
states. Thus, Sigismund Augustus' death saw Henri of Valois, the
brother of the French King, elected to the throne for two years, to
be followed by the Hungarian, Duke Stefan Bator, who took the
throne after Henri of Valois had returned to rule France as King
Henry III. However, the reign of Stefan Bator witnessed the establishment of Vilnius University, the first university in the Baltic

region, by the Jesuits in 1579, which brought the culture of the Counter-Reformation to Lithuania. It came without its religious turmoil, as he had protected Didžiosios Lietuvos Kunigaikštystės Statutą, the Statute of the Grand Duchy of Lithuania of 1573, which established the state's attitude to personal religious attachments, and is noteworthy as the first statute of complete religious tolerance in European history.

The dawn of the eighteenth century, which saw the beginning of major tensions with the emergent Russian state, and which structured the later determination of the nation, never to be finally absorbed by its Slavic eastern neighbor. During the first decades of the century, the Swedish King Sigismund III Vasa, the son of a sister of Stefan Bator's wife Anna, took the throne of Lithuania. His election, however, triggered Muscovite invasions into Lithuanian territory. Vilnius was twice occupied by the Russians, first in 1613, and again in 1655, when the Lithuanian-Polish Commonwealth was embroiled in war with the King's Lutheran enemies in Sweden. This first incursion was reversed in 1629, when the new protestant Swedish ruler, Gustavus Adolphus, occupied Livonia, then a vassal state of the Lithuanian-Polish Commonwealth and repulsed the Russian invasion. However, twenty-six years later, in 1655, they invaded again and devastated the Grand Duchy. In response, the Lithuanians and Swedes entered into a dynastic union in Kėdainiai to consolidate their response, but by the end of the 1650s, the Swedes were again in retreat. Between then and the end of the century domestic chaos increased in Lithuania as the power of the aristocracy increased at the expense of the elected kings. Lithuanian interests became progressively subsumed in the terminal confusion of the Union.

Decline and disintegration

By the eighteenth century, internal disorder had increased, as the nobles battled for influence. The election of Augustus II in 1506 promised a profitable economic union of the territories of which he was sovereign, but he was indebted to Russia and Denmark for supporting his election. His vision was lost when they dragged him into a war with Sweden, which lasted for twenty-one years. The Swedes succeeded in removing him and replaced him with Stanislaw I Leszczynski (1704-1709), who was nothing more than a puppet of the Poles, and though Augustus II eventually regained his position with the support of Tsar Peter the Great, the result was that the state became a Russian protectorate. When he died in 1733, the former Swedish puppet was re-elected with French support, and the Russian and Saxon armies retaliated by invading again. A series of plagues then ravaged the Commonwealth, which was already devastated by these wars. In East Prussia almost half of the Lithuanian population died, leaving vast areas open for colonization by Germans. All attempts to end this political anarchy during the reign of the last Lithuanian-Polish monarch Stanislaw August Poniatowski (1764-1795) were opposed by Russia, which was determined to frustrate his attempt to establish effective government by introducing significant constitutional reform. He sought to abolish the liberum veto, a convention that allowed even a single member of the Seimas, Parliament to veto any measure put before it. It was a convention which effectively paralyzed executive power in the country but the move to strengthen the monarchy precipitated the anger of Catherine the Great, who saw great advantages in the continued weakness of her neighbor. She was unscrupulous in her manipulations toward ensuring that the Seimas passed a 'fundamental law' that protected the privileges which the King planned to remove. It also made the Empress of Russia the guarantor of these 'Polish liberties.' While her obvious interference led to an anti-Russian uprising in 1768; the conflict ended in 1772 in the first partition of the Lithuanian-Polish Union, when Russia, Prussia, and Austria seized substantial parts of its territory. The Grand Duchy of Lithuania now lost about a third of its territories, losing regions that Lithuanians had ruled for centuries.

This partition was the first of three, although twenty-one years passed before the process recommenced. During this period, new structures of government and a modernized taxation system were installed in the reduced territories by Stanislaus II and these helped commercial and industrial modernization to follow. The ideas of the Enlightenment also spread with royal patronage, and a government department of education was established, which undertook the reform of Vilnius University and the supervision of high schools. These developments were the first of their kind in Europe and were the product of intense discussion of the concepts of reform and democracy that enjoyed official support throughout Lithuania.

Nevertheless, the developments of this period led to the dismantling of the Lithuanian-Polish state and, eventually, the assimilation of the Grand Duchy into Tsarist dominions. However, many of the political characteristics and dispositions of the later Lithuanian state were formed as these ideas of reform and democracy permeated the middle and upper classes. Under these influences many landowners emancipated the peasants on their estates and the wide interest in democracy was stimulated by reports coming from the fledgling United States of America. These trends resulted in the adoption in May 1791 of a modern Constitution, embracing the Grand Duchy of Lithuania and Poland, the first of its kind in any part of Europe. It is important to note that this Constitution was a model that was emulated in revolutionary France two years afterwards. Its provisions were enlightened and forward-looking. Notably, it ended the liberum veto and expressed a 'people's sovereignty,' with the separation of executive, legislative and judicial power, and a government, answerable to parliament. The educated urban class was given the right to vote.

Unsurprisingly, the Russian Empress, the supreme autocrat, was stung by this development, which provoked Russia and Prussia to carry out the second partition of the Lithuanian and Polish Union in 1793, when opponents of the Constitution, supported by Russian forces, attacked the Union. Claiming that the government itself was threatened by these political developments, the Empress had sent an army to suppress the reform. In the following year, she and the Prussian King took further advantage of this oppressive intrusion, preparing a treaty which reduced the territories of the Lithuanian and Polish states by half. Lithuania then lost most of Byelorussia, including the city of Minsk, but the disaster provoked an uprising against Russian domination. Anti-Russian forces seized Warsaw and Vilnius, but the military forces of Prussia and Russia crushed the revolt. They occupied Warsaw in 1794, when Catherine called a conference to dismantle these two states. In the subsequent agreement Russia took all lands east of the river Nemunas, while Prussia and Austria divided the rest between them. In this carve-up Prussia gained the regions adjacent to East Prussia, including the ethnic Lithuanian lands south and west of the Nemunas river, but most of the Grand Duchy of Lithuania was incorporated into the Russian Empire. The Treaty of Partition was signed in January 1797 in St. Petersburg. As a result, Lithuania, Poland, and the Union between them were removed from the political map.

The significance of this phase of Lithuanian history for the subsequent development of the present discussion is that it determines the historical memories of Lithuanian national identity and demonstrates long periods of tension with the emerging Russian state. This ended in that phase of history with Lithuania being absorbed into the territories of what had become a Russian Empire, one which was to become greatly extended eastward. However, it remained highly protective of those western provinces which gave it access to the Baltic Sea. That these provinces were largely inhabited by native populations whose language and identity were not Russian was regarded by that power only as being an excuse for cultural suppression. It was the misfortune of the Lithuanian people to be caught up, along with their neighbors, in these persistent tensions. Thus, Lithuania remained an oppressed 'internal colony' of the Tsarist regime throughout the nineteenth century and even into the twentieth century. Though the Tsarist regime disappeared from history in the dramatic events of the 1917 Bolshevik revolution, the attitudes of the new communist rulers continued to embody the earlier policies of russification which emphatically denied any right of self-determination to its subject peoples. As will be seen, this present account reflects this fundamental theme and the Lithuanian determination to oppose it, which framed the struggle for liberation and independence.

National Self-awareness

Although the state apparatus of Lithuania had disappeared with the partition of the Lithuanian and Polish states, the oppression which followed did not suppress the Lithuanian nation's sense of distinctiveness. Indeed, it may even have sharpened the latent sense of national being as there was widespread popular resentment, accompanied by uprisings which swept the country. The first of these took place in 1830 - 1831 and was followed by the closing of Vilnius University. The second was in 1863 when the occupiers reacted with intensified policing and even more radical policies of russification, which included an edict to prohibit all publication, except in the Cyrillic alphabet. While these restrictions mostly affected the Lithuanian middle classes, the common people were constrained in a different way by the extension of serfdom. Though this condition was removed during the 1870s, in the relative liberalization of the Tsarist regime, which reflected the general development of the economy toward the end of the nineteenth century, it inflicted a general impoverishment on rural life, delaying social progress for many decades.

Toward the end of the nineteenth century, Lithuania saw a growth of bourgeois cultural expression, which was common to the urban centers of the Russian Empire. This movement brought a new awareness of the linguistic distinctiveness of the Lithuanian language as the effects of the Western European "enlightenment" which had taken place a hundred years earlier began to penetrate the educated classes. This cultural self-consciousness became more apparent in Lithuania, where resentment of Russian rule now combined with a new national awareness to create the conditions in which patriotic movements, led by Dr. Jonas Basanavičius, Fr. Jonas Mačiulis – Maironis, and the poet Vincas Kudirka sprang into being. The appeal of these essentially nationalistic associations was limited at first but spread insistently. Ideas of liberal democracy and national self-expression fused in their activities, despite the brutal oppression by the Tsarist police. The stirrings of national consciousness were strengthened by the work of knygnešiai, or 'book-carriers', who risked exile in Siberia by smuggling books and newspapers printed in Lithuanian from the German-ruled area around the East Prussian university city of Königsberg (even women and children were among those patriots). These activities contributed to a linguistic renaissance among the cultivated urban class that had assimilated to polish influences at an earlier stage.

The ban on the Lithuanian press was finally lifted only in 1904. The relative relaxation of the Tsarist regime during the following decade created the conditions for a widespread patriotic revival, which was focused by a movement to repossess and standardize the ancient language of Lithuania and to give positive value to a cultural inheritance, previously interpreted as backward and rural. Those who were most active in this process were often the very intelligentsia whose education had been designed to alienate them from this background. Their commitment to the struggle for national identity was often intensified by a personal effort to repossess the language, which had been lost by an earlier generation, when speaking Lithuanian brought no social status or economic benefit. It was at this time that the foundation was laid which made a new Lithuanian state a practical possibility in the aftermath of the First World War.

Independence Achieved

The end of the First World War provided the opportunity to restore Lithuania's independence. The German army had occupied the country in 1915, after defeating the Tsarist armies in this region. In November 1914 a Committee to Assist the Victims of the War was founded in Vilnius. When the German occupation began, part of this group moved to St. Petersburg, where it began to perform the essential functions of a government-in-exile for Lithuanians displaced by the war. At first, the German military administration had planned to annex the country, but after the USA entered the war, the Kaiser began to respond to the national aspirations of the Central European nations. It was because of this shift in attitude that the German military administration allowed *Taryba*, or the National Council, to be convened in Vilnius on December 11, 1917. Its delegates, seizing the moment, proclaimed a resolution about the restoration of an independent Lithuanian state to rescue the nation from the chaotic forces which loomed in the face of the disintegration of the Russian autocracy and the impending defeat of Germany.

The *Taryba*, although it was at work on occupied territory, began to distance itself from Berlin as the war effort began to falter. When the war came to its end, it simply adapted its position in response to the changing circumstances, and on February 16, 1918, under the Chairmanship of Antanas Smetona, it proclaimed the restoration of the independent Lithuanian state based on democratic political structures. Germany recognized Lithuania on March 23, 1918, and during the next month complex political maneuvering took place between the Lithuanian authorities and the Germans, whose military forces were still present in Lithuania. However, the country received crucial financial support from Lithuanians in the United States and the Lithuanian intelligentsia in Western Europe lobbied the Allies for their country's independence. On November 11, 1918, the first Lithuanian cabinet took office under President Antanas Smetona with Augustinas Valdemaras as Prime Minister. Later the second Prime Minister, Mykolas Šleževičius, took further steps toward consolidating the new state by developing governmental structures at every level to fit the urgent need to defend the country.

The declaration of Lithuanian independence and the recognition of the new state did not bring sovereignty immediately. The situation was beset with danger, but it was necessary to defend what had been achieved, and this need brought the great achievements of Lithuania's past to the forefront in the minds of these political pioneers. Soon the growing military forces of Lithuania needed to defend the country against a Bolshevik invasion, attempting to establish a "Lithuanian-Belarus Soviet Republic." Fortunately, this experimental communist state named "Litbel" was short-lived but, while this threat was being dealt with, Lithuania was also attacked in the West by the well-equipped army of the so-called Bermondtists, who were attempting to recoup the Tsarist cause. No sooner than it had repulsed this attack, the new Republic of Lithuania was faced with a Polish invasion and an attempted coup d'état, as well as being beset by financial crisis. Again, the determined patriotism and military doggedness of the nation's leaders won through. The help of Latvian military support in the north of Lithuania must be noted, as it helped Lithuania to drive the Bolsheviks from the country. On July 12, 1920, a Peace Treaty was signed in Moscow between the Republic of Lithuania and Soviet Russia. In view of later developments, it is important to note here that the first Article of this Treaty stated that:

Russia recognizes without reservation the sovereign rights and independence of the Lithuanian State, with all the juridical consequences arising from such recognition, and voluntarily, and for all times abandons the sovereign rights of Russia over the Lithuanian people and their territory. The fact of the past subjection of Lithuania to Russia does not impose on the Lithuanian nation and its territory any liabilities whatsoever towards Russia.

The treaty was significant in legal terms because it was coordinated with the government which had succeeded the Tsarist regime and because it granted the regions of Gardinas, Suvalkai, and Augustavas to Lithuania. However, Lithuania was unable to secure the borders thus established. The Polish General Lucjan Zeligowski, acting under secret orders from his government, occupied the Lithuanian capital Vilnius and the surrounding region in September 1920. This occupation of Vilnius, the country's capital, complicated the relationship between Lithuania and Poland until the Second World War. It represented a major setback for the fledgling state.

The Years of the First Republic

Despite these troubled circumstances, the first Seimas, or Parliament of the Republic of Lithuania, began work on May 15, 1920. A new Constitution was adopted on August 1, 1922, having been drafted to reflect the democratic character and European identity of the Lithuanian Republic. Its preamble read:

In the name of Almighty God, the Lithuanian People, thankfully recalling the glorious efforts and noble sacrifices of its sons made to deliver the

Motherland, having recreated its state independence, and desiring to extend the firm democratic foundations of its independent life, to develop conditions of justice and equity, and to guarantee the equality, freedom, and well-being of all citizens, and suitable State protection for human labor and morality, through its authorized representatives.

The fundamentally democratic character of the principles guiding the Constitution's formation is apparent even from a brief selection of excerpts from its articles, e.g.:

(Art 1) The State of Lithuania is an independent democratic Republic. The sovereign power of the Republic belongs to the nation.

(Art 10) All Lithuanian citizens, men, and women, are equal before the law. Special privileges may not be accorded a citizen, nor his rights reduced on account of his origin, religion, or nationality.

(Art 97) Human labor is protected and safeguarded by special law. The State, by separate laws protects the workman in case of sickness, old age, and when work is insufficient.

(Art 100) Schools of all grades are accessible to all.

Yet, even as this Constitution was being written, the Polish occupation of Vilnius was being consolidated. Robbed of their capital city in this way, the Lithuanians established Kaunas as the state's temporary capital, and the government then faced major tasks in re-building the economy as well as in the creation of a national educational system. Now, for the first time, Lithuanian became the language of administration and of schooling, and every effort was directed toward the creation of a truly modern society. Rauch has observed of this period that "Lithuania made great strides in education. The number of primary schools increased from 1,036 in 1919 to 2,956 in 1939. The number of teachers increased, from 1,232 to 10,024, and the number of students from 45,540 to 379,233." Vytautas Magnus University was established in Kaunas at this time and a national press emerged, while literature, music, theatre, and other arts flourished. However, there were difficult undercurrents on the political front. The work of the legislators was necessarily rushed, and therefore somewhat chaotic, while the constant awareness of insidious underground activity by agents of Stalin's regime created an increasing security problem for the young democracy. Yet the political system was essentially rather weak and there was a threat of instability; the very existence of the state was at stake because it had its external enemies operating actively inside the country. Eventually, on December 17, 1926, to avoid the increasing possibility that left wing members of the Seimas would promote a communist takeover, a military coup took place in support of the Tautininkų, National Party and the Christian Democrats. As a result, Antanas Smetona, the leader of the Tautininkų Party, took control as President of the Republic.

The implications of this coup will be better understood if it is explained that during the period immediately before it took place, the Lithuanian intelligentsia who were opposed to Marxism and other extremes (socialism, national-socialism, and communism) had gathered around the periodical *Viltis*, "Hope" which had been established by President Antanas Smetona. The periodical *Viltis* was often controversial, not least because the Catholic Church was often suspicious of its liberal views in the atmosphere of the time. Antanas Smetona had served the Republic as its first President (between 1919 and 1920) and as its last one before the Soviet occupation (between 1926 and 1940). He had originally graduated in Law at St. Petersburg before returning to Vilnius as leader of the Lithuanian Democratic Party and had earlier been editor of the weekly *Lietuvos ūkininkas*, "the Lithuanian Farmer." Later Antanas Smetona became a famous contributor to the daily newspaper *Vilniaus naujienos*, "Vilnius News," and in 1907 he had founded a national liberation movement. During wartime in 1914-1915 he had established the fortnightly, *Vairas*, "The Steering Wheel".

Smetona was elected in 1917 as Chairman of the Lithuanian Council and from this position he went on to proclaim the Restoration of Lithuania, by declaring the establishment of the Independent Republic of Lithuania on February 16, 1918. He was elected as the first President of the Republic on April 4, 1919, and remained in that role until the convocation of the Constituent Assembly on June 19, 1920. His movement had failed to elect any representatives to Lithuania's parliament between 1920 and 1926, and Smetona, who was by now employed in teaching Greek at Vytautas Magnus University, became one of the loudest critics of the government. The crisis led him to the Presidency, when nationalist army officers took control of the President's residence, the Seimas, the Government House, and the headquarters of the army's General Staff on December 17, 1926. It was a pre-emptive action against the communist coup d'état and Stalin's take-over of the country as early as the late 1920s. The coalition government of President Kazys Grinius, who was faced with growing turmoil and rising pressure from the communists with little prospect of being successful, was removed from power. On being invited to take power by the officers of the Lithuanian army, Antanas Smetona became President for a second time. In 1927 he dismissed the Krikščioniai Demokratai (Christian Democrats) from government, dissolved the Parliament and initiated authoritarian governance. While these activities do not match our contemporary expectations of political leaders, it is important to read these historical developments in the context of a more authoritarian age. Smetona followed that authoritarian path even further in 1935, when all political parties were banned, but it should be noted that with few exceptions his government prosecuted only the extremes of right and left, the communists and the fascists, and indeed, Lithuania became the first European state to sentence Nazi activists to prison sentences. This was done with respect to offences committed in the Klaipėda region in 1935, where they were deeply involved in the process of separating this region from Lithuania in advancement of Nazi policies for expanding their recently announced Third Reich.

While the relationship of Lithuania with the Soviet Union had traditionally been good since the 1920 Treaty, Lithuania now found itself in a very unfavorable geopolitical situation at the crossroads of potential Russian-German confrontation. This worsening situation was complicated by Polish ambitions with respect to Lithuania. Lithuania's Soviet policy had developed in cognizance of this ambition and was based on hostility toward Poland, which was focused by the Vilnius question, following the Polish seizure of Lithuania's capital in 1920. The fact that the Soviet Union was the only power at that time to recognize the legitimate interests of Lithuania in Vilnius and the surrounding region was the basis of this stance. As a result, there were practically no relations between Lithuania and Poland, the countries being technically in a state of war, a situation which continued until Poland issued an ultimatum to establish diplomatic relations on March 17, 1938. It should be noted that this anti-Polish policy provided common ground for Lithuania's relationship with Germany. During the 1920s, Weimar Germany had been Lithuania's most important partner in many respects and Germany was still the major trading partner for Lithuania. The relationship clearly had mutual advantages, and it has been observed that "Germany and Lithuania had a unique opportunity for co-operation in the Klaipėda territory, which Lithuania had acquired with Berlin's tacit support." Indeed, because of German interest in Lithuania, the country was left to balance between the Soviet Union and Germany, for whom an anti-Polish Lithuania "was an important protection for East Prussia and a natural ally in case of war with Poland. Furthermore, Lithuanian hostility toward Poland prevented the formation of a cordon sanitaire under Polish leadership as a barrier between Germany and Russia. On this count, the policies of Berlin and Moscow concurred."

We must note that Poland's seizure of Vilnius in 1920 had not only spoiled Lithuanian-Polish relations, but now acted to prevent the formation of a closer Baltic alliance. It was a situation which increasingly worked not only against the interests of the Baltic States, but of Poland itself, as it created a permanent source of tension in the region. This was increasingly exploited by Moscow. While Latvia, Estonia, and Finland gravitated toward Warsaw to counter Soviet expansionism, Lithuania naturally looked for allies elsewhere. "The Lithuanians thus chose to play the Soviet card and shelved the idea of a Baltic entente." These dispositions were a dangerous feature in a developing situation. They were certainly influential when Lithuania concluded a non-aggression and neutrality treaty with the Soviet Union on September 28, 1926, when the Soviet Union recognized Lithuania's sovereignty in the Vilnius region. However, there were hidden implications in this agreement. Its negotiators had simultaneously and secretly assured Germany that the pact would not affect Germany's interest in the Klaipėda territory. This Treaty was twice renewed for five years on each occasion, in 1931 and in 1936, and its most notable provision was stated in its first Article: "The relations between the Union of Socialist Soviet Republics and the Lithuanian Republic shall continue to be based on the Treaty of Peace between Lithuania and Russia, concluded at Moscow on July 12, 1920, all the provisions of which shall remain in force and inviolability."

Baltic Cooperation

Other details of Lithuania's Non-Aggression Treaty with the Soviet Union are also worthy of attention. Under Article 2, the Soviet Union and Lithuania entered into a mutual agreement to guarantee the integrity and inviolability of their territories, while Article 3 stated that both parties mutually renounced every possible act of aggression which might be undertaken by one against the other and agreed to observe strict neutrality if either of them should be attacked by a third party. Under Article 4, both states undertook the obligation not to adhere to any agreement or coalition formed between the third parties with a view to the economic or financial boycott of either of the contracting parties. This non-aggression pact strengthened Lithuania's feeling of security, though its promulgation "occasioned great surprise throughout Europe" as "Lithuania was perceived as having weakened Europe's united front against Bolshevik Russia." Interestingly, however, similar non-aggression treaties with the Soviet Union were signed by Finland six years later in January 1932, and by Latvia and Estonia in February and in May of the same year. These details were, however, not the end of the story. Later in the 1930s Finland gravitated by degree towards the Scandinavian countries, while Estonia, Latvia, and Lithuania drew closer to each other. Following their admission as members of the League of Nations, each of these three countries, together with Finland, practiced a concerted policy in Geneva, and there was developing Baltic co-operation. On February 17, 1934, Estonia and Latvia signed a treaty of the Baltic Alliance, and on April 25 Lithuania sent a memorandum to those countries outlining principles for strengthening the solidarity of the Baltic States. Following this, and only five days later, Estonia and Latvia together invited

Lithuania to join in the Alliance, on May 1, 1934. Later in the same year, Ministers of Foreign Affairs conversed in Kaunas and Riga, and on September 12, 1934, Lithuania, Latvia, and Estonia jointly agreed to a "Treaty of Collaboration and Understanding" (known as the Charter of the Baltic Entente) in Geneva.

The declared purpose of this Baltic Entente was "to contribute to the maintenance and guarantee of peace, and to co-ordinate their foreign policy in the spirit of the principles of the Covenant of the League of Nations." Its signatories searched for unity in foreign policy and international relations, but also attempted to form an economic community, promoting collaboration in the administrative, judicial, and social spheres. After the Entente was signed on November 3, 1934, Lithuania, Latvia, and Estonia maintained regular mutual consultation through conferences of their Foreign Ministers to co-ordinate foreign and domestic policy, and nine of these were held between 1934 and 1940. As a result, the three states accepted the policy of neutrality, each of them adopting a new neutrality law modelled on the provisions already existing between the Nordic countries. In Estonia this was passed into law on December 6, 1938; and Latvian Parliament passed the provision on December 21, 1938. The Lithuanian Seimas repeated the proceedings on January 25, 1939. The Baltic States were idealistic enough to believe that they could maintain their independence by being neutral. History informs us that this was a naïve hope.

Klaipėda Lost

At the time this carefully formulated neutrality of the Baltic States was immediately recognized both by the Soviet Union and Germany, the major powers in the region. However, Lithuanian-German relations were increasingly strained throughout the 1930s over the Klaipėda region, and this tension came to a head when the Lithuanian Government concluded the first Nazi activist trial in Europe on March 26, 1935. No sooner had the verdicts been delivered than Nazi Germany responded with the introduction of economic sanctions against Lithuania, and on March 20, 1939, Joachim von Ribbentrop, the German Foreign Minister, presented an ultimatum to his Lithuanian counterpart Juozas Urbšys, requiring the cession of the territory of Klaipėda to the German Reich. The terms were thuggishly direct: "Either Lithuania surrenders Memel (the Klaipėda) region to Germany, or the Wermacht moves in" was the message. "In the latter case," Ribbentrop warned, "no one could say where the Wehrmacht would stop." Thomas Chase has described Lithuania's plight in clear terms: "In those days, when the appeasement policy flourished in European politics, the Lithuanian Government had little choice, but to accept this ultimatum." Thomas H. Preston, the British Chargé d'Affairs in Kaunas, summarized the Lithuanian situation as being "between the devil and the deep sea," but despite this sympathetic comment, there was no practical help to be obtained from London, and attempts to secure some military support from Great Britain failed. Bronius Kazys Balutis, the Lithuanian Ambassador in London, inquired of the British Government: "If now or in the future the Lithuanian Government were faced with far-reaching demands going beyond the question of Memel and affecting the political or economic independence of what remained of Lithuania, would the attitude of His Majesty's Government be the same as in the question of Memel, or could the Lithuanian Government hope for a greater measure of assistance from them?" To this Lord Halifax replied only: "That this was a part of the general question of the attitude to be adopted towards the German threat to the independence of other nations."

It might have been thought at this juncture that the issue between Lithuania and Germany had been resolved. As Bronis Kaslas has commented: "By settling the problem of Memel, Lithuania felt that she then was relieving all possible causes of conflict between Germany and herself." After all, Article 4 of the German-Lithuanian Treaty had stated: "To strengthen their decisions to assure amicable development of relations between Germany and Lithuania, the two countries undertake not to resort the use of force against each other and pledge not to support the use of force by an outside state against one of the two countries." Thus, Lithuania's new treaty with Germany by which Memel was relinquished, signed on March 22, 1939, was supposed to secure the German promise to respect Lithuania's neutral status. Indeed, if only briefly, Germany thereafter appeared to attempt to improve bilateral relations with Lithuania by taking Lithuania's economic interests in the region into account. However, Lithuania and the other Baltic States were only pawns in a Soviet–Nazi embrace, which was rapidly proceeding towards a horrifying conclusion.

The Soviet–Nazi pact

At this stage, in the first quarter of 1939, Soviet foreign policy expected German aggression to be directed towards the West, rather than the East. The Soviet Chargé d'Affaires in Berlin, Georgi Astakhov, expressed great interest in the Baltic region and insisted that "the question of spheres of influence was the essential component of any political agreement with the Reich." Ernst von Weizsäcker, German Secretary of the Foreign Ministry, wrote to the German Ambassador in Moscow Count Friedrich Werner von der Schulenburg stating that "if the talk (with Molotov) proceeds positively in the Baltic question too, the idea could be advanced that we will adjust our stand with regard to the Baltic in such a manner as to respect the vital Soviet interests in the Baltic." Later, on August 3, German Foreign Minister Joachim von Ribbentrop cabled Ambassador Count von der Schulenburg to say that "there was no problem from the Baltic to the Black Sea that could not be solved" between the Reich and the Soviet Union, and that "there was no room for the two of us on the Baltic and that Russian interests by no means needed to clash with ours there." Ambassador Schulenburg reported after this that he had stressed to Astakhov the absence of opposition of interests in foreign policy and mentioned German readiness thus to orient their behavior regarding the Baltic States, if the occasion arose, as to safeguard vital Soviet Baltic interests. At the mention of the Baltic States, Molotov was interested in learning "what states we meant by the term, and whether Lithuania was one of them."

It would seem from these exchanges that there was a developing rapport between the two sides, and indeed this is confirmed by the fact that on August 23, 1939, the Soviet Union and Nazi

Germany signed the now notorious "mutual Non-Aggression Pact," which divided the continent of Europe into zones of communist and Nazi influence. It is now known that during Ribbentrop's visit to Moscow, "the settlement of spheres of interest in the Baltic area" had been at the forefront of issues to be resolved. Thus, Lithuania was assigned to the German sphere, while the other Baltic States went to the USSR, the concluding factor perhaps being that Lithuania did not have a border with the USSR. Once Klaipėda had been seized by Germany, the Soviets possibly did not perceive their immediate vital security interests as lying there. So, the first secret protocol provided for the delineation of the partners' respective spheres of interest in the Baltic States (Lithuania, Latvia, Estonia, and Finland), Poland, and South-eastern Europe. The Lithuanian-Latvian border was defined as forming "the boundary of the spheres of influence of Germany and USSR," and both sides recognized "the interest of Lithuania in the Vilnius area." Although it was agreed that Poland was to be divided along the Narva, Vistula, and San rivers, there was agreement that there were further issues to be settled. In fact, Germany was preparing to incorporate Lithuania into its protectorate system. Thus, on August 29, 1939, Germany's Government demanded from Lithuania "unimpeachable neutrality," asking that Germany and Lithuania conclude a military convention, that a permanent German military commission be dispatched to Lithuania and that the strength and distribution, as well as the equipment, of the Lithuanian army be regularly determined in close agreement with the High Command of the Wehrmacht. Contrary, Lithuania continued its policy of strict neutrality towards Germany as well as Poland.

The German Government now invited the Lithuanian Foreign Minister Juozas Urbšys for a secret visit to encourage Lithuania's take-over of the Vilnius region. Von Weizsäcker directed the German Ambassador in Vilnius:

> In conversations with the Lithuanian Government, you are requested to express still more clearly than has already been done … our sympathies with Lithuanian aspirations to the Vilna area, and to state the view that, in the event of a territorial rearrangement taking place between Germany and

Poland, any Lithuanian claims to the Vilna area might also to a large extent
be taken into consideration.

Despite this prompting, the Lithuanian Government did not
wish to abrogate its policy of strict neutrality. For this reason, its
Foreign Minister's trip to Germany was delayed. Further, even
though the German Ambassador had told the Lithuanian Foreign
Ministry that he was aware "as General Raštikis has informed [our]
Military Attaché in the strictest confidence, the military measures
taken consisted almost exclusively of troop reinforcements along
the Polish frontier," the Lithuanian army did not move further. The
situation was clearly a very difficult one, but as the Lithuanian Foreign Minister of that time Juozas Urbšys told the author personally
in 1989: "We did everything we could to swim out of a rocky river."
The important fact remains, however, that Lithuania did not move
to regain its capital Vilnius from neighboring Poland, despite having full knowledge of German approval and indeed inducement.
Alternative opinions are still held about whether Lithuania might
have prevented the subsequent occupation of that region by the Soviet Union if she had sent her forces into the Vilnius region when
the Poles were forced to withdraw their army to fight the Germans
in the West. Some have also suggested that Lithuania might have
escaped the Soviet occupation, which came in 1940, had she remained in the German zone of influence at that time. However,
these interesting speculations serve only to emphasise the importance of the issues which lay in the balance at that most difficult
stage.

On September 17, 1939, Soviet troops crossed the Polish-So-
viet border and marched toward Vilnius, which was quickly occupied along with its region. When the Lithuanian Envoy in Moscow
Dr. Ladas Natkevičius met Molotov to enquire into the situation
two days later, the Soviet Foreign Commissar laconically explained
that "Soviet Russia never forgot Vilnius, and she will also not forget
friendly Lithuania…". Meanwhile, in Germany, Lithuanian Envoy
Colonel Kazys Škirpa met Joachim von Ribbentrop on September
20, 1939, and he was told that the question of Vilnius would be
raised in the discussions with Stalin and Molotov, based on the

agreement by both sides that the Vilnius region should be returned to Lithuania. However, Ribbentrop also stated that Lithuania remained in the German sphere of interests, indicating that he wanted to invite Lithuanian Foreign Minister Juozas Urbšys to visit him in Poland. His Foreign Ministry then drafted a defense agreement between the German Reich and the Republic of Lithuania, but, according to Kazys Škirpa, Lithuania failed to seize this last fragile chance to save the independence. Juozas Urbšys replied by written note to Joachim von Ribbentrop, affirming Lithuania's continuing neutrality. He also gave information about a planned visit to Sopot to Nikolai Pozdniakov, the Soviet Representative in Kaunas. As a result, the Germans asked Urbšys to delay this visit which in fact never took place.

At this juncture, a new dynamic manifested itself suddenly, when Stalin proposed that Hitler should give up the German claim to Lithuania in exchange for a strip of Polish territory, previously assigned to the Russian sphere. Being agreed, this proposal was incorporated in another secret protocol, signed on September 28, 1939 and following immediately after the Soviet Union's occupation of eastern Poland on September 17, 1939. Initially, this protocol provided that the region around Marijampolė, a small portion of Lithuania with an area of around 1,800 square kilometers, should still belong to Germany (see Map 5 in the Appendices). Later however, after protracted negotiations, the Germans relinquished the Lithuanian territory, when Russia paid 7,500,000 golden dollars for this transfer. Viacheslav Molotov and Ambassador Count von der Schulenburg then signed the "third secret protocol" on January 10, 1941, but by then the Soviet Union had already occupied Lithuania.

Soviet occupation

The process, which ended with Lithuania's incorporation into the Soviet Union, started on October 3, 1939, with an ultimatum demanding that the Lithuanian Government should sign three treaties; the first of which was a pact of mutual assistance; the second, an acceptance of the transfer of Vilnius and its region to Lithuania. The third concerned the cession of a part of south-western

Lithuania, known as the 'Marijampolė strip,' to Germany. To accomplish this, Stalin called Foreign Minister Juozas Urbšys to Moscow, where he was faced with the further demand that Lithuania admit about 50,000 Red Army troops to her territory to establish Soviet military bases there. Even though the Soviet Union had proposed to return the Vilnius region to Lithuania, President Antanas Smetona objected the Soviet ultimatum advising that the costs were too high and suggesting that it should be declined, but the Government had accepted the ultimatum, facing complete occupation of the country. Lithuania was not alone in facing this indignity, as treaties of the same character had already been imposed on Estonia on September 28, 1939, and on Latvia on October 5, 1939. Although a united Baltic anti-Bolshevik front could be imagined, it did not emerge. In Lithuania's case, there were protracted negotiations in the Kremlin, and the number of the troops to be based in Lithuania was reduced to 20,000 as a result. Also, the Soviet Union undertook the obligation "to respect Lithuania's independence and neutrality." Despite this, it was passed barely six months later, when Moscow suddenly accused Lithuania of kidnapping Soviet soldiers from the military bases and demanded a change of government. On June 14, 1940, at the time when the German army reached Paris, Foreign Minister Juozas Urbšys was confronted with the further ultimatum "that free entry into the territory of Lithuania be immediately assured for units of the army of the Soviet Union, which will be stationed in the most important centers of Lithuania." Bronis Kaslas has observed of Lithuania's response, that she "accepted the ultimatum on condition that her President will be able to designate the person whom he considered most qualified to head the new government" but in reality the President left the meeting of the Government in protest. It appointed, early on the morning of June 15, General Stasys Raštikis the new Prime Minister. Molotov informed Urbšys within hours that "this choice would be unacceptable." The President of Lithuania, Molotov dictated, "must consult with Deputy-Commissar of Foreign Affairs Vladimir Dekanozov." Dekanozov was on his way to Kaunas before another selection was made, but President Antanas Smetona refused to accept the Soviet ultimatum. He left the country in protest later that afternoon on the same day, June 15, 1940. The Soviet army formally occupied the country, and Commissar Dekanozov appointed both the new "Peoples' Government," and only two days later its Prime Minister Justas Paleckis became an acting President of Lithuania. He faithfully obeyed all the Kremlin's instructions for the country's incorporation into the Soviet Union and the deportation of a large number of the population to Soviet concentration camps in Siberia. Parallel ultimatums were simultaneously presented to the governments of Latvia and Estonia. By June 17 the Soviet army had invaded all the Baltic States.

Stalin's system was fully poised and wholly ruthless. A program of Socialization was immediately launched. The Communist Party was established as the single controlling force in the country. Organized chiefly from non-Lithuanian elements, and with many of its leading figures imported from Moscow, it took over the public affairs of Lithuania without delay. Persecutions and purges were immediately initiated, and the Communist Party leader Antanas Sniečkus was appointed Director of the State Security Department. Other communists were given leading positions in the Ministry of Internal Affairs, and in district administrations. All Lithuanian organizations and societies were closed, and communist collaborators gradually changed the experienced state apparatus. The first series of mass arrests began during the night of July 11 and 12, 1940, as a prelude to what were called elections, which took place on July 14. Succeeding events were programmed to move quickly. The opening session of what was dubbed the "Sovereign Peoples' Parliament" was held on July 21, 1940, when its opening sessions "unanimously agreed" that Joseph Stalin, the General Secretary of the Communist Party of the USSR, should be sent unanimous resolution, requesting that the Soviet Union should immediately accept Lithuania into "the Soviet family of nations." Lithuania's diplomats in the West actively protested this precipitate incorporation into the Soviet Union. Lithuania was not alone in being treated with such indignity: Latvia and Estonia had to follow the same path of misery, and in those countries the deportations to concentration camps in Siberia were soon started as well. In the week of June 14-21, 1941, only days before the German invasion, about 30,000 people (one percent of the total Lithuanian population) were brutally arrested and deported to Siberia with no previous notice and no possessions. It has since come to light that the Soviets had planned beforehand to dispose of approximately one-third of the entire Lithuanian nation at the beginning of this occupation, by destroying "700,000 Counter-Revolutionaries." However, the German invasion, which began on June 23, 1941, forced the postponement of this malignant plan.

3. Lithuanian Resistance and the Determination to Remain in Europe
Lithuania's Resistance against the First Soviet Occupation

Outside Lithuania there are few, whether in political circles or among the general public in Western Europe, who remember much about Lithuania's resistance to the Soviet Empire, even if they recall how the country became a victim of the secret Molotov-Ribbentrop pact between Soviet Russia and Nazi Germany and was occupied by the Soviet Union in 1940 as a result.[26] The fact is that Lithuania rebelled a year later and succeeded in liberating herself both from the Soviet troops, who were withdrawing in panic, having feared the Lithuanian insurgents and an incoming German attack.[27] Although now scarcely remembered elsewhere, this National Revolt of 1941 was seen as "the first crack" in the structure of the Soviet Union, as commented *The Times* then.[28] However, although Lithuania established a Provisional Government, Hitler was not prepared to contemplate the existence of any buffer state between Nazi Germany and the Soviet Union, and so the country was occupied, Lithuanian independent government being summarily and quickly dissolved by the German authorities.[29]

The first Soviet invasion had begun on October 10, 1939, when the Soviet army moved to secure their zone of influence, forcing Lithuania to receive twenty thousand military personnel. Though this was clearly a cynical abrogation of the 1920 Treaty between Lithuania and the Soviet Union, and an annihilation of the rights and privileges of an independent state, this brutal maneuver was somewhat surprisingly accompanied by the news that Vilnius and

---

26 See e.g., Adolfas Damušis, *Lithuania against the Nazi and Soviet aggression* (Chicago: The American Foundation for Lithuanian Research, 1998), p. 1
27 Damušis, *Lithuania*, pp. 2-3.
28 "Baltic Revolts," *The Times*, June 24, 1941; "Germany disposes of Baltic States," *The Times*, August 12, 1941.
29 Damušis, *Lithuania*, p. 3.

its region, which had been captured only days previously by the Red Army, was to be ceded to Lithuania.[30] Moscow demanded the formation of a new government on June 14, 1940. Another one hundred thousand Soviet troops were sent virtually overnight into the country to reinforce the message. Once Lithuania was occupied, the left-wing journalist Justas Paleckis formed what the Soviets called, a "People's Government" on June 17, and announced a "general election" for the middle of July.[31] This resulted in what was cynically called a *Liaudies Seimas*, "People's Parliament," an essentially quisling body, whose first resolution on July 21 was to declare Lithuania to be a "Soviet Socialist Republic" and to announce that the country was an applicant for membership in the Soviet Union. This

---

30   Lithuania's capital Vilnius was occupied by Poland in October 1920 and remained incorporated into it before the Second World War. The implemented plan by Stalin was the return of Vilnius to Lithuania but the eventual annexation of the whole of Lithuania to the Soviet Union (see Chapter 2).

31   The fraudulent nature of the "elections" of July 1940 is well revealed by Misiūnas and Taagepera: "In Lithuania, no lists of eligible voters were drawn up; in effect, anyone could vote, and several times if he so desired." See Romualdas Misiunas and Rein Taagepera, *The Baltic states. Years of Dependence, 1940 – 1990* (London: Hurst & Company, 1993), p. 27. In all three Baltic countries the internal passports were stamped to identify those who had voted. However, even with this threat, the turnout was low. "Officially, the results were to the Kremlin's satisfaction: in Lithuania, 95.5 percent of the electorate allegedly voted and gave 99.2 percent of its vote to the League. [...] Privately, several leading members of the Lithuanian administration were quoted as having claimed a real total turnout not exceeding 32 percent." See Misiunas, *The Baltic states*, p. 27. "Acting President Paleckis of Lithuania is supposed to have expressed privately his opinion that the actual voter turnout in Lithuania stood at 15 – 16 percent." See Juozas Brazaitis, "Pirmoji sovietinė okupacija (1940 – 1941)" *Lietuvių enciklopedija*, Boston, vol. XV, 1968, pp. 356–370, quoted Misiunas, *The Baltic states*, p. 27. "The ballot carried only the Soviet – assigned candidate's name. The only way to register opposition was to strike it out. Use of an isolated booth was discouraged or prevented; in many places, open ballots had to be handed to an official who dropped it in the box. The vote count was often cynical. [...] The obvious intention was the staging of a Soviet-style election with the unanimous victory of a single slate of candidates." See Misiunas, *The Baltic states*, p. 26. "In Lithuania, at least two candidates appeared on the slate without the knowledge of the individuals involved; it is unlikely that they were an exception." See Misiunas, *The Baltic states*, p. 26. Such is the evidence of intimidation, ballot rigging, as well as the fundamentally undemocratic nature of the electoral process, and it is central to disproving Soviet (and subsequent Russian) claims that the Baltic nations "joined" the USSR in 1940 voluntarily.

application was speedily accepted. The Supreme Soviet then acknowledged the "Lithuanian Soviet Socialist Republic" as a Soviet Union Republic on August 3. With little further ceremony, totalitarian structures were immediately installed, and the process of socialization of the culture and economy began in earnest, backed by a program of intimidation, which involved the immediate imprisonment and deportation to the Gulag (Soviet concentration camps) of around 2,000 leading Lithuanian personalities, followed by 6,500 military personnel, and the mass murder of 9,500 political prisoners from 15,000 arrested people. Over 34,260 Lithuanian citizens were deported to concentration camps in Siberia and to the other extreme northern regions beyond the Arctic Circle, without trial, during the first mass deportation between June 14 and June 17, 1941.[32]

It was not surprising that having been treated in this manner the Lithuanians rebelled again, as they already had many times in their earlier history. Algirdas Martin Budreckis has portrayed the uprising of 1941 as a continuation of the Lithuanian tradition of rebellion established in the uprisings of 1795, 1807, 1812, 1813, 1863, and 1905, and the liberation war for independence between 1918 and 1920. He commented that the brevity of the national revolt is what might strike a neutral observer, as the active or culminating phase of the revolt lasted a mere nine days. According to his account, the invading Nazis attempted to dismiss the episode as a minor outburst of chaos and violence at the start of the war between the major European powers. Although the Soviets, ever ready to seize a propaganda opportunity, characterized this reclamation of the Lithuanian state as the activity of Hitler's gangs, both conflicting powers were in fact angry about this unexpected rebellion.[33] Molotov, speaking on Radio Moscow, furiously decried "the Lithuanian rebels" as "enemies of the people". By contrast, Germany was silent, even though media reports in London, Stockholm, Paris

---

32   Damušis, *Lithuania*, p. 50. Total loss of population during first Soviet occupation is estimated as 135,860. See Table 3 "Population Loss in Lithuania during the First Soviet Occupation" in the Appendices.

33   Algirdas M. Budreckis, *The Lithuanian National Revolt of 1941* (Chicago: Lithuanian Encyclopedia Press, 1968).

and elsewhere had cheerfully announced the proclamation of independent Lithuania and the formation of a new government as "the first crack in the Russian bloc".[34]

Although short-lived, the uprising of 1941 was of great significance. Vytautas Vardys has claimed that the "militarily successful insurrection of 1941 showed that, under the right circumstances, the Red Army and its communist leaders were not invincible."[35] He has also observed about the partisan war, which began in reaction to these events, that "although the partisans did not achieve their ultimate goal of Lithuanian independence, the historical legacy of their struggle belied the legitimacy of the official regime," because "the making of the 'Soviet man' in Lithuania was now made more difficult."[36] Adolfas Damušis, a member of the Provisional Government of 1941, has highlighted another important aspect, suggesting that it helped create and develop the strategy and tactics of resistance carefully directed towards the restoration of the independence of the Lithuanian state.[37] However, its leaders were careful to avoid provoking a military response against the nation as a whole. They tried, therefore, to avoid actions such as the destruction of military trains or bridges. Their favored method was to respond directly and specifically whenever possible to acts of violence against the Lithuanian nation, such as deportation, persecution, and the confiscation of property, which were the characteristic features of the occupation. Professor Juozas Brazaitis, a philologist, became one of the leaders of the resistance at this time. He was elected Prime Minister of Lithuania's Provisional Government, fulfilling the duties of the Lithuanian Envoy Colonel Kazys Škirpa, kept under arrest in Berlin, after he was selected as Prime Minister of the Provisional Government. It is clear that, in developing the movement's strategy and tactics, Juozas Brazaitis consciously attempted

---

34   See e.g., Baltic "Revolts," *The Times*, June 24, 1941; "Germany disposes of Baltic States," *The Times*, August 12, 1941.

35   Vytautas S. Vardys and Judith Sedaitis, *Lithuania. The Rebel Nation* (Boston: Westview Press, 1997), pp. 83 – 84.

36   Adolfas Damušis, "Rezistencijos gairės," key-note paper, presented at the 10th Lithuanian Symposium of Science and Creativity, Chicago, November 27–30, 1998, and interview with Adolfas Damušis in Chicago on November 27, 1998.

37   Interview with Adolfas Damušis in Chicago on November 27, 1998.

to intensify the defiant mood of the country, trying to direct the nation towards the restoration of its independence with the lowest possible number of casualties.[38] Kęstutis Girnius has argued that without the partisan war, the question of whether the Lithuanian nation really esteemed its sovereignty would have been an open one.[39] Yet, conducted against overwhelming odds and clearly commanding much broader support than the numbers who took up arms would suggest, this war became the clearest answer to this question. It provided a compelling contradiction of the communist claims about the free entry of Lithuania to the Soviet Union and remains an example of sacrifice for future generations of the continuation of Lithuania's immemorial traditions of resistance.[40]

Nijolė Gaškaitė, a historian of the partisan war, has observed that the vigorous quality of this armed resistance contributed significantly to the establishment of the U.S. policy of non-recognition of the incorporation of the Baltic States into the Soviet Union.[41] Documents that the partisan Juozas Lukša had smuggled to the West through the Iron Curtain had confirmed the determination of the Lithuanian people to defend their homeland and illustrated the wider threat of the Soviet system to humanity as a whole. Gaškaitė says that Juozas Lukša provided the evidence that Lithuania had been coerced into joining the Soviet Union and that Bolshevism was "ready to destroy Western civilization, culture and Christianity."[42] Contrary to the claims of Soviet propaganda, the vigor of the partisan effort, and the esteem it attracted, also diminished the russification process in Lithuania, but it carried a heavy cost, because more than twenty thousand of Lithuanian most courageous men and women were lost in the early years of the partisan war. Also, the Russian special services succeeded in infiltrating into many

---

38   Interview with Damušis.

39   Kęstutis Girnius, *Partizanų kovos Lietuvoje* (Chicago: Į Laisvę Fondas, 1987), p. 404.

40   Girnius, *Partizanų kovos*, p. 405.

41   Nijolė Gaškaitė, Dalia Kuodytė, Algis Kašėta, and Bonifacas Ulevičius, *Lietuvos partizanai: 1944 – 1953* (Kaunas: Lietuvos politinių kalinių ir tremtinių sąjunga, 1996).

42   "Lietuvos Respublikos katalikų laiškas Šv. Tėvui Pijui XII Vatikane," in Juozas Daumantas, *Partizanai* (Vilnius : 1990), p. 420.

partisan districts within the four years of the partisan war (1945-
1949). For example, Vytautas Ivanauskas Gintautas, a Chief Commander of Jūra partisan district, wrote to Juozas Žemaitis, a Supreme Commander of the *Lietuvos Laisvės Kovų Sąjudis*, the Lithuanian Freedom Fight Movement, on July 20, 1949, that "the recent
deaths occurred exceptionally due to spies."[43] This dreadful statis-
tic brought about a significant shift in the national character in the
direction of accommodation and caution.[44]

In contrast to the attitudes taken by Lithuanian writers, Soviet
historians showed no respect for the Uprising of 1941 or the subsequent partisan war. Analyzing events from their Marxist stand-
point, they sweepingly condemned the uprising, the Provisional
Government of 1941, and the partisan war purely in terms of their
being "an episode in the class struggle." Indeed, Boleslovas Baranauskas, Povilas Štaras, Julius Būtėnas, and Aldona Gaigalaitė described the participants and organizers of the uprising simply as
"the German fifth column."[45] The men whom Lithuanians refer to
as the "forest brotherhood" were, therefore, dismissed as "bourgeois nationalists, collaborators, and fascists." More recently, however, Valentinas Brandišauskas has castigated those views as reflecting the crudities of the political outlook of the Soviet period
rather than being any consistent or scientific analysis of the
events.[46]

---

43   "LLKS Jūros srities vado V. Ivanausko-Gintauto raštas LLKS Tarybos prezidiumo pirmininkui J. Žemaičiui-Vytautui apie partizanų didelių nuostolių
priežastis ir pasiūlymai, kaip jų išvengti," in *Laisvės kovos 1944-1953 metais*
(Kaunas : Lietuvos politinių kalinių ir tremtinių sąjunga & Pasaulio lietuvių
sąjunga, 1996), pp. 385-386.

44   More analysis about the partisan war in Lithuania will follow in the next subchapter.

45   See e.g., Boleslovas Baranauskas, "Penktoji kolona Lietuvoje," *Mokslas ir gyven-
imas*, 4 (1960): 33-35; Povilas Štaras, *Lietuvių tautos kova už Tėvynės laisvę Didži-
ajame Tėvynės kare* (Vilnius: Vaga, 1956), pp. 7-8; Julius Butėnas, "Buržuaziniai
nacionalistai - hitlerinių okupantų talkininkai" in *Hitlerinė okupacija Lietuvoje*
(Vilnius: Vaga, 1961), pp. 159-182; Aldona Gaigalaitė, "Buržuaziniai nacionalistai hitlerinės Vokietijos tarnyboje," *Mada*, 2 (1960): 133-149.

46   Valentinas Brandišauskas, *Siekiai atkurti Lietuvos valstybingumą* (Vilnius :
Valstybinis leidybos centras, 1996).

In his memoirs, Juozas Brazaitis, Professor of Lithuanian Literature at Vytautas Magnus University in Kaunas, but later Minister of Education and Acting Prime Minister of the Provisional Government, described the events of the time as a "highly coordinated and well prepared action which aimed at the restoration of independent Lithuania."[47] The uprising consisted of two major stages: the first involving the establishment of *Lietuvių Aktyvistų Frontas*, the Lithuanian Activist Front, which was headed by Colonel Kazys Škirpa, Lithuania's Ambassador in Germany; and the second, the active organization of underground groups inside the country. According to Pilypas Narutis, the Front embodied the reaction of many Lithuanian organizations dissolved by the Soviets. Vytautas Bulvyčius, its organizer, was supported by members of the disbanded patriotic voluntary organization *"Šauliai,"* established during the brief lifespan of the Provisional Government, and by members of the various student groups and organizations, which had continued their work underground.[48] These groups now acted under a centralized leadership in order to optimize local resistance, by warning individual citizens of impending arrest, and providing information to protect the wider population from Soviet army violence. The front had headquarters and staff in Kaunas and Vilnius, who were charged with maintaining communications with the Free World, to collect and spread reliable information, and prepare the movement for the eventual seizure of those major cities.

The actual uprising started simultaneously in Kaunas and Vilnius following the receipt of a signal that the German army had crossed the Soviet Union's border. The main Russian military telephone exchange in Vilijampolė near Kaunas was then seized by the rebels, while the civil telephone exchange located in the Kaunas Post Office was also seized by its employees and handed over to the rebels, who then allowed only those telephone lines, useful for

---

47   Juozas Brazaitis, "Insurrection against the Soviets," *Lituanus*, 3, 1955: 8 - 10; Juozas Brazaitis, *Raštai. VI tomas. Vienų vieni.* (Chicago: Į Laisvę fondas lietuviškai kultūrai ugdyti, 1990).

48   Interview with Dr. Pilypas Narutis, *Lithuanian Activist Front*, Chicago, November 28, 1997.

the impending uprising, to operate.[49] The group's leader Leonas Prapuolenis then deliberately misled the Soviets by notifying them that German paratroopers had landed near Kaunas. Once the telephone lines were disconnected, severe panic broke out among the Soviet ranks.

Dr. Adolfas Damušis, a Minister of the Provisional Government, has given a personal description of the revolt:

> At 3.00 a.m. on June 23, we gathered at our headquarters (located in a Kaunas home for the aged) [...] where we drafted a Declaration for the Restitution of Lithuanian Independence, and a short statement which was also to be broadcast later that day. Meanwhile, the broadcasting studios were being secretly prepared for the announcement, and a fleet of Red Cross ambulances collected materials which had been kept by Kaunas University students under their beds and set to work, putting homemade mines along the roads to the broadcasting transmitter. At 9 a.m. the studios were ready to start the broadcast, and as the Ąžuolynas[50] in Kaunas, close to the transmitter, was full of Soviet troops, it was decided not to use loudspeakers in the streets to reduce the possibility of an attack. The radio broadcast was transmitted to Lithuania and the world at half past nine, and it was followed by the National Anthem of which a recording was fortunately found in the studio.[51]

Once Leonas Prapuolenis had announced the restoration of Lithuanian independence and the formation of a new government, the revolt spread spontaneously across the whole of Lithuania.

Adolfas Damušis described the uprising as an "expression of the legal indignation of the nation against the Soviet terror, with its killings and mass deportations to Siberia's concentration camps."[52] He also regarded the uprising as embodying a brave confrontation with Nazi Germany and a "fight for freedom and for human rights against the genocide and holocaust." The NKVD, Stalin's secret police, had however already taken notice of the armed underground organization, and of the couriers who crossed the Soviet borders. Fyodor Gladkov, the Commissar of Security in occupied Lithuania,

---

49   Interview with Damušis.
50   The Oak Park.
51   Interview with Damušis.
52   Adolfas Damušis, "1941 metų sukilimo reikšmė," Į Laisvę, no. 96 (133) (April, 1986): 4-5.

had reported in sinister mode: "We know that the counter-revolutionary element possesses large numbers of weapons in the territory of the Lithuanian S.S.R."[53] However, despite mass deportations on June 14, 1941, the organizational structure of the Lithuanian Activist Front was quickly rebuilt and the uprising was therefore successfully organized with more than 100,000 people participating directly between June 22 and 29, 1941 (i.e. approximately three percent of the total population). However, more than 4,000 people died during this time. Unfortunately, the successful outcome was all too short-lived, and the six-week long existence of the Provisional Government of Lithuania was denied by the Nazi regime. When the General Commissioner Dr. Adrian von Renteln arrived on August 5, 1941, he simply announced that the Lithuanian Government was dissolved. In response, the Provisional Government repeatedly rejected the German demand that its members should abandon their titles as "Ministers of Government" to become mere "advisors of the German civil government." Damušis states that Heinz Greffe, the representative of the Gestapo, responded by warning they would all be sent to concentration camps if this requirement was not met. The reasons why this did not happen, continue to be obscure, but it is believed that General von Rocque, who was the Supreme Commander of the German Army in Lithuania but who himself had critical views towards Nazi policies in Lithuania, conceded to the appeals of Lithuania's Defense Minister, General Stasys Raštikis, saving the members of the Provisional Government from this fate.[54]

In assessing the importance of the 1941 uprising, Dr. Juozas Girnius observed that the events connected with this short-lived government had "restored the self-confidence of the nation."[55] It certainly helped Lithuanians in a general determination not to give

---

53   *Hearing before the Select Committee to Investigate the Incorporation of the Baltic States into the U.S.S.R.* (Washington, D.C.: House of Representatives, 1953).

54   General Stasys Raštikis, the former Commander-in-Chief of the Lithuanian Army and its Minister of Defense was highly regarded by many German military leaders and was successful in defending Lithuanian interests during the first months of the German occupation of Lithuania.

55   Juozas Girnius, *Aidai*, no. 6 (1966): 241.

in to the Nazi occupation and laid the foundation for the partisan movement of later years. Juozas Damušis has documented the work of the Provisional Government and its restoration of Lithuania's administration.[56] Fifteen ministries were re-established[57] and a serious attempt was made to restore the Litas as the state currency[58] as well as to return sequestered land to private ownership, by allowing peasants to return to their farms which had been forcibly collectivized by the Soviets.[59] An attempt was also begun to restore houses,[60] factories,[61] restaurants and shops,[62] pharmacies,[63]

---

56   Adolfas Damušis, "Rezistencijos siekis - Valstybinis suverenumas," *Į Laisvę*, no. 111 (1991): 7–8.

57   The membership of the Provisional Government in June 1941 included: Vytautas Landsbergis-Žemkalnis (Minister of Communal Economy), General Stasys Raštikis (Minister of Defense), Professor Juozas Ambrazevičius (Acting Prime Minister and Minister of Education), Dr. Juozas Pajaujis (Minister of Labor and Social Security), Antanas Novickis (Minister of Communications), Professor Balys Vitkus (Minister of Agriculture), Dr. Ksaveras Vencius (Minister of Health), Juozas Senkus (Director of Information), Dr. Adolfas Damušis (Minister of Industry), Vladas Nasevičius (Minister of Internal Affairs), Jonas Matulionis (Minister of Finance), Mečys Mackevičius (Minister of Justice), Pranas Vainauskas (Minister of State Control), Vytautas Statkus (Minister of Trade), Levas Prapuolenis (Representative of the Lithuanian Activist Front), Colonel Kazimieras Škirpa (Prime Minister), Rapolas Skipaitis (Minister of Foreign Affairs). Škirpa and Skipaitis were prevented by the German authorities from assuming duties, and the arrested minister of internal affairs Colonel Šlepetys was nominated to this post. Then the Minister of Trade, Vainauskas, took the joint position of Minister of Trade and State Control.

58   Lietuvos Laikinosios Vyriausybės kreipimasis į Vokiečių karo vyriausybę. Lithuania's State Archive, *Lietuvos generalinės srities finansų valdyba*, Kaunas, 1940 - 1941, Part 2, Case 448, p. 125.

59   Lietuvos Laikinojo Ministerių Kabineto nutarimas dėl žiemkenčių ir dobilų sėjos bei dėl žemės iki 30 ha gražinimo. Lithuania's State Archive, *Laikinoji Lietuvos vyriausybė*, 1941 - 1943, Part 1, Case 6, p. 11; Žemės denacionalizacijos įstatymas. Lithuania's State Archive, *Laikinoji Lietuvos vyriausybė*, p. 12.

60   Miestų namų ir žemės sklypų denacionalizacijos įstatymas. *Laikinoji Lietuvos vyriausybė*, p. 9.

61   Pramonės įmonių denacionalizacijos įstatymas. Lithuania's State Archive, *Lietuvos generalinės srities Zarasų apskrities viršininkas*. Zarasai, 1941 - 1944, p. 62.

62   Prekybos ir viešojo maitinimo įmonių denacionalizavimo įstatymas. *Laikinoji Lietuvos vyriausybė*, p. 3.

63   Įstatymai, įsakai ir potvarkiai, išleisti Lietuvoje bolševikinės okupacijos metu, dėl turtų nacionalizacijos ir konfiskacijos. Lithuania's State Archive, *Lietuvos generalinės srities Darbo ir socialines apsaugos vadyba, Kaunas, 1926 - 1961*, Part 1, Case 26, p. 69.

and shipping to their rightful ownership.[64] Stasys Raštikis, who was Defense Minister during those six weeks, said that the administration tried to do everything in its power to restore all alienated properties.[65] According to Mečislovas Mackevičius, who was a Minister of Justice in the Provisional Government, the revolt "rescinded all Bolshevik Parliament decisions" and clearly demonstrated Lithuania's commitment to freedom and independence to the World.[66] A memorandum of the Provisional Government, prepared by Professor Juozas Ambrazevičius-Brazaitis, stated bluntly that "the Provisional Government was removed against its will and against the will of the Lithuanian nation."[67] Despite this major effort to maintain independence and the continuing Lithuanian resistance, the nation's economy was integrated into the war economy of the German Reich rather quickly.

Regardless its short-lived nature, the uprising of 1941 was a significant episode in Lithuania's history. It was an investment in idealism which was finally realized by the successful liberation of Lithuania in the early 1990s. In trying to assess the long-term impact of the revolt of 1941 on the contemporary history and politics of Lithuania, one can identify political, military, historical, and economic factors which remained influential. The political aspects include the continuing inspiration which the memory of the revolt provided, and the accompanying perception that the Soviet army could be forced to evacuate the country, if ever a favorable international situation were to be achieved. It was this vision which encouraged the Lithuanian partisans in the 1950s to continue with their military struggle in anticipation that the tension between the Soviet Union and the West would lead to actual hostilities, providing opportunity for the restoration of an independent state. This did not happen at that time, but eventually in the 1980s, Lithuania's *Sąjūdis* was able to exploit the Soviet policy of *perestroika* and

---

64   Lietuvos jūros ir upių prekybos laivyno denacionalizacijos įstatymas. *Laikinoji Lietuvos vyriausybė*, pp. 8 - 9
65   Stasys Raštikis, "The relations of the provisional government of Lithuania with the German authorities," *Lituanus*, no. 1-2 (1962): 16–22.
66   Mečislovas Mackevičius, "1941-jų metų sukilimas," *Sėja*, no. 4–5 (1961).
67   Raštikis, "Relations of the provisional government," p. 22.

glasnost successfully by actively drawing on the memories of their struggle. The Lithuanians then demanded that their constitutional right of self-determination should be returned, and that the Soviet troops should be swiftly returned to their homeland. These demands contributed decisively to the collapse of the Soviet Union.

The political importance of the 1941 Declaration of Independence was directly related to the earlier Declaration of Independence, on February 16, 1918. In both cases the declaration spurred the nation to fight for its freedom. When *Sąjūdis* declared on Lithuania's Independence Day, February 16, 1989, that "despite the brutal ultimatum and mutual agreement between Germany and USSR in 1939-1940 Lithuania was annexed by the Soviet Union but its legal international recognition as a state still exists and that *Sąjūdis* expresses the nation's commitment to restore its rights in a peaceful way and to live independently from any dictate," it drew heavily on these earlier declarations and the sense of pride which they engendered, allowing a weakened and terrorized nation to find the strength to leave aside fear and uncertainty and to recover its hope for freedom.[68] This hope was based on historical experience and a living memory of the past, of the achievement of the Provisional Government which provided a conscious model for *Sąjūdis*, and which was followed faithfully as soon as the movement achieved power. There were conscious parallels between the performance of the *Sąjūdis* governments and that of the Provisional Government. Under the Provisional Government decisions about the restoration of private property and the democratization of the state institutions was accomplished within six short weeks, despite the presence of the German army on Lithuanian territory. Similarly, *Sąjūdis* implemented laws about the restoration of the state and a free market economy after the Declaration of Independence on March 11, 1990, despite the continued presence of the Soviet army. Fortunately, then, the international situation was considerably more favorable for Lithuania than it had been in 1941.

---

[68]   Arvydas Kšanavičius, "Vasario 16-oji – neišsenkantis tautos stiprybės šaltinis," *XXI Amžius*, February 14, 2003. http://www.xxiamzius.lt/archyvas/xxiamzius/20030214/istving_01.html.

In both 1941 and 1990 the broad support of the people lay behind the movement for independence. *Sąjūdis* recalled the experience of the spontaneous (but eventually centralized) group structure of the Lithuanian Activist Front when creating its own nation-
wide organization. There was often a family link between generations, which gave a sense of purpose to the process. Perhaps this
was most clearly expressed in the case of the Landsbergis family, in
which Vytautas Žemkalnis-Landsbergis was a Minister in the Provisional Government, and his son Vytautas Landsbergis became
the leader of *Sąjūdis*. It should be stressed that such personal leadership was vital both in the Provisional Government and in the
Sąjūdis Parliament. The Provisional Government, under Juozas
Ambrazevičius, had established the need to fight for the *complete
independence* of the country, and this insistence was riveted firmly
in the national consciousness when the next opportunity came.[69]
The resoluteness of Landsbergis' leadership of *Sąjūdis* came from
this source, the family aspiration coinciding with the national aspiration, as in so many other cases.

Lithuania's diplomatic corps played an essential role in the
preparatory phase of the uprising of 1941. The founding meeting of
the Lithuanian Activist Front, which took place at the initiative of
Kazys Škirpa, Lithuanian Envoy in Germany on November 17,
1940, invited "joining all active forces of the nation to the Lithuanian Activist Front for the liberation of Lithuania."[70] This too was a
precedent for later reference, and Lithuania's surviving diplomacy
once again stimulated active support for *Sąjūdis* at the beginning of
the 1990s. However, in the *Sąjūdis* period the leaders favored a
gradualist "evolution rather than revolution" approach to independence. This approach had not been present among the leaders
of the uprising. Adolfas Damušis has said of his colleagues in the
Provisional Government, emphasizing a collective ideal, which
perhaps belonged to an age which was more naïve: "we were

---

69   Adolfas Damušis, "Juozas Ambrazevičius - Brazaitis archyvų dokumentuose,"
      Į Laisvę, no. 107 (1989 – 1990): 38.
70   Kazys Škirpa, *Sukilimas Lietuvos suverenumui atstatyti* (Chicago, Lietuvių
      Fronto Bičiulių Klubas: 1980).

idealists, under the influence of the great humanists, Professor Brazaitis, Professor Ivinskis, and others." He distinguished this style
of action "[...] in contrast to current development of affairs [in the
1990s], when everybody looks for his own benefit. That was not acceptable during our times. I liked that. Brazaitis had a very good
character. He spoke, discussed with everybody in the Cabinet and
only then did he draw conclusions. Some say, he was too mild, but
I liked that approach very much."[71] Clearly, there are parallels and
differences between the courses taken by the two governments, but
the later one was perhaps more wary of its path because of the way
in which the earlier one had been outlawed by circumstances beyond its control.

In sum, the relationship between the 1941 Provisional Government and the *Sąjūdis* governments can be expressed by the proverb
"a word teaches, and hope attracts." The earlier revolt provided the
later generation of Lithuanians with inspiration and aspiration. In
Adolfas Damušis, words, "we were very successful. We survived.
We had bright ideas and a very good advisory group. In such cases
you survive or die."[72] Professor Juozas Meškauskas argued that the
uprising revealed the true strength of the Lithuanian nation.[73] It
laid the background for the post-war resistance. It is amazing, that
when Hungary revolted in 1956, Lithuania was still fighting the
longest partisan war in contemporary European history. After he
had defected from the Russian MVD, Colonel Burlichi testified to
the Kersten Committee of the U.S. House of Representatives in June
1954, that the underground in Lithuania "remained unbroken."[74]
From this evidence we may conclude that, as another saying puts
it, "it is easy to light a new fire on an old hearth." Though the em-
bers of struggle in the cause of freedom appeared to have been

---

[71]   Interview with Dr. Adolfas Damušis, Chicago, November 30, 1997.

[72]   Interview with Damušis.

[73]   Interview with Prof. Juozas Meškauskas, former Dean of Kaunas Medical Faculty and a member of the *Lietuvių Aktyvistų Frontas*, Lithuanian Activist Front,
Chicago, November 28, 1997.

[74]   MVD, Soviet Ministry of Interior Affairs. Grigorijaus Stepanovičiaus Burlickio
parodymai in *Baltijos Valstybių Užgrobimo Byla. JAV Kongreso Ch. J. Kersteno
komiteto dokumentai 1953-1954 metai* (Vilnius: Du Ka, 1997), p. 793.

extinguished by the end of the 1960s, the inspiration of the 1941 uprising remained active in the hearts of the Lithuanian people in the later 1990s.

Resistance against Nazi Germany

Dr. Adolfas Damušis has explained: "The Lithuanian resistance was convinced that Soviet communism and German National Socialism, because of their similar imperialistic intentions, were equal enemies of Lithuania."[75] Professor Zenonas Ivinskis explicitly highlighted the national socialist policies in Lithuania: "Independence for Lithuania did not figure in their plans."[76] The plans for political autonomy of the Baltic nations drawn up before the Barbarossa operation were abandoned by German officials and Hitler himself.[77] Lithuania was once again trapped between the ambitions of German and Slavic expansionism, repeating the experience of earlier centuries. However, while Lithuania had been able to defend herself effectively during the mediaeval period, and had even managed to stop the German *"Drang nach Osten"* for five centuries as the Tartar *"Drang nach Westen"* in the past, the German military might was significantly stronger than Lithuania's during the period of the Nazi occupation, 1941-1944.[78] It was this recognition which underlay the Lithuanian Government's decision that resistance to Nazi Germany had to be non-violent.[79] The strategy deployed was designed, as Damušis has pointed out, on the principle of "[…] furthering national esteem, promoting the recovery of independence, and guarding against collaboration with oppressors."[80] One of the main principles of this resistance was "to refuse to answer calls for

---

75 Adolfas Damušis, *Lithuania against Soviet and Nazi aggression* (Chicago: The American Foundation for Lithuanian Research, 1998), p. 107.
76 Zenonas Ivinskis, "Lithuania During the War: Resistance Against the Soviet and the Nazi Occupants" in Vytautas Vardys, *Lithuania Under the Soviets* (New York: Praeger, 1965), p. 73.
77 Ivinskis, "Lithuania During the War," p. 73.
78 See Chapter 2 of this book "Lithuania's European roots."
79 Adolfas Damušis, "Juozas Brazaitis Lietuvos Rezistencijoje," *Į Laisvę,* no. 65 (1975): 42-50.
80 Damušis, "Juozas Brazaitis," pp. 42-50.

mobilization in order to minimize losses during occupation."[81] Further aspects of this determination to resist Nazism non-violently were to develop with time. They included the emergence of an underground press, the avoidance of taxes, refusal to participate in labor and military units, refusal to mobilize, and the establishment of underground Lithuanian schools.[82]

The Nazi plans for the occupation of Lithuania were contemptuous of any concept of national independence and would have allowed no provision for the continuation of the Lithuanian state once the invasion had been consolidated. Although directed against the Soviets, the Lithuanian uprising of June 1941 therefore immediately assumed the character of a confrontation with the Nazis. This was, however, very short-lived as the Provisional Government exercised its authority only until August 5, when it was summarily displaced by the incoming German occupation, which immediately imposed a 'General District' administration on the country. The first act of this regime was to deprive Jews of their citizenship, a move which was soon to lead to more terrible measures intended to terrorize the whole population as well as to address "the Jewish problem". In the meantime, the Lithuanians were heavily repressed, and many people were taken for forced labor. "Recruitment of Manpower" started in the spring of 1942 after Marshal Göring and other high Nazi officials repeatedly accused Heinrich Lohse, the Ostland Reichskomissar, for his alleged failure to provide the necessary manpower from the Baltic States. On May 2, 1942, it was decided to register all Lithuanians between the ages of seventeen and forty-five to mobilize 100,000 workers. Those failing to register were subject to a 1,000 Reichsmarks fine and a three-month sentence in the Pravieniškės, Dimitravas, and Pabradė forced labor camps.[83] Despite this, a resistance movement came into being which achieved some success in disrupting Nazi plans, particularly for recruiting young men into the army. The occupiers

---

81   Damušis, *Lithuania*, p. 107.
82   Bronius Kviklys, *Lietuvių kova su naciais* (Memmingenas: Mintis, 1946).
83   Ivinskis, "Lithuania During the War," p. 75-76.

were also unsuccessful in their projected establishment of a specifically Lithuanian corps of the SS.[84]

There is useful contemporary documentation of the character of the resistance which survives in the National Archives in Washington, D.C. The American Ambassador in Stockholm reported the Nazi failure to organize an SS legion in Lithuania in the following way:

> Lithuania's press uncovered this attempt to deceive the country and expressed strong opposition to any Lithuanian involvement. To attract Lithuanians, the Nazis promised good food, SS uniforms, equal rights, and property privileges. There was a universal boycott by Lithuanian youth of this German attempt at organizing an SS Legion. Recruiters sat idly by waiting at mobilization centers. The few who were attracted by the Nazi offers were intercepted by members of the Lithuanian underground before they got to the mobilization centers and were persuaded not to register. The organization of a Lithuanian SS Legion under German supervision was a complete fiasco.[85]

This response was so widespread that it must be regarded as having been an effectively organized boycott. As such it caused outrage in Nazi circles.[86]

It is now evident that there were five main reasons for this Lithuanian reluctance to join an SS Legion:

First, National Socialism was ideologically unacceptable to the Lithuanian people. There is no evidence of a Nazi movement in the country prepared to welcome the occupation, or of any reception of the invaders which was more than a passive acknowledgement of their military superiority. A nation which had just seen the withdrawal of a Soviet regime was in no position to contend against the more powerful army, but there is no evidence of its being welcomed, still less of a population prepared to welcome its radical ideology.[87]

---

84   Damušis, *Lithuania*, pp. 149-160.
85   "Boycott of SS Legion in Lithuania," Report of the Ambassador of the United States in Stockholm, Sweden, sent to the State Department in Washington, D.C., May 11, 1943. *National Archives*, Washington, D.C., R.G. 226, Records Office. Strat. Service, 38226, 30 pages. Quoted in Damušis, *Lithuania*, p. 159.
86   Damušis, *Lithuania*, p. 149.
87   Damušis, *Lithuania*, p. 150.

Second, it was well known that SS forces were intended to be sent to both the southern and western fronts, which were rapidly opening at this stage of the war, to act as an oppressive force in support of the occupational regime of other occupied states. A publication, which circulated in Lithuania in 1943, drew its readers' attention to this, observing that "Lithuanians understand the value of freedom and do not wish to repress it for others, but they have only one intention: to fight against the invasion of bolshevism."[88] There is little doubt that this sentiment was widespread.

Third, the brutal treatment and frequent killings of farmers who were unable to deliver requisitions of food for the German army was well known throughout the country and there was widespread sympathy for them based on a recognition of the impossibility of fulfilling the quotas imposed by the occupants.[89]

Fourth, the arrests of Lithuanian youth for compulsory deportation to Germany or for forced labor within Lithuania maintained an atmosphere of resentment which militated against recruitment.

Fifth, the widespread desecration of Lithuanian religious and cultural centers had done nothing to endear the occupation to Lithuanian nationals.[90]

A wide underground anti-Nazi press quickly sprang into being. In October 1941, an underground *Laisvės kovotojai* group, the Freedom Fighters, began the publication of a widely read paper *Laisvės kovotojas* ("The Freedom Fighter"). In early 1944 it organized a secret radio station *Laisvosios Lietuvos Vilniaus radijas* ("Free Lithuania's Radio Vilnius"). The remaining part of the *Lietuvos Aktyvistų Frontas,* the Lithuanian Activist Front, reformed and renamed itself to *Lietuvių Frontas,* the Lithuanian Front. Its leadership was dominated by *Ateitininkai,* a Catholic activist group, outlawed by the Nazi regime. In January 1943 they began to publish papers *Į Laisvę* ("Toward Freedom"), *Lietuvių biuletenis* ("Lithuanian Bulletin"), and individual groups of the Lithuanian Front published

---

88   "Lietuviai ir SS Legijonas," *Į Laisvę*, underground publication, November 23, 1943, p. 2. Quoted in Damušis, *Lithuania*, p. 150.
89   Damušis, *Lithuania*, p. 151.
90   Damušis, *Lithuania*, pp. 149-150.

papers *Vardan tiesos* ("In the Name of Truth"), a satirical publication *Pogrindžio kuntaplis* ("The Underground Pantofle"), and a publication *Lietuvos Judas* ("The Lithuanian Judas"), giving the names of Nazi collaborators. The students and lecturers of Vilnius and Kaunas universities published a paper *Atžalynas* ("The Sapling"). Publications appeared in the provincial towns as well, e.g. *Lietuva* ("Lithuania") was published in Šiauliai. Former members of various other organizations, such as the Riflemen's Association, printed their newspapers, *Lietuvos laisvės trimitas* ("Lithuania's Freedom Trumpet"), others published *Laisvės žodis* ("Word of Freedom"), *Lietuvos kelias* ("Lithuania's Way"), *Baltija* ("The Baltic"), *Jaunime, budėk* ("Youth Be Prepared"). *Valstiečiai liaudininkai* ("Farmers People's Party") published the popular and influential *Nepriklausoma Lietuva* ("Independent Lithuania").[91]

In the second half of 1943 the unification of the resistance against Nazi occupation took place. The leftist *Vyriausias Lietuvių Komitetas*, the Supreme Lithuanian Committee, and the Catholic-oriented *Lietuvos Taryba*, the Council of Lithuania, merged into one central organization *Vyriausias Lietuvos Išlaisvinimo Komitetas*, the Supreme Committee for Lithuania's Liberation. On February 16, 1944, the Supreme Committee for Lithuania's Liberation declared:

> The sovereign Lithuanian state did not disappear either because of the Soviet or the present occupation of the Reich; only the functioning of the organs of the sovereign state has been temporarily impaired. This functioning, interrupted by the Soviet occupation of June 15, 1940, and by acts committed by force and fraud under the violent pressures of this occupation, was temporarily restored by the national insurrection of June 23, 1941, and by the work of the Provisional Government.[92]

The Committee united all underground political forces and included representatives from all political parties (*Krikščionių demokratų partija*, Christian Democrats; *Darbo federacija*, Labour Federation; *Valstiečių sąjunga*, Farmers Union; *Valstiečių liaudininkų partija*, the Peasant People's Party; *Socialdemokratai*, the Social Democrats; *Tautininkai*, the Lithuanian National League) and delegates from

---

91   Ivinskis, "Lithuania During the War," p. 78.
92   Quoted in Ivinskis, "Lithuania During the War," p. 82.

the four most prominent paramilitary resistance organizations (*Lietuvių frontas*, the Lithuanian Front; *Laisvės kovotojai*, Freedom Fighters; *Tautininkų partija*, the National Party; *Lietuvos sąjungos lyga*, the Lithuanian Union League).[93]

Lithuanian universities and institutes were an early victim of the new regime. They were immediately closed, and eighty of their teaching staff were sent to Stutthof concentration camp, a move which was clearly consistent with Nazi policies toward potential sources of intellectual resistance in other occupied countries.[94] The pattern of brutal suppression was widespread: eight members of Lithuania's Supreme Liberation Committee were imprisoned, and some two hundred Lithuanian soldiers were shot without further question for refusing to join the German army. The tragedy of the Lithuanian Territorial Defense Force is well described by Professor Zenonas Ivinskis.[95] Intensified activities by Soviet partisans inspired the Germans to allow the establishment of a permanent Lithuanian military force for dealing with them. Popular Lithuanian General Povilas Plechavičius agreed to form twenty battalions of the *Litauische Sonderverbände*, the Lithuanian Territorial Defence Force, and they were formed immediately. However, the Germans pressed for more troops not only for the defense of Lithuania but also for the Eastern front and the SS. This was refused as well as the order to surrender to the SS to be sent to the Western front. As a result, on May 1944 General Povilas Plechavičius and all commanding officers were sent to the Salaspils concentration camp, near Riga in Latvia. The Nazis executed one hundred soldiers as a warning for the necessity to obey the German masters, but most of the troops fled into hiding, and the Germans succeeded in detaining only

---

93   Ivinskis, "Lithuania During the War," p. 82.
94   In addition, 46 Lithuanian intellectuals were arrested and sent to Stutthoff concentration camp. These included three Councilors to the Zivilverwaltung whom General von Renteln himself had appointed: Mečislovas Mackevičius (Justice), Pranas Germanas-Meškauskas (Education, died in concentration camp), Stasys Puodžius (Administrative Control, died in concentration camp). At the same time former Counselor Professor Vladas Jurgutis was sent to Stutthof concentration camp as well. See Ivinskis, "Lithuania During the War," p. 80.
95   Ivinskis, "Lithuania During the War," pp. 85-86.

3,500 troops, who were sent to the Luftwaffe for various duties in West German military airports.[96]

The Nazis also implemented an extermination program which was to massacre approximately 150,000 Lithuanian Jews. This meant that the rich Jewish life of Vilnius and Kaunas, both acknowledged centers of Jewish scholarship, was ended. In the first days of the occupation representatives from the Provisional Government made attempts to save the Jews. The Jewish community leaders had applied to them for help, and General Raštikis met General von Pohl on their behalf, informing him that the Lithuanian Government and the Lithuanian community were very much concerned about the German action against the Jews. General von Pohl stated that he could not do anything in this matter and suggested that General Raštikis talk with General von Rocques. The meeting between General Raštikis and General von Rocques then took place in the presence of General von Rocques' Chief of Staff. Lieutenant Colonel Kriegsheim, his adjutant, took stenographic notes. General Raštikis explained the displeasure and worry of the Lithuanian community and Government at the persecution and destruction of Lithuanian Jews, but these local German commanders replied that "the issue was decided in Berlin by Hitler himself."[97] "Herr General, do not fret and worry, this action will soon be over," was the chilling answer to the Lithuanian Provisional Government.

While some Lithuanian individuals collaborated with the Nazis in the Holocaust, the Lithuanian Provisional Government, which attempted to save the Lithuanian Jews, is clearly exempt from this charge.[98] In the same way that *Sąjūdis* declared support

---

96   Ivinskis, "Lithuania During the War," pp. 83-84.
97   Adolfas Damušis, "1941 metų sukilimo reikšmė," *Į Laisvę*, no. 96 (133), (April 1986): 4-5.
98   Apie Birželio Sukilimą ir Laikinąją Vyriausybę. Interview with Dr. Algimantas Liekis http://news.mireba.lt/ml/207/birzelio.htm. Alexander Slavin, a former KGB agent, published a book about the Holocaust in Lithuania in the Russian language in Israel, alleging that the Lithuanian Provisional Government passed a decree ordering the annihilation of the Lithuanian Jews. Dr. Algimantas Liekis argues that the document on which these accusations were based in fact is a falsification (it is even unsigned, while all other documents of the

for Gorbachev's perestroika during its earlier period of activities, *the Lithuanian Activist Front* also declared for support of Hitler's anti-communist war against the Soviet Union. This, however, does not mean that both anti-communist movements supported Russian or German dictators. These declarations were made in attempts to be perceived by the occupying authorities as pro-Nazi or pro-Soviet movements in their earlier periods of existence and thus to be tolerated by the occupying authorities in Lithuania. However, if *Sąjūdis* succeeded in winning elections and establishing the pro-independence government, the Provisional Government of *Lietuvų Aktyvistų Frontas,* Lithuanian Activist Front, was abolished by the Nazi regime, as was mentioned earlier.

During the remainder of the occupation period, many Lithuanians risked their own lives to save innocent people. The Vilnius State Jewish Gaon museum has a list of 3,000 who saved Jews there and almost the same number of their rescuers, and according to Alfonsas Eidintas this is not a complete list since several families had to co-operate to save one Jew.[99] Some 474 Lithuanians have been named by Israel's Yad Vashem Institute as "Righteous Gentiles" and the Canadian Lithuanian Journalist Society has published the impressive "List of A. Gurevičius," which contains 6,271 Lithuanians, who rescued those thousands of Lithuanian Jews (10,137) who survived the Second World War.[100] The family of Vytautas Landsbergis, later to become President of Lithuania, is among them.[101]

The attitudes struck both by the Nazis, and by these significant members of the Lithuanian population, clearly reflected established dispositions in Lithuanian public life during the period

---

Provisional Government are signed). He claims that both the KGB and the Gestapo used to make falsifications of many even more complicated signed documents in the past.

99   See Alfonsas Eidintas, "Remembering the Jewish Catastrophe: 60th Anniversary of the Holocaust." Speech at the Lithuanian Seimas special session, September 20, 2001.

100   See *A. Gurevičiaus sąrašai. Tūkstančiai lietuvių, kurie gelbėjo tūkstančius Lietuvos žydų Antrojo pasaulinio karo metais* (Vilnius: Protėvių Kardas, 1999), p. 152 and p. 188.

101   See Vytautas Landsbergis, *Lithuania independent again* (Cardiff: University of Wales Press, 2000), p. 19.

preceding the occupation. Damušis has emphasized that the sentencing of the Nazi activists in 1935 by a court in Klaipėda, as well as the declaration of strict neutrality issued by the government of independent Lithuania on the outbreak of the Second World War had given Hitler particular displeasure. In reflection, the Nazi administration decided to limit severely the numbers of Lithuanians who were to be deemed to be of the so-called Nordic race, and therefore suitable to become citizens of the Reich. This was done despite the Lithuanian mythological claim to have roots in the Aryan phenomenon, which figured so largely in the racial ideology of the Nazi creed.[102]

The Nazis had planned the destruction of both Lithuanian society and its Jewry in advance. The key personnel responsible for the Holocaust in Lithuania were General Franz Stahlecker, who arrived in Kaunas on the fourth day of the occupation, and Karl Jaeger, head of the secret police.[103] Stahlecker was charged with kick-starting the process and getting the local Lithuanians to participate.[104] He was assisted in this by Jaeger, Lieutenant Guenther Hamann, and Sergeant Rauca, and they tried to recruit the local population to participate in the mass killings which followed.

---

102 See Tables 4-6 (Appendices) for the number of victims of Nazi crimes in *Lithuania*.

103 Standartenfuehrer, Befehlshaber der Sicherheitspolizei und des SD.

104 In a letter to Heinrich Himmler of October 15, 1941 General Franz W. Stahlecker wrote: "[…] considering that the population of the Baltic countries suffered heavily under the government of Bolshevism and Jewry while Lithuania was occupied by the U.S.S.R., it was to be expected that after the liberation from the foreign government they, i.e., the populace itself, would render harmless most of the enemies left behind after the retreat of the Red Army. It was the duty of the secret police to set into motion these cleansing movements and to direct them in the correct channels in order to accomplish the purpose of the cleansing operation as quickly as possible. It was no less important in the view of the future to establish the unshakeable and provable facts that the liberated population themselves took the most severe measures against the Bolshevik and Jewish enemy quite on their own, so that the direction by the German authorities could not be found out." Franz W. Stahlecker, report to Heinrich Himmler of October 15, 1941. Helmut Krausnick, *The Truppe des Weltanschauungskrieges, Teil 1* in Helmut Krausnick and Hans-Heinrich Wilhelm *Die Truppe des Weltanschauungskrieges. Die Einsatzgruppen der Sicherheitspolizei und des SD 1938-1942* (Stuttgart: Deutsche Verlags-Anstalt, 1981), pp. 206-209, quoted in Damušis, *Lithuania*, p. 128.

However, there is evidence of Stahlecker having complained to Himmler that "it was not a simple matter to organize an effective action against Jews."[105] Yet, while there is much evidence of attempts made by members of the Provisional Lithuanian Government to avoid the impending tragedy, and of individual Lithuanians protecting Jews, there is still controversy regarding the local participation in the Holocaust. The Jewish researcher Dina Porat has argued that there was an "intense involvement of the local population in large numbers in the murder of the Jews," alleging that this "entailed a fatal combination of Lithuanian motivation and German organization and thoroughness."[106] The same author, though, admits that many Jews in Lithuania supported Stalin's regime.[107] Prof. Thomas Remeikis argues that "the strategic policy of passive resistance was almost universally accepted by the clandestine anti-German groups" in Lithuania but "the remaining fragments of the Lithuanian Communist Party, the red partisans and the Jewish underground" all were controlled by Moscow.[108] However, Adolfas Damušis, who was himself a member of the Provisional Government, and was arrested and moved through a series of German prisons, including Isterburg, Allenstein, Landberg an der Wharte, Berlin Tegel, and Bayreuth in Bavaria, asserts that the Germans fraudulently accused the Lithuanians of the extermination of Jews, and that their documents reflect this determination to implicate the Lithuanian population. Helmut Krausnick has described the pogroms in Kaunas of June 25-29, 1941, quoting Stahlecker, and Dina Porat also notes Stahlecker as having reported that "Lithuanian partisans" had liquidated approximately 1,500 Jewish people on the night of June 25, 1941, after burning some

---

105   Damušis, *Lithuania*, p. 128.
106   See e.g., Dina Porat, "The Holocaust in Lithuania" in David Cesarani, (ed.) *The Final Solution. Origins and Implementation* (London: Routlege, 1994).
107   Porat, "Holocaust."
108   Thomas Remeikis (ed.), *Lithuania under German occupation 1941-1945. Despatches from US Legation in Stockholm* (Vilnius: Vilnius University Press, 2005), p. 10.

sixty homes and a few synagogues.[109] However, both these observations of alleged atrocities are based on German sources.

Damušis contradicts their reports. He says that "neither executions nor fires occurred in Kaunas at the time," and bluntly described the report to which they were referring as "misinformation
[...] one of Stahlecker's many deceptions to cover up his crimes and
fraudulently incriminate Lithuanian nationals."[110] Indeed, it is not
possible to find any Lithuanian primary or secondary source mentioning these events of June 25, 1941. Further, interviews of two
Lithuanians, who were resident in Kaunas at that time, clearly
shows that such things did not happen in Kaunas on that night or
near that time.[111] However, in the end, this argument is about the
numbers involved, or the levels of popular support, indifference,
active or passive opposition to the genocide organized by the Nazis. While some Lithuanians did contribute, there is no evidence of
general enthusiasm for the Nazi crimes, still less of active participation by the general population. Adolfas Eidintas, a holocaust researcher, has argued with every appearance of being objective that
some 2,000-3,000 Lithuanians can realistically be estimated to have
participated in these appalling events, but he also acknowledges
that the full facts of the matter are currently unresolved.[112] Modern
Lithuania has, however, acknowledged that these questions are
ones which need to be laid to rest. In 1998, a special commission
was formed by the President of Lithuania which is currently inves-
tigating both Soviet and Nazi crimes in the country to determine
the statistics which alone can settle these arguments finally.[113]

---

109 Helmut Krausnick, "Die Einsatzgruppen vom Anschluss Osterreichs bis zum
     Feldzug gegen die Sowjetunion Entwicklung und Verhaltnis zur Wehrmacht"
     Teil I in Krausnick, *Die Truppe*, pp. 205-206.
110 Krausnick, *Die Truppe*, p. 129.
111 Interviews with Mr. Danielius Gintas & Mr. Bronius Čiudiškis, residents of
     Kaunas on June 25, 1940, Nottingham, December 15, 2001.
112 Alfonsas Eidintas, *Lietuvos žydų žudynių byla. Dokumentų ir straipsnių rinkinys*.
     (The Case of the Massacre of the Lithuanian Jews: Selected documents and ar-
     ticles) (Vilnius: Vaga, 2001). See also Alfonsas Eidintas, "Remembering the
     Jewish Catastrophe: 60th Anniversary of the Holocaust," speech at the Lithua-
     nian Seimas special session on September 20, 2001.
113 Eidintas, "Remembering the Jewish Catastrophe."

Although opinion in Lithuania has tended to regard the level of citizen participation in Nazi atrocities as having been small, and in fact minor, the final resolution of this painful question will have to await the outcome of this commission's work. The level of German participation and responsibility in these crimes is much easier to determine, and there can be no doubt that the prime mover in the genocide was the occupying power. Lieutenant Hamann's direct responsibility for the organization and direction of the *Roll commandos* used in carrying out Final Solution assignments is well-documented, and it is indisputable that these units, which consisted of eight to ten 'dependable SS men' (recruited from the infamous EK3 Einsatz group A Commando 3) represented the cutting edge of the Nazi attack on the Jewish community.[114] If there were Lithuanians who took part in these events, examination of the command structures of the SS will make it plain that their contribution was as a supporting cast, thus essentially marginal. The SS regarded the destruction of Jewry as its special mission, and while it may have involved others in its evil deeds, willing or unwilling, they were not allocated key roles. When Standartenfuehrer Karl Jaeger reported the executions of Jews carried out under his command and direction in the Seventh Fort at Kaunas on July 4 and 6, 1941, he added "with the co-operation of Lithuanian partisans."[115] However, while his Einsatz group habitually called their organized irregulars "Lithuanian partisans," this was a fraudulent identification which did not necessarily imply enthusiastic support for the occupation. It was a designation of enforced participation, or of what was described elsewhere in the occupied territories as "quisling" participation, which must be seen in the context of Stahlecker's instructions "[...] to implicate as much as possible the local population in

---

114   Karl Jaeger, report to Franz W. Stahlecker: Karl Jaeger, der Befehlshaber der Sicherheitspolizei u. der SD Einsatzkommando 3, Report an die Einsatzgruppe A SS-Brigadefuehrer Dr. Stahlecker, in Riga, of December 1, 1941, pp. 472-480. Geheime Reichsache PS-2076/41 (no. 1 and 2). Also incorporated in the R. Heydrich file on January 25, 1942. Zentrale Stelle der LJV'en., Gestapo Archive, Ludwigsburg, Germany. Quoted in Damušis, *Lithuania*, p. 147.

115   Karl Jaeger, report to Franz W. Stahlecker. Quoted in Damušis, *Lithuania*, p. 147.

his atrocities."[116] Damušis explains that "the documented state-ments of General Stahlecker clarify that most Lithuanians resisted German suggestions of revenge."[117] His observations on Stahlecker's attempts to smear Lithuanians by false association, or at least by creating the impression of a much wider support for his activities, are supported by Prunskis' reports of identifiable in-stances when Nazis dressed their own executioners in Lithuanian uniforms and then filmed them, to give the impression that the an-nihilation of Jews was being carried out by Lithuanian units.[118]

Standartenfuehrer Jaeger's own reports are perhaps clear evi-dence to indicate that this gruesome criminal operation was not a pogrom carried out by a local population, but a concerted cam-paign incited and carried out by the occupying power.[119] Prunskis gives evidence for the Einsatz group "conducting a planned mas-sacre day by day, moving from town to town". He describes how Guenther Hamann and his Roll commandos travelled to eighteen Lithuanian localities during the month of July 1941, thirty-two in August, thirty in September, eleven in October, and ten in Novem-ber. "In five months, he visited one hundred nine localities and ex-ecuted 147,346 Jews, and some communists."[120]

It is perhaps significant to mention that Soviet, as well as some German and Jewish sources, often describe the progress of the Hol-ocaust in Lithuania without making the necessary distinction be-tween the Gestapo's irregular helpers, and members of the Lithua-nian Activist Front, who were true Lithuanian partisans and patri-ots, who involved themselves in action against the Nazis and the Soviets equally to restore an independent state. Damušis explains that this results "either intentionally or without the benefit of more painstaking research, [...in the assumption...] that Stahlecker's plan to involve the local population in the extermination of the

---

116   Damušis, *Lithuania*, p. 130.
117   Damušis, *Lithuania*.
118   Juozas Prunskis, *Lithuania's Jews and the Holocaust* (Chicago: Lithuanian Amer-ican Council, 1979), p. 19.
119   Prunskis, *Lithuania's Jews*.
120   Prunskis, *Lithuania's Jews*.

Jewish people was easily put into practice." He adds "this ill-conceived assumption accepts at face value the highly misleading statements that local partisan groups acquiesced to the demands of the Einsatz groups and participated in their crimes."[121] The advantage to Soviet historiography of this substitution will be obvious, because the thrust of Stalin's propaganda for the reoccupation of the Baltic countries after the Second World War was based on allegations of Baltic complicity with Nazism (and it continues to be the background of Putin's Russian propaganda!) but the truth is that the Lithuanian partisans and activists were passionate fighters for national freedom. They were as much opposed to Nazi aggression as they had been to the Soviet one, and it is necessary here to attempt to redress the balance. Damušis makes it plain that the true Lithuanian partisans neither supported the activities of the Nazi occupying forces, nor did they participate in the gruesome atrocities of the Einsatz groups. A similar opinion was expressed by Dr. Petras Kisielius who drew my attention to a dozen books written by Jewish authors, who argue rather differently.[122] In fact Lithuanian partisans risked their lives in combat with both occupying forces. An estimated 1,600 were killed in the uprising which led to the establishment of the Lithuanian Provisional Government and approximately 2,000 more fell in battles with NKVD squads, local communist units and their collaborators, and certain Red Army detachments that were terrorizing the civilian population. Although their activities did not achieve an open profile under the Nazi occupation, there were a number of occasions when the Lithuanian partisans defended themselves and the headquarters of the Lithuanian Activist Front from the attacks by Nazi troops.[123] Lithuanians treasure the memory of the activists, partisans, and *baltaraiščiai* ("white-bandaged" irregulars), who courageously fought in the

---

121   Damušis, *Lithuania*, p. 133.
122   Interview with Dr. Petras Kisielius, December 13, 2001.
123   Two stories of an attack of the headquarters in Kaunas after the dilution of the Provisional Government were told by Škirpa. See e.g., Kazys Škirpa, *Sukilimas*, (Chicago: Lietuvių Fronto Bičiuliai, 1986).

face of insurmountable odds, and they should never be confused with the irregulars organized by the Einsatz leadership.[124]

In fact, a large proportion of these Einsatz irregulars were criminals who had been released from prison indiscriminately during the uprising.[125] However, there is additional evidence that the Gestapo recruited criminals directly from within the prisons in order to involve them in terrorizing the population and the Jews in particular. In a single month of July 1941, twenty-one criminals were released by them from Kaunas prison and enrolled for these purposes.[126] In addition, it is important to note that Lithuanian Germans were recruited into the SS units. As in other occupied countries, these people were of particular interest to the invading force, to whom they could be particularly useful as they spoke Lithuanian perfectly, an attribute which clearly made them ideally suited for spying and other nefarious assignments within the occupied country.[127]

SS Obersturmbahnfuehrer Ehrlinger's report on the current "Situation and Conditions" to the Reichssicherheitshauptmann, dated July 1, 1941, indicated that Nazis had succeeded in recruiting only five men who had previously fought as partisans against the Soviets. Two of these were subsequently enrolled in the Einsatz group. One of these served as a guard in Fort VII, a prison, in Kaunas and the other joined a Commando Kompanie with the agreement of the Fieldkommandant, and was mainly deployed also in guarding the prisons of Kaunas.[128] The report, written for administrative rather than propaganda purposes, provides useful evidence that the Lithuanian partisans were not involved in executions at Fort VII, and adds strength to the case that the Germans completely failed to organize an SS unit in Lithuania.

---

124   Damušis, *Lithuania*, pp. 133-134.
125   Damušis, *Lithuania*, p. 134. Similarly, the Soviets planned to release 6,000 of criminals after Lithuania's declaration of independence, using them in a crackdown of the independent country during the planned communist coup d'état.
126   Damušis, *Lithuania*, p. 134.
127   Damušis, *Lithuania*, p. 134.
128   "Report of Ehrlinger, SS Obersturmbannfuehrer of the Sicherheits Police" quoted in Damušis, *Lithuania*, p. 135.

This was not for lack of attempting to do so, but when it is considered that German recruitment yielded 50,000 volunteers in the Netherlands, 40,000 among the Belgians (half Flemish, half Walloon), 6,000 Danes, 6,000 Norwegians, and even 1,000 Finns (though their country was unoccupied), the fact that only approximately 8,000 Lithuanians probably served in the defense battalions (but not in the SS) seems comparatively creditable, and is certainly an effective repudiation of Soviet propaganda, which suggested mass involvement.[129] Though the Nazi authorities promised that these units would only be used within the respective homelands, most ended up serving on the Eastern Front, and some Lithuanian units ended up serving in Poland, and also further away, in Yugoslavia. Their exact contribution to the German war effort remains debatable. Some of these contingents may have become involved because they saw military involvement as being a way of undoing the injustice of the earlier Russian invasion. It is, however, obvious that the tragedy of the massacre of many of the Lithuanian Jews would not have occurred if there had been no Nazi occupation of Lithuania. Roger Petersen of the University of Chicago has said that "the issue of Lithuanian collaboration with the Germans remains controversial even in the year 2000."[130] He has helpfully observed that the continued controversy over the actual level of national involvement in Nazi criminality has more to do with inadequate apologies, failure to pursue suspected war criminals, and varying interpretations of the many other events which took place around June 1941, than with the actual numbers of Lithuanian collaborators.[131]

The arguments over this issue are important, but it will be necessary to await many updated reports from the International Commission for the Evaluation of the Crimes of the Nazi and Soviet Occupation Regimes in Lithuania, which was established under the

---

129   George H. Stein, *The Waffen SS: Hitler's Elite Guard at War, 1939 – 1945* (Ihaca: Cornell University Press, 1966), p. 156, quoted in Roger D. Petersen, *Resistance and Rebellion. Lessons from Eastern Europe* (Cambridge: Cambridge University Press, 2001), p. 156.

130   Petersen, *Resistance and Rebellion*.

131   Petersen, *Resistance and Rebellion*.

President of the Republic in 1998, before they can be resolved satisfactorily. Scholars from Lithuania, the United States, the United Kingdom, Israel, Russia, and other countries are currently sharing in its activity, and many recent academic papers have addressed the legacy of the Second World War in Lithuania on the basis of its work.[132] This section has addressed these issues briefly and has tended to support the argument that Lithuanian complicity was limited and restricted to informal groups of citizens. The commission has made its in-depth reports about both communist and fascist crimes in occupied Lithuania that the matter can be settled.[133]

Himmler's Generalplan Ost of 1942, which "envisaged that half the Estonians, over half the Latvians and 85 per cent of the Lithuanians would be deported," was undoubtedly brutal. But because "these large-scale deportations were not scheduled to take place until after the capitulation of the Soviet Union," according to Thomas Lane, the Soviet occupation of the Baltic States was more brutal than the Nazi occupation.[134] He is not alone in this conclusion: for example, Professor Andrei Zubov, a senior historian at the Moscow Institute of International Relations, argues that "communism was more terrible than Nazism and fascism because it destroyed society down to its foundations."[135] The Baltic people's "sufferings were acute and very long-lasting since they remained under Soviet occupation until the restoration of their independence

---

132   See e.g., Saulius Sužiedėlis, "Thoughts on Lithuania's Shadows of the Past: A Historical Essay on the Legacy of War" and "Thoughts on Lithuania's Shadows of the Past: A Historical Essay on the Legacy of War, Part II," *Artium*, www.artium.lt/4/journal.html.

133   The author is aware that the U.S. Department of State applied pressure on Lithuania to transform the International Commission for the Evaluation of the Crimes of the Nazi and Soviet Occupation Regimes in Lithuania into two separate commissions. Lithuania resisted that pressure, confirming that both Communist and Nazi crimes were parallel and, in fact, equal crimes against Lithuania, Western civilization and humanity. It is important to note that the monument for 100 millions of victims of Communism across the world was built in Washington, D.C. and it was be dedicated on June 12, 2007. See http://www.victimsofcommunism.org/.

134   Thomas Lane, *Victims of Stalin and Hitler: the Exodus of Poles and Balts to Britain.* (New York: Palgrave, 2004), p. 44.

135   http://jbanc.org/mgimo.html.

after the collapse of communism in the Soviet Union in 1991."[136] The Soviet regime, according to Thomas Lane, was particularly brutal in the Baltic States and in Poland, where approximately 1.6-1.7 million people were deported to Soviet concentration camps.[137]

The partisan war against the Soviets

In 1944 the Nazi occupation was replaced by the second Soviet occupation and the Lithuanians continued their struggle for freedom. Lithuanian historians have reviewed the history of the Partisan War, discerning the phases of its development in relationship to the establishment of centralized leadership, and the strategy and tactics of the struggle itself, with respect to its changing organizational structure. Nijolė Gaškaitė has recently assessed the progress of Lithuania's partisan war against the second Soviet occupation, dividing this into three main periods.[138] The first, which began in June 1944 to May 1946, saw the establishment of district organizations. Between May 1946 and November 1948 these districts were responsible for the conduct of the war. Finally, between November 1948 and May 1953 centralized structures were created, although they were then destroyed by the regime. Kęstutis Girnius, however, has used a different schema to assess the development of the partisan war according to the intensity of partisan activity.[139] Thus, the period from 1944 to 1946 saw extended recruitment and the movement gathering strength. The next two years, from 1946 to 1948, was a period of consolidation, while from 1949 to 1952 there was a weakening of activity and eventual defeat. Similarly, Vytautas Vardys distinguishes two four-year periods, which he describes first as the years of struggle (1944-1948), followed by gradual

---

136   Lane, *Victims of Stalin and Hitler*, p. 55.
137   See Darius Furmonavičius, "Victims of Stalin and Hitler: the exodus of Poles and Balts to Britain. By Thomas Lane" in *International Affairs*, 82, no. 4 (July 2006): 811-812.
138   Gaškaitė, etc., *Lietuvos partizanai: 1944 – 1953*, pp. 16-22.
139   Girnius, *Partizanų kovos Lietuvoje*.

decline (1949-1952).[140] The later years into the 1960s were marked by continued individual partisan activity rather than a partisan war.

The earlier discussion of the partisan war was developed in the absence of access to the Soviet archival material, which only became available after 1990. Now that much of this key documentation has been published, it is possible to refine the scheme, and it might be better to consider the time between July 1944 and April 1948 as being one of formation in which the activities of a district organizational structure emerged. The movement shifted toward a centralized organizational structure, and the adoption of the name, expressed this. *Lietuvos Laisvės Kovų Sąjūdis*, Lithuania's Fight for Freedom Movement, was formed into being between April 1948 and February 1949. The next period, between February 1949 and May 1953, was marked by the centrally organized partisan war throughout Lithuania. Between May 1953 and 1965 the activities of partisan groups were still diverse and widespread, although they gradually declined, in the face of Soviet superiority. The last Lithuanian partisans perished in battle in 1965 or else faded away. It is worth repeating here that at its peak the movement involved about one percent of Lithuania's total population. In the spring of 1945, some 30,000 partisans were already fighting the Soviet army and the NKVD forces. As we have mentioned earlier, the struggle was exceedingly fierce and Misiūnas and Taagepera estimate the average life span of partisans as having been a little less than two years. The human costs of the nine years of intense partisan activity between 1944 and 1953 were extremely high. About 100,000 people seem to have been directly involved in partisan fighting in Lithuania, and the estimated ultimate figure for partisan casualties was probably 50,000.[141]

Throughout the time the partisan war was under way, the Soviet ground and air forces were used against the supporters of the

140   Vytautas S. Vardys, "The partisan Movement in Postwar Lithuania" in Vytautas S. Vardys, (ed.) *Lithuania Under the Soviets* (Washington: Frederick A. Praeger, 1965).
141   Misiunas, *The Baltic states*, p. 86.

movement on many occasions. At the very beginning of the war, between July 1944 and April 1948, the partisan districts of *Vyčio, Didžiosios kovos, Vytauto, Tauro, Dainavos, Žemaičių, Kęstučio, Algimanto, Prisikėlimo* were formed and named. After 1945 the strategy had shifted from defensive tactics to outright partisan war, and the nine separate partisan districts which emerged were grouped into three military regions (Northeast, Northwest, and the Nemunas area) with joint military and political staff. The final consolidation of the freedom movement under the name *Lietuvos Laisvės Kovų Sąjūdis* was established formally on the anniversary of Lithuania's independence, February 16, 1949, after which the leadership passed into the hands of former officers of the Lithuanian army.

From an early date in their activity the partisans maintained an underground press, which published items ranging from irregular leaflets to substantial printed periodicals. The main newspapers were: *Aukštaičių kova* ("Aukštaičių fight" published in Vytautas district); *Laisvės talka* ("Supporting freedom," in Liūto division); *Žalioji giria* ("The Green Forest," in Didžiosios kovos district and Dzūkija); *Aukuras* ("The Altar," in Dainavos district); *Mylėk tėvynę* ("Love the Homeland," in the Merkio area headquarters), *Partizanas* ("The Partisan," in Southern Lithuania's area, which contained the Nemunas area headquarters); *Už tėvų žemę* ("For the Fatherland," in Dainavos district); *Girios balsas* ("Forest Voice," in the Marijampolė region); *Kovos keliu* ("Facing the Battle," in Tauras district); *Laisvės žvalgas* ("Freedom's scout," in Tauras region); *Alio* ("Hello," in Joint command of Kęstučio district); and *Laisvės varpas* ("The Bell of Freedom," serving all of Lithuania). This last publication had at least 127 issues between 1944 and 1951. The distribution of each of these newspapers was decentralized to the district level, with approximately 1,000 copies each. This partisan press diligently attempted to reflect the international situation of Lithuania, publishing the documents prepared by the movement's leadership, as well as reporting major world news. It is important to observe that the discovery of the secret documents of the Molotov-Ribbentrop pact, when they were taken from the German archives and published by the Americans, was particularly well documented in these newspapers. Major international developments, notably the establishment of the North Atlantic Treaty Organization, were well covered and the work of Lithuania's legations in the West was regularly reported. Thus, readers were able to understand that Lithuania's struggle was being conducted in both a diplomatic and a military way.[142]

The leadership of *Lietuvos Laisvės Kovų Sąjūdis* even organized training courses for partisan officers. In the summer of 1947 there were 72 graduates, whose training was accomplished mainly through surprise raids by small groups against the Soviet NKVD repression units. The chief tactics used by the partisans were to liberate arrested people; to warn collaborators; to order colonists to move out from Lithuania; and to prevent or disturb the organization of Soviet elections, which would be used to justify the occupation of the country. But the international contacts of the partisans were limited. One of the partisan leaders, Juozas Lukša-Daumantas, broke through the Iron Curtain of the heavily guarded border between occupied Lithuania and Poland with the support of his group in December 1947, and travelled across Polish territory before sailing across the Baltic Sea and finally reaching Stockholm in March 1948. He was searching for material support for the Lithuanian Freedom Fighters in the West. Unfortunately, his desperate mission was unsuccessful: while the western governments and intelligence services offered him promises, they gave no real help.[143] Daumantas settled briefly outside Lithuania, completing the manuscript of the book *Partizanai už Geležinės uždangos* ("Partisans behind the Iron Curtain") in Paris, where he married before returning

---

142 "Vasario šešioliktosios dienos proga," *Rytų Lietuva* February 15, 1949 in Algimantas Liekis (ed.), *Nenugalėtoji Lietuva: Lietuvos partizanų spauda (1944 - 1949)* (Vilnius: Valstybinis leidybos centras, 1995).

143 Britain's SIS initiated limited, though ineffective, operations in the three Baltic states. The KGB first compromised, and then controlled, MI6's entire intelligence network in the occupied Baltic states, completely deceiving the British and Americans. See Tom Bower, *The Red Web. MI6 and the KGB Master Coup* (London: Aurum Press, 1989). American attempts to infiltrate small numbers of selected anticommunist nationals into the Baltic states are described by Peter Grose, in Peter Grose, *Operation Rollback: America's Secret War Behind the Iron Curtain* (New York: Houghton Mifflin, 2000).

to Lithuania to continue fighting.[144] He used these opportunities to establish contacts with the Supreme Committee for the Liberation of Lithuania, and free Lithuanian diplomatic legations abroad, which were to serve as the chief information channel for explaining the real situation about the struggle in Lithuania to the outside world. He insisted on the necessity of external radio broadcasts to his country and explained the value of other moral support. He also brought an address to the Pope from the Lithuanian Catholics, which was delivered by Father Feliksas Kapočius, the National Delegate of the Third Pontifical Mission in Germany, informing the Pope fully about the mass murdering of the Lithuanians at the hand of the Soviet communists, and the Soviet Union's pervasive campaign to destroy the Catholic Church. Parallel communications were also sent to the Western governments. Eventually, Daumantas was parachuted back into Lithuania with CIA help, where he perished in 1951.

It is important to reflect on why people joined the partisans, and the reasons for the persistence of their resistance, despite the much less favorable conditions of the post-war occupation. Brazaitis' writing in 1961 gave five explanations for the recruitment of volunteers in the partisan war against the Soviet occupation.[145] He stated, first, that the experience of life under the 1940-1941 occupation had made it abundantly clear that Lithuania's aspirations for independence, economic prosperity, and freedom of conscience were incompatible with life under a Soviet regime. Second, he noted that the experience of organized resistance to the Nazi occupation encouraged a comparable response to the Soviet occupation. Third, there was the factor of public opinion, which felt that the comparative brevity of the Nazi occupation meant that the second Soviet occupation would also not last long, because the West would eventually realize the promises of the "Atlantic Charter," and act to

---

144   Juozas Daumantas, *Partizanai* (Chicago: Į Laisvę Fondas Lietuviškai Kultūrai ugdyti, 1950), or see the abbreviated edition of this book in English: K. V. Tauras, *Guerilla Warfare on the Amber Coast* (Chicago: Į Laisvę Fondas Lietuviškai Kultūrai ugdyti, 1962).

145   Juozas Brazaitis, "Partizanai antrosios sovietų okupacijos metu," *Į Laisvę*, no. 24 (61), 1961.

restore the independence which had been lost during the Second World War. Fourth, there was the practical and moral need to defend Lithuanian citizens from the Red Army and NKVD troops, and finally, many men had been forced to hide in the forests to avoid arrest or mobilization by the Soviet army. It was a combination of all these factors which had encouraged or driven men to take cover in the forests. A little later, Vytautas Vardys also discerned five aspects to activist participation in the partisan war against the Soviets. He did not, however, place so much emphasis on the necessity to defend citizens, as on the idealism and patriotism of the intelligentsia, and their positive attitude towards the West.[146] Similarly Thomas Remeikis, a political scientist, stressed that the hope that the West would eventually help the Baltic States was the most important factor in the motivation to 'go underground.' He was convinced that the original vision of the partisans involved the idea of resisting for a limited period, pending the victory of the West. It was felt that the restoration of independence to the Baltic States would play a major part in this achievement.[147] It is hugely unfortunate that the western states were eventually to be driven by a much more cynical policy. Their appeasement toward the Soviet Union can be blamed for this, though of course the real or imagined fear of nuclear war was to become a major factor in determining the twist of policy in this matter.

These varied factors were clearly at play in the individual decisions to join the partisan movement. However, what is very clear is that the movement, as it developed, would not have come into being without very widespread and continuing support in the wider community. Of course, while the whole community could not actively take to the forest, it could support those that did. Kęstutis Girnius writing in the 1980s felt that the majority of the Lithuanians believed there was a real possibility of war breaking out between the West and the Soviet Union, and that such a conflict

---

146   Vardys, "The Partisan Movement."
147   Thomas Remeikis, "The Armed struggle against the Sovietization of Lithuania after 1944," *Lituanus* 8, no. 1-2, (1962).

would see the Soviet Union driven from the Baltic States.[148] The memory of the Soviet terror during the 1940-1941 occupation and its intensification after the reoccupation was enough to inspire this hope.[149] This terror was directed at everybody with democratic views or who had voiced support for national independence at any time. It was extended to include those who complained of any aspect of the Soviet bureaucracy, or failed to adjust to its demands, and there is evidence that these demands (e.g., in relation to farm produce deliveries) were manipulated to put people at a deliberate disadvantage so that the officialdom could more effectively order their removal from the local scene. In fact, everyone was a potential target of the NKVD (later KGB) repression units. Thus, people went into the forests when they could no longer tolerate the insecurity of civilian life or were threatened with prison or deportation to the Gulag. While the first wave of partisans consisted of anti-German national underground members, they were joined by people avoiding enlistment in the Soviet army. The Stalinist collectivization and deportation programs produced further waves of partisans. Finally, the severe and unrelenting persecution of the Catholic Church added its own dimension to resistance in Lithuania, so priests and parish sacristans, organists, and women serving and cleaning churches, were often to be found among the main helpers of the partisan movement in Lithuania. They developed the necessary communications networks, helping to provide supplies, medication, treating and hiding wounded partisans.

It is possible to group the psychological, political, historical, and economic factors which motivated this reaction to the Soviet terror in the Baltic States. Natural human indignation in response to the brutalizing program of arrests, killings, and deportations was prominent, and the wish to defend family property and land was also important. The major political factors were patriotism, love of the homeland and its way of life, the yearning for independence, the eager anticipation of the demise of the Soviet regime, and the perception of its temporality; all these played their part. Historical

---

148   Girnius, *Partizanų kovos.*
149   Misiunas, *The Baltic states,* p. 84.

reasoning was also a factor, because there were many who had participated in the successful fight for freedom between 1918 and 1920. Behind this lay the longer historical memory of revolts in 1863 and 1905 against the Russian Tsarist regime. This recollection was itself spurred by closer reference to the successful but short-lived revolt against the Soviets in 1940-1941 and the anti-Nazi resistance of 1941-1944. Finally, we must consider the economic pressure on individuals, which resulted from their inability to pay the enormous taxes imposed on those who still retained private or family property as well as the unrelenting indignities imposed by collectivization and the confiscation of private property. Each of these factors contributed to individual decisions. However, the documents of the Lithuanian Freedom Fighters indicate that its Supreme Command originally intended only to keep the resistance active for a period between three and five years, in expectation of a conflict between the USSR and the West.[150] It was, of course, believed that the successful outcome of such a conflict would leave them in a position to take control in a restored and independent Lithuania.

It is important to recall that the memory of the partisan war played a significant part in establishing the moral resolve which carried through the liberation of Lithuania in the late 1980s and the beginning of the 1990s. On November 23, 1994, during the celebration of Lithuanian Army Day, President Vytautas Landsbergis said in a major public speech that the Parliament would have included a sentence commemorating the memory of *Lietuvos Laisvės Kovų Sąjūdis* in the Declaration of Independence (made on March 11, 1990), if more had been known about the partisan war at the time it was drafted. His acknowledgement was a public recognition, for the first time, of how heavily the details of their opposition had been suppressed by the Soviet system. Though many people carried profound memories of family associations, it was only after the achievement of independence that the story of their bravery began to be expressed coherently. However, these families, together with

---

150   E.g., "Prapuolenio - J. Deksnio ir Skrajūno - J. Lukšos raportas BDPS Prezidiumo pirmininkui apie pavestų uždavinių ir įgaliojimų vykdymą, 1948 m. balandžio mėn. 27 d." in *Laisvės kovos 1944-1953 metais*, p. 485.

the political prisoners and exiles who had survived the ordeal of those years, had organized themselves along with *Sąjūdis*, and had come to rejoice in its fulfillment of their long-held ambitions. Those who had participated in resistance movements, together with their children and grandchildren, had interpreted the *Sąjūdis*, as a movement directed to the same primary goal of national independence for Lithuania, and the expulsion of the Soviet army.[151] This movement, *Lietuvos Laisvės Kovų Sąjūdis*, can therefore be credited with having prepared the ground for all later anti-Soviet dissident activity in Lithuania.

Anti-Soviet Dissident Activity

Lithuanian resistance to the Soviet system was consistent, and we have reviewed its major phases: the uprising in 1941; the partisan war of 1944 to 1953; and the underground dissident anti-Soviet activity between 1953 and 1987. Opposition to the Soviet system found its expression, after the partisan movement was destroyed, in the peaceful defense of national, religious, and human rights.[152] Despite its brutality, the Soviet system was unable to crush the independence of Lithuanian opinion, though at first, the opportunities to express this were necessarily private or covert. However, strong religious and dissident feelings flowed beneath the surface of public life, overlapping with, and nourishing patriotic

---

151 My own grandfather Stanislovas Lazauskas was a political prisoner who was sent to the Soviet concentration camp in Vorkuta, Siberia in 1945, and I joined *Sąjūdis*, the Lithuanian independence movement, as did many grandsons of the Lithuanian partisans and deportees, with his memory in mind.

152 See Vytautas S. Vardys, *The Catholic Church: Dissent and Nationality in Soviet Lithuania* (New York: Columbia University Press, 1978); Vytautas S. Vardys, "Lithuania's Catholic Movement Reappraised," *Survey* 25 (1980); Vytautas S. Vardys, "Human Rights Issues in Estonia, Latvia, and Lithuania," *Journal of Baltic Studies*, 12 (1981); Vytautas Vardys, "Pogrindžio rezistencija Lietuvoje," *Ateitis* no. 4 (1982); Thomas A. Oleszczuk, *Political Justice in the USSR: Disent and Repression in Lithuania, 1969 – 1978* (New York: Columbia University Press, 1988); Thomas Remeikis, *Opposition to Soviet Rule in Lithuania* (Chicago: Institute of Lithuanian Studies Press, 1980); Alexander R. Alexiev, *Dissent and Nationalism in the Soviet Baltic* (Santa Monica: Rand, 1983); Nijolė Sadunaitė, *A Radiance in the Gulag* (Manassas: Trinity Communications, 1987).

sentiments, which resurfaced more insistently after Stalin's death.[153] In 1956 these feelings boiled over for the first time, when students in Kaunas and Vilnius held massive demonstrations of solidarity with the Hungarian revolution on All Souls' Day, November 2. This is the time at which Lithuanians have traditionally commemorated their dead family members, and this deeply religious occasion turned into a patriotic demonstration.[154] Significantly, the national anthem was sung, and the Lithuanian tricolor flag was then produced and paraded along the main street of Kaunas before the gathering was summarily dispersed by the police. A similar protest was held in the famous Rasos cemetery of Vilnius, when hundreds of young people were either arrested immediately, or tracked down even years later. Those who were identified as having participated in these demonstrations were thrown out of the universities and others lost their jobs.

The political consciousness in Lithuania between the end of the partisan war and before the beginning of *perestroika* is described in the words of political scientist Aleksandras Štromas:

> the nation as such decided to end active resistance to the occupation and to accept the condition of existence forced on the country, [...] it accepted a partial conformism [but] such a conformist position does not mean capitulation; it means just a change of tactics to seek the same goals [...] in order that the nation could pursue any goals, it is necessary first to protect its life.[155]

The implication was that it had become widely recognized that the time of active resistance had passed, but internal resistance, often intellectual and for most purposes hidden, became the order of the day. Of course, the world was changing, and Stalin's death was the first marker of major change, but as time passed, the communications revolution was beginning to influence communist societies to some degree. In the 1970s national protest again became a big issue, but by means of public demonstration, rather than by

---

153   See Vardys, *Lithuania.*
154   See e.g., Thomas Remeikis, *Opposition to Soviet Rule in Lithuania* (Chicago: Institute of Lithuanian Studies Press, 1980).
155   Aleksandras Štromas, *Politinė sąmonė Lietuvoje* (Political consciousness in Lithuania) (London: Nida, 1980), p. 20.

force of arms. On November 23, 1970, Simas Kudirka, a forty-year-old Lithuanian radio operator on a Soviet fishing vessel, jumped aboard the American coast guard cutter *Vigilant*, when it came alongside the *Sovetskaia Litva* at Martha's Vineyard, on the Massachusetts coast.[156] The defection failed, because the Coast Guard admiral allowed the Soviets to board the Vigilant and arrest him. Kudirka was to receive a ten-year prison sentence in occupied Lithuania, but he had declared before an open court the dedication of his generation to Lithuania's independence and to democracy, and his case received wide international attention. His stand then offered a role model for a generation of young Lithuanians, which many were happy to aspire to. The incident marked the beginning of a period of change during the later 1960s and the 1970s, which, according to Vytautas Vardys, saw three new types of dissident movement being formed. These were the movement in defense of the rights of the Catholic Church and of believers of any denomination; movements advocating national rights and self-determination; and those concerned with the advancement of human rights, and the monitoring of their violation by the regime.[157] It is worth noting the observation of David Kowalewski that approximately two-thirds of all dissident demonstrations in Lithuania between 1970 and 1977 were of a religious nature. Most of the remaining third were related to the issue of national rights.[158]

The scale of these movements, when viewed retrospectively, appears to have been quite remarkable. In comparison with the activity of dissident movements elsewhere in the Soviet Union, the level in occupied Lithuania was between five and ten times more intense than in other regions. Indeed, between 1965 and 1978 approximately 10 percent of all the demonstrations and protests which affected the entire former Soviet territories took place in Lithuania. This fact is even more remarkable when it is noted that

---

157   See Vardys, *Lithuania*.
158   David Kowalewski, "Dissent in the Baltic Republics: Characteristics and Consequences," *Journal of Baltic Studies*, 10, no. 4 (1979): 309-319.

the country had only 1.3 percent of the whole Soviet population.[159] In similar vein, Lithuania had the greatest number of underground periodicals per capita. The most famous of these was *Lietuvos katalikų bažnyčios kronika* ("The Chronicle of the Catholic Church of Lithuania"), which the KGB failed to prevent from being published throughout the 18 years before the Declaration of Independence in 1990.[160] Periodically there appeared more than a dozen other underground journals: *Aušra* ("The Dawn"); *Rūpintojėlis* ("The Sorrowful Christ"); *Lietuvos ateitis* ("Lithuania's Future"); *Dievas ir tėvynė* ("God and Country"); *Tiesos kelias* ("Way of Truth"); *Vytis* ("The Knight"); *Laisvės šauklys* ("Herald of Freedom"); *Pastogė* ("Shelter"); *Lietuvos archyvas* ("Lithuanian Archive"); *Varpas* ("The Bell"); *Alma mater; Perspektyvos* ("Perspectives"), and others, which reflected a primarily patriotic and Catholic orientation. While *Laisvės šauklys* and *Vytis* placed greater emphasis on national issues, the underground academic journal *Perspektyvos* was edited by a Lecturer at Vilnius University, Dr. Vytautas Skuodis, and two of his friends: Povilas Pečeliūnas, a secondary school teacher, and Gintautas Iešmantas, a journalist and a poet. They published essentially ideological articles, and the vigor of this journal was such that it included frequent papers written by members of the Lithuanian Communist Association, a dissident communist group that advocated Lithuania's secession from the Soviet Empire. Other articles discussing the ideas of Euro-communism and the secession of Lithuania were provided by Gintautas Iešmantas himself, a former editor of the communist journal.

It is a striking fact that the Lithuanian dissident movement included not only intellectuals, but also workers and peasants. It was this broad appeal which helped the Lithuanian underground to develop rapidly into a widespread social mass movement. However,

---

159   David Kowalewski, "Lithuanian Protest for Human Rights in the 1970s: Characteristics and Consequences," *Lituanus*, vol. 25 (1979).

160   Joshua Rubenstein, *Soviet Dissidents: Their Struggle for Human Rights* (Boston: Beacon Press, 1980). See *Lietuvių Katalikų Bažnyčios Kronika*. vol. 1 – 10 (Chicago: Lietuvos Kronikos Sąjunga, 1974 – 1992); Vytautas Vardys, "LKB Kronika," *Laiškai lietuviams*, vol. 18, 1992; Saulius Suziedelis, *The Sword and the Cross* (Huntington: Our Sunday Visitor Publication Department, 1988).

it was religious dissent which broadened the popular support of the opposition, especially when fresh Soviet anti-religious legislation was introduced in 1961 under Nikita Krushchev, which extended the criminal code to those engaged in teaching religion to children.[161] During the two years from 1970 to 1972 three priests and one woman were sentenced for this activity, but the persecution of the clergy was increased in other ways. Limits were set to enrolment in the single Catholic theological seminary serving Lithuania, located in Kaunas. It was allowed to enroll only 24 students between 1965 and 1966. More priests died than were ordained in this period, and in 1968 several parish pastors launched an initiative demanding permission to increase the number of students in the seminary. On this occasion, they appealed to the highest Soviet authority with the widest possible support, a tactic, which had previously been employed by Bishop Valančius in response to similar repression of the Catholic Church during the nineteenth century. This new development took immediate advantage of a Soviet law passed in 1968, which allowed public petition of government for the first time. Yet despite its legality, the Soviet authorities attempted to arrest the petitioners. However, the process of submitting petitions spread quickly after this first opportunity, and others followed, embracing various topics, and being endorsed by many thousands of people, not all of whom could be imprisoned. Among the more famous of these petitions was a letter to Secretary General Leonid Brezhnev, which demanded guarantees for the freedom of individual conscience. This was sent to him in December 1971 and to the Secretary General of the United Nations, Kurt Waldheim. It was the first biggest memorandum in the Soviet Union signed by 17,054 people and its submission became an international event.[162]

---

161 Suziedelis, *Sword and Cross*.
162 Can. Michael Bourdeaux, founder of the Keston Institute in Oxford, calls the Memorandum the founding document of the Lithuanian independence. Interview with Can. Michael Bourdeaux, Oxford, July 7, 2007. E.g. Darius Furmonavičius, "Septyniolikos tūkstančių parašų "Memorandumas". Pašnekesys su dr. Michael Bourdeaux, Kestono instituto įkūrėju," *XXI Amžius*, no. 58 (1555), August 1, 2007, p. 1 & 3. The author's grandmother Ona Lazauskienė signed it. Her signature was spotted by the author on one of the pages of the Memorandum during his visit to Can. Michael Bourdeaux in Oxford on July 7, 2007.

The way this petition was directed is instructive of the new mood in Lithuanian dissidence. According to Vytautas Vardys, "the routing of this petition indicated that the new generation of dissidents well understood not only the value of using Soviet laws for promoting their objectives but also the importance of public opinion for getting satisfaction of their grievances."[163] They were, of course, consistently supported by Lithuanian radio broadcasts from the West, which disseminated news about their activities and which were widely listened to as sources of reliable information by a broad number of people, who would otherwise have been wholly dependent on the Soviet media. It is proper to recall the important contribution of the Lithuanian programs of "Radio Free Europe/Radio Liberty" (based in Munich and later in Prague) and the "Voice of America" (in Washington, D.C.), both of which were financed by the U.S. Congress, or also the Russian broadcasts of the British Broadcasting Corporation (BBC).

The petition device was used with increased frequency, and the largest number of signatures collected was 148,149 for a petition presented in 1979. It requested the return of a newly built church in the port city of Klaipėda to religious use, after it had been summarily nationalized in 1961 to serve the local community as a cinema, only a short while after its construction was completed. The authorities, however, soon found ways of disregarding virtually all the petitions which came their way and Catholic dissidents therefore began to switch their attention to the process of monitoring the frequent violation of human rights, which was regularly taking place in all parts of occupied Lithuania. They therefore began to publish the *Chronicle of the Catholic Church of Lithuania* on March 19, 1972.[164] In the same vein, close contact was developed and maintained with the leading liberal Russian dissidents, notably the Academician Andrei Sakharov. The Russian biologist Sergej Kovoliov, who was later to become Boris Yeltsin's adviser for human rights, helped

---

163   See Vardys, *Lithuania*.
164   See *Lietuvių Katalikų Bažnyčios Kronika*, Vol. 1 – 10 (Chicago: Lietuvos Kronikos Sąjunga, 1974 – 1992); Vytautas Vardys, "LKB Kronika;" Sužiedėlis, *Sword and Cross*.

personally to transfer microfilms of the Chronicle to the West. It was a major venture as more than eighty volumes were published in the eighteen years between 1972 and 1990, and its importance was such that Vytautas Vardys has called the Chronicle the "uncensored voice of Lithuania."[165] When the Chronicle's twentieth anniversary was celebrated in 1992, it was publicly revealed that it had been edited (until he was uncovered and arrested by the KGB in 1983) by Father Sigitas Tamkevičius, S.J. (a Jesuit priest), who later in 1990 became Bishop of Kaunas. After Father Tamkevičius' arrest, Father Jonas Boruta, S.J., a young physicist, who had become a priest after graduating from an underground theological seminary, took his place. The KGB was never again successful in discovering who edited the Chronicle, but sister Nijolė Sadūnaitė, who had helped with the production, reproduction, and distribution of the Chronicle, was subsequently sentenced to a particularly long term of labor camp and exile for these "crimes."[166]

After the election of Pope John Paul II in 1978, five Catholic priests took the initiative in establishing *Komitetą tikinčiųjų žmogaus teisėms ginti*, the Catholic Committee for the Defense of Believers' Rights. This group had the stated goal of enabling believers to achieve equal rights with atheists, both in constitutional and practical terms. This committee published extensive materials on discrimination against believers and organized petitions as well as demonstrations. One of its leaders, Father Alfonsas Svarinskas, was arrested and sentenced in the spring of 1984 at the same time as Father Sigitas Tamkevičius. Around that time too, Father Juozas Zdebskis, who had earlier been sentenced for teaching religion to children, was mysteriously killed in a car accident, a fate which affected dissident leaders with an unnaturally high frequency during these years of occupation.

The largest nationalist upheaval of the post-partisan period began in Kaunas on March 14, 1972, after Romas Kalanta, a nineteen-year-old high school pupil, immolated himself in protest

---

165   See Vardys, *Lithuania*.
166   See Nijolė Sadūnaitė, *A Radiance in the Gulag* (Manassas: Trinity Communications, 1987).

against the Soviet occupation, hoping to attract the world's attention to Lithuania's plight. Though formally a member of the *komsomol*, he had adopted a nonconformist "longhaired hippie" style. When he burned himself to death at the centrally located theatre park in Kaunas, it was an act which had a deep political context as members of the Lithuanian hippie groups had contemplated such an act long before it took place, and had even drawn lots for the deed.[167] The police responded to the perceived challenge by insisting that this funeral must take place privately, but when the news was circulated that there would be no public event thousands of people took to the streets and marched down the central avenue of the city, overturning police cars, waving the Lithuanian flags and singing the national anthem. Special troops were immediately called to dissolve the crowd and approximately 500 people were arrested, while others were tracked down later according to well-established procedures.[168] Again, the official response meant that many of those who were students were removed from universities, while others lost their jobs. *Lituanus* reported approximately three thousand participants in these events.[169] This uprising, as the inhabitants of Kaunas called it, continued for five days until May 19 and it was reported that other young people in several provincial towns had repeated Kalanta's act. Shortly afterwards the youth of

---

167   Barbara W. Jancar, "Religious Dissent in the Soviet Union" in Rudolf L. Tokes (ed.), *Dissent in the USSR.* (Baltimore: Johns Hopkins University Press, 1975).

168   "Konferencija, skirta Romo Kalantos aukos ir politinių protestų 30-osioms metinėms bei mitingo prie Adomo Mickevičiaus paminklo 15-osioms metinėms paminėti" (Conference to commemorate the 30th anniversary of the death of Romas Kalanta and the 15th anniversary of the demonstration near Adomas Mickevičius monument) http://www.genocid.lt/GRTD/Konferencijos/lietuva.htm. The proceedings of the conference mention that at least 400 people were arrested because of this action. "Armed Conflict Events Data: Young People's Rebellion in Lithuania" reports the arrests of 200 to 500 people. See http://www.onwar.com/aced/data/lima/flithuania1972.htm.

169   "Furthermore, the fact that a simple miscalculation by the authorities could set off widespread disorders, involving several thousand participants, extensive property damage, at least one dead policeman, the arrests of reportedly 200 to 500 persons, and the intervention of internal security troops to quell the demonstrations, indicates the fragility of loyalty to the Soviet regime." See "Self-Immolations and National Protest in Lithuania," *Lituanus* 18, no. 4 (Winter 1972), http://www.lituanus.org/.

Vilnius reacted again at an international football competition, first refusing to stand up for the Soviet anthem, and later attempting to march on the city center. At these signs of unrest Moscow became anxious and representatives of the Central Committee of the Communist Party were sent to investigate the events. Initially, the response of the Communist Party First Secretary in occupied Lithuania Antanas Sniečkus was calm, but shortly afterwards several officials, school directors, and journal editors were either transferred to other duties, or lost their jobs. Eight leaders of the Vilnius demonstration were held in prison, and when they were sent for trial in October, the KGB attempted to close several groups dedicated to Lithuanian folk culture, because Communist Party opinion held that they were essentially concerned with nationalist activity. As a result, their members too were arrested, imprisoned, lost their jobs, or were dismissed from universities and schools. As dissidence became more widespread, the tariff imposed by the authorities became more predictable.

The heavy-handed nature of Soviet state reaction to these demonstrators served to encourage religious and nationalist dissent, and a significant group of human rights activists emerged, dedicated to the process of monitoring the police repression systematically. The first such monitoring group emerged late in 1977, just a year after President Ford and communist leader Brezhnev had signed the Helsinki agreements with other world leaders. In 1978, however, after all leaders of the Lithuanian Helsinki group were arrested, the group dissolved. Its members' intention had been to monitor Moscow's behavior according to the terms of the Helsinki agreement on human rights. By registering violations as they occurred, this Lithuanian group clearly incurred the severest official displeasure because it had become one of the most active of its kind in the whole Soviet Empire. Its organizer Viktoras Petkus was a twice-imprisoned activist of the Catholic movement, and other leading members included Father Karolis Garuckas, S.J.; the poet Ona Lukauskaitė-Poškienė; Eithan Finkelstein, an activist of the Jewish emigration movement; and Tomas Venclova, another poet. They had successfully published documents on individual cases of human rights violations, and several papers on the extensive religious oppression of the Catholic Church before being suppressed. According to Vytautas Vardys, "after the arrest of Petkus, the silencing of Finkelstein, the deaths of Garuckas and Poškienė and the departure of Venclova, dissident activity became less prominent."[170] However, this time the pause was not to be as prolonged as the regime may have hoped.

Despite this, the co-operation between Baltic dissidents manifestly increased in the 1970s. In 1979 leaders of the various streams of activity published a joint statement boldly articulating the legal and political basis for the restoration of an independent Lithuania, Latvia, and Estonia. Prepared in commemoration of the fortieth anniversary of the signature of the secret Molotov-Ribbentrop pact of August 23, 1939, there were 44 signatories to this statement, which was signed by 37 Lithuanians, 4 Latvians, and 4 Estonians. Among the Lithuanian signatories were four priests, as well as Antanas Terleckas, the future leader of the Lithuanian Freedom League. Among the Estonians were university professor Juri Kukk and ornithologist Mart Niklus. Academician Andrei Sakharov and some other prominent dissidents in Moscow also endorsed this Baltic declaration, which was especially unwelcome to the Soviets because it mentioned the Stalin-Hitler secret partition of Europe. It was a magnificent rebuff to the Soviet Union, and the formulation of the document stated that the Baltic countries rejected Soviet rule as having been imposed by force and demanded the reversal of the consequences of the 1939 Molotov-Ribbentrop pact. This, it declared, "was a conspiracy between the two greatest tyrants in history, Stalin and Hitler, against peace and humanity," and affirmed that the pact effectively inaugurated World War II, declaring "we consider the date of August 23rd as the day of shame." Depending on one's viewpoint, this was either an act of the greatest disobedience and effrontery toward the Soviet system, or a statement that its whole machinery was established upon an historical lie. Whichever way it was interpreted, this first pan-Baltic declaration of a

---

170   Vardys, *Lithuania.*

new era heralded a new phase in the struggle for national liberties in the region.

The text of this well-argued appeal is historically significant as it showed familiarity with the secret documents of the Molotov-Ribbentrop Pact, which the Soviets had always denied had even existed, as well as knowledge of more recent international legal documentation. It demanded action from the world community of nations, directing this appeal to:

First, the Soviet Union, which was asked to publish the full contents of the Molotov-Ribbentrop pact together with all the supplementary secret documents.

Second, the governments of East and West Germany who were called on to "pronounce the Molotov-Ribbentrop pact to be void from the moment of its signing, to help the USSR to 'liquidate' the consequences of the pact."

Third, the signatories of the Atlantic Charter were also asked to condemn the pact and its consequences "from the position of their moral responsibility."

Fourth, UN Secretary General Kurt Waldheim was asked to raise the question of Baltic freedom at the United Nations.

Therefore, the greatest implication of the Declaration perhaps was the fact that its appeal was directed both to the highest echelons of the Soviet state and to an international audience. The text of this declaration was like the resolution which was passed in the US House of Representatives in 1965 and in the US Senate in 1966, because of the initiative of the American Congressional Action to Free the Baltic States.[171] Although the response to the appeal was slow, we may acknowledge that its publication heralded a re-contextualization of the "Baltic problem" on the international scene.

Despite the noble conception and the gentle appeal of this declaration, its drafters and other dissidents paid a heavy price for their free speech. At least fourteen "collaborators," including the secretarial staff and distributors of the *Chronicle of the Catholic*

---

171   Interview with Juozas Kojelis, a member of the Congressional Action to Free the Baltic States and a founding member of the Baltic American Freedom League, in Santa Monica, California, February 2004.

Church of Lithuania, were sentenced to long prison terms or exile because of the subsequent police activity. So too were the editors of the Journal *Perspektyvos.* Several other members of the Catholic Committee for the Defense of the Rights of Believers and the Helsinki Monitoring Committee were killed, imprisoned, or confined to psychiatric hospitals. Altogether, during the 1970s and early 1980s the communist authorities imprisoned more than 150 Lithuanian men and women over what are now called matters of conscience. The KGB also destroyed many other rebellious people in various ways: they had car accidents with heavy trucks, for example, or they simply disappeared.[172]

Cumulative Patterns of Lithuania's Resistance

Although the communist system endured for much longer than the Nazi occupation after it was imposed on Lithuania by the Soviet Union, both totalitarian regimes were sullenly received, and both met with specific and active resistance. Lithuania's anti-Nazi resistance both before and following the German invasion indicates the commitment of the Lithuanians towards both freedom and independence. It is, therefore, patently untrue that the continuation of the underground war against the invader which followed the communist take-over of the Lithuanian state by apparatchiks and criminals in 1944 was inspired by pro-Nazi or pro-fascist sentiment, as was long suggested by the Soviet media. For them the word "fascist" was a term of convenience which included every sentiment that did not fit into the Soviet mentality of Marxism-Leninism-Stalinism. Non-violent forms of resistance, the underground press, avoidance of labor and military service, tax evasion, the blockade on mobilization, and non-cooperation in relation to the attempted establishment of an SS legion were the main forms of the struggle.

---

172   See e.g., Vardys, *Lithuania* as well as Thomas Remeikis (ed.), *The Violations of Human Rights in Soviet Occupied Lithuania: A Report for 1971* and 1972-1981 (Chicago: American Lithuanian Community, 1972-1981), Gintė Damušis, Casimir Pugevičius and M. Skabeikis, *The Violations of Human Rights in Soviet Occupied Lithuania: A Report for 1982* (Chicago: American Lithuanian Community, 1981) and other yearly reports (see Bibliography).

Lithuania had been the first European state to organize a Nazi trial process as early as 1935.[173] When the judgment of history is fully formed it will be widely acknowledged that Lithuania never identified its purposes with those of its historic enemies either from the east or from the west.

It must be considered that the flight westward of many thousands of Lithuanian intellectuals and their families at the end of the war was also a display of resistance. Even though it may have seemed a counsel of despair, those who left the homeland at this time knew full well from the experience of the first murderous Soviet occupation that there would be a world of difference between a self-imposed exile in the west and forced deportation to Siberia, even in the context of the huge dislocation which followed the German collapse. It is again totally untrue that this was a flight of collaborators and pro-Nazi elements, as the Soviet propaganda tried often to present them. Most of those who left were well-educated university graduates, teachers, farmers, doctors, businessmen, lawyers, and statesmen, who would have had some real stake in the building of civil society in a free Lithuania. They knew that they would be repressed or destroyed by the brutal forces of Stalinism. Many of them continued to struggle for Lithuania's cause of freedom in their long exile, betraying neither their loyalty nor their language and the hope of eventual return.

If we are to formalize the pattern of Lithuania's resistance against the Evil Empire, we can perceive the consistent character of the major phases: from the uprising of 1941, through the partisan war of 1944-1953, and consequent periods of dissident activity between 1953 and 1987. A cumulative statement can be made that this nation never accepted the Soviet regime. The communist system with its atheistic ideology was essentially foreign to Lithuania as a Christian, predominantly Catholic, and Western-oriented nation. Though the forces of repression and the succeeding inertia of the Soviet totalitarian bureaucratic regime left many in apathetic dependence on that system, the unanimity with which the whole

---

173   See subchapter "Klaipėda lost" in the previous Chapter 2, footnote 39 which describes Hitler's outrage at the trial and its outcome.

communist dictatorship was rejected when the opportunity finally presented itself, speaks volumes for the extent and the density of its popular dislike. That Soviet communist system suppressed the Lithuanian state and its symbols, but the active resistance inside the occupied country suggests three main conclusions.

First, that occupation, russification, and terror had never destroyed the general longing for an independent democratic Lithuania among the population at large.

Second, that the Lithuanians continued to explore every possibility toward the goal of restoring an independent, democratic Western state.

Third, the fifty years of struggle against the Soviet communist system eventually taught the Lithuanians how to manipulate it to their own ends.

The Lithuanians were more likely to succeed in these objectives because the nation knew its own history. This knowledge provided them with sufficient inspiration, and the know-how to exploit the weaknesses of the Soviet regime and eventually to destroy it.

Despite the great danger which so frequently pursued those men and women who took this stand in occupied Lithuania and who fought for these objectives, they constantly emphasized the western and democratic identity of their aspirations. When the break finally came with the Soviet system, the Lithuanian people lost no opportunity in choosing parliamentary and peaceful ways to liberate themselves from the Soviet Empire. This phase of the struggle began in the late 1980s and was, in effect, a more public continuation of the third phase of dissident resistance.

4. Winning the West

A generalized view of the revolutionary changes in the European political scene, which saw the collapse of what had long been discerned as the virtually impregnable Soviet system, might suggest that the changes which occurred in the Baltic States at that time were consequential to the processes of upheaval which were under way throughout Central Europe, and that the tactics of the Lithuanian leadership at this time were a mere reflection or localized expression of these broader processes. However, as John Hiden has perceptively observed, "Gorbachev's reforms *occasioned* rather than caused the remarkable contemporary reawakening of the Baltic republics," and this suggests an alternative explanation.[174] The truth is that the national awakening in all these Baltic countries and in Lithuania in particular, was essentially pro-active rather than reactive. It was clear from the first that the Lithuanians, as the closest neighbours of Poland, and as a nation which has shared much of their political history with the Poles, would take particular notice of *Solidarnosz* as its movement began to make its mark.[175] In Lithuania the general response to the *perestroika* process, therefore, went quickly beyond what Gorbachev intended to offer. Vytautas Vardys has observed that whereas Gorbachev sought "pluralistic socialism," the Lithuanians moved subtly but decisively forward and sought a "pluralistic society" instead. They were encouraged in this by the recognition that this was a possibility which was already being realized to a larger extent in some of those former "Soviet bloc" countries, like Poland, having a westward looking historical identity.[176] This recognition was fundamental to Lithuanian

---

174 John Hiden and Patrick Salmon, *The Baltic Nations and Europe. Estonia, Latvia, and Lithuania in the Twentieth Century* (London and New York: Longman, 1991), p. 147.

175 For a discussion of the peaceful revolutions in Central and Eastern Europe see Timothy Garton Ash, *We the people: the revolution of 89' witnessed in Warsaw, Budapest, Berlin, and Prague* (Cambridge: Granta Books, 1989).

176 Vytautas S. Vardys, "Sajudis. National Revolution in Lithuania" in Jan A. Trapans (ed.) *Toward Independence: The Baltic Popular Movements* (Oxford: Westview Press, 1991), p. 101.

aspirations. The ideological difference between the Soviet "reform-ers" and the objectives of *Sąjūdis* lay in the implicit demands of the Lithuanian movement with respect to the questions of national sov-ereignty and the free market economy, which in Lithuanian eyes, were essentially non-negotiable and inseparable.

While Gorbachev "in restructuring the economy, intended to intro-duce a degree of reform, *Sąjūdis*, like the other Baltic popular move-ments, [...] made radical demands concerning private ownership and management."[177] Gorbachev proposed political reform, but the discussion of these changes necessarily proceeded "in a charged at-mosphere of Lithuanian consciousness," which was driven by more radical determinations.[178] Many Western observers have argued that Gorbachev hoped to channel the energies of popular move-ments such as *Sąjūdis* into support for his own designs, but an ina-bility to annex the mood of the Baltic populations to this ambition, and particularly to control the mass-movement processes in Lithu-ania, was to become his most striking failure.[179] Indeed, it can be argued that his whole reform program eventually unravelled as a result. In this sense, the Lithuanian revolution can be seen as the essential catalytic element in the final destruction of the Soviet sys-tem, and it can reasonably be claimed that the actions of the Lithu-anian people in support for *Sąjūdis* were instrumental to the Soviet collapse.[180]

In many ways, the Lithuanian *Atgimimas* (Reawakening), be-ginning in 1988 can be defined in terms of increased public political activity on the part of its citizens, which was directed towards the restoration of an independent state. International circumstances provided the background for this activity, and particularly the in-creasing public awareness and the growing international recogni-tion of the actual illegality, indeed criminality, of the Molotov-

---

177   Vardys, "Sajudis," p. 101.
178   Vardys, "Sajudis," p. 101.
179   Vardys, "Sajudis," p. 101.
180   The English nursery rhyme: "for want of a nail a shoe was lost, for want of a shoe a horse was lost, for want of a horse, the battle was lost, for want of a battle, the war was lost, and all for the want of a nail" comes to mind in this association.

Ribbentrop pact by which Lithuania and the other Baltic States as well as eastern Poland had been incorporated into the Soviet Union. Further, the knowledge that the Western states had still not abandoned the policy of formal non-recognition of the incorporation of the Baltic States into the Soviet Union now became a major encouragement in the growth of public political activity. In this atmosphere, Gorbachev's announcement of *perestroika* and *glasnost* was seized on as providing an opportunity to test how far the Soviet system was willing to change. The first **public** challenge to the regime was the commemoration in Vilnius of the anniversary of the secret Molotov-Ribbentrop pact on August 23, 1987, when the Lithuanian Freedom League arranged a gathering in Vilnius near the monument for Adomas Mickevičius, the great Lithuanian and Polish poet. Despite the announcement of changes in public policy toward demonstrations and open speech, the Soviet regime reverted to its characteristic form and persecuted the participants of the demonstration.

Among the victims of their habitual behavior on that day was Petras Gražulis, who was sent off to military duty for having attended the meeting. However, times were changing, and the Petras Gražulis case was very well publicized internationally by the World Lithuanian Community, which reported the case widely to show how the KGB persecuted and attempted to control underground activists, even acting against people who were demonstrating against the secret deal between Stalin and Hitler, which had divided Europe in 1939, and, indeed, had led to the Second World War.[181] Gražulis himself responded to his oppressors with an open letter to Dmitri T. Jazov, the Soviet Defense Minister, which fully explained his reasons for refusing the imposed military duty. Copies of this letter were sent to Amnesty International and to the *Frankfurter Allgemeine Zeitung*. It stated that "he could not in conscience defend a regime which occupied and forcibly held the country, persecuted his faith, and violated his principles as a

---

181   Interview with Petras Gražulis, Lithuanian MP, Nottingham, September 26, 1997.

Christian."[182] Gražulis' trial on January 26, 1988 was the first political trial to be held in occupied Lithuania since Gorbachev's announcement of *perestroika* and *glasnost*, and over 200 demonstrators gathered near the court, including dissidents who had come from Moscow and Leningrad. Many of these demonstrations carried banners that read "Freedom for Lithuania," "KGB hands off Petras Gražulis," "Soviet aggressors get out of Lithuania," or "Freedom for Petras Gražulis." It was in this unprecedented atmosphere that Gražulis was sentenced to 10 months of labor camp, despite Gorbachev's discussions about *glasnost*, on February 2. It was a sign that the public statements of this regime did not correspond with its public behavior.

Celebrating Lithuania's Independence Day, February 16, 1987, another dissident, Antanas Terleckas, reported the attitudes of the Soviet state to the public mood to the Lithuanian Information Centre in Washington, informing how people were "being intimidated in all kinds of ways. Students showing up will be expelled. Workers will be discharged."[183] The militia appeared in large numbers during this day on the streets of Kaunas, the former capital of independent Lithuania, and some of its members were seen accompanying well-known KGB officers who were busy observing and filming the demonstration of a few hundred people, marching through the Old Town, and along the main street, which has now recovered its pre-war name of *Laisvės Alėja*, Freedom Avenue. Many in the crowd were pre-war graduates of independent Lithuania's gymnasiums in Kaunas and of the old Vytautas Magnus University, who made this an occasion for gathering. This anniversary of Lithuania's independence was being celebrated with great joy knowing that this was being done in public for the first time in many years. For many families it was also marked at home by listening to the radio, where they could hear the Voice of America or Radio Free Europe broadcasting the speech given to mark the anniversary by the head of free Lithuania's continuing diplomacy, Mr. Stasys

---

182   Interview with Gražulis.
183   Quoted in Dalia Katilius - Boydstun, "Six Months of "Glasnost" in Lithuania," *The Observer* (April 1988): 8.

Lozoraitis, Jr., Representative to the United States and to the Holy See. It was a memorable statement, and even today almost everybody in Lithuania, who was interested in politics at that time, can recall his optimistic speech, in which his belief in freedom, full democracy and the independence of the country, was unambiguously stated. His suggestions were, however, rather cautiously phrased as he carefully weighed his words in the hope that his influence might encourage steps which could lead to the restoration of an independent state.

These developments signaled the beginning of real changes in the domestic atmosphere in Lithuania and in the international climate too, particularly in the United States. Thirty-two Senators, who had been concerned by reports of reprisals against participants in the demonstration in Lithuania, delivered a letter to the Soviet Embassy in Washington, D.C. on February 11, 1988, requesting that Mikhail Gorbachev "act with restraint toward the Baltic peoples as they seek peacefully to express their aspirations for human rights and self-determination."[184] They expressed "concern about reports that the Soviets will move to block the flower-laying ceremonies at various historical sites in Lithuania's two major cities, Vilnius and Kaunas," and urged Gorbachev "to emulate the policy of Lenin, not Stalin," in dealing with the Baltic States, "taking into account that the founder of the USSR renounced forever all Soviet claims to Baltic territory in 1920, a pledge that his successor violated two decades later."[185] It will be noted that this formulation gets very close to the heart of the matter in dispute between the people of Lithuania and the Kremlin. It was, of course, a public sign that the wider world had at last begun fully to recognize the indignity and injustice that the Baltic countries had long endured.

This letter was one of the more important factors that have influenced the significant, but perhaps ultimately useful for Lithuania, over-reaction of the Soviet authorities in what was an occupied country to the seventieth anniversary commemoration of Lithuania's Independence which was planned for February 16, 1988. The

---

184   Quoted in Katilius, ""Glasnost" in Lithuania," p. 8.
185   Katilius, ""Glasnost" in Lithuania," p. 8.

Red Army troops were put into the streets in large numbers in advance with the obvious intention of preventing people from gathering or demonstrating against the occupation of their country. This activity, however, produced the reverse of its desired effect, as the intensity of this Soviet reaction served only to focus the Lithuanian public's attention on the actual meaning of the celebration. It encouraged them to take a greater interest in the history of Lithuania. The fact that this knowledge was still prohibited by the Soviet authorities also greatly contributed to the growth of international public attention and awareness of what was happening in the country. Indeed, it could be said that this obviously hostile military presence contributed its own confirming statement to the political environment, emphasizing everyone's awareness of living in an occupied state. The resentment it engendered created an atmosphere which provided the condition for the emergence of the new mass movement for Lithuania's independence from the Soviet Union, namely *Sąjūdis*.

Despite the over-reaction by the Soviet regime in 1988, it did not escape notice that this was, in fact, the first *public* commemoration of Lithuania's Independence Day which had taken place since 1940. Also, the enthusiasm with which it was embraced by the multitudes clearly indicated that the population's fear of the Soviet regime had vanished. It is interesting to speculate why so many thousands of troops were deployed in the streets in response to a letter from thirty-two American Senators and why thousands of KGB and militia officers were so busy around the towns and cities observing the crowds, using cameras to film participants in a demonstration, which had been arranged by only a few hundred of independent Lithuania's intelligentsia. So obvious was this over-reaction that many Lithuanians now began to perceive intuitively that "something big was coming." This intuition was carefully noted by the emerging *Sąjūdis* leadership, which now knew that the stakes had been greatly raised and that each further step towards liberation must be taken not only with the most careful calculation but with greater courage and vision.

Sąjūdis in Lithuanian means "movement." Initially *Sąjūdis* was called *Lietuvos persitvarkymo Sąjūdis* (i.e., Lithuania's movement in support of *perestroika*), but later the words "in support of *perestroika*" were dropped. Indeed, they were used for diplomatic and persuasive reasons only when they were first chosen, because *Sąjūdis* set the symbolic goal of a "free and independent country" from the beginning. In this the Lithuanian movement differed from the Latvian and Estonian popular fronts, whose inception as intellectual movements of national reawakening and economic independence was much more closely marked by the support given by their communist elites to Gorbachev's *perestroika* program.[186] In Lithuania the cut of the movement was different from the start. Already in September 1988, the famous Lithuanian poet Justinas Marcinkevičius had written an article which appeared on the front page of the first number of the *Sąjūdis* bulletin *Atgimimas* ("Rebirth") stating that "the country which we inherited from our ancestors belongs to us. We call it Lithuania and we desire that this country shall not disappear from the map of the World."[187] Standing immediately beneath the title of the new newspaper, this message was a statement that the country must be born again. It was, therefore, a formulation which was profoundly at odds with everything the Communist Party had ever stood for and was a word from the core of the *Sąjūdis* movement.

Despite these profound undercurrents, it was necessary to prevent the Soviet system from demanding *Sąjūdis'* extinction in the earliest days of its existence, for the *Iniciatyvinė grupė,* the Founding Group of *Sąjūdis*, to secure its legitimacy within the process of *perestroika* in the Soviet Union. Most members of this Founding Group were prominent intellectuals, and even though some of them were members of the Lithuanian Communist Party, Professor Vytautas Landsbergis was elected as its chairman. Landsbergis was known not to be a member of the Communist Party. His selection was thus perceived as a means of steering the movement away from direct Soviet control. It was a clear signal of the strategy being

---

186   Vardys, "Sąjūdis."
187   Justinas Marcinkevičius, *Atgimimas*, no. 1, September 16, 1988, p. 1.

unfolded. Landsbergis' own description is evidence of the mind of the movements' leaders: "We called it Restructuring" ("*Perestroika do konca*," he explained - using the Russian phrase – which means "Restructuring until the end.") This implied "Restructuring until Lithuania's victory," i.e., until Lithuania's liberation from Soviet occupation was complete.[188]

It is of interest to explore the reasons for Landsbergis' election to this fateful position. It gave him the privilege of becoming the leader of the liberation movement and eventually the Head of State, who took his people through several crises and crucial negotiations, which finally and probably against the expectation of many external observers, saw Lithuania becoming a free, independent, and sovereign state, and eventually a member of the United Nations and NATO. Landsbergis himself has commented, in an interview with the Lithuanian daily newspaper *Lietuvos aidas*: "It is most likely that I was elected as Chairman, because I was successful in settling quarrels between people with different views."[189] This is a modest response. Other opinions suggest that the repressive Soviet structures underestimated this ability for compromise, interpreting it as "softness." They, therefore, failed to attack him effectively initially, even though this would have been well within their capability.[190] Indeed, appearances were deceptive, and the *Washington Post* commented at the time "Landsbergis is a soft-spoken professor of music at the Vilnius Conservatory where he specializes in early 20th century avant-garde Lithuanian composers. His family is a mixture

---

188   Interview with Professor Vytautas Landsbergis, May 19, 1998, London. See also Vytautas Landsbergis, *Lithuania independent again* (Cardiff: University of Wales Press, 2000) for the story of Lithuania's liberation from the Soviet occupation, as witnessed by *Sąjūdis'* Chairman, the President of Lithuania's Parliament.

189   He was referring to the other members of the Founding Group such as Artūras Skučas, who represented the right-wing position in the spectrum of views held within the group, and the writer Vytautas Petkevičius who had ambitions to become leader (as indeed, the Soviet authorities expected). Vytautas Landsbergis: "Sugrįš Sąjūdžio gebėjimas atskirti tiesa nuo melo. Šiandien sukanka 10 metų, kai 1988 m. Mokslų akademijoje buvo įkurta Sąjūdžio iniciatyvinė grupė," *Lietuvos Aidas*, June 3, 1998, p. 7.

190   Private communication with Professor Vytautas Landsbergis, February 20, 2000.

of old Lithuanian nobility and modern intellectuals. His father fought against the Bolsheviks and the Poles for independence in 1918, and the family helped to hide Jewish families during the Nazi occupation."[191] This is scarcely a prescription for the David and Goliath drama which was eventually to unfold.

In effect, the history of the decision to elect Vytautas Landsbergis as Chairman of the *Sąjūdis* movement, which was taken on June 2, 1988, lay in Lithuania's earlier resistance to the Soviet occupation. The Lithuanians were focused on the decision by the Lithuanian Freedom League to commemorate the forty-eighth anniversary of the Molotov-Ribbentrop pact by a gathering near the monument to Adomas Mickevičius, the Lithuanian and Polish poet, on August 23, 1987. Over-reaction by the Soviet authorities to the celebration of this event, like their response to the later commemoration of the seventieth anniversary of Lithuania's National Independence Day, gave out signals that raised wide public attention to the possibility of confronting the Soviet police state. These events had been instrumental in defining the issues which the new movement needed to face. Its selection of Landsbergis may be seen either as an intuitive choice or as the calculated selection of a leader, whose career had already seen him picking his way through difficult issues without precipitating premature confrontation. We now have Landsbergis' autobiography, which explains both the personal and the political dimensions of this process. It is sufficient to state here that he had steered a series of national cultural heritage protection protests through the late 1970s and 1980s in association with his father, the architect Vytautas Landsbergis-Žemkalnis, which had steadily enlarged the space where dissenting opinions could be expressed safely.[192] For instance, they successfully protested the anticipated large scale destruction of medieval Vilnius for the purpose of the building of a motorway and underground car parks in 1978, involving branches of the Architects' Society and

191   David Remnick, "Lithuania Votes Independence; Legislature Seeks Soviet Secession; Non-Communist Is Elected President," *The Washington Post*, March 12, 1990, p. 7.
192   Landsbergis, *Lithuania*, pp. 23-28.

the Writers' Union, distributing leaflets and influencing the communist government. His earlier career had anticipated *Sąjūdis'* goals as it set out to restore an active appreciation of Lithuania's history to the nation's academic life, and to free public life of the perverse interpretations which had become endemic during half a century of deliberate Soviet falsification.[193] Being a researcher of the works of Mikalojus Konstantinas Čiurlionis, the Lithuanian impressionist artist and composer, Vytautas Landsbergis succeeded in publicizing his works, thus preserving them from communist destruction and contributing to their recognition.[194]

The emergence of *Sąjūdis* encouraged many affiliated discussion clubs and societies to emerge throughout Lithuania, a feature of life which was all the more welcome for the fact that it would not have been tolerated in earlier decades.[195] It is interesting to note how the Soviet authorities reacted in their characteristic attempt to ban the discussions of one of the more prominent of these societies, *Istorija ir kultūra*, the History and Culture Club, which had begun meeting on the premises of the *Žinijos draugija*, Knowledge Society, in Vilnius. The club dealt with threatened closure by simply relocating its discussions, moving into the hall of the Artists' Union, where it carried on as before. Its discussions were influential, and during a meeting of the club held in April 1988 the philosopher Arvydas Juozaitis, who also happened to be an Olympic Medalist in swimming, read a courageous paper on the necessity of restoring Lithuania's independence, which naturally was well-received.[196] Similar intellectual discussions on the economic situation and the possibilities of independence took place between the economists who were members of the Lithuanian Academy of Sciences. The group included Professors Kazimira Prunskienė, Kazimieras Antanavičius, Antanas Buračas and Eduardas Vilkas. Elsewhere, at the premises of the Cultural Foundation, which was headed by

---

193   See *Atgimimas*, no. 1, September 16, 1988, p. 1.

194   Landsbergis, *Lithuania*, pp. 67-77.

195   See e.g., Bronius Genzelis, *Sąjūdis. Priešistorė ir istorija* (Vilnius: Pradai, 1999) or Danutė Blažytė and Vanda Kašauskienė (eds.) *Lietuvos Sąjūdis ir valstybės idealų įgyvendinimas* (Vilnius: LII Leidykla, 1998).

196   Genzelis, *Sąjūdis*, p. 65.

Professor Česlovas Kudaba, other societies sprang into being, concerned with the preservation of nature and the conservation of historical monuments. Discussion began to develop freely as a result,
and outside the control of the communist authorities. As time
moved on, this trickle of free expression became a river, and then a
flood.

Sąjūdis naturally also aimed at re-establishing Lithuanian to
its proper place in public life as the state language, at putting an
end to the process of russification of public and academic life which
had been rampant since 1944. From 1978 on, after the infamous
Tashkent Conference, all doctoral dissertations were required to be
presented under the Soviet rules of candidature for higher degrees
and had to be written in Russian. The degrees were then confirmed
by Moscow through Soviet institutions rather than by the universities within the Soviet republic. These language requirements, and
the system within which the degrees were confirmed, caused anger
in the Lithuanian academic community, as it did in Latvia and Estonia. To add insult to injury, the business of the Lithuanian Communist Party was conducted in Russian, which was the required
language of all meetings of its Central Committee. As non-party
members could not progress in their careers, this was another cause
for anger. Thus, the aspirations of *Sąjūdis* to restore the nation's language to its proper place had widespread support throughout professional circles. Indeed, the case for this restoration of its dignity
was integral to *Sąjūdis'* campaign to restore justice and to respect
the ability of Lithuanian people to decide how their life and work
should be conducted. The language question became a particular
reflection of people's attitudes toward moral values in the context
of the feeling, which was endemic in Soviet times, that the moral
values of public life had been lost. It had become a habit to do one
thing, to say something else, and to think one's thoughts in secret.
Plagiarism, false statistics, evasion, theft, and denunciation had in
fact become the norm throughout Soviet society, while duplicity
and deception were, in the same vein, common in municipal and
public life.[197] Neither personal autonomy nor individual opinion

---

197   "Writings," i.e., false statistics.

was much respected by the Soviet system, if people had views which differed in any way from those demanded by officialdom. These difficulties had caused major problems that would have to be overcome in the new society, which *Sąjūdis* hoped would develop when the Soviet communist dream had exhausted itself.

Sąjūdis also set out to encourage a deep respect for nature and the environment. It called loudly for a clean-up of the polluted rivers and landscapes which could be found in many places throughout Lithuania, where the ruthlessly exploitative industrial process of the command economy had damaged the environment, without putting anything back. Many rivers had become almost dead due to the absence of measures to clean up pollution, and much of the soil was badly affected by excessive use of artificial fertilizers or was contaminated by the chemical industry in such places as the fertilizer factories at Kėdainiai and Jonava. The worst case was the Chernobyl-type atomic energy power station at Ignalina, one of the most powerful stations in Europe. It played an important role in the Soviet nuclear defense plans, with two reactors which had been built in the lake district of the Ignalina National Park of Lithuania. Open discussion of the problems and firm opposition to these matters was the basis for the broad public support which emerged for *Sąjūdis'* environmental policy. Eventually, the birth of a party of the Greens, *Žaliųjų partija*, succeeded in stopping the building by the Kremlin of the third nuclear reactor of the Ignalina power station as well as the construction of the Kaišiadorių hydro-accumulative power station, which threatened the existence of life in *Kauno marios*, the great artificial lake which stands on the Nemunas river near Kaunas.

The key words of the *Sąjūdis* movement, often repeated, were "honesty," "wisdom", and "spirituality". Indeed, the movement campaigned openly for the spiritual revival of the people, and for a better and more honest way of life.[198] *Sąjūdis* was, therefore, responsible for introducing the policy of public moral integrity, which requested that the political culture should be based on Christian principles. It was a stance that distinguished its activities

---

198   Genzelis, *Sąjūdis*, p. 3.

radically from the existing Soviet outlook, which was based on the fear of persecution. This commitment by the intellectual elite of the *Sąjūdis* movement inspired people to throw off the profound fear that had gripped the entire country since the Stalinist period. It was accomplished through a strategy of personal example and by taking the personal risk of gathering. Their technique won through because it opened hearts. In this way, *Sąjūdis* aroused public enthusiasm for the restoration of Lithuanian independence, based on an understanding of democratic values, embracing the vision of a restored state, a parliamentary republic and true independence from the Soviet Union to be achieved by means of the ballot box. [199] This vision was grounded in a call for historical justice. It suggested that the Soviet-Nazi agreement, which had divided Europe into zones of influence reflecting the imagination of Stalin and Hitler that all small states would have to disappear in future, had finally to be annulled. Thus, the resulting illegal occupation of Lithuania by the Soviet Union would have to end.[200] *Sąjūdis'* civilized understanding of the need for the peaceful expression of ideas stood in sharp contrast to the brutality of the totalitarian regime. At first, it offered a challenge which the system felt it could assimilate, but eventually its moral force was such that the regime was unable to ignore the large-scale *Sąjūdis* peaceful demonstrations and gatherings. The movement's emphasis on a "cool, calm, and coherent" disposition held firm even when faced by the brutal power of the Soviet state institutions, including the KGB. In the face of its provocations the movement turned to the example of Gandhi and other cases of peaceful liberation and non-violent resistance. At times this was directly articulated by Landsbergis, who was one of the most intellectual and well-read of the leaders.[201] In the final analysis, it was this method which saw the Soviet Russian intruders off Lithuanian

---

199   Genzelis, Sąjūdis, p. 3. *Sąjūdis* called this way of liberation the "parliamentary way of freedom."

200   See description of the largest gathering in Vingis park in commemoration of the secret Molotov-Ribbentrop pact later in this chapter.

201   The reader would greatly benefit from also reading an autobiography of Vytautas Landsbergis, *Lithuania Independent Again* (Cardiff or Seattle: University of Wales Press or University of Washington Press, 2000).

territory as surely as the British Raj was seen out of India half a century earlier, though the Soviet communist occupier was much more brutal and much more reluctant to leave.

We need to recall at this point how Lithuania's *Sąjūdis* movement first materialized in the summer of 1988, under some inspiration derived from the emergence of the Estonian National Front, which took advantage of a certain relaxation of the communist regime in the occupied Baltic States.[202] *Sąjūdis* actually came into being on June 3, 1988, at a time when public life was dominated by discussions about the drafting of a new constitution for Soviet Lithuania and a plan for the country's future economic development. The occasion was a meeting in the Small Conference Hall of Lithuania's Academy of Sciences.[203] Only a day earlier, a monthly discussion on the situation in the country, organized by Professor Bronius Genzelis, had taken place in *Mokslininkų rūmai*, the Palace of Scholars, in the village of Verkiai in the Vilnius region. The participants in that discussion, recognizing the significance of the moment, formally resolved to re-designate the following day's session as a broader national meeting to discuss the country's future systematically. This meeting then became, without any real previous planning, the effective founding meeting of *Sąjūdis*, as participants then went on to elect the *Iniciatyvinė grupė*, Founding Group, for *Sąjūdis*, which embraced the most prominent intellectual figures present, representatives of the nation's cultural and scholarly organizations and institutions.[204] The hope was expressed at this first

---

202 For international causes of such relaxation see Chapter 5.
203 See e.g., Genzelis, Sąjūdis, pp. 55-98; Eduardas Vilkas, "Birželio 3-oji Mokslo Akademijoje" in Blažytė, *Lietuvos Sąjūdis*, pp. 13-16.
204 See Genzelis, *Sąjūdis*, p. 66, They were Regimantas Adomaitis, Juozas Bulavas, Vytautas Bubnys, Antanas Buračas, Algimantas Čekuolis, Virgilijus Čepaitis, Vaclovas Daunoras, Sigitas Geda, Bronius Genzelis, Arvydas Juozaitis, Julius Juzeliūnas, Algimantas Kaušpėdas, Česlovas Kudaba, Bronius Kuzmickas, Vytautas Landsbergis, Bronius Leonavičius, Meilė Lukšienė, Alfonsas Maldonis, Justinas Marcinkevičius, Alvydas Medalinskas, Jokūbas Minkevičius, Algimantas Nasvytis, Romualdas Ozolas, Romas Pakalnis, Saulius Pečiulis, Vytautas Petkevičius, Kazimira Prunskienė, Vytautas Radžvilas, Raimundas Rajackas, Artūras Skučas, Gintaras Songaila, Arvydas Šaltenis, Vitas Tomkus, Zigmas Vaišvila, Arūnas Žebriūnas. Many members of the Founding Group

meeting that these people "could unite those institutions and raise foundations for new and powerful movement able to take responsibility for the restoration of Lithuania's independence." It was with this charge that *Sąjūdis* came into being.

Professor Vytautas Landsbergis has recalled the significance of that day in his interview for the BBC documentary film "The Second Russian Revolution":

> The most important moment was when we were elected. I wasn't there, but the next day I was told that the Committee had been elected and that I was on it. I was at that meeting at the beginning but then had to speak on television. There I said that the movement should be created, we shouldn't wait any longer; we are already late. Even the first meeting of the group went off without me; I wasn't informed in time. After that I was at every meeting of the committee. They were quite unusual; there were also meetings with the people, they lasted for many hours, in stuffy rooms, but nobody cared. There we formulated ideas that were to become a program of action and our methods.[205]

The fact that the Estonians had moved earlier to create a popular front undoubtedly gave an impulse to the Lithuanians at this stage. When the Estonian Popular Front was established in May 1988, Arvydas Juozaitis participated in its inaugural meeting as a representative of Lithuania's emerging movement for independence.[206] Later in the month the prominent Estonian economists Mikhail Bronstein and Ivar Raig visited Lithuania on May 26 – 27, 1988 to describe the political developments in their country. They were the acknowledged authors of Estonia's economic independence and had explained the constitution of their recently established Estonian Popular Front and its program to the members of the Lithuanian Academy of Sciences. The reaction was enthusiastically positive, and it was agreed that a similar movement must emerge in Lithuania as soon as possible.[207] The meeting chaired by Professor

---

of *Sąjūdis* many of them later went on to become candidates to the Supreme Soviet of the USSR and won seats in the General election which took place on March 26, 1989.

205 Interview with Prof. Vytautas Landsbergis, Second Russian Revolution. 2RR 1/1/15, British Library of Political and Economic Science.

206 Genzelis, *Sąjūdis*, pp. 65–66.

207 *Sąjūdžio žinios*, no. 2, June 13, 1988, p. 2.

Bronius Genzelis on June 2 took place, which led directly to the founding of *Sąjūdis* on June 3, and it is interesting to note that Lithuanian physicists were the instigators and among the most active supporters of the new political processes which were emerging in this way.[208]

These leading scholars were well known both for their scientific work and for their critical thinking about the Soviet system. The Empire had tolerated them despite their humorous deprecation of its workings, probably because most of them related to research contracts for the Soviet military industry. They were a sophisticated constituency, and their tactics were subtle. One of their ploys was to challenge the Central Committee of the Communist Party in Lithuania by producing an "informal" list of candidates to the Communist Party conference in Moscow. The list, purporting to be in support of Gorbachev's attempts at *perestroika* was published on May 27, 1988, in *Vakarinės naujienos* ("The Evening News"), a Vilnius newspaper, by members of the Academy of Sciences' Institute of Semiconductor Physics.[209] The move was a masterstroke, conceived by well-honed minds, and the Central Committee of the Communist Party in occupied Lithuania was really cornered by this carefully considered tactic. It was a maneuver which faced the Central Committee with a major dilemma, as now they had either to accept the physicists' proposal, which required it to follow Gorbachev's public instruction that candidates to the

---

208 A physicist Ms. Angonita Rupšytė became the head of the Secretarial Committee, administrative apparatus of the *Sąjūdis* movement, and was actively involved in the creation of its structures. She was instrumental in the achievement of *Sąjūdis'* victory in the first elections in still occupied Lithuania in 1989, when *Sąjūdis* won most allocated seats to the Supreme Soviet of the USSR. See Angonita Rupšytė, "Sąjūdžio dėka laimėti pirmieji demokratiniai rinkimai," *XXI Amžius, Horizontai*, p. 1, http://www.xxiamzius.lt/archyvas/priedai/horizontai/20040428/2-1.html.

209 "Atviras laiškas LKP CK" (Open letter to the Central Committee of the Communist Party in Lithuania), *Vakarinės naujienos*, May 27, 1988, p. 1. The Institute of the Semiconductor Physics suggested academics Juras Požėla, Jokūbas Minkevičius, Eduardas Vilkas, writers Vytautas Petkevičius, Vytautas Bubnys, Romas Gudaitis, journalist Algimantas Čekuolis, architect Algirdas Kaušpėdas to be representatives in the 19th conference of the Communist Party of the USSR.

conference had to be elected by secret ballot by Communist Party members in various organizations or continue with its habitual method of nominating its own candidates without reference to any wider consultations. If the first path was followed, it was now obvious that the mood of the country was such that the Central Committee's nominees were very likely to lose the elections. Alternatively, the Central Committee could neglect Gorbachev's instruction and send its own candidates to Moscow without holding elections. It was, of course, unable to change its corrupt habits, so its response was to adopt the latter course, following a pattern of behavior, which had become second nature to its members. But they had been smoked out and the fact that the Central Committee of the Communist Party had ignored the list of candidates provided by the physicists of the Lithuanian Academy of Science exposed it to public opinion. Thus, immediate charges of flagrant abuse of the electoral process were loudly voiced. It had, of course, been indulging in such cynical manipulation for decades, but now it was seriously wrong-footed by a vigorous public outcry directed against its unseemly behavior.

These developments in the nomination of candidates for the all-Union conference of the Communist Party in Moscow marked a critical stage in the change of popular attitudes. The reaction of the Central Committee of the Lithuanian Communist Party damaged its reputation not only in Lithuania, but at the Kremlin, as it demonstrated its inability to react effectively to the challenges of contemporary society and showed its incompetence "to play the *perestroika* game" in occupied Lithuania. From the viewpoint of *Sąjūdis* this was the first successful step in discrediting the Central Committee of the Communist Party in Lithuania. It was a significant boost to its self-confidence, and it suggested that the best tactics were ones of "push and wait." This policy meant that the movement would be well advised to make radical demands, and then simply wait for the Communist Party leadership to make a mistake. It would then be advertised widely in a manner which would further discredit the communists in the public eye.[210]

Almost as soon as it was established, the *Sąjūdis* movement began to lay out a program for national reconstruction, which was virtually an election program for an alternative government. When the first public meeting of the Founding Group took place on June 13, 1988, it was announced that commissions would be established to investigate national ecological, social, economic, cultural, and legal issues as well as the "national question" itself. Bronius Genzelis was then appointed to head the Social Commission, which quickly set to work in highlighting violations of justice in Lithuania and in the Soviet Union.[211] According to Genzelis, *Sąjūdis'* social program must first set out to abolish the privileges of the *nomenklatura*, "the new class of exploiters and idlers, on which the bureaucratic state apparatus was formed," then raise the living standards of ordinary people and improve conditions of work for workers in state

---

210 According to this policy of "push and wait," three major periods of *Sąjūdis* political activity can be found in its relations with the Communist Party. At first, its "target" was the Central Committee of the local Communist Party. During this period *Sąjūdis* emphasized its support for Gorbachev's policy of *perestroika*, and therefore emphasized the "lack of *perestroika*" in Lithuania. Developing this policy of demonstrating support for the Kremlin led to an increased confrontation with the party bureaucracy in Lithuania. As a result, *Sąjūdis* managed to achieve change in the communist leadership in Lithuania when (as a compromise between the Kremlin and *Sąjūdis* leadership), Songaila was ejected from his position in favor of Brazauskas, who was a good speaker and administrator, and a pro-Lithuanian communist. The change of the communist leadership and its subsequent rather co-operative behavior led to the full legalization of *Sąjūdis* in Soviet Lithuania. This occurred in time to enable it to present its own list of candidates to the Supreme Soviet of the Soviet Union in the run-up to the elections of March 26, 1989. The second phase followed *Sąjūdis'* victory in those elections, which took pro-independence candidates to the Supreme Soviet of the USSR and allowed Lithuania's representatives to take the fight for their country's independence to the Soviet capital itself (see the next chapter "The Parliamentary Way to Freedom"). The third period was marked by *Sąjūdis'* influence on the pro-Lithuanian part of the Communist Party, which eventually directed it to formal separation from the Soviet Party. *Sąjūdis'* victory in the elections to the Lithuanian Supreme Soviet then permitted Lithuania's independence from the Soviet Union to be declared. See also the next chapter The Parliamentary Way to Freedom.

211 Lietuvos Persitvarkymo Sąjūdžio Informacinis Pranešimas, no. 3, June 28, 1988, p. 1.

institutions. The idea was to introduce strict controls on public spending, both in the industrial and the social sectors.[212] The parallel Cultural Commission was led by the writer Vytautas Bubnys, who advised "on the necessity of unifying the work of all the cultural societies for the struggle to preserve the Lithuanian national heritage."[213] The filmmaker Arūnas Žebriūnas, head of the Commission of Nationalities, spoke similarly of the need to recognize the Lithuanian language as the state language even in the Constitution of Soviet Lithuania. He argued that the problems of minority cultural groups other than the Russian or Polish population, also needed to be examined and resolved. The primary argument was that "national history must be returned to the Lithuanian nation," and that source materials must be published systematically to correct the distortions of "Soviet history," which had deliberately been interposed in the attempt to suppress national awareness in Lithuania.[214]

The records of this first meeting reflect an impressive unanimity of purpose. Antanas Buračas, an economist, spoke about the economic and political implications of "Soviet self-government" in Lithuania, opening questions of the future reform of prices and how standards of living would be maintained, and other issues such as the mobility of labor, and of economic development, which would take full account of environmental issues and the demands of trade with other republics.[215] Kazimira Prunskienė, another economist, then discussed the budgetary implications of reform, and the journalist Vytautas Tomkus spoke on legal issues, calling for a Lithuanian Ministry of Justice to be brought into existence after insisting that a strong economic mafia existed in Lithuania. He explained that the Soviet constitution was formulated in such a way that the legal system of the republic could not operate differently from the Soviet one. Finally, Vytautas Landsbergis spoke about

---

212 *Nomenklatura*, i.e., Soviet bureaucracy (in Russian).
213 Sąjūdžio Informacinis Pranešimas, no. 3, June 28, 1988, p. 1.
214 Sąjūdžio Informacinis Pranešimas, 3, p. 1.
215 Sąjūdžio Informacinis Pranešimas, 3, p. 1.

Lithuania's vulnerability to the machinations of the Soviet central bureaucracy.[216]

Once it had got down to business in this way, *Sąjūdis* established its own news bulletin *Sąjūdžio žinios*, ("Sąjūdis News"), which was produced without the approval of Soviet censorship. Its own duplicating machine was used for the earlier copies, though later it was distributed and multiplied by the various local *Sąjūdis* groups. Then *Sąjūdis* information boards also sprang up in the town centers and in the offices of various organizations. Soon an independent press began to flourish. *Atgimimas* ("Rebirth") appeared weekly in Vilnius; *Kauno aidas* ("Echo of Kaunas") in Kaunas; *Mažoji Lietuva* ("Lithuania Minor") in Klaipėda, while other periodicals followed in many other towns. The most important achievement, however, was *Sąjūdis'* success in gaining access to the republic's television with the establishment of a one-hour weekly program *Atgimimo banga* ("the Wave of Reawakening") which soon became the most influential and popular TV program, not least because *Sąjūdis* was able to ensure that its major meetings, demonstrations and gatherings were reported live, or recorded to be shown to the Lithuanian people on this program. With this energetic publicity drive, *Sąjūdis* was able to educate the public, and so began to achieve significant results within a few months of its establishment.

The progress of the movement was rapid, and its momentum astonishing. Osvaldas Balakauskas, a professional composer and member of *Sąjūdis'* Founding Group, who was subsequently appointed Lithuanian Ambassador to France, has described the year 1988 in the following terms:

there was a quiet start between January and May, while the establishment of *Sąjūdis* was being worked at. The first of three large meetings took place in June. The second meeting was in July; and the third, which was the first high point of its activity, was held in August. The reaction, and the strengthening of the revolution occurred in September, but the highest point of the year came with the General Meeting of *Sąjūdis* representatives in October. After

---

216   Sąjūdžio Informacinis Pranešimas, 3, p. 2.

experiencing its first defeat in November, the 'political advent' then followed in December.[217]

This rather sparse overview describes the stages in the growth of *Sąjūdis'* political strength during its first year of existence rather well, but the comments of Farther Vaclovas Aliulis, MIC, a Marian Fathers priest, and another member of the Founding Group, on the major achievements of 1988 are needed to fill out the picture. In his opinion, the public, and particularly the younger generation, became fully aware of the truth about the current situation and the real facts of the recent history of Lithuania only after details of the numbers of innocent people who had been deported to Siberia between 1941 and 1952 were brought into public view. Further, as Lithuanian was given the status of the republic's language, the will of the nation for independence from the Soviet Union became more clearly expressed. These developments were eventually to become firmly focused by the national petition which protested against Soviet constitutional amendments designed to limit the rights of republics to secede from the USSR in the summer of 1989. In the space of a single week, *Sąjūdis* was able to collect 1,650,000 signatures from amongst a total population of nearly 4 million.[218] It was a decisive moment, which showed the extent of the demand for change.

The strategy of the movement was already embodied in embryonic form in the statement (made at the first general meeting of its representatives held on October 22, 1988) that its objective was to employ "all constitutional means of struggle for Lithuania's sovereignty."[219] The formulation of seeking a "constitutional way for the restoration of Lithuania's state" was proposed by the Kaunas *Sąjūdis* group, which was more radical in its views at that stage than the branches in Vilnius and elsewhere.[220] Shortly after this, Vytautas Landsbergis' formula "what was stolen, must be returned"

217 Osvaldas Balakauskas, "Mums reikia visos teisybės," *Kauno aidas*, December 29, 1988, p. 3.

218 Vaclovas Aliulis, "Linkiu tiesumo ir tolerancijos," *Kauno aidas*, December 29, 1988, p. 2. See also Antanas Terleckas, "LLL-bekompromisinė konfrontacija su Sovietų valdžia" in Blažytė, *Lietuvos Sąjūdis*, p. 38.

219 *Sąjūdžio Informacinis Pranešimas*, 3, p. 2.

220 *Sąjūdžio Informacinis Pranešimas*, 3, p. 2.

emerged following his discussions with Stasys Lozoraitis, Lithuanian Ambassador to Washington, and Dr. Bill Hough, an expert in International Law in New York.[221] It became a slogan of some genius in this context, as the simplicity of its understatement was compelling enough to bring those who might otherwise have wavered into line with the Kaunas group's formulation. Sentiments on the constitutional nature of the struggle, and the realization that its goal was the hope for return of stolen independence, were fused to become an unequivocal demand and a non-negotiable reality.[222] Lithuanians would henceforth emphasize at every possible opportunity that they had never joined the Soviet Union freely and were in fact the victims of the secret Soviet-Nazi pact. They used the moral force of this argument as a wedge with which to split the Soviet system, exploiting the opportunities offered by both the western policy of non-recognition and the right of a Soviet republic to withdraw from the Union under the Constitution of the USSR. When the implications of its defined position were fully absorbed, *Sąjūdis* then adopted a stance which declared that it is "not we who should withdraw from the Union but the Soviets who must withdraw from Lithuania, because we never entered it on our own free will."[223]

In this situation even the activists of *Sąjūdis* felt the best way to restore Lithuania's independence was evolutionary rather than revolutionary. They knew that according to the Soviet Constitution, any republic could (at least in theory) withdraw from the Soviet Union. They were also aware that despite this formal position, the Communist Party, and the KGB both existed to guarantee Soviet unity. It is interesting in this respect to note that when a two and a half hour long discussion took place on August 31, 1988 between the *Sąjūdis* leaders and General Eduardas Eismuntas (the head of

---

221 See William J. H. Hough, III, The Annexation of the Baltic States and its effect on the Development of Law Prohibiting Forcible Seizure of Territory," *New York Law School Journal of International and Comparative Law*, 6, no. 2 (Winter 1985).

222 Vytautas Landsbergis, "Sugrįš Sąjūdžio gebėjimas atskirti tiesą nuo melo. Šiandien sukanka 10 metų, kai 1988 m. Mokslų akademijoje buvo įkurta Sąjūdžio iniciatyvinė grupė," *Lietuvos Aidas*, June 3, 1998, p. 1 & 5.

223 Landsbergis, "Sugrįš Sąjūdžio gebėjimas," p. 1 & 5.

the KGB in Lithuania) and Edmundas Baltin (his deputy), the question of the constitutional right of the Lithuanian Soviet Republic to withdraw from the Soviet Union was both raised and admitted.[224] In reality, however, the Communist Party regarded it as its prime duty to ensure that the republic would never exercise that right, and General Eismuntas confirmed this fact in the same discussion by telling the *Sąjūdis'* leaders:

If you wish to leave the Soviet Union by implementing this constitutional right, and if you use the slogan that you wish to exploit your constitutional right to leave the Soviet Union, I will have no objections, nor will anybody else. That is your constitutional right. You can exercise it, please, but [...] as a communist, I will fight for Soviet Lithuania, for the socialist system, and for Soviet Lithuania to remain within the Soviet Union.[225]

To publicize its goals *Sąjūdis* organized public meetings and demonstrations. A few smaller, environmental demonstrations took place near controversial industrial enterprises, all of them peaceful. Many were opposed to the construction of a third reactor at the Chernobyl-type nuclear power station at Ignalina, the largest of its type in Europe. Many demanded a reduction in the scale of the hydro-accumulative power station at Kaišiadorys and intensified their protests against a whole series of highly polluting Soviet chemical factories.[226] It is also important to record that the ruling elite also attempted to resist further environmental pollution of the country by the Soviet chemical industry. The environmentalist Česlovas Kudaba was prominent in his attempts to attract local and international public attention to problems of pollution from chemical plants, and to other issues such as excessive land-drainage

---

224   *Sąjūdis'* leaders A. Buračas, V. Petkevičius, J. Juzeliūnas, B. Genzelis, G. Songaila, V. Antanaitis, A. Skučas, A. Medalinskas, K. Prunskienė, R. Ozolas, Z. Vaišvila, A. Juozaitis, V. Bubnys, S. Geda, A. Žebriūnas, S. Pečiulis, M. Laurinkus, Č. Stankevičius, V. Valiušaitis, M. Kontrimaitė, as well as KGB General Edmundas Eismuntas participated in the discussion about Lithuania's independence from the USSR. See transcript of the meeting of KGB General Eismuntas with *Sąjūdis*: "Kas yra politinis nusikaltėlis," *Kauno aidas*, August 31, 1988, p. 2.

225   "Kas yra politinis nusikaltėlis," *Kauno aidas*, p. 2.

226   "Kas yra politinis nusikaltėlis," *Kauno aidas*, p. 2.

schemes which were destructive of the natural beauty of Lithuania's landscape. These consistent protests struck a deep chord within the Lithuanian community. The political scientist Vytautas Vardys has rightly said: "Moscow's insistence on further expanding Lithuania's chemical industries was a major factor in uniting the communist intellectual elite in their support for [...] *Sąjūdis* in the summer of 1988."[227]

As time went on, publicly expressed environmental demands toward the Soviet authorities assumed a more overtly political dimension. An example of this was the public meeting which took place in the central Gediminas Square in Vilnius on July 9, 1988, organized by the *Sąjūdis* Founding Group. It invited all the Lithuanian delegates to the nineteenth conference of the Communist Party in Moscow to attend. When the day came, it was very evident that the First Secretary of the Communist Party Algirdas Brazauskas was troubled by the sight of the Lithuanian national flag flying in this public place and was clearly in a dilemma as to whether to address the meeting or not. His perplexity must have been compounded by the fact that *Sąjūdis* had passed a special resolution anticipating this occasion demanding that delegates of the Moscow Conference should express the interests of Lithuania there, rather than simply being puppets of the Kremlin on that occasion. The leaders of the Communist Party were again obviously wrong-footed about these events, and inevitably they had to turn to their masters in Moscow for advice. It was not until August 18, 1988, following a high-level visit by Alexander Yakovlev, a member of the Moscow Politburo, that the prohibition against flying the national flag and singing the Lithuanian national anthem were withdrawn. In Soviet terms this was a concession. They could now be used publicly and were indeed granted co-existence alongside the symbols of the communist state. While this was a step in a victory for the *Sąjūdis* movement, it was clear that Moscow was becoming deeply concerned about the growing conflict between *Sąjūdis* and the Communist Party. This was what lay behind Yakovlev's visit. However, his review of the situation produced positive results

---

227   Vardys, *Lithuania*.

because it was announced that *Sąjūdis'* existence was legal, on the grounds "that *Sąjūdis* was not an opposition party" but a movement in support of Gorbachev's *perestroika*. The Kremlin was hoping to increase Communist Party influence in *Sąjūdis* and the course of events in Lithuania. In consequence of his visit and advice, communist officials were ordered not to resist the election of "*Sąjūdis* communists" to leading positions inside the party, and television coverage of *Sąjūdis* meetings and events was allowed on the Republic's TV channel.[228]

These events marked a significant amelioration. "It was good that it was Yakovlev who came and not somebody who was more narrow-minded," said Vytautas Landsbergis during his interview for the BBC, and he added:

> Yakovlev managed to understand a lot of things in the right way. After all, he was a supporter of the reforms, and of course he has seen the world, and he's not a narrow-minded party functionary who's spent all his life in Moscow, and he understood that the changes were necessary and needed. [...] From these meetings with Yakovlev the main conclusion was that *Sąjūdis* is not a bad thing. It should not be abolished. It should not be persecuted. That at least partially it was working in the right direction. There was a warning that something bad can come of it, but that there was a need to reasonably develop this movement, and for the governing bodies to use this movement for their own purposes.[229]

While these observations reflect the truth of the situation, it is also evident, with hindsight, that the Kremlin's strategists had seriously underestimated the role of *Sąjūdis*, and its influence on the Lithuanian population. Soon after Yakovlev's visit, its largest event was organized, when the Founding Group planned another public rally under the title *Istorinė teisingumo diena*, Historical Day of Justice. This gathering, which will be described in more detail below, can be the most crucial turning-point in *Sąjūdis'* history. Indeed, it has been said that the nation became unified for its march to national independence during this very meeting because the participants included not just the leaders of *Sąjūdis*, but also some

---

228   Vardys, *Lithuania.*
229   Interview with Vytautas Landsbergis, Second Russian Revolution, 2RR 3/5/2, British Library of Political and Economic Science.

Lithuanian members of the Soviet communist elite. The presence and the support of those members, who were tending to favour *Sąjūdis*, were becoming increasingly important. Vytautas Vardys, commenting on what was taking place, wrote "the Lithuanians are like radishes - they are red on the outside and white inside."[230] The event was organized by *Sąjūdis* to be held in Vingis Park, Vilnius, on August 23, 1988, and was advertised as an occasion to mark the forty-ninth anniversary of the secret Molotov-Ribbentrop pact. Nearly 150,000 people participated. The occasion was presided over by the Chairman of the *Sąjūdis* Founding Group, Vytautas Landsbergis, and many other members of the Founding Group, together with many prominent intellectuals and some members of local Communist Party elite participated in the gathering. The live transmission of the events by Lithuanian TV also rallied the entire nation behind the quest for independence, which emerged forcefully from the gathering.[231]

The true significance of the Vingis Park rally was the fact that the whole truth about the secret division of Europe between Soviet Union and Nazi Germany was expressed there in public, for the first time since the Soviet occupation of Lithuania in 1944. In his speech, Vytautas Landsbergis explained how Lithuania had become the victim of two criminal regimes, Stalinism and Nazism. He called everybody's attention to the fact that the attempted commemoration of the anniversary of the pact one year earlier had been disbanded by the Soviet authorities on the grounds that it "constituted an anti-Soviet activity."[232] This action was a candid exposure of the way in which the communist system had conspired to hide the truth. It was an observation which served to reinforce the impact of the poet Justinas Marcinkevičius' contribution to the debate in which he called loudly for the open publication of the secret documents of the Molotov-Ribbentrop pact. These documents, he said,

---

230 Vytautas Vardys, "Išeivija," *Draugas*, October 26, 1985, p. 7.
231 Vardys, "Išeivija."
232 "Istorinės Tiesos Diena. Protesto mitingo Lietuvoje, Vilniuje, Vingio parke Prieš Vokietijos ir Tarybų Sąjungos Nepuolimo sutarties (Ribentropo-Molotovo pakto) pasirašymą 1939 m. rugpjūčio 23 d. stenograma. 1988 m. rugpjūčio 23 d.," *Atgimimas*, no. 1, September 16, 1988, p. 7.

had been hidden from the public gaze for half a century. He also condemned the pact not just for its secrecy but for its brutal violation of international law, and for the fact that it had led to the outbreak of the war. He then demanded the opening of all the Soviet archives to scientists, historians, journalists and anyone interested in history, in order to set the record straight, so that a new and honest school textbook of Lithuanian history could be published, which would be free from Soviet falsification.[233] When he had finished speaking, another academician, Antanas Buračas, spoke about the need to restore the flag of independent Lithuania.[234] Lionginas Šepetys, Secretary of the Central Committee of Soviet Lithuania's Communist Party, then said that if the Soviet News Agency TASS continued to spread disinformation claiming that *Sąjūdis* had no popular support, he would be the first to deny such claims.[235] He was followed by Edmundas Atkočiūnas, a priest, who mentioned that Father Alfonsas Svarinskas and Father Sigitas Tamkevičius, as well as Petras Gražulis, were still held in Russian gulags as political prisoners, despite *perestroika*.[236] Next the historian Gediminas Rudis spoke about the direct consequences of the deal "between the two most reactionary and brutal dictatorships of the twentieth century," explaining in particular just how Lithuania's occupation by the Soviet Union had been a product of this pact.[237] Finally, the philosopher Arvydas Juozaitis expressed the wish that there would be no more falsifications of Lithuania's history, whether in academic research or in the press.[238] It was a call to the nation to face truths which had long been suppressed.

These progressive revelations gathered to build a positive tension in the huge crowd which had gathered and following these momentous statements Vytautas Landsbergis invited the audience to listen to the testimony of Juozas Urbšys, who had been independent Lithuania's last Foreign Minister between 1938 and 1940.

---

233   "Istorinės Tiesos Diena," p. 8.
234   "Istorinės Tiesos Diena," pp. 8-9.
235   "Istorinės Tiesos Diena," p. 10.
236   "Istorinės Tiesos Diena," p. 10.
237   "Istorinės Tiesos Diena," p. 11.
238   "Istorinės Tiesos Diena," p. 11.

He had recorded a speech especially for this rally from his flat in Kaunas. Juozas Urbšys' message announced how "during Lithuanian-Soviet negotiations in Moscow about the transfer of Vilnius to Lithuania in October 1939, Stalin had openly admitted that the USSR had made a deal with Germany, yes, the same fascist Germany, that the largest part of Lithuania should belong to the Soviet Union and a narrow strip along its borders, to Germany. He had laid a map of Lithuania on the table and showed the division line drawn on the territory of independent Lithuania, separating the possessions of Germany from those of the USSR."[239] He added: "I tried to protest against such a partition of an independent state, saying that Lithuania could never have expected that from a friendly USSR."[240] Doubt as to whether the agreement of 1939 had ever really served the best interests of the Soviet Union, as Soviet historians claimed, were then voiced by the historian Liudas Truska. He pointed out the heavy cost of the pact for the Baltic States and Poland, arguing that Stalin had been engaged in an attempt to secure the return of the lands which had belonged to the Russian Empire until the First World War, and had therefore pursued a carefully crafted scenario for the re-occupation of Lithuania. In doing this, Truska also mentioned that when Vincas Krėvė-Mickevičius, briefly Lithuanian Prime Minister, had arrived in Moscow in 1939, Molotov had openly said that Russia would "use any opportunity to get back to the Baltic Sea" and that "all small states would disappear in the future."[241]

It was now the turn of Vladislovas Mikučiauskas, Soviet Lithuanian Foreign Minister, to speak and he too urged the necessity of condemning the crimes of Stalinism. However, he then moved at once to praise the achievements of Soviet Lithuania. At this, the crowd started to indicate that they repudiated his message and were unwilling to listen anymore.[242] The poet Sigitas Geda then took the stage. He discussed the meaning of Lithuania's annexation

---

239   "Istorinės Tiesos Diena," p. 11.
240   "Istorinės Tiesos Diena," p. 11.
241   "Istorinės Tiesos Diena," pp. 11-12.
242   "Istorinės Tiesos Diena," p. 12.

and the need to inform "the more powerful nations of Europe and Asia" about Lithuania's hopes and intentions. His meaning was quite unmistakable, as the term "more powerful nation of Asia" in Lithuanian idiom is a reference to Russia. He added that "there will be no twenty-first century, without reconciliation amongst nations." It was clear to all that he was stressing the necessity of respecting the right of all nations to self-determination. "Lithuania has awakened, has risen, and will rise again," he declared. It was a bold announcement of faith and hope in the restoration of an independent Lithuania, and was perceived as such by the applauding crowd.[243] Mentioning efforts currently being made by Lithuania's authorities to help Artūras Sakalauskas, a Lithuanian soldier in the Soviet army, who had been crippled due to the criminally brutal treatment he had received, Landsbergis then asked the composer Julius Juzeliūnas, Chairman of the Commission for the Investigation of Stalinist crimes in Lithuania, to speak.[244] Juzeliūnas then testified that more than 300,000 people had been deported from Lithuania during the Stalinist terror of the 1940s. He then described the social achievements of independent Lithuania during the 20 years of freedom before the occupation of 1940, describing them as having amounted to a miracle. Citing Antanas Sniečkus, the First Secretary of the Lithuanian Communist Party, he pointed to the paradoxical fact that the communists who had been imprisoned by the authorities in Lithuania, had been saved by that fact from dying under Stalin's terror in Moscow, and appealed that reports made to the Commission in future should provide details about the victims as well as the perpetrators of the Stalinist crimes. This material, he said, now needed to be published openly to make sure that such events would not be repeated in future. He insisted that people should stop being afraid of breaking promises made to their oppressors under duress to keep quiet about what they had seen in the Soviet prisons and concentration camps. He ended his speech with an appeal:

---

243   "Istorinės Tiesos Diena," p. 13.
244   "Istorinės Tiesos Diena," p. 13.

> on this, the eve of the forty-ninth anniversary of the amoral deal between the world's two most brutal criminals Stalin and Hitler, we invite the people of Lithuania, calling the whole Lithuanian nation to attention by appealing to the sound of *Varpas* (The Bell) of Vincas Kudirka who had spoken for the nation's freedom a century ago with the cry: "Arise! Arise! Arise!"[245]

At this, tens of thousands of people lit candles in memory of the victims of Stalinist and Nazi crimes, holding them up in silent protest and in hope.[246]

The subsequent speaker was the writer Kazys Saja, who announced the names of Balys Gajauskas, Viktoras Petkus, Father Sigitas Tamkevičius, Gintautas Iešmantas and many others, who were still held in jail for holding views exactly like those expressed publicly in the present meeting. The only "crime" of these prisoners, he said, was that they had been brave enough to give this news openly at an earlier date. He then demanded freedom for all political prisoners currently held throughout the whole Soviet Union, and the crowd responded with exultant shouts of: "Freedom for the prisoners of conscience!"[247] This cry provided a signal for this momentous gathering to end with an invitation to sing the previously banned National Anthem, while the equally forbidden National Flags and State emblems of independent Lithuania were waved before the crowd. *Sąjūdis* then announced its demands for the complete publication of the secret protocols of the Soviet-Nazi pact; for the opening of the secret and hidden archives; for the rewriting of school history textbooks; and for the restoration of Lithuania's independence. As Vytautas Vardys has put it: "By making all the demands that it did, *Sąjūdis* placed itself squarely in the tradition of the dissidents who had demanded both Soviet and German denunciation of this pact as early as 1979."[248]

In less than three months, "priorities had shifted from the needs of *perestroika*, as defined by Moscow, to the requirements of

---

245   Vincas Kudirka, the famous Lithuanian physician and writer (1858-1899), the author of the National Anthem.

246   "Istorinės Tiesos Diena," p. 14.

247   "Istorinės Tiesos Diena," p. 14.

248   Vardys, *Lithuania*, pp. 127-128.

political reform as perceived by the Lithuanians."[249] Events were moving at an unexpected pace, but the enthusiasm, which had developed, had yet to be put to the test.

---

[249]   Vardys, *Lithuania*, pp. 127-128.

5. The Parliamentary Road to Freedom

The growing impatience for national independence which was manifest in Lithuania from the time of the Vingis Park rally was paralleled in the other Baltic countries, where the Latvian and Estonian Popular Fronts had similarly affirmed their commitment to the peaceful parliamentary route to the restoration of national independence.[250] However, neither the formulation of constitutional propositions, nor the preparation of political platforms, nor yet the creation of a popular mood, would be sufficient to move the monolithic impediments to national freedom which the Soviet Union and its constitution, totalitarian apparatus, its Communist Party, its censored press and media system, and exploitative command economy presented to the would-be reformers. To bring about, then win, free elections in order to liberate Lithuania from Soviet occupation would be merely a first step for *Sąjūdis*. Indeed, in the event, two important sets of general elections needed to be won at differing levels of Soviet constitutional practice even to reach that point. The first of these to be faced as the general election to the Supreme Soviet of the Soviet Union, and the second, the general election to the Supreme Soviet of occupied Lithuania, the Lithuanian Soviet Socialist Republic, as it was called in Soviet terminology. The three important dates which mark our description of the progression of these events were: the declaration of moral independence for Lithuania on February 16, 1989; secondly "The Baltic Way," the largest freedom demonstration the world had yet seen, when the peoples of Lithuania, Latvia, and Estonia linked their hands along the highway running from Tallinn, through Riga, to Vilnius in a huge protest gathering against the continuing consequences of the secret Molotov-Ribbentrop pact on August 23, 1989. Finally, there was the celebration of Lithuania's Independence Day on February 16, 1990.

---

250 See e.g., Romas Batūra, *Baltijos kelias - kelias į laisvę. 1989.08.23. Dešimtmetį minint* (Vilnius: Lietuvos Sąjūdis, 1999), p. 14.

These all proved to be occasions that mobilized support for *Sąjūdis* both in Lithuania and in the West.[251]

We have already seen that the initial tactics of *Lietuvos persitvarkymo Sąjūdis*, the Lithuanian Restructuring Movement, were two-fold, in keeping with its title.[252] First of all, the movement declared its support for Gorbachev's policies of *perestroika* and *glasnost* and demanded the full introduction of these purported new realities into Soviet Lithuania. Second, *Sąjūdis* set out to act as a *de facto* movement for the liberation of Lithuania from Soviet occupation. In Soviet constitutional terminology, the movement could therefore be described as an expression of the legitimate right of a republic to leave the Soviet Union, while from an international perspective, it was a legitimate movement for national self-determination, a principle protected and guaranteed by the United Nations Charter of Human Rights. Third, it was a movement for the restoration of independent Lithuania, which still existed internationally as a legal entity. Finally, *Sąjūdis* existed as a protest movement to demand Soviet withdrawal from Lithuania, which emphasized the fact that Lithuania and the other Baltic States had been illegally occupied by the Soviet Union.

Within less than five months from the first meeting of the *Sąjūdis* Founding Group, the movement had fully developed its structure, becoming an active, well-organized, and effective political body with its major goal clearly defined as the restoration of Lithuanian independence. Thus, it emerged rapidly on the political scene of occupied Lithuania as a highly motivated political institution and was soon to suggest its alternative candidates for the general elections to the Supreme Soviet of the Soviet Union and to the Supreme Soviet in occupied Lithuania. *Sąjūdis* candidates were fielded at both levels, focusing their campaign unequivocally on the goal of future independence for Lithuania. The official Communist Party candidates in these contests still viewed the country's future

---

251 See e.g., Romas Batūra, *Lietuvos Sąjūdis ir valstybės atkūrimas. Panorama* (Vilnius: Valstybės žinios, 1998), pp. 24–25.

252 "Restructuring" (in Lithuanian) means "perestroika" (in Russian).

as remaining within the changing Soviet Union and, therefore, they were cast as the opponents of this policy.

Initially, the *Sąjūdis* organization had no formal membership requirements. Anyone could, thus, join a local *Sąjūdis* group and could show support for Lithuania's independence simply by performing voluntary work. The movement's structure was simple: *Sąjūdis'* followers elected representatives to district meetings, and these in turn elected *Sąjūdis* councils in the cities and regions, although only after full consultation among the different representative groups. *Sąjūdžio Taryba*, the Council of *Sąjūdis*, was elected as we have seen during a general founding meeting and later *Sąjūdžio Seimas*, the Parliament of *Sąjūdis*, was elected during the annual general meetings. Many members of this Council and this Parliament later became the movement's candidates in elections both for the Supreme Soviet of the Soviet Union and for the Supreme Soviet in occupied Lithuania. When they were elected to the Kremlin's Supreme Soviet in March 1989 with a great majority in most instances, *Sąjūdis* became the winning and dominant political force in the first free election in the history of the Soviet Union. This was achieved despite the threatening and ubiquitous presence of the KGB, the Red Army, the Soviet militia and the Communist Party, all institutions of Soviet totalitarian power.

The major initial tactic employed by *Sąjūdis* was to exploit the Kremlin's mistakes.[253] It is ironic to suggest that the biggest of these was that body's acceptance of *Sąjūdis* as "the Lithuanian movement for *perestroika*." An examination of the events will confirm that the Kremlin had no choice other than to promote *perestroika* in occupied Lithuania if it was not to lose credibility in the eyes of reformers everywhere. It is also fair to observe that the *Sąjūdis* movement was sometimes given more space than might be expected by its opponents even though the objectives of the two sides were radically different. An example of this was the outcome of the visit of Aleksandr Yakovlev, a member of the Politburo of the all-Union Communist Party and the chief ideologist of perestroika in the Soviet Union, who came to Lithuania August 11 - 14, 1988. This visit was

---

253   See the previous chapter.

a turning point in *Sąjūdis'* relationship with the party. Indeed, Romualdas Ozolas, a member of the Founding Group of *Sąjūdis* and later deputy Prime Minister of Lithuania, even said after he had left that "we are still alive due to the visit of Alexandr Yakovlev."[254] Yakovlev had delivered a lengthy speech to the Lithuanian communists in May 1988 entitled "In the Interests of the Country and Every Nationality," part of which was shown on national television, in which he examined many of the problems of Soviet society from "economic stagnation" to "bureaucratism." It is interesting at this distance in time to note that this appraisal included references toward Lenin's attitude to "national consciousness," which, he said, allowed that "ethnic and nation-state differences [...] would [...] remain for an indefinitely long time after the victory of socialism on a world-wide scale."[255]

This visit had rather unexpectedly eased pressure on the *Sąjūdis* leaders at a critical stage and had given them both freedom and time to match their actions more effectively to a speedily changing situation. Alexander Yakovlev has since remembered his meetings with the Lithuanian leaders in the following way:

> The reasons that there weren't any difficulties with them then was that the questions we discussed then were not about independence, or the split of the Party. We talked about sovereignty, economic independence [...] If we had acted in time, if we had introduced the principle of confederation then, we would not have these problems now. But our machine, the dictates of its central apparatus, that did not take the national interests into consideration created the problem.[256]

When asked: "Did you try to persuade the Central Committee, the Politburo, to change its attitude? Did you encounter resistance?" Yakovlev answered: "It never stopped. The Empire mentality is very well developed."[257] He explained that Gorbachev had also understood the situation perfectly well, but "he had to take the

---

254   Interview with Alexander Yakovlev for the BBC, *The Second Russian Revolution.* 2RR 1/2/18, British Library of Political and Economic Science, London, 1990.

255   Alexander Yakovlev, *The October Revolution and Perestroika* (Moscow: Novosti Press Agency Publishing House, 1989), p. 62.

256   Interview with Yakovlev for BBC.

257   Interview with Yakovlev for BBC.

level of understanding in the country into account."[258] He added ironically: "Do you think General Makashov is the only one who thinks that we left Eastern Europe without a fight?"[259]

Richard Krickus has described how Yakovlev accepted an observation from the Soviet Lithuanian writer Vytautas Petkevičius at one of the public hearings in which he attempted to sound out his feelings. He said: "Isn't it paradoxical? I know three ethnic languages and I'm being called a nationalist. The person who calls me this knows only one language, Russian. Although he has lived in this republic for several decades, he calls himself an internationalist!"[260] Interestingly, this exchange was entirely cut from the program which reported the meeting on national television. However, the remark, which was in fact directed against the Russian Nikolai Mitkin, the Second Secretary of the Communist Party and the Kremlin's chief watchdog in occupied Lithuania, was widely publicized in other ways. It reflected a shift in opinion which Yakovlev recognized, and one of the major outcomes of his visit was also the replacement of the rigid and reactionary First Secretary of the Communist Party Rimgaudas Songaila by the more flexible Algirdas Brazauskas. The Second Secretary was also changed and Vladimiras Beriozovas, a Lithuanian-born Russian, was given the post. It was clear from these moves that the Kremlin hoped that Yakovlev's visit would enable it to better control *Sąjūdis* which had undoubtedly remained a target of the Soviet secret security forces. Now, because of his appearance, it temporarily seemed that *Sąjūdis* had been supported, indeed even legitimized, by the Kremlin. For a period, Moscow encouraged communist membership of *Sąjūdis*, in the hope that its contribution would improve the situation in the republic. Moscow clearly hoped by this device to divert the energy of the population towards the idea that managed change for the Soviet system in Lithuania would be a better alternative than the unpredictable process of pushing for independence. However, the

---

258   Interview with Yakovlev for BBC.
259   Interview with Yakovlev for BBC.
260   Richard Krickus, *Showdown. The Lithuanian Rebellion and the Breakup of the Soviet Empire* (Washington and London: Brassey's, 1997), p. 60.

reality proved to be different. Contrary to the Kremlin's expectations, the *Sąjūdis* movement managed to win some influence within the Communist Party in occupied Lithuania itself, a process which eventually enabled its separation from the Communist Party of the Soviet Union (CPSU). Although a small part of the party remained faithful to its Moscow masters when this happened, the greater part of the membership of the Communist Party in occupied Lithuania was effectively already in a state of schism from the CPSU before the end of 1989. Though the Lithuanian Communist Party senior members were 'not prepared to follow Landsbergis wherever he wished to go' and were sometimes subject to a severe strain in their loyalties, the fact remains that they were unwilling from this stage onward to offer active resistance to the expressed will of the Lithuanian people. Nevertheless, despite this improvement, they remained an ambiguous force, not least afterwards, when *Sąjūdis* had formed the national government and was facing great international pressure, and eventually a full economic blockade.

Three major stages of *Sąjūdis'* activity can be identified as it took its planned peaceful and parliamentary route towards the achievement of independence. Initially, as we have already seen, *Sąjūdis* presented itself as a movement on behalf of *perestroika* but its real goals and aims at that stage were implicit rather than explicit. They could, nevertheless, be seen in its symbols or "read between the lines of its text." Its mode reflected the style of literature written during the Soviet period. The reasons for this subterfuge were prudential, as was the perception that it was necessary to increase political demands on the Soviet authorities gradually. There was also the need to achieve legitimacy to avoid the movement being treated as anti-Soviet, and thus being disbanded while in its early stages, just as a written text had to satisfy the Soviet censorship before it was published. For these reasons, *Sąjūdis* can be understood retrospectively as having used the Soviet lexicon rather widely, while conducting its activity within the borders, or, in fact, on the edge, of what was legal within the Soviet framework. Even Landsbergis, the leader of *Sąjūdis'* Founding Group, used phrases like *"Soviet Lithuania"* in the beginning of his speeches, although he always finished them with the expression "*Lithuania.*" Gorbachev's portraits were also carried in the public demonstrations in support of perestroika and glasnost, and leading members of occupied Lithuania's ruling bodies were invited to participate and talk at *Sąjūdis'* meetings. Meanwhile, *Sąjūdis* policy was essentially one of "push and wait." During a trip to the United States in June 1989 its leader Vytautas Landsbergis stated that "our way is incremental - you push, and you wait and see. This policy was a conscious one. In order to become independent, we started passing laws, and pulled away step by step. The Baltic States are in a special category, of trying to decolonize gradually."[261]

History has since confirmed how the Baltic States continued to make clear their claim of a non-violent path for liberation from Soviet occupation with a steady and cumulative determination. The three most important factors in persuading the Kremlin to view *Sąjūdis* as an organization of managed change rather than the liberation movement which it really was were: the acceptance of communists into membership of *Sąjūdis*; the flexibility of Landsbergis' leadership in the Founding Group, and the continuing dialogue between the movement and the Soviet authorities. Thus, it had every appearance of acceptability. Organizing the public meeting with the delegates attending the nineteenth Communist Party conference before their trip to Moscow was one such deception, done to display commitment to *perestroika* and change within the Soviet system, but at the same time, to seek public assurances of the delegates that they would commit themselves to Lithuanian interests.

It was in this context that the demand for the resignation of Songaila, the First Secretary of the Communist Party in occupied Lithuania, was voiced by Professor Bronius Genzelis, a member of the Founding Group of *Sąjūdis* and a prominent member of the Lithuanian Communist Party, being its leader in the University of Vilnius. We have seen how *Sąjūdis'* position changed following the Vingis Park gathering on August 23, 1988, in which 150,000 people commemorated the anniversary of the Molotov-Ribbentrop pact.

261   "*Sąjūdis* leader comments on vital issues. The fight for independence has to be non-violent and evolutionary," *The Observer* no. 7-8 (July–August 1989): 6–7.

Sąjūdis had seized an opportunity. It openly stressed the illegality of the incorporation of the Baltic States into the USSR. It denounced, because of incontrovertible evidence, the international crime committed by two dictators, Stalin and Hitler. *Sąjūdis'* position now was that justice had to be restored and that the means of implementation would be the withdrawal of the Soviet Union from Lithuania and the other Baltic States as soon as possible.

The second stage of *Sąjūdis'* activity involved the electoral effort to win a majority of the seats allocated to the Lithuanian Soviet Socialist Republic in the Supreme Soviet of the Soviet Union. Though there had been some changes in the Soviet system since Brezhnev's days it would be a mistake to suggest that these elections were intended to resemble the electoral process of democratic society in any way. Within occupied Lithuania, the Communist Party showed great reluctance to implement any changes in the nomination of candidates for the electoral lists. It was *Sąjūdis* which forced its hand in ensuring that *Sąjūdis* candidates were able to stand against its lists. It was the first-ever election in the Soviet Union to allow any element of opposition politics. The Kremlin clearly overestimated its ability to control the outcome of the election, e.g., the counting of ballots in its own favor, achieving 99 percent of "yes" votes, as it used to be in the past. One could perhaps argue, that the announcement and holding of general elections in the USSR in a more or less democratic way was a mistake by the Kremlin, at least in the sense that the demonstration of the beginnings of the democratic process were perceived by the Kremlin as being an adequate response to what the country desired. Lithuania wanted democracy, but the nation had reached the point where this demand and that of national self-determination were inseparable in the public mind. Thus, the election offered an opportunity which was exploited effectively by *Sąjūdis*. It opened the parliamentary way to freedom and the movement succeeded in wining a majority of seats.[262] The Lithuanian Freedom League had initially suggested a boycott of the election to the USSR Supreme Soviet on the

---

262　See Chapter 8 for analysis of international pressure to the Soviet Union to achieve real change in the Soviet system.

grounds that such elections might legitimize Soviet rule in occupied Lithuania. *Sąjūdis* had disagreed, perceiving these elections precisely as a means of steering occupied Lithuania out of Soviet control. *Sąjūdis'* leadership, in effect, opted to use the opportunities which the Soviet system offered for its own dismantling. Indeed, as politics is the art of the possible, that was probably the only realistic way under prevailing conditions to achieve the goal of Lithuania's independence from the Soviet Union.

The beginning of 1989 was marked by a major demonstration calling for the withdrawal of the Red Army, which was initiated by *Lietuvos Laisvės Lyga*, the Lithuanian Freedom League, a more radical organization than *Sąjūdis*. To mark Independence Day on February 16 the Lithuanian Freedom monument in Kaunas, which had been destroyed by the Stalinist Soviet authorities on Lithuania's incorporation into the Soviet Union, was publicly reinstated. In anticipation of the occasion, *Sąjūdžio Seimas*, the Parliament of *Sąjūdis*, issued its most radical statement to date, calling unequivocally for the re-establishment of an independent, democratic and neutral Lithuanian state. From that moment onward, the declaration "Independence - for a Reborn Lithuania, democracy - for an Independent Lithuania, a decent life - for a Democratic Lithuania!" became *Sąjūdis'* main slogan for its election campaign.

The reaction of Moscow and the local Communist Party in occupied Lithuania to these developments was particularly angry. There were ominous rumblings on Moscow radio, when Kriuchkov, the KGB boss, claimed that a "fascist dictatorship was taking power in Lithuania." Locally, the First Secretary of the Communist Party Algirdas Brazauskas threatened to tighten restrictions on the increasingly independent press as well as to clamp down on Communist Party members' activities and participation in the leadership of *Sąjūdis*. The broadcasting of *Sąjūdis'* ninety-minute weekly television program *Atgimimo banga* was then summarily suspended and communist officials began furiously to denounce *Sąjūdis'* support for political independence, accusing it of deviating from its original intention to support *perestroika*. Despite these developments and perhaps helped by them, *Sąjūdis* won 36 of the 41 seats allocated to the Lithuanian Soviet Socialist Republic in the election to the Supreme Soviet of the Soviet Union on March 26, 1989. It was obvious that this victory was a clear manifestation of the Lithuanian people's support for national independence and their wish to put an end to communist ideology and Soviet colonialism. Then, to drive the reflected message home to those who controlled the Soviet system, the new *Sąjūdis* deputies disseminated a book in the Russian language with the documentary evidence about the secret Molotov-Ribbentrop pact, which had been printed in Vilnius[263]. When they arrived at the Kremlin, some 100,000 copies of the book which included full texts of the secret protocols of the Soviet-Nazi deal were distributed in Moscow and elsewhere in Russia. They were effectively posting a public notice that the Soviet occupation of Lithuania was based on a fundamentally illegal and criminal treaty.

The general election to the Supreme Soviet of the Soviet Union was perceived by *Sąjūdis* as providing the opportunity for the election of representatives of occupied Lithuania to negotiate with the Kremlin on the restoration of an independent state. The representatives it sent to Moscow in 1989 were supporters of Lithuania's independence, a fact which marked the election as standing in stark contrast with the events of 1940, when Moscow had manipulated a general election in Lithuania unscrupulously in order to have its own representatives nominated to a hastily re-named Parliament to the "Supreme Soviet of the Lithuanian Soviet Socialist Republic," which had then arbitrarily announced that it was "the will of the nation" to join the Soviet Union. However, we must note that in 1989 *Sąjūdis* itself had also not been above some manipulation in the national interest. The former communist leader Algirdas Brazauskas owed his election to the fact that the *Sąjūdis* leadership regarded him as being potentially useful in the forthcoming negotiation process with Moscow. *Sąjūdis* had withdrawn its own candidate so that he could be returned unopposed. However, the

---

263   The Kremlin's officials denied the existence of the Molotov-Ribbentrop pact by saying that they did not find its original. *Sąjūdis* stated that it will help Moscow to find the pact by getting many Russian people become familiar with its text.

situation was changing, even in Moscow, in a favorable way and because of this, the Lithuanian and other Baltic delegations were able to persuade the USSR Supreme Soviet to set up a Commission to investigate the Molotov-Ribbentrop pact and its secret protocols. Once nominated, this commission set to work quickly and on August 22, 1989, fourteen of its twenty-six members reported their conviction that the pact should be annulled. Responding to pressure from the Balts, they had declared that relations between the Baltic States and the Soviet Union should be governed not by the Molotov-Ribbentrop agreement but by the earlier treaties, signed by Lenin in 1920, under which the Soviet Union had guaranteed the independence and territorial integrity of all three states. It was very soon after this report was made that *Sąjūdis* and its allies in the neighboring countries arranged the huge *Baltijos kelias* (Baltic Way), demonstration in which over a million Lithuanians, Latvians and Estonians accepted the invitation to join hands peacefully along a 650 km route, connecting the capitals of the three Baltic States, Vilnius, Riga, and Tallinn. This was, of course, a graphic expression of the rejection by the people of these nations of the evil deal which had robbed their countries of both the right to existence and independence as well as all normal democratic rights for over half a century, despite the persistent Soviet propaganda that they had joined the USSR freely.

The Baltic representatives in the Kremlin's Supreme Soviet, including *Sąjūdis* members, made the most of the initiative now created. They stated that this demonstration was in effect 'the first referendum in the occupied Baltic states,' announcing that its scale 'demonstrated the manifest wish of the Lithuanians, Latvians and Estonians to restore their states, and to be independent from the Soviet Union.' Naturally, this impressive demonstration was reported on the major television news programs across the world, and even within the Soviet Union, despite a campaign of disinformation by TASS. Thus, it served the intention of its organizers well indeed because it ensured that full western attention was drawn towards the illegality of the secret pact and the need to annul its consequences, ending the Soviet occupation of the Baltic States. The climate of international public opinion was beginning to flow in the direction desired by the three Baltic countries.

Despite Moscow's fury at these developments, the regime refrained from the use of military force. It did, however, attempt to provoke violence by movements of Soviet troops. For example, many more than the normal quota of Soviet soldiers was seen in the streets of Kaunas and although they avoided causing provocation, troops in civilian dress and KGB officers holding weapons were sent to Sąjūdis meetings. They were often identified by Sąjūdis' volunteer stewards or by members of the movement's developing information and intelligence agency, Sąjūdžio Informacinė Agentūra. Naturally, they were often asked to leave as soon as possible. Invariably, these people were alarmed by the presence of television or other cameras and would often disappear soon after being noticed. Moscow also sent troops dressed in civilian clothes to increase the support for communists, by voting in the USSR Supreme Soviet election in some constituencies. However, this campaign ended almost as soon as it started because Lithuanian television played with the situation by filming these men all with identical civilian clothes and short hair, arriving to vote on military trucks. The radio networks also commented extensively on this and other similar attempts at fraud. This tactic of ironic exposure was much used and served as a valuable weapon in the war of lies waged by the Kremlin's propaganda machine. Of course, the fact that its work had backfired became strikingly obvious with Sąjūdis' victory in the general election to the Supreme Soviet of the Soviet Union. This event briefly shifted the major scene of political events from Vilnius to Moscow, where the deputies of occupied Lithuania were widely regarded as "poisoned tomatoes," who had come spreading ideas of democracy in the Kremlin. These "separatists," who against all the expectations of the communist elite had become deputies of the supreme legislative body of the Soviet Union, were now well placed to begin what was perhaps the greatest manipulation of the Soviet system since its establishment in 1917 - the destruction of the Soviet system from the top.

At this stage, *Sąjūdis* began work to encourage the local Supreme Soviet in occupied Lithuania to proclaim the superiority of the republic's laws over the Soviet ones, to establish Lithuanian citizenship as a status distinct from Soviet citizenship, and to guarantee these Lithuanian citizens the benefits of the rights which are defined by the Universal Declaration of Human Rights.[264] Thus, the *Sąjūdis* deputies in the Supreme Soviet of the Soviet Union began to act decisively at the local level, using their authority to encourage the Supreme Soviet in the occupied country to prepare laws which would smooth the restitution of the Lithuanian state. This campaign had, of course, begun with reference to the coming election to the Supreme Soviet in occupied Lithuania, expected to take place on February 24, 1990.[265] Underlying this political strategy, *Sąjūdis* activists understood the economic stranglehold of the command Soviet economy would have to be broken if political separation was to become in any way feasible. A few months earlier, Baltic economic experts had worked out a model for economic independence and the key provisions of this so-called *Baltic Model* included demands that economic reforms must be based on the principles of a market economy. This implied that the Baltic economies must be firmly under the control of their governments, and that their natural resources must come under the control of the republics and not belong to the Kremlin. It also required that the occupied Baltic republics must become distinct entities, even within the Soviet Union's budget, with powers to raise their own taxes.[266]

During the last months of 1988, occupied Estonia began to move more rapidly along this path toward self-determination than the other occupied Baltic States. On November 17 the Supreme Soviet in occupied Estonia confirmed these economic principles and declared the superiority of the republic's legislation over the Soviet laws. At this stage the reform process was moving more slowly in

---

264 "LPS Seimo nutarimas," *Atgimimas*, no. 17, 28 April 1989, p. 2.
265 "LPS Seimo rezoliucija," LPS Seimo nutarimas. *Atgimimas*, no. 17, April 28, 1989, p. 2.
266 Vytautas S. Vardys, "Sąjūdis: National Revolution in Lithuania" in Jan A. Trapans (ed.) *Toward Independence: The Baltic Popular Movements* (Oxford: Westview Press, 1991).

occupied Lithuania, where the local Supreme Soviet refused to implement parallel legislation, despite great pressure from *Sąjūdis* to
do so. However, these matters were tabled for debate. Algirdas Brazauskas, the new First Secretary of the Communist Party, was recalled urgently to Moscow to meet Gorbachev. On his return to Vilnius, he delivered an apologetic speech in a television appearance
in which he gave excuses for failing to lead the republic on a path
like that taken by Estonia. It was clear that he had accepted Moscow's orders rather than attempting to resist them. His weakness
was fully exposed a few days later, when *Sąjūdis* declared on November 20, 1988, that "henceforth only those laws should be honored, that do not limit Lithuania's independence." This announcement increased the conflict with the Communist Party, not least because *Sąjūdis* had also declared the *moral* independence of Lithuania the same day. Although it did not yet have the power to pass
the necessary legislation, the movement had now shown an initiative which it clearly intended to use to the full. Within a week, it
had gathered signatures from almost half the entire population of
Lithuania to mark its protest against changes in the Soviet constitution, which had been proposed in clear design to centralize
power in Moscow even further. The prepared constitutional
amendments seemed designed explicitly to prevent the separation
of the Baltic republics from the Soviet Union. A petition with 1.8
million signatures was presented to the Supreme Soviet of the Soviet Union on November 24, 1988.

The similarity of the political processes in occupied Lithuania,
Latvia and Estonia encouraged unanimity and increased co-operation between the independence movements. The representatives of
the Lithuanian *Sąjūdis* and of the Latvian and Estonian Popular
Fronts maintained a close liaison, affirming their belief in the peaceful, parliamentary way for the restoration of national independence. The joint meeting of the representatives of all three national
movements in Tallinn on May 13-14, 1989, formed the Baltic Assembly, a joint representative and coordinative body of the three
liberation movements for their deeper co-ordination and co-operation. It passed the Declaration of Rights of the Baltic Nations, which

announced the right of each of the three peoples to live in its historically defined territory; the right to self-determination; and the
right of each of the Baltic nations to define its own political status
freely. The declaration also emphasized the right of independent
collaboration with other states and nations and expressed the collective will to regain state sovereignty in a neutral and demilita-
rized Baltic and Scandinavian region.[267] Having passed this important declaration, the Baltic Assembly also sent letters to the
heads of the member states of the Conference for Security and Co-
operation in Europe; the Secretary General of the United Nations;
and the Chairman of the Presidium of the USSR Supreme Soviet,
which emphasized that Lithuanian, Latvian and Estonian independence were established with all the privileges of international
recognition between 1918 and 1940. They referred explicitly to the
criminal secret deal between Stalin and Hitler which had divided
Europe into the zones of Soviet and Nazi influence and had led directly to the destruction of the independence of the Baltic States and
expressed a formal confidence that the Soviet Union would condemn its policy pursued towards the Baltic States between 1939 and
1940 and would therefore declare the agreements contained in
those secret protocols to be invalid. They further expressed the
hope that the Soviet Union would no longer impede the negotiation
process of the restoration of state sovereignty to Lithuania, Latvia
and Estonia. The formulation also stressed that the nations wished
to re-establish their independence within a neutral and demilita-
rized zone of Europe. They then passed a "Resolution on Stalinist
crimes," which demanded that the international community
should acknowledge that the Soviet policies toward the Baltic
States, and the Stalinist terror, which accompanied their incorporation into the Soviet system had been acts of genocide and a crime
against humanity. The resolution demanded that the initiators and
executors of those communist crimes then committed should be uncovered; that the communist institutions involved should be recognized as having been criminal organizations; and that an international legal mechanism should be established on the Nuremberg

---

267   "Baltijos tautų deklaracija," *Atgimimas,* no. 20, May 23, 1989, p. 1.

model to investigate those crimes against humanity as it had dealt with Nazi crimes in the past.

At around this time Maati Hint, a representative of the Estonian Popular Front, delivered a lecture entitled "The Baltic Way" in Tallinn, which briefly reviewed the relationship between the Estonian, Latvian and Lithuanian nations, who had lived near the Baltic Sea in common destiny for thousands of years, at the crossroads of northern and eastern Europe. Maati Hint spoke of how the foundations for independence laid down between 1920 and 1940 had been cruelly undermined by the totalitarian regimes of the Soviet Union and Nazi Germany. Despite having been allocated to the sphere of the Stalinist aggressor under the secret protocols of August 23 and September 28, 1939, and the terror, mass deportations, and forced migration which followed, they had remained faithful to their languages, culture, national and religious traditions. He claimed that "the Baltic Way is the European Way. There must be neither linguistic, nor cultural isolation, but free relationships, free development. The Baltic Way is the way of negotiations, persuasions, and proofs."[268] It was a proclamation of the confident determination of all three Baltic nations that their history, culture, political will, and hope for the future lay with Western Europe. Within weeks of the speech, his formula "the Baltic Way is the European Way" was endorsed publicly and internationally by the largest ever hand-linking demonstration on August 23, 1989. No similar declaration of the democratic will of three nations had previously been witnessed in this form by history. These peoples were clearly determined to rejoin democratic Europe as sovereign nations.

On the home front, *Sąjūdis* was fully engaged in encouraging the Communist Party in occupied Lithuania to separate from the Soviet Communist Party. Already during the fourth session in April of the *Sąjūdžio Seimas*, Sąjūdis' Parliament, a resolution had been passed, inviting the Lithuanian Communist Party to call an extraordinary meeting and to adopt a party program independent

---

268   Romas Batūra, *"Baltijos kelias" - kelias į laisvę. 1989.08.23. Dešimtmetį minint* (Vilnius: Lietuvos Sąjūdis, 1999), p. 15.

from Moscow.[269] When this advice was accepted, it became evident that the fact that membership in the party had suddenly begun to drop sharply was among the reasons for the split from Moscow. Its leadership had finally realized that independence from Moscow could not be avoided if it was to retain its influence in Lithuania. That the decision was taken in defiance of warnings from Mikhail Gorbachev and the Soviet Politburo was evident, because Lithuanian reporters acquired the text of an unpublished resolution of the Soviet Politburo which accused the Lithuanian Communist Party and its First Secretary Algirdas Brazauskas of allowing "hesitations, inconsistencies and deviations from the resolutions of the Communist Party of the Soviet Union." It went on to declare that the Lithuanian Communist Party must "fulfill without delay" the CPSU policy "against federalization of the party and for preserving the party as one united whole."

Moscow followed up this by dispatching its chief ideologist, Politburo member Vadim A. Medvedev, to Lithuania. According to TASS, he warned the Lithuanian Communist Party on November 30 that their independence move was actively harming Gorbachev's *perestroika*. Moscow's television then publicized Medvedev's statement that self-determination and secession were two different things: "There are many problems that can be solved only if all republics work together." His plea was followed by an appeal from Gorbachev himself, published in the pages of the Lithuanian communist newspaper *Tiesa* ("Truth") in which he wrote that the "common house of Europe" can be built "only on the foundation of the acceptance of the realities of European politics." The article asserted that Soviet society and the Soviet state had become a "single organism" long ago. He also said, exposing a fundamental assumption, that the peaceful coexistence of the USSR with the West and Europe was dependent on a continuing Soviet presence in Lithuania and the other Baltic States. The actual limits of his openness were neatly expressed by the concurrent and carefully coordinated attack on Lithuania by Moscow's Central Television. Further confirmation that official communist control of the media was "alive and well"

---

269   "Ketvirtoji Seimo Sesija," *Atgimimas*, no. 17, April 28, 1989, p. 1.

came within days when the rather open television program *Vzglyad* ("View") was suddenly withdrawn from the Soviet television program schedule.

Despite these threats from the Kremlin, the Supreme Soviet of the Lithuanian Soviet Socialist Republic voted to strip the Communist Party of its leading role in society on December 7, 1989. This decision had already been taken in most central European countries, but occupied Lithuania was the first republic in the Soviet Union to legalize alternative political parties. It was a historic decision of great significance, and the first of the newly registered parties was the 2000-member *Lietuvos demokratų partija*, Lithuanian Democratic Party, which advocated full independence as its central principle. This push for the legalization of a multi-party system was a further factor which helped to orient the republic's Communist Party towards its break with the Soviet one and the Lithuanian precedent-setting action encouraged other republics to follow suit. The issue was discussed in the USSR Supreme Soviet, but by then both Estonian and Armenian Supreme Soviets had passed similar provisions and embodied them in their national constitutions. These changes were now moving very quickly with a self-confirming momentum. At the extraordinary meeting of the Lithuanian Communist Party held on December 19-20, 1989, 855 delegates voted in favor of complete separation from the Kremlin, in distinction from those 160 delegates who were for autonomy within a reformed Soviet party. Twelve abstained. Following the vote, Vytautas Stakvilevičius, a member of the Lithuanian Communist Party and of *Sąjūdis*, stated that the Lithuanian nation wants independence and statehood," adding "whether our party is independent or not will also decide whether Lithuania will be independent or not."[270]

It was now clear to the leader of the Lithuanian Communist Party Algirdas Brazauskas that the party could retain its popularity only by supporting independence. Choosing his words carefully, and perhaps reserving a certain ambivalence on the matter, he observed that "although Lithuania's experience with independence

---

270   "Ketvirtoji Seimo Sesija," p. 1.

was brief, it left a deep mark in our people's consciousness," adding that the restoration of Lithuanian statehood "was the top priority of the party." "We are in favor of a sovereign Lithuanian state," he said. "Sovereignty means political independence, and the independence of the state in its domestic and foreign policy."[271] It is clear from these formulations that *Sąjūdis'* stance had now entered the *realpolitik* of even the most senior echelon of the Communist Party in occupied Lithuania. Speaking before the vote of December 20, Raimundas Kašauskas, a writer, who was also a member of both the party and *Sąjūdis*, reminded the conference that Gorbachev had said when describing the changes in Eastern Europe: "Every nation has the right to choose its own way to develop its social structure." Kašauskas then emphasized that the expression "***all European nations*** includes us," adding: "We are no worse than anyone else in Eastern Europe." It was this sentiment which carried the day, but it had consequences. Gorbachev's reaction was furious. He responded by calling a two-day emergency meeting of the Soviet Communist Party on December 25-26, 1989, and Algirdas Brazauskas was heavily pressed during this meeting. However, his explanation of his position was honest:

> I am not a grand master in politics, but I must stress that the main reason for what we've done was the desire to strengthen our position in the republic as a political force. That should be remembered in further actions, when we start talking about the structural changes in the Party. Our main aim should be to preserve the leading role of the Party. And I am going towards that aim. ... The Federation of Soviet Republics and the relations between the republics will not be static. They will change. The republics will be establishing new direct links with each other, with neighboring states.[272]

Brazauskas' declaration was not received highly. Yegor Ligachev, a hardline member of the Politburo, commented later:

> Even before the plenum and during the plenum, I was sure that we were dealing with people who had betrayed their fellow communists, I am talking about the Lithuanian Communist Party [...] The former leaders of the Communist Party of Lithuania had broken the Party in half, and had created

---

271   "Ketvirtoji Seimo Sesija," p. 1.
272   Interview with Algirdas Brazauskas, Second Russian Revolution, 2RR 1/3/8, British Library of Political and Economic Sciences.

> a break-away party that was designed to service Sąjūdis, the current leaders
> of Lithuania. That was sectarianism, pure and simple, and I said that at my
> speech at the plenum, and the time that has elapsed since has confirmed the
> truth of my words. They have defected to the other side, the other camp,
> they lost the influence they had had in Lithuania.[273]

Though they knew the strength of feeling against them and could feel the resentment, few Lithuanian political leaders expected Moscow to use force against Lithuania. Arvydas Juozaitis said publicly: "It is difficult to imagine, and I would say highly improbable, that while Gorbachev is talking about non-interference in Eastern Europe, he would send tanks into Vilnius."[274] For the time being he was right as that reaction did not come until more than a year afterward, but the vote in Vilnius had left the first visible crack in the Soviet Communist Party since Lenin's revolution. The *Los Angeles Times* commented that "the defection by one of the Soviet Union's tinier republics seems to have rocked the Kremlin more than the collapse of communism in all six Warsaw Pact nations since August."[275] The wound was of course serious, because it ran counter to the deepest delusions which were embodied in the world – the dominance expectations of Marxist ideology. The Communist Party which had held the Soviet Empire together since the Soviets abandoned Stalinist terror had expected to continue to do so. Gorbachev thus called the separation "illegitimate" and emphasized that "the current party and state leadership [in Moscow] will not permit the break-up of the state."[276] Eventually, in the hope of encouraging a reversal, the infuriated Kremlin Central Committee decided to send a 250-member delegation to Lithuania, as the *Los Angeles Times* humorously described it at the time, "to talk with virtually every one of the 200,000 members of the Lithuanian [Communist] party."[277] It was President Mikhail Gorbachev, who was also the CPSU General Secretary, and who personally led this

273   Interview with Yegor Ligachev, Second Russian Revolution. 2RR 3/5/5, British Library of Political and Economic Sciences.
274   "Ketvirtoji Seimo Sesija," p. 1.
275   "Man of the Decade's Challenge," *Los Angeles Times*, December 29, 1989.
276   "Man of the Decade's Challenge."
277   "Soviets plan to stump Lithuania for support," *Los Angeles Times Service*, December 30, 1989.

unprecedented explanatory mission to Lithuania. Landsbergis' laconic response to the news that it was coming was that Gorbachev would get a "warm reception in Lithuania" and would be greeted "as the leader of a friendly foreign state."[278] He was, as ever, master of the necessary understatement.

On Christmas Eve, 1989 the deputies of the Supreme Soviet of the Soviet Union finally adopted a resolution, which acknowledged that the Soviet-Nazi pact of 1939 had violated the sovereignty and independence of the Baltic States. The statement also clarified the fact that the agreement then made was legally untenable and was therefore invalid from the moment it was signed. That the resolution was passed in this form was due to a great extent to the influence and hard work of deputies from the occupied Baltic States, particularly the *Sąjūdis* representatives. The underlying situation was now gathering momentum as Latvia too was about to reject Communist Party supremacy. This was done a few days later on December 28, after a stormy debate in Riga's Parliament, when members voted 220 to 50 to eliminate a section of the constitution that declared the Communist Party to be the "leading and guiding force of Soviet society." The Latvian vote was further evidence of the strongly flowing tide of freedom. On the same day in Vilnius, tens of thousands of Lithuanians rallied to support the Lithuanian communists' stand against the Kremlin. This rally was widely reported, and even the Soviet television program *Vremya* ("Time") showed scenes of the demonstration on Gediminas Square numbering more than 50,000 and commented that "thousands of people gathered to hear bold, uncompromising speeches" supporting party independence.[279] Gorbachev responded to these events by angrily denouncing the Lithuanian Communist Party, and the movement for independence, in one breath, but his speech also revealed that some of his own Central Committee members felt the Lithuanian Communist Party decision must be recognized as a *fait*

---

278   See Vytautas Landsbergis, *Lithuania Independent Again* (Cardiff: University of Wales Press, 2000), p. 167.
279   "Latvia Rejects Communist Party Supremacy," *Associated Press*, December 29, 1989.

accompli, and that the Soviet party should give a 'political assessment' only. This made it clear that the reform process had reached the politicians at this level, but he then went on to make it ominously plain that the majority had nevertheless argued in favor of "strong measures to preserve the integrity of the party and state." In other words, he was showing a heavy hand.

Gorbachev now unleashed a bitter attack against *Sąjūdis,* accusing it of "inflaming national sentiments" and "fomenting separatism" by attempting to "internationalize the so-called Baltic question." This accusation implied the accompanying threat that the Soviet government would not permit the break-up of the Soviet Union. The speech was followed up by his three-day visit to Lithuania which only served to strengthen support for the Lithuanian drive for independence. When he arrived, he met people in the squares and in the streets, but "the people very simply told him that they didn't want to be within the Soviet Union."[280] Landsbergis recalled an episode in Šiauliai, when Gorbachev "was talking to a worker, using empty phrases and as the phrases were having no result, he just went away, and gave in."[281] Landsbergis added that "in fact, it was his defeat in Lithuania, and perhaps the first such defeat in his voyages in foreign countries."[282] Ligachev remembered in the BBC documentary "The Second Russian Revolution," that he had talked with Gorbachev before his trip to Lithuania and after it:

> I insisted on my very clear views, and at some point I began to feel that we would not be able to save the situation by simple talk, by simple advice and recommendations. I felt that Brazauskas and I held different positions. Brazauskas was holding social democratic positions whereas we were true communists. [...] It became quite clear to me at some point in that talk, that recommendations, advice, would not help, that we had to say to our Party honestly and clearly and to the Communist Party of Lithuania what was happening, and what was happening was a disintegration of our Party from within. Incidentally, [...] I mentioned to Gorbachev that what began to happen in Lithuania was a drive towards the secession of Lithuania from the Soviet Union. The process began within the Party, first they destroyed and split the Party, and then they tried to get out of the Soviet Union. Why?

---

280   Interview with Vytautas Landsbergis for BBC, Second Russian Revolution. 2RR 3/5/2, British Library of Political and Economic Science.
281   Interview with Landsbergis for BBC.
282   Interview with Landsbergis for BBC.

> Because the Party had been the only force that could bring people together, organise people, it was this cohesive force that held people together. They wanted to remove that political force, by dividing it, by splitting it.[283]

Both during and after his work Gorbachev warned that the cost of secession would be high, and that the Lithuanian republic would have to pay Moscow 33 billion dollars in compensation for Soviet investment.[284] His blackmailing threats did not, however, pass without being parried. Julius Juzeliūnas retorted:

> I think this remark by Gorbachev is child's talk, it is not serious ... if they can present us with a bill, we can give them a bill, too. What about the 350,000 Lithuanians deported by Stalin to Siberia, half of whom died in exile or deportation? What about the industries here that produce only for Moscow and leave us only pollution? We are one hundred percent colonized. These bills from Gorbachev are not serious, they would be modest compared to the bills we would present to Moscow.[285]

His response clearly voiced the prevailing public opinion in Lithuania at this point, and it is not surprising that only a few weeks later *Sąjūdis* won an overwhelming majority of seats in the Supreme Soviet of occupied Lithuania in the first multi-party election, which was held on February 24, and a "run-off" on March 4, 1990.[286] This election presaged a major breakthrough in the process of reclaiming national independence, and on March 11, 1990 *Sąjūdis'* Chairman Vytautas Landsbergis was elected President of the Supreme Council of the Republic of Lithuania, which was later called *Atkūriamasis Seimas*, or Founding Parliament, by a vote of 91 over Brazauskas' 38 votes. The legislature was now expected to steer the republic through the independence process. It was originally supposed to have convened later in the month, but *Sąjūdis'* leaders decided to move the opening session forward urgently because they had learned that a special meeting of the USSR Supreme Soviet had been called for March 12. Not unrealistically they feared

---

283   Interview with Ligachev for BBC.
284   "Lithuania lawmakers meet, prepare to break free from Soviet rule," *Knight-Ridder News Service*, March 11, 1990, e.g., in *The Sun Diego Union-Tribune*, March 11, 1990.
285   Ibid.
286   Ibid.

that the Supreme Soviet in the Kremlin would pass laws restricting the rights of republics to withdraw from the Soviet Union that could seriously interfere with the drive for Lithuania's secession, unless Lithuanian independence had been declared beforehand. The *Sąjūdis* legislator Vladas Terleckas said that "we must not miss the moment for action, and this is the chance."[287] The crucial importance of the timing of the Declaration of Independence as a factor in the Lithuanian success has also been confirmed by President Vytautas Landsbergis who presided over the fateful session of the nation's Supreme Council, when the Lithuanian Parliament declared the restoration of Lithuania's independence by 124 votes and 6 abstentions.[288]

---

287 Ibid.
288 Interview with President Vytautas Landsbergis, May 19, 1998, London. The text of Lithuania's declaration of independence on March 11, 1990, is as follows:
   "The Supreme Council of the Republic of Lithuania, expressing the will of the nation, resolves and solemnly proclaims that the execution of the sovereign power of the Lithuanian state, heretofore constrained by alien forces in 1940, is restored, and henceforth Lithuania is once again an independent state.
   The February 16, 1918, Act of Independence of the Supreme Council of Lithuania and the May 15, 1920, Constituent Assembly Resolution on the restoration of a democratic Lithuanian state have never lost their legal force and are the constitutional foundation of the Lithuanian state.
   The territory of Lithuania is integral and indivisible, and the constitution of any other State has no jurisdiction within it.
   The Lithuanian state emphasizes its adherence to universally recognized principles of international law, recognizes the principles of the inviolability of borders as formulated in Helsinki in 1975 in the Final Act of the Conference on Security and Co-operation in Europe, and guarantees rights of individuals, citizens and ethnic communities.
   The Supreme Council of the Republic of Lithuania, expressing sovereign power, by this act begins to achieve the State's full sovereignty."
   Extracted from the Text of the Lithuanian Declaration of Independence 11th March 1990. *The Associated Press*, March 12, 1990.

6. Sąjūdis' Peaceful Revolution

Although, there is room for debate about the way in which the process developed, it is quite clear that the struggle which *Sąjūdis* developed in Lithuania toward the end of the 1980s was of crucial importance in the events, which led to the collapse of the Soviet Union in August 1991. Anthony Packer, Lithuania's Honorary Consul in Wales and the editor of the English language version of Vytautas Landsbergis biography, referring to the "tense maneuvering on the last decade of communist influence," places Lithuania's suffering in its wider European context with reference to:

> four events, selected to suggest the momentum of those years, and to illustrate how the Lithuanian experience contributed to the global outcome. We first recall the strikes organized in the Polish shipyards by Lech Walesa in the early 1980s; then the scenes in 1989 when the people of Berlin ripped down the Wall, which had divided their city, with bare hands and hammers. The Vilnius nightmare of January 1991 follows, but the last scene is that of Boris Yeltsin, standing on a tank near the White House (the parliamentary home of the infant Russian democracy) in Moscow in August of the same year. Defiant, and inviting the people to dismiss the putschist threat to reinstate Stalinism, he said: 'Remember the people of Vilnius. They showed us the way!'[289]

These remarks provide a further context for the sharply worded observation by Richard Krickus in his study of the contribution of the Lithuanian rebellion to the breakdown of the Soviet Empire: "Historians may one day conclude that the final chapter in the collapse of the Soviet order began on October 22, 1988, when *Sąjūdis* held a two-day-long founding congress."[290]

Although, the fact is not widely recognized, Yeltsin's spontaneous formulation, at a critical point in Russian history and virtually at the moment, when the reactionary attempt at a coup d'état within the Kremlin hierarchy began to collapse, serves to highlight the assertion that Lithuania's independence movement, which

---

289 Anthony Packer, "Editor's Preface," in Vytautas Landsbergis, *Lithuania Independent Again* (Cardiff: University of Wales Press, 2000), p. x.
290 Richard J. Krickus, *Showdown. The Lithuanian Rebellion and the Breakup of the Soviet Empire* (Washington and London: Brassey's, 1997), p. 62.

succeeded in winning freedom for Lithuania, was also one of the most important factors in the collapse of the Soviet Union. It is, however, apparent that many commentators fail to understand the importance of the events that took place in Lithuania, while some even omit to mention *Sąjūdis* or Lithuania in their books.[291] According to Professor Alfred Erich Senn, the majority of commentators have overlooked the living memory of the independence struggle, which is reiterated by the Lithuanians, Latvians, and Estonians, and so, fail to recognize why the Lithuanians, particularly, acted as the icebreakers of the Soviet Empire.[292] According to Senn the historical consciousness of the Lithuanians played a particularly important role in that process.[293] That consciousness had two important elements: the living memory of their state's existence before the Second World War and the recollection of the state-building achievements of Grand Duke Vytautas Magnus and the medieval glory of the largest European state of the fifteenth century.[294]

Professor Walter Clemens has argued, that "the Baltic independence movements were as weighty as any [other] factors in subverting the USSR." [295] The major international impact of *Sąjūdis* peaceful revolution, which was the more radical and more advanced of the processes in the three Baltic countries, was therefore nothing less than the collapse of the Soviet Union. Clemens has also argued that "the key role played by the Baltic independence movements in undermining the Soviet system is attested in the memoirs of Gorbachev." Similar statements can also be found in subsequent comments by Eduard Shevardnadze, the Soviet Foreign Minister (1985-1990), in the memoirs of Jack Matlock, the American

---

291 E.g. Geoffrey A. Hosking, Jonathan Aves and Peter J. S. Duncan, *The Road to Post-Communism. Independent Political Movements in the Soviet Union*, 1985 – 1991 (London and New York: Pinter Publishers, 1992). See also Wisla Suraska, *How the Soviet Union Disappeared* (Durham: Duke University Press, 1998).

292 Alfred E. Senn, *Gorbachev's Failure in Lithuania* (New York: St. Martin's Press, 1995), pp. xii-xiii.

293 Senn, *Gorbachev's Failure*, p. xiv.

294 See also Chapter 2 - Lithuania's European Roots.

295 Walter C. Clemens, "Who or What killed the Soviet Union? How three Davids undermined Goliath," *Nationalism & Ethnic Politics* 3, no. 1 (1997): 136 & 138–139.

ambassador in Moscow (1987-1991), and in the memoirs and papers of James A. Baker, the U.S. Secretary of State (1989-1992).

According to Clemens, the Balts effectively exploited the Kremlin's perestroika and glasnost initiatives, as well as the Soviet constitutional framework. Under that Soviet constitution every republic had the theoretical right of withdrawal from the Union, and the Balts mobilized a certain moral power to work toward this goal, emphasizing this moral stance by eschewing violence.[296] When the twin policies of *perestroika* and *glasnost* were declared in the Soviet Union, an opportunity was provided that could not be missed, but the major goal of *Sąjūdis'* peaceful revolution from the start was, as we have seen, the restoration of Lithuania's independence and her return to Europe, to democracy, freedom, and prosperity. The eagerness of *Sąjūdis* to lead the country into the European community of states is attested by the question put to the emissary of a British political party, who visited the movement's headquarters in July 1991, after his credentials had been established:

> What are Lithuania's chances of admission into the European Community?[297]

The question was deeply rooted in *Sąjūdis* fundamental philosophy and its understanding of the nation's place in history. In addressing a Swedish Moderate Party conference in 1989, Vytautas Landsbergis, leader of *Sąjūdis*, had stated:

> We were (and legally we are) an ancient European state, temporarily removed from Europe's map, and to the large extent, also from European cultural processes.[298]

In the same vein, the Sąjūdis philosopher Arvydas Juozaitis wrote, when inviting people to the Vingis Park rally held on August 23,

---

296   Clemens, "Who or What killed the Soviet Union?" *Nationalism & Ethnic Politics* 3, no. 1 (1997): 142–145.
297   Packer, "Editor's preface," p. viii.
298   Vytautas Landsbergis, "Teisingumas - taika - žalioji taika" (Speech in Moderate Party Conference, Stockholm, December 8, 1989). Cited in Vytautas Landsbergis, *Atgavę viltį* (Vilnius: Sąjūdis, 1990), p. 44.

1988 to commemorate the forty-ninth anniversary and the dire consequences of the iniquitous Soviet-Nazi pact:

> We will arise, together with the community of European nations. Let's talk to the world![299]

Vytautas Landsbergis said at the gathering of *Sąjūdis* on January 11, 1990, just two days before the killings of innocent peope by Soviet troops:

> Our stability was violated in 1940. We would like to restore it for ourselves, and for Europe, where we want to have the right to return as an independent state.[300]

From this moment on and propelled by the collective effect of the subsequent rally, the nation's largest ever demonstration. Lithuania was a major player, even the catalyst, of the liberation process, which swept inexorably through Central and Eastern Europe. Landsbergis observed:

> We feel that we have influenced Eastern Germany, Czechoslovakia, our neighbor Byelorussia, Ukraine, and the distant Caucasus. We keep our relations and collaborate with Russia's democratic movement.[301]

Moscow's destabilizing tactics

Gorbachev's reaction to the Declaration of Independence by the Lithuanian Parliament was again one of fury, and he immediately informed Brazauskas that "should Lithuania wish to separate," it would be faced with a series of financial and territorial demands.[302] At their next meeting he shouted at Landsbergis, saying: *"Nobody*

---

299 Arvydas Juozaitis, "Tautos ir Europos vardan," *Sąjūdžio žinios*, August 23, 1988, p. 2.

300 Vytautas Landsbergis, "Kalba Sąjūdžio mitinge. Vilnius, Katedros aikštė" (Speech in the gathering of Sąjūdis in Cathedral Square, Vilnius, January 11, 1990). In Landsbergis, *Atgavę viltį*, p. 46.

301 Vytautas Landsbergis, "Teisingumas - taika - žalioji taika," (Speech to the Moderate Party Conference, Stockholm, December 8, 1989). Cited in Landsbergis, *Atgavę viltį*, p. 44.

302 Landsbergis, *Lithuanian Independent Again*, p. 173.

will recognize you, *everybody* is laughing at you!"[303] His political response as a leader of the Communist Party and as Supreme Commander of the Soviet military forces had three main characteristics. First, he ordered "all necessary steps" to be taken for the return of Lithuania to the Soviet Union. These included an economic blockade, intelligence operations, a military build-up, and military operations inside the country. Certain major buildings in Vilnius, the Lithuanian capital, were occupied by troops within days of the Declaration of Independence,[304] and Soviet military helicopters began to drop leaflets urging people not to listen to their democratically elected government.[305] Four weeks after the declaration of independence, Soviet troops attacked the headquarters of the International Red Cross in Vilnius, where some young people were hiding to avoid recruitment to the Soviet army.[306] The Soviet Government then passed decrees designed to abolish Lithuania's free press.[307] Despite these steps Lithuania's media and institutions attempted to continue working as if nothing major had happened, informing people about events, the Kremlin's reaction, Lithuania's stand, and the brutalities of the occupying regime.

In hindsight, these activities, directed from Moscow, can be seen to be preparations for the attempted communist *coup d'état* that took place in Lithuania during January 1991. That action too was initiated by the Kremlin in an operation designed to gain the maximum advantage from the distraction of the world's attention by the Gulf war. It was a practiced tactic, just as the invasion of Hungary in 1956 had been conducted in parallel with the Suez crisis. Gorbachev, as Chairman of the Presidium of the USSR Supreme Soviet then initiated a law on the secession of republics from the Soviet Union which was designed to keep the Baltic States within the USSR. The proposal foresaw that the crucial vote on any

---

303 Landsbergis, *Lithuanian Independent Again*, pp. 173-174.
304 "Ne laisvam žodžiui," *Atgimimas*, no. 14, April 4-11, 1990, p. 1.
305 Audrius Ažubalis, "Jau okupavo ir mūsų dangų," *Atgimimas*, no. 14, April 4-11, 1990, p. 1.
306 Audrius Ažubalis, "Kraujas raudonas ir naktį," *Atgimimas*, no. 14, April 4-11, 1990, p. 1.
307 "Ne laisvam žodžiui," p. 1.

proposal for succession would be taken in the Supreme Soviet, where it required a two-thirds majority. Under this law the "constitutionally guaranteed" right of the republics to withdraw from the Soviet Union, would be practically impossible to realize. At the same time, a widespread disinformation program was initiated by the Soviet information agencies and in the media about events in Lithuania. The all-Soviet Union news program *Vremia* ("Time") and other news programs of the Central Soviet television network now set out to demonstrate "the people's resistance to the decision of independence" and the alleged "violation of Soviet citizens" rights in Lithuania. Their newspapers claimed that *Sąjūdis* persecuted Russians and was aiming to reintroduce capitalism and bourgeois order. *Sovietskaja Rosija* ("Soviet Russia") declared, that workers had asked General Valentin Varenikov, the Supreme Commander of the Soviet army, to assure their civil rights and guarantee continued freedom by "restoring order" in the republic.[308] The quality of the campaign can be judged by the fact that *Pravda* and *Izvestia* published pictures of Landsbergis standing in Cathedral Square in Vilnius with a uniformed group of boy scouts, announcing this to be "the reappearance of fascist youth!" Another Moscow television program similarly denounced the world Scout movement as a "fascist organization."[309] Leaflets attacking national minorities were produced by the KGB, which were then distributed in a number of places by *agents-provocateurs* and were claimed to have been prepared by the *Sąjūdis* movement.

This "war of nerves," as it was called by Soviet President Mikhail Gorbachev (the phrase was also used by the Lithuanian President Vytautas Landsbergis), began immediately after the publication of the Declaration of Independence.[310] Its motivation was rooted in a mounting indignation which the Russian newspaper *Literaturnaja Rossija* summed up in a bitter denunciation of the secession which protested:

---

308   "Iš dvivaldystės į diktatūrą," p. 1.
309   In fact, only two countries in Europe have ever forbidden the Scout Movement - the Soviet Union and Hitler's Germany.
310   Vytautas Landsbergis, *Lūžis prie Baltijos* (Vilnius: Vaga, 1998), p. 168.

Russia may lose those lands, which have given her geopolitical access to the Baltic waters and were won with such difficulty during seven hundred years of struggle against the Teutonic Order, Livonia, Sweden, and the always antagonistic Rszeschpospolita.[311]

The meaning of these formulations may need explanation to the western reader, but in brief they clearly implied that the Soviet leadership did not want the separation of Lithuania from the Soviet Union and would resist the project with every means at its disposal.[312] Despite these clear signs Lithuania's leadership was undeterred. It sought negotiations with the Soviet Union as soon as possible after independence had been declared. Indeed, Landsbergis sent a letter to the Soviet leader on March 12, officially proposing 'to begin negotiation for solving all questions, related to the re-establishment of the independent state of Lithuania.'

In their correspondence with the Kremlin's rulers the Lithuanian leadership expressed the hope that 'the Union of Soviet Socialist Republics will recognize the re-established independent Republic of Lithuania' and will begin negotiations but circumstances quickly developed in a manner which revealed that this was a rather naïve underestimation of the Soviet reaction. According to

---

311   *Literaturnaja Rosija* cited in "Iš dvivaldystės į diktatūrą," p. 1.

312   Secretary James Francis Byrnes in his memoirs Speaking Frankly tried to answer the question "What are the Russians after?": "Despite the violence of the Russian revolution, the aims of Bolshevik diplomacy differ very little from those of the Czars. And the aims that Stalin and Molotov have pursued since the end of the war vary little from the demands they made of Adolf Hitler.
In 1939 the Soviet Union embarked upon an active policy of expansion. Between December 4, 1939, and the end of 1945, the Soviet Union took control of the territories of Latvia, Lithuania, Estonia, Bessarabia, south Sakhalin and the Kuriles, parts of Finland and of Poland, the Konigsberg area in East Prussia, the Transcarpathian Ukraine, and Tannu Tuva. It also took over Port Arthur where although it did not acquire sovereignty, it did acquire the right for thirty years to maintain a naval base jointly with China. In all, nearly 300,000 square miles of territory have been acquired since 1939, bringing the area of the Soviet Union to 8,455,939 square miles, only slightly less than the greatest extent of czarist Russia.
It is clear, then, that expansionism is not an innovation of the Communist regime. It is rooted in Russian history. Only the personalities and the tactics have changed". James Francis Byrnes, *Speaking Frankly* (Reprint. Westport, CT: Greenwood Press, 1974). See also James Francis Byrnes Papers, Special Collections, Clemson University Libraries, MSS90, ser. 5, box 2, folder 7, pp. 426-429.

Landsbergis, it was later discovered that the KGB in Vilnius, had sent a special agent to Moscow on the very day that the Declaration of Independence was announced to ask advice on a military plan designed to remove Lithuania's "independence seekers" by force. He informs us in his memoirs that this plan had been prepared by General Zhitnikov, Commanding Officer of the Soviet Division, garrisoned in Vilnius in co-operation with Vytautas Sakalauskas, a former Soviet Prime Minister of occupied Lithuania. It included clauses allowing the release of 6,000 criminal prisoners, who no doubt would have been expected to pay for their new freedoms by joining in the mayhem which was being contemplated. It only needed permission from Moscow to put this plan into operation but sanction at that level was refused because it was known that Washington would not have remained silent.[313] The proposed plan closely resembled the exploits of the Nazis after Lithuania's occupation in 1941, when criminals were released from prison by the German authorities to "participate in the creation of a new Europe."[314] This time however Gorbachev chose not to follow the Nazis' example for pragmatic reasons, but on April 20 (coincidentally the birthday of Adolf Hitler), Soviet troops occupied the offices of many Lithuanian newspapers, beating up the editorial staff. As they were busy beating the employees of one editorial house, a crowd gathered nearby shouting "fascists, fascists!" Subsequent comment in the independent press took up this theme, suggesting that the Soviets had in effect, paid their respects to their former ally,

---

313   Landsbergis, *Lūžis*, p. 160. See also Landsbergis, *Lithuania Independent Again*, p. 167. In fact, on March 24 James Baker sent a letter to Eduard Schevarnadze saying that "I am very troubled by recent developments in Lithuania. [...] President Bush has said that use of force, or coercion, is bound to backfire. Both the President and I hope that you will find a way to move from a path of coercion to a path of dialogue and negotiation. There is no acceptable alternative to setting this matter peacefully." James A. Baker III Papers, Seeley G. Mudd Manuscript Library, Princeton University, MC#197, Series B: Secretary of State Box 108.

314   Interview with Pilypas Narutis, leading member of the Lithuanian Activist Front, Chicago, November 28, 1997.

Adolf Hitler, by their brutal behavior in beating the staff of the Vilnius Publishing House.[315]

Moscow's campaign was unrelenting, multi-leveled and well-orchestrated. Though, he did not accept Zhitnikov's proposal, Gorbachev said that Lithuania's declaration of independence was "illegal and invalid." It is evident however that he feared that increased violence in Lithuania might attract too much Western attention, probably because of unfavorable response to recent events in Tbilisi (Georgia) and elsewhere.[316] Despite this, he continued to reject the notion of any negotiations with the newly elected government in Vilnius, advising the Supreme Soviet that this implied "negotiations with a foreign country." The Supreme Soviet responded by voting instructions to Gorbachev "to ensure that Soviet laws were enforced in Lithuania." It was, of course, a mandate to allow him to impose his will by military force. Shortly thereafter the Chief of the Soviet military forces in Lithuania met Landsbergis for the first time on March 14 at his Parliamentary Office. During subsequent meetings he was accompanied by three other senior officers, one of whom was the Commander of the Special Forces (OMON), located in Lithuania. Landsbergis, remembering these meetings said, that the faces of the generals "showed anger from the moment of their arrival," and that they backed up the meetings with military maneuvers and the movement of tanks and armored vehicles around the country. A visit to Lithuania by General Varenikov, the Supreme Commander of the Soviet army, also implied a further supposedly veiled threat.

Landsbergis described the Soviet generals, who visited him, as having assumed an authoritarian and threatening tone, and as punctuating the discussion with dogmatic phrases. They announced, that the Soviet constitution charged them with protecting

---

315   Audrius Ažubalis, "Ar įmanoma nuplėšti garbę Lietuvai," *Atgimimas*, no. 17, April 25 - May 2, 1990, p. 1.

316   People were brutally killed by special forces during the peaceful demonstration in Tbilisi, Georgia on April 9, 1989, when soldiers under the command of General Rodionov committed atrocities, murdering twenty demonstrators and wounding a further two hundred people. Other places in the region, such as Karabah, Abkhasia, and Moldova also experienced Soviet military violence.

the indivisibility of Soviet territory and that they were, therefore, responsible for conscripting the youth of Lithuania to the armed forces. Landsbergis' response had been to explain repeatedly, that any orders they gave or were given had no more legal right in Lithuania than they might have in Finland, Poland, or any other country. Further, they had no right whatsoever to conscript the young men of another nation into their own forces. Landsbergis was of course aware that his visitors were military men, who had enough force to crush Lithuania at any time of their choosing, but he firmly pointed out that such an action would have been a continuation of Stalin's aggression. He told them he was convinced that the present government of the Soviet Union would neither wish nor dare to adopt Stalin's methods and advised them that their current dilemma was, in the end, a political problem which had to be resolved by political means. Gorbachev himself had already been advised of this. Meanwhile, Landsbergis sought to do everything possible to reduce the tension between his people and the Soviet garrisons. He asked Lithuanians to exercise caution, and avoid all provocations, because a conflict would benefit neither Lithuania, nor the Soviet Union. In Landsbergis' account these talks with the military began with cold, strained formality, but ended with a normal business-like atmosphere. Yet, despite this, they did not proceed to business-like conclusions, because Moscow intended to continue in the same manner until the Lithuanians were quite worn down. Landsbergis referred to the process as a "creeping occupation," and in the end it had tragic results.[317]

Late in 1989 a summit meeting took place in Malta, where the Soviet and American leaders concluded a verbal agreement, in which Bush promised not to press the question of Baltic independence if Gorbachev held back from the use of military force in the Baltic States. This deal constrained Gorbachev from using military force to crack down on Lithuania's democracy directly. He clearly did not understand it as restricting the demonstration of military

---

317   Landsbergis, *Lūžis*, p. 176.

force which started almost straight away.[318] On March 15, 1990, Gorbachev became the first Soviet "Executive President," under a new Soviet constitutional amendment, and his first public decision in this capacity was to issue an ultimatum to Lithuania.[319] Over the weekend of Sunday, March 18, 1990, he demanded the renunciation of the country's Declaration of Independence. One day before he delivered this ultimatum, the Soviet military forces began unscheduled military maneuvers all over Lithuania, which were accompanied by the spreading of leaflets dropped from military helicopters, accusing the Lithuanian leadership of rebuilding "bourgeois Lithuania." Being aware of their opponent's capacity for force, Lithuania's leadership naturally feared that this activity might be leading up to *coup d'état*. On the evening of March 23, 1990, this concern reached a high level when it was learned that army units had been issued live ammunition and that tanks were being moved from Kaunas to Vilnius. Shortly after hearing this news, Landsbergis received reports that around a hundred armored troop carriers filled with soldiers were also on the move. In this critical situation, he took the decision "to emphasize the continuity of the Lithuanian state" and to renew "his authority to speak on behalf of our country as it was being reborn and as it faced these direct threats," by formally re-appointing Stasys Lozoraitis, Lithuania's representative in Washington and to the Holy See, as Lithuanian Ambassador in Washington.[320] It was a symbolic act because the Lithuanian Embassy in the United States had continued its diplomatic work throughout the entire period of occupation in virtue of the authority conferred upon it by the pre-war independent Lithuanian state.

---

318 During the Malta Summit held on December 2-3, 1989 the Soviet and American leaders concluded a verbal deal over the Baltics. In this meeting (which was called the "Seasick Summit," because it took place in a ship during stormy weather), "Bush and Gorbachev make a secret compact on the Baltics: Gorbachev pledged to avoid violence, while Bush promises not to "create big problems" for him." See Michael R. Beschloss, and Strobe Talbott, *At the Highest Levels. The Inside Story of the End of the Cold War* (London: Little, Brown & Co, 1993), p. 500.

319 Gorbachev appointed himself president rather than being democratically elected.

320 See also Landsbergis, *Lithuania Independent Again*, p. 171.

The new letters of credential, issued to Mr. Lozoraitis, made him the first accredited diplomat of the re-born state.

The United States followed the events in Lithuania closely. Lithuania was a top priority in a meeting between President George H. W. Bush and Secretary of State James A. Baker III on March 9, 1990.[321] The reaction of the United States to Lithuania's Declaration of Independence was immediate, supportive but rather cautious. George Bush had weighed the situation and had directed his aides and the Department of State to use delicate language in order to allow a balance to be struck between the policy of non-recognition of Lithuania's annexation and his wish not to create troubles for Gorbachev.[322] His spokesman told the press that the United States

---

321 'Proposed Agenda for Meeting with the President, Friday March 9, 1990, ' James A. Baker III Papers, Seeley G. Mudd Manuscript Library, Princeton University, MC#197, Series B: Secretary of State Box 115, Folder 7: "I. Lithuania
   ○ The Lithuanian nationalist majority in the Lithuanian legislature will probably issue *a unilateral declaration of independence from the USSR, possibly as early as* this weekend, March 10-11.
   ○ The Lithuanians intend to convene the first session of the new Sajudis–dominated Lithuanian Supreme Soviet before the opening of a special session of the USSR Congress of People's Deputies in Moscow, March 12-13.
   ○ That latter session has been called to consider Gorbachev's *proposal to create a strong executive Presidency*, with Gorbachev its near-certain occupant, and possibly a restrict new law on secession.
   ○ Lithuanian nationalists fear that Gorbachev might at once try to use his power (or the new secession law) to prevent independence, and so want to be in a position to forestall such a move, if necessary, by formally declaring independence first and seeking international recognition.
   ○ If the Lithuanians sense, however, that Moscow will refrain from taking immediate measures designed to impede independence, they too may hold off as well.
   ○ We nevertheless need to be prepared to respond to a unilateral declaration of independence by the Lithuanians, should mutual restrain break down.
   ○ You may wish to discuss with the President the 1) contingency draft private message to Gorbachev and 2) White House Department press statement".
322 The U.S. Department of State also drafted the letter of the President of the United States to Mikhail Gorbachev. James A. Baker III Papers, Seeley G. Mudd Manuscript Library, Princeton University, MC#197, Series B: Secretary of State Box 115, Folder 7:
Dear Mr. President,
   Our fruitful discussions in Malta in December enabled me to understand better the challenges and opportunities you face. […]

could not offer Vilnius fresh diplomatic recognition, because a government must be "in control of its own territory." However, the White House press release of the same day invited "a peaceful solution of the issue" and called on "the Soviet government to address its concerns and interests through immediate constructive negotiations with the government of Lithuania."[323]

Secretary Baker has kept me informed of the content of his discussions with Minister Shevarnadze and you on the future of Estonia, Latvia and Lithuania. As you know, the United States has maintained a consistent position with respect to the status of the three Baltic States for more than four decades. From 1922-1940, we and many other nations, including the Soviet Union, recognized Estonia, Latvia and Lithuania as independent states. Regrettably, their status was forcibly changed in 1940 after an agreement between Stalin and Hitler. Their continued incorporation in the Soviet Union is therefore a unique legacy of that dark period in history of Europe. As a mater of conviction and legal obligation, the United States and other countries have therefore never recognized their incorporation into the U.S.S.R. Our views on this point are firm.

Let me assure you that we understand that the aspirations of the Lithuanian and other Baltic peoples for self-determination present a very sensitive issue for the Soviet Union. The United States has no intention to exacerbate tensions in the Baltics, nor to gain unilateral advantage or threatened Soviet security interests through this avenue. We have stressed in public statements our interests in a peaceful, evolutionary process.

I am mindful of both the historical legacies and the gravity of the dilemma you confront in seeking to resolve the question of Baltic self-determination. I urge that you persevere on the peaceful approach that you have taken to this point. I strongly believe that the best way to resolve this issue peacefully and wisely would be negotiated outcome which satisfies both the Baltic peoples' desire for self-determination and legitimate Soviet interests in securing guarantees, economic cooperation, and the cultural and human rights of minority nationalities.

Sincerely,

George Bush.

323 Beschloss, *At the Highest Levels*, p. 194. Office of the Assistant Secretary of the U.S. Department of State drafted the following press statement of the White House:

-- The United States has never recognized the forcible incorporation of the independent states of Estonia, Latvia, or Lithuania into the USSR in 1940. We have consistently supported the Baltic peoples' inalienable right to peaceful self-determination.

-- The new parliament has declared its intention to restore Lithuanian independence. The United States calls upon the Soviet Government to respect the will of the Lithuanian people as expressed through their freely elected representatives.

Lithuania's predicament was now raised high in the international agenda; Gorbachev meantime repeated in Moscow that he would not bargain with Landsbergis and the Kremlin ministries were ordered to increase their "protection" of Soviet installations in Lithuania. The country was also warned against the plans for issuing its own currency, establishing independent foreign trade relations, or attempting to seize Soviet property. In Vilnius, Landsbergis complained that Bush had "sold Lithuania" in favor of relations with Gorbachev, as Bush had indeed sided with Gorbachev rather than with Landsbergis, perhaps because he believed that his friend's success in *perestroika* of the USSR was more important for international stability and peace than independent Lithuania. Despite this, and the tactics adopted by Gorbachev, Lithuania's commitment for freedom did not weaken. Indeed, Landsbergis writes in his memoirs that Gorbachev's arrogant invalidation of Lithuania's position helped people to face the fact that Lithuania must express herself differently. A new formula needed to be found quickly, and so it was announced that the real issue was "not so much to leave the Soviet Union as persuading the Soviet Union to leave us."[324] This idea had been emphasized by 'an old man,' who had visited Landsbergis at his office at the Lithuanian Supreme Council in the spring of 1990, and who had remarked casually before he left: "Why do they make all this fuss about us, it is *they who must leave our country!*"[325]

-- The United States believes it is in the mutual interest of Lithuania, the Soviet Union, and all CSCE countries to resolve this issue peacefully.

-- We note that the Soviet Union maintains troops and personnel in Lithuania, that there is a non-Lithuanian population whose rights must be considered, and that the USSR has significant interests in the Baltic States.

-- We call upon the Soviet Government to address its concerns through immediate, constructive negotiations with the Government of Lithuania.

-- We expect the Soviet Union to refrain from any act of intimidation, coercion, or repression against the Lithuanian people. We reaffirm our strong opposition to any initiation or encouragement of violence by any party.

James A. Baker III Papers, Seeley G. Mudd Manuscript Library, Princeton University, MC#197, Series B: Secretary of State Box 115, Folder 7.

324   Landsbergis, *Lūžis*, p. 314.

325   Landsbergis, *Lūžis*, p. 314.

Meanwhile Lithuania's diplomatic correspondence continued the search for a peaceful solution of the problem. Lithuania's Parliament, led by Landsbergis, applied to the Western governments for "political and moral support," and Czechoslovakia's President Vaclav Havel offered his country as a neutral place for talks between the USSR and Lithuania. He wrote to Vytautas Landsbergis, stating that the intensifying situation in Lithuania was being followed with concern, as any form of violence, even simple threats, might hinder efforts toward peaceful coexistence in Europe. He observed that the only solution to this complex situation lay in open political dialogue between representatives of the Soviet Union and Lithuania and offered facilities for negotiating a settlement. "Czechoslovakia, a country which actively seeks participation in the peaceful process of all of Europe," he said, "is prepared to offer its assistance and neutral ground for such dialogue."[326] Landsbergis' reply gratefully accepted this proposal, noting the fact that Havel was the first head of state to offer such positive assistance: "Lithuania will not forget this."[327] Havel's offer was a gesture which helped Vytautas Landsbergis and Kazimira Prunskienė, the Prime Minister of Lithuania, to request the Soviet and the American governments to allow negotiations to begin on neutral territory. Neither Moscow, nor the United States reacted to the proposal, and no pressure was applied to ensure that the Soviets should use the idea.

Despite this lack of outcome, the Soviets decided not to use force now. Even Yegor Ligachev, a known reactionary member of the Politburo, publicly announced that "tanks will not help in this matter." It was not as if this solution had not been considered. During a private meeting in Moscow with American Admiral William Crowe, Chairman of the Joint Chiefs of Staff, the Soviet Defense Minister Dimitri Yazov, said that the Soviet army was "ready to crush Lithuania" but he had also added: "If even one republic

326   Letter to Vytautas Landsbergis from Vaclav Havel, March 29, 1990. Cited in *The road to negotiations with the U.S.S.R.* (Vilnius: Supreme Council of the Republic of Lithuania, 1990), p. 127.
327   Letter to Vaclav Havel from Vytautas Landsbergis, March 31, 1990. Cited in *The road to negotiations*, p. 128.

secedes, Gorbachev is through, and if he has to use force to prevent one of them from leaving, he's out, too."[328]

The attitudes of the Congress and of the press as well as the lobbying activities of the American Baltic communities were increasingly putting pressure on Bush to support Lithuania. Indeed, many Senators and Congressmen had already publicly demanded the immediate restoration of full diplomatic relations with Lithuania. Under pressure from the American legislators, Brent Scowcroft, National Security Advisor to the President, warned the Soviet Ambassador Dubinin that if the Kremlin used force against Lithuania, President Bush might well cancel his June summit with Gorbachev. The tension over the issue was succinctly expressed by William Safire, who wrote in the *New York Times*: "We are playing out one of the great moral moments in modern history."[329]

It is now evident that the Kremlin was willing to test just how far the Americans were ready to go in their support of Lithuania. The Soviet government, therefore, ordered their power ministries to increase its military protection of vital installations throughout Lithuania. On March 21, 1990, Gorbachev himself ordered that Lithuanian citizens must surrender all weapons and instructed the KGB to tighten border controls. Landsbergis responded by rejecting the order as "intimidation by a foreign power," which was enforceable "only through brutal, armed force." He added that the "ghost of Stalinism [...] was [...] walking in the Kremlin," and sent a letter to Anatoly Lukyanov, Chairman of the Supreme Soviet of the USSR, objecting to a resolution, which had been passed by an extraordinary session of the Supreme Soviet, which had asserted the supremacy of Soviet laws above those of Lithuania. The letter objected emphatically to the description of the country as a "republic of the USSR" on the grounds that:

> Lithuania was an internationally recognized member of the League of Nations until its forcible occupation by the armed forces of the USSR in June 1940, pursuant to the secret protocols of the Nazi-Soviet Non-Aggression Pact of 23 August 1939. The annexation of Lithuania by the USSR violated

---

328   Beschloss, *At the Highest Levels*, p. 195.
329   *New York Times*, April 4, 1990.

the terms of Lenin's Declaration of Rights of the Peoples of Russia of 15 November 1917; the Soviet-Lithuanian Peace Treaty of 12 July, 1920; the Lithuanian-Soviet Treaty of Non-Aggression of September 28, 1926; the Kellogg-Briand Pact of 1929; the Lithuanian-Soviet Mutual Assistance Pact of October 10, 1939; and the Covenant of the League of Nations.[330]

It added that this "annexation and occupation of Lithuania, and of its neighbors Estonia and Latvia, has been reviewed and denounced as a flagrant breach of international law by the former Supreme Soviet of Lithuania, as well as the Supreme Soviets of Estonia and Latvia; the Parliament of the Republic of Poland; the Assembly of the Council of Europe, and by the European Parliament."[331] Furthermore, it advised that a similar action had been taken by the USSR Supreme Soviet on December 24, 1989.[332]

Thus, Lithuania reminded the USSR Supreme Soviet of the great array of definitive international legal opinion, which stood united against its continued failure to acknowledge the country's formal independence, and further pointed out that Soviet Russia itself had declared in its 1920 Peace Treaty that it recognized without reservation and "for all time" the sovereign rights and independence of the Lithuanian state, a statement which made it quite clear in itself that Lithuania was never legally part of the territory of the USSR and that there "could be no legal justification for extending the validity of the Soviet Constitution [passed in 1977] or other Soviet laws over Lithuanian territory." It also emphasized that:

> although the USSR Constitution does not apply to Lithuania, Article 72 of that Constitution does in fact provide for the unqualified right of each Soviet republic to secede from the USSR, and indeed that the well-known Soviet Constitutional expert, Alexander Lukyanov and other scholars had written in connection with this provision that: "This right of Soviet republics to secede is unconditional, and for such right to be effectuated, the approval of the highest organs of the Soviet Government is not necessary; nor is the approval of the other Soviet republics."[333]

---

330   Letter to the Supreme Soviet of the USSR from Vytautas Landsbergis, March 21, 1990. Cited in *The Road to Negotiations*, pp. 38-40.
331   Letter to the Supreme Soviet from Landsbergis, pp. 38-40.
332   Letter to the Supreme Soviet from Landsbergis, pp. 38-40.
333   Letter to the Supreme Soviet from Landsbergis, p. 39.

This letter of Landsbergis clearly formulated what is called "an open and shut case." Precedent after precedent, treaty after treaty had been cited, *causa finita!* But the conclusion of the argument was also pressed. Lithuania's Parliament now informed the Supreme Soviet that:

> [the Lithuanian Parliament] is vested with all legitimate legal authority in Lithuania, and that any attempt by the government or military organs of the USSR to interfere with the enforcement of Lithuanian law in Lithuania will be viewed as a violation of generally-recognized principles of international law, including Article 2(4) of the Charter of the United Nations, the International Human Rights Covenants, the General Treaty for the Renunciation of War of 1928, the United Nations 1974 Declaration with respect to the Definition of Aggression, and the 1970 United Nations General Assembly Declaration on Principles of International Law Concerning Friendly Relations and Co-operation Among States.[334]

Finally, the Lithuanian Parliament also urged the Soviet Union to respect the right of Lithuania to control and regulate all customs and passport formalities on its frontiers with the Kingdom of Sweden; the Russian SFSR; Poland; Latvia, and the Byelorussian SSR.[335]

Senator Jesse Helms in Washington demanded immediate recognition for the Lithuanian independence in the U.S. Senate. However, the resolution failed by a vote of 59 to 36. Nevertheless, on March 22 President Bush reiterated the principle that the United States had never recognized the Soviet annexation of Lithuania, stating that "there are certain realities in life – the Lithuanians are well aware of them – and they should talk as they are, with the Soviet officials about these differences." He continued:

---

334   Letter to the Supreme Soviet from Landsbergis, p. 39.
335   Letter to the Supreme Soviet from Landsbergis, p. 40:
in accordance with the terms of the Helsinki Final Act, and universally accepted principles of international law, including Article 13 of the Universal Declaration of Human Rights, all Lithuanian citizens have the right to leave Lithuania and return at any time. Thus, any efforts by Soviet personnel stationed on and near the frontiers of Lithuania to harass or to impede the legal right of Lithuanians to cross into states other than the RSFSR or Byelorussia would be viewed as a serious breach of international legal and human rights norms.

> We're not here to sit here and say, who in Lithuania ought to talk to whom in Moscow. How presumptuous and arrogant that would be for any President! Lithuanians have got elected leaders, and clearly the Soviets have a strong leader. They can figure that out without fine-tuning from the United States.[336]

Although this formulation was opaque, he was clearly urging negotiations by the Soviets with the Lithuanians. Such negotiations had not taken place yet. Interestingly, a large section of former President Landsbergis' memoirs reflect the tedious Soviet avoidance of negotiations, presumably because of the principle stated by Gorbachev that such negotiations would confirm their autonomous status. But Bush's statement at this point emphasizes a simple rule which can be established: as soon as the Americans made concessions to the Kremlin over the contention about Lithuania, or even appeared as though they were about to make a concession, the Soviets then increased pressure on Lithuania.

Only a day after Bush's speech, the Soviets ordered two American diplomats to leave Lithuania, and imposed limits on travel and access to Lithuania by foreign diplomats and the press. On that same day the Commander of Soviet army ground forces General Varennikov promised Lithuania's leader Vytautas Landsbergis in a telephone conversation that his men would not seize the Lithuanian parliament building that night. So, it was now clear that the Soviets had decided to move to confrontation. Secretary James A. Baker III stated in his letter to Foreign Minister Eduard Schevardnadze that he is "very troubled by recent developments in Lithuania:"[337]

> President Bush has said that use of force, or coercion, is bound to backfire. Both the President and I hope that you will find a way to move from a path of coercion to a path of dialogue and negotiation.
>
> There is no acceptable alternative to setting this matter peacefully.

---

336   Beschloss, *At the Highest Levels*, p. 199.
337   James A. Baker message to Shevardnadze, March 24, 1990. James A. Baker III Papers, Seeley G. Mudd Manuscript Library, Princeton University, MC#197, Series B: Secretary of State Box 108, Folder 1.

The necessary psychological pressure on the Lithuanians was strengthened by a driving convoy of Soviet tanks near the Parliament building the next day, March 25, 1990. It was a continuous pressure and a threat. Soviet troops then seized and occupied two Communist Party leadership schools and took possession of the former local headquarters of the Communist Party in Vilnius.

Gorbachev received Senator Edward Kennedy in the Kremlin on the following day, March 26. Senator Kennedy had been charged by President Bush to pose the question to Gorbachev: "Under which circumstances would the Soviet Union use force against Lithuania?" Gorbachev had replied, suggesting that the Lithuanians themselves would be to blame for any violence. Force he said "would be used only if there is violence that threatens the lives of others." Kennedy had then warned Gorbachev that the Soviet-American relationship would be "at high risk" "if there is a Tiananmen Square in Vilnius." Gorbachev responded saying that he was "committed" to a peaceful resolution of the conflict, but then significantly asserted that Lithuania was an "internal matter" for the Soviet Union.[338] A day later, Soviet soldiers occupied two more buildings, which belonged to the independent Lithuanian Communist Party and handed them over to the Moscow loyalists. Soviet soldiers also seized and brutally beat a dozen Lithuanian soldiers, who had deserted from the Soviet army. No written reply had yet been received to several Landsbergis' letters, although he as the Head of State and Prime Minister Kazimira Prunskienė had both signed a note sent to Mikhail Gorbachev, which protested vigorously against these actions by the Soviet armed forces, because they "grossly violated Lithuania's sovereignty." The protest stated:

> constant demonstration of military force, blackmail through armed interference, illegal seizures of civilian buildings by soldiers, and especially the kidnapping of Lithuanian citizens who were under the protection of the State and Red Cross, in the early morning of March 27, 1990, resulting in bloodshed, clearly demonstrate that Lithuania remains a country on whose territory an occupying power can run, rampant but unpunished. This is completely unjustifiable aggression and at the same time a continuation of the 1940 aggression against the State of Lithuania. Based on the above, the

---

338   Beschloss, *At the Highest Levels*, p. 199.

Government of Lithuania demands the return of abducted citizens, recalls its delegates – the former USSR Peoples' Deputies – from Moscow, and demands negotiation on neutral territory with the Government of the USSR. Lithuania is an unarmed, peaceful state; it can resist an aggressor only with moral strength and not resist evil with violence.[339]

Again, Gorbachev did not reply, but Bush told Republican leaders that he intended to hold Gorbachev to his pledge not to use force against Lithuania. He was still cautious, however, adding: "Let's give the situation a chance to work itself out peacefully." However, according to Strobe Talbot, Bush recalled the case of President Eisenhower and Hungary in 1956 in several conversations with his advisers. He said: "I am not going to be a President who gives subject peoples the false impression that if they rebel, they are going to get help." During a telephone conversation at this juncture, George H. W. Bush and Margaret Thatcher agreed that further public pressure on Gorbachev would not yield results. The President therefore ordered Fitzwater to slow down the currently escalating criticism of the Soviet actions in Lithuania.[340] In keeping with this disposition President Bush sent a letter to Gorbachev on the day after the meeting with Kennedy, emphasizing that he was not trying to make Gorbachev's dilemma more difficult. In other words, he reiterated that he was keeping his side of the Malta deal. However, he expressed his hope that Gorbachev would keep his word and not use military force in Lithuania, no doubt emphasizing this aspect because Kennedy had informed him that Gorbachev was keeping the option of using force open. Jack Matlock, American Ambassador in Moscow, was told, when asked to deliver the letter, "to pursue the notion that the Soviets might solve the Baltic problem by endorsing the results of a plebiscite on independence."[341]

Meanwhile, in Lithuania, the New Vilnia hospital was being attacked by Soviet troops. Some Lithuanian young people, who had absconded from the Soviet army, were hidden there, and a dozen

---

339 High Governmental Note to Mikhail Gorbachev from Vytautas Landsbergis and Kazimira Prunskienė, March 27, 1990. In *The Road to Negotiations*, p. 41.

340 Beschloss, *At the Highest Levels*, pp. 200–201.

341 Beschloss, *At the Highest Levels*, p. 202.

of them were captured and beaten. The policemen, who had been protecting them, were also heavily beaten. A similar attack occurred in Kaunas a few hours later. The Supreme Council of Lithuania had then protested against these Soviet actions, and on March 30, Soviet forces occupied the State Prosecutor's office in Vilnius, and installed Moscow loyalists in the positions held by Lithuanian nominees. On the next day, March 31, responding somewhat to Washington's pressure, Gorbachev sent two appeals to Lithuania. The first of these was addressed to the Supreme Council of Lithuania, requesting "that the adopted illegal decrees be repealed immediately in a session of the Supreme Soviet of the Lithuanian SSR. Such a step would present an opportunity for the discussion of the entire complex of questions, which has arisen, on the only acceptable basis – adherence to the USSR Constitution."[342] The second, addressed to the people announced that "the actions being resorted to in Lithuania have no logical basis," and expressed the hope "that citizens of the Lithuanian SSR would support" his appeal for adherence to the USSR Constitution.[343] In both cases, his appeal asked for too much. Lithuania could not return back to the Soviet Union. To have accepted these invitations to submit to the Soviet constitution would have been to abandon the entire progress which had been achieved to date and to undermine the legal basis of Lithuania's right to independence, even to revert to the position determined by Stalin under his secret deal with Hitler.

In response to these blandishments Lithuania's leader Vytautas Landsbergis replied:

> the Supreme Council of Lithuania has asserted that the basis for re-establishment of Lithuania's independence is the de jure continuity of the Lithuanian state pursuant to international law, and the December 1989 declaration of the Second USSR Congress of Peoples' Deputies as to the invalidity

---

342   Appeal of Mikhail Gorbachev to the Supreme Council of the Republic of Lithuania. Cited in *The Road to negotiations*, p. 46.

343   Appeal of Mikhail Gorbachev to the Lithuanian people, *The Road to negotiations*, pp. 46-48.

of the 1939 Molotov-Ribbentrop pact, condemning the resulting policy of ultimatums and violation of international law. [344]

He also stated that "Lithuania's representatives are ready and willing to enter into talks and discussions of any level with the USSR Government or its representatives at any time to discuss Lithuania's legal status from the Soviet Constitutional and international legal perspective."[345] On the same day April 2, 1990, Kazimira Prunskienė, the Prime Minister, sent a letter to D.T. Yazov, Minister of Defense of the USSR, urgently requesting him to receive representatives of the Supreme Council and the Council of Ministers.[346] Neither letter received a reply.

The next day, April 3, the Soviet Foreign Minister Eduard Shevardnadze met with U.S. Secretary of State James A. Baker, who asked whether the Soviets would be ready to "lift sanctions" and "start meaningful, serious dialogue," if Vilnius were to suspend its independence decree. Shevardnadze had replied that "the Lithuanians will come around. There is a split in the Lithuanian leadership. Things will work themselves out."[347] However, he assured Washington that Moscow would not use military force in Lithuania. Baker seized the opportunity and said: "That's not enough. We have to have a real dialogue. What would it take to get you to agree to one?" To this Shevardnadze gave no clear answer. However shortly after the meeting, his assistant, Tarasenko, said to Dennis Ross, Baker's aide: "We're willing to go along with your idea of a suspension of the independence decree, but the Lithuanians have

---

344   Response of the Presidium of the Supreme Council of the Republic of Lithuania to President Mikhail Gorbachev's Appeal of March 31, 1991. *The Road to negotiations*, p. 49.

345   *The Road to negotiations*, p. 50.

346   High Governmental Note to D.T.Yazov from Kazimiera Prunskienė. Cited in *The Road to Negotiations*, p. 51.

347   The Kremlin hoped that Kazimiera Prunskienė, the Prime Minister, and Vytautas Landsbergis, the President of the Lithuanian Parliament, would split apart. It would then be easier for the Kremlin to deal with the rebellious country.

to be willing to come to Moscow."[348] Baker passed this message back to Landsbergis, who was relieved that the Soviets had finally shown signs of flexibility, although, he remained as firm as ever about his own position, because suspension of the Declaration of Independence would mean that Lithuania would have to accept Soviet law. He was however able to see that if the Soviets were willing to agree to a "temporary" suspension of consequences following the Declaration of Independence "that might be a way to resolve the problem." Therefore, on April 5, 1990, Landsbergis responded to Gorbachev, saying that "the people of Lithuania are met with a desire to understand your point of view," adding "the Supreme Council of Lithuania is prepared for a dialogue in which the essence and letter of the Acts and Decrees of the Supreme Council of the Republic of Lithuania would be discussed from the perspective of international law, as well as the Constitution of the USSR."[349]

As always, Gorbachev's response to this communication was to have a dual character, and he moved towards confrontation and the possibility of compromise at the same time. On April 9, 1990, the Presidential Council discussed the situation in Lithuania. It noted that:

> the reply of the Supreme Council of the Republic to the address of the President of the USSR is not constructive, does not open any realistic ways to

---

348   Beschloss, *At the Highest Levels*, p. 202. In his handwritten note President George Bush asked Secretary James Baker in relation with "two plus four" meeting on the re-unification of Germany on April 4, 1990:
Have you told the Lithuanians directly and authoritatively what is required to begin a dialogue and what you will do in response to those steps (e.g. end boycott)?
Secretary Baker noted (the other side of the hand-written note):
SUGGESTION HAS TO COME FROM LITHS [abbreviation of Lithuanians]
                  | MUST
  Liths (1) Suspend for indeterminate time – dealt | COME
  Liths (2) Come to Moscow – begin dialogue alongside Fed. Council
| FROM
  USSR (3) Suspend too economic [?] blockade [?] [interpretation of the last two words in the note] | THEM.
James A. Baker III Papers, Seeley G. Mudd Manuscript Library, Princeton University, MC#197, Series B: Secretary of State Box 109, Folder 1.
349   Response of the Supreme Council of the Republic of Lithuania to the Appeals of March 31, 1990, by Mikhail Gorbachev. Cited in The Road to Negotiations, p. 55.

solve the problem and in fact leads to a deadlock. The present government of Lithuania, by its unconstitutional actions and escalation of unlawful acts, blocks the possibilities of resolving the crisis, strains the situation in the Republic, and therefore bears full responsibility.[350]

It continued,

members of the Presidential Council, following the mandate of the Third Congress of the People's Deputies of the USSR, concluded that it is necessary to resort to further economic, political and other means to protect the interests of the Constitution of the USSR, citizens residing on the territory of the Republic, and interests of all the country.[351]

This portentous statement gave Gorbachev the authority for the crackdown on Lithuania, and he signed a secret plan for this the next day. He also confirmed the membership of a new "rapid reaction group to the events in Soviet Lithuania," its members being Yevgeny Primakov, Yuri Masliukov, Andrei N. Girenko, Valentin M. Falin, Vladimir Kriuchkov, Grigory I. Revenko (coordinator), all of whom were top officials of the KGB.[352] The major task delegated to them was "the regulation of the political crisis in Lithuania." Thus, they set to work first, developing a general strategy for applying pressure on Lithuania, and afterwards, devising a precise timetable for the crackdown, which would use every possible economic, propaganda, and military means. While this blunt implement was being prepared, Gorbachev's spokesman Arkadi Maslennikov announced that the Soviet Government "would not insist that Vilnius repeal its declaration of independence," though the Lithuanians "must stop passing laws that contradicted the Soviet Constitution."[353]

At this point, at least two members of the Soviet Presidential Council, Alexander Yakovlev and Vadim V. Bakatin, failed to agree

---

350   Response, p. 55.
351   TASS-ELTA report: "A meeting of the Presidential Council" April 9. Cited in *The Road to negotiations*, p. 57. The same day Landsbergis sent an appeal to the Danish and Norwegian nations saying, "we hold up our hands to you from our political prison."
352   Edmundas Ganusauskas, "Maskva sprendė, kaip sutramdyti nepaklusnią Lietuvą," *Lietuvos rytas*, May 2, 1997, pp. 1-2.
353   Ganusauskas, "Maskva sprendė," pp. 1-2.

to the plan for a crackdown, when Gorbachev presented it during one of its the meetings. They attempted to persuade other members of the Council to reject the proposed scenario. As a result, the meeting of the Council reached no decision. Nevertheless, the Soviet President issued a secret unilateral decree without further discussion or their knowledge just the next morning. This confirmed the plan, ordering its immediate realization.[354] As a result the first elements of a detailed plan for economic sanctions against Lithuania emerged. This was designed to stop the supply of gas and oil, building materials, and the import of wood, and many other industrial products, and the means of implementation consisted of decrees issued by the Soviet Foreign Ministry, the KGB, Soviet Radio and Television, and the Soviet news agencies TASS and APN.[355] Also, the propaganda institutions were to deliver the Soviet view on the forthcoming crackdown to the leaders of states, and the world's television and press information agencies.[356] The disposition of Soviet policy towards national minorities and the neighboring countries can be inferred from fact that the Soviet Ambassador in Poland was instructed "to exchange views about the Lithuanian Poles "in a spirit of trust," and to discover the interest in possibilities of ensuring that Lithuania will remain in the Soviet Union by support of their various organizations."[357] The KGB had to ensure that all aspects of the Soviet administration were set in gear for the forthcoming confrontation, and the personnel of all Soviet institutions in Lithuania were instructed to facilitate the organization of the twenty first meeting of the Communist Party, which was planned to be held in Vilnius.[358] A new "Soviet Lithuania" radio station was established, and propaganda programs were launched, while the local pro-Kremlin communist leader Mykolas Burokevičius was ordered to organize a public meeting in support of the Communist Party. Other "representatives of Soviet society" were also prepared to travel in northern and Western Europe, and to the United States

---

354   Ganusauskas, "Maskva sprendė," pp. 1-2.
355   Ganusauskas, "Maskva sprendė," pp. 1-2.
356   Ganusauskas, "Maskva sprendė," pp. 1-2.
357   Ganusauskas, "Maskva sprendė," pp. 1-2.
358   Ganusauskas, "Maskva sprendė," pp. 1-2.

to explain "the problems in Soviet Lithuania" from the Kremlin's viewpoint. Finally, the military element of the plan gave orders "to keep control of key installations, the main communication systems, and radio transmission networks."[359]

The intention of the plan was to commandeer all aspects of Lithuanian society, including its international reputation, swiftly and stealthily, and with brute force, where this seemed relevant. The demonstration of Soviet willingness to use military force started in a curious way, when the Kaunas city Council dismantled a monument to Lenin, which had stood in a central square, the original name of which *Nepriklausomybės aikštė,* Independence Square, was restored. The immediate response of the Soviet army was to place all the monuments to Lenin in Lithuania under armed guard. Next, attempts to provoke violence followed in the traditional Soviet fashion. Then, in Klaipėda, again paint was daubed on a monument, erected to the Soviet soldiers who had fallen when the Red army had arrived in the city late in 1944. When this came to the attention of the occupying Soviet military, troops arrived to guard the site. But no Lithuanian official was allowed to investigate the case or to enter the area until after the Soviet Central television had reported the incident. Naturally, the facts were presented in a manner which suggested that *Sajūdis* was hostile to all Russians, and shortly afterward leaflets appeared in Klaipėda and other places, published anonymously by "someone" and purporting printed on behalf of *Sajūdis*, calling for the Soviet barracks in the city to be blockaded.[360] The Soviet army, having probably engineered the entire scenario on a "provocateur" basis, then announced that its reaction would be terrible if this happened. Similar threatening provocations occurred every day in many places. The Lithuanians, however, maintained their peaceful approach, even though the propaganda offensive continued to build up. On April 10, 1990, Gorbachev told delegates to the 21st Komsomol Congress:

> it is my firm belief that we should not, under any circumstances, allow a
> new delineation of borders. [...] We are trying to convince the government

359   Ganusauskas, "Maskva sprendė," pp. 1-2.
360   "Someone," i.e. a KGB provocateur.

of the local republic that they must annul their decisions contradicting the USSR *Constitution and* return to the situation which existed on March 10. [...] Yet if the situation develops in such a way that only presidential rule can guarantee the people's *well-being and* control the situation so that it would not take on a violent nature and evolve into civil strife or confrontation, then we will have to resort to presidential rule.[361]

The same speech also justified the idea of economic sanctions against Lithuania, and he also accused Lithuania of breaking its economic ties.

Some days after this speech, on April 14, the day before Easter, Mikhail Gorbachev and Nikolai Ryzhkov sent a telegram, delivering an ultimatum to the Lithuanian Parliament and Council of Ministers, which demanded the promulgation of *"decrees that would re-establish the situation of the Republic as of March 10, 1990."*[362] Their communication made it clear that they objected particularly to Lithuania's new Law on Citizenship, and the issue was stated in peremptory form:

if within two days the Supreme Soviet and the Council of Ministers [of Lithuania] do not revoke their [...] decisions, orders will be given to suspend deliveries from other Union republics of the type of production that is sold on the foreign market for hard currency.[363]

Making a point in full knowledge that his devotions would probably not be appreciated in the Kremlin, Landsbergis told journalists that "Lithuania was celebrating Easter" and that an answer to the ultimatum would not be given until "after the end of this Christian holiday."[364] However, the ultimatum was in fact taken very seriously, and both Kazimira Prunskienė, the Prime Minister at that time, and Vytautas Landsbergis sent telegrams by return to Gorbachev and Ryzhkov, urging the Soviets to begin negotiations.

---

361 Elta report: USSR President Mikhail Gorbachev on Lithuania, April 11, 1990. In *The Road to Negotiations*, pp. 59–61.

362 According to this law the Lithuanian citizens were to receive "Identity Cards as Citizens of the Republic of Lithuania." See also Telegram of Mikhail Gorbachev and Nikolai Ryzhkov to the Supreme Council of Ministers of the Republic of Lithuania, published April 14, 1990. Cited in *The Road to negotiations*, pp. 61–62.

363 Telegram of Gorbachev and Ryzhkov, *The Road to Negotiations*, pp. 61–62.

364 *The Road to Negotiations*, pp. 61–62.

Moscow acted at 9.30 pm on April 18, 1990, when it finally imposed economic blockade on Lithuania, cutting the supply of oil abruptly, and reducing the supply of gas by eighty percent. The threat was very real, but Landsbergis sent a letter to Gorbachev, stating that "the re-establishment of the independent state of Lithuania, based on the condemnation of the Molotov-Ribbentrop pact and its effects on the USSR and the entire world, cannot harm the reform you are executing in the Soviet Union [...]."[365] He explained that:

> [Lithuania] stressed its readiness for consultations, a dialogue, or other contacts which would help to avoid confrontations and make it possible to harmonize the vital interests of both countries through an avenue of constructive negotiations. [...] Both large and small countries, those that are powerfully armed and those that are unarmed, if they guide themselves by principles of humanism, can and must find a solution to any sort of complications which are worthy of civilized societies, and search for the wisest of decisions only through political dialogue.[366]

His was a voice of reason, attempting to calm a spirit of revenge.

As the crisis developed, it was swiftly noted, both inside and outside Lithuania, that the Soviet Government's decision to impose economic sanctions against one of its own (as it perceived the matter) republics was itself, in a paradoxical way, a form of recognition of Lithuanian statehood. Moscow clearly expected that the imposition of sanctions would lead to Lithuania's capitulation within weeks, and its consequent return to the USSR (or, as the demand was put to the government of Lithuania, "to the situation existing on March 10, 1990;" the day next before the declaration of independence). Moscow intended that its blockade would demonstrate to the world, and impress on the Balts, that they were wholly dependent economically on the Soviets and would need to remain so. The Kremlin had acted in the belief that these harsh impositions would give "a good lesson" to Lithuania, but, the results of the

---

365   Letter to Mikhail Gorbachev from the Presidium of the Supreme Council of the Republic of Lithuania - April 20, 1990. Cited in The *Road to Negotiations*, pp. 66–67.
366   Letter to Gorbachev, *The Road to Negotiations*, pp. 66–67.

blockade were quite contrary to those expected by the Kremlin, because its economic pressure attracted significant global attention and huge Western political support for Lithuania. On this occasion, Washington reacted rather sharply: Secretary Baker had telephoned Soviet Foreign Minister Shevardnadze to tell him that there were limits to the patience of the United States.[367] Indeed, as the blockade deepened, the American administration even discussed the possibility of implementing economic sanctions against the Soviet Union, and the economic blockade against Lithuania was condemned generally in European capitals as well. The blockade also had the effect of encouraging closer Baltic collaboration. On May 12, the leaders of the three Baltic countries agreed to establish the Baltic Council, which consisted of the Chairmen of the three Supreme Councils, and the Prime Ministers of all three Baltic States. The major goal of the new Council was the co-ordination of activity directed towards the restoration of the complete independence of all the Baltic countries from the Soviet Union. The creation of this regional body provided, in due course a new momentum to the internationalization of the Baltic question, demonstrating to the world that the goals of the other two Baltic States were precisely parallel with those of Lithuania.[368]

The Baltic Council's existence was a statement of the growing realization that full independence from the Soviet Union was the only acceptable goal for the citizens of these Baltic States. In this climate, the application of blockade had the reverse effect of what its architects intended. In effect, it stimulated the development of reciprocal relations between Lithuanian enterprises and those in other republics, which though remaining within the Soviet Union had been developing their own autonomy, and other independent states such as Poland, which had recently discarded the shackles of communism. Thus, supplies of petrol, oil, and other raw materials

---

367 "JAB notes from 4/18/90 phone call w/USSR FM Shevardnadze." James A. Baker III Papers, Seeley G. Mudd Manuscript Library, Princeton University, MC#197, Series B: Secretary of State Box 108, Folder 16.
368 "Deklaracija dėl Lietuvos respublikos, Latvijos Respublikos ir Estijos Respublikos santarvės ir bendradarbiavimo," *Atgimimas*, no. 19, May 16 - 23, 1990, p. 1.

obtained privately from these places helped to undermine the Kremlin's economic sanctions, even though Moscow had forbidden the Soviet railways and other transport agencies from carrying supplies into Lithuania. It is also interesting to record that Soviet army officers sold substantial quantities of petrol, oil, and diesel fuel to the Lithuanians secretly, from the army's own supplies. Even the KGB was unable to stop the emerging market.[369]

Finally, the Soviet economic blockade can now be seen to have also worked against the economic interests of the USSR, as Lithuania had some unique enterprises, producing for instance, electronic components and integrated circuits for military and civilian use. Cutting off supplies to Lithuania, thus, meant closing off the supplies of these valuable production elements to factories in the Soviet Union. As a result, the Lithuanians have often remarked that the economic harm, achieved by Gorbachev's blockade on them was finally much less for Lithuania than the Soviet Union itself. While the blockade did effect of psychological pressure in Lithuania, the dramatic reduction of the national economy, which Moscow predicted, did not come. However, there was a definite decrease in the standard of living and unemployment rose. This provided the background, which assisted the destabilizing activities, carried out by the Soviet intelligence forces. These actions were often directed towards provoking division in the Lithuanian leadership, and it was no accident that an extra-parliamentary organization, which called itself *Ateities forumas*, the Forum for the Future, was created. This body attempted to "unite the left" in opposition to the activity of the Supreme Council. Prime Minister Kazimira Prunskienė herself played an important role in its creation by opposing the "*Sąjūdis*' Supreme Council" and lending all her support. The fact, that this body was pro-Soviet in its direction was highlighted by Vytautas Landsbergis in his memoirs, where he dryly comments: "What I did not realize was that Prunskienė, the Prime Minister herself, had been a KGB agent."[370]

---

369   Landsbergis, *Lūžis prie Baltijos*, p. 181.
370   Landsbergis, *Lūžis prie Baltijos*, p. 162.

These difficult circumstances clearly did strain the loyalty of some Lithuanians, sometimes to the breaking point, and some of the communist leadership was particularly susceptible, even though their party had moved to a position of independence from the Communist Party of the Soviet Union for pragmatic reasons. Thus, the "left" in the parliament, which was led by former Communist Party First Secretary Algirdas Brazauskas, now the deputy Prime Minister and head of anti-blockade measures, resisted the passage of virtually any law that would have strengthened Lithuania's independence. Openly criticizing what they called "paper laws" introduced in the Supreme Council of Lithuania, they demanded a "more realistic approach" towards the relationship with the Kremlin. Their words had the ring of appeasement, yet in Russia Boris Yeltsin, the country's leader, was prepared to condemn economic sanctions against Lithuania with vigor. Also, not a few of the deputies of the Russian Supreme Soviet, as indeed of the USSR Supreme Soviet, sent telegrams to Lithuania expressing support *"for your and our freedom."* Meanwhile, inside Lithuania a "Blockade Fund" was created to which people and organizations donated money, gold, and other valuable items. The Lithuanian Foundation in the United States presented Lithuania with one million dollars, and upon receiving it, Landsbergis stated, that though it was not enough to buy oil, it was still a large sum when the situation of the Lithuanian people and the country's organizations was considered.[371] However, even when Lithuania was able to offer Moscow hard currency for raw materials, Moscow did not answer.

The implementation of the military part of Gorbachev's plan began on April 19, 1990, the day after the imposition of economic sanctions, when fifty key buildings and installations in Vilnius were staked out to be invaded by military intelligence. On April 21, a coded message was sent from the headquarters of Soviet military intelligence in Vilnius, to General Achalov, the Commander of the

---

371   "In the 40 years since its inception, the Lithuanian Foundation has advanced its goals by awarding over $11,000,000 in grants and scholarships, including a special, one-time capital fund disbursement of $1,150,212 to aid Lithuania's educational and cultural institutions after the country declared independence from the Soviet Union in 1990," http://www.lithfund.org/about_us_lf.html.

Soviet airborne forces, who was holding three units in readiness for action. These troops had already completed a reconnaissance of the Lithuanian security systems and had surrounded a series of key targets. Their observations had been thorough, and had included such detail, as e.g., the height of walls and fences together with calculations about the numbers of personnel and the material equipment needed to capture them. The *Seimas* (the buildings of the Lithuanian Parliament) and the *Sajūdis* headquarters were marked in these documents as particularly important targets. There was a list of Lithuanian citizens, who were to be "interned and transferred to Russia" in a move, which was planned to be reminiscent of the Soviet deportations to Siberia during the 1940s.[372] The home addresses and other precise details of each anticipated victim, together with coded instructions to the executives of these operations complemented every name. According to these directives, all heads and prominent members of the leading Lithuanian organizations and movements needed to be charged.[373] According to Oleg Kalugin, the former head of the KGB in the United States at the time, when the Soviet Union had invaded Czechoslovakia, "the same units that went to Czechoslovakia in civilian dress have also come to the Baltic States and they are organizing political meetings."[374] His observation is a useful confirmation of how the standard destabilizing tactics, first used in Czechoslovakia in 1968, but later applied in other states of the Soviet Empire, were again being repeated in Lithuania and the other Baltic States in 1990-91.

According to Landsbergis, among the reasons why Gorbachev postponed military measures against Lithuania was the fact that he had received misleading intelligence information from the KGB. It had wrongly calculated that the Lithuanian economy would collapse under the pressure of the sanctions by the middle of May. This view is corroborated by evidence of a telephone call which deputy Prime Minister Algirdas Brazauskas made at this time to

372   Ganušauskas, "Maskva sprendė," pp. 1-2.
373   Ganušauskas, "Maskva sprendė," pp. 1-2.
374   L. Trey, "KGB at work in the Baltic States," *The Estonian Independent*, January 24, 1991, p. 7.

Vaclovas Sakalauskas, a former Soviet Prime Minister of occupied Lithuania. The record of the call, which was secretly recorded and reported by the head of the KGB in Lithuania to Gorbachev himself shows that Brazauskas believed that there would be a crisis in Lithuania by the middle of May, to which "the only solution would be presidential rule." In this way, it was anticipated that Gorbachev could present himself as a "savior of Lithuania" without the use of military violence.[375] It is interesting to reflect that the reaction of the West, while these developments were afoot, was moderate. On April 21, the European Community foreign ministers, meeting in Dublin, asked the Soviet Union to lift the blockade, though they refused to send supplies themselves because of "the very difficult position of President Gorbachev." Two days after this, on April 23, President Bush organized a National Security Council meeting to discuss the situation in the Baltic States, at which Secretary of State James A. Baker reported that none of the American European allies favored punitive sanctions against the Kremlin. Baker had argued earlier, along with Treasurer Nicholas Brady, Minister of Agriculture Clayton Yeutter, and the President's Special Trade Representative Clara Hills, that "economic sanctions against the USSR would be an "excessive response," unless Gorbachev resorted to large-scale violence."[376] President Bush had accepted this advice, although he decided to inform Gorbachev that if the economic blockade had not been lifted by the time of the Washington Summit, the United States would withhold approval from the anticipated American-Soviet commercial trade agreement, an agreement which held a much greater importance for the Soviets than the Americans.

Landsbergis' response to the situation at this stage was to inform American journalists that Lithuania had become the victim of a "second Münich." It was a shrewd formulation, and according to Strobe Talbot, "this reference to Neville Chamberlain's appeasement of Hitler further reduced Bush's sympathy for Landsbergis, as, like many of his generation, Bush regarded Münich as one of the

---

375 Landsbergis, *Lūžis prie Baltijos*, p. 180.
376 Beschloss, *At the Highest Levels*, p. 205.

greatest political follies of the century."[377] Preoccupied with the issues of the reunification of Germany, George H.W. Bush now encouraged François Mitterrand and Helmut Kohl to write a letter to Vytautas Landsbergis, urging that Lithuania should temporally suspend the effects of the Declaration of Independence, and then negotiate with Moscow. The actual letter stated that:

> the Lithuanian nation [has] unequivocally announced its will to realize the right to independence. [...] Yet, history has created a complex situation, one, which is bound together by many political, legal, and economic ties. Their undoing will take patience and time, and traditional modes of dialogue will have to be used. We also suggest that discussions begin immediately between you and the Soviet leadership, so that the present crisis would be solved in an acceptable manner for both sides. Without a doubt, it would become easier to begin such negotiations by temporarily delaying the results of your parliament's decisions, which would not lose their worth because they are based on universally accepted principles – the right to self-determination.[378]

Reacting to information about this intervention, the Soviet information agency TASS claimed that the letter from Mitterand and Kohl had "demanded that the Lithuanians renounce independence." However, the French Ministry of Foreign Affairs rejected this interpretation as being a distortion, commenting:

> the letter from the Republic's President and Chancellor Kohl to President Landsbergis does not imply any demands to renounce Lithuanian independence. Quite the contrary, this letter is a reminder of the Lithuanian nation's "unwavering" choice and emphasizes the universally accepted right to self-determination, on which the declaration of independence is based. What is being suggested is a suspension of their chosen means, "delaying the results," so that negotiations could begin. The Vilnius government, with which the diplomatic corps keeps in constant touch, understands this viewpoint.[379]

---

377   Beschloss, *At the Highest Levels*, p. 206. An agreement reached on September 29, 1938, between Germany, the United Kingdom, France, and Italy is known as the Münich agreement. The allies agreed not to resist the Nazi aggression against Czechoslovakia.

378   Letter to President Landsbergis from President Mitterrand and Chancellor Kohl, April 26, 1990. Cited in *The Road to Negotiations*, p. 68.

379   Letter to Landsbergis from Mitterrand and Kohl, cited in *The Road to Negotiations*, p. 68.

Meanwhile within Lithuania, Prime Minister Kazimira Prunskienė publicly endorsed the Kohl-Mitterrand proposal, and the Minister of Justice, Pranas Kūris, also suggested acceptance of its suggestion for a "moratorium." The Supreme Council of the Republic of Lithuania demonstrated its flexibility by passing a decree *On the Expansion of Relations between the Republic of Lithuania and the Union of Soviet Socialist Republics,* which offered a legal "moratorium," for acts undertaken in consequence of the Declaration of Independence, for a period of "up to one hundred days if the Soviet Union agrees to start negotiations with Lithuania about the restoration of statehood."[380] This decree was controversially evaluated in different Lithuanian political circles. It had emerged as a shadow initiative of the White House and the Department of State, which had indicated that the Kremlin was ready to accept the suspension, as a precondition for the start of negotiations.[381] The proposal then was taken up on Landsbergis' suggestion, and the Supreme Council was able to agree "not to adopt new political legislative acts during the period of preliminary parliamentary consultations between Lithuania and the USSR, if they were to begin before May 1, 1990."[382] This time limit, added to the decree at Landsbergis' suggestion, provided an additional safeguard because it implied that any lack of progress in the discussions would allow the Lithuanian side a safe continuity of passing decrees and legislation of the independent state which had been re-established by the Declaration of Independence of March 11, 1990. It is important however to emphasize that the expression "moratorium" meant only the temporary suspension of passing of new legislation, rather than a return to the constitutional position as it existed on the day before this declaration was made.

---

380   Supreme Council of the Republic of Lithuania Decree on the Expansion of Relations between the Republic of Lithuania and the Union of Soviet Socialist Republics, April 18, 1990. Cited in *The Road to Negotiations*, p. 64.

381   "JAB notes from 4/18/90 phone call w/USSR FM Shevardnadze." James A. Baker III Papers, Seeley G. Mudd Manuscript Library, Princeton University, MC#197, Series B: Secretary of State Box 108, Folder 16.

382   Decree on the Expansion of Relations, April 18, 1990. Cited in *The Road to Negotiations*, p. 64.

It is notable that Moscow did not respond to these suggestions of the Lithuanian Parliament, despite privately Shevardnadze assured Baker that the Soviets "are for a very suspensible approach." "Suspension?" Soviet Foreign Minister said, "Meeting between Gorby and Landsbergis. I don't think that's a bad solution or basis for a dialogue."[383] At this point in time the Kremlin was the prime beneficiary of American diplomatic initiatives. Indeed, as we mentioned earlier, Bush appeared to be "more on Gorbachev's side than on Landsbergis," and as Beschloss has observed, "Gorbachev knew that the more Landsbergis listened to the cautionary advice he was getting from Washington, the more time there would be to work out a compromise that might keep the union together."[384] There was, therefore, a sense in which neither side was in any great hurry to begin negotiations, as the Lithuanians also believed that the passage of time would probably favor independence on the assumption, that the longer their state lasted independently of the Soviet Union, the more secure the experience of statehood and deeper the sense of national identity would become.

The Bush administration, which at the time saw Prunskienė's position as "a more reasonable alternative to Landsbergis," received her privately in the White House on May 3. During this meeting, the President told her that he could not believe that so deep a sense of statehood existed in such a small nation. In reply, Prunskienė expressed "regret" for Landsbergis' comment about "the second Münich" and then, according to Strobe Talbot, "offered to postpone the full implementation of independence until 1992 if negotiations with Moscow were proceeding constructively. Bush praised her patience and foresight."[385] Prime Minister Prunskienė then went on to visit Canada, the UK, France, and Germany, meeting the Canadian Prime Minister Brian Mulroney, British Prime

---

383   "JAB notes from 4/18/90 phone call w/USSR FM Shevardnadze." James A. Baker III Papers, Seeley G. Mudd Manuscript Library, Princeton University, MC#197, Series B: Secretary of State Box 108, Folder 16.

384   Beschloss, *At the Highest Levels*, p. 203. Also, "JAB notes from 4/21/90 phone call w/USSR FM Shevardnadze," James A. Baker III Papers, Seeley G. Mudd Manuscript Library, Princeton University, MC#197, Series B: Secretary of State Box 108, Folder 16.

385   Beschloss, *At the Highest Levels*, p. 207.

Minister Margaret Thatcher, French President François Mitterrand, and German Chancellor Helmut Kohl on the way.

On May 1, 1990, the U.S. Senate voted 73 against 24 to uphold President Bush's earlier indication that America would withhold the American-Soviet trade treaty until the economic sanctions against Lithuania were lifted and negotiations with Vilnius begun. It meant that the United States had threatened to freeze all economic relations if the blockade of Lithuania continued. On the following day, Vytautas Landsbergis replied to the earlier letter from Chancellor Kohl and President Mitterrand:

> Relying upon France and the Federal Republic of Germany as well as the other Western democracies to support the democracy of Lithuania, we request you to convey to the government of the Soviet Union our consent to discuss the idea of temporarily suspending those consequences of the adopted decrees of the sovereign parliament of the Republic of Lithuania which present the greatest obstacle to the government of the Soviet Union.[386]

At this juncture, the European leaders made no reply to Landsbergis, and neither did George H. W. Bush. This may have been because Eduard Shevardnadze had told James Baker on May 4, in Bonn: "We need a little more time on Lithuania. We'll be patient. We won't use force. We'll find a political solution."[387] At this stage, the powers seemed to be of a common mind, sharing an assumption that Lithuania's hand would soon be played out. Indeed Shevardnadze's personal aide Tarasenko commented, in conversation with Secretary of State Baker's aide Ross: "Shevardnadze almost seemed to feel that everything will work itself out now."[388] Ross concluded that at last the "Soviets were seeing a fissure in the Lithuanian leadership between Landsbergis and the more accommodating Prunskienė."[389] It should however be made clear to the reader that the implication of these opinions at this stage was that Lithuania's future was to be resolved within the orbit of continuing Soviet rule, as this "fissure" was ultimately along the line which

---

386 Letter to Francois Mitterrand from Vytautas Landsbergis of May 2, 1990. Cited in *The Road to Negotiations*, p. 164.
387 See Beschloss, *At the Highest Levels*, p. 206.
388 Beschloss, *At the Highest Levels*, p. 206.
389 Beschloss, *At the Highest Levels*, p. 206.

marked the essential difference between compliance with the USSR and continuing defiance.

On May 11, Gorbachev welcomed Lithuania's Prime Minister Prunskienė, just one day before he was to meet with Secretary Baker, in the Kremlin. Under the pressure from both the Kremlin and Washington before her trip to Moscow, President Landsbergis and Prime Minister Prunskienė signed a statement on behalf of and with the full approval of the Lithuanian Parliament and Government, clarifying Lithuania's position in advance of a negotiated settlement, and in preparation for negotiations to begin:

> [...] Lithuania, in consideration of the situation that has factually developed, and seeking to avoid escalation of tension and negative social and political effects, [is] prepared: to temporarily suspend the unilateral realisation of those decrees of the Supreme Council of the Republic of Lithuania arising from the Acts on the Restoration of the Independent State of Lithuania.[390]

In order to take Russian interests into account, even though these matters were debatable, a list of proposals was attached concerning the safeguarding of borders with the Kaliningrad region, military responsibilities, the co-ordination of economic relations, and the establishment of guarantees for Soviet citizens living in Lithuania. President Landsbergis wanted to be quite sure that only proposals previously known to him would be discussed and that a concealed deal between the Kremlin and the left-wing Lithuanian Government, headed by Kazimira Prunskienė, was precluded by the mandate for negotiations.

TASS reported on the same evening that "upon examination of the documents it became clear that certain steps have been made toward the normalization of the situation." The report however prevaricated by adding:

> they do not, however solve the main issue: they do not annul the Act of the Supreme Council of the Lithuanian SSR on the Re-establishment of the State of Lithuania which, by a decision of the Extraordinary Congress of the USSR People's Deputies, was deemed illegal. Mrs. Prunskienė was asked to take notice of the fact that the Supreme Council of the Lithuanian SSR must annul

---

390   Statement by the Supreme Council and Government of the Republic of Lithuania. In *The Road to Negotiations*, p. 75.

this Act, or at least suspend it and all legislation adopted thereafter which contradicts the Constitution of the USSR.[391]

When Secretary Baker met Gorbachev in the Kremlin the day after these letters were sent, there was, according to Strobe Talbot, "a strained meeting." However, Gorbachev promised to open direct talks between Moscow and Vilnius, although with the usual pre-attached condition that this could happen only if the Lithuanian Parliament suspended its Declaration of Independence. At this, Gorbachev told Baker: "I had a good discussion with Mrs. Prunskienė. She will go back to her Parliament and argue for suspension of the Declaration of Independence. I hope she'll manage to get it through."[392] Baker then told Gorbachev firmly that the American-Soviet trade agreement would remain in jeopardy for as long as the Kremlin was using pressure against the Baltic republics.[393]

While Baker and Gorbachev were thus engaged in marking their positions with each other, Kazimira Prunskienė returned to Vilnius to inform the Supreme Council of the outcome of her trip to Moscow. She reported that the Kremlin had "expressed concern" about the treatment of the pro-Kremlin Communist Party in Lithuania, which had been proscribed by the parliament along with the KGB as an organization which was suspected, or proved to have engaged in activities likely to undermine the Lithuanian state, and took the opportunity of saying that she herself felt that communist political forces should be legalized in Lithuania.[394] "If you agree,"

---

391 Discussion at the Kremlin. In *The Road to Negotiations*, p. 76.
392 Michael R. Beschloss, and Strobe Talbott, *At the Highest Levels. The Inside Story of the End of the Cold War* (London: Little, Brown & Co, 1993), p. 211.
393 Beschloss, *At the Highest Levels*, p. 211.
394 The Communist Party had split into two organizations in Lithuania. One, which supported the restoration of Lithuania's independence had adopted the name *Lietuvos Socialdemokratinė Darbo Partija* (the Lithuanian Social Democratic Labour Party), while and the second minor group, which continued as the pro-Kremlin Communist Party, called itself *Lietuvos Komunistų Partija TSKP platformoje* (Lithuanian Communist Party on the platform of the Soviet Union Communist Party). They were subsequently known colloquially as "the Platformists." This party was a clear fifth column of the Kremlin, and the Lithuanian Parliament and the Government reacted by making their activities in

she informed the Parliament, "I could take the initiative of entering into contact with the Communist Party in Lithuania. We must discuss the possibility of printing their newspaper in Lithuania, not in Byelorussia. We need to discuss Moscow's demand to make it possible for them to appear in television and other media."[395] It should be noted that these words of the Prime Minister were hardly conducive to the unity of the state at this point in time, because they contributed to the existing division in the Parliament, and exacerbated the political tensions between the Parliament and the Government.[396] Indeed, the internal political tensions between the Parliament and the Government had become rather, even dangerously, acute. Juozas Urbšys, the former Foreign Minister of Independent Lithuania (1938-1940), expressed the prevailing mood in the country at this point, when he sent a letter to the Supreme Council, warning that "[…] The hand of the centre *(i.e. the Kremlin)* can be felt everywhere: "divide and rule" […] Please do not respond to these provocations."[397]

Against this background, the Supreme Council met on May 23 in order to resolve "the complex of issues related to the consolidation of the re-established independent State of Lithuania."[398] Also a decree was issued "temporarily to suspend, for the period of official interstate negotiations, those actions and decisions arising from realization of the Acts of March 11, 1990 of the Supreme Council of the Republic of Lithuania related to interests that could be defined

---

Lithuania illegal in the same way as the KGB in Lithuania. Soviet army recruitment offices and various branches of *DOSAF* (Society in Support of Military Fleet and Army) were also closed for the same reasons.

395   This proposal by the Prime Minister to legalize activity of the pro-Kremlin's Communist Party in Lithuania was a very strange one. However, it is understandable in the context of the later decision of the Supreme Court of Lithuania, which eventually acknowledged the fact that the Prime Minister herself was indeed an agent of the KGB. *Lietuvos Aidas*, May 23, 1990, p. 7.

396   At this stage the Parliament had become divided more and more between the supporters of President Landsbergis and those supporting the left-wing Government headed by Kazimira Prunskienė. These growing political tensions were rather destructive in their character, and on many occasions disturbed the normal activity of the Parliament.

397   Supreme Council of the Republic of Lithuania. Decree, May 23, 1990. In *The Road to Negotiations*.

398   Decree. In *The Road to Negotiations*.

by both parties as objects of negotiation."[399] It added that "this decree enters into force with the start of interstate negotiations between the Republic of Lithuania and the USSR and is valid during
the period of negotiations determined by the parties, and according
to rules approved by them."[400] The formulation had, however, been
carefully drafted in order to ensure that the "temporary suspension" of the implementation of new legislation applied only to the
brief "period of interstate negotiations." The purpose of this move
was another attempt to get the Soviet Union closer to the negotiation table. It was, however, designed so that this proposal would be
revoked if these negotiations about the reestablishment of Lithuania's independence had not begun within one hundred days.

The device worked as the response to this move was instant.
Indeed, shortly before midnight on the same day Gorbachev telephoned Egidijus Bičkauskas, the Lithuanian Government's Representative in Moscow, indicating his readiness to meet for talks. On
the following day, Egidijus Bičkauskas, with Romas Gudaitis and
Nikolai Medvedev, both Lithuanian MPs, visited Moscow and
were received by Gorbachev who stated that while he was "not
against a secession of Lithuania from the USSR in principle" that
negotiations on the matter "could begin only, when the Act of
March 11 was suspended." However, he also made plain that he
did not accept the resolution of the Supreme Council of Lithuania
only to "suspend actions and decisions," arising from the Act. He
also showed that he anticipated that there would need to be several
years of negotiations between Lithuania and the USSR over the secession.[401] Nevertheless, he did not object to information about the
meeting being passed to the media, and it was obvious to the Lithuanians by this time that he was engaged in maneuvering. Some
demonstration of dialogue having taken place was necessary for
him at this point in order that he should be cast in the best light for
the planned Washington summit, where the issue of Lithuania

399   Decree. In *The Road to Negotiations*.
400   Decree. In *The Road to Negotiations*.
401   Balys Bučelis, "A Meeting with Mikhail Gorbachev." In *The Road to Negotiations*, pp. 79-80.

would be one of the more acute matters of negotiation. Gorbachev was, of course, now on the horns of a dilemma as he urgently needed Western financial aid. Nevertheless, he did not want to lose the Baltic States.

The stakes were already high, and on May 30 during his visit to Czechoslovakia, Landsbergis emphasized this by saying that he believed the Soviet Union would disintegrate:

> If the processes there are peaceful, as we have seen in Lithuania, Latvia, and Estonia, there could arise a free association of free states in place of the USSR, and then the states themselves will decide this question of whether the central monopolies and the all-encompassing military-industrial complex will be necessary.[402]

He added, "I'm sure the old Soviet Union will not be needed by anyone then."[403] It was, of course a prophetic statement, although it would be nearly fifteen months before it was verified as such. President Bush administration cautiously has encouraged peaceful disintegration of the Soviet Union by economic means as well: "If the USSR and the Republics continue on the reform path, we will work with them to achieve the political ends. (E.g. Baltic independence could evolve out of 1+9)."[404] In the meantime, Gorbachev met Bush in the White House on May 31, where Bush told him that it would be "extremely difficult" to persuade the Senate to approve the trade agreement unless economic sanctions against Lithuania were terminated. In reply Gorbachev said that he 'did not intend to use force against the Baltic States and that he hoped the crisis could be solved through dialogue.'[405] Baker then was more

---

402   Voice of America, June 1, 1990, quoted in Vytautas S.Vardys, and Judith Sedaitis, *Lithuania: The Rebel Nation* (Oxford: Westview Press, 1997), p. 188.

403   Voice of America, June 1, 1990, quoted in Vardys, *Lithuania: The Rebel Nation*, p. 188.

404   Notes for June 3 [1991] NSC Principals Meeting (without POTUS) on U.S. Economic Relationship with the USSR. James A. Baker III Papers, Seeley G. Mudd Manuscript Library, Princeton University, MC#197, Series B: Secretary of State, Box 110, Folder 4.

405   See Beschloss, *At the Highest Levels*, p. 217. Soviet leader Mikhail Gorbachev wrote to President George Bush saying that "I only wish to confirm that from the very outset we made up our mind to solve this problem peacefully, in the

specific and told Shevardnadze that it would be very difficult for him even to send the agreement to Congress, unless Moscow changed the situation regarding Lithuania, to which Shevardnadze replied that it was "extremely important for Gorbachev that the agreement is signed, and he begged the Americans to do so."[406] President Bush was then advised by Baker to sign the agreement, and he agreed to do so, but on the condition that Gorbachev promised to lift the economic blockade of Lithuania and that he passed an emigration law.[407] The Soviet President then requested that his linking of the agreement to the settlement of the Lithuanian issue should not be made public.

This rather tense exchange appeared to offer a sign of hope that this complex process might be coming to an end. On June 6, Arnold Rüütel, Anatolijs Gorbunovs, and Vytautas Landsbergis, all Presidents of the Supreme Councils of the Baltic States, sent a further letter to Mikhail Gorbachev asking him to convene a joint meeting "in which the themes, period, and agenda of future negotiations would be foreseen."[408] This was an attempt to ensure that an agenda was agreed in advance and to prevent later filibustering tactics which could be used to delay the real independence for many years. Gorbachev did not reply, but he did respond to Arnold Rüütel's independent proposal to meet by inviting the three Baltic Heads of States to a meeting of the Council of the Federation, which was planned for June 12. They would attend along with the leaders of other Soviet republics, but they were also promised a subsequent separate meeting as the Baltic leaders.[409] Gorbachev clearly intended that the acceptance of these invitations would suggest to the world that the Baltic States were returning to the "family of Soviet

framework of our Constitution and the existing laws, of course," […] "ruling out any outside interference." Letter of Mikhail Gorbachev to POTUS, May 2, 1990. James A. Baker III Papers, Seeley G. Mudd Manuscript Library, Princeton University, MC#197, Series B: Secretary of State, Box 19, Folder 1.

406   Beschloss, *At the Highest Levels*, p. 217.

407   The United States pressed the Soviet Union to facilitate the permissions for emigration, with regard for the re-unification of families.

408   "Joint telegram to USSR President Mikhail Gorbachev." In *The Road to Negotiations*.

409   Landsbergis, *Lūžis prie Baltijos*, p. 189.

states," but the Baltic Presidents themselves perceived the moves as a sign that Gorbachev was at last willing to start negotiations.[410]

It was for this last reason that the Baltic Heads of States decided to attend the meeting. However, they avoided taking part with the leaders of the Soviet Republics in the earlier discussion. Their silence at this stage was intended to emphasize their different status and their independence from the Soviets. When they met Gorbachev, they were asked a series of questions which were clearly designed to ferret out the prospects for a change of heart on their part, but Landsbergis replied bluntly that there was no question whatever of Lithuania's participation in the Soviet Union. He then raised the issue of the continuing economic blockade against Lithuania, a concern which was echoed also by the administrations of the other republics.

At this juncture, Gorbachev and Ryzhkov used the opportunity to demand again that Lithuania's Act of Independence should be rescinded before a further meeting on June 26. The meeting then ended fruitlessly, but Landsbergis was now prepared for a further meeting, which he attended with his deputy, Česlovas Stankevičius, and Lithuania's representative in Moscow, Egidijus Bičkauskas. According to Landsbergis, Gorbachev and Lukjanov acknowledged "the wish of the Lithuanians to save face" in this further meeting and suggested how this might be achieved. It was now a case of the Soviet leaders, suggesting how a political retreat over independence might be "sold" to the people of Lithuania. There was of course a certain unreality in Gorbachev's proposals, as if he was unaware of the implications of flouting public opinion so brazenly in a free and independent society. When he again asked Landsbergis to return his country to the situation as it was on

---

410   Landsbergis, *Lūžis prie Baltijos*, p. 189. The pressure to the Soviets for the negotiations came from the United States. Notes for June 3 NSC Principals Meeting (without POTUS) on U.S. Economic Relationship with the USSR, James A. Baker III Papers, Seeley G. Mudd Manuscript Library, Princeton University, MC#197, Series B: Secretary of State, Box 108, Folder 16. JAB notes from 7/29-31 mtgs. w/USSR FM Besmertnykh & Pres. Gorbachev – in conjunction w Bush – Gorbachev summit (& START signing) Moscow, USSR, James A. Baker III Papers, Seeley G. Mudd Manuscript Library, Princeton University, MC#197, Series B: Secretary of State, Box 110, Folder 4.

March 10, if he wanted to begin negotiations, Landsbergis bluntly informed him that the current Supreme Council of Lithuania was the first to have been elected democratically since the Second World War, and that if it should turn its back on the decisions taken on March 11, the Lithuanian people would interpret the actions as being an agreement that Lithuania remained, after all, a part of the Soviet Union. This they would regard as being a simple betrayal.[411] Despite this assertion, Gorbachev remained totally impervious. He continued to insist on a return to the situation that had existed before the declaration of Lithuania's independence. The positions were deadlocked, and the situation remained tense during the remainder of 1990, even though the Kremlin did finally revoke its economic blockade against Lithuania at the end of June because of the pressure from the United States. 'After the blockade had been introduced it became clear that it was not giving the political effect, all the sympathies were on the side of Lithuania, and the Moscow leadership was seen in a very bad light, besides we said that no state could be blockading itself, and that the blockade of Lithuania was, in fact, recognition of Lithuania as an independent state,' commented Vytautas Landsbergis.[412] However, it had now become clear to the Lithuanian Parliament that the Kremlin would increase military pressure in its attempts to return Lithuania to the Soviet Union.

It is important to remind the reader once again that each time the Americans took side of the Soviets, the Soviets applied pressure on Lithuania. It is also important to emphasize that the timing of the demand to suspend Lithuania's Declaration of Independence was related with the negotiations between the United States, the United Kingdom, France and the Soviet Union as well as Federal Republic of Germany and German Democratic Republic on the reunification of Germany. It clearly highlights the Soviet hopes and actions related to the reunification of Germany that Lithuania would stay within the Soviet Union for undetermined period of

---

411   Landsbergis, *Lūžis prie Baltijos*, p. 197.
412   Interview with Vytautas Landsbergis for BBC. The Second Russian Revolution, 2RR 3/5/2, British Library of Political and Economic Science.

time. The fact that Lithuania in fact has never suspended its declaration of independence, as it was demanded by the Kremlin and encouraged to do so by the United States to facilitate the negotiations with the Soviets, eventually essentially contributed to the collapse of the Soviet Union. On the other hand, both President George H. W. Bush and Secretary James A. Baker attempted to discourage the Soviets from using the military force against Lithuania.

7. Legality or Brutality
The Road Towards Negotiations

The legal continuity of the Lithuanian state was one of the most important factors in the process of Lithuania's liberation. Both Vytautas Landsbergis, President of the Lithuanian Parliament, and Algirdas Saudargas, Foreign Minister, when independence was renewed, made much of this fact in personal interviews. Both explained its symbolic and practical implications by reference to the fact that the Lithuanian state, though annexed by the Soviet Union, had continued to exist as a legal entity in international affairs despite the occupation of the homeland by the Soviet Union.[413] The U.S. policy of non-recognition of the incorporation of Lithuania and the Baltic States into the Soviet Union was the backbone of this legal continuity. In 1965-1966 the U.S. Congress had passed series of resolutions reaffirming the illegality of Soviet occupation. Further, President Reagan's administration had joyfully emphasized this policy in 1982-1988 by explaining to other world leaders why the United States never recognized the Soviet take-over of the Baltic States, applying diplomatic pressure to the Soviets to withdraw. This pro-Baltic and anti-communist policy would really have been unthinkable without the successful daily activities of the American Baltic organizations: the American Lithuanian Council, the American Baltic communities as well as newly established organization at that time: the Congressional Committee to Free the Baltic States. Later, the Baltic American Freedom League and the Joint Baltic American National Committee, representing the American Lithuanian, Latvian, and Estonian Councils were established, and they remained the most effective Baltic political and lobbying organizations.[414] An important further contribution to this struggle was the

---

413 Interview with President Vytautas Landsbergis, London, May 22, 1998, and interview with Foreign Minister Algirdas Saudargas, London, November 11, 1998.

414 See *Baltic American Freedom League Baltic Bulletins 1982-1992*. Los Angeles, BAFL, 1994 and the JBANC Bulletins: http://www.jbanc.org/chronicle.html

annual national commemoration by the U.S. Congress of Baltic Freedom Day on June 14, which was begun in 1982, on the day of mass deportations from the Baltic States to Siberia in 1940. The next year, on June 14, 1983, President Ronald Reagan invited two hundred Baltic Americans to the White House to witness the Baltic Freedom Day proclamation ceremonies, sending his letter to each Head of State, represented in the United Nations, which explained clearly why the United States had not recognized the forcible incorporation of the Baltic States into the Soviet Union.[415] In Europe, the 500th anniversary of the death of St. Casimir, who had ruled as Grand Duke of Lithuania for fifty two years between 1440 and 1492, was marked by the Holy See on March 4, 1984 by special ceremonies which proclaimed him as Patron of Lithuania. Diplomats and the representatives of National Bishops Conferences were invited to this special event, which implicitly emphasized internationally the policy of non-recognition of the incorporation of Lithuania into the Soviet Union.[416]

The translation from a situation in which this legal existence had seemed increasingly frail to one where the nation's presence could be confidently renewed in the practice of international diplomacy was the task of independent Lithuania's embassies and consulates in the Free World, which had kept the nation's flag flying during the fifty years of occupation. It was now the objective of the freely elected government to give substance to the mission which many observers until very recently had seen increasingly as an assertion of frail values. Now, with the resurgence of national pride, and with a democratically elected parliament in place, it was time to realize that there was practical value to the diplomatic effort in the years which had passed since 1940, as now there was a real

---

as well as Leonardas Šimutis, *Amerikos Lietuvių Taryba. 30 metų Lietuvos laisvės kovoje. 1940-1970* (Chicago: American Lithuanian Council, 1971) (Lithuanian American Council. 30 Years Struggle for the Liberation of Lithuania).

415   Juozas Kojelis, Keynote speech at the Baltic American Freedom League's Annual Banquet, March 19, 1994.

416   Lecture of Rev. Vaclovas Aliulis, MIC about the role of the Catholic Church in liberation of Lithuania from the Soviet occupation on the occasion of the commemoration of the 520th anniversary of the death of St. Casimir in the Lithuanian Catholic Centre – Židinys in Nottingham, England on March 7, 2004.

possibility that the issue of Lithuania's liberation could be resolved in a legal and constitutional manner, rather than through military confrontation with the Soviet Union. The strategy was eventually realized under Vytautas Landsbergis' leadership of *Sąjūdis* and through the crucial years of 1990 - 1991, fifty years after the first Soviet invasion of Lithuania.

Many references to the concept of the continuity of the national state were made in the text of Lithuania's Declaration of Independence. They are also to be found in the speeches by Lithuanian statesmen, both before and after the declaration, as well as being mentioned in all the important diplomatic correspondence throughout this period. The Act on the Restoration of the Lithuanian State declared unequivocally that "the Supreme Council of the Republic of Lithuania, expressing the will of the nation, resolves and solemnly proclaims that the execution of the sovereign power of the Lithuanian State, heretofore constrained by alien forces in 1940, is restored, and henceforth Lithuania is once again an independent state."[417] What was being restored was, therefore, the embodiment of a national being which had been suppressed, but never extinguished.

Important technical issues were tackled in the session of the Supreme Council of Lithuania held on March 11, 1990, when this Declaration of Independence was passed. Its effect was the formal reinstatement of the Lithuanian Constitution, as originally enacted on May 12, 1938, with the statement that the Constitution "was suspended illegally when, on June 15, 1940, the Soviet Union committed aggression against the independent state of Lithuania and annexed it."[418] The new law included the annulment of the effect of the October 7, 1977, Soviet Constitution on the soil of the Republic of Lithuania. This sweeping measure included the Basic Law of the Soviet Union, and all fundamental legislation which had been

---

417   Supreme Council of the Republic of Lithuania. Act on the Restoration of the Lithuanian State in Povilas Žumbakis (ed.), *Lithuanian Independence. The Re-Establishment of the Rule of Law* (Chicago: Ethnic Community Services, 1990), p. 60.

418   Law of the Republic of Lithuania on the reinstatement of the May 12, 1938, Lithuanian Constitution in Žumbakis, *Lithuanian Independence*, p. 61.

applied by the USSR to Union Republics. The Lithuanian Soviet Socialist Republic ceased to exist. The effect of these procedures was to assert, with the fullest authority of the nation, that its sovereign Constitution had not been truly abrogated by either usurping the Soviet Constitution applicable at the time of the invasion, nor by its 1977 successor, nor by any of their derivative protocols and procedures. However, as the whole framework of the existing Lithuanian Government was wholly predicated on the Soviet arrangements, and because the 1938 Lithuanian Constitution was not adequate to deal with immediate practicalities, the Supreme Council then moved to suspend those of its clauses which governed the status and powers of the President of the Republic, the Assembly, the State Council, and the State Supervisory body. It enacted that the Basic Law of the Lithuanian Republic should be retained as the effective framework of governance, until such time as a Constitutional Convention had provided a workable constitution which could be passed into law.[419]

This rather complex procedure had the simple effect of giving the state an effective working Constitution which was stripped of all Soviet reference, and which could operate as a provisional arrangement until such time as a new major law could be fully drafted and implemented. The aim of the legislation was to affirm the continuity of the state, despite the Soviet invasion and the Stalinist terror, and to ensure the continuity of governance at a time of social and political change. The continuity of the state was also a significant factor in Lithuania's negotiations with the Kremlin, and this can be clearly seen in the letters which were sent at this crucial time by the Lithuanian President both to the heads of Western states and to Moscow. Thus, Landsbergis' first letter to Gorbachev emphasized the themes of *restoration* and *legality*:

> We, the Deputies of the Supreme Council of the Republic of Lithuania, elected democratically and freely by the people of Lithuania, who for decades have striven to restore the independent statehood of their country, inform you that on March 11, 1990, the Supreme Council of the Republic of

---

419   Law on the reinstatement of the Lithuanian Constitution in Žumbakis, *Lithuanian Independence*, p. 61.

> Lithuania adopted legal acts and political resolutions affirming the restora-
> tion of the independent Lithuanian state.[420]

The repeated emphasis of the continuity of the Lithuanian state was also an important factor in Soviet - American relations. From the Lithuanian viewpoint, this internationally recognized continuity of state was wholly non-negotiable. This adamant stance was necessary because its concession would have made the case for independence an aspiration rather than the assertion of a *de jure* principle. Moscow's attempts to demonstrate to the United States its "wish for dialogue" with Lithuania was based on an insincerity because the Soviet authorities were constant in their attempts to avoid acknowledging the integrity of the legal arguments which Lithuania was putting forward on this point. This apparent Soviet willingness to negotiate with Lithuania reflected only Gorbachev's hopes of signing the American-Soviet trade agreement, which implied assistance for economic liberalization.[421]

Meanwhile, Lithuania attempted to explore the Kremlin's stated wish to begin discussions by pushing for real negotiations. Landsbergis told the Supreme Council:

> We see ourselves, and our homeland in intensive interaction with the inter-
> ests of the East and the West. … Lithuania is a participant in the process. …
> We have emphasized that we are part of Europe. … We see clearly expressed
> a new factor – the attention of the European leaders [focused] towards Lith-
> uania. … Our main task now is to remain united among ourselves.[422]

---

420   Letter to the Chairman of the Supreme Soviet of the Union of Soviet Socialist Republics in Žumbakis, *Lithuanian Independence*, p. 66.

421   Gorbachev desperately needed American money for the stagnating Soviet economy, but the Bush administration deliberately attempted to bankrupt the Soviets by refusing further loans and suggesting the withdrawal of the Soviet regime from Cuba and elsewhere. For instance, during the Malta conference in December 1989 the Soviets were given a document which clarified that the Soviet assistance to Cuba and Cambodia was $12 billion and $15 billion; and Secretary Baker stated during his meeting with the Soviet Finance Minister Pavlov that "Cessation of such aid would of course free those funds for other uses." Memorandum of Conversation, March 14, 1990. James A. Baker III Papers, Seeley G. Mudd Manuscript Library, Princeton University, MC#197, Series B: Secretary of State, Box 108, Folder 15.

422   Interview with Vytautas Landsbergis, London, May 22, 1998.

This statement was then followed on May 9, 1990, by the Supreme Council's decision to form a Parliamentary Commission "to examine ties with the Supreme Soviet of the USSR." This was a careful formulation which was designed to allow the nomination of a group of negotiators to be ready to seize the moment, if Moscow should relent and permit negotiations to begin.

Landsbergis has called this phase of the process "the rocky road to negotiations," and he explains the bluff and procrastination of the Soviet tactics at this time. It was a protracted process, in which it must often have been difficult to decide when to take the initiative.[423] Vytautas Landsbergis, Anatolijs Gorbunovs, and Arnold Rüütel, the three leaders of the Baltic States meeting in Tallinn, appealed to both Mikhail Gorbachev and George H. W. Bush jointly by sending letters, emphasizing the legal continuity of these states. On May 12, 1990, they prepared a joint declaration which stated:

> During the Second World War several European states lost their independence. Their independence is now re-established; the last vestiges of the Second World War are being successfully liquidated. The question of German unification is being resolved. The only countries, which (continue to) bear the difficult legacy of the past war, are the Republic of Estonia, the Republic of Latvia and the Republic of Lithuania, the independence of which has endured de jure but not de facto. We ask you to take note of this legacy of the Second World War, which has lasted until the present. The realization of international law in all of Europe, and with respect to the Baltic States, formerly full members of the League of Nations, will create preconditions for the strengthening of peace, disarmament, and development in Europe. Our nations, through their elected parliaments, express the resolute will and capability to fulfill their state independence.[424]

The three Presidents of the Baltic parliaments then simultaneously issued a further communiqué, which said:

> As fellow members of the League of Nations, the Republic of Lithuania, the Republic of Estonia, and the Republic of Latvia were universally recognized and active subjects of world politics. Their relations with the Russian Soviet Federal Socialist Republic and the Union of Soviet Socialist Republics were,

---

423   Vytautas Landsbergis, *Lithuania Independent Again* (Cardiff: University of Wales Press), pp. 193-214.

424   Joint letter to Mikhail Gorbachev of May 12, 1990, in *The Road to Negotiations with the U.S.S.R.* (Vilnius: Supreme Council of the Republic of Lithuania, 1990), p. 74.

and in the future must be, founded on the bilateral peace treaties signed in 1920, and the legal documents stemming from these treaties. The forced incorporation of the Baltic republics into the Soviet Union following the 1939 Soviet-German Non-Aggression Pact, and its secret protocols, was an act of occupation and annexation. The Supreme Councils of Lithuania, Estonia, and Latvia have adopted decrees, which declare the decisions of 1940 on membership in the Union of Soviet Socialist Republics null and void. A majority of states and UN members do not recognize the annexation of the Baltic States, and maintain that the Republics of Lithuania, Estonia, and Latvia continue to exist de jure. [...] the Baltic States now seek to take part in international life. Their goal is full membership in the United Nations and other international organizations. The Baltic States are determined to add their contribution to the Helsinki process and will therefore, seek participation in Helsinki II. It is their belief that the question of Baltic independence must be included in the agenda of a new summit meeting and the Conference on Security and Co-operation in Europe. ... the Baltic States value their return to world politics as a step which can only strengthen international trust, security, and co-operation.[425]

Failure of communist coup d'état

The precarious situation in which Lithuania was now placed had all the appearances of being an endgame, where the initiative taken by the Lithuanians had been blocked at every move by the Kremlin. No initiative whatever came from that quarter, and the static threat remained unrelieved, except for the reduction of the blockade which has been noted. The major consideration in Moscow had been to "let the Lithuanians stew in their own juices," but it is now evident that there was a buildup, masterminded by the KGB and other reactionary forces within the Soviet hierarchy, to destroy Lithuania's democratic revolution by arranging a *coup d'état*. It is now clear that this reactionary *coup d'état* failed catastrophically, but the brutal military power displayed by the Soviet special forces in Vilnius on January 13, 1991, in what became the high point of the Lithuanian liberation struggle, was intended to reach a radically different conclusion. The actual remarkable outcome was the result of an astonishing calmness and self-organization by a significant

---

425   Communiqué from the meeting of the Presidents of the Supreme Councils of the Republic of Lithuania, the Republic of Estonia and the Republic of Latvia in *The Road to Negotiations*, pp. 72–73.

majority of the country's population.[426] The Soviet reaction to this heroic stance manifested at that time was, however, typically cynical. Mikhail Gorbachev's own reaction to the event was "only fourteen killed and all that fuss!" It is a convenient measure for the civilized observer of how far Gorbachev's entire career as a Soviet politician had kept him from the values which are embodied in the Universal Declaration of Human Rights and are common in western democracy.[427]

The scenario of the *coup d'état* was simple. The Soviets hoped to convey the fiction that the massacre they had planned for Sunday January 13 had started as a mass revolt against "authoritarian rule" by the democratic Lithuanian Parliament. It was intended that Soviet troops, and the local Russian Yedinstvo organisation which was active in their support, would represent themselves as a benevolent supporting cast for a revolt by the masses against "Landsbergis' Parliament."[428] In this "through the looking-glass scenario," it was intended that the Soviet Army would intervene as a "pacifier," and crush the Parliament "in order to protect the Lithuanian capital from serious civil disorder," on the pretext that crowds organized by the pro-communist organizations Yedinstvo and the Salvation Committee "might get out of hand." The plans for the materialization of the event were carefully developed, using public relations techniques and specific Soviet electronic equipment for crowd management. The direction of events had been perfected in other Soviet cities. In Vilnius, however, the Yedinstvo crowd failed to mobilize the mass support they had hoped for. The number of people demonstrating against the Parliament was relatively small, and, in any case, it was outmatched by the response of ordinary Lithuanians whose reaction was to turn out in large numbers to

---

426   Vytautas Landsbergis, "Sausio Tryliktoji po šešerių metų. Kalba iškilmingame Seimo posėdyje 1997 m. sausio 13 d.," *Lietuvos Aidas*, January 14, 1997, p. 5.

427   Quote in Richard J. Krickus, *Showdown. The Lithuanian Rebellion and the breakup of the Soviet Empire* (Washington: Brassey's, 1997), p. 136.

428   Yedinstvo - i.e., a highly reactionary pro-Soviet organization sponsored by Moscow.

show unmistakable support for their own singing revolution against the occupation.[429]

The Lithuanian Parliament had known far in advance that the Soviet leaders were preparing a military attack of this kind. President Landsbergis, for instance, had already been made aware that the Kremlin was contemplating its military action against Lithuania at the end of November. Indeed, he had responded by warning the population in a speech on Lithuanian Television and Radio, in which he suggested that Gorbachev had become an ally of the reactionary forces in the Soviet Union.[430] His observations were prescient, and indeed, he even claimed that Gorbachev had decided to support the United States and other Western democracies against Iraq in the cynical expectation of getting a free hand to use Soviet military force in the Baltic States as a trade-off. According to President Landsbergis, preparation for such actions had already begun, and indeed, the Russians did finally strike at a time when it might appear that the eyes of the world would be fully taken up with the events in the Middle East. Unexpectedly for the Moscow strategists, the reaction of the West on this occasion was serious and brought a measured response.

As the threat of violence loomed, there were many small signs of what might come. During the months of build-up, leading Lithuanian figures made a common declaration of intent. In November 1990, the Deputy Prime Minister Romualdas Ozolas said that "the diplomatic games" were "over," and warned that armed resistance would be an effective means of self-defense in the event of a crackdown by the Soviet Union. He said that the Lithuanian nation would not allow a repetition of the events of 1940, observing that "my children will not be able to accuse me that nobody shot back,

---

429   A few hundred Yedinstvo demonstrators attempted to get into the Parliament building.

430   Vytautas Landsbergis, "Smurtą naudos, kai viskas bus gerai parengta. 1990 m. lapkričio 24 d. Kalba per Lietuvos radiją ir televiziją" ("Violence will be used as soon as it will prepare well for it." Speech on the Lithuanian radio and television, November 24, 1990) in Vytautas Landsbergis, *Laisvės byla* (Vilnius: Lietuvos Aidas, 1990), p. 156.

as in 1940."[431] As a result of this wide-spread feeling, there was a general preparedness and the organization of volunteers for the defense of the homeland was speeded-up. The movements of Soviet troops were monitored and reported back to the Lithuanian Parliament. However, it passed a resolution stating its commitment to peaceful non-violent resistance and it began a steady diplomatic campaign against the expected crackdown. The heads of the other Baltic States also declared that their homelands would defend themselves against force, and a joint session of the three Baltic Parliaments was held in Vilnius on December 1, 1990, which issued "An Appeal to the Parliaments of the World." In anticipation that there would be some sort of showdown Kazimira Prunskienė, Lithuanian Prime Minister, visited both Australia and Japan, and Vytautas Landsbergis, the President of the Lithuanian Parliament, went to Canada, the United States, and Norway searching for support. On this journey he met President Bush, who observed that the United States hoped the Soviet government would work constructively with Baltic leaders "without resorting to threats, intimidation, or the use of force."[432]

However, Moscow's message to the Balts was to be different. Potential channels for communication were closed rather than opened. For example, the Soviet Deputy Prime Minister Vitaly Doguzhyev told the Lithuanian Government that a consultative meeting, scheduled for December 14, 1990, could not take place. Just before Christmas, the Soviet postal services prevented Lithuanian mail from being sent to the West. The Soviets hoped to prevent the flow of information to the West and to isolate in this way, preparing for a crackdown. As so often before, the Lithuanian Parliament called on the Kremlin to negotiate. This time they even dropped the earlier demand for an initial protocol to discuss the agenda and purpose of negotiations, but again the Soviets made no response to Lithuania's suggestions, except to send supplementary troops to Lithuania on January 7, 1991. It was officially announced

431 Romualdas Ozolas, "Apie Tėvynės meilę ir išgyvenimą," *Gimtasis kraštas*, November 22-28, 1990, pp. 1-2.

432 White House press release, December 22, 1991.

that these reinforcements had been sent to catch Lithuanian military deserters, but it was obvious that the development had more sinister purposes. According to Vytautas Landsbergis:

> Soviet influences were obviously at work, encouraging the opponents of our independence to revolt and to collaborate with the Soviet Army which was being prepared for an offensive. The tension was extreme [...] (Eventually) the resignation of the Prime Minister herself completed the scene. It was a crisis which left us struggling to decide who should be appointed to ministerial office, what kind of administration we would now get, and wondering whether we would after all be able to keep the affairs of state in our hands.[433]

Before she left office, Prime Minister Prunskienė had contributed to the mobilization of those who were against Parliament, with the decision of the cabinet to organize a major increase in prices. The move may have had some economic rationale, but it was ill-timed - though, of course, well-timed from the viewpoint of those who wanted to weaken the case for the strengthening of true independence. However, public reaction forced her resignation, which was followed by a parliamentary decision to rescind the damaging policy. Public opinion then remained supportive of the parliamentary thrust towards national sovereignty, established without fear of Soviet intrusion. She resigned because of that determination by the Parliament and the Government.

On December 20, 1990, the Soviet military authorities had introduced armed patrols in Lithuania's third city Klaipėda, attempting "to guard the monument for liberators." The incident recaptures an earlier one, when the monument for an unknown Soviet soldier was painted during the night as a provocation and military patrols were sent into the city. Aware of the potential these maneuvers had for provocation of the local population, Landsbergis issued a statement inviting Lithuanians to refrain from responding to violence and asking them to be vigilant, and report every single aggressive incident to Lithuania's own police.[434] The Presidium of the Supreme Council also appealed directly to Mikhail Gorbachev,

---

433 Landsbergis, *Lūžis prie Baltijos*, p. 223.
434 Lietuvos Respublikos Aukščiausios Tarybos prezidiumo pareiškimas. Vilnius, December 20, 1990.

asking him to denounce this order by the military command as an infringement of the rights of the civilian authorities and of the state of Lithuania. However, no response was received either to this appeal, or to the parallel requests for informal meetings about the start of negotiations.[435] The only Soviet response was to announce plans to recapture some ten thousand Lithuanian conscripts who had left the Soviet Army, many out of conviction that they should no longer serve in a foreign army and some because they had become the objects of brutal treatment, simply because of their nationality. In typical Soviet style, these moves had been calculated for their psychological impact on society, and meanwhile the Soviet military build-up increased steadily. Aware of the dangerous undercurrent, the leaders of the three Baltic States, Landsbergis, Gorbunovs, and Rüütel, together with their Prime Ministers, appealed to the international community asking all members of parliaments and governments to condemn the rising tension. The Danish Foreign Minister Elleman-Jensen was the first to respond, with reply saying that he intended to raise the question of whether it was right to continue supporting the Soviet Union economically when this policy was being applied to the Baltic States, in the next meeting of the Foreign Ministers of the European Community countries.[436]

At around this time Landsbergis received information from General Fiodor Kuzmin, the Supreme Commander of the Soviet Army in the Baltic States, that Dmitry Yazov, the Soviet Defence Minister, had ordered a special paratrooper division to enforce the recruitment of Lithuanian youth into the Soviet Army.[437] Simultaneously, the Yedinstvo movement again attempted to storm the Lithuanian Parliament to protest rising prices. A nasty scene had developed until an even larger Lithuanian crowd managed to push these Soviet supporters away from the Parliament, singing

---

435   Lietuvos Respublikos Aukščiausiosios Tarybos prezidiumo kreipimasis į Tarybų Sąjungos prezidentą M. Gorbačiovą. Vilnius, December 20, 1990. On January 7, 1991, Vytautas Landsbergis sent a telegram to Gorbachev asking informal meeting with the issue of negotiations. "Dėl padėties Baltijos valstybėse. Apie JAV valstybės departamento Baučerio ir Danijos užsienio reikalų ministro Elemano-Enseno pareiškimą," *Lietuvos Aidas*, January 5, 1991, p. 1.

436   "Dėl padėties Baltijos valstybėse," *Lietuvos Aidas*, p. 1.

437   "SSSR ir vėl žada naudoti ginkluotą jėgą," *Lietuvos Aidas*, January 8, 1991, p. 1.

Lithuanian songs as they did so.[438] The threat of intrusion upon, and even the occupation, of the Parliament by Yedinstvo, supported by the KGB, operating as a vanguard for Soviet Army action, was obvious indeed. Consequently, thousands of people massed around the Lithuanian Parliament at night, in response to President Vytautas Landsbergis' call to defend this bastion of independence. Meanwhile, the United States reacted sharply to the growing build-up of tension. The State Department declared that the United Sates had never recognized the incorporation of the Baltic States into the Soviet Union and it supported the current wish of the Baltic peoples to decide their future for themselves. The statement also cited press reports that the Soviet Army had been sent to the Baltic States. The American Ambassador in Moscow Jack Matlock then met Soviet Foreign Minister Eduard Shevardnadze and reiterated the United States' demand for peaceful negotiations.[439]

President Bush now criticized the Soviet Union even more sharply for attempting to intimidate the Baltic States by military means. The White House Press Secretary Marlin Fitzwater openly described the Soviet decision to send troops to the Baltics as "provocative and counterproductive" and he urged the Kremlin "to cease attempts at intimidation and turn back to negotiations" in dealing with Lithuania. He also criticized the Soviet decision to send troops to four other republics outside the Baltics, but the criticism of this military imposition in the other republics was more restrained. According to the views of the American administration, they did not share the special case status of the Baltic States which essentially hinged on the fact that the United States and other sovereign Western states had never recognized their forced incorporation into the Soviet Union. It is, therefore, likely that the White House statement was provoked by a concern that an internal crisis in the Soviet Union could jeopardize American-Soviet relations at a time when the co-operation of Moscow was especially important

---

438 Jonas Baranauskas, "Ateikite ir paremkite savo valdžią - kitaip galite turėti svetimą," *Lietuvos Aidas,* January 9, 1991, p. 1.
439 "JAV valstybės departamento pareiškimas dėl pranešimų, kad sovietų kariuomenė siunčiama į Baltijos valstybes," *Lietuvos Aidas,* January 8, 1991, p. 2.

to the Gulf operation concerning the liberation of Kuwait which was in preparation. Indeed, one official characterized his statements as "laying down a marker to the Soviet Union about the U.S. national interest in averting such a crisis."[440]

The situation in Lithuania remained particularly tense and Landsbergis, ever a realist, was prompted to say "the only power that can save us is Lithuania itself."[441] At this point, the Kremlin covertly encouraged the establishment of a "National Committee of Salvation" which purported to be an association of those who were "opposed to Landsbergis' extremism," but who nevertheless imagined themselves capable of offering an alternative government for "socialist" Lithuania within the Soviet Union. It was clearly another ploy to divert public opinion and to subvert the democratic will of the Lithuanian people, while Soviet troops were simultaneously being deployed to occupy a series of key buildings, including the Press House in Vilnius which they captured by military force.[442] Juozas Jermalavičius, who was now the chief secretary of the pro-Moscow "platformist" Communist Party in Lithuania, took this opportunity to state bluntly that their "National Committee of Salvation" had been created to "take all power into its hands." It was a formulation which removed any ambiguity that may have remained for foreign observers at this stage of the reasons for the increasing tension and the involvement of the military. The administration he envisaged would have repeated under modern conditions exactly what the Paleckis and Sniečkus Soviet regime had done in 1940.[443] The composition of this reactionary committee was, however, kept out of the public eye, though all suggestions were

---

440   "Soviet troops enter capital of Lithuania," *Star - Tribune*, January 9, 1991.

441   Vytautas Landsbergis, *Lietuvos Aidas*, January 10, 1991, p. 1.

442   The Press House, the building in Vilnius, where many of newspapers and journals were edited and printed; Dainis Kupčikas, "Kulkų suvarpytos sienos," *Lietuvos Aidas*, January 12, 1991, p. 4.

443   The reader is again reminded that the Communist Party in Lithuania had split into two parties. One declared its support to the idea of Lithuania's independence, *Lietuvos Socialdemokratinė Darbo Partija*, the Lithuanian Social Democratic Labour Party. The other was a pro-Kremlin party, which was called the "Communist Party on a Soviet Platform." "Nauja iškaba," *Lietuvos Aidas*, January 12, 1991, p. 2.

that it included the cream of the communist apparatchiks and the generals of the Red Army, and that the whole Soviet communist state apparatus was on a state of alert in order to further its purposes. Clearly all was prepared and finally the machine, which the Soviets had built up so painstakingly, began to move into action.

On Sunday night January 13, 1991, beginning at 1:35 a.m. local time, Soviet Special Forces, using tanks and armored personnel carriers, attacked the Lithuanian Television and Radio transmission tower which dominates the skyline of the northern suburbs of Vilnius. Fourteen innocent people were killed by Soviet troops that night and over 500 were wounded during this brutal operation, when the tanks drove through crowds of unarmed civilians who had gathered to guard the tower in defense of Lithuanian broadcasting, and as a symbol of the country's Independence.[444] Vytautas Landsbergis recalled:

> I tried to call Moscow, President Gorbachev, but only his aide answered the telephone call and said that President Gorbachev couldn't be reached or couldn't come to the telephone and I asked that aide [...] very precisely and with great intensity that he should by all means pass the news to the President that the Army with tanks is being put against an unarmed people, and that I asked the President that very moment by his order to stop these actions, and this campaign.[445]

It was a fateful act, and the *Frankfurter Allgemeine Zeitung* of January 14, 1991, commented:

> Lithuania's freedom is broken, and the world has reason to worry about other Baltic republics. The answer to the question, 'Is Gorbachev still master of the situation' - be the answer yes or no - is equally frightening. In the first case it is clear from the events of the military intervention on Sunday night that the will to reform has been crippled. Were perestroika and glasnost only

---

444 "Didvyriškai žuvusiųjų Lietuvos radijo ir televizijos gynėjų vardai," *Lietuvos Aidas*, January 15, 1991, p. 1.

445 Interview with Prof. Vytautas Landsbergis, The Second Russian Revolution. 2RR 3/5/2, British Library of Political and Economic Science.

temporary measures of a politics whose goal remained unchanged, namely the preservation of Soviet power?[446]

The recognition of the cynical character of Soviet brutality and its accompanying propaganda was universal. The *Financial Times* in London observed on January 14, 1991:

> If the west were to decide that the military murders in Vilnius this weekend were a deliberate act of presidential authority, and if this is a harbinger of more to come, then the western states must open an examination of phased withdrawal of its aid to the Soviet Union. It must re-examine its posture on arms-control agreements and on further arms cuts. It must reassure at least those central European countries which are building democratic structures from the collapse of Soviet and domestic communist tutelage that it now regards them as inviolable ... But the terrible choice will be inescapable if the sky continues to darken. As it becomes clear that reaction has gripped the structures of Soviet power, so we cannot continue collaboration with it.[447]

Elsewhere, Czeslaw Milosz, the American Nobel prize-winning poet of Polish and Lithuanian origin, wrote that:

> the thrashing tail of the wounded totalitarian beast has hit Lithuania, and our concern with Middle Eastern events should not make us indifferent to the tragedy of this small nation. The military and the KGB have made a mistake by sending troops. If there was a chance the Baltic states would remain part of a federation with its center in Moscow, that chance is now lost. Without exaggeration, one can say that the blood spilled in Vilnius is the gauge of Lithuania's future as an independent country.[448]

This last sentiment was expressive of a real change in attitudes toward the *de facto* character of the Soviet presence in Lithuania and the other two Baltic States which was now generalized at the highest levels. World opinion had, in fact, reacted with revulsion. The former U.S. Secretary of State George Shultz said that "we should be very strong in our statements about the Baltics. The Baltics, as

---

446 From the editorial "The will to reform is broken," Frankfurter Allgemeine Zeitung, January 14, 1991, in *The Gift of Vilnius. A Photographic Document in Defense of Freedom. January 13, 1991. A Terrible Beauty is Born* (Chicago: Public Affairs Council, Lithuanian American Community, 1991), p. 46.

447 From the editorial "Consequences of Vilnius," *Financial Times*, January 14, 1991 in The *Gift of Vilnius*, p. 52.

448 Czeslaw Milosz, "Moscow's poisoned tomato" in *The Gift of Vilnius*, p. 5.

far as we are concerned, are independent countries. We've never recognized that they are a part of the Soviet Union. The flags of the Baltics hang in the lobby of the State Department to this day. So that is our posture, and we should say so."[449] In the same vein Henry Kissinger wrote that if the Soviet government intervened militarily in Lithuania on a larger scale, "this might have a bigger influence on the international situation than the war in the Persian Gulf."[450] It was against this background of international condemnation that Lithuania gave her own evaluation of the Soviet military actions as an "open military aggression that must immediately be stopped."[451]

Other political steps were taken which emphasized the cynical illegality of the Soviet military action when Lithuania, Latvia, Estonia and Russia recognized each other's sovereignty in a concerted action on January 14, 1991.[452] Russia's contribution at this junction should be noted as having been particularly important, since it contributed to the later Soviet collapse, when the largest Soviet republic was choosing its own path towards sovereignty and independence from the Soviet Union by recognizing the three Baltic States as independent countries. Lithuania, Latvia, Estonia and Russia then applied collectively to Javier Perez de Cuellar, the Secretary-General of the United Nations, requesting the immediate convention of an international conference for the regulation of the Baltic Problem.[453] In moving this action, Landsbergis was effectively telling the West that "if you want to help us, please support Yeltsin, not

449   Quoted in *The Gift of Vilnius*, p. 64.
450   "Nesutarimus lydės smurtas," *Lietuvos Aidas*, January 31, 1991, p. 3.
451   "Lietuvos Respublikos Aukščiausiosios Tarybos nutarimas dėl priemonių Lietuvos respublikai ginti," *Lietuvos Aidas*, January 15, 1991, p. 1.
452   "Pareiškimas," *Lietuvos Aidas*, January 15, 1991, p. 1.
453   Landsbergis was convinced that Lithuania would be attacked under the smokescreen provided by the Gulf war. So, he asked the western nations to postpone the beginning of the Gulf war; "Kreipimasis į Jungtinių Tautų Generalinį Sekretorių Jo Prakilnybę poną Ksavierą Peresą de Kueljarą" (Appeal to the Secretary General of the United Nations), *Lietuvos Aidas*, January 15, 1991, p. 1.

Gorbachev," and at last he could be quite confident that the world was really aware of the burdens he had been carrying.[454]

The Supreme Council of Lithuania now appealed to all the peoples of the Soviet Union, reminding them that the unfolding tragedy in Lithuania was also a tragedy for them, and inviting them to do everything possible to stop Soviet aggression.[455] On January 13, 1991 the Supreme Council issued a further appeal to the states of the world, informing them that the USSR had declared war on Lithuania, and inviting them to recognize that the Soviet Union had, in fact, attacked another sovereign state.[456] These external actions heralded to the world that the Lithuanians were preparing to continue the work of their Parliament and the Government under any circumstances that could be foreseen, even the darkest situation. The Parliament, therefore, passed a law providing for the organization of a Government in Exile in the event that the Supreme Council should become unable to work in Vilnius because of Soviet military intervention.[457] In step with this action, Russia's leader Boris Yeltsin issued an appeal to Russian soldiers in the Baltic States, stating that the sending of soldiers outside the borders of the Russian Federation was an illegal act, and inviting them to think about their own families left at home.[458]

The Lithuanian Parliament passed a decree deeming the activity of the Committee for the National Salvation criminal, and on January 14, 1991 it issued its own appeal to Soviet army officers and soldiers in Lithuania, reminding them that often they had been pushed into crimes against humanity by the Soviet authorities, and informing them that their oath to defend the state did not entail an obligation to kill innocent people abroad, who loved their own

---

454   Interview with Prof. Vytautas Landsbergis, the President of Lithuanian Parliament, Cardiff, May 10, 2000.

455   "Lietuvos Respublikos Aukščiausiosios Tarybos Kreipimasis," *Lietuvos Aidas*, January 16, 1991, p. 1.

456   "Kreipimasis," *Lietuvos Aidas*, January 16, 1991, p. 1.

457   "Lietuvos Respublikos Įstatymas dėl Lietuvos Respublikos vyriausybės emigracijoje," *Lietuvos Aidas*, January 15, 1991, p. 4.

458   "Boriso Jelcino kreipimasis į Rusijos kareivius," *Lietuvos Aidas*, January 16, 1991, p. 1.

homeland.[459] It was accompanied by a statement explaining the illegal actions of Soviet military forces who had captured and were occupying the Press House in Vilnius - the home of many editorial boards of the Lithuanian national press, and the studios of the Lithuanian National Television and Radio Service, and other key buildings, pillaging the premises, destroying equipment, and even wounding and killing peaceful people, who were protecting these places. This protest against these brutal actions included the demand that the army should be withdrawn from these buildings and sought compensation for the damage and the punishment of the initiators of the operation, no matter how high their rank.[460]

The intense Soviet military activity continued. The Lithuanian Ministry of Internal Affairs regularly informed the press how Soviet troops stopped cars and fired on civilians. One person was shot at night for having attempted to film soldiers from a car, and three deliberate collisions between civilian cars and military vehicles were recorded during another night.[461] On January 17 the car of Vidmantas Povilionis, a Member of the Lithuanian Parliament, was stopped by Soviet officers on the Kaunas-Vilnius highway. They ordered him to raise his hands above his head, and then kept him standing in the cold for two and a half hours while threatening to shoot him.[462] These stories were circulated widely, and no one could remain in doubt about the real policies of the Soviet Empire.

There were some positive steps at this stage in the response of the United States which now applied pressure on the Soviet Union, demanding a halt to these military actions. The Department of State stated publicly that the United States was deeply concerned over the situation in the Baltic States, and that peaceful dialogue was the only way to stabilize the situation in Lithuania. Indeed, Secretary Baker invited the Soviet Ambassador to discuss the situation in

---

459 "Lietuvos Respublikos Aukščiausiosios Tarybos nutarimas dėl vadinamojo "Nacionalinio gelbėjimo komiteto" veiklos politinio ir teisinio įvertinimo," *Lietuvos Aidas*, January 16, 1991, p. 1. Also "Kreipimasis," *Lietuvos Aidas*, January 16, 1991, p. 1.

460 "Lietuvos Respublikos Aukščiausiosios Tarybos Pareiškimas dėl TSRS ginkluotųjų pajėgų neteisėtų veiksmų. " *Lietuvos Aidas*, January 17, 1991, p. 1.

461 "Vyriausybėje," *Lietuvos Aidas*, January 17, 1991, p. 1.

462 "Pareiškimas," *Lietuvos Aidas*, January 19, 1991, p. 1.

Lithuania, despite being busy with the Gulf crisis.[463] However, *quid pro quo*, the Soviets also stepped up the propaganda war against Lithuania as Soviet officers attempted to deny responsibility for killing innocent people by the Lithuanian Television and Radio Tower in Vilnius. They fabricated stories, claiming that the people who died there had been killed by the Lithuanian Defense Department, and that the bodies had been laid before the tanks to be photographed to provide fascist anti-Soviet propaganda.[464] The government responded in protest, stating that it was totally untrue to argue that Lithuania was divided into two opposing sides, and that the Soviet claims that unarmed Lithuanian people had attacked the Soviet troops were simply unfounded.

With the eyes of the world on the country and the passions of the nation engaged in indignation at what had occurred, the state funerals of the men and women who had died while guarding the Vilnius Television and Radio Tower took place on January 16, 1991. In his eulogy Father Robertas Grigas, one of the most prominent defenders of the Parliament, said simply: "The tanks will not force us to behave against our conscience."[465] The new Lithuanian Prime Minister Gediminas Vagnorius told the mourners that Soviet military forces had learned nothing from their aggression in Hungary, Czechoslovakia, and Afghanistan. "We demand the establishment of an international commission to investigate the crimes of the Soviet Army," he said.[466] The Secretary of the Latvian Supreme Soviet was also present and declared that these Lithuanian brothers and sisters had died not only for Lithuania but also for Latvian independence. Other participants at the state funeral, including many members of parliament and senators from the neighboring states, who also made statements, saying that the Soviet Union had attempted to perform a *coup d'état* in Lithuania, using military force.

---

463   "Pasaulio naujienos," *Lietuvos Aidas*, January 17, 1991, p. 2.
464   Lina Baltrukonytė, "Šlykštus spektaklis tęsiasi," *Lietuvos Aidas*, January 19, 1991, p. 2.
465   "Vardan tos Lietuvos," interview with Fr. Robertas Grigas, http://www.aus ra.pl/a0101/grigas.html.
466   Prime Minister Kazimira Prunskienė had resigned on the eve of Bloody Sunday. The abortive increase in prices by her government has coincided with the Soviet attempts at *coup d'état*.

They affirmed that there had been no internal conflict despite the Soviet leadership's attempt to describe events in those terms. The truth was that it was a struggle which had pitted Soviet military force against a democratically elected Lithuanian Parliament and a validly appointed Government.[467]

The ripple effect from the events in Vilnius continued. In an address on January 29, President Bush revealed that the Soviets had promised to withdraw troops and reopen dialogue with the Baltic States.[468] In his key letter to Gorbachev, President Bush stated on January 23:

> Last June, during the Washington Summit, we talked about the effect of Soviet actions in the Baltic States at great length. I explained that I appreciated the constraints under which you were operating but that I too faced certain pressures. Nonetheless, I honored your personal request and signed the Trade Agreement in spite of the economic blockade that the Soviet Union had imposed on Lithuania. You gave me assurances that you would take steps to settle peacefully all differences with the Baltic leaders. Several weeks later, you lifted that blockade and began a dialogue with Lithuanian and other Baltic leaders. From that time on, our cooperation in the economic sphere has expanded, culminating in the steps that I took on December 12 in response to the difficult circumstances that your country faced as winter approached. I said then that I wanted to do something to help the Soviet Union stay on the course of political and economic reform.
>
> Unfortunately, in view of the events of the last two weeks – resulting in the deaths of at least twenty people in the Baltic States – I cannot in good conscience, and indeed, will not continue along this path. I believe that the leaders of the Baltic States have acted with restraint, particularly in the last two weeks, and did not deserve to have their quest for negotiations met with force. The unrelenting intimidation, pressure, and armed force to which these democratically elected leaders have been subjected is something that I frankly cannot understand.
>
> I had hoped to see positive steps toward the peaceful resolution of this conflict with the elected leaders of the Baltic States. But in the absence of that and in the absence of a positive change in the situation I would have no choice but to respond. Thus, unless you can take these positive steps very soon, I will freeze many elements of our economic relationship including Export-Import credit guarantees, Commodity Credit Cooperation credit guarantees, support for "Special Associate Status" for the Soviet Union in

---

467   "RTFSR, Ukrainos Respublikos, Moldovos Respublikos, Gruzijos Respublikos ir TSRS liaudies deputatų, Lenkijos senatorių ir parlamento deputatų - įvykių Vilniuje liudininkų pareiškimas," *Lietuvos Aidas*, January 19, 1991, p. 4.
468   See Vardys, *Lithuania. The Rebel Nation*, p. 180.

the International Monetary Fund and World Bank; and most of our technical assistance programs. Further, I would not submit the Bilateral Investment Treaty for Consent to ratification when and if they are completed.[469]

However, despite Gorbachev's promise to Bush, the Soviet Army continued its activities in Vilnius, and on the night of January 24-25, they blocked almost all entries to the city, stopping cars by shooting into the air. Some of their troops had attacked a car belonging to the Supreme Council, wounding an accountant, and seizing money which he was taking back to the Parliament from the bank. They also fired on security staff and a group of four English journalists, who had already been detained for hours in a Soviet military area near Vilnius as they were arriving at Parliament.[470] Again, in cynical contradiction to the promise given to the President of the United States, Gorbachev gave a directive requiring Soviet troops to patrol the streets of Lithuania with authority to enter any premises. Ostensibly, this was to search for "criminals" but as it was linked to the question of patriotic demonstrations of any kind, it gave a new meaning to that word. An unannounced decree of the Soviet Defense Ministry and Ministry of Internal Affairs, permitting this activity, had been signed in readiness on December 29, 1990, and now on January 26, it was implemented at the initiative of the Soviet President Mikhail Gorbachev. The Lithuanian Supreme Council protested against this arbitrary action immediately and appealed to the democratic states, asking for help in stopping these renewed moves towards dictatorship in the Soviet Union.[471]

The reaction in the West to the killings in Vilnius was serious. There was a real sense of shock and this time the positions were firm. Perhaps it had dawned on people what really underlay the genial *bonhomie* which they associated with Comrade Gorbachev. The Soviet actions were therefore reflected on endlessly in the press

469   Letter of POTUS to President Gorbachev, January 23, 1990. James A. Baker III Papers, Seeley G. Mudd Manuscript Library, Princeton University, MC#197, Series B: Secretary of State, Box 109.

470   "Sovietų kariuomenė siautėja," *Lietuvos Aidas*, January 26, 1991, p. 1 and *Lietuvos Aidas*, January 31, 1991, p. 1.

471   "Lietuvos Respublikos Aukščiausiosios Tarybos pareiškimas dėl agresijos prieš Lietuvą plėtimo ir karinės diktatūros grėsmės TSR Sąjungoje," *Lietuvos Aidas*, January 29, 1991, p. 2.

and were found wholly unacceptable on moral grounds. In Washington President Bush said openly that he had found "the turn of events deeply disturbing," and asked the Soviets to withdraw troops. Speaking in Congress later he said that the United States "remained committed to helping the Baltic States." Meanwhile, the German Chancellor Helmut Kohl had sent a confidential message to Gorbachev demanding the withdrawal of the troops.[472] Both the U.S. Senate and the Bundestag then passed resolutions asking the Soviet President "to refrain from using force," calling upon him "to withdraw Soviet troops from Lithuania."[473] Similar reactions came from the majority of Western governments but Iceland's Foreign Minister Jón Baldvin Hannibalsson, who headed the official delegation of Iceland to Lithuania on January 20, stated that "my government is seriously considering the possibility of establishing diplomatic relations with the Republic of Lithuania." The *Allting* (Parliament) of Iceland then informed the Supreme Council of Lithuania just three weeks after the Soviet attacks that the recognition of the Lithuanian state originally made in 1922 was still valid, and that Iceland intended to restore full diplomatic relations with Lithuania as soon as possible.[474]

The European Parliament now made a special statement regarding the situation in the Baltic States, which expressed a categorical demand for an end to military actions in Lithuania, Latvia, and Estonia. It condemned military aggression against the Baltic nations and stated that this aggression violated the principles of the Helsinki agreements, which had been confirmed only a few weeks before in Paris. The document also invited the Council of Ministers of the European Community to include the Baltic problem on the agenda of the next meeting of the CSCE and declared that it would halt all programs of technical assistance to the Soviet Union, keeping the situation under careful review until all military units had been withdrawn from the Baltic States. It also demanded that the

---

472   "JAV prezidento nuomonė ir jos komentaras," *Lietuvos Aidas*, January 31, 1991, p. 1.

473   Quoted in Vardys, *The Rebel Nation*, p. 179.

474   "Pripažinimas," *Lietuvos Aidas*, February 13, 1991, p. 1.

dialogue between the Baltic States and the Kremlin regarding the future of the three states should be renewed immediately and condemned all the current attempts to limit freedom of the press in the Soviet Union. Finally, it invited Mikhail Gorbachev to identify the persons responsible for this military aggression, and to draw the necessary conclusions. It also resolved to block a one-billion-dollar European Community food aid package which had originally been prepared at the request of the Soviet Union, until these matters had been dealt with.[475]

These acts of solidarity by the West helped Lithuania greatly. Even Japan withheld delivery of 100 million dollars' worth of food supplies which had been intended for the Soviets. The U.S. Secretary of State James A. Baker announced that "the use of force by the Soviet government in the Baltics fundamentally and tragically contradicts the basic principles of *perestroika*, *glasnost*, and democratization."[476] He reiterated his earlier statement that "partnership is impossible in the absence of shared values."[477] This extended Western reaction ensured that there was no further bloodshed in Lithuania. The expected attack on the Parliament, so closely anticipated and expected to come with little notice, never materialized. Nevertheless, the Soviets continued their program of violence and intimidation for weeks after this, though it was done at the cost of considerable damage to Gorbachev, whose former reputation as a reformer was now irrecoverable. The Nobel Prize winning poets Czeslaw Milosz and Josef Brodsky went so far as to suggest that Gorbachev's Nobel Prize be revoked. The Norwegians collected a half million-dollar peace prize for the Lithuanian people and entrusted it to Vytautas Landsbergis. According to Professor Vytautas Vardys, Gorbachev, formally the shining hero of historic reforms, was now regarded with anger, disappointment, and sadness[478].

---

475   "Europos parlamento bendras pareiškimas apie padėtį Baltijos valstybėse," *Lietuvos Aidas*, January 30, 1991, p. 3.

476   BATUN News, January 21, 1991, p. 9. Quoted in Vardys, *Lithuania. the Rebel Nation*, p. 179.

477   BATUN News, quoted in Vardys, *Lithuania. the Rebel Nation*, p. 179.

478   It is worthy to observe that in his notes Secretary Baker changed the abbreviated name "Gorby" into "Gorbo."

Even though no one assumed responsibility for the Soviet military actions, it was clear that they had been well orchestrated, and probably from the highest level. Although Gorbachev claimed that he had heard about the massacre "only the next morning," it was common knowledge that the Soviet system worked in a such manner that his prior agreement would have been needed. This supposition was confirmed when a commission of military experts from the independent organization *"Shchit"* (Shield), which had come into being to gather the opinions of experts who were opposed to the gross abuses of military force and of personnel in the Soviet Army, delivered a report which concluded that a *coup d'état* had been attempted in Lithuania, "with the help of the army, the internal forces of the Interior Ministry, and the KGB of the Soviet Union, for the purpose of restoring political rule by the Communist Party of the Soviet Union [to be exercised] by its constituent part, the Lithuanian Communist Party." The report continued: "The President of the USSR had to know about the planned concomitant actions of the Soviet Army, the internal forces of the Ministry of the Interior, and the KGB. Such actions could not be taken without his personal permission."[479] However, instead of acknowledging his responsibility, Mikhail Gorbachev blamed local military commanders for "choosing the wrong type of response" to demands which had come in from the National Committee of Salvation asking them to intervene in order "to protect human rights in Lithuania." "If you want to find out [...] who gave their response, there is one way to do that, it's [...] the President, who is also the chief leader of their army, he could demand [...] he could demand reports from his three ministers: Yazov, Pugo and Kruchkov," commented Vytautas Landsbergis.[480] As ever the Soviet system continued to manipulate truth to its own advantage, but its credibility since January 13 was now thin and it was clear that the Baltic region had become an

---

479 "Shchit" was an independent organization of military experts in Moscow set up to investigate the abuse of military force, etc. See "Zaklyuchenie nezavisimykh voennykh expertov obshchestvenoi organizatsii "Schit" na sobytiya v Vilnyuse 11 - 13 yanvarya 1991 goda." Quoted in Vardys, *Lithuania. The Rebel Nation*, p. 181.

480 Interview with Landsbergis for BBC.

international problem rather than a domestic one, despite Gorbachev's arguments.

Effectively, the Soviet system had blown its luck. Its brutality continued to be faced with Lithuanian firmness and calmness. The Kremlin had immediately followed the debacle of January 13 with preparations for a referendum to be held on Lithuanian territory. It was a crude attempt to gain popular backing over the question of a new Union Treaty. In response, the Lithuanians prepared their own national referendum, which raised the single significant question: "Do you favor the idea that the Lithuanian state should be an independent democratic republic?" The ballot was held on February 9, 1991, and its outcome demonstrated clearly to the world that an absolute majority of the Lithuanian people believed that Lithuania must continue on its chosen path of independence and democracy.[481] The evidence was unarguable: of the total of 2,652,738 voters in Lithuania, 2,247,810 (84.74 per cent) voted. Out of these 2,028,339 (90.47 per cent) voted *yes*, i.e., supporting the proposition of independence and democracy.[482] The result was therefore crystal clear, but Gorbachev had denounced this referendum even before the voting took place. He now pushed on to organize a further "All Union referendum" on March 17, on 'the question of the territorial integrity of the USSR.' Interestingly, only an extremely small minority of Lithuania's population participated in this event, which was in effect conducted illegally on Lithuanian territory.[483] This outcome demonstrated satisfactorily to the world that the Lithuanian Parliament and Government had solid popular support for its position, and that the case for continued political ties with the USSR was a purely unilateral policy of the Kremlin's creation.

The results of the Lithuanian referendum and the total failure of the attempted Soviet referendum did not, however, lead to negotiations beginning between Lithuania and the Soviet Union, though the Kremlin now did start to pay some lip-service to the

---

481 "Lietuvos valstybė yra nepriklausoma demokratinė respublika," *Lietuvos Aidas*, January 29, 1991, p. 1.

482 "Ar jūs už tai, kad Lietuvos valstybė būtų nepriklausoma demokratinė respublika," *Lietuvos Aidas*, February 14, 1991, p. 4.

483 See Vardys, *Lithuania. The Rebel nation*, p. 183.

idea of negotiations. It is evident that it wished to demonstrate some sort of willingness about the Soviet-Lithuanian dialogue, if only because it needed to play up to Washington to avoid the cancellation of the planned Soviet-American summit. Even before Lithuania had conducted the February 9 referendum, Gorbachev announced the formation of the "negotiating group" whose first meeting took place on April 4, 1991. The discussion went rather well and both sides declared themselves satisfied with this discussion on the "regulation of the relationships between the Republic of Lithuania and the USSR." The discussion covered the principles, goals, and procedures of future discussions but the formulas used carefully excluded any mention either of "independence," or of the "Soviet Socialist Republic of Lithuania."[484] It is difficult to see what this blandness implied because this procedural negotiation, which can be interpreted as the opening of the Soviet-Lithuanian discussions, did not develop into a full negotiation. Essentially, the position was one of stalemate until the Moscow putsch took place on August 19, 1991, although the situation in Lithuania remained tense. The killings of six Lithuanian customs officials by OMON special troops on the eve of the Soviet-American summit, during the "3 on 3" meeting between Gorbachev, Besmertnij, and Chernomyrden and George Bush, James Baker, and Brent Scowcroft on July 31, 1991 at Gorbachev's *Dacha* at 11:30 am, were no doubt an indication that either the Soviet leadership was attempting to test the American reaction in a rather brutal way, or that it was is losing control of its power structures.[485]

---

484   Vardys, *Lithuania. The Rebel nation*, p. 184.
485   Hand-written message to POTUS "Deaths of Lithuanian Border Guards" by James A. Baker III informed that:
This morning the Lithuanian government discovered the bodies of six border guards, plus two other seriously wounded guards, at a customs post on the border with Byelorussia.
The Lithuanian Government has not as of 12:30 p.m. – charged anyone with the crime.
U.S. Embassy notes this looks like an OMON operation.
James A. Baker III Papers, Seeley G. Mudd Manuscript Library, Princeton University, MC#197, Series B: Secretary of State, Box 108, Folder 5.

The international implications of the attempted *coup d'état* in Moscow which took place in August 1991 have been well documented. Much of the discussion has focused on the internal inertia of the communist hegemony which had patently worsened during the Brezhnev era, and on the superficial attempts at reform under Mikhail Gorbachev. If there was indeed any sense of "historical necessity" in the changes which came about as a result of the *coup*, it was because the communist system was unsuitable in a world of increasing freedom of communication and economic liberalization. The clumsy conclusion of the plot to turn the Soviet state back on its course by repudiating Gorbachev and the ambiguous course which he had taken in the direction of reform in August 1991 touches on the real question whether the communist state was ever transformable. Gorbachev's failures had opened up the issues which Landsbergis had then put effectively. In fact, he had asserted that the only answer to the problem was to disintegrate the Evil Empire. Gorbachev's maneuvers were unsuccessful, and the most devoted Soviet *apparatchiks* were driven in the opposite direction, seeking to turn the clock back to Stalinism. The significance of the Lithuanian contribution to the demise of this perverse revanchism lies in the Lithuanian nation's path to freedom and its place in history as a catalyst for the momentous change which was then poised to sweep through Eastern European politics and, indeed, it still deserves wider and more unmistakable recognition.

International Recognition Again

International recognition of Lithuania's renewed independence cascaded following the failure of the Moscow putsch on August 19-21, 1991. Iceland was the first country to recognize Lithuania's newly reconfirmed sovereignty by establishing diplomatic relations well before the August Putsch. Iceland's Parliament had already passed a resolution on February 11 stating that its recognition of the Republic of Lithuania of 1922 remained valid and encouraged its government to establish full diplomatic relations as soon as possible. Many Lithuanians said at the time that "Iceland broke the ice!" by doing this.[486] It was a good beginning, but the full establishment of diplomatic relations by most states did not follow until after the failure of the putsch.[487]

Denmark confirmed its recognition of the Republic of Lithuania on August 24 and two days later it followed this by signing a joint communiqué confirming the full renewal of diplomatic relations with all three Baltic States.[488] Norway became the third country to follow, and its Foreign Minister Thorvald Stoltenberg took the process further by suggesting that Lithuania should enjoy free trade with the EFTA states.[489] On the same day Hungary and Argentina moved to recognize Lithuania, and the German and French Foreign Ministers suggested that the European Community states should collectively recognize Baltic independence in a joint statement. France recognized the restored Republic of Lithuania on August 25 and its Foreign Minister Roland Dumas used the announcement to emphasize that France had never recognized the incorporation of Lithuania into the Soviet Union. He then became the first Foreign Minister of a Western state to visit Lithuania, and by August 29 France and Lithuania had renewed their diplomatic relations in full.[490]

The re-establishment of diplomatic relations by other states now followed in a torrent.[491] On August 26 the Italian government congratulated the Baltic States on the restoration of their independence, again emphasizing that it had not recognized the Soviet incorporation of the Baltic States. On the same day Canada announced that it was re-establishing diplomatic relations with the Baltic States, pointing out that it had never recognized the

---

486   "Žvilgsnis iš šalies," *Lietuvos Aidas*, September 6, 1991, p. 6.

487   Iceland established rather than a *renewed diplomatic relation* with Lithuania as the two countries (though recognizing each other) had no formal diplomatic ties before 1940, despite their bilateral collaboration agreements signed in 1923 and 1930. See *Lietuvos užsienio politikos dokumentai*, 1 sąsiuvinys (Vilnius: Lietuvos Respublikos Aukščiausiosios Tarybos leidykla, 1992), p. 9.

488   *Lietuvos užsienio politikos dokumentai*, p. 7.

489   "Žvilgsnis iš šalies," *Lietuvos Aidas*, p. 6.

490   See "R. Dumas Vilniuje," *Lietuvos Aidas*, August 30, 1991, p. 1 as well as *Lietuvos užsienio politikos dokumentai*, p. 20.

491   See the Table 2 in the Appendices for dates of the re-establishment of diplomatic relations in 1991 and the sequence.

annexation of the Baltic countries and had continued with their recognition *de jure* till the restoration of their independence. On August 27 the countries of the European Community re-established diplomatic relations, all member states of the EC warmly congratulating the country on its restoration of independence. Australia's Foreign Minister announced his country's restoration of mutual relations on the same day, in a speech which also encouraged the Russian leader Boris Yeltsin to finalize his country's response to the question of Baltic independence.

Sweden was the first country to re-open its embassy in Vilnius. This was done on August 29, 1991.[492] A letter was received from the Swedish King on August 27 which stated that his government had agreed formally and officially to recognize Lithuania as an independent and sovereign state. The country's rush to help Lithuania at this point may have reflected its regret at having recognized Lithuania's annexation in 1940. However, it had been firmly associated with the meeting of the Nordic Council on August 28, when it had joined with Denmark to suggest the Council's expansion to include the three Baltic States.[493] All these moves were very promising and indicated the enormous reservoir of goodwill towards the three countries. On August 30 Algirdas Saudargas, Lithuanian Foreign Minister, and Dr. Claudio Vitalone, the First Deputy Foreign Minister of Italy, signed the agreement for re-established diplomatic relations.[494] Then Cardinal Angelo Sodano, the Secretary of State at the Vatican, sent a letter to the Republic of Lithuania, and Gediminas Vagnorius, Prime Minister of Lithuania, who replied expressing eagerness for the re-establishment of full diplomatic relations with the acceptance of the appointment of an Apostolic Nuncio to the Republic.[495] This was followed up on

---

492   "Švedijos ambasada – pirmoji." *Lietuvos Aidas*, August 30, 1991, p. 1.

493   "Šiaurės taryba ir mes: bendradarbiauti žmonių labui," *Lietuvos Aidas*, September 26, 1991, p. 1.

494   "Lietuva – Italija," *Lietuvos Aidas*, August 31, 1991, p. 1. Also *Lietuvos užsienio politikos dokumentai*, p. 21.

495   "Jo Ekscelencijai Gediminui Vagnoriui Lietuvos Respublikos Ministrui Pirmininkui," *Lietuvos Aidas*, August 31, 1991, p. 1.

September 31 when a joint declaration was signed.[496] Although the Vatican had allowed the Lithuanian legation continued accreditation at the Holy See since 1940, this was the first time in half a century that the Catholic Church had been able to place its diplomatic representative in the country.

On September 1, 1991, John Major, British Prime Minister, met the three Prime Ministers Gediminas Vagnorius of Lithuania, Ivars Godmanis of Latvia, and Edgar Savisaar of Estonia at the British Embassy in Moscow.[497] He confirmed that the United Kingdom recognized Lithuania, Latvia and Estonia as independent states and discussed the current situation in the three states, as well as their relationship with Russia. During a press conference Gediminas Vagnorius was asked to give his opinion why Britain, like the United States, had delayed the renewal of its recognition of Lithuania, Latvia, and Estonia, and he answered that perhaps Britain did not want to encourage the separation of other republics from the Soviet Union. He was convinced, however, that the delay had no negative implications for Lithuania.[498] Interestingly, in a later interview with BBC Radio Douglas Hogg, the Minister of State in the British Foreign and Commonwealth Office, said that NATO had no intention of guaranteeing the security of the borders of Lithuania, Latvia and Estonia, who would therefore have to establish their own relationships with Moscow and all the other Soviet republics for themselves.[499]

Later, on September 2, the Canadian and Lithuanian Governments signed a memorandum about the establishment of diplomatic relations.[500] Similarly, on the same day, the President of the United States George H. W. Bush welcomed Lithuania's return to the international community of free nations. Vytautas Landsbergis immediately responded, observing that the American President's statement provided political protection to the Baltic States, and

496 "Atkurti diplomatiniai santykiai su Vatikanu," *Lietuvos Aidas*, October 1, 1991, p. 1.
497 "Didžiosios Britanijos atstovybėje," *Lietuvos Aidas*, September 3, 1991, p. 1.
498 "Didžiosios Britanijos atstovybėje," *Lietuvos Aidas*, p. 1.
499 "NATO negarantuoja sienų apsaugos," *Lietuvos Aidas*, September 4, 1991, p. 1.
500 *Lietuvos užsienio politikos dokumentai*, p. 27.

would therefore contribute to the stabilization of the international situation in the Baltic region. He also expressed hope that the United States would support Lithuania in its efforts to join the United Nations Organization.[501] A little while later, when asked whether the United States would recognize other seceding republics, President Bush told a press conference that the Baltic States were an exception, because "we never recognized the forceful incorporation of the Baltic States into the USSR."[502] He added that "the United States recognized Lithuania in 1922 and did not withdraw this recognition."[503] In a subtle move Lithuania herself emphasized this continuity of state by appointing Stasys Lozoraitis as Lithuania's Ambassador in Washington on September 6, 1991 when it responded to the confirmation of recognition by the United States.[504] Until then he headed the Lithuanian Embassy in Washington, D.C., which still functioned during all the years of occupation of the homeland, having succeeded Stasys Bačkis in 1987 and his father Stasys Lozoraitis (Foreign Minister of Lithuania between 1934 and 1938), who was in charge of Lithuania's still-functioning diplomacy in the West until his death in 1983.

Germany also restored diplomatic relations with Lithuania and the other Baltic States at the end of August, and on September 2, a German Special Representative, Gottfried Albrecht, arrived in Lithuania. A few days later the Chairman of the Bundestag, Professor Dr. Rita von Suessmuth, headed a visiting delegation to Lithuania which included Hans-Dietrich Genscher, the German Federal Minister for Foreign Affairs and Deputy Federal Chancellor.[505] Lithuania's Prime Minister Gediminas Vagnorius then paid the first official visit to Germany on September 15-19, 1991, to meet Chancellor Helmut Kohl, the Foreign Minister Hans Dietrich

---

501   "Vytauto Landsbergio komentaras," *Lietuvos Aidas*, September 5, 1991, p. 1.

502   "Bushas pripažįsta Baltijos šalis, bet kartu remia Gorbačiovą ir jo Sąjungą," *Lietuvos Aidas*, September 6, 1991, p. 6.

503   "Letter of President G. Bush to President of Lithuania Vytautas Landsbergis, August 31, 1991," *Lietuvos Aidas*, September 7, 1991, p. 1.

504   "Lietuvos Respublikos Aukščiausiosios Tarybos Prezidiumo Nutarimas," *Lietuvos Aidas*, September 11, 1991, p. 1.

505   "Lietuva ir Vokietija: vakar ir šiandien," *Lietuvos Aidas*, September 11, 1991, p. 3.

Genscher, and other statesmen. In the consequent meeting Germany expressed clear support for Lithuania's participation in the European Community, beginning with her admission as an Associate Member state of the EC. Chancellor Kohl also promised to try to influence other European states in winning their support for Lithuania, and expressed Germany's support for the early withdrawal of Soviet troops from the country as soon as possible.[506] The signature of a declaration about the re-establishment of diplomatic relations between Switzerland and Lithuania by Swiss Ambassador Jen Stahelin and Lithuanian Deputy Foreign Minister Gediminas Šerksnys, followed on September 5, 1991.[507]

On September 14 U.S. Secretary of State James A. Baker visited Lithuania.[508] He came bearing gifts, using the visit to announce a donation of 16 million dollars of aid to the Baltic States. While in Vilnius, he also announced a substantial package of assistance programs in a few areas: the strengthening of state institutions; education; English language learning; and the reform of banks, the economy, and agriculture.[509] On October 2 the United States opened its Embassy in Vilnius.[510]

The Soviet Union's recognition of the Republic of Lithuania came on September 6, 1991, the same day as the confirmation of recognition by the United States, and the renewal of diplomatic relations was completed on October 9.[511] Having annulled the secret

---

506 "Sėkmingas vizitas Vokietijoje," *Lietuvos Aidas*, September 25, 1991, p. 1; "Pirmas oficialus," *Lietuvos Aidas*, September 21, 1991, pp. 1-2; "Bona kaip ant delno," *Lietuvos Aidas*, September 25, 1991, p. 6 and *Lietuvos Aidas*, September 26, 1991, p. 14.

507 "'Lietuvos aido' informacija," *Lietuvos Aidas*, September 6, 1991, p. 1.

508 "J. Bakeris Vilniuje," *Lietuvos Aidas*, September 14, 1991, p. 1; "Baltics trip went fine, but one country acts almost as if the coup had <u>not</u> been <u>unsuccessful</u>. I'll talk to you about this – and follow your advice to take a nap," commented Secretary Baker to President Bush straight after the one-day visit of Estonia, Latvia, and Lithuania on a route via St. Petersburg (underlined by Secretary Baker). James A. Baker III Papers, Seeley G. Mudd Manuscript Library, Princeton University, MC#197, Series B: Secretary of State, Box 115, Folder 10.

509 "J. Bakeris Lietuvoje," *Lietuvos Aidas*, September 17, 1991, p. 1.

510 "Atidaryta JAV ambasada," *Lietuvos Aidas*, October 3, 1991, p. 1.

511 See "Maskva pripažįsta Baltijos valstybes," *Lietuvos Aidas*, September 7, 1991, p. 2 and Virgilijus Kizas, "Lietuva ir SSSR atnaujino diplomatinius santykius," *Lietuvos Aidas*, October 10, 1991, p. 1.

protocols of the Molotov-Ribbentrop pact, it had finally recognized that Lithuania had been illegally incorporated into the Soviet Union. The USSR Council of State then also announced its decision to support Lithuania's applications to join the United Nations and the Conference for Security and Co-operation in Europe.[512] After the failure of the coup in Moscow, the Soviet Ministry of Defence also ordered Soviet troops in Lithuania to return to their permanent bases.[513] This did not, however, mean that they left the country, but the Lithuanian Television and Radio Tower in Vilnius and other major buildings were at last returned to Lithuania. The issue of the withdrawal of Soviet troops from the country became a major subject in the negotiations of Lithuania with Russia after the collapse of the Soviet Union and the top priority of Lithuanian foreign and security policy for the next two years.

On September 17, 1991 Lithuania was formally admitted to the United Nations, and the President of Lithuania's Parliament Professor Vytautas Landsbergis addressed the General Assembly, saying that "Lithuania's belief in justice, and her refusal to be afraid or to lie turned out to be stronger than knives, rockets, automatic rifles, or moving iron boxes."[514] He also stated that Lithuania wished "to expand non-nuclear and confidence zones, and thus demanded the withdrawal of all foreign troops from her territory."[515]

It is interesting to note how at this stage Russia itself encouraged the recognition of Lithuania's independence. The Russian Foreign Minister Andrei Kozyrev and Boris Yeltsin's assistant Starovoitova's interview broadcasted by the BBC encouraged the West to recognize the independence of the Baltic States.[516] The fact that Lithuania had recognized Russia's sovereignty on January 14, 1991, had of course been useful to the general recognition of Russia's own independence from the Soviet Union. This mutual

---

512   "SSSR Valstybės tarybos nutarimas dėl Lietuvos Respublikos nepriklauso-
      mybės pripažinimo," *Lietuvos Aidas*, September 10, 1991, p. 1.
513   See *Lietuvos užsienio politikos dokumentai*, p. 68 and "Perversmas žlugo," *Lietu-
      vos Aidas*, August 22, 1991, p. 1.
514   "Vytauto Landsbergio kalba Jungtinese Tautose," *Lietuvos Aidas*, September
      19, 1991, p. 1.
515   "Vytauto Landsbergio kalba," p. 1.
516   "Praneša Užsienio reikalų ministerija," *Lietuvos Aidas*, August 22, 1991, p. 1.

support proved to be successful. On Christmas Eve 1991 the Soviet Union ceased to exist and Russia, formerly the largest Soviet Republic, finally became an independent country as well.

This process was, of course, of major international significance, but the outcome was far from being secure, as there were political forces in Moscow which evaluated the developing situation totally differently. Vladimir Zhirinovski, who was something of a loose cannon in contemporary Russian politics, a representative of what might be termed the fascist-like tendency, who was feared in the West and elsewhere, and showed populist capabilities which were xenophobic and indeed fascist in practice, told the correspondent of the Lithuanian News Agency ELTA that "in future there will be a different regime in Russia. The Empire that existed before 1917 must be restored. Then only one Baltic province will exist, with its capital in Riga [...] There will be silence and order in the Baltic [...] The Russian authorities will rule from the Baltic Sea to the Pacific Ocean."[517] The voices and growing influence of "empire restorers" like Zhirinovski and Putin seemed to be the more threatening because the country's Stalinists, who included many senior military leaders, were also calling for an "assertive policy" towards the Baltic States. This chorus grew more powerful during 1992 and 1993 and became more influential as Yeltsin and his government was increasingly moved away from their budding "Atlanticism" in the direction of a "new Russian nationalism". Out of this distorted perspective emerged the new doctrine of the "Near Abroad," which was highlighted in full form in a speech made by Andrei Kozyrev, Russia's Foreign Minister, to the CSCE in Stockholm in December 1992, who "shocked his audience by denouncing Western interference in the Baltic States."[518] He told the West: "to keep their noses out of the states of the former Soviet Union" and stated that "the territory of the former Soviet Union could not be considered a zone in which CSCE norms were wholly applicable

---

517 "Du komediantai Kremliaus suvažiavimų rūmuose," *Lietuvos Aidas,* September 4, 1991, p. 4.
518 See Peter Truscott, *Russia First. Breaking with the West* (London: I.B. Tauris Publishers, 1997), p. 37.

[…] (as) *It* was essentially *a post-imperial area in which Russia had to protect its own interests by all available means, including military and economic ones.*"[519] Already in October 1992, two months before this speech, Boris Yeltsin had told Russian Foreign Ministry officials that Russia was still "a great world power," which should not "shy away from defending" its own interests. Yeltsin had also said that "he was disappointed with the attitude of the West, particularly the United States, which often saw Russia as a state that always said *yes*, forgetting that Russia was a great power, albeit with temporary difficulties."[520] Considered together, these indications brought little comfort to the fledgling Baltic States.

The emergence of Lithuanian sovereignty from its long period of occlusion was not an arrival of any kind at a promised land of comfortable reconstruction and equable relationships with her neighbors based on the principles of concord, harmony, and mutual respect. Despite the promising start given by Yeltsin's confirmation of Lithuania's independence, the situation with respect to Russia became progressively entangled. This became particularly evident after that country had itself disengaged from the incubus of its constitutional relationship with the Soviet Union and when a rather significant immigrant population of Russians in Lithuania (7%) fell prey to anxieties about a 'nationalist' takeover. The groundwork for this fear was a result of Soviet propaganda but it now gave scope for the likes of Zhirinovsky who was only too pleased to use them as a cynically manipulated vehicle in the service of his imperial dream. This occurred despite every attempt by Lithuania, constitutionally and otherwise, to show its care for all its ethnic minorities, and to emphasize their equality before the law, and the value of the new situation for their democratic rights, both at the ballot box and in the promotion of human rights. The developing situation was less easy to deal with in the new context of Russia's accusations against the Baltic States of alleged violations of the human rights of its compatriots.

---

519   Truscott, *Russia First*, p. 37.
520   Truscott, *Russia First*, p. 38.

Further, there was the presence in Lithuania, and the other Baltic countries, of a substantial element of the Soviet Army. Now, it was technically subject to the Russian state which was, however, not yet declared to be securely in control of this body, which retained the capacity for massive military force, and whose senior officers had been appointed by the now formally non-existent Soviet Union. The situation was likely to be exploited as the dynamic of Yeltsin's administration was affected by turbulent and nostalgic forces in economics, public opinion, and political manipulation. However, the diplomatic recognition of Lithuania meant that the essential struggle for freedom and independence had been won. Bronislovas Kuzmickas, the Vice-President of the Supreme Council, opined that the Second World War finally finished when Lithuania, Latvia and Estonia became independent countries.[521] Kuzmickas also wrote that "the practical task of the restoration of independence has begun now that the heroic period is over."[522] It is to this new period that we will now turn.

---

521   Bronius Kuzmickas, "Europos diena Šveicarijoje," *Lietuvos Aidas*, September 13, 1991, p. 6. However, we might better say that the real end of the Second World War for Lithuania started to emerge with the final withdrawal of Russian troops in 1993, though Lithuania's major security problem with respect to Russia was finally resolved after Lithuania's joining NATO and the European Union. Excessive militarization of the Russian occupied Lithuania Minor (Königsberg, Karaliaučius, or Kaliningrad region) remains one of the major security problems for Lithuania, and therefore this occupation also seriously threatens European and Transatlantic security for Europe as a whole (see the Chapter 10).

522   Bronius Kuzmickas, "Ateina pragmatiškasis metas," *Lietuvos Aidas*, September 5, 1991, pp. 1-2.

8. Lithuania's Success in the Helsinki Process

The achievement of independence for Lithuania was a process which can be claimed to have grown out of the nation's history. Its achievement reflected a resistance which was lodged deeply in the collective consciousness of the Lithuanian people. Certainly, the accumulated sense of grievance at the indignity and the prolonged oppression of the Soviet occupation, the lack of freedom, the economic inflexibility and the denial of human rights which had been a part of everyday life under Soviet occupation had sharpened the wish of many of the people for better things. The memory of dispossession from family lands; the experience of exile, whether one's own or that of a near relative; and the memories of the struggle by the Lithuanian resistance often rankled and certainly remained active in the reflections of the multitude of individuals and families for whom the Soviet experience had often been a culture of death, punishment, injustice, and deportations. Vytautas Landsbergis has written well of these emotions and how they affected his own family, and those close to them, and of how these experiences reflected a common condition to which his passionate response released the call for national liberation for the whole nation.[523]

This liberation process involved most of the Lithuanian population when the nation was finally ready to stand up and declare that enough was enough. The Baltic Way, the unprecedented demonstration on August 23, 1989, involved approximately a third of the entire population of three countries. It reflected the passionate emotional engagement of the Baltic people in the process of unstitching the vicious agreements which Molotov and Ribbentrop had served up for their respective masters in 1939. These levels of popular emotion, directed soberly and without violence, addressed issues of historical truth and natural political justice in seeking disengagement from the communist superpower.

---

523 Vytautas Landsbergis, *Lithuania Independent Again* (Cardiff: University of Wales Press, 2000).

Much of our discussion up till now has noted the cautious initial response of the Western powers. We have also noted now the flood of recognition, and the general rejoicing at the collapse of the Soviet super-state, which came in the later months of 1991. It is perhaps disappointing to notice that the 'attitude lag' in Western support for Lithuania's progress toward freedom seems not to have changed greatly once this euphoria of international acknowledgment vanished. Indeed, in surveying the development of Lithuania's relationship with Russia in the immediate post-independence period, it will be seen that the fledging Russian state which had taken such positive action with Boris Yeltsin's help in laying the foundation for state-to-state relationships with the three Baltic nations during the final phases of Gorbachev's ascendancy, reverted rapidly to the hectoring, threatening, and controlling mode of its Soviet precursor. It is a phenomenon which can only be explained by observing that expressions of the Russian state embodied dispositions which have clear roots in Russian history going back to Tsarist times.

As these trends are analyzed, however, it is possible to perceive a different process at work among the Western states, and in international relations, which expressed a spirit that became progressively more supportive of Lithuanian national ambitions and that of the other Baltic States. This process was vital in giving an audience which paid increasing attention to the needs of these nations in the later part of the Cold War age. The international action and support which accompanied this movement of opinion helped build confidence in the Baltic States. It became increasingly significant as a moral counterbalance to Soviet calculations. This was never more apparent than when the Soviets chose briefly to ignore what had been achieved, when they took the desperate measures which unfolded on the night of January 13, 1991, when the activity of their forces rapidly dispersed any positive capital which they had acquired in world public opinion.

The context to which we refer is that of the "Helsinki Process," or the activity of the Conference for Security and Co-operation in Europe (CSCE), which was renamed the Organization for Security and Co-operation in Europe (OSCE) in 1992. This organization, which is an important part of the European security framework, complements the work of NATO, which is the organization at the highest level of hierarchy in the European and Transatlantic security framework, dealing primarily with collective defense and political co-operation. The CSCE was originally established in 1975, essentially as an organization of co-operative security intended to project Western values and norms onto the Soviet bloc countries. It was grounded from the start in the concept of *co-operative security,* and its task is now redefined in terms of the prevention of the conditions that make war likely.[524] This objective is pursued through building an institutionalized community between states, through co-operation over political, economic, and cultural affairs, as well as arms control, and Confidence and Security Building Measures (CSBM), and it is important in evaluating the context of co-operative security to note that this differs from the concept of *collective security*, which is less concerned with *prevention*, than with providing a mechanism for punishment by member states of a state breaching international law and exercising aggression against a third party.[525]

In practice, these concepts of *collective* and *co-operative security* overlap in the activities of the three major international security organizations serving Europe, i.e. the North Atlantic Treaty Organization (NATO), the European Union (EU), and the Organization for Security and Cooperation in Europe (OSCE).[526] Together these bodies constitute a developing European "Security Architecture," its "interlocking institutions" forming the background to a "Western European security community" which first emerged in the Cold War era. These bodies continue to adapt themselves, and were recently engaged in enlargement, embracing new member states in

---

524   See Gülnur Aybet, *The Development of a European Security Architecture in the Post-Cold War Era.* PhD thesis. University of Nottingham, 1997.

525   The United Nations is more an organization of collective security than of co-operative on these terms.

526   Professor Christopher Hill defined the EU as a diplomatic alliance which attempts to manage American power but after the EU enlargement, embracing the Central and Eastern European countries, its core "Franco-German engine" was replaced by an increased Anglo-Franco-German collaboration.

Central and Eastern Europe. Within and between these interlocking institutions a hierarchy can be identified, which is structured by the balance of influence and power, in which the decisive role belongs to NATO, and to the United States within NATO. The North Atlantic Alliance is therefore the largest and the most significant European security organization, representing the defensive alliance of all the major Western democracies.[527] Lower in this hierarchy lies the EU, essentially a "soft-security" organization, which is primarily concerned with the unification of economic rules and the consolidation of a single economic space. The OSCE membership embraces states in a vast "Euro-Atlantic area". Like all these organizations, it reflects a projection of Western values, and is closely related to the fundamental concepts of democracy, free market economy, and society governed by principles of law, which are the binding forces of the Western family of nations. Collectively, NATO and the EU embody what Karl Deutsch termed the "Western security community," and the eastward enlargements of these organizations

---

527   For the rationale of why the countries of Central and Eastern Europe have the desire to join NATO see: Zbigniew Brzezinski, "Living with a New Europe," *The National Interest*, no. 60 (Summer 2000): pp. 17-33, which comments: "In spite of the vanishing of the Soviet military threat, after the dissolution of the Warsaw Pact Organization and the withdrawal of the Russian troops from the front lines they occupied during the Cold War, the North Atlantic Treaty Organization (NATO) remains the defense and security framework for the Western world." See also, Jean Klein, "Interface Between NATO/WEU and UN/OSCE," in Michael J. Brenner, *NATO and Collective Security* (London: Macmillan, 1998, p. 249): "NATO is the most inclusive military organization in Europe, provides the institutional mechanism for military cooperation with the United States, has elaborate structures and standards already in place, and happens to be the organization deployed in Europe's war zones;" and Philip H. Gordon, "Their Own Army? Making European Defense Work," *Foreign Affairs* 79, no. 4 (July/August 2000): 16. The members of NATO are protected by the Article 5 security guarantee of the North Atlantic Treaty: "The Parties agree that an armed attack against one or more of them in Europe or North America shall be considered an attack against them all and consequently they agree that, if such an armed attack occurs, each of them, in exercise of the right of individual or collective self-defense recognized by Article 51 of the Charter of the United Nations, will assist the Party or Parties so attacked by taking forthwith, individually and in concert with the other Parties, such action as it deems necessary, including the use of armed force, to restore and maintain the security of the North Atlantic area." See e.g., Robert Hunter, *Security in Europe* (London: Elek Books, 1969), p. 159.

therefore imply an extension of the area of security and stability. Thus, Lithuania's Declaration of Independence, and the maturing of her position in relation to her western neighbors, has raised very important questions about her future contribution to this abstract, but at the same time real and rather well-functioning European and transatlantic security framework.[528] These questions are sharpened by Lithuania's participation, and its influence on European security as a whole, and it is important also to analyze the extent to which the European and transatlantic security framework has both influenced the development of the domestic security agenda inside Lithuania, as well as how Lithuania has contributed to European security as a whole.

The Helsinki Process

Having contributed significantly to the creation of pre-conditions for the emergence of mass movements for independence by pressing the Soviets to respect human rights and allow freedom in the exchange of information across and within state borders, the Helsinki Process also played a significant role in the withdrawal of Russian troops from Lithuania and the other Baltic States. Paul Cerjan, a former President of the National Defense University in the United States, has argued that these achievements have "earned a place in history as one of the most successful campaigns of the Cold War," as they laid the foundations of an acceptable framework for dialogue between the West and the East, which was accompanied by the "steady drumbeat of respect for human rights."[529] At its inception the major aim of the process was to abolish the Stalinist

---

528 Lithuania's Declaration of Independence explicitly mentioned the Helsinki process saying that "the Lithuanian state emphasizes its adherence to universally recognized principles of international law, recognizes the principles of the inviolability of borders as formulated in Helsinki in 1975 in the Final Act of the Conference on Security and Cooperation in Europe, and guarantees the rights of individuals, citizens and ethnic communities." See endnote 38 of the Chapter 5 for the full text of the Declaration.

529 Paul G. Cerjan, Foreword. In John Fry, *The Helsinki Process. Negotiating Security and Cooperation in Europe* (Washington: National Defense University Press, 1993), p. xii.

division of Europe, and it later became a major vehicle through which the CSCE built up moral pressure on the communist regimes in respect of human rights.[530] Its human dimension was reflected in the insistent demand that the Soviet authorities must respect fundamental human rights, including freedom of movement, and from 1975 onwards Western governments were able to urge the communist regimes to comply with the international agreement which had been signed by Leonid Brezhnev in Helsinki on August 1, 1975. It was a process of great significance and, indeed, Michael Novak, the American Ambassador who was the Head of the U.S. delegation to the CSCE Human Dimension Experts Meeting in Bern in 1986 (and who was Slovak by origin), has claimed that the Helsinki Process helped to dismantle the justifications advanced by the Soviet regime for devoting a disproportionate share of the national wealth to military purposes.[531] He pointed out that the CSCE had begun its existence in the search for collective security as "a child of the Cold War" which by the 1990s might seem to have become "in many ways a victim of its own success." Whatever truth these assertions may hold, it is still true to say, without doubt, that the multilateral diplomacy, it espoused through the Helsinki Process, became an important instrument in the eventual peaceful transformation of the Soviet Union.[532]

The first Helsinki Summit took place in 1975 and the second in 1992. A sequence of follow-up meetings between these dates helped develop the aim of opening up Soviet society and was successful in relaxing the military tension between the USSR and the Free World. Each CSCE follow-up meeting encouraged the Soviet government to take further specific steps toward complying with promises made during the signing of the Helsinki Final Act on freedom of movement and communication between East and West.[533]

---

530 "A club for all Europe. Don't build too much on the CSCE," *The Economist*, November 17, 1990.

531 Michael Novak, *Taking Glasnost Seriously. Toward an Open Soviet Union* (Washington: American Enterprise Institute for Public Policy Research, 1988), pp. 2-3.

532 Novak, *Taking Glasnost Seriously*, pp. 2-3.

533 "The long, slow, muddy road from Helsinki," *The Economist*, May 31, 1986.

A series of documents published by the organization reflected the process by which the experts of both sides progressively defined the fields of practical cooperation. The most significant of these were "Principles Guiding Relations Between Participating States," "Co-operation in the Field of Economics, of Science and Technology and of the Environment" and "Co-operation in Humanitarian and Other Fields." These achievements were all important milestones in the relaxation of East-West relations. Indeed, the Helsinki Process can now be interpreted as an extended institutionalized struggle for Western values, reflecting a cumulative process which enabled a progressive improvement of relationships and a validation of viewpoints, which if not wholeheartedly embraced by the *apparatchiks* of the Kremlin system, were fully appreciated, and absorbed by many in the populations of which they had so long been overlords.

Falk Lange has suggested that the Balts found in the Helsinki conferences "a forum for addressing their lawful claims" from the start.[534] The Baltic émigré organizations were to explore early on the opportunities, which the process offered for raising the question of Baltic freedom. At first, their efforts had little success, and indeed, during the first Helsinki Summit, the Soviets had successfully insisted that Baltic lobbyists were to be arrested upon arrival in Helsinki.[535] The Latvians Uldis Grava, Aina Teivens and Joseph Valiūnas, a Lithuanian, were subjected to this indignity, though they were eventually released after the intervention of the American Embassy in Helsinki. Yet, despite this promising intervention by the U.S. delegation at that conference, it still failed to keep the promise made on the eve of the proceedings to call for the independence of Lithuania, Latvia and Estonia.[536] Indeed, the Soviets repeatedly attempted to use the Helsinki Process to freeze the

---

534   Falk Lange, "The Baltic States and the CSCE," *Journal of Baltic Studies* 25, no. 3 (Fall 1994): 233–248.

535   Die Balten und die Sicherheitskonferenz. In *Mitteilungen aus dem baltischen Leben*, no. 3, September 1975, p. 6-10. Quote in Lange, "The Baltic States and the CSCE," pp. 233 – 248.

536   Die Balten und die Sicherheitskonferenz, p. 9. Quoted in Lange, "The Baltic States and the CSCE," pp. 233 – 248.

existing borders in Europe by advancing arguments for legitimiz-
ing the division of Germany, their occupation of certain Polish and
Romanian territories, and their incorporation of Lithuania, Latvia,
and Estonia into the Soviet Union. Yet, while the United States and
many other Western states failed to advance strong arguments for
the reversal of these historic injustices, they refused to renege on
their doctrine of non-recognition of the incorporation of the Baltic
States into the Soviet Union. However, while they did not provide
the support that the Baltic peoples had hoped for their case, at least
they did not concede the principle of the continuity of their sovereignty, which was eventually so crucial to their reassertion of national independence.[537]

John Hiden and Patrick Salmon have usefully argued that the
signing of the Helsinki Declaration on Human Rights by the Soviet
government in 1975 provoked a new wave of dissent inside the Soviet Empire.[538] They commented that Lithuania "produced more
dissident publications per capita than any other Soviet republic" in

---

537   President of the United States Gerald Ford stated before the beginning of these
negotiations (which involved all thirty-five states, signatories to the Helsinki
Agreements): "Specifically addressing the understandable concern about the
effect of the Helsinki Declarations on the Baltic nations, I can assure you, as
one who has long been interested in this question, that the United States has
never recognized the Soviet incorporation of Lithuania, Latvia, and Estonia
and is not doing so now". Quoted in *ELTA Information bulletin*, no. 4 (377)
(April 1990): 14.
   British Prime Minister Margaret Thatcher emphasized that the United Kingdom and other Western states had never recognized the illegal incorporation
of the Baltic States into the Soviet Union on multiple occasions. Later she said
at a Hoover Institution lunch in Washington in 1991: "In particular, we cannot
overlook or condone the disgraceful abuses of those rights which we've seen
in the Baltic States. These States were seized by the Soviet Union not by law
but by fraud and violence. That seizure has never been regarded as legal by
the West. We fully support the right of the Baltic States to determine their own
future. And we must make it clear to the Soviet Union that it is not a question
of whether they will be free — but only of when they will be free. And they
will — they will be free." Margaret Thatcher, Speech at Hoover Institution
Lunch, Four Seasons Hotel, Washington, D.C., March 8, 1991, http://www.ma
rgaretthatcher.org/Speeches/displaydocument.asp?docid=108264.
538   John Hiden, and Patrick Salmon, *The Baltic Nations and Europe. Estonia, Latvia
and Lithuania in the Twentieth Century* (London and New York: Longman, 1995).

the subsequent decade.[539] Indeed, a Lithuanian "Helsinki Group" established on November 25, 1976 by five underground activists became a focal point in the defense of human rights in the country.[540] Two intensive periods of its activity can be identified: the first, lasting from the establishment of the group until August 1977, when the authorities imprisoned Viktoras Petkus, its most active member.[541] The second began in 1979, when Father Bronius Laurinavičius joined the movement, and continued until 1981, when he was killed in a car accident.[542] The Group condemned the Soviet invasion of Afghanistan, protested against the deportation of Professor Andrei Sakharov, and forwarded appeals to the Soviet and German governments during the commemoration of the 40th anniversary of Molotov-Ribbentrop pact on August 23, 1979 requesting that they should denounce the Soviet-Nazi pact in order to bring final closure to its consequences. The membership of the Helsinki Group in Lithuania, included Nijolė Sadunaitė, Father Bronius Laurinavičius, Eitanas Finkelsteinas, Vytautas Vaičiūnas, Mečislovas Jurevičius, Balys Gajauskas, Povilas Pečeliūnas, Tomas Venclova and together they can be recognized as having pioneered the

---

539   Vytautas S. Vardys, "Lithuanian national politics," *Problems of Communism* 38, (July-August 1989): 54, quoted in Hiden, *The Baltic Nations and Europe.*

540   The Helsinki Group's founders were the dissident Viktoras Petkus, the writer Tomas Venclova (son of the famous communist writer Antanas Venclova), Farther Karolis Garuckas, a Catholic priest, and the Jewish scientist Eitanas Finkelsteinas.

541   Viktoras Petkus had received an earlier sentence of ten years at the age of 17 for his activities in the Catholic youth organization *Ateitis* (Future). Released in 1953 under the post-Stalin amnesty, he was sentenced again in 1957 "for disseminating anti-Soviet propaganda." See Richard Krickus, *Showdown. The Lithuanian Rebellion and the Breakup of the Soviet Empire* (Washington and London: Brassey's, 1997).

542   Farther Bronius Laurinavičius, a graduate of the University of Vilnius Faculty of Philosophy and Theology, was born in 1913 in the parish of Gervėčiai a Lithuanian area of Byelorussia. He joined the Lithuanian Helsinki Group following the death of Fr. Karolis Garuckas. Eventually the KGB followed him, and twice attempted to run him down. Not long before he was killed the Communist newspaper *Tiesa* (The Truth) published a paper attacking Father Laurinavičius for drawing schoolchildren into the Church. (See "On the "accidental" death of Helsinki Group member Rev. Laurinavičius," in Thomas Remeikis (ed.), *Violations of Human Rights in Soviet Occupied Lithuania. A Report for 1981* (London: The Lithuanian Association in Great Britain, 1982).

struggle against the communist empire.[543] Their appeal in respect of the Molotov-Ribbentrop pact was the forerunner of the world's largest-ever demonstration, the Baltic Way, ten years later.[544] The Soviet authorities continuously monitored and persecuted the members of the Group, but its activities and its persecution were reported regularly to the CSCE Human Rights Meetings by *Vyriausiasis Lietuvos Išlaisvinimo Komitetas* ("the Supreme Committee for the Liberation of Lithuania"), a Lithuanian émigré community organization, which also used these international opportunities to reflect on the independence issue as it affected all three Baltic countries.

Cardinal Vincentas Sladkevičius, MIC, Archbishop of Kaunas and Primate of the Catholic Church in Lithuania, once shrewdly observed that a major factor in Lithuania's liberation from the Soviet occupation was the way in which "the people and society themselves began to behave as if they were free."[545] Indeed, this attitude increasingly permeated the community, perhaps in reflection of the emphasis which Vytautas Landsbergis put on the most prominent element of his campaign through his insistence that the legal continuity of the Lithuanian state was unbroken. There was an increasing recognition that the Soviet system was weakening, and the Helsinki Process contributed to this significant achievement by pressing the Soviets to relax their regime. *Sąjūdis*, the Lithuanian Independence movement, could certainly not have emerged without the preliminary relaxation of the Soviet communist regime, which was in no small degree a consequence of the Helsinki Process. The role of international factors in the liberation of Lithuania from the Soviet occupation therefore interrelates and correlates with broader questions of how the Soviet collapse was linked to the end of the Cold War. Although most Sovietologists

---

543   See Vytautas S. Vardys, *Krikščionybė Lietuvoje* (Chicago: Lietuvos krikščionybės jubiliejaus komitetas, 1997).

544   Nijolė Sadūnaitė, a nun and Catholic activist, and the author of several books, the most prominent of which are "KGB akiratyje" (In the Focus of the KGB) and "Gerojo Dievo Globoje" (Under the Care of a Good God).

545   Lithuania's Cardinal Sladkevičius quoted in "Leidėjų žodis," publishers introduction, in Nijolė Sadūnaitė, *Gerojo Dievo Globoje* (Chicago: Ateitis, 1989), p. 5.

failed to perceive the impending Soviet collapse, many keen observers of Lithuanian origin, and notably the members of Lithuania's diplomatic service, were convinced that it would come. Even
as early as 1985 they knew that the foundations of the system were
crumbling.[546]

Michael Cox has concisely summarized the customary explanations for the end of the Cold War. The first was the role played
by Ronald Reagan's revitalization of the doctrine of containment.
He indicates that after 1985 the Kremlin, being confronted with the
U.S. Administration's determination to struggle for victory with
greater vigor than at any time since the Second World War was
"forced to the negotiating table."[547] However, the *Reaganauts* argue
that for "those of us honored to have served in his administration
the old formula of 'containment' was not satisfactory."[548] They insisted "on 'roll back' – a policy to force Soviet and Soviet proxy le-
gions out of areas they had already occupied or into which they

---

546 For example, Lithuanian diplomats Stasys Lozoraitis in Washington, and Bronius Balutis in London, predicted the eventual liberation of Lithuania and continuously worked towards this goal throughout their lives, embracing the
Lithuanian communities both in the USA and the UK. The American political
scientist Richard J. Krickus (who is a third generation American Lithuanian)
foresaw the collapse of the Soviet Union in a book written in the middle of the
1980s, see Richard J. Krickus, *The Superpowers in Crisis: Implications of Domestic
Discord* (Washington: Pergamon-Brassey's International Defense Publishers,
1987), p. 220. In addition, Professor Aleksandras Štromas, the political scientist
of Lithuanian origin, who had emigrated from the Soviet Union, organized an
international conference about the Soviet Union in Geneva in 1985, which delivered the main conclusion that the collapse of the Soviet Union is inevitable
and imminent. See proceedings of the conference: Alexander Shtromas, and
Morton A. Kaplan (eds.), *The Soviet Union and the Challenge of the Future* (New
York: Paragon House, 1988). Professor Walter Clemens (Boston and Harvard
Universities) also predicted the collapse of the Soviet Union. See his mono-
graphs, Walter Clemens, *The U.S.S.R. and Global Interdependence: Alternative Fu-
tures* (Washington, DC: American Enterprise Institute, 1978), Walter Clemens,
Can Russia Change? The USSR Confronts Global Interdependence (New York:
Routledge, 1990), Walter Clemens, *Baltic Independence and Russian Empire* (New
York: St. Martin's, 1991), Walter Clemens, *Dynamics of International Relations:
Conflict and Mutual Gain in an Era of Global Interdependence* (Lanham: Rowman
& Littlefield, 1998).

547 Michael Cox, "Rethinking the End of The Cold War," *Review of International
Studies* 20, no. 2 (1994): 187-200.

548 Linas J. Kojelis, "He liberated the World: the global legacy of Ronald Reagan,"
June 28, 2004.

were expanding *worldwide*."[549] On the other hand, some other scholars have suggested that Reagan's hawkish policies may have slowed down the collapse,[550] but Professor Laurence Freedman has suggested that the "new German issue" which followed the collapse of the Berlin Wall, and the rise of "the new Right" in Europe were further factors. He pointed out, however, that these explanations have a certain cause and effect relationship.[551] Some argued that the role of Mikhail Gorbachev, the new Secretary of the Soviet Communist Party, was particularly important as well. They believed that since he was much younger than his predecessors, he wished to change the face of the Soviet system. Although the extent of his contribution will long be debated, it is likely that it may have been more ambiguous then has been widely recognized. Certainly, Vytautas Landsbergis' comments in his memoirs provide a stimulating alternative to many widely held views, revealing Gorbachev's actions as being directed to the preservation of the Soviet Empire.[552] What however is certain, that his policy of *glasnost* was, as Michael Novak put it, "taken seriously by the West." Once the concept was in the public realm, the United States and other Western democracies pressed the Soviet authorities to stick to the words about *glasnost* and *perestroika* particularly seriously. The tool was ready and "the Helsinki Process helped to turn the promises into reality."[553] However, it is important to point out that the Lithuanian nation itself, both the major part in the occupied country and the smaller Lithuanian expatriate community in the West, played a vitally important role in the Soviet collapse. Alfred Senn has

---

549   Kojelis, "He liberated the World."

550   Richard Davy (ed.), *European Détente: A Reappraisal* (London: Royal Institute of International Affairs, 1992); Vojtech Mastny (ed.) *The Helsinki Process and the Reintegration of Europe: 1989-1991. Analysis and Documentation* (Wahington: the National Academies Press, 1992).

551   See, e.g., Lawrence Freedman (ed.) *Europe Transformed: Documents on the End of the Cold War* (New York: St. Martin's Press, 1990 and Michael Cox, "After Stalinism: The Extreme Right in Russia, East Germany and Eastern Europe," in Paul Hainsworth (ed.), *The Extreme Right in Europe and the USA* (London: Pinter, 1992).

552   Vytautas Landsbergis, *Lithuania Independent Again* (Cardiff: University of Wales Press, 2000).

553   Novak, *Taking Glasnost Seriously.*

described its national stance as having been "the nut that Gorbachev was unable to crack,"[554] and it is a matter of historical fact that the country's Declaration of Independence influenced the Latvians and Estonians to follow the example set. Later the Ukrainians, the Byelorussians, and finally even the Russians themselves followed. Even some East Germans have said they were inspired by Lithuanian actions when they set out to break down the Berlin Wall because they were less afraid when they saw how a small nation had rebelled against its oppressor so bravely. It was indeed a matter of note for many other nations when Lithuania's population stood up peacefully before the colossus of the Soviet Union, and defiantly announced "We are a free people."

The Helsinki Process helped to pave the way for the peaceful revolutions that took place in the Soviet Empire. While the debates in the security arena emphasized questions of confidence building and military transparency, the persistence with which the 'Baltic issue' was raised ensured that this agenda did not avoid questions of territorial integrity, self-determination, or peaceful border changes through negotiations. The cumulative effect of this was vital and it is reflected in the fact that respect for the fundamental Helsinki principles was embodied in the formulations adopted by Lithuania's Declaration of Independence, passed on March 11, 1990, the phrasing of which included the sentence:

> The State of Lithuania stresses its adherence to universally recognized principles of international law, recognizes the principle of inviolability of borders as formulated in the Final Act of the Conference on Security and Co-operation in Europe in Helsinki in 1975, and guarantees human, civil, and ethnic community rights.[555]

It was in this way that the Lithuanians demonstrated that they viewed the Helsinki Process as a tool for peaceful change in Europe. They had benefited from its deliberations and so were prepared to capture a tide which was now flowing rapidly toward the

---

554   Alfred Senn, *Gorbachev's Failure in Lithuania* (New York: St. Martin's Press, 1995).

555   Act on the Re-establishment of the State of Lithuania. In *The Road to Negotiations with the U.S.S.R.* (Vilnius: Supreme Council of the Republic of Lithuania, 1990), p. 164.

reunification of Germany, the independence of the Baltic States, and the dismantling of the Soviet Empire. The White House in Washington had already hinted that the Helsinki Process might become one of the tools for a peaceful resolution of the issues from the restoration of Lithuanian state to the withdrawal of Russian troops. The first White House statement made after Lithuania's Declaration of Independence which declared that the "United States believes it is in the mutual interest of Lithuania, the Soviet Union, and all CSCE countries to resolve this issue peacefully."[556]

Joining the CSCE

The wish for full participation in the thirty-five-nation Conference on Security and Co-operation in Europe became an immediate priority for the foreign policy of Lithuania and her neighbors after the restoration of independence.[557] This move was an extension of the search for international recognition, as the normalization of their international relations was symbolic of the "return to Europe," but membership in international organizations was also a practical step which would assist in obtaining "international tools" for the increase in the security of these still vulnerable democracies. Lithuania's Parliament and Government perceived their country's participation in the Helsinki Process both as a logical continuation of the achievement of an independent state and then as an instrument for ensuring the withdrawal of the Soviet Army from its territory. Active diplomatic attempts to gain observer status in the CSCE were therefore initiated soon after the Declaration of Independence. Though these efforts were not rewarded with early success, this recognition was soon accorded once diplomatic relations were renewed.

To mark the 51st anniversary of the Molotov-Ribbentrop pact, *Sąjūdis* organized a major event on August 23-24, 1990, "The Way

---

556 "Statement by the Press Secretary," Office of the Press Secretary, the White House, March 11, 1990. See special issue: "Lithuanians Declare Independence. March 11, 1990" *Lituanus* 36, no. 2 (1990): 13.

557 Česlovas Stankevičius, "Baltijos šalių nepriklausomybė ir Europos saugumas," *Lietuvos Aidas*, May 30, 1990, pp. 1-2.

to Europe" rally at Lazdijai, near the Lithuanian-Polish border, in the form of a weekend camp. It ended with a demonstration and an attempt to cross the Polish border, which was then still patrolled on the Lithuanian side by troops under the command of the Soviet Army and the KGB.[558] Despite this, the local border-control staff was persuaded to allow the participants to cross into Poland, and then to return, without formal permission from the Soviet authorities. The symbolic importance of this was huge. It meant that this "Soviet border" (as it was deemed by the Kremlin) had been crossed by the Lithuanians in large numbers without reference to their alleged authority. Many Lithuanian MPs, Lithuanian and foreign academics, and several highly influential commentators had been invited to this "European week," at which lectures, and seminars were given on Lithuania's European roots and the European aspirations of its people. This "first time event" was therefore heralded as a significant triumph and received widespread and favorable publicity. Soon after it, the Baltic Council made a statement "On the future political resolution of the German problem and the development of the Helsinki Process," which invited the United States, the United Kingdom, France, and particularly the USSR, "as the victors of the Second World War, to make determined efforts to help resolve the Baltic and German problems via the Helsinki Process." The basis of its argument was that a Second World War occupation persisted for the Baltic nations, thus the Baltic leaders invited the victors of the Second World War to use their meetings not only to solve the problem of German reunification, but to restore the independence of their three countries at the same time.

At a meeting with the Baltic leaders in Moscow on May 12, 1990, Secretary Baker had promised American support in their quest for CSCE membership.[559] However, the built-in contradictions of the Helsinki Process related to the decision making which requires so many members with different political systems, both democracies and totalitarian states, to find a consensus for common

---

558   "Kelias į Europą prasidėjo," *Lietuvos Aidas*, August 24, 1990, p. 1; "Mes turim grįžti į Europą," *Lietuvos Aidas*, August 24, 1990, pp.1-2.
559   Stankevičius, "Baltijos šalių nepriklausomybė," pp. 1-2.

policies, became more apparent, even before the Copenhagen "Human Dimension" meeting of the CSCE in June 1990. Thus, the request of the Baltic Foreign Ministers for their countries to be given observer status was politely denied. This occurred even though Lithuania and the other Baltic states had been invited as guests by Denmark.[560] It was a rebuff, as an earlier application by Lithuania had been rejected, on the grounds that it would not get the necessary consensus from the thirty-five CSCE *members because of Soviet objections*. Nevertheless, that status was promptly granted to Albania.

However, all the signatories to the 1975 Helsinki Final Act, the Soviet Union and the United States being among them, now committed themselves to "respect the equal rights of peoples and their right to self-determination." When the Baltic issue was raised, despite the "new style" in which the Soviets spoke, they acted exactly as their precursors had done. Their Deputy Foreign Minister Vladimir Petrovski indeed even used the occasion to advise that the Baltic States had "no legal grounds" for requesting such membership "because they are part of the Soviet Union."[561] At a joint Press Conference on June 28 the question was asked as to whether the Soviet blockade against the Lithuanian people was a violation of human rights, and thus worthy of extensive discussion at the CSCE Conference. In responding, the Soviet Ambassador, Yuri Reshetov, again resorted to the traditional "Big Lie" routines, by accusing the Baltic Governments of large-scale "violations of human rights," "segregation policies," and "the plundering of state property." He insisted, against the evidence, that no "economic blockade" had been imposed on Lithuania, saying rather that "certain economic measures" had been undertaken, and went on to deny that Lithuania's 1940 annexation had been carried out by force.[562] Despite this crude filibustering the Baltic cause received verbal support from the United States at the succeeding Copenhagen meeting. On June

---

560   Lennart Meri, Foreign Minister of Estonia; Janis Jurkans, Foreign Minister of Latvia; and Algirdas Saudargas, Foreign Minister of Lithuania.
561   A press briefing in Copenhagen on June 8, 1990.
562   For more about the "economic blockade" see Chapter 5.

6 U.S. Secretary of State James A. Baker expressed concern over Soviet policy in the Baltic States, and at the plenary session on June 12 the American Ambassador Max Kampelman elaborated on this by making a strong statement in favor for freedom of the Baltic States. Later, on June 14, 1990, John Evans, another American delegate, reminded the participants that it was 50 years ago "to the day" that the Soviet Union had occupied the Baltic States. He added that he wished to remind the Soviet Union that Principle Five of the 1975 Helsinki Accords stated that "no country shall occupy another or use direct or indirect force against another state, and that any occupation or acquisition of another state by force would not be recognized as having legal effect." Later, on June 27, the Deputy Head of the U.S. Delegation Jane Fisher criticized Soviet restrictions on travel to the Baltic States.

Yet, while the United States was playing this close game, important support was also given by delegates from the smaller countries, in particular Iceland, whose Foreign Minister Jon Baldvin Hannibalsson had said on June 6 that any use of force by the Soviets against the Baltic States could endanger further general progress towards European security. He then emphasized that the only solution to the Baltic problem compatible with the Helsinki Process was "full recognition of these nations' right to independence." Further help came from the other Scandinavian nations when shortly thereafter Kjell Magne Bondevik, Norway's Foreign Minister, invited the Baltic Foreign Ministers to Oslo on June 9 where they were received together with representatives of the Baltic World Council. During these discussions Kjell Magne Bondevik announced that he would take responsibility for raising the question of Baltic observer status before the next CSCE Conference, which was planned for late November in Paris. He was confident that this request would now be granted and promised that the Baltic issue would also be raised at the next Nordic Council meeting.[563] On June 12 Uffe Elleman-Jensen, Denmark's Foreign Minister, expressed similar sentiments when he received the Baltic Foreign Ministers and other

---

563   The Nordic Council comprises Iceland, Norway, Denmark, Sweden, and Finland.

representatives in a private audience. He emphasized the international importance of the restoration of their independence and recalled that Denmark had never recognized the legality of the occupation. He now promised Denmark's wholehearted support for the Baltic effort to gain observer status with the CSCE and discussed economic assistance for Lithuania in positive terms.

Further support for the independence of the Baltic States and their admission to CSCE membership was voiced by the Austrian, British, Canadian, Dutch, Irish and other delegates. On July 19, Lithuania, Latvia, and Estonia applied once again for observer status at a CSCE preparatory meeting in Vienna. The request was signed on behalf of the three states by Estonian Minister Endel Lipmaa, who informed the meeting that the Baltic States saw "no alternative" to full independence from the Soviet Union. It was by now an appeal to a sympathetic audience, which was well-informed of the human rights issues and the legal grounds of the claim for renewed independence. Only a few days earlier on June 15, 1990, Steny H. Hoyer, Co-Chairman of the U.S. Helsinki Commission, had told the Copenhagen Conference that:

> The CSCE as an institution must also take a stand. Human dignity, tolerance, mutual respect – let these enduring and fundamental values be our standards as we enter the 1990s, a decade in which the number of participating CSCE states will grow. Lithuania, Latvia, Estonia, and Albania have all expressed an interest in participating in the CSCE. We welcome their request to join in our ongoing search for security and co-operation among states, and in developing policies, which guarantee the rights of communities and individuals.[564]

This promising statement was evidence that the ground was beginning to move, and the signs became even more promising when the question of why the Baltic States had not yet been granted CSCE observer status was raised in the U.S. Congress Helsinki Commission Hearing, which was held in Washington on July 18. At this meeting Ambassador Max Kampelman, Chairman of the American Delegation at Copenhagen, presented a written report

---

[564]   "Hoyer welcomes Baltic countries to CSCE," *ELTA information bulletin*, no. 8 (382), August 1990, p. 17.

which mentioned the visit of the Baltic Foreign Ministers. Notifying his listeners that observer status was impossible without a full consensus of CSCE members, he announced that the U.S. delegation had expressed its hope that the Baltic States would one day be able to take part in CSCE conferences.

At this congressional hearing Ambassador Kampelman answered questions from Senators Alfonse D'Amato, Dennis DeConcini, Frank Lautenberg, and Congressman Steny Hoyer. His replies disclosed that he had asked the Danish Secretary General to distribute the Baltic letter requesting observer status to all 35 participating delegations. This had been done despite strong Soviet objections. He then indicated regret that the Baltic Foreign Ministers had not yet raised the question of observer status, either with him directly or with the other members of the American delegation. After he had spoken, the Commission called Dr. Kazys Bobelis, Vice-Chairman of the Baltic World Council and Chairman of the Supreme Committee for the Liberation of Lithuania, who provided a Lithuanian perspective on the Copenhagen meeting, expressing gratitude to the U.S. Delegation for its "compassion and assistance," and complimenting the host country Denmark for the way in which it had responded to the NGOs which he represented. Then, after voicing "great disappointment" that the conference had failed to discuss Mikhail Gorbachev's "blatant human rights violations" in Lithuania, he criticized its consequent "deviations from the rules of procedure," drawing attention to the fact that Albania's request for observer status had been placed on the agenda without previous consultation and granted with little discussion despite its having "one of the most abysmal human rights records in Europe." He pointed out that Lithuania's parallel request had been denied, with no explanation being given.[565] Dr. Bobelis suggested that there were obvious contradictions, and appealed to the U.S. Government "not to inflate Mr. Gorbachev's importance in the changes taking place throughout Eastern Europe and the Soviet Union," but rather to begin a dialogue with the democratic leaders of the newly elected

---

565   "Balts receive CSCE moral support, but no observer status," *ELTA Information bulletin*, no. 8 (382), (August 1990), p. 16.

governments in Lithuania, Latvia and Estonia, and even in the Russian Republic, beginning with immediate recognition of Lithuania's claim to independence.[566]

Dr. Bobelis' contribution reflected a wider concern about the impediment to recognition then being experienced by each of the Baltic nations. A complementary incident occurred during the Paris CSCE Summit in 1991 when Mikhail Gorbachev threatened to leave the hall unless the Baltic Foreign Ministers, who had been invited to Paris as guests of the French Government, left the meeting. The French hosts had responded by asking the Baltic delegates to leave the Conference. It was a significant moment, and the problem of the Baltic States at this time was later described by Professor François Thom who wrote sharply:

> The Baltic representatives were subjected to a shameful treatment ... We talk about the common European home, but it is managed by the Soviets... Instead of taking advantage of our privileged political position as leaders, we are trying to augment our generosity with redoubled servitude: the more we finance the Soviet Union, the more we bow to the Soviet dictated position.
>
> This paradox is especially obvious in the French position... Before us is a strange picture of Europe, one part of which is trying to free itself from the Soviet regime, while the other one is trying to prop it up, to ensure its existence, sometimes even resorting to dishonorable actions which we are witnessing. Freedom is not something that is given once for perpetuity. History shows that the slide to slavery often begins with actions of cowardice that appear to be innocent.[567]

British Prime Minister Margaret Thatcher spoke at the summit and her words reinforced this theme, although perhaps more ambiguously:

> Now that democracy is returning to Eastern Europe, those national feelings are surfacing as people regain pride in their own country. And with them are reappearing problems of minorities and of people and nations who have been divided or annexed as a result of the territorial changes of the 1930s and 1940s. And we need to have in mind the particular position of the Baltic Republics. We welcome the fact that negotiations have started between

---

566   "Balts receive CSCE moral support," p. 16.
567   "Balts receive CSCE moral support," p. 16.

them, and the Soviet government and we hope for a successful outcome acceptable to both sides.[568]

Indeed, but the Soviets were only "playing at" negotiations at this time, and the real outcome was the attempted communist *coup d'état*, and the tragic January events which were described in the previous chapter.

The ambiguous situation continued with only little relief in the waiting period when, despite Soviet objections, Lithuania was invited as a guest of Poland to the CSCE cultural conference held in Krakow. The blockage reflected the standing regulations of the CSCE which required a total consensus among the members when issues of membership were being voted upon. This system would not in fact even permit the question of Baltic membership to be opened up until the existence of Lithuania and the other Baltic States as independent states had been reconfirmed by formal international recognition. Only when the coup had failed in the Kremlin could this process begin to take off, and it was then when the diplomatic relations were renewed, that Lithuania and the other Baltic States were invited to take up CSCE membership. Even at that stage a small but real doubt about the eligibility of Lithuania, Latvia, and Estonia for CSCE membership was raised, when the Head of the U.S. delegation to the CSCE unexpectedly asked: 'Where does Europe end?'

On September 10, 1991 the three Baltic States were at last admitted to full membership in the CSCE, ironically enough, during the CSCE Conference on the Human Dimension held in Moscow.[569] Algirdas Saudargas, Lithuania's Foreign Minister, marked the occasion by thanking those who had given consistent support to his country, and to Latvia and Estonia, and expressed his readiness to sign the Helsinki Final Act and the Paris Charter for a New Europe

---

568   Margaret Thatcher, Speech at Paris CSCE Summit, Kleber Centre, Paris, November 19, 1990, http://www.margaretthatcher.org/Speeches/displaydocument.asp?docid=108250.

569   "ESB konferencija Maskvoje," *Lietuvos Aidas*, September 10, 1991, p. 1.

on behalf of Lithuania.[570] A month after this Lithuania and the other Baltic States finally became signatories to the Helsinki Final Act on October 15, and when this was done, Vytautas Landsbergis said that the ultimate restoration of his country and the other two Baltic States to full independence had been intrinsic to the whole Helsinki Process. He added that Lithuania's major foreign policy goal was now to ensure the final withdrawal of the Soviet Army from its soil.[571] Before the end of the year Lithuania and the other Baltic States also became signatories of the Charter of Paris for a New Europe. This was achieved on December 6, 1991 and represented a final step in the joining of the Helsinki process.[572]

The withdrawal of former Soviet troops

The major security problem left for Lithuania at the close of 1991 was, as Vytautas Landsbergis had declared, the withdrawal of the former Soviet Army from the country's soil. This was achieved with great difficulty on Lithuania's side and with great resistance on the Russian side. Česlovas Stankevičius, who chaired the Lithuanian

---

570   See Algirdas Saudargas, "Jau ne svečiai," *Lietuvos Aidas*, September 18, 1991, p. 1. In recognition of the historic changes taking place in Europe effecting the end of the Cold War, and the role of the Helsinki process in bringing them about, the CSCE convened a summit of its Heads of State or Government in Paris in November 19-21, 1990. Its final document, known as "The Charter of Paris for a New Europe," established the framework for the conduct of North Atlantic-Eurasian relations for the foreseeable future. See also Erika B. Schlager, "The Challenges of Change: An Introduction on Helsinki-II," in Arie Bloed (ed.), *The Challenges of change. The Helsinki Summit of the CSCE and its Aftermath* (Dordrecht: Martinus Nijhoff Publishers, 1994), p. 3.

571   "Siekimas tiesos. Vytauto Landsbergio kalba pasirašius Helsinkio susitarimo Baigiamąjį aktą," *Lietuvos Aidas*, 16 October 1991, p. 1; "Helsinkis, 1991 spalio 15," *Lietuvos Aidas*, October 17, 1991, p. 1. "Svarbiausias Lietuvos užsienio politikos uždavinys. Lietuvos užsienio reikalų ministras Algirdas Saudargas šnekasi su korespondentu Virginijum Kizu," *Lietuvos Aidas*, October 18, 1991, p. 1.

572   The Charter was effectively an attempt to "codify" the process of democratization of Eastern and Central European societies by providing a political framework to guide its progress. It attempted to "institutionalize" aspects of the Helsinki process, and marked the end of the division of Germany, and of the Cold War. See G. J. Tanja, "Peaceful Settlement of Disputes within the Framework of the CSCE: a Legal Novelty in a Political – Diplomatic Environment," in Bloed, *The Challenges of change*, pp. 73 – 74.

delegation, rightly observed that "the negotiations were the main and essential means which helped achieve an orderly withdrawal of the occupation forces from Lithuania and the other Baltic States."[573] Two factors framed this process, of which the first was the continued firmness of the Lithuanian leadership in its position that "in negotiations with Russia, Lithuania preserved to the very end the principle that the obligation to withdraw the occupation troops from Lithuania immediately was not an object for negotiations [...] This was considered an absolute and unconditional international obligation of Russia which sprang from the violation of international law committed by the Soviet Union; i.e., Lithuania's occupation. Therefore, Lithuania negotiated with Russia not on whether the Soviet troops would be removed, but only on the timetable and procedure of the withdrawal."[574] The second was the

---

573 Česlovas Stankevičius, "Enhancing Security of Lithuania and Other Baltic States in 1992-94 and Future Guidelines," NATO Research Fellowship report, http://www.nato.int/acad/fellow/94-96/stankevi/01.htm. He explains that "the issue of negotiations encompasses several stages and aspects: initiation of negotiations and international assistance facilitating the negotiations; legal and political positions of the negotiating parties and crucial differences between them; transparency during negotiations and international assistance in the course of negotiations; negotiation outcomes and the procedure of the withdrawal of the armed forces; and the attention shown by the international community."

574 Stankevičius, "Enhancing Security of Lithuania." www.nato.int/acad/fellow/94-96/stankevi/summ.htm. Česlovas Stankevičius explains that "in the signed agreements with Russia on the withdrawal of the occupation troops Lithuania did not grant any temporary legal status to these troops and did not recognize them as a legal subject. Until the very moment of their withdrawal, the presence of the occupation troops on the Lithuanian territory was illegal." He further emphasizes, that "during negotiations Lithuania did not recognize any rights to these occupation forces to the buildings or any other real estate used or built by them in Lithuania." It is interesting to note that "during the negotiations on the procedure of removal of the occupation troops, Lithuania claimed reimbursement for the damage sustained to Lithuania and its citizens during the occupation" and that "the Lithuanian citizens demanded compensation for this damage at a referendum in 1992." This demand was also included in the official Interpretative Statement of Lithuania attached to the 1992 Helsinki Summit Declaration. Russia has not denied Lithuania's right to them but during negotiations no agreements were signed on the procedure of damages. However, "Lithuania has not abrogated its claim, thus the claim remains valid," stated Dr. Česlovas Stankevičius. See Stankevičius, "Enhancing Security of Lithuania."

growing support of the international community for this common objective of all the Baltic States and the existence of the European and transatlantic security framework, including the continuing multilateral diplomacy of the CSCE.[575] Despite these convergent factors the Russian army did not finally leave Lithuania until August 31, 1993. However, this was a whole year earlier than its departure from Latvia, Estonia, Germany, and Poland.

The explanation of why the Russians left Lithuania first embraces a few major factors but it is not unrealistic to say that it was an achievement which can be attributed to the firm leadership of the negotiating team headed by the President of the Lithuanian Parliament Vytautas Landsbergis, his deputy Dr. Česlovas Stankevičius, Foreign Minister Algirdas Saudargas and his deputy Dr. Gediminas Šerkšnys. Anatol Lieven has claimed that the Russian Army left the Baltic States because its military commanders so decided in St. Petersburg in 1992. [576] This interpretation contradicts the actual events, which suggest that the Russians attempted to stay as long as possible. Despite the fact an agreement with Russia on the procedure and deadlines of withdrawal of the troops from Lithuania was reached on September 8, 1992, Russia attempted to avoid its completion until August 1993 by seeking to legalize the presence of the withdrawing troops and by exerting pressure, suspending the troop withdrawal and applying other measures.[577] They certainly wished to retain their military bases in the Baltic States and would have stayed even longer if they had not been urgently pressed to go home by the international community. Help from the United States was particularly important. President Bill Clinton recalls in his memoirs about July 1994:

> In early July, I returned to Europe for the G-7 summit in Naples. On the way, I stopped in Riga, Latvia, to meet with the leaders of the Baltic states and celebrate the withdrawal of Russian troops from Lithuania and Latvia, a

575   See Darius Furmonavičius, "The Northern European Security Community," *Lithuanian Papers* 10 (1996): 16.

576   Anatol Lieven, "The Baltic iceberg dead ahead: NATO beware," *The World Today* 52 (July 1996): 176.

577   Stankevičius, "Enhancing Security of Lithuania," www.nato.int/acad/fellow/94-96/stankevi/summ.htm.

move we had helped to speed up by providing a large number of housing vouchers for Russian officers who wanted to go home. There were still Russian troops in Estonia, and President Lennart Meri, a filmmaker who had always opposed Russian domination of his country, was determined to get them out as soon as possible. After the meeting there was a moving celebration in Riga's Freedom Square, where I was welcomed by about forty thousand people waving flags in gratitude for America 's steadfast support of their newfound freedom.578

The Latvians and Estonians managed to agree on the deadline of the withdrawal one year later than the Lithuanians, on August 31, 1994. In the agreements with Latvia and Estonia, Russia succeeded in achieving some significant concessions of recognition of some temporary legal status for the troops as well as certain rights of the occupational forces to the real estate. Russia succeeded in receiving Latvia's concession to allow Russia to exploit the Skrunda military radar station until the end of 1998 and in agreements with Latvia and Estonia "Russia succeeded in establishing certain rights and privileges for the military pensioners left in these two countries."579 Lithuania in particular had insisted on pursuing an extremely active foreign policy toward this goal, and the withdrawal of the Russian Army "as soon as possible," and certainly before there was any chance of a "second coup in Moscow." It was the undeniable priority of Lithuanian national security policy from the outset, and it was pursued with single-minded determination.580 Every single document signed by the Lithuanians with Russia at that time contained carefully thought through paragraphs excluding any possibility for the inaccurate interpretation of what was achieved during the negotiation process.581

The situation regarding the Soviet Army was explosive. Lithuania was in a hurry to avoid the development of any situation in which relationships with the Russians might deteriorate. At one

---

578   Bill Clinton, *My Life* (London: Hutchinson, 2004), p. 607.
579   Stankevičius, "Enhancing Security of Lithuania," www.nato.int/acad/fellow/94-96/stankevi/summ.htm.
580   Vytautas Landsbergis, "Lietuva ir Maskva," *Lietuvos Aidas*, October 9, 1993, p. 5.
581   See NATO Research Fellowship report by former Minister of Defense Česlovas Stankevičius, "Enhancing Security of Lithuania," www.nato.int/acad/fellow/94-96/stankevi/summ.htm.

point, the Russians explained their inertia on the matter by claiming that they were unable to exercise control over the still considerable body of Soviet forces stationed in the Baltic territories, and such an alarming scenario was all too feasible as there was active memory among older citizens of similar things happening between 1919 and 1921. The truth is that the Soviet Army was the relic of a now no-longer-existing state. Even though the new Russian state had assumed responsibility for it, the relationship was an uneasy one and was fraught with very great difficulties because the new economic exigencies of the "new Russia" raised questions even about its ability to pay military salaries.

In this context, Lithuania's immediate tactic was to press for Russia to accept full legal responsibility for the troops stationed in the Baltic States, though Yeltsin was wary of the proposition. He was fully aware of the links between the leaders of the army and the men who had designed the failed *coup d'état*, and it was by no means clear that his own position in Russia would remain secure if a second communist coup were to be attempted by the military chiefs of staff of the Northwestern army in the Baltics. In the end, however during a visit by Landsbergis to Moscow, he finally agreed to take these troops under Russian jurisdiction. Landsbergis has since recalled how his "slow process of persuasion" was eventually rewarded by an agreement. This accord was finally signed in Moscow on September 8, 1992.

The story behind the treaty is of major importance. The process which led to it had received a solid background on June 14, 1992, when a referendum was held in Lithuania on two questions: first, "Should the Russian military forces have been withdrawn from our country before the end of the year?", and second, "Should the Government of Lithuania seek reparations for the damage done during the Soviet occupation?" The nation had answered both questions in the affirmative. "This "double Yes" response," as Landsbergis described it, "obviously strengthened our position because international pressure for the withdrawal of foreign forces from all three Baltic States became much more obvious in the weeks which followed."[582]

Lithuania now won its biggest diplomatic victory since regaining independence. This occurred when the CSCE at its summit meeting in Helsinki on July 9-10, 1992, called firmly for the early withdrawal of Russian troops from Estonia, Latvia, and Lithuania. The CSCE Final Act, Article 15 had explicitly mentioned "the stationing of foreign armed forces on the territories of the Baltic States," as a "problem to be resolved." Its formulation was discussed in the Baltic Independent, a Vilnius newspaper, as follows:

> Even where violence has been contained, the sovereignty and independence of some States still needs to be upheld. We express support for efforts by CSCE participating States to remove, in a peaceful manner and through negotiations, the problems that remain from the past, like the stationing of foreign armed forces on the territories of the Baltic States without the required consent of those countries. Therefore, in line with basic principles of international law and in order to prevent any possible conflict, we call on the participating States concerned to conclude without delay appropriate bilateral agreements, including timetables, for the early, orderly and complete withdrawal of such foreign troops from the territories of the Baltic States.[583]

The importance of this declaration is emphasized by the fact that this was the single specific issue to be highlighted in the final document. It was agreed to by all members of the CSCE except for Yugoslavia which was excluded from the organization at that moment because of the continuing Bosnia-Herzegovina war. The issue of the troops was placed on the agenda after four months of intense negotiations in Helsinki by the senior Lithuanian officials in the teeth of highly vigorous opposition from Russia, which had made strong objections to Article 15 from the drafting stage onward by urging that this issue should be regarded as a purely bilateral matter rather than one with an international dimension. The Russian representatives had consistently attempted to demand that there should be no reference either to the context of international law, nor explicit mention of Russia itself. However, the effort put in was not entirely fruitless, because this position was finally relinquished

---

only days before the summit began. To offer a compromise to the Russians, the name of the occupying country was not mentioned in the text of the Final Act.

At the end of the conference, confusion continued to surround the CSCE stance on Yugoslavia, but the Baltic States were able to celebrate a diplomatic victory over Russia. A last-minute compromise had been arranged by which the Kremlin succeeded in having the wording softened so that the term "violation" had been replaced. This blunted appeal called on the Baltic States, and an unnamed third country, to act in respect of basic principles of international law. The somewhat elliptical prose which this compromise embedded, however, gave the Lithuanian leader Vytautas Landsbergis an opportunity to score a most successful point for the Baltic States. Confessing himself to be fascinated by what he called the "diplomatic metalanguage" of the document, he asked ironically if the reference to "all parties concerned" might mean that Lithuania should withdraw its troops from its neighbors' territory. It was unfortunate that his remarks were being made at a moment when the arrival of Milan Panic, the new Yugoslav premier, distracted from his statement. It was therefore not widely reported in the media, yet it was not without effect, as must have been noted by some at the gathering. Landsbergis had gone on to say that Lithuania regarded the formulation of "bilateral agreements" (as used in the text) to mean agreements concluded with Russia alone as it was her troops which were present on Lithuanian soil and "not with Latvia or Estonia, who have no armed forces in Lithuania." The point was quite clear, and at the final ceremony of the gathering he reinforced it further by taking advantage of a procedural device already deployed by the United States at the first Helsinki Conference to protect its policy of not recognizing the Soviet annexation of the Baltic States by adding an interpretative statement. This read: "This situation is not anonymous. It did not arise from nowhere. It came from the state whose rights and obligations were assumed by Russia when it was admitted into the UN."[584] It was a further maneuver to

---

584   *The Baltic Independent*, July 17 - 23, 1992, p. 8.

ensure that the Russians could not continue to evade their obligations.

The Baltic States under Lithuanian leadership now threatened to veto the Summit 's final declaration if their concerns remained unmet. They received strong moral support from Sweden in this and were encouraged by the attitudes struck at the G-7 Summit in Munich which had preceded the Helsinki meeting, and which had supported the legitimate Baltic aspirations. Despite earlier differences over how hard they should press their case, the three Baltic countries were now obviously acting together. Carl Bildt, the Swedish Prime Minister, confirmed their stance by saying "when we call for the conclusion 'without delay' of bilateral agreements on the 'early, orderly, and complete' withdrawal of (the Russian) forces, we do so in the interest of the stability of all of Europe."[585] However, in responding to them, the Russian leader Boris Yeltsin launched a counter attack which replicated elements of the former Soviet propaganda, which again had discerned Baltic nationalism as being "aggressive." He said:

> aggressive nationalism is now replacing the ideological confrontation of the past. This disease may become the real plague of the twenty-first century. For many years it was demanded that Russia observe human rights. Now Russia itself demands it. We see several countries are strengthening provisions that establish standards of discrimination along ethnic lines. We decisively reject such actions because they infringe on the interests of millions of our fellow-Russians.[586]

These words had dampened the mood of the gathering, as Yeltsin's speech made no mention of troop withdrawal. Instead, an attack had been launched on the newly invited independent Baltic States, accusing them of abusing the human rights of their Russian inhabitants. From the Baltic nations' point of view his speech carried all the implications of psychological reversal which a lawyer might observe in the behavior of an abusive relationship where the abuser accuses the abused of carrying the responsibility for the attacks which have occurred. "Such an approach is alien to the

---

585   *Baltic Independent*, p. 8.
586   *Baltic Independent*, p. 8.

elementary norms of our civilization," Yeltsin had said, appealing to the benchmark concept of "reasonable human behavior" but projecting it onto the Baltic nations (each of whom had lost whole swathes of their population during the deportations to Siberian concentration camps, and whose freedoms had been crushed for decades by Soviet Russian communist oppression). But his aides went even further than the Russian leader himself, expressing criticism of the Baltic governments' treatment of Russians in the region as being "a cause of constant concern for the Russian President personally, and the Russian Parliament," accusing them of the abuse of civil rights of their compatriots, in contradiction of the great effort which all three Baltic States were taking to ensure the rule of law and an impartial protection of the rights of all ethnic groups after the pattern of the conventions to the United Nations and other international bodies to which they were newly subscribed, and of the European Union to which they were all aspirant.[587]

The harsh Russian propaganda was echoed by Yedinstvo in Lithuania and the Interfronts, the Russian organizations in the other Baltic States, which remained what could still be called "pro-Soviet." The fact that these statements were being made by the Russian Foreign Ministry gave them credence, which was reinforced by the publication of a "White Book." It contained a few biographies of Russians who were allegedly being discriminated against in the Baltic States, and an unattributed Soviet-style "history of the Estonian SSR" which claimed that the country had belonged to Russia historically. It ludicrously described Estonia's recent drive towards independence and its national revival as the "falsification of history." This Russian propaganda appeal, which was aimed at influencing the international press, even included a plea, published in the name of Sergei Dimanis, Latvia's leading hardline communist, that the CSCE should convene a conference entitled "Apartheid in Latvia."[588]

These extraordinary protestations were in fact frenetic efforts to distract attention from a studied policy of delay on the vital

---

587   *Baltic Independent*, p. 8.
588   *Baltic Independent*, p. 9.

question of moving troops out of the Baltic States. At high level meetings with Western leaders during the Helsinki-2 Summit in 1992, the Baltic Presidents reiterated their concern, both at the continuing delay in producing a timetable for the withdrawal and at the unruly behavior of the occupying forces. President Bush told them that Yeltsin had assured him that no new troops were being sent to the Baltic States. He asked: "Is this true?" and received the reply: "Unfortunately not." The Baltic leaders added that they were essentially unsure of the Russian leadership's commitment to the issue.[589] Bush was then quoted as saying: "Yeltsin will have no doubts about the U.S. position on the troop pull-out" to the three Presidents, and Vytautas Landsbergis as having remarked: "Russia today is an inheritor of the Soviet Union's violations of legal agreements, which Russia is willing to put right. It is mere coincidence that the style of some of its generals is reminiscent of that of Vyacheslav Molotov." [590] With even more cutting skepticism he added: "There is one more coincidence that can be observed in their comments – the mention of 'semi-foreign countries' and 'zones of special interest.'[591]" He was, of course, giving warning of the nostalgic attitudes within the Kremlin toward the Baltic countries. Landsbergis chose to sit near Yeltsin after he had made his speech: "I did not want to be regarded by Yeltsin as a bad boy," he subsequently commented. "I wanted to give him a feeling of political alliance, so I sat near him." The maneuver did not go unrewarded, as Yeltsin had said "*Ladno* ("O.K." in Russian). We need to sign an agreement."[592] Knowing this story, one might claim that the decision about the Russian withdrawal from Lithuania was in fact precipitately achieved in Helsinki. The Helsinki-2 Summit opened a chance for another step forward, extending the international framework for it and suggesting to Russia an acceptance of Western values of civilized behavior between states.

---

589   Ibid.
590   *Baltic Independent*, p. 9.
591   *The Baltic Independent*, p. 9.
592   Interview with Vytautas Landsbergis, the President of Lithuania's Parliament, May 19, 1998, London.

Despite this positive advance the situation became explosive again with the beginning of the war in Bosnia later the same year, when Russia's Foreign Minister Alexander Kozyrev returned in an aggressive stance when he reiterated his view that there was much similarity between the situation in the Balkans and that of Lithuania and the other Baltic States. His pronunciation was once again interpretable as a renewed threat to their statehood and independence, especially when the troop withdrawals were stopped for periods on multiple occasions. At this juncture, a firm position was again taken by the Lithuanians, and they again received the support of the international community. The linking of western financial help to Russia and the withdrawal of its military forces from the Baltic States had, however, become a reality at this stage. As a response, Russia now related the issue of the withdrawal of the Russian army from the Baltic States to the "questions of treatment" of the Russian-speaking population in Lithuania, Latvia, and Estonia. The Russian allegations toward Lithuania were, however, sharply rejected by the Lithuanian Government as "not truthful." The level of Russia's expressed reluctance to withdraw its forces varied in respect of the demands being raised. At first, it accused Lithuania and the other Baltic States of violations of the human rights of its compatriots. It then attempted to legitimize the presence of the army by demanding permission to privatize at least some of its military holdings and openly claiming the right to retain military bases. Finally, it attempted to stop the withdrawal by claiming that it lacked the material resources for the technical operation, saying variously that funding for the project was not available or that there was too little housing for the returning troops in their homeland. A particularly firm stand was required by the Baltic States to maintain resistance to this behavior.

Again, the Lithuanians took the lead. They refused to allow the Russian Army any possibility of staying in the country. In the end, this forceful refusal helped achieve the results hoped for by all the Baltic countries, when the troops finally left Lithuania on

August 31, 1993, and Latvia and Estonia a year later.[593] The firm support of the United States and the rest of the international community in demanding that Russia must comply with the Helsinki Final Act of 1992 contributed greatly to its success by requiring "early, orderly, and complete withdrawal," an achievement which was eventually facilitated by the offer of financial help being conditional on the withdrawal. Without the existence of the CSCE as a tool for multilateral diplomacy this achievement would have probably been more complicated, and thus the withdrawal of the former Soviet Army from Lithuania is among the best examples of the effectiveness of the CSCE's multilateral diplomacy yet experienced in Europe. In retrospect, if the process is to be viewed objectively, it will be seen that Russia did not demonstrate willingness to comply with the norms and ethics of international behavior in signing the agreement so much as a reluctance to exclude itself from the process of European security development. Finally, Yeltsin had no real choice other than to sign (under the friendly pressure of the international community) an agreement about the withdrawal of the troops or, as the "Baltic Independent" put it sharply in July 1992, "to miss a chance for photo opportunities."[594] Effectively, a situation had been achieved in which Russia could no longer afford to ignore world opinion or the opinions of its neighbors. The Kremlin's hegemony over Central and Eastern Europe was finally overthrown, and Lithuania's participation in the Helsinki Process had contributed greatly to the wresting of the jealously guarded remains of its former supremacy in the Baltic region away from the Soviet Empire's grip.

However, in examining the process, one can see that Western governments   accepted   Baltic   arguments   for   their   own

---

593   Lithuania's approach to securing troop withdrawal differed from that of Estonia and Latvia whose larger problems with a Russian settler population placed them in a different category. Eventually, both nations were forced to compromise over the issue of Soviet "military pensioners" continuing to live in their countries. Latvia was even forced to allow the military base in Skrunda to remain in Russian hands until the end of the century. In contrast, Lithuania refused to allow permission for the military bases to remain in her territory and refused permission for military pensioners to remain in the country.

594   See *Baltic Independent*, pp. 7-8.

independence only with reluctance and that the nations at the western end of the former Soviet Empire were on the edge of extinction. Suslov's Soviet policy "We would have Lithuania, although without Lithuanians" was not ultimately successful in the country he referred to, but it *was* to a larger extent successful in Latvia and Estonia. Meanwhile, Russia linked the issues of the withdrawal of the army with its bogus claims for "respect of minorities' rights." Finally, the OSCE was to a large extent made to serve Russian foreign policy goals in Latvia and Estonia, where the Russian speakers constituted more than one third of the population. However, the OSCE's role of multilateral diplomacy was constructive during the withdrawal of the former Soviet troops from Lithuania and its successful outcome there was a considerable spur to the achievement of the same goal in the partner countries.

The acceptance by the OSCE of the link between the "treatment" of the Russian minorities in Latvia and Estonia and the timing of Russian Army's final withdrawal from those states greatly lessened the constructive role for the Helsinki Process in this region, and to that extent was a success for Russian diplomacy.[595] Even now the Helsinki Process can continue to have a beneficial effect particularly with respect to the still occupied Königsberg (Kaliningrad) region, which the Lithuanians call *Mažoji Lietuva* or Lithuania Minor, although the current foreign policy of Lithuania and the other EU states has not yet fully explored the existing mechanisms of the OSCE toward this area (see Chapter 10). It would be necessary to demand the fulfilment of Russia's obligation to give advance notice of its military maneuvers to neighboring states.

The Helsinki Process: its Limits and Benefits

The enduring non-recognition of Lithuania's incorporation into the Soviet Union presented a background for its liberation, and the Helsinki Process provided the tools that helped the international community use diplomatic methods in promoting peaceful changes within the Soviet Empire. This facilitated the eventual

---

595   See *Baltic Independent*, pp. 7-8.

withdrawal of Soviet (Russian) military forces from Lithuania and the other Baltic States, thus ending their occupation. Eventually, the mounting pressure to respect the fundamental human rights of oppressed people along with the policy of non-recognition of the incorporation of the Baltic States were major international sources of global political change and the collapse of the communist Evil Empire.[596] The Soviet Union's disintegration can also be interpreted as an outcome of attempts by the Free World to encourage the political changes within the Soviet Empire. Ideals, embodied in the United Nation's Declaration of Human Rights and spread by the Helsinki Process, had never been permitted to take root in the Soviet Union, where Stalin's rule had perpetuated a distorted mirror-image of the perverse characteristics of the Nazi state.

It is easy in retrospect to persuade oneself that the international tools provided by the Helsinki Process were inevitably going to produce the successful results which we have noted. At first, it was an uncertain tool but there is great significance in the way in which diplomatic exploration of the recurrent problems it was invoked to deal with made constant reference to essential human values. In the end it was perhaps this appeal which finally penetrated because it mobilized forces which the repressive ideology of the communist system could not integrate, but also could not refuse. Eventually, however, the limits of the process also became obvious, as the very flexibility of its *modus operandi* left it an apparent playground for Russian ambitions in Europe. For a time, the OSCE became a virtual tool of Russian foreign policy, almost helping to realize its ambitions in what it called its "near abroad." The Russian authorities took over the wording used by the West toward the Soviet Union and turned it to their own purposes, even suggesting that the major violators of human rights in Europe before the Soviet troops were withdrawn from their countries were Lithuania and its neighbors, Latvia, and Estonia. This outcome is of course not an

---

596   These policies were first developed by the United States and in particular by the Reagan administration. The name of the Evil Empire was used in the documents of the National Security Council at that time. See e.g., NSC document collections at the Ronald Reagan Presidential Library in Simi Valley, California.

enigma to the student of Russia's imperial history, as the geopolitical themes manifested in the attitudes and policies of the Russian
state since 1991 can be demonstrated to have exceedingly long an-
tecedents in Russian foreign policy, going back hundreds of years
to Tsarist times. Indeed, the social psychology of Russian attitudes
toward the nations of the Baltic region is fused in the national consciousness of these peoples. It makes their commitment to a western European identity the more comprehensible, as it represents an
established countervailing process in their national and international aspirations, as they turn to the Western countries and away
from a neighbor whose ambitions have long threatened them with
annihilation.

It is against this background that we must now turn to examine the second phase of Lithuanian, and by implication the other
Baltic States', foreign policy, and international diplomacy. This
phase follows from their achievement of international recognition,
which disburdened the national community of Lithuanians. It leads
us towards the next chapter about how the recovered state has
aligned itself within the western orbit of alliances in such a way that
the threat of absorption "from the east," which had been a constant
for over five hundred years, may be obviated forever. In practical
terms, this has involved the ambition of Lithuania and her neighbors to participate as full members of the consensual collective defense and security arrangements of Western Europe at the highest
level, by joining NATO.

9. Lithuania's Integration into NATO
Adding Value to the Alliance

The Place of Lithuania in the Changing European and Transatlantic Security Framework

We must now examine the place of Lithuania in the changing European and Transatlantic security framework. Its context is given by President Valdas Adamkus, who emphasized that "most importantly, we are all members of the same family. Our values are common, and the basic principles of freedom, democracy, and the free-market economy are widely shared both in the East and the West of the continent. Above all, people [...] are well aware of the value of commitment and responsibility. They have proven this, persistently and outspokenly, during the turbulent years of reform and transition."[597] As Jonas Kronkaitis, former Supreme Commander of the Lithuanian army, has similarly pointed out: "NATO's values are Lithuania's values and the political leadership of Lithuania would be doing an injustice to its citizens if it did not seek membership in this western defense alliance."[598] Thus, Lithuania is committed to the European - Atlantic values of democracy, free market economy, and of respect for human rights which are shared across the Alliance. In this perspective, as Ambassador Klaus-Peter Klaiber has observed, "the commitment of the Baltic States to European and Atlantic values and their commitment to continue on the path of ever closer cooperation, both regionally and internationally, is beyond doubt."[599]

We have affirmed that Lithuania is defined by history, culture, geography, and its neighbors as an indivisible part of the West, and

---

597 Valdas Adamkus, "Lithuania's Contribution to the Euro-Atlantic Security," *Lithuanian Foreign Policy Review* no. 1 (9) (2002): 11.

598 Jonas Kronkaitis, "Development of the Lithuanian Armed Forces – an Important Step for Regional Security and Stability," *Lithuanian Foreign Policy Review* no. 2 (10) (1998): 140.

599 Klaus Peter Klaiber, "The Baltic States in NATO's Enlargement Strategy," *Lithuanian Foreign Policy Review* no. 2 (1998): 138.

of Europe. As a White Paper, prepared by the Centre for Strategic and International Studies, Washington D.C. and the Institute of International Relations and Political Science, Vilnius University, states: "[geographically,] Lithuania straddles two important European sub-regions: the Nordic-Baltic and the Central European, and it borders on the Russian centered Commonwealth of Independent States (CIS)."[600] This White Paper argues that Lithuania forms a link between North and Central Europe: "It is a position which enables the country to play a major role both in North-South and West-East relations. Unlike the West-East division that has engendered persistent conflict between Europe and Russia, northern and central Europe have remained closely interconnected throughout modern history."[601] Vytautas Landsbergis, the former President of the Lithuanian Parliament, has often said that if the place of Lithuania in the European and Transatlantic security framework is understandable as a function, or as a role that can be played. Lithuania's achievement of independence and statehood is making a particularly important contribution in the Baltic region. As a result, "Sweden feels the difference, and Poland is significantly safer. The new security is expressed in the following clear formula: "Lithuania's security is a part of Poland's security, and Lithuania's security is crucially important for Poland's security. The principle can be extended to include Latvia and Estonia. If Lithuania had not withstood pressure from the East, pressure between Byelorussia and the Kaliningrad region, there would have been a catastrophe not only for Lithuania, but for her neighbors as well."[602]

The re-establishment of Lithuania's statehood and its strengthening was a particularly important development for all of Europe. Now, when Lithuania is a member of NATO, it is free to contribute to European security more than ever. Experts have recognized that its defense preparation is serious by the invitation to join the Alliance. Although the country has increased its defense

600   "Lithuania's Security and Foreign Policy Strategy," *Lithuanian Foreign Policy Review* no. 1 (9) (2002): 86.
601   "Lithuania's Security and Foreign Policy Strategy," p. 86.
602   Interview with Prof. Vytautas Landsbergis, London, May 19, 1998.

spending, and in terms of military preparation Lithuania leads among the Baltic States, even more efforts are required, particularly a further increase in defense spending. NATO, by ensuring security in the Baltic region, can therefore possibly influence Russia's politics in a positive long-term direction. As Landsbergis has observed before Baltic NATO membership was achieved, "our decision about integration into Western structures is a positive thing, because it will finally put everything in its place and that will create conditions for good neighborhood relations."[603]

The importance of Lithuania and the other two Baltic states for European security and stability can be clearly read in Carl Bildt's words. As far back as 1994 the former Swedish Prime Minister called the Baltic States "the litmus test of Russia's real intentions for Europe,"[604] and subsequently Vytautas Landsbergis claimed that "the key to European security lies in the Baltic States."[605] Dr. Ronald Asmus, Executive Director, Transatlantic Centre (German Marshall Fund) and former Deputy Assistant Secretary of State for Europe, observed that "a strategy towards the Baltic States should be a top priority," because "history has shown that events in the Baltics often have repercussions well beyond the region,"[606] a view successfully summarized by Vėjas Gabriel – Liulevičius, Professor of History of the University of Tennessee, who has claimed "As go the Baltics, so goes Europe."[607]

We have claimed, and it is widely accepted, that the withdrawal of the Russian Army from the Baltic States undoubtedly transformed the security environment in the Baltic Sea region, and in Europe as a whole.[608] As a direct result, the security environment has improved significantly for Finland, Sweden, and Denmark as

---

603 Interview with Prof. Vytautas Landsbergis.
604 Carl Bildt, "The Baltic Litmus Test," *Foreign Affairs* (Autumn 1994): 72 – 85.
605 Vytautas Landsbergis, "Baltijos kraštai - Europos saugumo raktas," *Lietuvos Aidas*, October 10, 1995, p. 5.
606 Ronald Asmus and Robert Nurick, "NATO enlargement and the Baltic states," *Survival* 38, no. 2 (Summer 1996): 121–142.
607 Vėjas G. Liulevicius, "As go the Baltics, so goes Europe," *Orbis* (Autumn 1995): 387–402.
608 E.g. N. Blanc – Noel, *Changement de cap en mer Baltique.* (Paris : Fondation pour les études de defense nationale, 1992).

well as for Poland, Germany, and the Baltic States themselves. The other European states also feel more secure because of Russia's departure from the Baltic countries. However, to assure the irreversibility of the security development described above as well as to sustain economic growth, Lithuania, Latvia, and Estonia spent the decade of 1993-2003 after the Russian Army withdrawal in seeking full membership in NATO and the EU. Joining NATO was the priority of their foreign and national security policy. They were finally invited to join NATO during the Prague summit in November 2002. This decision was received with joy when they completed accession negotiations, and ratified the Washington Treaty, when the U.S. Senate unanimously ratified their membership on May 8, 2003 and other NATO states completed the ratification shortly afterwards as well as when the Treaty was finally deposited at the State Department on March 28, 2004. The first European country to ratify this new wave of NATO enlargement was Denmark (May 15, 2003), followed by Canada (March 28, 2003), Norway (April 10, 2003), Hungary (June 3, 2003), Germany (July 11, 2003), and the other NATO allies. The Baltic States finally became full members of the Alliance on April 2, 2004, when all the Parliaments of NATO member states ratified their accession treaties.

The Transatlantic Security Community in North Central Europe

Immediately upon the restoration of independence, Lithuania and the other Baltic states, Latvia, and Estonia, faced enormous security problems. These included the withdrawal of the Soviet Army, the reorientation of their economies to the West, the resolution of sensitive questions concerning minorities, and the need to resolve the serious environmental problems caused by Soviet colonization. The resolution of the major security problem of troop withdrawal has been dealt with in the previous chapter. In this one we shall examine the formation and the enlargement of the security community in the Baltic Sea region.

Once the withdrawal of the Soviet Army was completed, the Transatlantic security community can be said to have expanded to the eastern shores of the Baltic Sea. In this new situation it can be affirmed that a war is now unthinkable between any of the Baltic and Nordic or other Central European and Western European states. However, the Baltic States and to a differing degree many other Central European states share a common historical experience of Russian aggression. The Baltic States also enjoy common goals and values, and share a similar political culture, and these factors lead to their peaceful collaboration. Thus, it is inconceivable that any conflict or disagreement between Estonia, Finland, Lithuania, Latvia, or Poland would ever be resolved by force of arms. This is not necessarily a state of affairs that needs to be formalized by treaties as institutional ties, and the sense of habitual co-operative behavior between individuals, social groups, and between the Baltic countries and other Central European states already indicates that a Transatlantic security community ("Western European security community" in Carl Deutsch's terms) has been formed in the Baltic Sea area.[609] Moreover the Northern European states emphasize the indivisibility of their security from that of Lithuania, Latvia, and Estonia. Zbigniew Brzezinski has claimed that the Baltic States have become an "indivisible" part of the broader Nordic-Baltic region, and similar ideas apply to Poland and Lithuania, as Poland has emphasized that its security is indivisible from Lithuania's security. [610] One can therefore argue that the Baltic States' independence achieved in 1991 "closed the missing link around the Baltic Sea," becoming members of the Transatlantic security community, despite the grudging attitudes of the re-emergent authoritarian Russian state.

In the eyes of millions of Central Europeans, Byelorussians, Ukrainians, and even Russians or East Germans, Lithuania's and the other Baltic States' independence symbolized the ultimate

---

609   The concept of a "security community" was first developed in the 1950s by Karl Deutsch. It means that "there is real assurance that the members of that community will not fight each other physically but will settle their disputes in some other way." See Karl W. Deutsch *Political Community and the North Atlantic Area* (Princeton: Princeton University Press, 1957), p. 5.

610   "Zbigniew Brzezinski teigia, kad Baltijos kraštai yra Šiaurės Europos dalis," *Europos Lietuvis*, December 17, 1997, p. 5.

collapse of the Soviet Union. Lithuania's own declaration of independence certainly influenced the Latvians and Estonians, later the Byelorussians and Ukrainians, and even the Russians themselves to follow the same course, and it was soon recognized by the Balts that if the Baltic States were to be offered early full membership in NATO, it would mean the acknowledgement of their political influence and role at a time of crucial transition. "We saved you billions of dollars in the arms race," said Vytautas Landsbergis, President of the Lithuanian Parliament.[611]

It will be helpful to briefly recapitulate the history of Lithuania's joining the Alliance. Well in advance of the main wave of the re-establishment of Lithuania's diplomatic relations in August 1991, the government of Iceland consulted Manfred Wörner, NATO, Secretary General, and he privately encouraged the establishment of diplomatic relations with Lithuania. This was done on February 11, 1991, approximately a month after the Soviet attempts at a *coup d'état* in Lithuania. Just before the end of the same year the North Atlantic Co-operation Council was established on December 20, 1991. It embraced all 16 NATO states, six former Warsaw pact states, and the three Baltic States. Following this, NATO Secretary General Manfred Wörner visited the Baltic States on March 13-16, 1992, on the second anniversary of the re-establishment of the Lithuanian state, and the Allied Forces Northern Europe Commander General Garry Johnson followed this up by visiting Lithuania on February 9, 1993. Lithuania's Parliament passed a resolution on December 23, 1993, which recommended that the Lithuanian Government should apply for NATO membership. Lithuania's decision to join NATO was reached by a consensus of all parliamentary parties, and as a result Lithuania became the first Central European country to apply for full NATO membership on January 4, 1994. It was admitted to the newly established NATO Partnership for Peace later the same month, on January 27, 1994, and the celebration of the third anniversary of the restoration of Independence on March 11 the same year was marked by the signing of the first military

---

611   Vytautas Landsbergis' speech in the Conference of the Euro-Atlantic Integration in Vilnius, September 3-4, 1998.

collaboration agreement with another NATO state, Denmark. In December 1996, Lithuania's Parliament passed a new law laying down the basis of the nation's security and announced that integration into the European and Trans-Atlantic security framework was to be the top priority of Lithuania's foreign and national security policy.

The end of the Cold War and the movement of the Baltic States toward NATO membership also emphasized the resulting democratic reforms which emerged in Russia itself. Zbigniew Brzezinski emphasized, saying in 1997 that Baltic membership in NATO would assist Russia "to define itself as a nation instead of an empire," and Vytautas Landsbergis has confirmed the matter, saying "I formulate this idea in a similar way. Polish membership of NATO creates conditions for a normal and friendly relationship with Russia. The same is valid for Lithuania."[612]

The major arguments for the Baltic States, entry to NATO are now resolved, but until very recently the issues were under contention. Not to have ratified the NATO treaty would have given a completely wrong signal to Russia, particularly to its expansionist political forces and its influential Soviet intelligence and military caucus. It would also have undermined embryonic democratic developments in Russia itself, because influential fascist and nationalist as well as communist political forces would have perceived it as their own victory or taken it as the acquiescence of the Western states to their hopes of the restoration of the western limits of the Tsarist Empire. Historically, of course, the Baltic States, even when they were enmeshed in the Soviet Union, were always an example for Russia's democratic political forces and it is on this basis that we can assume that Baltic NATO membership will significantly improve Baltic-Russian relations in the long term, as it confirms that the Baltic States are securely anchored in their democratic choice.

It must be stressed that the Baltic States' search for NATO membership was not a move *against* Russia but embodied a search for *improved* relations with their expansionist neighbor as the element of fear of absorption by military means at some future time

---

612   Interview with Prof. Vytautas Landsbergis, London, May 19, 1998.

by Russian interests was envisaged as having been removed by this determination. The model for this transition was perhaps the example of Norway, which was already a NATO member with a common border with Russia, but also enjoying respectful relations with Moscow. Russia has always tended to consider firm and clear decisions by its neighbors. In this context NATO enlargement to the Baltic States increased stability in the Baltic Sea region and it therefore also increased the security of Europe as a whole.

The NATO alliance embodies in its treaty the basis of the principle of the indivisibility of European security. President Bill Clinton said in a letter to the Estonian President Lennart Meri in 1996 that "a new Europe is united by common values," where there is no room for "spheres of influence." Lithuania's view, expressed by Česlovas Stankevičius, the country's former Defense Minister, has strongly supported that concept, and it was on this formulation that Lithuania, Latvia and Estonia consistently and firmly rejected Russia's attempts to put the Baltic States within Russia's sphere of influence prior to the signing of the U.S.-Baltic Charter in Washington in 1998. [613] They also resolutely rejected Russia's offer of so-called "security guarantees" which were made in attempt to distract from the negotiations toward these countries' entry into NATO.[614]

Some of the arguments against Baltic membership in NATO were expressed in terms of the Baltic States being "undefendable." However, this concept of "undefendable European states," can be seen not to accord with the principles of democracy once it is examined thoroughly. In fact, according to Česlovas Stankevičius, to divide European democracies into "defensible" and "non-defensible states" would be to create new lines of division precisely the sort which it was sought to avoid in enlarging NATO.[615]

The consent arguments to the interests which confronted Lithuania's application to join NATO were neatly dealt with by Vytautas Landsbergis when he observed that:

---

613   Česlovas Stankevičius, "NATO enlargement and the indivisibility of security of Europe: A view from Lithuania," *NATO Review* (September 1996).

614   Stankevičius, "NATO enlargement."

615   Stankevičius, "NATO enlargement."

When we are told "you are indefensible," we identify in this postulate a strangely pre-established presumption of the aggression of Russia. However, there is another way of evaluating the situation. We believe that the political protection - of being very close to, or already in the Alliance - is the most reliable method of maintaining good relations with our biggest neighbor. It also helps to avoid the possible dilemma of military defense. These are the benefits which security brings to all of us. Insecurity, as an alternative, causes instability and even stimulates aggression.[616]

In offering this opinion he was confirming his conviction, shared by all the governments of the re-established Lithuania, that after the liberation from Soviet occupation the country had become an indivisible part of the "project of a Europe whole and free." It was this conclusion which was finally fulfilled when Lithuania, Latvia, Estonia, Slovenia, and Slovakia, along with Romania and Bulgaria, were invited to join NATO during its Prague summit on November 22-23, 2002, as we recalled earlier. Lithuania and other invited states became full members of the North Atlantic Alliance on April 2, 2004.

Lithuania also started accession negotiations for European Union membership in January 2000, and its full membership was achieved on May 1, 2004. In addition, Lithuania later became a member of the World Trade Organization at the end of 2000 and has been a member of the World Bank since 1993. Thus, the country is now an active member of the major international and regional security organizations, which also include her participation in the UN, the OSCE, the Council of Europe, and the Council of the Baltic Sea States.

Lithuania's Achievements in the NATO Integration Process

Lithuania was a leader among the Baltic States and other invited countries as well as the Vilnius-10 (or V-10) group of states in the

---

616   Vytautas Landsbergis, "Security Problems of Central and Eastern Europe," speech delivered at the European - Atlantic Group Meeting, House of Commons, July 12, 2000, London.

push for NATO membership.[617] The painful historical lessons of the past have made the leaders and shapers of the re-embodied Lithuanian state adopt "the concept of "total defense" which assists in preparing its public for an unconditional defense of its country by mobilizing all available national resources."[618] Thus, in recent years Lithuania's Parliament has passed a number of laws related to the nation's search for integration into the Western system of self-defense. "The Law on the Fundamentals of National Security" which asserts that national security is to be developed as a part of the Transatlantic defense system was passed in December 1996. Another law on national defense organization and military service was passed in May 1998, and it outlined the concept of military command harmonized in accordance with NATO principles as follows: "Regardless of its prospects for NATO membership, Lithuania is committed to maintaining its defense capability based on universal military conscription, the readiness to mobilize reserves and the preparedness of its citizens to resist aggression." According to a 1999 statement of Lithuania's Ministry of Defense, "Lithuania believes in total and unconditional defense of its freedom."[619]

These observations provide a framework in which the stance of Lithuania's Government has been defined, i.e., "The Lithuanian military strategy is based on the principle that Lithuania is defendable and shall be defended."[620] It was based on this recognition that the Law on the Strategy of Financing of the National Defense System was passed in January of 1999. According to this law, the national defense budget was increased to 2 per cent of the national GDP (i.e. $292 million in 2002).[621] The Conservative Seimas (Parliament) (a center-right coalition of the Conservative Party and the

---

617   Vilnius' group of states, NATO candidate states that were united by Lithuania to speak in one voice in search for their NATO membership.
618   Jonas Kronkaitis, "Lithuanian armed forces ready for interaction and self-defense," *NATO's Nations* 47 (2002).
619   Česlovas Stankevičius, "Lithuania on its way to NATO," in *NATO's Nations and Partners for Peace. Getting Ready for NATO: The Baltic States*, Special Issue 1999.
620   Stankevičius, "Lithuania on its way to NATO."
621   "146 DSCFC 03 E - Invited NATO members' progress on military reforms", http://www.nato-pa.int/default.asp?SHORTCUT=364.

Christian Democratic Party) also approved budget targets in January 1999 that sought to bring total defense spending up to 2.5 percent of GDP by the year 2005 but the left-wing Social-Democratic government failed to achieve those targets. Lithuania has, though, worked hard on creating armed forces which are firmly based on a Western model and can function independently, but are wholly compatible with NATO, and available to be integrated into NATO. The main priorities of the government's development of these defense structures were to enhance self-defense capabilities and to make its armed forces fully inter-operable with those of NATO. The government also formed a permanent Commission for Lithuania's integration into NATO which produced a National NATO Integration Program as was required by the NATO Membership Action Plan.[622] Lithuania's Ambassador to NATO in 2002 Gintė Damušis emphasized, shortly after full accession to the organization had been agreed, that Lithuania "has already found her 'niche of capabilities' within NATO", and "Lithuania has foreseen areas where it could demonstrate high competence, such as engineering units, military medical doctors, and special forces," a statement which clearly emphasized its areas of specialization and its usefulness immediately upon integration.[623]

Lithuania has been an active contributor to NATO missions when the opportunity has arisen. More than 1,000 servicemen have served in NATO-led, OSCE and UN missions, including the UN Protection Force (UNPROFOR II) in Croatia, the Implementation Force (IFOR) and Stabilization Force (SFOR) in Bosnia-Herzegovina; in the Force in Kosovo (KFOR), and in Albania (AFOR).[624] Since August 1994 Lithuania has also actively participated in peacekeeping missions of UNPROFOR, later IFOR, and it remains an active participant of the SFOR mission in Bosnia-Herzegovina. Seven

---

622   Andrius Kubilius, "Seeking integration into the Alliance," in NATO's Nations and Partners for Peace. Getting Ready for NATO: The Baltic States, Special Issue 1999.

623   Interview with H.E. Gintė Damušis, Lithuania's Ambassador to NATO, December 6, 2002.

624   *Lithuania: Adding Value to the NATO Alliance. 2002,* (Vilnius: Ministry of National Defense, Republic of Lithuania, December 2001), p. 6.

Lithuanian platoons and an entire company have also served in Croatia and Bosnia, where 41 Lithuanian military personnel served in all. In 1999 Lithuania engaged almost 200 men in SFOR Bosnia and contributed 2 ambulance teams to the NATO-led humanitarian operation "Allied Harbor." A Lithuanian peacekeeper Normundas Valteris died in the peacekeeping mission in Bosnia-Herzegovina, where two other Lithuanian soldiers were injured. Some 30 Lithuanian soldiers have also served alongside Polish troops as part of KFOR since autumn 2001, and 95 servicemen were deployed with Danish forces as part of SFOR in February 2002. Also since 1999, 30 Lithuanian peacekeepers have served in Kosovo's southeastern city of Kachanik alongside the U.S. Falcon Brigade and the Polish-Ukrainian battalion POLUKRBAT. Lithuania has also provided a fully maintained AN-26 transport aircraft and crew to NATO-led KFOR and SFOR missions since April 2001, while in the second half of 2003 two groups of Lithuanian soldiers - a total of 120 troops - served in an international peacekeeping operation in the same area. Elsewhere, around 40 troops of Special Forces have served in the anti-terrorist mission "Enduring Freedom" in Afghanistan since November 2002, while four Lithuanian war physicians also served there in the UN-led forces ISAF.[625]

Since 1995 Lithuania has hosted numerous international military exercises, including the "Amber Hope" and "Baltic Challenge" series. In 1998 the country hosted a large-scale exercise "in the spirit of Partnership for Peace" known as the "Baltic Challenge 98," with the participation of 5,000 troops from 12 NATO and NATO Partnership for Peace (PfP) countries.[626] In 1999 Lithuania hosted further PFP exercises "Amber Hope 99" and "Baltic Hope 99" as well as contributing to 28 exercises, e.g., "Co-operative Nugget 99," "Co-operative Guard 99." "Amber Hope 2001" brought together over

---

625   "Lithuanian peacekeepers return to Kosovo after vacation," BNS, January 23, 2003. See also *Lithuania: Adding Value to NATO*, p. 6.
626   PFP-NATO Partnership for Peace program "could be seen as a path into NATO for those who became "active" partners in choosing for themselves the extent of their engagement with NATO." See e.g., in Gerald B. H. Solomon, *The NATO Enlargement Debate, 1990 – 1997. Blessings of Liberty* (London: Praeger, 1998), p. 34.

2,800 military and civilian personnel from 14 foreign countries. The objectives of these exercises of which most of the planning and organization was conducted by the Lithuanian Ministry of Defense, were "to teach and practice the NATO Operational planning processes, apply the Rules of Engagement, and gain experience in conducting peace support operations within a multinational framework."[627]

Lithuania has also established state borders which are fully protected using modern European equipment and the use of new communications equipment, anti-tank, and anti-aircraft weapons. Lithuania is "sharing the burden of building Euro-Atlantic security, and by co-operating in implementing the concept of non-Article 5 operations, included in the missions of the Alliance, Lithuania is thus already acting as a NATO ally," stated the Lithuanian Defense Minister in 1999.[628] The report of the Kosovo peacekeepers on their return expresses the spirit of Lithuanian contribution to these ventures. "By increasing self-defense capabilities, participating in peace implementation operations and exploiting partnership initiatives we contribute to the implementation of Alliance core functions."[629] In addition, Lithuania has concentrated particular attention towards the development of a regional air surveillance system which ensures the effective co-ordination and exchange of a regionally integrated air picture with her neighboring states and with NATO. The Regional Air Surveillance Co-ordination Centre (RASCC) near Kaunas was established in the framework of the BALTNET project, originally launched by the United States Regional Airspace Initiative. "This system is really fully compatible with the NATO standards, and it could be connected to NATO air space control system within a few hours, as we are waiting for that moment," was Ambassador Gintė Damušis' comment in December 2002.[630]

---

627   *Lithuania: Adding Value to the NATO Alliance*, p. 10.
628   Stankevičius, "Lithuania on its way to NATO," p. 79.
629   Ibid., p. 81.
630   Interview with Ambassador Gintė Damušis.

Lithuania's military crisis management capabilities are fostered by the BALTBAT, the joint Baltic Battalion, which is wholly capable of peacekeeping and peace implementation missions, and by the LITPOLBAT, the joint Lithuanian and Polish peacekeeping battalion. According to Česlovas Stankevičius, Lithuania's former Minister of Defense, the "LITPOLBAT, above all, strengthens Lithuania's strategic partnership with Poland, a new NATO member and the only NATO country having a common border with Lithuania."[631] In addition to these arrangements, the BALTRON, a joint Baltic Squadron of naval vessels, is fully interoperable with NATO. It can perform mine-clearance tasks and can provide support to international peacekeeping operations. The Baltic States have also cooperated to establish the Baltic Defense College, the BALTDEF-COL, in Tartu, Estonia, which teaches senior staff officers a curriculum based on NATO-compatible doctrines, with coursework adjusted to the geopolitical, geographical, and military situation of the Baltic region.

Lithuania is willing to share its expertise and experience with other NATO partners and sponsors the studies of Georgian students at the Baltic Defense College. Lithuania consults Georgia in the Caucasus on issues of the withdrawal of Russian troops, and the development of its armed forces. In February 2001 Georgia and Lithuania signed a Defense Co-operation Agreement. Georgia has welcomed Lithuania's NATO membership and is itself committed to reforms aimed at eventual future membership in the Alliance. Lithuania also signed a Defense Co-operation Agreement with Ukraine in autumn 2000. "All these projects are very well evaluated by NATO states, and the American Ambassador to NATO even said that they could serve as an example for other NATO members to demonstrate how to join resources, to combine capabilities for the development of well-aimed effective new programs."[632]

In addition, Lithuania has organized three major "Vilnius Conferences" to emphasize its commitment to good relations with its neighbors as well as integration into the Transatlantic

---

631   Ibid.
632   Interview with Ambassador Gintė Damušis.

Community. Vilnius hosted visits by the Heads of State of Poland, Latvia and Estonia, Ukraine, Russia, and Byelorussia in the year 1998, and in September 1999, it welcomed a major international conference discussing the Euro-Atlantic integration of the Baltic States as a key to European security and stability. The year 2000 was marked by the attendance of Lord Robertson, NATO Secretary General, at the Vilnius Conference of that year held on May 18-19 as well as by the participation of Foreign Ministers of NATO candidate countries. The conference passed the Vilnius Statement, in which the Foreign Ministers of the candidate countries invited NATO to enlarge its membership during the next summit in 2002, by inviting all the candidate countries to join the Alliance. "Only through NATO membership extending the zone of democratic reforms, stability, security, and prosperity will it be possible to deter the proliferation of instability."[633] Lithuania also started what has been called the "Vilnius process," which united all NATO candidate members to speak with one voice. This began on May 10-11, 2001, during the meeting of the Prime Ministers when the Vilnius Group was formed, calling itself the Vilnius-ten (or V-10), when Croatia was invited to join the group. The joint statement on NATO enlargement was passed at that meeting.

On May 27-31, 2001, the Spring Session of the NATO Parliamentary Assembly took place in Vilnius, and "it was the largest international event in Lithuania in a decade and the first such meeting held outside NATO territory. Some 270 parliamentarians from NATO and NATO-associated states gathered in the Lithuanian capital. The assembly approved a declaration on NATO enlargement, and Lithuania once again declared its commitment to join the organization during its 2002 summit in Prague."[634] In the same week, on May 29-30, the meeting of Foreign Ministers of the European-Atlantic Partnership Council took place in Budapest, and the Foreign Ministers of the Vilnius-10 Group held a meeting with the

---

633 Algirdas Saudargas, "Not only a Consumer of Security," in *NATO's Nations and Partners for Peace. Getting Ready for NATO: The Baltic States.* Special Issue 1999.

634 Darius Furmonavičius, "Lithuania," *2002 Britannica Book of the Year* (Chicago: Encyclopaedia Britannica, 2002), p. 459.

U.S. Secretary of State Colin Powell. During another meeting of the Foreign Ministers of the Vilnius-10 Group, held in Tallinn on July 1-2, 2002, the conviction was expressed that NATO would adhere to the principle of widening the common zone of security and stability in Europe, and would invite all the qualified democracies to join the Alliance in 2002. By reaffirming their commitment to the Membership Action Plan, the Ministers encouraged transparency and co-operation within the Vilnius Group.

On October 5, 2001, a meeting of the heads of the Vilnius Group states took place in Sofia, where they:

> □ stated that Europeans have viewed the Atlantic Alliance as the expression of a European commitment to America's security;
> □ reiterated their full support for the war against terrorism;
> □ shared the vision outlined by President George W. Bush in June 2001, at Warsaw University, that "all of Europe's new democracies, from the Baltic to the Black Sea and all that lie between, should have the same chance for security and freedom and the same chance to join the institutions of Europe – as Europe's old democracies have;"
> □ stated that they looked forward to the historic decisions to be taken at the Prague Summit in 2002.

A day earlier, on October 4, the meeting of Foreign Ministers of the Vilnius-10 Group had taken place in Bled, Slovenia. Their joint statement reiterated support for the United States and the Alliance in its anti-terrorist campaign and pledged their willingness to engage in further co-operation and exchange of experience in their efforts to join NATO. At the end of the year, on December 6-7, the meeting of the Foreign Ministers of the European Atlantic Partnership Council took place in Brussels. The Foreign Ministers of the Vilnius-10 Group again made a joint statement on terrorism and met with Secretary Powell.

On March 8, 2002, at the meeting of Foreign Ministers of the Vilnius-10 Group in Skopje, Macedonia, a joint statement was made, which:

> □ called on NATO to accept Croatia formally into the Membership Action Plan process at the NATO Foreign Ministers meeting in Reykjavik;
> □ emphasized the historic opportunity for the Alliance to encourage "robust enlargement" at its next meeting in Prague;

□ stressed the importance of NATO enlargement for the Vilnius group countries as well as its contribution to peace and stability in the Atlantic region and in strengthening Alliance efforts in the fight against terrorism;

□ welcomed the positive developments in South-Eastearn Europe, aimed at building a peaceful, stable, democratic and prosperous region; and expressed support for the efforts of Macedonia to overcome the crises and threats to its territorial integrity and sovereignty.

Later the same month, the meeting of the Prime Ministers of the Vilnius-10 Group in Bucharest held on March 25-26, adopted a declaration which expressed certainty that NATO enlargement would strengthen the foundations of the organization and its ability to deal with future challenges. The meeting also welcomed increased NATO-Russia co-operation; it stated that global efforts were needed to rein in terrorism and encouraged NATO to complete its building of Europe whole and free, as well as to consolidate the stability of South-Eastern Europe. At the Reykjavik meeting in May 2002 the NATO Foreign Ministers agreed that the Prague Summit would proceed with the enlargement.

President Valdas Adamkus has said on Lithuania's contribution to the Euro-Atlantic security:

ten years ago, Lithuania and some other Central and Eastern European countries started from ground zero, but today they can offer fully operational units capable of joining NATO missions! Moreover, our countries have shown an impressive aptitude for the application of the latest technologies.

We often omit the crucial fact that one soldier from a candidate country can replace one NATO soldier who can be sent on another mission. For example, during the last decade, almost 1,000 Lithuanian soldiers have taken part in various peace-keeping missions in Balkans. Accordingly, 1,000 NATO soldiers have been freed up to other assignments including the on-going campaign in Afganistan.

My country is also committed to send its military and medical units to join the Operation Enduring Freedom within the Czech and Danish forces.
Today, we should focus more on mobility, interoperability, and cutting-edge technologies. I have no doubts that my country with its 10,000 strong, well-equipped regular forces, trained to Western standards, as well as its 2 percent of GDP for defence spending, will make a tangible contribution to NATO's collective defence.[635]

---

635   Valdas Adamkus, "Lithuania's Contribution to the Euro-Atlantic Security," *Lithuanian Foreign Policy Review* no. 1 (9), (2002): 10.

Lithuania's role in the enlargement of NATO was further emphasized by President Valdas Adamkus during his lecture "Lithuania in an Integrated World," given at the meeting at Chatham House in London on March 27, 2002:

> I remember that after the first round of the enlargement many thought that the countries not taken in were too weak and divided to ever make it.
> However, our countries joined in a group also known as the "Vilnius Ten" and, I believe, successfully championed their cause. Now, three years after Washington, discussions focus on a largest possible wave of enlargement. This lesson of solidarity is indeed invaluable.
> I have no doubts that our countries will continue to co-operate after Prague. We share so much - our geography, history, and the experience of transition. Even the challenges before us are ... similar. Together, we can be more effective in the European Union and in NATO.[636]

Lithuania in the NATO Enlargement Debate

As the United States is the major decision-maker in the NATO alliance, American support for the invitation of the Baltic States to join NATO was of key importance at the crucial NATO Prague Summit meeting held in November 2002. Undoubtedly, Lithuania's diplomacy, the important influence of the one-million-strong American-Lithuanian community, and of the Baltic as well as other Central European communities in the United States, and even the fact of the election of Valdas Adamkus, an American Lithuanian, as the President of Lithuania, were all key factors which played an essential role in securing the commitment of the United States to invite all of the Baltic States to join NATO together, and in persuading both President William J. Clinton's and President George W. Bush's administrations to commit themselves firmly to the "vision of Europe whole and free," with no new lines of division of the continent. Dr. Ronald D. Asmus, the former Deputy Assistant Secretary of State for Europe (1997-2000) has confirmed in his book "Opening NATO's Door" that "the Baltic-American community was small but well organized and worked closely with other groups to build

---

636   Valdas Adamkus, "Lithuania in an Integrated World." Speech by H.E. Mr Valdas Adamkus, President of the Republic of Lithuania, at the Royal Institute of International Affairs, Chatham House, London, March 27, 2002.

political support for NATO membership. When State Department officials briefed Congress on U.S. policy, they often found that Baltic-American representatives had either just preceded them or were standing outside ready to make the case for the U.S. to provide more security assistance. They were relentless and single-minded in their focus on getting into NATO."[637]

Undoubtedly, many American Lithuanians supported the election of President George W. Bush, and he has since supported Lithuania by making the historic first visit of an American President to Lithuania. In his speech in Vilnius, he observed:

> Many doubted that freedom would come to this country, but the United States always recognized an independent Lithuania. We knew that this continent would not remain divided. We knew that arbitrary lines drawn by dictators would be erased, and those lines are now gone. No more Munichs. No more Yaltas. The long night of fear, uncertainty and loneliness is over. You're joining the strong and growing family of NATO. Our Alliance has made a solemn pledge of protection, and anyone who would choose Lithuania as an enemy has also made an enemy of the United States of America. In the face of aggression, the brave people of Lithuania, Latvia and Estonia will never again stand alone [...].
>
> You are needed in the NATO Alliance. You will contribute to our common security. Yet the strength of NATO does not only depend on the might of armies, but on the character of men and women.
>
> We must be willing to stand in the face of evil, to have the courage to always face danger. The people of the Baltic states have shown these qualities to the world. You have known cruel oppression and withstood it. You were held captive by an empire, and you outlived it. And because you have paid its cost you know the value of human freedom.[638]

The encouragement and lobbying activity of the Baltic-American organizations, particularly the Joint Baltic American National Committee in Washington D.C. which embraced the major Baltic political organizations in the United States: the American Lithuanian Council, the American Latvian Council, and the American Estonian Council, as well as the Baltic American Freedom League in California with its representative in the capital, gained a positive

---

637   Ronald D. Asmus, "*Opening NATO's Door. How the Alliance Remade itself for a New Era*" (New York: Columbia University Press, 2002), p. 159.

638   "Alliance of Freedom Being Tested by 'New and Terrible Dangers'," Remarks by the President to the Citizens of Vilnius Rotušė, Vilnius, Lithuania November 23, 2002. See e.g., http://www.jbanc.org/nofear.html.

response from President Bill Clinton who met with the Presidents of Lithuania, Latvia, and Estonia in Washington, on June 25, 1996. On March 28, 1997, a U.S. Congress delegation travelled to Vilnius where it confirmed that NATO doors would not be shut to the Baltic States. This was followed by a visit by Professor Vytautas Landsbergis, then President of Lithuania's Parliament, to the United States. During their meetings with Landsbergis Vice-President Al Gore and Secretary of State Madeleine Albright confirmed that Lithuania would not stay in a "gray zone of security" if it was not accepted by NATO in the first round of its enlargement which was by then already being planned. They made it plain that the United States was committed to a wave of NATO enlargement, which would embrace Poland, the Czech Republic and Hungary at this stage. However, as Madeleine Albright put it, the United States already wanted to create the conditions which would allow the Baltic States to walk through an open NATO door. Obviously, the United States was still encountering rather strong internal resistance to the concept of this NATO enlargement.

The discussion at this stage reflected a significant debate and resistance by "Old Europe," the British, French and the Italian leaders, at the NATO Madrid Summit. However, finally NATO leaders recognized "the progress achieved towards greater stability and cooperation by the states in the Baltic region which are also aspiring members."[639] They then emphasized that "as we look to the future

---

639   "Madrid Declaration on Euro-Atlantic Security and Cooperation. Issued by the Heads of State and Governments," Press Release M-1 (97) 81, Meeting of the North Atlantic Council, Madrid, July 8, 1997, http://www.nato.int/docu/pr/1997/p97-081e.htm. For the debate during the Madrid Summit see Ronald D. Asmus, *Opening NATO's Door. How the Alliance Remade Itself for a New Era* (New York: Columbia University Press, 2002), pp. 238-250. "The British were the most cautious on the open door – they wanted to say as little as possible. The U.S. wanted to be forward leaning on the open door in principle, but to avoid language that either tied its hands for the future or created a de facto pecking order of preferred future candidates. The French and Italians were at the other end of the spectrum. They wanted a firm commitment to bring in Romania and Slovenia in 1999 while avoiding any mention of the Baltic states. The other Southern European states supported the Franco-Italian position while the Nordics were in our corner out of shared desire to not discriminate against the Baltic states." Asmus, *Opening NATO's Door*, p. 245.

of the Alliance, progress towards these objectives will be important for our overall goal of a free, prosperous and undivided Europe at peace."[640] Their statement was published in July 1997. After this Madrid Summit Madeleine Albright visited Vilnius, where she declared that the Baltic States were serious candidates for NATO membership, and the new U.S. administration then supported the preparation of the Baltic States for NATO membership. President Clinton said that the United States wanted to create conditions which would permit the Baltic States to "walk in through open doors." Madeleine Albright then invited Dr. Ronald Asmus to take the position of Assistant for Europe to develop the strategy for NATO enlargement. Thus, three important initiatives emerged in the Baltic Sea region, related to the process of NATO enlargement, embracing the idea of "strategic homes." The first was the "U.S.-Baltic Charter," signed by the Presidents of the four states; the "U.S. Northern European initiative," facilitating co-operation in the Baltic Sea region; and the "NATO Membership Action Plan," which prepared for the candidate countries to do their homework in preparation for NATO membership.

The U.S.-Baltic Charter was signed by the President of the United States William J. Clinton, President of Estonia Lennart Meri, President of Latvia Guntis Ulmanis, and President of Lithuania Algirdas Brazauskas in the White House on January 16, 1998. Though it avoided offering any security guarantees to the Baltic States at this stage, it created the conditions for increased U.S.-Baltic collaboration which would lead to full NATO membership. As Dr. Ronald D. Asmus put it: "We needed a strategy to create the conditions that would make it possible to one day bring the Baltic states into NATO – not as a precipitous, isolated act that would sour relations with Moscow but as part of an overall strategy for building security and stability in the region. But for that strategy to work, we first needed to agree with leaders of the Baltic states on what we were trying to achieve, embrace a common strategy on how to

---

640   Asmus, *Opening NATO's Door*, p. 24.

achieve it, and create the mechanisms to follow up with practical steps."[641]

Earlier in the 1990s, the American attitude was like its earlier disposition toward the Soviet Army's withdrawal from the Baltic States, which was finally completed by the dismantling of the Skrunda radar station in Latvia. The Baltic States were already members of the Organization for Security and Co-operation in Europe, and according to the principles of the OSCE every state could choose the international security organizations they wished to join. This meant that the Baltic States, if they wanted to become NATO members, could not be prevented from making attempts to join. Indeed, even Russia had earlier recognized this right of Lithuania when it signed the withdrawal treaty which led the former Soviet Army out of the Lithuanian state in 1992.[642]

The Northern European Initiative was directed to help the Baltic States to become NATO members in both political and military

---

641 Asmus, *Opening NATO's Door*, pp. 231-232. As an insider Dr. Ronald Asmus observes: "The Clinton Administration's Baltic commitment took many people by surprise. And not everyone was happy. Primakov hated it and repeatedly warned us against taking steps to bring the Baltic states closer to NATO. It was unpopular with some of our key European allies as well. The exception was our Nordic allies who were, if anything, even more supportive in word and deed than the U.S. We looked to them for advice and ideas on how to craft our strategy. They knew the region better than we did and understood the importance of getting the U.S. more involved – and often lobbied for more U.S. involvement vis-à-vis more skeptical Europeans. The convergence of U.S. – Nordic thinking on the Baltic issue led to a kind of implicit strategic alliance and cooperation in the region that would, in turn, play a key role at the NATO Madrid summit. The Clinton Administration was often accused of pursuing a strong Baltic policy for domestic political reasons. The reality was that we were being criticized at home from both the right and the left. I would sometimes amuse my Nordic and Baltic counterparts by explaining the U.S. political lineup on this issue with four wine glasses at dinner. My staff soon dubbed it the "Asmus Four Glass Theory on the Politics of Baltic NATO Membership." As I described it to Talbot in a memo, "Right-wing Republicans want to bring them in now, Bush Republicans and Democratic defense hawks say never; Democratic internationalists such you and me say yes in principle but not now; and liberal Democratic arms controllers say it is not worth risking the arms control agenda with Moscow because of the Baltic issue." Fashioning the two-thirds majority required for Senate ratification required a good strategy and enough time," Asmus, *Opening NATO's Door*, p. 231.
642 See the previous chapter on the Russian army withdrawal from Lithuania.

terms. First, the United States helped to develop Lithuanian military forces to a level compatible with NATO standards. Second, the United States backed EU membership for the Baltics and their collaboration with Nordic EU states as a means of integrating them into the family of European states. Third, the United States supported strengthening the collaboration of Russia's northern parts with the EU by strengthening NATO-Russian collaboration, in an attempt to enhance Russia's trust in NATO.

However, at this stage Russia played at delaying the signing of agreements on its borders with Estonia and Latvia and constantly accused both states of the violation of human rights of its compatriots. These actions exacerbated suspicions that Russia still harbored imperial ambitions in the Baltic Sea region. When the Russian Foreign Minister Primakov organized a conference in Moscow for Members of Parliament of the European states in April, 1998, he delivered a one and a half hour speech about "the Red Line in Europe." This use of the Stalinist terminology "Red Line" was also employed by Boris Yeltsin in an interview for "The Guardian" newspaper at the beginning of June 1998, and Russia continued to make diplomatic attempts to clarify its so-called "legitimate security concerns," using some carefully formulated propaganda phrases, to influence Western decision makers and media.[643] To give an example, its diplomacy claimed that if the Baltic States were to be part of NATO, it would feel isolated in the way that Germany felt isolated after the Versailles Treaty. In defensive terms, however, the isolation of such a large state is unthinkable, and the whole campaign ignored the obvious truth that NATO is a defensive Alliance, and that its enlargement has nothing to do with what Russia called "its legitimate security concerns." The concept of isolation in this context had no rational foundation.

When NATO Secretary Javier Solana visited the Baltic States a little later, on June 17-18, 1998, he confirmed that the NATO door would remain open for the Baltic States, and Lithuania's President Valdas Adamkus met President Bill Clinton on October 22-23, 1998. The delegation of American Senators headed by William Roth, the

---

643   The Guardian Foreign Page, *Guardian*, May 15, 1998.

Chairman of the North Atlantic Assembly, visited Lithuania on November 17-18 of the same year. A new Membership Action Plan for candidate countries was subsequently launched during the NATO Golden Jubilee meeting held in Washington on April 23, 1999, to help the candidate states in their preparation for admission to NATO.

Even though Russia was opposed to Baltic membership in NATO, it eventually admitted the fact that this was unavoidable. Russian President Vladimir Putin told listeners in a live television interview while he was visiting the United States, that "every country has the right to choose its alliances" and he also told his hosts while visiting Finland that it was their choice, "but we do not see any objective reasons for NATO expansion."[644] However, during the subsequent meeting between President Adamkus and President Putin in the Kremlin, the Russian President agreed that Lithuania and the other Baltic States had a right to choose their own alliances. We can see in this that the nostalgic Russian position had changed its previous form since the time when Russia had offered its own unilateral "security guarantees" to the three Baltic countries in 1998. The offer was of course firmly rejected then. It was all too reminiscent of "security guarantees" given unilaterally by Stalin in 1939[645].

However, Russia's diplomatic attempts to play its "Europe versus America" strategy still continued. Strangely, the United Kingdom was cultivated as one of the major intermediaries between Russia's foreign policy in Europe and that of the United States. It was the United Kingdom which introduced the proposal to invite Russia into membership of a new NATO-Russia Council,

---

644   "Russian President expresses understanding for Karelia demands and NATO hopes of Baltic States," *Helsingin Sanomat*, International Edition, September 4, 2001.

645   Prof. Raimundas Lopata, Director of the Institute of International Relations and Political Science, Vilnius University reveals that the rumors were spread by the Russians (before President Adamkus visit to Moscow in March 2001) that they would offer nearly half of the Kaliningrad region in exchange for Lithuania's refusal to join NATO. See Raimundas Lopata, "Geopolitical hostage: the case of Kaliningrad oblast of the Russian Federation." www.tspmi. vu.lt/files/mokslkonfer/kaliningrad-stokholm.doc.

a position which granted invitee almost all the rights of a full member. This proposal was vetoed by the Americans and the Czechs, and finally after protracted negotiations, a consensus was found within NATO for the establishment of this new body, though without granting Russia any veto right to interfere with the NATO enlargement process. NATO Secretary General Lord Robertson said at the Royal Institute of International Affairs during the Conference "Europe and America: A New Strategic Partnership - Future defense and industrial relations" held on February 18, 2002: "[It is] our determination to go beyond consultation, and to work constructively together on all the issues where we have what President Putin calls 'the logic of common interests.' A new forum for this cooperation, in which we can decide and act 'at 20,' should be ready well before Prague. Our aim is to have it operational, with myself in the chair and Russia seated between Portugal and Spain, by the time Foreign Ministers meet in Iceland in May."[646] His perspective was clear but we may now observe that the idea of the new NATO body "at 20" was rather strange and perhaps was only an attempt to engage Russia and dissolve concerns over NATO enlargement, but what about Ukraine, Georgia, and the other PfP partner countries? Such a new body, say "at 35," to include the nineteen NATO members, plus the ten "Vilnius Group" candidate members, together with the three neutral PfP member countries (Sweden, Finland, and Austria), plus three partners (Russia, Ukraine, Georgia) would be future-oriented. Such a Council could eventually be open to other emerging democracies from the former Tsarist Russian Empire, such as Belorussia, an authoritarian regime at present, but a country which has a growing opposition and a dissident movement, particularly among the youth.[647] We might also suggest that the major aim of that Council could be to facilitate the peaceful and

---

646 "NATO: Enlarging and redefining itself." Speech by Secretary General the Rt. Hon. Lord Robertson of Port Ellen at Chatham House on February 18, 2002. "20" - 19 NATO states plus Russia.
647 Erick Jarvis, "Almost Baltic: Belarusian Nationalism and the Search for Non-Russian Identity," conference paper at the 19th Conference on Baltic Studies "Dynamics of Integration and Identity: the Baltics in Europe and the World," University of Toronto, Ontario, Canada, June 3-5, 2004.

final transformation of the former Tsarist Russian Empire into a friendly alliance of non-nuclear democracies.

The United States and the international community are, of course, interested in collaboration with Russia. This is not because it has demonstrated some westward turn after the malignant events of September 11 in joining efforts to combat terrorism or continued to support international terrorism as the Soviets used to do in the past, but also because it still possesses 15,000 nuclear warhead capabilities. These, in the words of General Joseph Ralston, former SACEUR, "can be compared with tennis balls [...] if one tennis ball is lost in the game it is a minor problem, however, if one nuclear rocket is lost, it is a major problem." As Leon Fuerth (former National Security Advisor to Vice President Al Gore) put it, "we should also be looking for ways to promote the downsizing of Russia's huge plant for the production of nuclear weapons."[648] However, in practical terms, it is going to be much easier to integrate smaller states into the European and Transatlantic security framework. In the face of growing anxieties about Communist China or the Islamic world this step offers an immediate increase in security in distinct from the vaguer possibilities of reforming the huge and still unpredictable successor to the former Russian Tsarist Empire.

According to Paul Goble, former Director of Radio Free Europe/Radio Liberty for Public Communications, speaking to the Joint Baltic American National Committee Conference in Washington, D.C. in March 2001, in addition to its attempts to prevent the Baltic States from full integration with the West, Russia has chosen to continue to conduct acts of subversion. 'Subversion' is however in this case "the weapon of the weak, just as it was for the Soviets in the 1930s."[649] The case for this viewpoint is strengthened when we consider that "according to RFE/RL reports, Mr. Putin has asked the Russian Duma for $50 million to conduct a campaign in the media against enlargement in Europe and the United States. This certainly smacks of the Soviet disinformation campaigns of the 1980s, first against the intermediate range nuclear missiles in

648   Leon Fuerth, "On Russia, think bigger," *Washington Post,* May 1, 2002.
649   Helle Bering, "A Russian game of chess," *Washington Times,* March 14, 2001.

Europe and later against Ronald Reagan's Strategic Defence Initiative."[650] Yet despite these Russian attempts to manipulate opinions and events their results were miserable and unsuccessful. They have now become clearly overshadowed by the beginning of the war against terror. For the first time the Alliance invoked the Article Five guarantee of the NATO Treaty to defend the United States against the terrorist attacks, and NATO AWACS planes joined the patrolling of the airspace of the United States after the September 11 events. The mass media has been fully submerged in the coverage of the war against terror, and later the Israeli-Palestine conflict, rather than being involved in this Russian-encouraged discussion of the evil intentions of the "NATO candidate countries."

We must now examine the position of another European state, Germany, which has moved its position from being a mere advocate of Baltic integration into NATO to becoming an active supporter. During a meeting with President George W. Bush in February 2002 German Chancellor Gerhard Schröder emphasized that the German position had changed in a supportive direction, indicating that a decision not to invite the Baltic States into NATO would send entirely the wrong signal to those states which were opposed to the enlargement process.[651] Germany then confirmed this "active" position of support for the Baltic NATO membership in a joint statement made by the Foreign Ministers of the Baltic States and Germany, issued in Riga on February 11, 2002.[652] The Bundestag then adopted a resolution on the NATO enlargement, voicing support for the admission of all seven NATO candidate countries into the Alliance in the forthcoming round of enlargement. The German Foreign Minister Joschka Fischer, in his address to German legislators, underscored the need to affirm the Transatlantic interests by this NATO enlargement: "speaking about specific countries the debate singled out the Baltic States, both over their positive assessment [with regard to the] implementation of

---

650   Bering, "A Russian game."
651   "Baltijos šalių narystės NATO nukėlimas būtų klaidingas ženklas," BNS, February 2, 2002.
652   "Vokietija pritaria Baltijos šalių narystei NATO ir ES," BNS, February 12, 2002.

accession criteria by them, as well as Germany's historic responsibility for the Baltic states in the context of Molotov-Ribbentrop pact of 1939." There was active support for this stance in the Bundestag from the German-Baltic Parliamentary Cooperation Group and its Chairman Baron Wolfgang von Stetten.[653]

Another major European country, France, has also eventually actively supported NATO enlargement to include the Baltic States. They have made progress in their position since the 1997 Madrid Summit and French President Jacques Chirac became one of the strongest supporters of Baltic NATO membership in Europe. During his visit to Lithuania in 2001 he stated at Vilnius University:

> La securité en Europe repose également sur le lien transatlantique, incarné par l'OTAN. Je sais l'aspiration de la Lituanie, et aussi de ses voisins baltes, à entrer dans l'Alliance. Cette aspiration est legitime. Je la comprends et je l'accueille favorablement. [...] La France estime que, pour chaque pays, le choix des alliances auxquelles il souhaite appartenir est un attribut essentiel de sa souveraineté.[654]

In this context the election of Mr. Jacques Chirac for a second term as President of France was important for the success of the NATO Prague summit which issued the invitation to the Baltic States to join NATO.

The Nordic countries have also been active supporters of Baltic NATO membership since the idea was first introduced in NATO circles by Denmark in 1995. Then, at the start of the real debate about the enlargement of NATO, Denmark suggested that the Baltic States should be invited to join NATO first, and Lithuania responded by taking the position that "at least one of the Baltic States" needed to be invited to join NATO in the first round of enlargement. However, despite these favorable tendencies among

---

653   "German Bundestag supports admission of seven countries," BNS, April 26, 2002.

654   Speech of President Jacques Chirac delivered at Vilnius University, quoted in President Jacques Chirac's letter to Dr Darius Furmonavičius of January 30, 2002. "European security depends on the transatlantic link, expressed by NATO. I understand the aspiration of Lithuania and other Balts to join the Alliance. This is a legitimate aspiration. I understand and I favorably support it. France regards that the choice of alliances is an important expression of every state's sovereignty."

Nordic states, other European states, particularly the United Kingdom, expressed real concern about NATO development. Although John Hiden and Patrick Salmon commented after Prime Minister John Major's visit to Moscow and his meeting with the Baltic leaders in the British Embassy there in 1991 that "the tradition of appeasing the Soviet Union, maintained by British leaders from Anthony Eden to Margaret Thatcher, seems at last to have been broken," the British Government remained less supportive than the Balts had expected in the NATO enlargement debate this time.[655] It is clear today that even the Rt. Hon. Malcolm Rifkind, a former Conservative Foreign Secretary (whose family originated in Lithuania) and later the Honorary President of the British-Lithuanian Society, remained highly cautious about the idea of Baltic NATO membership. Following the election of a Labor government the British government became even less accessible for the Balts, though a clear change in the British position on this issue would eventually be observed. This occurred during the trip of Geoff Hoon, British Defense Secretary, to Lithuania at the end of February 2002. He then stated, in Vilnius on February 26: "Great Britain wants Lithuania to be in NATO," this being the first official British Government statement to express clear support for Lithuania's aim to join NATO.[656] The Baltic News Service commented the next day: "Official London earlier gave vague phrases about support for NATO enlargement."[657] Geoff Hoon stated: "My visit here, and all that I have learned about the remarkable progress that Lithuania has made, reinforces my determination that NATO should see an enlargement, and the United Kingdom is looking forward to Lithuania being one of those countries to join."[658] A subsequent meeting between President Valdas Adamkus and Prime Minister Tony Blair took place in Downing Street on March 26, 2002, and the British Prime Minister assured him of Her Majesty's Government's

---

655   John Hiden, and Patrick Salmon, *The Baltic Nations and Europe. Estonia, Latvia and Lithuania in the Twentieth Century* (London: Longman, 1991), p. 191.
656   "Britain wants to see Lithuania in NATO: Hoon," BNS, February 27, 2002.
657   "Britain wants to see Lithuania in NATO."
658   "Britain wants to see Lithuania in NATO."

support for the invitation to join NATO which would be considered during the Prague summit in November.[659]

Integration into NATO was of course essential to the national interests of the Baltic States. It was perceived as a necessity by the Baltic societies from an early point in the developing debate, but of all three Baltic countries, the Lithuanian population was the most supportive of the country's efforts to join the Alliance. According to Baltic Surveys Ltd. (a member of Gallup International), in a report published in March 1998, some 55 percent of the Lithuanian population, 47 percent of the Latvians and 54 percent of the Estonians approved of these efforts. Later, research by *Vilmorus*, the Lithuanian public opinion register, in February 2002 showed a significant increase in public support for NATO membership, as 60 percent of the population were favorably disposed toward the invitation to Lithuania to join NATO (some 21 percent were "against," and 18 percent were "undecided").[660] The majority of Lithuanians clearly believed NATO membership to be the best way to guarantee the country's future security and stability.

On May 23, 2001, on the eve of the NATO parliamentary session in Vilnius, all eleven political parties represented in the Lithuanian Parliament concluded an agreement on the national defense policy budget for 2001-2004. The Parliament restated joining NATO as Lithuania's priority and agreed that "in 2002 the defense budget of Lithuania shall be 2 percent of GDP, and in 2003-2004 this percentage will not be decreased." The agreement confirmed Lithuania's place as an active participant in NATO's Membership Action Plan (MAP) process, which had been initiated at the Washington NATO summit of 1999 and which assisted Lithuania in its practical preparations for NATO membership.

Furthermore, when President Valdas Adamkus met President George W. Bush at the White House on January 17, 2002, the President of the United States affirmed American support for "all those

---

659   Lecture of H.E. Mr. Valdas Adamkus, President of Republic of Lithuania "Lithuania in an integrated world," in Royal Institute of International Affairs, March 27, 2002.

660   "Už narystę NATO balsuotų dauguma Lietuvos gyventojų. NATO naujienos," URM, February 20, 2002.

nations ready to meet NATO's requirements and contribute to common security." President Adamkus replied by congratulating President Bush on the particularly successful speech he had made in Warsaw. In response the President of the United States congratulated the real author of the speech, Ambassador Daniel Fried, Senior Director and Special Assistant to the President for European and Eurasian Affairs, National Security Council, who was sitting nearby. It is worth remembering a few paragraphs from that historic speech:

> Yalta did not ratify a natural divide, it divided a living civilization. The partition of Europe was not a fact of geography, it was an act of violence. And wise leaders for decades have found the hope of European peace in the hope of greater unity. In the same speech that described an "iron curtain," Winston Churchill called for "a new unity in Europe, from which no nation should be permanently outcast."
>
> Consider how far we have come since that speech. Through trenches and shellfire, through death camps and bombed-out cities, through gulags and food lines men and women have dreamed of what my father called a Europe 'whole and free.' This free Europe is no longer a dream. It is the Europe that is rising around us. It is the work that you and I are called on to complete. [...]
>
> I believe in NATO membership for all of Europe's democracies that seek it and are ready to share the responsibilities that NATO brings. [...] As we plan to enlarge NATO, no nation should be used as a pawn in the agendas of others. We will not trade away the fate of free European peoples. No more Munichs. No more Yaltas. Let us tell all those who have struggled to build democracy and free markets what we have told the Poles: from now on, what you build, you keep. No one can take away your freedom or your country.[661]

After this meeting Lithuanian President Valdas Adamkus told the journalists that all doubts as to whether Lithuania would be invited to join NATO had now been dissolved. It is important to mention that he had met Latvian President Vaira Vike-Freiberga and Estonian President Aronld Rüütel on the eve of his visit to Washington and that both had authorized him to speak for them in his discussions with the President of the United States. In November

---

661   Remarks made by the President in address to Faculty and students at Warsaw University, Warsaw University, Poland, June 15, 2001. The White House Office of the Press Secretary.

2001 the House of Representatives passed the Freedom Consolidation Act (H. R. 3167), by the overwhelming margin of 372-46 (over 85 percent support for authorizing Congress to grant the assistance for the countries designated under the NATO Participation Act of 1994). This authorization now allocated $6.5 million for Estonian foreign military financing; $7 million for Latvia; $7.5 million for Lithuania; $8.5 million for Slovakia; $4.5 million for Slovenia; $10 million for Bulgaria; $11.5 million for Romania, the Bill being designated the "Gerald B. H. Solomon Freedom Consolidation Act of 2001," after the late New York Congressman who had been a great supporter of NATO enlargement.[662]

The U.S. Senate also debated and passed the Bill in May 2002, despite some minor opposition.[663]

When endorsing the Baltic bid for NATO enlargement, Senator Jesse Helms, then Chairman of the Foreign Relations Committee, stated:

> With the collapse of Communism those nations finally achieved their rightful independence from Russian occupation and domination. Yet Russia still looms menacingly over these countries. In looking at the current Russian government, one gets the distinct impression that the Russian leadership

---

662 Freedom Consolidation Act of 2001 (Introduced in the Senate). http://expand-nato.org/senact2001.html. Algis Rimas, former American diplomat, who served as a Deputy Chief of Mission of the United States in Vilnius before his retirement and was later the Chairman of the Public Affairs Commission of the American Lithuanian Community, as well as the Representative of the American Lithuanian Council in Washington, D.C., and a member of the Board of the Directors of the JBANC, played a vitally important role in passing the Freedom Consolidation Act in the Congress. Therefore, he was one of the key personalities in persuading the Senate to commit to the second wave of NATO enlargement, embracing Estonia, Latvia, Lithuania, Slovakia, Slovenia, Bulgaria, and Romania.

663 Republican Senator John Warner from Virginia, a member of the Armed Services Committee was skeptical towards the enlargement of NATO. It is not surprising that he voted against the first round of NATO enlargement in 1998, against the admission of Poland, Hungry and the Czech Republic. His colleague Republican Senator James Inhofe from Oklahoma, also a member of the Armed Services Committee, also voted against the first wave of NATO enlargement on the grounds of its potential costs to U.S. taxpayers and to the U.S. military. See "Inhofe opposes NATO expansion," April 29, 1998. In fact, NATO enlargement is within the interests of American taxpayers since it is within the defense interests of the United States.

considers Baltic independence to be a temporary phenomenon. That is an impression that the Russians cannot be allowed to long entertain.

Just as we never recognized the Soviet annexation of the Baltic states, we must not repeat the mistakes of the 1940s today by acknowledging a Russian sphere of influence in what Russian leaders ominously call the "near abroad." These nations' independence will never be fully secure until they are safe from the threat of Russian domination and are fully integrated into the community of Western democracies.

I intend to work with the Bush Administration to ensure that the Baltic states are invited to join their neighbors Poland, Hungary, and the Czech Republic as members of the NATO alliance. This is vital not only for their security, but for ours as well. If we want good relations with Russia, we must show Russia's leaders an open path to good relations, while at the same time closing off their avenues to destructive behavior. That means taking the next step in the process of NATO expansion, by issuing invitations to the Baltic nations when NATO's leaders meet for the next alliance summit planned for 2002. [664]

The incorporation of these views into the legislative process of the U.S. Congress' European Security Act affirmed that the security of the United States was discerned as inseparable from the security of Europe. By doing so the United States designated Lithuania, and her neighbors, as eligible to receive assistance under the program established under Section 203 (a) of the NATO Participation Act of 1994. The importance of these determinations is evident in the wording of the statement made by the Senate in passing congratulations to Lithuania on the tenth anniversary of its independence:

Whereas the United States had never recognized the forcible incorporation of the Baltic states of Estonia, Latvia, and Lithuania into the former Soviet Union; Whereas the declaration on March 11, 1990, of the re-establishment of full sovereignty and independence of the Republic of Lithuania led to the disintegration of the former Soviet Union; Whereas Lithuania since then has successfully built democracy, ensured human and minority rights, the rule of law, developed a free market economy, implemented exemplary relations with neighboring countries, and consistently pursued a course of integration into the community of free and democratic nations by seeking membership in the European Union and the North Atlantic Treaty Organization; and Whereas Lithuania, as a result of the progress of its political and economic reforms, has made, and continues to make, a significant contribution toward the maintenance of international peace and stability by, among other actions, its participation in NATO-led peacekeeping operations in Bosnia

---

664   Address by Senator Jesse Helms, Chairman, U.S. Senate Committee on Foreign Relations at the American Enterprise Institute, January 11, 2001.

and Kosovo: Now, therefore, be it *Resolved by the Senate (the House of Representatives concurring)*, That Congress hereby-- (1) congratulates Lithuania on the occasion of the tenth anniversary of the reestablishment of its independence and the leading role it played in the disintegration of the former Soviet Union; and (2) commends Lithuania for its success in implementing political and economic reforms, which may further speed the process of that country's integration into European and Western institutions.[665]

However, in reporting these positive words and in rethinking the history of the accompanying events, we must not overlook the fact that the path to NATO membership was at times beset with serious difficulties. President Vytautas Landsbergis stated that "Lithuania [...] has no wish to once again find itself as a commodity on a counter where the great traders conduct their bargaining."[666] That explains why Lithuania put itself at the forefront of European - Atlantic integration by the initiation of the "Vilnius Process," uniting all ten new candidate countries to speak with one voice. Following their meeting in Vilnius on May 18 – 19, 2000, the Foreign Ministers of the NATO applicant countries issued the "Vilnius Statement" which reaffirmed their commitment to the completion of the historic project of a Europe whole and free:

> We recognize that NATO and the European Union are the two central foundations of the Euro-Atlantic community and that we must pursue accession in both institutions if we are to fully reintegrate our democracies into the community we share. We recognize that these aspirations are complementary, and we are committed to pursuing both objectives in parallel.
> We are firmly convinced that the integration of our democracies into NATO and the EU will facilitate the creation of a free, prosperous, and undivided Europe. Today, we reiterate our common commitment to work together cooperatively to achieve this goal. Our goal will not be reached until each of us, as well as other European democracies sharing the values of the Euro-Atlantic community and able to bear its common responsibilities, has been fully integrated into these institutions. We call upon the member states of NATO to fulfill the promise of the Washington Summit to build a Europe whole and free. We call upon the member states at the next NATO Summit in 2002 to invite our democracies to join NATO. [667]

---

665   Congratulating the Republic of Lithuania on the tenth anniversary of the reestablishment of its independence, U.S. Senate, March 2, 2000.
666   Vytautas Landsbergis' speech in the Conference "Euro-Atlantic Integration as a Key Aspect of Stability," in Vilnius, September 3-4, 1998.
667   "Vilnius Statement," May 19, 2000, Vilnius, Lithuania.

We can move forward the conclusions of this account by recalling the forceful statement of Vaclav Havel, President of the Czech Republic, on the importance of Baltic NATO membership:

> I fail to understand why these three free countries should not be offered membership as soon as possible, especially as they are working hard to be ready for it. Yielding to some geopolitical or geostrategic interests of Russia, or perhaps merely to its concern for its own prestige, would be the worst thing that the Alliance could do in this respect. It would amount to returning to the Ribbentrop-Molotov pact; to confirming its legitimacy; to recognizing Russia's right to surround itself with a cordon sanitaire, or with a sphere of its interests euphemistically called the "near abroad;" in short, to rededicating ourselves to the old principle of dividing the world and nations regardless of their will. It would, in fact, be a denial of the underlying concept of the Washington Treaty, NATO's fundamental document, that is, of the conviction that democratic countries of the Euro-Atlantic region have the right to freely choose the way in which they wish to protect their freedom and that the Alliance should be made accessible to them if they opt for collective defense. There is not much time left: any further delay would make admission of these countries more difficult. I therefore believe that the invitation to join the Alliance should be extended to them at the next NATO summit in Prague.[668]

The conclusion of the historic debate was invitations for Lithuania, Latvia, and Estonia, together with the other candidate states of Slovenia, Slovakia, Romania, and Bulgaria to join NATO at the historic Prague NATO Summit. Ambassador Gintė Damušis then said in December 2002 that "MAP will continue until we [...] become full members. We are implementing very specific tasks in every area: e.g., in the security area, we must ensure that secret documentation would be kept and circulated in an orderly manner; in the military sphere - that military reform would be implemented as it was planned; in the economy – that a certain level of economic stability would be reached; in the sphere of resources – that adequate funding would be assigned for defense."[669]

The evolution of a common viewpoint of Saddam's Iraq as a Stalinist-like dictatorship brings both satisfaction and obligations

---

668 Address by Vaclav Havel, President of the Czech Republic, at the Conference "Europe's New Democracies: Leadership and Responsibility," Bratislava, May 11, 2001.
669 Inteview with Ambassador Gintė Damušis.

to those who find themselves in the Western partnership of defense. The resulting security obligations are very clear, as is witnessed by the fact that all Vilnius-10 states unequivocally supported the firm stance of the United States against Iraq, and signed their declaration on February 5, 2003, after the United States had presented evidence to the United Nations General Assembly and Security Council: "Our countries understand the dangers posed by tyranny and the special responsibility of democracies to defend our shared values. The Transatlantic community, of which we are a part, must stand together to face the threat posed by the nexus of terrorism, and dictators with weapons of mass destruction."[670]

Authoritarian Russia is becoming such a dictatorship with a huge stockpile of weapons of mass destruction once again. Soviet farms, equipped with factories to produce of biological weapons and their storage facilities; the usage of chemical weapons in the mass murder of the Chechens, in parallel with the crimes against the Kurds committed by Saddam Husein in Iraq; modernization programs for nuclear weapons and stockpiles of nuclear warheads and nuclear materials; the involvement at state level in drug dealership worldwide; and the lack of civilian control of military forces and lack of respect for freedom and human rights by the current Russian regime resembles the development of a fascist state which possesses or will possess in the near future a serious challenge to the United States and to Europe as a whole, i.e. to the whole Transatlantic Community. The North Atlantic Alliance succeeded in keeping the Russian leopard within its cage for more than fifty years, but it is also important to keep it safely inside its cage in the future as well.

---

670   Statement of the Vilnius group countries in response to the presentation by the United States Secretary of State to the United Nations Security Council concerning Iraq, February 5, 2002.

10. European Enlargement and the Königsberg Question
Stalin's Legacy Within an Enlarged Europe

This chapter argues that the territory of the present Kaliningrad region historically was never part of Russia, and that its continued occupation by Russian military and security forces implies a "right of conquest" which is not sustainable in international agreement or international law. Indeed, the present status of the Königsberg region is not defined well at the international level. The Soviet Union broke an agreement of the Potsdam conference, namely its undertaking not to mark its western borders and not to incorporate Königsberg and the adjacent area into the USSR in advance of the final peace settlement. In addition, the Soviet Union no longer exists, but Russia retains its hold on this illegally occupied territory, a trophy of the Second World War.

The neighboring states of Lithuania, Poland, and Germany, as well as the Scandinavian states, are deeply interested in the demilitarization of the region. The Balts welcomed the U.S. House of Representatives resolution demanding the withdrawal of Russian troops from the region, which was unanimously passed in 1996. However, almost nothing appears to have happened since, as the Russian Army is still there, and the pollution of the Baltic Sea continues on a critical scale. The international community, particularly the European Union, whose economic aid to Russia totaled more than $1billion, must attach conditions to this aid to require that Russia withdraw its army and allow the people of the region to decide their own future in a referendum. Indeed, the Second World War will at last be over when the Königsberg region is liberated from Russian occupation.

With the recent enlargement of NATO and the EU, the question of the Königsberg region has inevitably become a part of the international agenda, not least because this region, which contains a rusting Soviet fortress, the legacy of Russian Stalinist expansionism into Europe, found itself located as its exclave within the territory of NATO and the EU since April 2 and May 1, 2004.[671]

The region of Königsberg/Karaliaučius is a separate territory (Kaliningradskaya oblast) which is currently administered as part of the Russian Federation.[672] It lies on the Baltic shore between Poland and Lithuania and is separated from Sweden by the Baltic Sea. Until the Second World War this region was a part of Germany, known as East Prussia. When the German frontiers were redrawn after 1945, the Allies agreed to assign the southern part of East Prussia to Poland, but the northern part was annexed by the Soviet Union, despite the agreement of the Soviet delegation at Potsdam, described in detail below, not to mark the western borders of the USSR and not to incorporate Königsberg and the adjacent area into the Soviet Union in advance of a peace settlement.[673] Thus, it is

---

671   The Baltic States were invited to join NATO during the Prague Summit on November 21, 2002, and they became full NATO members on April 2, 2004. They also completed their negotiations for joining the European Union and they were invited to join it together with other ten candidate states during the Copenhagen summit of December 12 – 13, 2002. Lithuania, Poland, Estonia, and Latvia overwhelmingly voted "for" in their EU referendums. (In Lithuania 89.95 percent of voters voted for joining the EU on May 13 and 14, 2003 and 8.82 percent were "against" from among the 63.37 percent of the electorate who voted. In Poland 74.77 percent voted for joining the EU on June 7 and 8, 2003, while 25.23 percent were "against" from 57.34 percent of all eligible voters. In Estonia 64.1 percent of eligible voters took part in the referendum on September 14, 2003, 66.8 percent of voters voted in favor of joining the EU, and 33.2 percent were against. In Latvia 72.5 percent of voters participated in the referendum on September 20, 2003, and 67 percent voted for the joining of the EU with 32.3 percent of voters "against"). The Baltic States became full EU members on May 1, 2004.

672   We will use the historic name Königsberg but we will not change other spelling (Koenigsberg, Königsburg, Konigsberg) used in the quotations from the archival material. The Lithuanians call the area the Karaliaučius region or Mažoji Lietuva, Lithuania Minor. The Russians still call it the Kaliningrad region from the name of Kalinin, Soviet Commissar and President of the Stalinist Soviet State.

673   Although the documents of the unification of Germany contain the "Elements of a Final Settlement," a member of the American delegation assured me that the Königsberg issue was left aside on purpose so that the Soviets would not be able to claim that the United States recognized the region as being a part of the Soviet Union. JAB notes from 5/4/90 mtg. w/USSR FM Shevardnadze (in conjunction w/2+4 mtgs.) Bonn, FRG. James A. Baker III Papers, Seeley G. Mudd Manuscript Library, Princeton University, MC#197, Series B: Secretary of State, Box 108, Folder 1.

important to emphasize that though the region is currently administered by Russia, it can be argued that it is not a *legal* part of Russia.[674]

The Königsberg Issue at the World War II Conferences

Foreign Secretary Anthony Robert Eden wrote to his American
counterpart James Francis Byrnes that in December 1941 Stalin had
informed him that he regarded the question of the western frontiers
of the Soviet Union as "the main question for us in the war."[675] In
preliminary talks, the possible border along the so-called Curzon
Line of the Paris Peace Conference was discussed between Stalin
and Eden during his visit to Moscow in 1941 and with Molotov in
London in 1942. In the Teheran conference (28 November 28 – December 1, 1943) Anthony Eden said that it was the line known as
the Ribbentrop-Molotov Line.[676] After substantial discussion on
the future of Germany and its partition, Stalin was seeking a deal
on East Prussia at the Teheran conference in 1943, himself drawing
the line with a red pencil on a map "to illustrate the fact that if part
of eastern Prussia, including the ports of Könisburg and Tilsit, were
given to the Soviet Union he would be prepared to accept the Curzon line [...] as the frontier between the Soviet Union and

---

674   See Richard J. Krickus, *The Kaliningrad Question* (Lanham: Rowman & Little-
      field, 2002), pp. 172-174. Professor Krickus argues that the United States should
      now recognize Kaliningrad as a *de jure* part of Russia, while the author of this
      book argues that it is now the right time for the United States to emphasize the
      policy of non-recognition of the incorporation of this region into the USSR and
      to raise the issue of the illegality of the Russian presence in the region interna-
      tionally.

675   The British Foreign Secretary (Eden) to the Secretary of State, Quebec, August
      23, 1943. *Foreign Relations of the United States. The Conferences at Washington and
      Quebec, 1943* (Washington: United States Government Printing Office, 1970), p.
      1113.

676   *The Teheran Conference. Proceedings of the Conference. Foreign Relations of the
      United States. The Conferences at Cairo and Teheran, 1943* (Washington: United
      States Government Printing Office, 1961), p. 599.

Poland."[677] This line goes roughly along the current border between the Kaliningrad region and Poland, but Stalin's red line on the map went virtually through the cities of Königsberg and Insterburg.[678] Charles E. Bolen, the interpreter for the American delegation, says in his memoirs that during their discussion Stalin and Churchill virtually agreed on the future borders of Poland but the official American record of the conversation says that "although nothing was stated, it was apparent that the British were going to take this suggestion back to London to the Poles."[679] On February 11, 1945, at the Crimea (Yalta) Conference the Big Three agreed on the boundary between Poland and the USSR as being the Curzon Line (with minor deviations from the Line surrendering a few miles in favor of Poland).[680] However, the archival material clearly shows that there had not been any legally binding agreement made between the allies about the transfer of the Königsberg region to the Soviet Union at any conference.[681] This is why Stalin attempted to secure his gains at the *Potsdam* conference in Berlin, which took place from July 17 to August 2, 1945. (The conference was named the *Terminal conference* in the British diplomatic correspondence or alternatively the *Berlin conference*).

---

677   RG43 Records of International Conferences, Commissions, and expositions. World War II Conferences. Pre-Yalta Conferences. Teheran Conference, Minutes of Meetings, November - December 1943, General Records, 1943, E. 290, National Archive II, Washington, D.C.

678   The original of the map is missing in its envelope in the State Department's collection of the documents of the World War II Conferences (Box 1a) in the National Archive, Washington, D.C., but it is published in the page facing p. 601, *The Teheran Conference. Proceedings of the Conference. Foreign Relations of the United States. The Conferences at Cairo and Teheran, 1943* (Washington: United States Government Printing Office, 1961), p. 601.

679   Foreign Relations, p. 604. Charles E. Bohlen wrote in his memoirs "the division that Churchill and Stalin agreed to is the one that still exists." See Charles E. Bohlen, *Witness to History 1929 – 1969* (New York: W.W. Norton, 1973), p. 152

680   "Eastern Poland between the Riga line and Curzon line," 740.00119 Potsdam / 5 – 2446 National Archive II, Washington, D.C.

681   World War II conferences material (Boxes 1A-10b), National Archive II, Washington, D.C.

The Königsberg Question at the Potsdam Conference

"At plenary session on July 22nd Marshal Stalin circulated a draft paper [...] seeking the approval of the Conference for a proposal that pending the final settlement of territorial questions at the Peace Congress the boundary of the U.S.S.R. should embrace the northern half of East Prussia including Konigsberg."[682] The Soviet delegation presented the following draft of the document entitled "On shaping the decision of the Three Heads of Government regarding the transfer to the Soviet Union of the Königsberg area":

> The Conference approved the proposal of the Soviet Union that pending the final settlement of territorial questions at the Peace Congress, the part of the western border of U.S.S.R. adjoining the Baltic Sea should follow the line from the point on the eastern shore of the Danzig Bay indicated on the map, annexed hereto, eastward - north of Braunsberg - Goldap to the junction of the frontiers of the Lithuanian S.S.R., the Polish Republic and the former East Prussia.[683]

The British preparatory material for the Potsdam conference clearly states that "the Soviet draft is not acceptable in its present form" because it would commit His Majesty's Government to:

- admitting that the Königsberg area is not under the authority of the Allied Control Council in Germany;
- admitting that East Prussia no longer exists;
- recognising the incorporation of Lithuania into the U.S.S.R. as the Lithuanian Soviet Socialist republic.[684]

"It would seem preferable that we should not ourselves propose a redraft at this stage but should first see whether the Russians cannot be persuaded to withdraw their proposal," stated the British Foreign Office document entitled "Königsberg."[685] However, the British protocol of July 24 reports that:

> At plenary session on July 23rd Prime Minister explained that Soviet Delegation's draft would in effect require His Majesty's Government to

---

682   PRO FO 10 (37).
683   PRO FO 10 (37).
684   PRO FO 934/2, p. 508.
685   PRO FO 934/2, p. 508.

recognise (a) that East Prussia no longer existed and that this area had been withdrawn from the authority of the Control Council in Germany, and (b) the incorporation of Lithuania in the U.S.S.R. On the other hand, he had already made it clear that His Majesty's Government were in full sympathy with this Soviet claim. President Truman stated that the United States Government likewise saw no objection in principle to this part of Germany being transferred to the Soviet Union in due course. It was agreed that the Conference should record understanding that His Majesty's Government and the United States Government would support the Soviet claim at the peace settlement.[686]

Stalin presented two main arguments why Russia had to have this port in its possession at the expense of Germany, when submitting the draft of a text on the western borders of the USSR:

First, Russia had shed so much blood and gone through untold suffering during the present war. Secondly, Russia was anxious to secure some piece of German territory, so as to give some small satisfaction to the tens of millions of her people who had suffered in the war.[687]

President Truman said that the American delegation was ready to agree to this proposal in principle, though they thought that "some examination of it on ethnological grounds might prove necessary. But he raised no objection to Russia acquiring a piece of German territory."[688] Mr Churchill agreed also in principle with the Soviet claim, but he emphasized that all legal issues had to be solved in a peace settlement:

The only question which now arose was what he might describe as the act of legal question of transfer. At present the Soviet draft involved an admission by us all that East Prussia no longer existed, and that Koenigsberg and the territory around it was under the authority of the Allied Control Commission for Germany, and that Lithuania was now one of the Soviet Republics. All these were really matters for the final peace settlement. But so far as His Majesty's Government were concerned, we were ready to support the

686   PRO FO 10 (37).
687   CHAR 20/209/6, Churchill Papers, Churchill Archives Centre, Churchill College, p. 186 (Prime Minister's printed personal minutes, June and July 1945. June 1, 1945 – July 23, 1945).
688   Minutes.

Soviet wish that the Peace Treaty should make provision for the U.S.S.R. acquiring the port of Koenigsberg.[689]

He also emphasized that "he made this statement as one of principle. He had not examined the exact line on the map, and this would be a question which would have to be examined at the Peace Conference. But he would like to assure Premier Stalin of a continuing support of the Russian position in this part of the world, when the Peace Conference came."[690]

Stalin agreed that a final settlement of this question would be made at the Peace Conference and he "was satisfied with the assurances given by the British and United States governments."[691] Churchill suggested the redrafting of the Russian statement "in somewhat more general terms" and that "meanwhile the understanding of the three Great Powers would be recorded in the conclusions of the present Conference."[692]

However, if we read the final document of the Potsdam conference without a deep analysis and knowledge of the context and without careful reading of the protocols of the British and American delegations, the impression can arise that the Potsdam conference agreed to the final transfer of Königsberg and adjacent areas to the Soviet Union and that the case is therefore closed. Indeed, many researchers wrongly take for granted that the region was "ceded to the Soviet Union by the Western allies" at the Potsdam conference in 1945.[693] The final text of the sixth paragraph of the Potsdam declaration says:

VI. CITY OF KOENIGSBERG AND THE ADJACENT AREA.

---

689   Minutes.
690   This is particularly important point because Churchill linked the Königsberg question with the question of the status of Lithuania, which was never ultimately recognized as part of the Soviet Union by the British Government. See Minutes.
691   Minutes.
692   Minutes.
693   See e.g., Ingmar Oldberg, "The Kaliningrad Oblast – a troublesome exclave," in Daniel Kempton and Terry D. Clark, *Unity or Separation. Center-Periphery Relations in the Former Soviet Union* (Westport, Connect. & London: Praeger, 2002), p. 143.

The Conference examined a proposal by the Soviet Government that pending the final determination of territorial questions at the peace settlement, the section of the western frontier of the Union of Soviet Socialist Republics which is adjacent to the Baltic Sea should pass from a point on the eastern shore of the Bay of Danzig to the east, north of Braunsberg-Goldep, to the meeting point of the frontiers of Lithuania, the Polish Republic and East Prussia.

The Conference has agreed in principle to the proposal of the Soviet Government concerning the ultimate transfer to the Soviet Union of the City of Koenigsberg and the area adjacent to it as described above subject to expert examination of the actual frontier.

The President of the United States and the British Prime Minister have declared that they will support the proposal of the Conference at the forthcoming peace settlement.[694]

This declaration was signed by Truman, Attlee, and Stalin. After Churchill lost the subsequent General Election to Attlee, the new British Prime Minister came to the Potsdam conference in Berlin.

The real agreement is, however, clearly, and thoroughly reflected in the protocol of the British delegation. It reports the agreement of the Soviet delegation to comply with the demand of the British and American delegations, its obligation not to incorporate the territory of the region and not to mark the western borders of the USSR in advance of the Peace Settlement:

M. MOLOTOV said that on the substance of this question there was no misunderstanding between the three Delegations. The Soviet Delegation fully accepted the position that there could be no actual transfer of territory in advance of the peace settlement and, further, that the actual frontier could not be delimited in detail without expert examination on the spot.[695]

The protocol of the American delegation also confirms the agreement by saying:

MR. BYRNES pointed out that the President had taken a position on all discussions such as this that it must be understood that the cession of territory would have to be left until the peace settlement.

---

694   The Potsdam Declaration, President Truman Library, Independence, Missouri.
695   CHAR 20/236, Churchill Papers, Churchill Archives Centre, Churchill College, p. 258 (Official: Prime Minister's "Terminal": record of the proceedings of the [Potsdam] Berlin Conference [Germany], 17 July to 1 August 1945).

MR. MOLOTOV stated that everyone agreed to this.[696]

Thus, it is important to emphasize once again that the Soviets agreed at Potsdam that their western borders would be subject to negotiation at the Peace Settlement by the Allies. It is interesting to note that Stalin signed up to the wording "the frontier of Lithuania" not to the wording "the frontier of the Lithuanian S.S.R," as originally suggested in the Soviet draft, thus also emphasizing the illegal nature of the incorporation of the Baltic States into the USSR.[697]

However, the Soviets broke the Potsdam agreement and incorporated Königsberg and the adjacent area into the Soviet Union in advance of the Peace Settlement. Stalin refused to negotiate the withdrawal from Europe. The speedy satisfaction of Russia's wishes was the naïve idea of Churchill himself. He wanted to persuade Stalin to agree to the withdrawal from Poland and the rest of Central and Eastern Europe, including possibly also the Baltic States, by accepting the Soviet claims to Königsberg and its adjacent area, but with the condition that the *Imperator* agree to negotiate the *Bear's* withdrawal from Europe (Churchill's terminology), to facilitate achieving the final Peace Settlement. Churchill wrote to President Truman in his top-secret telegram after the capitulation of Berlin on May 11, 1945, expressing his concern about Russia:

> [...] We may be able to please them [the Russians] about the exits from the Black Sea and the Baltic as part of a general settlement. All these matters can only be settled before the United States Armies in Europe are weakened. If they are not settled before the United States Armies withdraw from Europe [...] there are no prospects for satisfactory solution and very little of preventing a Third World War. It is to this early and speedy showdown and settlement with Russia that we must now turn our hopes.[698]

He also wrote to President Truman the next day, repeating his anxieties:

---

696   Minutes of the Eleventh Meeting of the Foreign Ministers, 11:25 A.M. August 1, 1945, President Truman Library, Independence, Missouri.

697   Lithuania and the other Baltic States, Latvia, and Estonia were incorporated into the Soviet Union in 1940 because of the Molotov-Ribbentrop pact of 1939.

698   CHAR 20/218/109-110, Churchill Papers, Churchill Archives Centre, Churchill College, p. 86 (Prime Minister to President Truman marked "Personal and Top Secret," May 11, 1945).

> I am profoundly concerned about the European situation. What about Russia? [...] The absolute combination of Russian power and the territories under their control or occupied, occupied with the communist technique in some other countries, and above all their power to maintain very large armies in the field for a long time. [...] An iron curtain is drawn down upon their front. We do not know what is going on behind.[699]

Despite this denial Churchill was in fact well informed about the communist terror, particularly in Poland. The people of the Königsberg region suffered even more intense terror. Indeed, after the Soviet Army entered the region in October 1944, the inhabitants experienced mass murder at the hands of the communists. Probably the most brutal ever mass rape and murder of German women and children took place in the Königsberg region. Almost all the Germans and Lithuanians living there were killed or deported to Soviet concentration camps in Siberia. It was not until the late 1980s that ethnic Germans from other parts of the Soviet Union were allowed to settle there again, and it now seems likely that some 10,000 Germans live there today, half of them in Kaliningrad, the capital.

Is the Königsberg Region Really an Ethnically Russian Region?

Before becoming German, this region was originally inhabited by the ancient Prussians, a Baltic tribe as well as by the Lithuanians. The Old Prussian language was closely related to Lithuanian but has long been extinct. Today approximately 40,000 Lithuanians continue to live in the region. They represent about 4 percent of the population of nearly a million, the majority of whom are Russians who settled there only during the last half century. This picture contrasts sharply with the situation a century ago when, despite prolonged and intensive Germanisation, there were still 170,000

---

699 CHAR 20/218/109-110, Churchill Papers, Churchill Archives Centre, Churchill College, p. 109 (Telegram from WSC to President Harry Truman marked "Personal and Top Secret" expressing his concern over the future strength of the Soviet Union in Europe and what is going on behind the "iron curtain" of the Soviet Front; and asserting the importance of them coming to an "understanding" with the Soviet Union before they withdraw significant forces from Europe and retire to their zones of occupation," May 12, 1945).

Lithuanians in the region, representing 9 percent of the total population of two million.

In fact, this region was always closely related to Lithuania culturally. The Königsberg region is the main part of what Germans called *Klein Litauen* or Lithuanians call *Mažoji Lietuva, Lithuania Minor*, which was important as having been the birthplace of the nation's literature, literary language, and national press. For example, the first Lithuanian book *The Catechism*, the translation of eleven of the most widely known Lutheran hymns by the Protestant Pastor Martynas Mažvydas, was published in Königsberg in 1547.[700]

It is appropriate to recall that Lithuania and the other Baltic States became victims of the secret Soviet-Nazi pact of August 23, 1939, known as the Molotov-Ribbentrop Pact, and that they were occupied by the Soviet Union in 1940.[701] The United States never agreed to recognize their incorporation into the Soviet Union, but privately President Roosevelt made a remark to Stalin on December 1, 1943, "that when the Soviet armies re-occupied *these areas* [italics mine, D.F.], he did not intend to go to war with the Soviet Union on this point,"[702] and that the State Department recommended for President Truman in the preparatory material for the Potsdam Conference that:

---

700   Trilupaitienė, J. M. Martynas Mažvydas and the first Lithuanian hymnals.
      http://pirmojiknyga.mch.mii.lt/Leidiniai/trilupait.en.htm.
701   See Chapter 2. Excellent sources for the Soviet-Nazi pact of 1939: Richard Sontag and John Beddin (eds.) *Nazi-Soviet Relations 1939 - 1941: Documents from the Archives of the German Foreign Office* (Washington, D.C.: Department of State, 1948); *Germany. Auswärtiges Amt: Documents on German Foreign Policy, 1918-1945. Series D, (1937-1945), vol. 7, The last days of peace, August 9 – September 3, 1939.* London, H.M.S.O, 1956; Bronis Kaslas, *The USSR - German Aggression Against Lithuania*, (Pittston: Euroamerica Press, 1973), the collection of documents related to the pact; Saulius Sužiedėlis, "The Molotov-Ribbentrop Pact and the Baltic States: an Introduction and Interpretation," *Lituanus* 35, no. 1 (Winter 1989): 8-46.
702   Memorandum of conversation. 3:20 P.M. December 1, 1943, The President, Ambassador Harriman, Mr. Bohlen; Marshal Stalin, Mr. Molotov, Mr. Pavlov. RG 43 Records of International Conferences, commissions, and expositions. World War II Conferences. Pre-Yalta Conferences material, Teheran Conference, Minutes of Meetings, Nov-Dec. 1943, General records, 1943, E. 290, National Archive II, Washington, D.C.

> on the one hand the United States government has declared its objections to the method by which the three Baltic states were incorporated into the Soviet Union, and on the other the Soviet Government insists that such incorporation was legally carried out and is not subject to question. Under these circumstances the United States government in connection with the final territorial settlement in Europe may formally recognize as a fact the inclusion of the three Baltic states in the Soviet Union.[703]

The British Government verbally recognized the incorporation as early as 1942 in the negotiation of the Anglo-Soviet Treaty, although that paragraph did not appear in the final signed text. The preparatory text for the Potsdam conference prepared by the British delegation did however observe:

> [...] Recognition of the incorporation of the Baltic States into the U.S.S.R.
>
> We hope that this question will not be raised at Terminal, and we have no reason to imagine that it will. If the Russians should however bring it up, it would be consistent with our past policy if we were to say that this is an issue which must await the Peace Settlement.
>
> It will be recalled that in the first stage of the negotiations for the Anglo-Soviet Treaty of 1942 we agreed to the insertion in the Treaty of a clause signifying that at the Peace Settlement we would not oppose the claim of the Soviet Government that the Baltic States are now constituent Republics of the Soviet Union. The Russians may consider that we are under at least a moral obligation to adhere to this agreement, even though it was omitted from the final text of the Treaty, but we are in no way committed to take any action before the Peace Settlement.
>
> The Americans have not recognized any change in the status of the Baltic States since 1940. They have not prejudiced their position in the way we did during the negotiations for the Anglo-Soviet Treaty. There is therefore good reason to expect that we shall have their support if we insist on the postponement of this issue until the final peace negotiations.[704]

Only later did the British Government correct that error, allowing the Lithuanian Embassy to continue its work in London, despite the occupation of the homeland of the country, taking a similar position to the policy of non-recognition by the United States. President Truman rightly noted in his diary, which is now on

---

703   Top Secret. Estonia, Latvia, and Lithuania. Recommendation. 740.00119 Potsdam/5 – 2446. Potsdam. "Territorial Studies," Berlin Meeting of Heads of Government, National Archive II, Washington, D.C.

704   FO 934/6, p. 22, PRO (Public Record Office, London. Preparatory material for the Potsdam Conference of the British Delegation).

exhibit at his Library in Independence, Missouri, that "the Soviets broke all agreements: Teheran, Yalta, Potsdam, they raped Bulgaria, Romania, Estonia, Latvia, and Lithuania."[705]

Unfortunately, the Russians still fail to understand that the withdrawal of their remaining military troops from Europe would not reduce their prestige but, on the contrary, would improve their "face" and their relations with the West. The Russians are still raping Lithuania Minor, as well as the eastern part of Estonia, Karelia, and the eastern part of Latvia, these all being border territories annexed from Finland, Estonia and Latvia which naturally belong to Europe. Speaking at the Kremlin on June 11, 2003, President Putin dismissed a suggestion that Moscow might be willing to surrender Russia's "rights" to the Kaliningrad Oblast in exchange for writing off foreign debt. According to Radio Free Europe quoting Russian TV, Putin said "Russia does not trade in its lands and never will," and he then noted that there is a Russian naval base in Kaliningrad, and that it will remain there.[706] He also arranged a meeting with the Polish President Alexander Kwasnewski on a naval cruiser in the Baltic Sea near Kaliningrad straight after his visit to London as a 'part of the celebration of the 300th Anniversary of St. Petersburg.' The demonstration of Russian military force in the Kaliningrad region as the 'Windows to the World' could only indicate for the neighboring countries and international community a necessity to demand Russian withdrawal.

The Kaliningrad Region is an Anomaly and an Anachronism

During a dinner-debate of the European-Atlantic Group held in London in October 2002, the Rt. Hon. Michael Ancram, then Shadow Foreign Secretary of the British Conservative Party, was asked: "Why cannot NATO and the EU leaders ask Russia to

---

705   See the diary of President Truman in the exhibition of his Presidential Museum in Independence, Missouri.

706   "Security and Foreign Policy in Russia and the Post-communist Region," RFE/RL, 4: 24, June 18, 2003.

withdraw its military forces from the Königsberg region as soon as possible, and allow the people there to decide their future themselves in a referendum?" He answered by saying that it is obvious that "the region is an anomaly, which the EU has to resolve," and that he "would like to see more debate about the future of this region in Europe."[707]

Inevitably the future of this region lies with Europe. President Vytautas Landsbergis, Member of the European Parliament, made a statement on the Karaliaučius-Kaliningrad region on May 23, 2002, which suggested that Europe should initiate a "real international debate on this issue." He asked in addition: "Will the European Union be responsible for this region in future, or will its neighbors, Poland, Lithuania or Sweden?"[708] In July 2004 he suggested the establishment of a parliamentary group in the European Parliament for the solution of the Königsberg problem, and thirty other members of the European Parliament have expressed interest in joining.[709] President Vytautas Landsbergis' book "Karaliaučius ir Lietuva" (Königsberg and Lithuania) is an important collection of documents and it is the most significant contribution to the debate on the future of this region in Europe.[710] As early as February 16, 1992 Vytautas Landsbergis, then President of the Lithuanian Parliament, called the region an anachronism, demanding the withdrawal of all Russian military troops. He also called for a change in the status of the region at the international conference organized by the Lithuanian Parliament in 2006, but the Russians are still

---

707   See the speech of Rt. Hon. Michael Ancram in the web page of the European-Atlantic group in London: www.eag.org.uk.

708   Tėvynės Sąjungos Pirmininko, Seimo nario Vytauto Landsbergio pareiškimas "Dėl dirbtinai kaitinamo Karaliaučiaus-Kaliningrado klausimo," May 23, 2002.

709   "V. Landsbergis inicijuoja specialios grupės Kaliningrado klausimais įsteigimą" (Vytautas Landsbergis initiates a special group for the solution of issues related to Kaliningrad), ELTA, July 26, 2004.

710   Vytautas Landsbergis, "Karaliaučius ir Lietuva" (Vilnius: Demokratinės Politikos Institutas, 2003).

keeping the region as a trophy of the Second World War, just as they keep the Northern territories of Japan.[711]

The Russian Military Fortress within the EU

Landsbergis' concern is well-founded. Currently Kaliningrad is an impoverished area which is the primary source of drug trafficking in the Baltic States and Europe, and it has the most severe AIDS problem in the continental region. The EU Report on Kaliningrad, which attempted to draw an in-depth picture of the difficult situation in the region, was right in stating that the strategic importance of the area had decreased during the 1990s, but it highlighted major problems. It stated: "Kaliningrad is the second worst source of pollution in the Baltic Sea region after St. Petersburg, generating more than 400,000 tons annually of domestic and industrial waste," and said: "Diseases such as tuberculosis, diphtheria, measles, and epidemic paratyphoid are widespread. [...] Drug use and prostitution have led to the alarming spread of other communicable diseases. For instance, Kaliningrad is among the worst regions in Russia for registered cases of HIV and is by far the most affected area in the Baltic Sea region."[712]

There are probably more Russian troops concentrated there than there are American army personnel in the remainder of Europe, a consideration which is magnified considering President

---

711   "Lithuania: Landsbergis promotes change in Kaliningrad's status," BBC Mon FS1 FsuPol grh/es, Source: Vilnius BNS www-text in English 1900 GMT February 3, 2006. Japan has never recognized Soviet annexation of its Northern Territories (Etorofu, Kunashiri, Shikotan and Habomai islands). The United States has always supported the Japanese position. On comparison of the cases of the Königsberg region and the Japanese Northern Territories see Darius Furmonavičius, "The liberation of the Königsberg/Kaliningrad region and the Northern territories/Southern Kuril Islands in comparative perspective," in the proceedings of the 6th Biennial Conference of ECSA-Canada, Victoria, British Columbia, 19-20 May 2006, http://www.ecsac2006.com/pdf/Darius-Furmonavicius.pdf#search=%22Darius%20Furmonavicius%22. Also, Darius Furmonavičius, "The liberation of the Königsberg/Kaliningrad region and the Northern territories/Southern Kuril Islands in comparative perspective," _Lituanus_, no. 4 (52), (2006): 5-15.

712   _The EU and Kaliningrad_, Commission of the European Communities, January 17, 2001, p. 14.

Bush's announced intention to phase out the American presence even further.[713] The Lithuanians still figure it as a force of at least 40,000 troops and approximately 200,000 military personnel. An accurate estimate of the total military accumulation in the region is probably considerably higher than the estimate made in the 2001 European Commission Report *"The EU and Kaliningrad,"* which said that the numbers had "fallen from 200,000 to only 18,000."[714]

However, the *Military Balance* of the International Institute of Strategic Studies (2006, 2007, 2008, 2009 and 2010) indicates a slight

---

713   The United States reduced the presence of American troops in Europe from 250,000 to 100,000 in 1997. Further withdrawal of more than 70,000 troops from Germany and South Korea is foreseen within ten years (2004-2014). See e.g. Roland Eggleston, "Germany: Dismay In Some Towns Over Planned U.S. Troop Withdrawal", RFE/RL HEADLINES, August 18, 2004. Also, the President of the United States, despite the deep concerns of the Government of Iceland, decided that Naval Air Station, Keflavik in Iceland "will begin a transition to a reduced "footprint" which will be completed by 30 September 2006." http://www.naskef.navy.mil/template5.asp?PageID=51&newsid=318. This ongoing American withdrawal from Europe undoubtedly contradicts the long-term national security interests of the United States, despite all justifications about the permanent relocation of troops closer to the war areas in the Middle East. It indirectly encourages the nostalgic authoritarian Russian regime to take up more adventurous policies towards Central Europe, including the Baltic States, thus increasing the chance that the present economic war in Europe between the expansionist Russian state oil and gas companies and the governments defending their key infrastructure will grow into a military confrontation not least because of the possibility of an accumulated perception by the Russians that the United States would choose to refuse to defend its NATO allies in Europe if Russia decides to attack the EU in future. Therefore, the fascist Russian regime can try to use its military forces in adventurous attempts to occupy a smaller NATO country, under various pretexts and explanations, checking the overall NATO response and imagining that such a step could contribute to the eventual dissolution of the North Atlantic Alliance, as some experts foresee within the next twenty years. On the other hand, if the Russian influence in Washington, D.C. continues to increase further and if the whole layer of short-sighted middle ranking officers, who think that "Putin is our ally," remains within the Pentagon and the Department of State, the repetition of the tragedy of 1939 in Europe will be more likely, particularly when the neo-conservatives have already succeeded in shifting all U.S. foreign policy from dismantling communist power structures in Russia to the development of democracy in the Middle East. President Obama's reset policy towards Russia was a naïve mistake and, in fact, it was further encouragement for the totalitarian Kremlin's regime to attempt to increase its influence in Europe.

714   *The EU and Kaliningrad*, Commission of the European Communities, January 17, 2001, p. 12.

increase in ground forces in 2006 in comparison with the numbers of military vehicles in 2001 (some 837 battle tanks (plus some 26 tanks of the naval infantry – 864 all together), 865 armored vehicles (plus some 220 armored vehicles of the naval infantry – 1,085 all together).

[i] In 2006, there were 51 Su-27 aircraft: 28 SU-27 aircraft Flanker (Baltic Fleet) coastal defense plus 23 Su-27 Flanker naval aviation and 26 Su-24 Fencer as well as 14 other planes (12 An-12 Cub / An-24 Coke / An-26 Curl; 2 An-12 Cub), all together 91 planes (Baltic Fleet) and 55 helicopters (including 11 Mi-24 Hind attack helicopters, 19 Ka-28 (Ka-27) Helix, 8 Ka-29 Helix, 17 Mi-8 Hip). The ground and airborne forces were backed by 18 SS-21 Scarab (Tochka) missiles and the coastal defense – by a regiment of 8 surface-to-surface SS-C-1B Sepal missiles. (These Sepal missiles (the so-called shorter-range missiles - up to 745 km rage with 350 kT conventional or nuclear warheads) are prohibited by the INF treaty).[715]

[ii] According to the ISSS, the Kaliningrad Oblast had in 2006 some 10,500 ground troops, 1,100 naval infantry plus four additional regiments (approximately four thousand men). So, it mentions about sixteen thousand troops altogether. The Swedes and Danes give a similar figure, and this figure is generally accepted. *The Military Balance* (2001-2015) indicates a slight increase in ground and air forces in 2008 in comparison with the numbers of military vehicles, planes, and helicopters in 2001.[716]

[iii] In 2008, there were 28 Su-27, 26 Su-26 aircraft (Baltic Fleet) and 11 attack as well as 44 transport helicopters. The ground forces in the Kaliningrad area were backed also by 18 SS-21 Tochka (Scarab) missiles and the coastal defense – by a regiment of 8 surface-to-surface SS-C-1b Sepal missiles.[717] Both type of missiles can be used as nuclear weapons.[718]

---

715 *The Military Balance 2006* (Oxford: Oxford University Press, 2007), p. 159 & 162.
716 *The Military Balance 2006* (Oxford: Oxford University Press, 2007), p. 159 & 162.
717 *The Military Balance 2008.*
718 Ibid., p. 218. Also, see Principle Warsaw Pact Tactical Missiles and Rockets. Presidential Library, Simi Valley, California.

[iv] In 2000, there were 74 aircraft and 41 helicopters in the region, although only one operational submarine.[719]

[v] In 1996, there were 5 naval aviation regiments: 102 aircrafts and 42 helicopters, and one army headquarters of 24,000 ground troops in the region.[720]

[vi] In 2010, there were 24 Su-27, 29 Su-26 aircraft (Baltic Fleet) and 14 transport planes plus 11 attack as well as 37 other helicopters; 811 tanks and 1,239 armed carrier vehicles, 345 peaces of artillery and 1 brigade with 12-18 SS-21 Tochka (Scarab) missiles capable of being used as nuclear weapons.[721] In addition, Coastal Defense contained of 2 regiments with 133 artillery peaces, 1 regiment with surface-to-surface 8 SS-C-1B *Sepal* missiles capable of being used as nuclear weapons. In 2010, the Kaliningrad Special Region had 11,600 troops (10,500 ground and airborne troops as well as 1,100 naval infantry).

[vii] Since July 2010 military forces of the Kaliningrad Special Region became part of the Western Military District with the headquarters of the Baltic Fleet in St. Petersburg. One can observe a decrease in numbers of aircraft and attack helicopters as well as troops in the region over the last decade; nevertheless, the exact number of military forces in Russia is still a state secret and probably totals between four and five million (officially 1.1 million). At least 12 agencies in Russia (including border troops, the railways, Interior Ministry, Presidential communications, etc.) have official military organizations. The border troops do not have heavy equipment, so they do not count in the balance of forces. And who can deny that this is all enormously large for this small area of 6,000 square miles (15,000 square kilometers)?[722] Substantial military tasks could be carried out, if necessary, by these border guards or other military personnel, including relatively young pensioners (age 40+), called back for duty, still residing in the region. Consequently, even a figure of two hundred thousand militarized personnel or roughly one

---

719   *The Military Balance 2000/2001* (Oxford: Oxford University Press, 2000), p. 123.

720   *The Military Balance 1996/1997* (Oxford: Oxford University Press, 1996), pp. 114-118.

721   *The Military Balance 2010* (Oxford: Oxford University Press, 2010), p. 228.

722   http://www.hkhamb-ahk-kaliningrad.com/en/chap01.html.

fourth of the population of the region, including women and children, is likely to be a modest one. Surprisingly, "the European Commission is not aware of any demands for the withdrawal of the Russian military presence in Kaliningrad" and it believes that "the Russian military presence in Kaliningrad amounts to a total of 16,500 men, with some 8,600 men due to leave by the end of 2003."[723]

It would be wise for the EU to check if this was the case, because unfortunately Russia remains "a wild-card in European and regional security scenarios."[724] According to the RAND study, Russia cannot represent even a part of:

> the threat the Soviet monolith posed and for which the United States prepared for decades. [...] if certain negative trends continue, [... it could] create a new set of dangers that can in some ways prove even more real, and therefore more frightening, than the far off specter of Russian attack ever was.
>
> As a weak state, Russia shares some attributes with "failed" or "failing" states, which the academic literature agrees increase the likelihood of internal and interstate conflict and upheaval. Tracing through the specifics of these processes in Russia reveals a great many additional dangers, both humanitarian and strategic.[725]

Indeed, one important feature of failed states, internal war, is explicitly present in Russia. Vytautas Landsbergis, MEP, former President of Lithuania, made a statement on July 21, 2003 entitled "Russia as a Failed State."[726] He said that mafia activity and murders, an authoritarian system of justice and the suppression of free media, the manipulation of elections, degradation of the army and

---

723   Letter of Gerhard Lohan, Head of Unit (Russia, Ukraine, Moldova, Belarus), Directorate Eastern Europe, Caucasus, Central Asian Republics, External Relations Directorate General, who quoted Jane's Sentinel security assessment from August 2002.

724   Dana Michael Linnet, *Denmark's Foreign and Security Policy Toward the Baltic States 1991-1995. A case study of Post-Cold War Policy Change,* University of Copenhagen, April 2000.

725   Olga Oliker and Tania Charlick-Paley, *Assessing Russia's decline: trends and implications for the United States and the U.S. air force RAND, December 2002.* http://www.rand.org/rnb/1202/mr1442.html.

726   "Seimo nario Vytauto Landsbergio Pastabos. Rusija kaip nepavykusi valstybė," remarks of Vytautas Landsbergis, MP "Russia as a Failed State." July 21, 2003.

the Palestinianisation of the war in Chechnya, plus the official state order as a "managed democracy" show the main attributes of such a failed state.[727] As a failed state, therefore, Russia is no less dangerous than it was during the Cold War period, despite the nature of the threat being of a different character.[728]

A Bone of Contention Between Russia and the Enlarged EU

The European Commission launched a debate on January 17, 2001 on the impact of its enlargement policies on occupied Königsberg. However, the initiative did not develop into a real discussion on the future of this region, as its effect had so far been confined to questions of economic help for this region. The more radical question of the nature of the continued Russian presence there has yet to be ventilated at that level. Chris Patten asserted, at the inception of the discussion, that "Kaliningrad should not become a bone of contention between Russia and the enlarged EU." While serving to truncate the debate, his statement was wholly remarkable for its failing to mention the historic name of the region Königsberg, the birthplace of the famous philosopher Immanuel Kant. Nor did he suggest that Russia's presence in the region is illegal, or note how the Soviet Union had broken the Potsdam agreements.[729] Still less did he point out Russia's insistence on retaining the naming of the region after Kalinin, a Commissar of the Stalinist Soviet state and eventually its President, and its continuing use of the name *Sovietsk* (for the city once known as Tilsit), reflecting the Soviet state's name itself, which serves only to emphasize Russia's lack of repentance for its Stalinist legacy in Europe, and its leaders' nostalgia for the former totalitarian regime.

It is noteworthy also that Chris Patten stated, during a plenary session of the European Parliament held in Strasbourg on May 14, 2002: "We share the Parliament's view that, as part of Russia,

---

727 Remarks of Vytautas Landsbergis.
728 See the final chapter "Concluding Remarks" in this book.
729 "Commission launches debate on impact of enlargement on Kaliningrad," IP/01/66, Brussels, January 17, 2001.

Kaliningrad is essentially a Russian responsibility. We also believe that EU enlargement is an opportunity from which Kaliningrad can greatly benefit, rather than a threat."[730] While we know that indeed the EU is no threat to anyone in the region, the present situation of Kaliningrad is likely to remain a significant threat to the EU and neighbors of the region for as long as the question of future Russian military withdrawal remains unresolved. It is therefore the right time to question the political background for the statements of the European Commissioner, and to ask whether they represent an historical ignorance, or a wish to appease. It is surprising that the EU has yet to take a decisive position on the necessity of resolving this vital issue, but it seems that the newly elected members of the European Parliament, representatives from a "new" Europe, including the Baltic States, are much more interested in the international debate on this important European and Transatlantic security question.

The official policy of Lithuania is that, while it does not have any territorial claims at present, "Lithuania has a potential claim to the Kaliningrad region."[731] Both Vytautas Landsbergis, former President of the Lithuanian Parliament, and Stasys Lozoraitis, former Lithuanian Ambassador in Washington, D.C. and the head of independent Lithuania's diplomacy in the West, indicated that this region should belong to Lithuania in future.[732] Lithuania raised her claim to this region in the past, when after World War I, the National Council of Prussian Lithuania issued the following declaration in Tilsit (Sovietsk) on November 30, 1918:

---

730 "EU-Russia Summit and Hoff Report on Kaliningrad," Speech by The Rt. Hon Chris Paten, European Parliament – Plenary session, Strasbourg, May 14, 2002 – SPEECH/02/201.

731 Algimantas P. Gureckas, "Lithuania's Boundaries and Territorial Claims between Lithuania and neighboring states," *New York Law School Journal of International and Comparative Law* 12, no. 1-2, p. 112.

732 "Pareiškimas dėl Karaliaučiaus srities," in Vytautas Landsbergis, Pusbrolis Motiejus, (Vilnius: Vaga, 2003), p. 283; Stasys Lozoraitis, "Lietuvos byla tarptautinėje plotmėje," *Dirva*, October 18, 1990, in Landsbergis, Pusbrolis Motiejus, p. 183; Vytautas Landsbergis, "Karaliaučiaus krašto priklausomybės teisiniai aspektai," in Vytautas Landsbergis, *Karaliaučius ir Lietuva. Nuostatos ir idėjos*, (Vilnius: Demokratinės Politikos Institutas, 2003), pp. 11-13; "Iš kalbos Vasario 16-ąją pasitinkant," in Landsbergis, *Karaliaučius ir Lietuva*, p. 14.

Considering that everything that exists has a right to continue existing and that we, Lithuanians who live here in Prussian Lithuania, are the majority of the population of this land, we demand, on the basis of Wilson's right of national self-determination, that Lithuania Minor be joined to Lithuania Major. All these, who with their signatures have adopted this declaration, pledge to dedicate all their capabilities for implementation of this goal.[733]

From 1998, by the vote of the Lithuanian Parliament, November 20 is officially celebrated as the commemoration day of the Act of the unification of Lithuania Minor with the Republic of Lithuania. In its Lithuanian-Russian Treaty of July 29, 1991, Lithuania recognized the Kaliningrad Oblast as part of the Russian Federation *de facto* but not *de jure*.[734] So, Lithuania still keeps an active claim to the northern part of East Prussia open, but at present it is more deeply interested in the demilitarization of the region. Despite the strong resolution of the U.S. House of Representatives, initiated by Christopher Cox, former Chairman of the Policy Committee and unanimously passed in the House of Representatives in 1996, demanding that Russia withdraw its military forces from the region almost nothing appears to have happened since. The Russian Army is still there, and the pollution of the Baltic Sea still advances on a critically high scale. However, there are important undercurrents which are equally relevant to an understanding of how the situation may be rectified. The Baltic Assembly, which embraces representatives of all three Baltic parliaments, has drafted an appeal to the European governments, and those of Russia and the regional government in Kaliningrad, to the effect that the future of this region is with Europe and that a referendum must be held to permit the citizens of that region to decide on their future for themselves.[735]

733   Op. cit. Algimantas P. Gureckas, "Lithuania's Boundaries and Territorial Claims between Lithuania and neighboring states," *New York Law School Journal of International and Comparative Law* 12, no. 1-2, p. 113.

734   Gureckas, "Lithuania's Boundaries and Territorial Claims," p. 115.

735   Interview with President Landsbergis, May 18, 2002. See also Vytautas Landsbergis, *Karaliaučius ir Lietuva. Nuostatos ir idėjos,* (Vilnius: Demokratinės politikos institutas, 2003) and a review of this book, whose title can be translated as *Koenigsberg and Lithuania: standpoints and ideas* by Dr. Darius Furmonavicius in *International Affairs* 80, no. 3 (May 2004): 557-558.

It is important to note that during the first meeting on April 24, 2002, between the Russian Prime Minister Mikhail Kasayanov and the European Union Commissioners, the Kaliningrad issue dominated the discussion. A major point in the discussion was Russia's request for "visa-free corridors" through the territories of the future EU members Poland and Lithuania, "to allow the free movement of people and goods." While it is known that the EU declined this request, it is highly significant that Russia also sought free access for "military personnel and material along these corridors."[736] It is also important to record that while Russia's President subsequently declined an invitation to participate in the EU-Russia Summit in Copenhagen, though demanding a meeting in Brussels, the European Commission made what must be interpreted as totally unacceptable and indeed immoral concessions to Russia, agreeing feasibility studies looking into non-stop visa-free trains running across Lithuanian territory, once Lithuania had joined the EU. The proposal for such "sealed trains" has of course deeply disturbing historical echoes of the famous sealed train in which Lenin was taken to Russia for the organization of the Communist revolution in St. Petersburg. The very proposal clearly violates the sovereignty of Lithuania, and it is very strange indeed that Putin's European friends in power at that time, notably Italy's Silvio Berlusconi, Spain's Jose Maria Aznar, France's Jacques Chirac and Greece's Constantin Simitis were all in favor of such a deal, which was crisply named by Vytautas Landsbergis, as "a new Ribbentrop-Molotov pact on the future of Lithuania."[737] However, it did not become a reality thanks to the firm position of Denmark, and the efforts of the Germans, aided not least by their drawing European attention to Russia's internal war in Chechnya, but Russia started putting pressure on Lithuania once again from June 2003, in the hope of gaining a new military transit agreement. Vytautas

---

736   Ahto Lobjakas, "Russia: Kaliningrad's Future A Topic of Kasayanov's Talks With EU," RFE, May 24, 2002.

737   See Judy Dempsey, "Diplomatic notebook: Putin's Schengen shenanigans," October 9, 2002, and the statement of Vytautas Landsbergis, MP, former Chairman of the Delegation of Lithuania for the Negotiations with the USSR, "About the Possibility of a New Ribbentrop-Molotov Pact," October 7, 2002.

Landsbergis has stated that Russia was exploiting the last opportunity before Lithuania's joining of NATO and the EU. It persisted but failed in its attempt to gain "supplementary rights in Lithuania" through the long-term military transit agreement.[738]

Despite this difference in positions, on November 11, 2002 an agreement was reached between the EU and Russia in Brussels on the issue of "Facilitated and Simplified Transit Documents" to residents of the occupied Königsberg region, and civilian inhabitants from Russia, under which both types of documents were to be controlled by Lithuania. According to the *Financial Times*, this agreement has effectively changed the status of the region. A further concession, though, was made by the EU Commission prior to the accession of Lithuania on May 1, 2004, which granted Russia a virtually customs-free transit regime to and from Kaliningrad. These agreements go far towards removing any risk of friction, but it is noteworthy that three issues, which are related to the environmental and administrative problems and particularly sensitive for Lithuania, have been left unanswered.

First, the extraction of oil in the Baltic Sea by Lukoil, the Russian company, from the D-6 platform in the Baltic Sea (approximately 3 miles from Lithuania's border) can transform the *Kuršių Nerija* (the Curonian Spit, a UNESCO recognized World Nature Heritage National Park) and the whole region into a potential disaster area. (Lithuanians thought that the international community, above all the EU, should demand the discontinuance of the building of these extraction facilities immediately, and the Lithuanian Conservative Party organized a successful week-long demonstration in September 2003 near Lukoil petrol stations in Lithuania, encouraging people to buy petrol in other stations, and to a greater effort attempts to attract international attention to the problem).

Second, using its sophisticated energy policy, Russia continues its attempts to force the Baltic States and Poland back into its zone of influence. A new deal has been concluded on the so-called

---

738   Vytautas Landsbergis, "Dėl Rusijos karinio tranzito per Lietuvą," Statement of Vytautas Ladsbergis, MP "On Russia's military transit across Lithuania," July 23, 2003.

North European gas pipeline through the Baltic Sea, which is planned to be funded partially by the European Union itself (!) and which will have branches to the Kaliningrad region as well as to Finland, Sweden, the Netherlands, Germany, and Britain but there was no plan to have branches to Lithuania, Latvia, Estonia, or to Poland, Slovakia or other Central and East European states. This was once again called the new Molotov-Ribbentrop pact by many politicians and commentators in Lithuania and in Poland. It was strongly criticized by Lithuanian President Valdas Adamkus and Lithuanian Prime Minister Algirdas Brazauskas, who attempted to reverse its provisions.[739] The pipeline caused controversy in Germany. Poland perceived it as a security threat but did little to oppose it.[740] In fact, the North European gas pipeline creates the possibility of an effective Russian economic blockade of Poland and the Baltic States at some time in the future. Up to now such blackmail, which has been known to be used by Russia in past times, has not been possible because any reduction in supplies to Lithuania and Poland would instantly reduce the supplies of natural gas to the Kaliningrad region (even the USSR found it could not afford to terminate the entire supply of gas to Lithuania during the economic blockade of 1990, but rather it decreased the supply to one third of the original level). At the same time the building of an independent pipeline from Norway to Poland and the Baltic States is a vital necessity. The Poles have already signed an agreement with the Danes about the building of 220 km (140 miles) pipeline under the Baltic sea to join the Polish and the Danish pipelines in order to import the Norwegian gas (if the natural gas supplies from Russia are stopped) or to export the natural gas.[741] Liquid Natural Gas terminal in Klaipeda, Lithuania which was launched at the end of 2014 was an important step in energy independence of Lithuania and the Baltic States.

---

739   "Gas Pipeline to Run to Russia's Kaliningrad Region-Report," Dow Jones International News, July 3, 2005.

740   "The Baltic Pipeline Will Seriously Impair Poland's Energy Security but Warsaw Is Doing Little About It," Economic Review, Polish News Bulletin, July 8, 2005.

741   Ibid.

In the meantime, President Putin stated (at a news conference following his talks with the French and German leaders) that Russia and Europe are "moving in the right direction" and that "natural large-scale changes are currently under way and will continue in Europe and Russia. ... Our colleagues and successors will have to take this into account."[742] In other words, this can be interpreted as saying that the rulers of the Kremlin have succeeded in increasing Russian influence in Europe, and deceiving the democratic states, since the national security interests of the Baltic States and Poland are being ignored in return for the supply of "cheap" Russian gas and the development of the Kaliningrad region (within the Russian Federation as a special economic zone). This therefore left Central European members of the EU, within the Russian energy influence zone. There are obvious hopes by the Kremlin that the United States would eventually accept such "large scale European changes" caused by German-Russian energy co-operation, and consequently abandon its defense commitments to Europe through NATO.

So, the Lithuanians believe that it should be particularly important for Europe to diversify its energy resources independently from Russia, thus abandoning plans for the Northern European pipeline.

Third, the Russians still fail to understand that the withdrawal of their remaining military troops from Europe as well as from Japan would not reduce their prestige but, on the contrary, would improve their 'face' and their relations with the West. Although half of the military forces were withdrawn from the occupied Japanese Northern Territories during the President Yeltsin period, as they were also reduced in the occupied Königsberg region, nevertheless, tactical nuclear weapons were redeployed in the region at the beginning of the presidency of Putin in 2001 and the further withdrawal of Soviet military hardware was postponed for an undefinite period. Despite the EU "Special program for the Kaliningrad Oblast" and the budget line B7-520 of 392 million euros for

---

742 "Putin says Russia, Europe 'moving in the right direction'," BBC Monitoring Newsfile, July 3, 2005.

2004-2006, excessive militarization continues; numerous military exercises such as Baltica-2005 also take place. There are constant and deliberate violations of Baltic and Finnish airspace by Russian spy-planes and other military planes flying to and from the Kaliningrad region, one of which, an SU-27, crashed in Lithuania in 2005, carrying four air-to-air missiles and at least 2 kg of radioactive metal.[743]

During the celebration of the 750th anniversary of Königsberg in July 2005, at the ceremonies renaming Kaliningrad University as Kant University, Vladimir Putin made some strong statements that "Kant was categorically opposed to settling any disputes between states through war" and that Russia was "trying to stick to his teaching in this respect." Despite this new type of presentation, Russia is continuing heavy militarization of the region.[744] The status quo is strengthened not only through bilateral diplomacy (so that, for example German Chancellor Gerhard Schröder and French President Jacques Chirac were invited to participate in these ceremonies while close neighbors, Lithuanian President Valdas Adamkus and Polish President Alexander Kwasniewski, were not welcomed[745]) but also by an increased military presence in the region.

The Baltic Assembly passed a resolution "Concerning the demilitarization of the Kaliningrad region and its future development," suggesting that "the demilitarization of the Kaliningrad Region should be treated as an essential element for the security process in Central Europe and the entire Continent."[746] On the eve of the EU-Russia summit, Prof. Tunne Kelam, Estonian Member of the

---

743 "Russia denies violation of Estonian airspace," BBC Monitoring Former Soviet Union, July 2, 2005. "Estonia alleges new air space violation by Russia," Agence France Presse, July 2, 2005. "Russian minister denies violation of Finnish airspace," BBC Monitoring Former Soviet Union, June 27, 2005.

744 "Russia will stick to Kant's teaching on peaceful settlement of disputes – Putin," Interfax, July 3, 2005.

745 "Putin, Chirac, Schroeder to meet at Kaliningrad 750th anniversary," ITAR-TASS, July 3, 2005. "Polish Leaders: Disappointed at Russia Anniversary Snub," Oster Dow Jones Commodity Wire, June 27, 2005.

746 "Resolution "Concerning the Demilitarization of the Kaliningrad region and its future development," Vilnius, November 13, 2004, http://www.litlex.lt/Litlex/Eng/Frames/Laws/Documents/16.HTM.

European Parliament, asked the European Commission "how systematic violation by Russian planes of the borders of EU Member States can be tallied with common values upon which the EU-Russia partnership is officially based. Is not the integrity of the EU's eastern borders part of our common foreign and security policy? As for Kaliningrad, is it not in the interests of all parties to start to find ways to demilitarize this last vestige of the Cold War in Europe?"[747] Lithuanian Foreign Minister Antanas Valionis stated that the crash of an SU-27 jetfighter in Lithuania had shown that it was necessary to urge the demilitarization of the Kaliningrad region: "Keeping such forces in such a place where they can cross the borders of a number of states in minutes is an anachronism. It will be difficult to avoid incidents in the future if such forces are further kept there."[748] The Lithuanian Parliament called for the demilitarization of the Kaliningrad region in its resolution on the crash of the Russian SU-27 fighter in Lithuania.[749] The Lithuanian American Council demanded full demilitarization of the region and that its future be resolved as part of the heritage of the Lithuanian nation.[750]

On the other hand, the EU's aid to Russia has totaled more than one billion euros since 1990. It does not seem inappropriate to request something in return for this, in the form of a rapid, orderly, and complete demilitarization of the Königsberg region. (This is an approach which worked well in the early 1990s when Russian officers received vouchers for housing in Russia, with American assistance, in return for the smooth withdrawal of military forces from the Baltic States).

---

747   Debates, One-minute speeches on matters of political importance, September 26, 2005 - Strasbourg, European Parliament, http://www.europarl.eu.int/om k/sipade3?PUBREF=//EP//TEXT+CRE+20050926+ITEM-012+DOC+XML+ V0//EN&LEVEL=2&NAV=S&L=EN.

748   Interview of Foreign Minister Antanas Valionis with Lithuanian National Radio, BBC Monitoring Newsfile, September 22, 2005.

749   Lietuvos Respublikos Seimas. Rezoliucija "Dėl incidento su Rusijos kariniu orlaiviu SU-27," Vilnius, October 13, 2005.

750   Amerikos Lietuvių Tarybos Kongreso Rezoliucijos, Chicago, October 23-21, 2005.

In addition, considering a broader picture of Central and Eastern Europe, it is particularly important that attempts should be made to facilitate regime change in Byelorussia, and to achieve the withdrawal of all Russian military forces from Moldova and Georgia as soon as possible. In this context, we are impelled to note that it is very strange indeed that the U.S. government decided to terminate the broadcasts of Radio Free Europe and Radio Liberty (RFE/RL) to the Baltic States and to Poland as well as other countries of Central Europe in January 2004, as well as to reduce them significantly to Byelorussia and Ukraine. It was a particular paradox at a time when Russia has made attempts to change the foreign policy orientation of Ukraine and to increase its significant influence in the region. It is suggested that this development alone makes it imperative that the U.S. Congress should act to increase assistance funding to the Baltic States, including military assistance programs, and indeed to expand radio broadcasts to other countries of the Baltic Sea region, including Belorussia and Ukraine, while creating a new broadcast, facilitating the liberation of the occupied Königsberg region.

It would also be wise in the long term for other governments to follow the lead of those in the Baltic States in demanding an international court on the crimes of communism, modeled on the Nuremberg trials of Nazism, as a means of cleansing Russia of the stains of the communist period and as a way of finally ending the Cold War, in the way that Nazism was purged from Germany. In the meantime, it would also be particularly important to encourage the international community to add pressure on Russia to get the Russians to pay back the grand total of damages to the Baltic States and other Central and Eastern European states related to their occupation ($32 billion to Lithuania alone).[751]

---

751   In 1999 Lithuania's Government (Prime Minister – Andrius Kubilius, Chairman of the Conservative Party) calculated Russia's debt as at least 80 billion litas (or $27 billion) due as a compensation for Lithuania's occupation (1940-1990).

Litmus Test of the European Union Itself

One can argue that the outcome of the Königsberg question is a litmus test of the European Union itself. Obviously, the EU can help the region (as we have mentioned earlier, during 2004-2006 this assistance totaled some €392 million or over $400 million), but the real question is whether the European Union can develop firm and clear policies regarding this region's future. Until it does, its effective stance will remain essentially pro-Russian. In fact, the European Union must create a common strategy toward the Kaliningrad region, replacing its currently ineffective strategy towards Russia.[752]

Professor Romano Prodi then, President of the European Commission, has stated in his address "A Wider Europe – A Proximity Policy as the key to stability" made in December 2002 to the 6th ECSA-World Conference Peace, Security and Stability: International Dialogue and the Role of the EU that we need to set benchmarks to measure what we expect our neighbors to do [...] We might even consider some kind of "Copenhagen proximity criteria."[753] He also mentioned that 58 percent of Russians wish to join the EU, according to opinion polls performed by the EU at the end of 2002. The percentage in the Kaliningrad region is undoubtedly much higher. Indeed, Russia must be persuaded to respect human rights and to acknowledge the wish of its people to join the EU, and to let the occupied Königsberg region become free by allowing its integration into the EU. This is the way to resolve the enormous problems of the region, rather than allowing the present clumsy situation to continue.

In her recent book *"Statecraft,"* former British Prime Minister Margaret Thatcher has argued that it is no longer possible to reform the EU. It can be suggested that the EU approach to the resolution

---

752 Sander Huisman, "Future of Kaliningrad," *ISS-EU Newsletter* 1 (February 2002), http://www.iss-eu.org.

753 "A Wider Europe - A Proximity Policy as the key to stability," Speech by Romano Prodi, President of the European Commission. "Peace, Security and Stability International Dialogue and the Role of the EU." Sixth ECSA-World Conference. Jean Monnet Project, Brussels, December 5-6, 2002. See: http://europa.eu.int/comm/external_relations/news/prodi/sp02_619.htm.

of the Königsberg issue will show clearly whether this is true or not. The question is whether the EU can find the strength to transform its present policies by issuing a clear demand for Russian withdrawal from the Königsberg region. This can be done by attaching conditions to economic aid to Russia and allowing the people of the region and their descendants (but not the colonists, in parallel to the UN case of West Sahara) to decide their own future in a referendum. If this were to happen, the Baltic nations would sincerely recognize that this organization has the genuine intention of playing a positive role in the Baltic Sea region.

An important role in the solution of the Königsberg question might also be imputed to the Council of the Baltic Sea States (CBSS), an organization of multilateral diplomacy and co-operation, established in 1992 at the initiative of Denmark and Germany, and which embraces all countries around the Baltic Sea, including Russia, with the United States participating as an observer. Also, the OSCE mechanism for peaceful change of borders could be used. We shall paraphrase the Prime Minister of Hungary, who charged Westerners with "not always understanding his people's profound longing for Europe," by saying that "Europe is like grandfather's watch that was taken away by a Russian soldier." We might also add that Königsberg, the birthplace of the famous philosopher Immanuel Kant, is like grandfather's watch, still in the possession of the Red Army.[754] Indeed, the Second World War will at last be over, when the Königsberg region is finally liberated from Russian occupation, and Russia will then be freer to pursue a destiny of peace with her immediate Western neighbors.

It would be wise for Russia to show its goodwill and to withdraw rapidly, orderly, and completely its military and security forces from former East Prussia as they were withdrawn from Denmark in the 1940s, or Austria in the 1950s or the Baltic States, Poland, and Germany in the 1990s.

---

754   Prof. John Hiden has observed that Viktor Orban's words apply equally to the Baltic States. The same is valid for Lithuania Minor. See John Hiden, "Regional Security: All or Nothing at All?" in Marko Lethi and David Smith, *Post-Cold War Identity Politics. Northern and Baltic Experiences* (London & Portland: Frank Cass, 2003), p. 180.

11. Concluding Remarks

The main argument of this study has been that Lithuania is an indivisible part of Europe and of the West. She was invited to join in the second wave of NATO enlargement in November 2002 as well as the new wave of EU enlargement in December of the same year. These invitations and their acceptance confirmed Lithuania's commitment to European-Atlantic values of democracy, free-market economy, and the rule of law. Her struggle to achieve this fulfillment of her destiny is emphasized by Lithuania's having fought the longest partisan war in European history against the Soviet occupation during the years 1945-1960. She did this to retain her freedom and to remain in Europe. Her peaceful liberation from Soviet occupation and her preparatory steps of full integration into the European and transatlantic security framework were a vindication of the bravery of Lithuania's sons and daughters who gave their lives in a spirit of sacrifice against the nation being swallowed once more by an enemy firmly committed to opposing those European-Atlantic values.

The policy of non-recognition by Western states of the incorporation of Lithuania into the Soviet Union, and the Helsinki process, were eventually found to be the major international tools that assisted the advent of peaceful change to the Soviet Union, and the eventual liberation of the Lithuanians from the communist regime. The policy of non-recognition by Western states of the incorporation of the Baltic States into the Soviet Empire by Western states gave an external legitimacy which was eventually to be of crucial importance to the legal confirmation of Lithuania's right to self-determination and independence. It was positively and actively expressed during the administration of U.S. President Ronald Reagan. The subtle pressure and urging of the Helsinki process to respect the fundamental human rights of oppressed people, which was started during President Gerald R. Ford's administration in 1975, eventually became the major international source for moral inspiration. Finally, President George Herbert Walker Bush's encouragement of peaceful process and discouragement of the Soviet leaders from using military force in Lithuania facilitated the collapse of the Soviet Union. President George W. Bush's commitment to his father's vision of a Europe whole and free, as well as to NATO enlargement, increased European and transatlantic security and stability.

Looking back, some clear patterns in the process of state restoration can be identified. This is best perceived when comparing the situation which emerged in the late 1980s and early 1990s with the conditions that Lithuania faced during the late 1910s and early 1920s. Three major similarities can be identified: in both scenarios the declaration of national independence came first. Next, there was a period of resistance against the enemies of independence, and finally there came the search for international recognition. However, as Alfred Erich Senn has noted, the military and diplomatic situations were strikingly different in these two cases. The struggle of 1918-1920 was much more difficult and uncertain, because Lithuania had to battle to find itself a place in the power vacuum that had emerged after the mutual destruction of the German and Russian empires. The Bolshevik Revolution had taken place and a strong and energetic nationalist neighbor had emerged in the form of Poland. The issue of determining Lithuania's borders immediately became the most important task of Lithuania's diplomacy, "ranging from the loss of Vilnius in 1920 to regaining it in 1939, from gaining Memel in 1923 to losing it in 1939, and of course from escaping Russia in 1918-1919 to being incorporated into the Soviet Union in 1940."[755] The historical anamnesis of these matters partly explains why in the 1990s the Lithuanians were so adamantly supportive of the Helsinki principle of the "non-violability" of borders in Europe. The borders of Lithuania in 1991 were the borders of the former Soviet Lithuanian Republic, rather than the pre-war borders of the Lithuanian Republic of the 1920s or 1930s, when the Vilnius region was occupied by Poland and the Klaipėda

---

755   Alfred E. Senn, "Comparing the circumstances of Lithuanian independence, 1918 - 1922 and 1988 – 1992," in Eberhard Demm, Roger Noël, R. and William Urban (eds.), *The Independence of the Baltic States: Origins, Causes, and Consequences. A Comparison of the Crucial Years 1918 - 1919 and 1990 – 1991* (Chicago: Lithuanian Research and Studies Center, 1996), p. 14.

region was taken away by Nazi Germany. Nevertheless, in the 1990s the major problem for Lithuanian diplomacy was not border issues but the presence of the former Soviet army.

With just one (albeit major) foreign threat - the Russian troops, the situation in the 1990s was very different from that of the 1920s, when Lithuania was struggling against three enemies at the same time: the Soviet Russian army in the east, the Bermondtist Army in the north, and the Polish Army in the south. According to Senn, the passive resistance with which the Lithuanians confronted the Soviet troops in the 1990s was a powerful weapon that the nation could not have used in the 1920s.[756] He emphasizes other interesting similarities too. The debate over the possible powers of the nation's President was as lively in the 1920s as in the 1990s, and in both periods, Lithuania had to wait long and anxiously for international recognition to be extended.

For Lithuania, the 1990s were marked by peaceful liberation from Soviet occupation and the completion of the withdrawal of Russian troops on August 1, 1993. The latter represents probably the best case of OSCE multilateral diplomacy in Europe as the result of a clear re-orientation of the state to the West. Nevertheless, it is often overlooked - and it is indeed quite remarkable - that a relatively small European country like Lithuania, which played a key role in the peaceful collapse of the Soviet Union, also played an important role in this process of building a Europe whole and free. Particularly noteworthy is the fact that it led the second round of NATO enlargement, uniting all candidate countries to speak with one voice. In May 2000, Lithuania initiated and led the Vilnius process, uniting nine NATO candidate countries, which subsequently grew to ten states in collaboration for seeking full NATO membership.[757]

---

756   Senn, "Comparing the circumstances of Lithuanian independence," in *The Independence of the Baltic States*, p. 14.

757   On May 19, 2000, the Foreign Ministers of NATO candidate countries Albania, Bulgaria, Estonia, Latvia, Lithuania, Macedonia, Slovenia, Slovakia, and Romania signed Vilnius' statement. A year later Croatia joined the V-9 during the Conference of Prime Ministers in Bratislava, thus it became V-10.

This study, which has elaborated on this vital process, clearly demonstrates why the European and transatlantic security framework needed to embrace Lithuania and take it into full membership. It has argued that Lithuania is crucially important for the security and stability of the Baltic region, Europe and the whole transatlantic community. We have noted that Lithuania's geographical location in proximity to the Russian occupied Königsberg-Kaliningrad region, on the shores of the Baltic Sea and her shared frontier with Belarus, might in future have tempted an adventurous Russian government to explore its imperial ambitions anew.

The presidential crisis in Lithuania in 2004, the first presidential impeachment in modern European history following the election of Rolandas Paksas, whose role was central to these events, exposed financial backing of alleged Russian related organized crime. Those events clearly indicate the level and the intensity of Russia's covert operations in Europe, particularly in the Baltic States.[758] Recently Vladimir Socor, an analyst of the Jamestown Foundation, commented at the NATO Istanbul summit, that "the Baltic States are welcomed into NATO but Russia still looms in the background," suggesting that NATO should help the Baltic States to counter the covert activities of Russia.[759] Analyzing the recent political situation in Lithuania he concluded that "first, Russia's overt attempts to gain a voice in [the] NATO decision-making process (e.g., via the NATO-Russia Council) are being accompanied by covert actions aiming to subvert political processes in certain NATO member countries and to penetrate their institutions. Second, NATO countries targeted by such actions need assistance in immunizing their institutions against this type of subversion."[760]

It is worth recalling recent history and the sudden disclosure of vast amounts of information about Soviet intelligence and

---

758   Three Russian diplomats were expelled from Lithuania in relation to the Presidential impeachment process. "Lithuania expels three Russian diplomats for spying," AFP, February 27, 2004.

759   Vladimir Socor, "The Baltic States are welcomed into NATO but Russia still Looms in the Background," *Eurasia Daily Monitor*, The Jamestown Foundation, vol. 1, issue 44, July 2, 2004.

760   Socor, "The Baltic States."

counter-espionage operations in Eastern Germany. This was the former area of responsibility of Vladimir Putin. As Mark Kramer rightly put it, "suspicions had long existed in the West about the bizarre nature and scale of East German and Soviet activities but the revelations went even beyond what had been expected, including elaborate support of extreme leftist and neo-Nazi terrorists in West Germany, the provisions of paramilitary training and weapons to Arab and Irish terrorist groups, international arms dealing, the subversion of foreign governments, the formation and maintenance of special "murder squads", and the complicity of Stasi officials in Syrian- and Libyan-sponsored terrorist attacks against American soldiers."[761]

Numerous military exercises were conducted in the Western part of Russia in the 1990s, including the occupied Königsberg region, in which the declared objective was "to capture the Baltic states." They were highly similar to exercises performed in the 1950s to "capture" Denmark, and their repetition only emphasizes the historical legacy of Stalinism in Europe.[762]

In February 2004, the Russian military performed the largest maneuvers of two decades in a massive simulation of an all-out nuclear war. This involved the test-firing of missiles and flights by dozens of bombers and closely resembled the 1982 Soviet exercise dubbed the "seven-hour nuclear war."[763] The Lithuanian government's concern resulted in a NATO E-3 AWACS plane landing in the country on February 24/25, 2004. Together with another AWACS plane above Northern Poland, it monitored the situation in the Kaliningrad region closely, helping to secure Baltic airspace

---

761   Michael Kramer, "The Collapse of East European Communism and the Repercussions within the Soviet Union (Part I)," *Journal of the Cold War Studies*, 5, no. 4, pp. 251-252.

762   The Polish officer recalls: "the capture of the line including Hamburg and the Kiel Canal was our first responsibility. A landing operation was to be carried out at Bornholm, the occupation of Bornholm. And as a further assignment for that Maritime Front was the opening of an offensive against the Jutland Peninsula. The occupation of the Danish straits and the closure of the Baltic." See http://www.isn.ethz.ch/php/documents/collection_9/texts/Stalin_Legacy.htm.

763   "Russia planning maneuvers of its nuclear forces next month," Associated Press, January 30, 2004.

during these exercises which coincided with covert actions in an attempt to destabilize the political situation in Lithuania and in Latvia, just a month before their joining NATO. According to the Jamestown Foundation Report, Latvian President Vaira Vike-Freiberga, "spoke for all the ten countries that joined NATO between 2002 and 2004 [when she] cautioned NATO against overlooking traditional-type threats to security while the alliance retools to deal with new types of threats." She said that a 'full capacity for collective military defense remains indispensable for shielding the member countries against any external pressures and coercion,'[764] and Vladimir Socor commented: "She looked back on these countries' recent history as captive nations from the 1945 Yalta agreements ("one of the 20th century's gravest mistakes") and noted the decades of Moscow-imposed totalitarianism, isolation, and lost generations, which had continued until their self-liberation and return to the West under NATO security guarantees."[765]

Thus, despite NATO and EU membership, there are still important internal and external security problems remaining for Lithuania and the other Baltic States. Internally, Lithuania's economy was dubbed "the Baltic Tiger" by *The Economist* in 2003 (with record GDP growth of 9.4 percent in the first quarter), but pensioners and people in rural areas found themselves in particularly difficult circumstances. One-fifth of the population was living in poverty, and the salaries of academics and physicians had been frozen for six years. The social-democratic government led by Algirdas Brazauskas failed to address social problems properly. Moreover, the vision of a strong middle class developed during the *Sąjūdis* peaceful revolution did not become a reality. Most of the wealth in Lithuania was concentrated in the hands of former communists and Russian-related businessmen. This allowed Russia to influence and manipulate election processes in Lithuania more easily. The radical raising of the standard of living for most of the population in Lithuania continues to be the top priority issue, vitally important for the internal security of the country.

---

764 Socor, "The Baltic States."
765 Socor, "The Baltic States."

An example of Russian covert activities in attempts to over-take a NATO and EU member state was the establishment of the Labor Party in Lithuania by the Russian Gazprom-related business-man Victor Uspaskych. He attempted to overtake the government by the winning of a General Election rather than with the help of external military force. After his failure and a sequence of serious allegations against his party as having links to Russian secret intel-ligence activities, solid evidence was found by the Lithuanian au-thorities proving his tax avoidance as well as his involvement in the corrupt distribution of EU funds. Labor leader Uspaskych departed to Russia without any notice, seeking to avoid justice, prior to his resignation as Chairman of the party.[766]

Externally, a major security problem remains – the Stalinist legacy within an enlarged Europe – namely, the Russian nuclear military base in the occupied Königsberg-Kaliningrad area and continuous Russian demands for having access to a visa-free "Dancing corridor" across Lithuania. One can only hope that NATO, the EU and the OSCE will eventually succeed in resisting these imperial ambitions and contribute to the solution of the Kö-nigsberg issue. However, the key decisions must be made in Wash-ington D.C. and in other NATO capitals as well as in Moscow. It would be a particularly serious error for the Lithuanian govern-ment and in fact, a real crime for the European Commission to agree with Russian demands that the feasibility studies for non-stop Russian trains across Lithuania - mentioned in the so-called Brussels EU-Russia Declaration of November 2002 - become a real-ity.[767] It would be a naïve step to open up the EU borders for possi-ble Russian transit of weapons of mass destruction to and from the occupied Königsberg region. Contrarily, both the Lithuanian Gov-ernment and the European Commission could demand rapid, or-derly and complete withdrawal of Russian troops from the Königs-berg area. This is not a new suggestion, as for instance Vytautas

---

766 "Lithuanian commentary praises foreign ministry for finding Russia's 'weak spot,'" *Kauno Diena*, August 21, 2006, in BBC Mon FsuPol amb.
767 *Lithuanian Railways* Ready for Fast Transit Train, *Newsfile Lithuania,* Issue No. 28 (818), July 12-18, 2004.

Landsbergis has stated on numerous occasions that the Russian army must leave this area.[768] In 1994, Algirdas Brazauskas proposed to the United Nations that "Lithuania, whose territory is used for transit to this Russian enclave, is not indifferent to the future of the Kaliningrad district and the Lithuanian minority residing there. [...] Lithuania proposes to examine issues pertaining to the Kaliningrad district as part of the round-table mechanism established by the European Stability Pact. We hope that all interested parties will give support to this initiative."[769] Despite this proposal being rejected by the Russians, it was a clearly visible attempt by the Lithuanian Government to contribute to international debate on the future of this region.

Against this background it would be wise for NATO leaders to remind President Putin of the U.S. House of Representatives resolution, passed unanimously in 1996, which asked Russia to withdraw its military forces from the Kaliningrad region. We must now enquire as to why NATO and the EU cannot ask Russia, as a sign of good will, to withdraw all of its military forces a few hundred miles to the East across the whole front: to return Karelia to Finland and the still occupied parts of Estonia (Jaanilinn, Petseri) and Latvia (Abrene) to the new EU member states, and finally to remove itself from the Königsberg region, which in effect remains a Soviet-occupied exclave within NATO and the EU.

Inevitably, the long-term future of the Königsberg region lies with Europe and Vytautas Landsbergis, former President of the Lithuanian Parliament and a Member of the European Parliament, has suggested that its integration into the EU should be by means of a referendum of self-determination.[770] On July 12, 2004, in his inaugural speech in the Lithuanian Parliament, President Valdas Adamkus expressed hope that Belarus will choose its democratic way of development once again, that the Kaliningrad region will

---

768   Vytautas Landsbergis, Apie Lietuvos užsienio politiką, <u>Horizontai</u> a supplement to *XXI Amžius*, Nr. 15, August 11, 2004, p.3.

769   BNS, September 30, 1994.

770   Vytautas Landsbergis, *Karaliaučius ir Lietuva. Nuostatos ir idejos (Koenigsberg and Lithuania. Standpoints and ideas)*. (Vilnius: Demokratines politikos Institutas, 2003), p. 231.

become more open to Europe and that Russia itself will become more engaged in European-Atlantic collaboration.[771] Thus, Lithuania is determined both to encourage and to contribute to the democratic process in Kaliningrad as well in Byelorussia. These processes are vitally important for security and stability in the Baltic Sea region and in Europe as a whole but can only be successful if the United States remains actively engaged in Europe, and particularly in the Baltic States.

Baltic States Change the Course of History – Again

"Anyone who would choose Lithuania as an enemy has also made an enemy of the United States of America," stated President George W. Bush during his visit to Lithuania in 2002. In 2022 Secretary Austin told Lithuanian Defense Minister Arvydas Anušauskas that by hosting exiled Russian and Belarusian opposition leaders, Lithuania had become "a beacon of democracy" and was setting an example for allies.

The Baltic States were occupied by the Soviet Union under the auspices of the notorious Moscow Pact of 1939-1941, also known as the Stalin-Hitler Pact or Molotov-Ribbentrop Pact between the Soviet Union and Nazi Germany. "A special military operation" began on June 14, 1940, and hundreds of thousands of Estonians, Latvians and Lithuanians were deported to Siberia.

At the time, U.S. Secretary of State Sumner Welles refused to accept the annexation of the Baltic States. Radio Free Europe and the Voice of America also kept alive the cause of freedom. Peaceful liberation of the Baltic States finally occurred with the collapse of the Soviet Union in 1991, and the withdrawal of Russian troops from Lithuania in 1993 and from Latvia and Estonia in 1994.

The Baltic States celebrated the centenary of diplomatic relations with the United States of America in 2022. Politically, they became an indivisible part of the West by joining NATO and the EU in 2004. Economically, however, despite all their attempts to achieve full energy independence from Russia during the last thirty

---

771   http://adamkus.321.lt/index.php?exp=10&s_id=10&n_id=267&lang=lt.

years and the opening of the natural gas import terminal "Independence" in Lithuania in 2014, thus ending their dependence on the Kremlin's natural gas and oil, they are regrettably still connected to Russia's electricity grid and the reliability of their electricity supply is still determined in Moscow.

The Baltic American Freedom League encourages the liberation of the Baltic states from the grip of Russian electricity and supports their full energy independence from the Kremlin's terrorist regime. Recently, the Prime Ministers of Estonia, Latvia and Lithuania agreed to complete their technical project of integration into the European electricity grid as soon as possible, and by 2025 at the latest.

The flow of illegal migrants organized by the Kremlin is another serious security challenge for the Baltic States. Estonia has a border with Russia, while Latvia borders Belarus as well as Russia. Lithuania has a border with both the Russian military base in the illegally occupied Königsberg area of East Prussia (the Kaliningrad region) and with Belarus.

Lloyd Austin said: "Meanwhile, Russia is conducting a continuous hybrid campaign of its own. And now China is also increasing its pressure on Lithuania. I commend your government for its firm policy regarding China, and we know that you have faced reprisals for your principled decisions." Lithuania allowed the opening of a Taiwanese trade representative office in Vilnius, despite all the contrary pressures from the Chinese Communist regime.

Permanent U.S. Military Presence in the Baltic States

The Baltic States have hosted rotational U.S. battalions in Lithuania since 2019, U.K.-led NATO troops in Estonia, Canadian-led NATO troops in Latvia and German-led NATO troops in Lithuania. The United Kingdom holds leadership of the Joint Expeditionary Force (JEF) and Standing Joint Force Headquarters, which are usually based in London, but now also operate in Lithuania and Latvia.

U.K. liaison officers stationed in Denmark, Estonia, Finland and Sweden coordinate military activities between JEF nations in the Baltic Sea region during this time of heightened regional security. According to U.K. Defence Secretary Ben Wallace, this deployment demonstrates the defensive partnerships within the ten-nation alliance of the JEF.

A permanent American presence in Estonia, Latvia and Lithuania would further bolster U.S. and transatlantic security by ensuring that the "Suwalki Corridor" from Poland to Lithuania remains open. A U.S. presence would also clearly indicate to both NATO allies and adversaries that the territorial integrity and independence of the Baltic States is of vital interest. A U.S. presence would fill gaps in Baltic defense capabilities and provide the Baltics with confidence, enabling stronger NATO deterrence of attacks from Russia.

Enhancing NATO's deterrent posture in the Baltic region would significantly reduce the probability of a Kremlin challenge.

Defense of the Baltic States

2022 defense budgets in the Baltics were 2.5% of GDP in Estonia, 2.2% of GDP in Latvia and 2.52% of GDP in Lithuania. Estonian Prime Minister Kaja Kallas, Latvian Prime Minister Krišjanis Kariņš and Lithuanian Prime Minister Ingrida Šimonytė agreed on the need to raise defense spending to 3% of GDP during 2023.

It is interesting to note that the Baltic States once again changed the course of history by supplying Ukraine with weapons *before* the February 24, 2022, invasion by Russia. The Kremlin's plan to capture Kiev and all of Ukraine in a few days failed partly because of this allocation of supplies.

Ukraine Must Win the War

Prior to the Kremlin's invasion of Ukraine on the 24th of February 2022, Estonia granted Ukraine over a third of its entire defense budget and Latvia granted close to a third. Lithuania was the first NATO state to supply ammunition to Ukraine following Russia's occupation of Crimea in 2014. In May 2022 it took Lithuanians just three days to collect over 5 million EUR to purchase the Turkish Bayraktar drone, as well as the Lithuanian government granting

Ukraine $300 million in defense assistance during 2022. Over the course of 2022, the Baltic States' total defense assistance of close to $1 billion was the highest per capita in the world.

The Kremlin must lose this current war. An ambivalent war outcome, says Lithuanian Foreign Minister Gabrielius Landsbergis, will not bring security to Europe. If Putin succeeds in achieving territorial gains, Russia will renew its war in Ukraine and elsewhere in the future. According to former Russian Prime Minister Kasyanov, if the Kremlin isn't stopped in Ukraine, its next target will be the Baltic States.

The Kremlin's threats are unacceptable. The movement of Putin's private terrorist Wagner army to Byelorussia is an additional serious security threat to the NATO's Eastern flank, particularly to Lithuania, Latvia and Poland.

Strategic Goals: NATO membership for Ukraine

Liberating the whole of Ukraine from Russian occupation and inviting Ukraine to join NATO must be key foreign policy priorities for the United States at the NATO summit in Washington in July 2024. This is the only way to deter a Russian attack on NATO, including the United States, in the future.

In addition, to truncate the funding of Putin's war, the United States must place an international embargo on all Kremlin oil exports. If the Kremlin is not stopped in Ukraine, the probability of a war between Russia and NATO will increases greatly. It is therefore also vitally important that the United States accomplishes a strategic victory over Russia by helping Ukraine to achieve full liberation of her territory as soon as possible.

Only the United States can provide Ukraine with all the required weapons, including long-range missiles, tanks and planes. According to Senator Jim Rish, the US administration should provide Ukraine with everything possible to protect against Russian aggression. Additionally, only the United States can adequately mobilize production.

In short, U.S. military assistance in the Baltic States is vital to the stability and security of Europe and of the whole transatlantic alliance and it is going to be cheaper to deter Russia from possible aggression than to engage with Russia in direct military conflict.

A new world order, according to President Zelenskyy, should be along these lines: Russia must withdraw all its military forces to a few hundred miles from its border, from all Ukrainian territories and from all the territories conquered and illegally annexed by the Soviet Union. Ukraine has also recognized the territorial integrity of Japan. Russia must eventually withdraw from the Northern Territories of Japan as well as from all other regions still occupied since the Second World War. It will be important to bring the Kremlin's war criminals to justice, and to dismantle its nuclear, biological and chemical weapons, facilitating the disintegration of the Russian Empire. All currency reserves of the Kremlin's terrorist regime must be used for the rebuilding of Ukraine and paying compensations to Estonia, Latvia, Lithuania and other neighboring states for the occupations and the illegal annexations of their territories in 1940-1941 and 1944-1990.

Selected Bibliography

I. Primary Sources

Unpublished Documents

Bizauskas, K. Memorandum, 1924. Hoover Institution Archives, Stanford University.

Bundeskanzeramt to Darius Furmonavičius, February 13, 2002.

CCG: notes on Potsdam conference, Public Record Office, London.

Coleman, Frederick W. B. Diaries, 1909-1938. Hoover Institution Archives, Stanford University.

Daužvardis, Petras P. Papers, 1931-1971, Hoover Institution Archives, Stanford University.

Eastern Europe: fighting in Konigsberg are on Jan 29 and Jan 30, Public Record Office, London.

"Įstatymai, įsakai ir potvarkiai, išleisti Lietuvoje bolševikinės okupacijos metu, dėl turtų nacionalizacijos ir konfiskacijos." Lithuania's State Archive, *Lietuvos generalinės srities Darbo ir socialines apsaugos vadyba, Kaunas, 1926 - 1961*, Part 1, Case 26, 69.

Kaslas, Bronis. Papers, 1918-1974. Hoover Institution Archives, Standord University.

Klimas, Petras. Diary excerpts, 1910-1939. Hoover Institution Archives, Stanford University.

"Lietuvos jūros ir upių prekybos laivyno denacionalizacijos įstatymas." Lithuania's State Archive, *Lietuvos generalinės srities Darbo ir socialinės apsaugos vadyba, Kaunas, 1926 - 1961*, Part 1, Case 26, 8 - 9.

"Lietuvos Laikinojo Ministerių Kabineto nutarimas dėl žiemkenčių ir dobilų sėjos bei dėl žemės iki 30 ha gražinimo." Lithuania's State Archive, *Laikinoji Lietuvos vyriausybe*, 1941 - 1943, Part 1, Case 6, 11.

"Lietuvos Laikinosios Vyriausybės kreipimasis į Vokiečių karo vyriausybę." Lithuania's State Archive, *Lietuvos generalinės srities finansų valdyba*, Kaunas, 1940 - 1941, Part 2, Case 448, 125.

Map Room files for the Potsdam Conference. Harry S. Truman Library, Independence, Missouri.

"Miestų namų ir žemės sklypų denacionalizacijos įstatymas." *Laikinoji Lietuvos vyriausybė*, 1941 - 1943, Part 1, Case 6, 9.

Lithuanian National Council of America, Miscellaneous records, 1918-1925. Hoover Institution Archives, Stanford University.

Lithuanian subject collection, 1918-2003. Hoover Institution Archives, Stanford University.

Naval Aid files for the Potsdam Conference. Harry S. Truman Library, Independence, Missouri.

Note communicated by the Charge d'Affairs at Kovno (Received in Foreign Office, April 5). Mr. Preston to Mr. Orde, Kovno, 28 March 1939. [N 1816/30/59]. Public Record Office, London.

Potsdam Conference. Public Record Office, London.

Potsdam conference 1945: UK Delegates, Records. Public Record Office, London.

Potsdam conference 1945 July-August: protocols, press, telegrams. Public Record Office, London.

"Pramonės įmonių denacionalizacijos įstatymas." Lithuania's State Archive, *Lietuvos generalinės srities Zarasų apskrities viršininkas. Zarasai*, 1941 - 1944, 62.

"Prekybos ir viešojo maitinimo įmonių denacionalizavimo įstatymas." Lithuania's State Archive, *Lietuvos generalinės srities Zarasų apskrities viršininkas. Zarasai*, 1941 - 1944, 3

President Jacques Chirac to Darius Furmonavičius, January 30, 2002.

Telegrams from Potsdam conference. Public Record Office, London.

Terminal (Potsdam) conference, records of meetings. Public Record Office, London.

Terminal (Potsdam) conference, telegrams. Public Record Office, London.

Viscount Halifax to Mr. Orde (Riga), Foreign Office, March 22, 1939, [N 1592/30/59] Public Record Office, London.

Vokietaitis, A., Papers, 1943-1944, Hoover Institution Archives, Stanford University.

"Žemės denacionalizacijos įstatymas." Lithuania's State Archive, *Laikinoji Lietuvos vyriausybė*, 1941 - 1943, Part 1, Case 6, 12.

Published Documents

Adamkus, Valdas "Lithuania's Contribution to the Euro-Atlantic Security." *Lithuanian Foreign Policy Review*, no. 1 (9) (2002).

Adamkus, Valdas. *Penkeri darbo metai. Kalbos, intervju, laiškai*. Vilnius: Baltos lankos, 2002.

Adamkus, Valdas. Speech of the President of Lithuania in the conference "The Baltic States: Co-operation and Search for a New Vision," Vilnius, April 24, 1998.

A. Gurevičiaus sąrašai. Tūkstančiai lietuvių, kurie gelbėjo tūkstančius Lietuvos žydų Antrojo pasaulinio karo metais. Vilnius: Protėvių Kardas, 1999.

"Act on the Re-establishment of the State of Lithuania." In: *The Road to Negotiations with the USSR. Vilnius*: Supreme Council of the Republic of Lithuania, 1990, p. 164.

Antikomunistinis Kongresas ir Tribunolo Procesas "Komunizmo nusikaltimų įvertinimas." Vilnius: Ramona, 2002.

"Appeal of Mikhail Gorbachev to the Lithuanian people." In: *The Road to negotiations with the USSR*. Vilnius: Supreme Council of the Republic of Lithuania, 1990, pp. 46-48.

"Appeal of Mikhail Gorbachev to the Supreme Council of the Republic of Lithuania." In: *The Road to negotiations with the USSR*. Vilnius: Supreme Council of the Republic of Lithuania, 1990, p. 46.

"Atviras laiškas Lietuvos komunistų partijos centro komitetui." *Vakarinės naujienos*, May 27, 1988, p. 1.

"Attempted Defection by Lithuanian Seamen Simas Kudirka." *Hearings Before the Subcommittee on State Department Organisation and Foreign Operations of the Committee on Foreign Affairs, 91st Congress, 1st session.* U.S.A. Congress. House of Representatives.

Baltijos valstybių užgrobimo byla. JAV Kongreso Ch. J. Kersteno komiteto dokumentai 1953 - 1954 metai. Vilnius: Du Ka, 1997.

"Baltijos tautų deklaracija". *Atgimimas*, May 23, 1989.

"Boriso Jelcino kreipimasis į Rusijos kareivius." *Lietuvos Aidas*, January 16, 1991, p. 1.

Bučelis, Balys. "A Meeting with Mikhail Gorbachev." In: *The road to negotiations with the USSR*. Vilnius: Supreme Council of the Republic of Lithuania, 1990, pp. 72-73.

"Congratulating the Republic of Lithuania on the tenth anniversary of the reestablishment of its independence." US Senate, Washington, USA, March 2, 2000.

"Communiqué from the meeting of the Presidents of the Supreme Councils of the Republic of Lithuania, the Republic of Estonia and the Republic of Latvia." In: *The road to negotiations with the USSR. Vilnius*: Supreme Council of the Republic of Lithuania, 1990.

Constitution of the Republic of Lithuania, Monee, U.S.A., 1990.

"Deklaracija dėl Lietuvos respublikos, Latvijos Respublikos ir Estijos Respublikos santarvės ir bendradarbiavimo." *Atgimimas*, May 16 - 23, 1990, p.1.

"Discussion at the Kremlin." In: *The road to negotiations with the USSR*. Vilnius: Supreme Council of the Republic of Lithuania, 1990, p. 76.

Documents on British Foreign policy, 1919 – 39. London: His Majesty's Stationery office, 1951.

Eidintas, Alfonsas. "Remembering the Jewish Catastrophe: 60th Anniversary of the Holocaust." Speech at the Lithuanian Seimas special session, September 20, 2001.

"ELTA report: USSR President Mikhail Gorbachev on Lithuania, April 11, 1990." In: *The Road to negotiations with the USSR.Vilnius*: Supreme Council of the Republic of Lithuania, 1990, pp. 59-61.

"Europos parlamento bendras pareiškimas apie padėtį Baltijos valstybėse." *Lietuvos Aidas*, January 30, 1991.

"Garbingam Cordell Hull, Valstybės Sekretoriui, Wasingtonas, D.C. P.Žadeikis, Lietuvos pasiuntinys, 1940 m. liepos 22 d." In: *Baltijos Valstybių Užgrobimo byla. JAV kongreso Ch. J. Kersteno komiteto dokumentai, 1953 - 1954 metai*. Vilnius: DuKa, 1997, pp. 357-360.

Garbingam Cordell Hull, Valstybės Sekretoriui, Wasingtonas, D.C. P.Žadeikis, Lietuvos pasiuntinys, 1940 m. rugpjūčio 3 d. In: *Baltijos Valstybių Užgrobimo byla. JAV kongreso Ch. J. Kersteno komiteto dokumentai, 1953 - 1954 metai*. Vilnius, DuKa, 1997, pp. 360-361.

Gedimino laiškai. Vilnius: Mintis, 1966.

Gruzdytė, I. (ed.) *Lietuvos Sąjūdis. Lietuvos sąjūdžio programa ir įstatai: priimta Lietuvos Sąjūdžio suvažiavime 1990 m. balandžio 22 d.* Vilnius: Lietuvos Sąjūdis, 1990.

Havel, Vaclav. Address by President of the Czech Republic, at the Conference "Europe's New Democracies: Leadership and Responsibility," Bratislava, May 11, 2001.

Hearing before the Select Committee to Investigate the Incorporation of the Baltic States into the USSR. Washington: House of Representatives, 1953.

Helms, Jesse. Address by the Chairman of the U.S. Senate Committee on Foreign Relations at the American Enterprise Institute, January 11, 2001.

"High Governmental Note to D.T.Yazov from Kazimira Prunskiene." In: *The Road to negotiations with the USSR*. Vilnius: Supreme Council of the Republic of Lithuania, 1990, p. 51.

"High Governmental Note to Mikhail Gorbachev from Vytautas Landsbergis and Kazimira Prunskiene, March 27, 1990." In: *The Road to negotiations with the USSR*. Vilnius: Supreme Council of the Republic of Lithuania, 1990, p. 41.

"Jo Ekscelencijai Gediminui Vagnoriui Lietuvos Respublikos Ministrui Pirmininkui." *Lietuvos Aidas*, August 31, 1991.

"Joint letter to Mikhail Gorbachev of May 12, 1990." In: *The road to negotiations with the USSR*. Vilnius: Supreme Council of the Republic of Lithuania, 1990, p. 74.

Juozaitis, A., Rupšytė A., Volungiavičiūtė. *Sąjūdžio veikla struktūra ir dokumentai*. Vilnius, 1989.

"Joint telegram to USSR President Mikhail Gorbachev." In: *The road to negotiations with the USSR*. Vilnius: Supreme Council of the Republic of Lithuania, 1990.

Kojelis, Linas J. "He liberated the World: the global legacy of Ronald Reagan," June 28, 2004.

"Kreipimasis į Jungtinių Tautų Generalinį Sekretorių Jo Prakilnybę poną Ksavierą Peresą de Kueljarą." *Lietuvos Aidas*, January 15, 1991.

Kronkaitis, Jonas "Development of the Lithuanian Armed Forces – an Important Step for Regional Security and Stability." *Lithuanian Foreign Policy Review*, no. 2 (1998).

Landsbergis, Vytautas. Kalba Sajūdžio mitinge. Vilnius, Katedros aikstė. Speech in the gathering of Sajudis in the Square of Cathedra, Vilnius, January 11, 1990. In: V. Landsbergis, *Atgave vilti*. Vilnius: Sąjūdis, 1990.

Landsbergis, Vytautas. *Karaliaučius ir Lietuva*. Vilnius: Demokratinės Politikos Institutas, 2003.

Landsbergis, Vytautas. *Lietuvos kelias į NATO*. Vilnius: Versus Aureus, 2005.

Landsbergis, Vytautas, "Lithuania Addresses the Subject of NATO," *Bridges*, no. 9, 1998.

Landsbergis, Vytautas. *Pusbrolis Motiejus. Knyga apie Stasį Lozoraitį iš jo laiškų ir pasisakymų*. Vilnius: Vaga, 2003.

Landsbergis, Vytautas. Sausio Tryliktoji po šešerių metų. Kalba iškilmingame Seimo posėdyje 1997 m. sausio 13 d. *Lietuvos Aidas*, January 14, 1997, p. 5.

Landsbergis, Vytautas. Teisingumas - taika - žalioji taika. Speech in Moderate Party Conference, Stockholm, December 8, 1989. In: V. Landsbergis, *Atgavę vilti*. Vilnius: Sąjūdis, 1990, pp. 41-46.

Landsbergis, Vytautas. Security Problems of Central and Eastern Europe. Speech delivered at the European - Atlantic Group Meeting, House of Commons, London, July 12, 2000.

Landsbergis, Vytautas. Vytauto Landsbergio kalba Jungtinėse Tautose. *Lietuvos Aidas*, September 19, 1991, p. 1.

Landsbergis, Vytautas. *Kryžkelė*. Vilnius: Lietuvos Aidas, 1996.

Landsbergis, Vytautas. *Laisvės byla*. Vilnius: Lietuvos Aidas, 1992.

Landsbergis, Vytautas. *Nauji dokumentai apie Sausio 13-ąją*. Vilnius: Baltijos kopija, 2003.

Landsbergis, Vytautas. *Europos Parlamente. 2003 birželis – 2004 lapkritis*. Vilnius: Baltijos kopija, 2005.

Landsbergis, Vytautas. *Europos Parlamente. 2004 lapkritis – 2005 lapkritis*. Vilnius: Baltijos kopija, 2005.

Landsbergis, Vytautas. *Būta ir pasakyta. Mintys*. Vilnius: Pasviręs pasaulis, 2002.

Landsbergis, Vytautas. Siekimas tiesos. Vytauto Landsbergio kalba pasirašius Helsinkio susitarimo Baigiamąjį aktą. Landsbergis' speech after the signing of the Helsinki Final Act. *Lietuvos Aidas,* October 16, 1991.

"Law of the Republic of Lithuania on the Provisional Basic Law of the Republic of Lithuania." In: P. S. Zumbakis, ed., *Lithuanian Independence. The Re-Establishment of the Rule of Law*. Chicago: Ethnic Community Services, 1990, p. 62.

"Law of the republic of Lithuania on the reinstatement of the May 12, 1938 Lithuanian Constitution." In: P. S. Zumbakis, ed., *Lithuanian Independence. The Re-Establishment of the Rule of Law*. Chicago: Ethnic Community Services, 1990, p. 61.

"Letter of President G. Bush to President of Lithuania Vytautas Landsbergis, August 31, 1991. *Lietuvos Aidas*, September 7, 1991.

"Letter to Francois Mitterrand from Vytautas Landsbergis of May 2, 1990." In: *The road to negotiations with the USSR*. Vilnius: Supreme Council of the Republic of Lithuania, 1990, p. 164.

"Letter to Mikhail Gorbachev from the Presidium of the Supreme Council of the Republic of Lithuania – April 20, 1990." In: *The Road to negotiations with the USSR*. Vilnius: Supreme Council of the Republic of Lithuania, 1990, pp. 66-67.

"Letter to President Landsbergis from President Mitterrand and Chancellor Kohl, 26 April 1990." In: *The Road to negotiations with the USSR*. Vilnius: Supreme Council of the Republic of Lithuania, 1990, p. 68.

"Letter to the Chairman of the Supreme Soviet of the Union of Soviet Socialist Republics." In: Paul S. Zumbakis, ed., *Lithuanian Independence. The Re-Establishment of the Rule of Law*. Chicago: Ethnic Community Services, 1990, p. 66.

"Letter to the Supreme Soviet of the USSR from Vytautas Landsbergis 21 March 1990." In: *The Road to negotiations with the USSR*. Vilnius: Supreme Council of the Republic of Lithuania, 1990, pp. 38-40.

"Letter to Vaclav Havel from Vytautas Landsbergis, March 31, 1990. In: *The road to negotiations with the USSR.*" Vilnius: Supreme Council of the Republic of Lithuania, 1990, p. 128.

"Letter to Vytautas Landsbergis from Vaclav Havel, March 29, 1990. In: *The road to negotiations with the USSR.*" Vilnius: Supreme Council of the Republic of Lithuania, 1990, p. 127.

"Lietuvos Respublikos katalikų laiškas Šv. Tėvui Pijui XII Vatikane." In: Daumantas, J. *Partizanai.* Vilnius: 1990, p. 420.

Lietuva. Dokumentai, Liudijimai, *Atgarsiai. 1991.01.13.* Vilnius: Spaudos Departamentas, 1991.

Lietuvių Katalikų Bažnyčios Kronika. Vol. 1–10. Chicago: Lietuvos Kronikos Sajunga, 1974 – 1992.

Lietuvos Respublikos Konstitucijos Projektas. Vilnius: Lietuvos Respublikos Aukščiausiosios Tarybos leidykla, 1992.

Lietuvos Laikinoji Vyriausybė. Posėdžių Protokolai. Vilnius: Lietuvos Gyventojų Genocido ir Rezistencijos Tyrimo Centras, 2001.

"Lietuvos Respublikos Aukščiausios Tarybos prezidiumo pareiškimas." Vilnius, December 20, 1990.

"Lietuvos Respublikos Aukščiausiosios Tarybos prezidiumo kreipimasis į Tarybų Sąjungos prezidentą M. Gorbachevą." Vilnius, December 20, 1990.

"LPS Seimo nutarimas." *Atgimimas,* April 28, 1989, p. 2.

Lietuvos Persitvarkymo Sąjūdžio bendroji programa: priimta LPS steigiamajame suvažiavime 1988 m. spalio 23 d. Vilnius: Mintis, 1988.

"Lietuvos Respublikos Aukščiausiosios Tarybos nutarimas dėl vadinamojo "Nacionalinio gelbėjimo komiteto" veiklos politinio ir teisinio įvertinimo." *Lietuvos Aidas,* January 16, 1991.

"Lietuvos Respublikos Aukščiausiosios Tarybos pareiškimas dėl agresijos prieš Lietuvą plėtimo ir karinės diktatūros grėsmės TSR Sąjungoje." *Lietuvos Aidas,* January 29, 1991.

"Lietuvos Respublikos Aukščiausiosios Tarybos Pareiškimas dėl TSRS ginkluotųjų pajėgų neteisėtų veiksmų." *Lietuvos Aidas,* January 17, 1991, p. 1.

"Lietuvos Respublikos Aukščiausiosios Tarybos Prezidiumo Nutarimas." *Lietuvos Aidas,* September 11, 1991.

"Lietuvos Respublikos Įstatymas Dėl Lietuvos Respublikos vyriausybės emigracijoje. *Lietuvos Aidas.*" January 15, 1991.

Lietuvos Sąjūdis. Steigiamasis suvažiavimas. Vilnius: Mintis, 1990.

Lietuvos užsienio politikos dokumentai. 1 sąsiuvinys. Vilnius: Lietuvos Respublikos Aukščiausiosios Tarybos leidykla, 1992.

"Prapuolenio - J. Deksnio ir Skrajūno - J. Lukšos raportas BDPS Prezidiumo pirmininkui apie pavestų uždavinių ir įgaliojimų vykdymą, 1948 m. balandžio mėn. 27 d." In: *Laisvės kovos 1944-1953 metais*. Kaunas: Lietuvos politinių kalinių ir tremtinių sąjunga, Pasaulio lietuvių bendruomenė, 1996, p. 485.

Remeikis, Thomas, ed. *Lithuania under German occupation 1941-1945. Despatches from US Legation in Stockholm*. Vilnius: Vilnius University Press, 2005.

Remeikis Thomas, ed. *The Violations of Human Rights in Soviet Occupied Lithuania. A Report for 1981*. London: the Lithuanian Association in Great Britain, 1982.

Remeikis, Thomas, ed. *The Violations of Human Rights in Soviet Occupied Lithuania. A Report for 1979/1980*. London: Lithuanian Association in Great Britain, 1981.

Remeikis, Thomas and Bronius Nainys, eds. *The Violations of Human Rights in Soviet Occupied Lithuania. A Report for 1978*. London: Lithuanian Association in Great Britain, 1979.

Remeikis, Thomas, ed. *The Violations of Human Rights in Soviet Occupied Lithuania. A Report for 1977*. London: Lithuanian Association in Great Britain, 1978.

Remeikis, Thomas, ed. *The Violations of Human Rights in Soviet Occupied Lithuania. A Report for 1976*. Lithuanian Association in Great Britain, 1977.

Remeikis, Thomas, ed. *The Violations of Human Rights in Soviet Occupied Lithuania. A Report for 1975*. Lithuanian Association in Great Britain, 1976.

Remeikis, Thomas, ed. *The Violations of Human Rights in Soviet Occupied Lithuania. A Report for 1974*. Lithuanian Association in Great Britain, 1975.

Remeikis, Thomas, ed. *The Violations of Human Rights in Soviet Occupied Lithuania. A Report for 1973*. Lithuanian Association in Great Britain, 1974.

Remeikis, Thomas, ed. *The Violations of Human Rights in Soviet Occupied Lithuania. A Report for 1972*. Lithuanian Association in Great Britain, 1973.

Remeikis, Thomas, ed. *The Violations of Human Rights in Soviet Occupied Lithuania. A Report for 1971*. Lithuanian Association in Great Britain, 1972.

"Response of the Presidium of the Supreme Council of the Republic of Lithuania to President Mikhail Gorbachev's Appeal of March 31, 1991." In: *The Road to negotiations with the USSR*. Vilnius: Supreme Council of the Republic of Lithuania, 1990, p. 49.

"RTFSR, Ukrainos Respublikos, Moldovos Respublikos, Gruzijos Respublikos ir TSRS liaudies deputatų, Lenkijos senatorių ir parlamento deputatų - įvykių Vilniuje liudininkų pareiškimas." *Lietuvos Aidas*, January 19, 1991.

"Rt. Gerb. Viskontui Halifax, K.G.P.C., G.S.C.I., G.C.I.E., Jo didenybės užsienio reikalų valstybės sekretoriui, Užsienio reikalų ministerija, Londonas, S.W.I. B.K. Balutis, 1940 m. liepos 23 d." In: *Baltijos Valstybių Užgrobimo byla. JAV kongreso Ch. J. Kersteno komiteto dokumentai, 1953 - 1954 metai*. Vilnius: DuKa, 1997, pp. 361-362.

Sontag, Richard J. and John S. Beddin, eds., *Nazi-Soviet Relations 1939 - 1941: Documents from the Archives of the German Foreign Office*. Washington, D.C.: Department of State, 1948.

"Statement by Supreme Council and Government of the Republic of Lithuania." In: *The road to negotiations with the USSR*. Vilnius: Supreme Council of the Republic of Lithuania, 1990, p. 75.

"Statement by the Press Secretary. The White House Office of the Press Secretary, March 11, 1990." In: *Lituanus*, 36:2, 1990 (Special issue "Lithuanians declare independence. March 11, 1990").

"Supreme Council of the Republic of Lithuania Decree on the Expansion of Relations between the Republic of Lithuania and the Union of Soviet Socialist Republics, 18 April, 1990." In: *The Road to negotiations with the USSR*. Vilnius: Supreme Council of the Republic of Lithuania, 1990, p. 64.

"Supreme Council of the Republic of Lithuania. Act on the Restoration of the Lithuanian State." In: P. S. Zumbakis (ed.) *Lithuanian Independence. The Re-Establishment of the Rule of Law*. Chicago: Ethnic Community Services, 1990, p. 60.

"Supreme Council of the Republic of Lithuania. Decree, May 23, 1990." In: *The road to negotiations with the USSR*. Vilnius: Supreme Council of the Republic of Lithuania, 1990.

"TASS-ELTA report: "A meeting of the Presidential Council" April 9." In: *The Road to negotiations with the USSR*. Vilnius: Supreme Council of the Republic of Lithuania, 1990, p. 57.

"Telegram of Mikhail Gorbachev and Nikolai Ryzhkov to the Supreme Council of Ministers of the Republic of Lithuania, published April 14, 1990." In: *The Road to negotiations with the USSR*. Vilnius: Supreme Council of the Republic of Lithuania, 1990, pp. 61-62.

Text of Lithuanian Declaration of Independence. *The Associated Press*, March 12, 1990.

Thatcher, Margaret. Speech at Hoover Institution Lunch, Four Seasons Hotel, Washington, D.C., March 8, 1991.

Thatcher, Margaret. Speech at Paris CSCE Summit, Kleber Centre, Paris, November 19, 1990.

"The Foreign Minister to the Legation in Lithuania. Berlin, August 29, 1939. *Germany. Auswärtiges Amt: Documents on German Foreign Policy, 1918-1945*. Series D, (1937-1945), vol. 7, The last days of peace, August 9 – September 3, 1939." London: H.M.S.O, 1956, p. 404.

"The Minister in Lithuania to the Foreign Ministry. Kovno, August 29, 1939. *Germany. Auswärtiges Amt: Documents on German Foreign Policy, 1918-1945*. Series D, (1937-1945), vol. 7, The last days of peace, August 9 – September 3, 1939." London: H.M.S.O, 1956, p. 411.

"The Minister in Lithuania to the Foreign Ministry. Kovno, August 31, 1939. *Germany. Auswärtiges Amt: Documents on German Foreign Policy, 1918-1945*. Series D, (1937-1945), vol. 7, The last days of peace, August 9 – September 3, 1939." London: H.M.S.O, 1956, p. 467.

"The State Secretary to the Legation in Lithuania. Berlin, August 30, 1939. *Germany. Auswärtiges Amt: Documents on German Foreign Policy, 1918-1945*. Series D, (1937-1945), vol. 7, The last days of peace, August 9 – September 3, 1939." London: H.M.S.O, 1956, p. 450.

Stankevičius, Česlovas "Enhancing Security of Lithuania and Other Baltic States in 1992-94 and Future Guidelines." NATO Research Fellowship report, 1995.

"Vilnius Statement". Vilnius, Lithuania, May 19, 2000.

White House press release, December 22, 1991.

"Zaklyuchenie nezavisimykh voennykh expertov obshchestvenoi organizatsii "Schit" na sobytiya v Vilnyuse 11 - 13 yanvarya 1991 goda." In: V. S. Vardys and J. Sedaitis, *Lithuania. The Rebel nation*. Oxford: Westview Press, 1997.

Newspapers

"A club for all Europe. Don't build too much on the CSCE." *The Economist*, November 17, 1990.

Aliulis, Vaclovas. "Linkiu tiesumo ir tolerancijos." *Kauno aidas*, December 29, 1988, p. 2.

"Ar jūs už tai, kad Lietuvos valstybė būtų nepriklausoma demokratinė respublika." *Lietuvos Aidas*, February 14, 1991.

"Ateikite ir paremkite savo valdžią - kitaip galite turėti svetimą." *Lietuvos Aidas*, January 9, 1991.

"Atidaryta JAV ambasada." *Lietuvos Aidas*, October 3, 1991, p. 1.

"Atkurti diplomatiniai santykiai su Vatikanu." *Lietuvos Aidas*, October 1, 1991.

Ažubalis, Audrius. "Ar įmanoma nuplėšti garbę Lietuvai." *Atgimimas*, April 25 - May 2, 1990, p. 1.

Ažubalis, Audrius. "Kraujas raudonas ir naktį." *Atgimimas*, April 4 - 11, 1990.

Ažubalis, Audrius. "Jau okupavo ir mūsų dangų." *Atgimimas*, April 4 - 11, 1990.

Balakauskas, Osvaldas. "Mums reikia visos teisybės." *Kauno aidas*, December 29, 1988, p. 3.

"Baltic "Revolts."" *The Times*, June 24, 1941.

"Bona kaip ant delno." *Lietuvos Aidas*, September 25, 1991.

"Bushas pripažįsta Baltijos šalis, bet kartu remia Gorbačiovą ir jo Sąjungą." *Lietuvos Aidas*, September 6, 1991.

"Dėl padėties Baltijos valstybėse." *Lietuvos Aidas*, January 5, 1991.

"Didvyriškai žuvusiųjų Lietuvos radijo ir televizijos gynėjų vardai." *Lietuvos Aidas*, January 15, 1991.

"Didžiosios Britanijos atstovybėje." *Lietuvos Aidas*, September 3, 1991.

"Du komediantai Kremliaus suvažiavimų rumuose." *Lietuvos Aidas*, September 4, 1991.

"ESB konferencija Maskvoje." *Lietuvos Aidas*, September 10, 1991.

From the editorial "Consequences of Vilnius." Financial Times for January 14, 1991. In: *The Gift of Vilnius. A Photographic Document in Defense of Freedom. January 13, 1991. A terrible beauty is born.* Chicago: Public Affairs Council, Lithuanian American Community, 1991.

From the editorial "The will to reform is broken." Frankfurter Allgemeine Zeitung for January 14, 1991. In: *The Gift of Vilnius. A Photographic Document in Defense of Freedom. January 13, 1991. A terrible beauty is born.* Chicago: Public Affairs Council, Lithuanian American Community, 1991.

Furmonavičius, Darius. "Baltijos valstybių nepriklausomybės išbandymas," *Draugas*, May 18, 2007.

Furmonavičius, Darius. "Karaliaučiaus kraštas tebėra problema" (The Königsberg region remains a problem). *Tėviškės Žiburiai* (Canada), March 23, 2004, pp. 1&3.

Furmonavičius, Darius. "Kas toliau? Išlaisvinkime Mažąją Lietuvą iš Rusijos okupacijos" (What 's next? Let 's liberate Lithuania Minor from Russian occupation), *Europos Lietuvis* (UK), March 23, 2004, pp. 7-10.

Furmonavičius, Darius. "Karaliaučiaus krašto problema." (The problem of Königsberg region), *Lietuvos Aidas* (Lithuania), September 2003.

Furmonavicius, Darius. "Neišspręsta Karaliaučiaus krašto problema." (An unresolved problem of Königsberg region), *XXI Amžius* (Lithuania), June 2003.

Furmonavičius, Darius. "Baltijos valstybės ir Karaliaučiaus kraštas." (The Baltic States and the Königsberg region), *Tėviškės Žiburiai* (Canada), July, 2002.

Furmonavičius, Darius. "Lietuvos tarptautinė padėtis ir perspektyvos" (International Lithuania's situation and perspectives), *XXI Amžius* (Lithuania), March 2002.

Furmonavičius, Darius. "Lietuvos tarptautinė būklė ir perspektyvos" (Lithuania's international position and perspectives), *Tėviškės Žiburiai* (Canada), March 2002.

Furmonavičius, Darius. "Lietuvos tarptautinė padėtis ir perspektyvos." (Lithuania's International situation and perspectives), *Europos Lietuvis* (UK), March, 2002.

Furmonavičius, Darius. "Lietuva bus pakviesta į NATO." (Lithuania will be invited to join NATO), *Britanijos Lietuvių Balsas* (UK), February, 2002.

Furmonavičius, Darius. "Lietuva žengia į Europą." (Lithuania rejoins Europe), *Britanijos Lietuviu Balsas*, May 2000 (UK).

Furmonavičius, Darius. "Europos saugumo raktas." (A key to European Security), *Lietuvos Aidas* (Lithuania), May 14, 1998.

Furmonavičius, Darius. "Europos saugumo raktas." (European security key), *Darbininkas* (USA), February 14, 1998.

Furmonavičius, Darius. "Lietuva grįžta į Europą." (Lithuania returns to Europe), *Draugas* (USA), June 5, 1998.

Furmonavičius, Darius. "Europos saugumo raktas." (A key to European security), *Europos Lietuvis* (UK), June 11, 1998.

Furmonavičius, Darius. "Settlement of sovereignty will end second world war," *Financial Times*, October 5, 2002.

Furmonavičius, Darius. "Lietuvos Topografiniai žemėlapiai."Lithuania's Topographic maps), *Draugas* (USA), September 14, 1998.

Furmonavičius, Darius. "Saugumo departamento darbas gali nulemti Lietuvos ateitį," *Draugas*, May 30, 2007.

Furmonavičius, Darius. "Septyniolikos tūkstančių parašų memorandumas. Pašnekesys su Keston institute įkūrėju Dr. Michael Bordeaux." (Seventeen thousand memorandum. Interview with Dr. Michael Bourdeaux, Founder of the Keston Institute), *Draugas*, July 25 and 26, 2007.

Furmonavičius, Darius. "Septyniolikos ūkstančių parašų memorandumas. Pašnekesys su Keston institute įkūrėju Dr. Michael Bordeaux." (Seventeen thousand memorandum. Interview with Dr. Michael Bourdeaux, Founder of the Keston Institute), *XXI amžius*, August 1, 2007.

Furmonavičius, Darius. "Šiaurės Europos saugumo bendruomenė." (Northern European security community), *Europos Lietuvis*, September 30, 1997 (UK).

Furmonavičius, Darius. "Karaliaučiaus krašto problema" (The problem of the Königsberg region), *Europos Lietuvis* (UK), February 5,1998.

Furmonavičius, Darius. "Lietuvos Laisvės ir Demokratijos garantas." (The guarantee of Lithuania's Freedom and democracy), *Europos Lietuvis* (UK), 21 February 1999.

Furmonavičius, Darius. "Vasario 16-osios reikšmė išsivaduojant Lietuvai iš Sovietų okupacijos." (The role of February 16th in liberation of Lithuania from the Soviet occupation) *Europos Lietuvis* (UK), March 5,1998.

Furmonavičius, Darius. "Vakaras su Vytautu Landsbergiu Lietuvių Namuose Londone." (Evening with Vytautas Landsbergis in the Lithuanian House in London), *Europos Lietuvis* (UK), 28 May 1998.

Furmonavičius, Darius. "Kas valdo Lietuvą šiandien." (Who rules Lithuania today), *Europos Lietuvis*, April 2, 1998 (UK).

Furmonavičius, Darius. "Niels von Redecker, 'The Baltic Question and the British Press, 1989-1991." *Europos Lietuvis* (UK), October 29, 1998.

Furmonavičius, Darius. "Lietuvos Topografiniai žemėlapiai." (Lithuania's Topographic Maps), *Europos Lietuvis* (UK), July 9, 1998.

Furmonavičius, Darius. "Amerikos spauda apie Lietuvos Prezidentą." (American press about Lithuania's President), *Europos Lietuvis* (UK), 30 April 1998.

Furmonavičius, Darius. "Susitikimas su Lietuvos Užsienio Reikalų Ministru Algirdu Saudargu." (Meeting with Lithuania's Foreign Minister Algirdas Saudargas), *Europos Lietuvis* (UK), 17 September 1998.

Furmonavičius, Darius. "Trečiuosius Lietuvos narystės NATO metus minint," *Draugas*, April 20, 2007.

Furmonavičius, Darius. "Interview with Vytautas Landsbergis," *Draugas News*, July 2015, p. 1, 4-5.

Furmonavicius, Darius. "We are doing revolution. How Believers won the Cold War," book review Bourdeaux, Michael. *One Word of Truth. The Cold War Memoir of Michael Bourdeaux and Keston College*, London: Darton, Longman and Todd Ltd, 2019 in *Draugas News*, June 2020.

Ganusauskas, Edmundas. "Maskva sprendė, kaip sutramdyti nepaklusnią Lietuvą." *Lietuvos rytas*, May 2, 1997, pp. 1-2.

"Germany disposes of Baltic States." *The Times*, August 12, 1941.

Goble, Paul. "Shots heard round the World." *RFE/RL Baltic States Report*, 2:1, January 15, 2001.

"Helsinkis, 1991 spalio 15." *Lietuvos Aidas*, October 17, 1991, p. 1.

"Iš dvivaldystės į diktatūrą." *Atgimimas*, April 11 - 18, 1990.

"Istorinės Tiesos Diena. Protesto mitingo Lietuvoje, Vilniuje, Vingio parke, 1988 m. rugpjūčio 23 d., Prieš Vokietijos ir Tarybų Sąjungos Nepuolimo sutarties pasirašymą 1939 m. rugpjūčio 23 d. Stenograma." *Atgimimas*, no. 1, September 16, 1988.

"J. Bakeris Vilniuje." *Lietuvos Aidas*, September 14, 1991.

"J. Bakeris Lietuvoje." *Lietuvos Aidas*, September 17, 1991.

"JAV prezidento nuomonė ir jos komentaras." *Lietuvos Aidas*, January 31, 1991.

"JAV valstybės departamento pareiškimas dėl pranešimų, kad sovietų kariuomenė siunčiama į Baltijos valstybes." *Lietuvos Aidas*, January 8, 1991.

Jockus, A. "Kodėl lietuviai neapdainavo Žalgirio mūšio" (interview with Alfredas Bumblauskas). *Lietuvos Aidas*, July 15, 1999.

Juozaitis, Arvydas. "Tautos ir Europos vardan." *Sąjūdžio žinios*, August 23, 1988.

"Kas yra politinis nusikaltėlis." *Kauno aidas*, August 31, 1988.

"Kelias į Europą prasidėjo." *Lietuvos Aidas*, August 24, 1990.

"Ketvirtoji Seimo Sesija." *Atgimimas*, April 28, 1989.

"Kreipimasis." *Lietuvos Aidas*, January 16, 1991.

"Kulkų suvarpytos sienos." *Lietuvos Aidas*, January 12, 1991.

Kuzmickas, Bronius. "Ateina pragmatiškasis metas." *Lietuvos Aidas*, September 5, 1991.

Kuzmickas, Bronius. "Europos diena Šveicarijoje." *Lietuvos Aidas*, September 13, 1991.

Landsbergis, Vytautas. "Baltijos kraštai - Europos saugumo raktas." *Lietuvos Aidas*, October 10, 1995.

Landsbergis, Vytautas. "Lietuva ir Maskva." *Lietuvos Aidas*, October 9, 1993.

Landsbergis, Vytautas. *Lietuvos Aidas*, January 10, 1991.

Landsbergis, Vytautas. "Lithuania Address the Subject of NATO," *Bridges*, 9, 1998.

Landsbergis, Vytautas. "Sugrįš Sąjūdžio gebėjimas atskirti tiesą nuo melo. Šiandien sukanka 10 metų, kai 1988 m. Mokslų akademijoje buvo įkurta Sąjūdžio iniciatyvinė grupė." *Lietuvos Aidas*, June 3, 1998, pp. 1 & 5.

"Latvia Rejects Communist Party Supremacy." *Associated Press*, December 29, 1989.

"Lietuva – Italija." *Lietuvos Aidas*, August 31, 1991.

"Lietuva ir SSSR atnaujino diplomatinius santykius." *Lietuvos Aidas*, October 10, 1991.

"Lietuva ir Vokietija: vakar ir šiandien." *Lietuvos Aidas*, September 11, 1991.

"Lietuvos aido" inf. *Lietuvos Aidas*, September 6, 1991.

"Lietuvos Respublikos Aukščiausiosios Tarybos nutarimas dėl priemonių Lietuvos respublikai ginti." *Lietuvos Aidas*, January 15, 1991.

Lietuvos Aukščiausiosios Tarybos (pirmo šaukimo) pirmoji sesija. Stenogramos. Vilnius: Lietuvos Respublikos Aukščiausioji Taryba, 1990.

"Lietuvos valstybė yra nepriklausoma demokratinė respublika." *Lietuvos Aidas*, January 29, 1991.

"Lithuania lawmakers meet, prepare to break free from Soviet rule." Knight-Ridder News Service, *The San Diego Union-Tribune*, March 11, 1990.

"Man of the Decade's Challenge." *Los Angeles Time*, December 29, 1989.

Marcinkevičius, Justinas. *Atgimimas'*, no. 1, September 16, 1988.

"Maskva pripažįsta Baltijos valstybes." *Lietuvos Aidas*, September 7, 1991.

"Mes turim grįžti į Europą." *Lietuvos Aidas*, August 24, 1990.

Milosz, Czeslaw. "Moscow's poisoned tomato." In: *The Gift of Vilnius. A Photographic Document in Defense of Freedom. January 13, 1991. A terrible beauty is born.* Chicago: Public Affairs Council of the Lithuanian American Community, 1991, p. 5.

"NATO negarantuoja sienų apsaugos." *Lietuvos Aidas*, September 4, 1991.

"Nauja iškaba." *Lietuvos Aidas*, January 12, 1991.

"Ne laisvam žodziui." *Atgimimas*, April 4 - 11, 1990.

"Neatidėliotini darbai rugsėjo menesį." *Lietuvos Aidas*, September 4, 1991.

"Nesutarimus lydės smurtas." *Lietuvos Aidas*, January 31, 1991.

Ozolas, Romualdas. *Gimtasis kraštas*, November 22-28, 1990.

"Pareiškimas." *Lietuvos Aidas*, January 15, 1991.

"Pareiškimas." *Lietuvos Aidas*, January 19, 1991.

"Pasaulio naujienos." *Lietuvos Aidas*, January 17, 1991.

"Perversmas žlugo." *Lietuvos Aidas*, August 22, 1991.

"Pirmas oficialus." *Lietuvos Aidas*, September 21, 1991.

"Praneša Užsienio reikalų ministerija." *Lietuvos Aidas*, August 22, 1991.

"Pripažinimas." *Lietuvos Aidas*, February 13, 1991.

"R. Dumas Vilniuje." *Lietuvos Aidas*, August 30, 1991.

Remnick, David. "Lithuania Votes Independence; Legislature Seeks Soviet Secession; Non-Communist Is Elected President." *The Washington Post*, March 12, 1990.

Rupšytė, Angonita. "Sąjūdžio dėka laimėti pirmieji demokratiniai rinkimai." *XXI Amžius, Horizontai*, p. 1.

"Sąjūdis leader comments on vital issues. The fight for independence has to be non-violent and evolutionary." *The Observer*, vol. 7 - 8, 1989.

Saudargas, Algirdas. "Jau ne svečiai." *Lietuvos Aidas*, September 18, 1991.

"Sėkmingas vizitas Vokietijoje." *Lietuvos Aidas*, September 20, 1991.

"Šiaurės taryba ir mes: bendradarbiauti žmonių labui." *Lietuvos Aidas*, September 26, 1991.

"Šlykstus spektaklis tęsiasi." *Lietuvos Aidas*, January 19, 1991.

"Soviet troops enter capital of Lithuania." *Star - Tribune*, January 9, 1991.

"Soviets plan to stump Lithuania for support." *Los Angeles Times Service*, December 30, 1989.

"Sovietų kariuomenė siautėja." *Lietuvos Aidas*, January 26, 1991.

"SSSR ir vėl žada naudoti ginkluotą jėgą." *Lietuvos Aidas*, January 8, 1991.

"SSSR Valstybės tarybos nutarimas dėl Lietuvos Respublikos nepriklausomybės pripažinimo." *Lietuvos Aidas*, September 10, 1991.

Stankevičius, Česlovas. "Baltijos šalių nepriklausomybė ir Europos saugumas." *Lietuvos Aidas*, May 30, 1990.

"Svarbiausias Lietuvos užsienio politikos uždavinys." *Lietuvos Aidas*, October 18, 1991.

"Švedijos ambasada – pirmoji." *Lietuvos Aidas*, August 30, 1991.

"The long, slow, muddy road from Helsinki." *The Economist*, May 31, 1986.

Tininis, V. "1972 metai: Gegužė, sudrebinusi Lietuvą." *Lietuvos rytas*, May 13, 1992.

Trey, L. "KGB at work in the Baltic States." *The Estonian Independent*, January 24, 1991.

Vardys, Vytautas S. "Išeivija." *Draugas*, October 26, 1985.

"Vasario šešioliktosios dienos proga," *Rytų Lietuva,* February 15, 1949. In: A. Liekis, ed., *Nenugalėtoji Lietuva: Lietuvos partizanų spauda (1944 - 1949).* Vilnius: Valstybinis leidybos centras, 1995.

"Vyriausybėje." *Lietuvos Aidas,* January 17, 1991.

Landsbergis, Vytautas. "Sugrįš Sąjūdžio gebėjimas atskirti tiesą nuo melo." Šiandien sukanka 10 metų, kai 1988 m. Mokslų akademijoje buvo įkurta Sąjūdžio iniciatyvinė grupė. *Lietuvos Aidas,* June 3, 1998.

"Vytauto Landsbergio komentaras." *Lietuvos Aidas,* September 5, 1991.

"Zbigniew Brzezinski teigia, kad Baltijos kraštai yra Šiaurės Europos dalis." *Europos Lietuvis,* December 17, 1997.

"Žvilgsnis iš šalies." *Lietuvos Aidas,* September 6, 1991.

OMRI - RFE/RL messages.

Lietuvos Aidas (1990-2004).

Kauno Aidas (1989-1989).

Sąjūdžio Žinios (1988-1989).

Atgimimas (1989-2004).

Films

"The Second Russian Revolution." BBC documentary film.

Memoirs

Adamkus, Valdas. *Likimo Vardas – Lietuva.* Kaunas: Santara, 1998.

Adamkus, Valdas. *Penkeri darbo metai.* Vilnius: Baltos lankos, 2002.

Aliulis, Vaclovas. *Vieno žąsiaganio istorija.* Vilnius: Aidai, 2007.

Baker, James Addison, III. *The Politics of Diplomacy: Revolution, War, and Peace, 1989-1992.* New York: G.P. Putnam's Sons, 1995.

Beschloss, Richard M. and Strobe Talbott. *At the highest levels. The Inside Story of the End of the Cold War.* London: Little, Brown & Co, 1993.

Brazaitis, Juozas. *Raštai. VI tomas. Vienų vieni.* Chicago: Į Laisvę fondas lietuviškai kultūrai ugdyti, 1986.

Brazauskas, Algirdas. *Lietuviškos Skyrybos.* Vilnius: Politika, 1992.

Bush, George and Brent Scowcroft. *A World Transformed.* New York: Knopf, 1998.

Clinton, Bill. *My Life.* London: Hutchinson, 2004.

Daumantas, Juozas. *Partizanai.* Chicago: Į Laisvę Fondas Lietuviškai Kultūrai ugdyti, 1950.

Genzelis, Bronius. *Sąjūdis. Priešistorė ir istorija.* Vilnius: Pradai, 1999.

Gorbachev, Mikhail. *Memoirs.* London: Doubleday, 1996.

Landsbergis, Vytautas. *Crossroad of Europe.* Vilnius, 2008.

Landsbergis, Vytautas. *Lithuania independent again.* Cardiff, University of Wales Press, 2000.

Landsbergis, Vytautas. *Lūžis prie Baltijos.* Vilnius: Vaga, 1998.

Landsbergis, Vytautas. *Kryžkelė.* Vilnius: Lietuvos Aidas, 1996.

Landsbergis, Vytautas. *Sunki Laisvė. 1991 m. ruduo – 1992 m. ruduo. I knyga. Statom valstybę.* Vilnius: Vaga, 2000.

Landsbergis, Vytautas. *Sunki Laisvė. 1991 m. ruduo – 1992 m. ruduo. II knyga. Sąjūdis Opozicijoj. Parlamentinės Demokratijos Mokykla.* Vilnius: Vaga, 2000.

Landsbergis, Vytautas. *Sunki Laisvė. Išvesti Rusijos Kariuomenę. Atvirame Pasaulyje. Lyg ir Godos.* Vilnius: Vaga, 2000.

Landsbergis, Vytautas. *Lietuvos Kelias į NATO. 1992-2004 m. idėjos, dokumentai, liudijimai.* Vilnius, Versus aureus, 2005.

Landsbergis, Vytautas. *Lapkričio knygelė: 1989 metų pabaigos įvykių ir idėjų užrašai.* Vilnius: Lietuvos nacionalinė Martyno Mažvydo biblioteka, 2021.

Matlock, Jack. *The End of the Soviet Empire.* London: Macmillan, 1995.

Ohman, Jonas. *Donbaso džiazas..* Vilnius: Alma Litera, 2021.

Raštikis, Stasys. *Kovose dėl Lietuvos. Kario Atsiminimai.* Vol. 1-2. Los Angeles: Lietuvių Dienos, 1957.

Sadūnaitė, Nijolė. *A Radiance in the Gulag.* Manassas: Trinity Communications, 1987.

Sadūnaitė, Nijolė. *Gerojo Dievo Globoje.* Chicago: Ateitis, 1989.

Šimutis, Leonardas. *Lithuanian American Council. 30 year struggle for the liberation of Lithuania. 1940 – 1970.* Chicago: Draugas, 1971.

Škirpa, Kazys. *Sukilimas Lietuvos suverenumui atstatyti.* Chicago: Lietuviu Fronto Bičiulių Klubas, 1980.

Škirpa, Kazys. *Lietuvos Nepriklausomybės sutemos.* Chicago: Lietuvos kronika, 1996.

Tauras, Kęstutis V. *Guerilla Warfare on the Amber Coast.* Chicago: Į Laisvę Fondas Lietuviškai Kultūrai ugdyti, 1962.

Urbšys, Juozas. *Atsiminimai.* Chicago: Tautos Fondas, 1988.

Zelikow, Philip and Condoleezza Rice. *Germany Unified and Europe Transformed. A Study in Statecraft. With a New Preface.* Cambridge, Massachusetts: Harvard University Press, 1998.

II. Secondary Sources

Books

Alexiev, Alexander R. *Dissent and Nationalism in the Soviet Baltic.* Santa Monica: Rand, 1983.

Andrew, Christopher and Vasili Mitrokhin. *The Mitrokhin Archive. The KGB in Europe and the West.* London: Penguin, 1999.

Ash, Timothy G. *We the people: the revolution of '89 witnessed in Warsaw: Budapest, Berlin and Prague.* Cambridge, Granta Books, 1990.

Asmus, Ronald D. *Opening NATO's Door. How the Alliance Remade Itself for a New Era.* New York: Columbia University Press, 2002.

Barėnas, Kazimieras. *Britanijos lietuviai. 1947-1973.* London: Nida, 1978.

Barėnas, Kazimieras. *Britanijos lietuviai. 1974 – 1994.* London: Lithuanian Association in Great Britain, 1997.

Batūra, Romas. *Baltijos kelias - kelias į laisvę. 1989.08.23. Dešimtmetį minint.* Vilnius: Lietuvos Sąjūdis, 1999.

Batūra, Romas. *Lietuvos Sąjūdis ir valstybės atkūrimas. Panorama.* Vilnius: Valstybės žinios, 1998.

Batūra, Romas. *Siekiant nepriklausomybės. Lietuvos Sąjūdžio spauda 1988-1991 m.* Vilnius: Valstybės žinios, 2005.

Bieliūnienė, Aldona, Birutė Kulnytė and Rūta Subatniekienė. <u>*Lithuania on the Map.*</u> Vilnius: National Museum of Lithuania, 2002.

Blanc – Noel, N. *Changement de cap en mer Baltique.* Paris: Fondation pour les etudes de defense nationale, 1992.

Blažytė, Danutė and Vanda Kašauskienė, ed., *Lietuvos Sąjūdis ir valstybės idealų įgyvendinimas.* Vilnius: LII Leidykla, 1998.

Borrow, George. *Wild Wales. Its people, language and scenery.* London: John Murray, 1919.

Bower, Tom. *The Red Web. MI6 and the KGB Master Coup.* London: Aurum Press, 1989.

Brandišauskas, Valentinas. *Siekiai atkurti Lietuvos valstybingumą.* Vilnius: Valstybinis leidybos centras, 1996.

Bourdeaux, Michael. *Land of crosses. The struggle for religious freedom in Lithuania, 1939-1978.* Devon: Augustine Publishing Company; Keston College, 1979.

Būčys, Žygintas, Birutė Kulnytė, Margarita Matulytė, Vida Nacickaitė and Tadas Šėma. *Lietuvos laisvės sąjūdis. The Lithuanian Freedom Movement.* Vilnius: Lietuvos nacionalinis muziejus, 1998.

Budreckis, Algirdas M. *The Lithuanian National Revolt of 1941*. Chicago: Lithuanian Encyclopedia Press, 1968.

Budreckis, Algirdas. *Algirdas. Senovės Lietuvos valstybininkas jo veikla ir laikai*. New York: the Lithuanian National Guard in Exile, 1981.

Chase, Thomas G. *The Story of Lithuania*. New York: Stratford House, 1946.

Christiansen, Eric. *The Northern Crusades: The Baltic and the Catholic Frontier, 1100 – 1525*. London: Macmillan, 1980.

Clemens, Walter C. *Can Russia Change? The USSR Confronts Global Interdependence*. New York: Routledge, 1990.

Clemens, Walter C. *Baltic Independence and Russian Empire*. New York: St. Martin's, 1991.

Clemens, Walter C. *Dynamics of International Relations. Conflict and Mutual Gain in an Era of Global Interdependence*. Lanham: Rowman & Littlefield Publishers, 1998.

Clemens, Walter C. *The Baltic Transformed. Complexity Theory and European Security*. Lanham: Rowman & Littlefield, 2001.

Clemens, Walter C. *The U.S.S.R. and Global Interdependence: Alternative Futures*. Washington, DC: American Enterprise Institute, 1978.

Courtois, Stéphane, Nicolas Werth, Jean-Louis Panné, Andrzej Paczkowski, Karel Bartosek, Jean-Louis Margolin. *Juodoji Komunizmo Knyga. Nusikaltimai, teroras, represijos*. Vilnius: Vaga, 2000.

Damušis, Adolfas. *Lithuania against Soviet and Nazi aggression*. Chicago: The American Foundation for Lithuanian Research, Inc., 1998.

Davy, Richard, ed. *European Détente: A Reappraisal*. London: Royal Institute of International Affairs, 1992.

Demm, Eberhard, Roger Noël, and William Urban, eds. *The Independence of the Baltic States: Origins, Causes, and Consequences. A Comparison of the Crucial Years 1918-1919 and 1990-1991*. Chicago: Lithuanian Research and Studies Center, 1996.

Detter, Ingrid. *The International Legal Order*. Stockholm: Gower, 1994.

Deutsch, Karl W. et al. *Political Community and the North Atlantic Area*. Princeton, Princeton University Press: 1957.

Eidintas, Alfonsas, Vytautas Žalys, Alfred E. Senn, and Edvardas Tuskenis, ed. *Lithuania in European Politics. The Years of the First Republic, 1918 – 1940*. London: Macmillan, 1997.

Eidintas, Alfonsas. *Lietuvos žydų žudynių byla. Dokumentų ir straipsnių rinkinys*. (The Case of the Massacre of the Lithuanian Jews: Selected documents and articles). Vilnius: Vaga, 2001.

Fry, John. *The Helsinki Process. Negotiating Security and Cooperation in Europe*. Washington: National Defense University Press, 1993.

Freedman, Laurence, ed. *Europe Transformed: Documents on the End of the Cold War.* London: 1990.

Gabrys, Juozas. *A Sketch of the Lithuanian Nation.* Paris: Imprimerie de la Cour d'Appel, 1911.

Gaškaitė, Nijolė, Dalia Kuodytė, Algis Kašėta, and Bonifacas Ulevičius. *Lietuvos partizanai: 1944 – 1953.* Kaunas, Lietuvos politinių kalinių ir tremtinių sąjunga: 1996.

Gerner, Kristian and Stefan Hedlund. *The Baltic States and the End of the Soviet Empire.* London: Routledge, 1993.

Gerutis, Albertas, ed. *700 years for Lithuania.* New York: Manyland Books, 1969.

Gimbutas, Marija. *The Balts.* London: Thames and Hudson, 1963.

Girnius, Kęstutis. *Partizanų kovos Lietuvoje.* Chicago: I Laisve Fondas, 1987.

Gražiūnas, Albinas. *Lietuva dviejų okupacijų replėse. 1940-1944.* Vilnius: Tėvynės Sargas, 1996.

Grose, Peter. *Operation Rollback: America's Secret War Behind the Iron Curtain.* New York: Houghton Mifflin, 2000.

Gudavičius, Edvardas. *Lietuvos Istorija. Nuo Seniausių Laikų iki 1569 metų.* Vilnius: Lietuvos Rašytojų Sąjungos Leidykla, 1999.

Harrison, E. J. *Lithuania's fight for freedom.* London: The Federation of Lithuanian Societies in Great Britain, 1944.

Hiden, John. *Germany and Europe 1919 – 1939.* London: Longman, 1993.

Hiden, John. *The Baltic States and Weimar Ostpolitik.* Cambridge: Cambridge University Press, 1987.

Hiden, John and Patrick Salmon. *The Baltic Nations and Europe. Estonia, Latvia and Lithuania in the Twentieth Century.* London: Longman, 1994.

Hosking G. A., J. Aves and P. J. S. Duncan. *The Road to Post-Communism. Independent political Movements in the Soviet Union, 1985 – 1991.* London: Pinter Publishers, 1992.

Ivinskis, Zenonas. *Lietuvos Istorija. Iki Vytauto Didžiojo Mirties.* Roma: Lietuvių Katalikų Mokslo Akademija, 1978.

Kaslas, Bronis J. *The USSR - German Aggression Against Lithuania.* Pittston: Euroamerica Press, 1973.

Kaslas, Bronis J. *The Baltic Nations. The Quest for Regional Integration and Political Liberty.* Pittston: Euramerica Press, 1976.

Katkus, Algirdas. *Nuo aušros iki sutemų.* Vilnius, 2008.

Kershaw, Ian. *Hitler. 1889 – 1936: Hubris.* London: Penguin Books, 1999.

Kiaupa, Zigmantas. *The History of Lithuania.* Vilnius: Baltos lankos, 2005.

Krickus, Richard. *Showdown. The Lithuanian Rebellion and the Breakup of the Soviet Empire.* Washington: Brassey's, 1997.

Krickus, Richard J. *The Superpowers in Crisis: Implications of Domestic Discord.* Washington: Pergamon-Brassey's International Defense Publishers, 1987.

Kviklys, Bronius. *Lietuvių kova su naciais. 1941 – 1944.* Memmingen: Mintis, 1946.

Kubilius, Andrius. *Kodėl krepšinis Lietuvoje gražesnis už politiką.* Vilnius, Versus aureus, 2004.

Lane, Thomas. *Lithuania: Stepping Westward.* Amsterdam: Harwood Academic Publishers, 2001.

Lehti, Marko and David J. Smith. *Post-Cold War Identity Politics. Northern and Baltic Experiences.* London: Frank Cass, 2003.

Liulevičius, Vėjas G. *War Land on the Eastern Front. Culture, National Identity, and German Occupation in World War I.* Cambridge: Cambridge University Press, 2000.

Lithuania at the Turn of the Centuries. Vilnius: Algimantas, 2000.

Lopata, Raimundas & Matonis, Audrius. *Prezidento suktukas.* Vilnius: Versus aureus, 2004.

Lucas, Edward. *Najasis Šaltasis Karas. Kremliaus keliama grėsmė Rusijai ir Vakarams.* Vilnius: Baltos lankos, 2008.

Lucas, Edward. *The New Cold War: How the Kremlin Menaces Russia and the West.* London: Bloomsbury, 2008.

Mačiulis, P. *Trys ultimatumai.* New York: Darbininkas, 1962.

Masteika, R. *Žalgirio musis.* Vilnius: RaMastas, 1999.

Mastny, Vojtech, ed. *The Helsinki Process and the Reintegration of Europe: Analysis and Documentation.* New York: 1992.

Misiunas, Romualdas and Taagepera, Rein. *The Baltic states. Years of Dependence, 1940 – 1990.* London: Hurst & Company, 1993.

Misiūnas, Remigijus. *Didi maža tauta: Lietuvos įaizdžio kampanija JAV 1919 metais. A Great Little Nation: Lithuania's Image Campaign of 1919 in the U.S.* Vilnius: Bonus Animus, 2008.

Namier, L. B. *Diplomatic prelude. 1938 – 1939.* London: MacMillan, 1948.

Novak, Michael. *Taking Glasnost Seriously. Toward an open Soviet Union.* Washington: American Enterprise Institute for Public Policy Research, 1988.

Oleszczuk, Teresa A. *Political Justice in the USSR: Dissent and Repression in Lithuania, 1969 – 1978.* New York: Columbia University Press, 1988.

Pajaujis-Javis, Joseph. *Soviet Genocide in Lithuania.* New York: Maryland Books, 1980.

Perry, Charles M., Michael J. Sweeney and Andrew C. Winner, *Strategic Dynamics in the Nordic-Baltic Region. Implications for U.S. Policy*. Dulles: Brassey's, 2000.

Petersen, Roger D. *Resistance and Rebellion. Lessons from Eastern Europe*. Cambridge: Cambridge University Press, 2001.

Plekis, K. *Genocide. Lithuania's threefold tragedy*. W. Germany: Venta, 1949.

Pleikys, Rimantas. *Jamming*. Vilnius: Rimantas Pleikys, 2000.

Prunskis, Juozas. *Lithuania's Jews and the Holocaust*. Chicago: Lithuanian American Council, 1979.

Radžvilas, Vytautas. *Sunki laisvė*. Vilnius: Tyto Alba, 2005.

Rauch, George v. *The Baltic States: The Years of Independence: Estonia, Latvia, Lithuania, 1917-1940*. New York: Palgrave, 1996.

Remeikis, Thomas. *Opposition to Soviet Rule in Lithuania*. Chicago: Institute of Lithuanian Studies Press, 1980.

Remeikis, Thomas (ed.) *Lithuania under German occupation 1941-1945. Despatches from US Legation in Stockholm*. Vilnius: Vilnius University Press, 2005.

Rubenstein, Joshua. *Soviet Dissidents: Their Struggle for Human Rights*. Boston, Beacon Press: 1980.

Rukšėnas, Algis. *Day of Shame*. New York: David McKay, 1973.

Sabaliūnas, Leonas. *Lithuania in Crisis. Nationalism to communism, 1939 – 1940*. Bloomington: Indiana University Press, 1972.

Senn, Alfred E. *Gorbachev's Failure in Lithuania*. New York: St. Martin's Press, 1995.

Senn, Alfred E. *The Great Powers, Lithuania and the Vilna Question 1920-1928*. Leiden: E. J. Brill, 1966.

Senn, Alfred E. *The Emergence of Modern Lithuania*. New York: Columbia University Press, 1959.

Senn, Alfred E. *Lithuania Awakening*. Berkeley: University of California Press, 1990.

Smith, David J., Artis Pabriks, Aldis Purs and Thomas Lane. *The Baltic States. Estonia, Latvia, Lithuania*. London: Routledge, 2002.

Solomon, Gerald B. *The NATO Enlargement Debate, 1990 – 1997. Blessings of Liberty*. London: Praeger, 1998.

Stein, George H. *The Waffen SS: Hitler's Elite Guard at War, 1939 – 1945*. Ihaca: Cornell University Press, 1966.

Shtromas, Alexander and Morton A. Kaplan, eds., *The Soviet Union and the challenge of the future*. New York: Paragon House, 1988.

Stepanianienė, Afimija. *Antisovietinis 1941 m. Lietuvių Sukilimas.* Kaunas: Projektavimas ir kompiuteriai, 1996.

Suraska, Wisla. *How the Soviet Union Disappeared.* Durham: Duke University Press, 1998.

Sužiedėlis, Saulius. *The Sword and the Cross.* Huntington: Our Sunday Visitor Publication Department, 1988.

Šapoka, Adolfas. *Lietuvos Istorija.* Fellbach: Patria, 1950.

Škirpa, Kazys. *Sukilimas.* Chicago: Lietuvių Frinto Bičiuliai, 1986.

Štromas, Aleksandras. *Politinė sąmonė Lietuvoje.* London: Nida, 1980.

Trapans, Jan A., ed. *Toward Independence: The Baltic Popular Movements.* Oxford: Westview Press, 1991.

Truscott, Peter. *Russia First. Breaking with the West.* London: I.B. Tauris Publishers, 1997.

Umiatowski, Roman. *Poland, Russia and Great Britain, 1941-45.* London: Hollis and Carter, 1946.

Vardys, Vytautas S., ed. *Lithuania Under the Soviets.* Washington: Frederick A. Praeger Publishers, 1965.

Vardys, Vytautas. S. and J. Sedaitis *Lithuania. The rebel nation.* Boston: Westview Press, 1997.

Vardys, Vytautas. S. *The Catholic Church: Dissent and Nationality in Soviet Lithuania.* New York: Columbia University Press, 1978.

Vardys, Vytautas. S. *Krikščionybė Lietuvoje.* Chicago: Lietuvos Krikščionybės Jubiliejaus Komitetas, 1997.

Vitas, Robert A. *The United States and Lithuania: Stimson doctrine of nonrecognition.* New York: Praeger, 1990.

XX amžius: Lietuvos valstybingumo problemos. Kaunas: Šviesa, 1990.

Yakovlev, Alexander. *The October Revolution and Perestroika.* Moscow: Novosti Press Agency Publishing House, 1989.

Žalimas, Dainius. *Lietuvos Respublikos atkūrimas. Pagrindiniai klausimai pagal tarptautinę teisę.* Vilnius: Atviros Lietuvos Fondas, 1997.

Articles

Asmus, Ronald and Robert Nurick. "NATO enlargement and the Baltic states." *Survival*, 38, no. 2 (Summer 1996): 121-142.

Bildt, Carl. "The Baltic Litmus Test." *Foreign Affairs*, vol. 73 (Autumn 1994): 72-85.

Brazaitis, Juozas. "Insurrection against the Soviets." *Lituanus*, no. 3, 1955, pp. 8-10.

Brazaitis, Juozas. "Partizanai antrosios sovietu okupacijos metu." *I Laisve*, no. 24 (61) (1961).

Brzezinski, Zbigniew. "Living With a New Europe." *The National Interest*, no. 60 (Summer 2000): 17-32.

Bumblauskas, Alfredas. "Dėl Lietuvos Didžiosios Kunigaikštystės civilizacijos pobūdžio." *Lietuvos istorijos studijos*, no. 3, 1996.

Clemens, Walter C. "Who or What killed the Soviet Union? How three Davids undermined Goliath." *Nationalism & Ethnic Politics*, 3, no. 1 (1997): 136-158.

Cox, Michael. "After Stalinism: The Extreme Right in Russia, East Germany and Eastern Europe." In: P. Hainsworth, ed., *The Extreme Right in Europe and the USA*. London: Pinter, 1992, pp. 269-285.

Cox, Michael. "Rethinking the End of the Cold War." *Review of International Studies*, 20, no. 2 (1994): 187-200.

Damušis, Adolfas. "1941 metų sukilimo reikšmė." *Į Laisvę*, no. 96 (133) (April 1986): 4-5.

Damušis, Adolfas. "Juozas Ambrazevičius - Brazaitis archyvų dokumentuose." *Į Laisvę*, no. 107 (144) (Winter 1989-90): 35-38.

Damušis, Adolfas. "Juozas Brazaitis Lietuvos Rezistencijoje." *Į Laisvę*, no. 65 (1975): 42-50.

Damušis, Adolfas. "Rezistencijos siekis - Valstybinis suverenumas." *Į Laisvę*, no. 111 (148) (Summer, 1991): 7-10.

Damušis, Adolfas. "Kaunas Tautos sukilimo dienomis." *Į Laisvę*, no. 91 (128) (September 1984): 51-61.

Damušis, Adolfas. "Rezistencijos gairės." The Xth Lithuanian symposium of science & creativity, Chicago, USA, November 27 – 30, 1998.

Damušis, Gintė, Casimir Pugevičius, and M. Skabeikis. *The Violations of Human Rights in Soviet Occupied Lithuania: A Report for 1982*. Chicago: American Lithuanian Community, 1983.

Furmonavičius, Darius. "January 13, 1991 in Lithuania." *Lituanus*, vol. 54, no. 1 (Spring, 2008): 5-20.

Furmonavicius, Darius. "Sąjūdis Peaceful Revolution, Part I." *Lituanus*, vol. 55, no. 1 (Spring, 2009): 5-25.

Furmonavicius, Darius. "Sąjūdis Peaceful Revolution, Part II." *Lituanus*, vol. 55, no. 2 (Summer, 2009): 5-37.

Furmonavičius, Darius. "Northern European Security Community." *Lithuanian Papers*, vol. 10 (1996): 36-37.

Furmonavičius, Darius. "The European Enlargement: the Koenigsberg/Kaliningrad issue." In the proceedings of the ECSA-Canada biannual conference, vol. 1, Montreal, May 27-29, 2004, pp. 353-376.

Furmonavičius, Darius. "Lithuania at the turn of the millenium," *Lithuanian Papers*, vol. 17 (2002): 7-11.

Furmonavičius, Darius. "Lithuania." In *Britannica Book of the Year 2001*. Chicago: Encyclopaedia Britannica, 2001, p. 461.

Furmonavičius, Darius. "Lithuania." In *Britannica Book of the Year 2002*. Chicago: Encyclopaedia Britannica, 2002, p. 459.

Furmonavičius, Darius. "Lithuania." In *Britannica Book of the Year 2003*. Chicago: Encyclopaedia Britannica, 2003, p. 462.

Furmonavičius, Darius. "Lithuania." In *Britannica Book of the Year 2004*. Chicago: Encyclopaedia Britannica, 2004, p. 431.

Furmonavičius, Darius. "President Rolandas Paksas." In *Britannica Book of the Year 2004*. Chicago: Encyclopaedia Britannica, 2004, p. 89.

Furmonavičius, Darius. "Lithuania." In *Britannica Book of the Year 2005*. Chicago: Encyclopaedia Britannica, 2005, p. 428-429.

Furmonavičius, Darius. "Lithuania." In *Britannica Book of the Year 2006*. Chicago: Encyclopaedia Britannica, 2006, p. 427.

Furmonavičius, Darius. "Lithuania." In *Britannica Book of the Year 2007*. Chicago: Encyclopaedia Britannica, 2007, p. 426.

Furmonavičius, Darius. "Lithuania." In *Britannica Book of the Year 2008*. Chicago: Encyclopaedia Britannica, 2008, p. 430.

Furmonavičius, Darius. "Lithuania." In *Britannica Book of the Year 2009*. Chicago: Encyclopaedia Britannica, 2009.

Furmonavičius, Darius. "Lithuania." In *Britannica Book of the Year 2010*. Chicago: Encyclopaedia Britannica, 2010.

Furmonavičius, Darius. "Lithuania." In *Britannica Book of the Year 2011*. Chicago: Encyclopaedia Britannica, 2011, p. 430.

Furmonavičius, Darius. "Lithuania." In *Britannica Book of the Year 2012*. Chicago: Encyclopaedia Britannica, 2012.

Furmonavičius, Darius. "Lithuania." In *Britannica Book of the Year 2013*. Chicago: Encyclopaedia Britannica, 2013, p. 453-454.

Furmonavičius, Darius. "Lithuania." In *Britannica Book of the Year 2014*. Chicago: Encyclopaedia Britannica, 2014, p. 453-454.

Furmonavičius, Darius. "Lithuania." In *Britannica Book of the Year 2010*. Chicago: Encyclopaedia Britannica, 2015, p. 453-454.

Furmonavičius, Darius. "The Lithuanians in Poland." In S. Wolff and K. Cordell, eds., *The Ethnopolitical Encyclopaedia of Europe*. London: Macmillan, 2004.

Furmonavičius, Darius. "Jonas Černius (1898-1977)." In *The Supplement to the Modern Encyclopedia of Russian, Soviet, and Eurasian History*. Gulf Breeze: Academic International Press, 2004.

Furmonavičius, Darius. *Post-Cold War Identity Politics. Northern and Baltic Experiences*. By M. Lehti and D. Smith, eds. London: Frank Cass. 2003 and *Constructing Post-Soviet Geopolitics in Estonia*. By P. Aalto. London: Frank Cass. 2003. In *International Affairs* (October 2003): 1157-1158.

Furmonavičius, Darius. *Karaliaučius ir Lietuva (Koenigsberg and Lithuania)*. By V. Landsbergis. Vilnius: Demokratines Politikos Institutas. 2003. In *International Affairs* (May 2004): 538-539.

Furmonavičius, Darius. "The Königsberg/Karaliaučius/Kaliningrad region – Stalin's legacy within an enlarged Europe," *Lituanus*, vol. 52, no. 4 (Winter 2006): 5-17.

Furmonavičius, Darius. "Memoir book by Canon Michael Bourdeaux," *Istorija* 118, no. 2 (2020), pp. 128-132.

Gureckas, Algimantas P. "Lithuania's boundaries and territorial claims between Lithuania and neighbouring states," New York Journal of International and Comparative Law, 12, no. 1 (1991).

Ivinskis, Zenonas. "Lithuania During the War: Resistance Against the Soviet and the Nazi Occupants." In V. Vardys, *Lithuanian Under the Soviets*. New York: Praeger, 1965.

Jancar, Barbara. "Religious Dissent in the Soviet Union." In: R. Tokes, ed., *Dissent in the USSR*. Baltimore: Johns Hopkins University Press, 1975, pp. 191-230.

Katilius-Boydstun, Dalia. "Six Months of "Glasnost" in Lithuania." *The Observer*, April 1988, pp. 8-9.

Kowalewski, David. "Dissent in the Baltic Republics: Characteristics and Consequences." *Journal of Baltic Studies*, 10, no. 4 (1979): 309-319.

Kowalewski, David. "Lithuanian Protest for Human Rights in the 1970s: Characteristics and Consequences." *Lituanus*, 25 (1979).

Krausnick, Helmut. *Die Truppe des Weltanschauungs-krieges, Teil 1*. In H. Krausnick and H. H. Wilhelm *Die Truppe des Weltanschauungskrieges. Die Einsatzgruppen der Sicherheitspolizei und des SD 1938-1942*. Stuttgart: Deutsche Verlags-Anstalt, 1981.

Krivickas, Domas. "The Molotov - Ribbentrop pact of 1939: legal and political consequences." *Lituanus*, 35, no. 2 (1989).

Kubilius, Andrius. "Seeking integration into the Alliance." In: *NATO's Nations and Partners for Peace. Getting Ready for NATO: The Baltic States*, Special Issue 1999, p. 75.

Kuleba, Dmytro. "Why NATO must admit Ukraine. Kyiv needs the Alliance and the Alliance needs Kyiv," *Foreign Affairs*, April 25, 2023.

Lange, Falk. "The Baltic States and the CSCE." *Journal of Baltic Studies*, 35, no. 3 (Fall 1994): 233 – 248.

Lieven, Anatol. "The Baltic iceberg dead ahead: NATO beware." *The World Today*, vol. 52 (July 1996): 175-179.

Liulevicius, Vėjas G. "As go the Baltics, so goes Europe." *Orbis*, 39, no. 3 (Summer 1995): 387- 402.

Mackevičius, M. "1941-jų metų sukilimas." *Sėja*, 1961.

Oleszczuk, Thomas A. *Political Justice in the USSR: Disent and Repression in Lithuania, 1969 – 1978.* New York: Columbia University Press, 1988.

Packer, Anthony and Darius Furmonavičius. "Brief history of Lithuania." In: V. Landsbergis, *Lithuania independent again.* Cardiff: University of Wales Press, 2000, pp. 353-377.

Pašuta, V. "Gedimino laiškai kaip istorijos šaltinis." In: V. Pašuta, ed., *Gedimino laiskai*, Vilnius: Mintis, 1966, pp. 7-18.

Raštikis, Stasys. "The relations of the provisional government of Lithuania with the German authorities." *Lituanus*, 8, no. 1-2 (1962): 16-22

Remeikis, Thomas. "The Armed struggle against the Sovietization of Lithuania after 1944." *Lituanus*, 8, no. 1-2 (1962): 29-40.

Saudargas, Algirdas. "Not only a consumer of security." In: *NATO's Nations and Partners for Peace. Getting Ready for NATO: The Baltic States*, Special Issue, 1999, pp. 77-78

Senn, Alfred E. "Comparing the circumstances of Lithuanian independence, 1918 - 1922 and 1988 – 1992." In: E. Demm, R. Noel, and W. Urban., eds., *The independence of the Baltic states: origins, causes, and consequences. A comparison of the crucial years 1918 - 1919 and 1990 – 1991.* Chicago: Lithuanian Research and Studies Center, 1996, pp. 12-20.

Stankevičius, Česlovas. "NATO enlargement and the indivisibility of security of Europe: A view from Lithuania." *NATO Review* (September 1996): 21-25.

Stankevičius, Česlovas. "Lithuania on its way to NATO." In: *NATO's Nations and Partners for Peace, Getting Ready for NATO: The Baltic States*, Special Issue, 1999, pp. 79-81.

Stankevičius, Česlovas. "Lietuvos nepriklausomos valstybės atstatymo veiksmų 1990 m. kovo mėn. 1-11 d. kronika," *Jurisprudencija* 29, no. 1 (2022), pp. 6-46.

Sužiedėlis, Saulius. "The Molotov-Ribbentrop Pact and the Baltic States: an Introduction and Interpretation." *Lituanus*, 35, no. 1, 1989, pp. 8-46.

Vardys, Vytautas S. "Lithuanian national politics." *Problems of Communism* 38, (July-August 1989): 53-76.

Vardys, Vytautas S. "Human Rights Issues in Estonia, Latvia, and Lithuania." *Journal of Baltic Studies*, 12, no. 3 (1981): 275-298.

Vardys, Vytautas S. "Lithuania's Catholic Movement Reappraised." *Survey*, 25, no. 3 (112) (1980): 49-73.

Vardys, Vytautas S. "Sajudis: National Revolution in Lithuania." In: J. A. Trapans, ed., *Toward Independence: The Baltic Popular Movements*. Oxford: Westview Press, 1991.

Vardys, Vytautas S. "The partisan Movement in Postwar Lithuania." In: V. S. Vardys, *Lithuania Under the Soviets*. Washington: Frederick A. Praeger Publishers, 1965, pp. 85-108.

Vardys, Vytautas. "Pogrindžio rezistencija Lietuvoje." *Ateitis*, no. 4 (1982).

Vardys, Vytautas. "LKB Kronika. *Laiškai lietuviams*." 18 (1992).

Vilkas, Eduardas. "Birželio 3-oji Mokslo Akademijoje." In: D. Blažytė and V. Kašauskienė, ed., *Lietuvos Sąjūdis ir valstybės idealų igyvendinimas*. Vilnius: LII Leidykla, 1998, pp. 13-16.

Illustrations

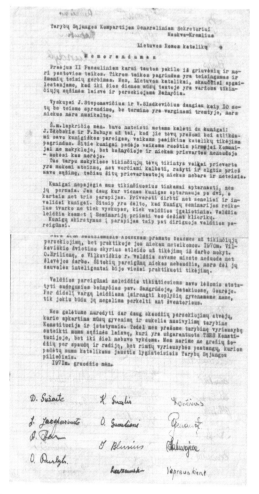

1. The Memorandum of the Seventeen Thousand. A sample page displaying my grandmother Ona Lazauskienė signature (the last signature in the middle column). *Courtesy of the Keston Institute, Oxford.*

To Angelé Nelsas
With best wishes,

Ronald Reagan

2. Angelé Katarina Nelsas, President of the Baltic American Free-
    dom League, meets with President Ronald Reagan in June 1987
    before his trip to Reykjavik for the Summit with Soviet leader
    Mikhail Gorbachev. *Courtesy of Mrs Angela Nelsas.*

3. Demonstration beside the monument to the poet Adomas
    Mickevičius in Vilnius on August 23, 1987, to condemn the se-
    cret Soviet - Nazi deal, the notorious Moscow pact of 1939 -
    1941 (called the Stalin – Hitler or Molotov - Ribbentrop pact)
    which assigned the Baltic States to the zone of Soviet influence.
    Courtesy of Kęstutis Jankauskas.

4.   Photographer Romualdas Pozerskis. The founding meeting of
     Sąjūdis in Vilnius Sports Hall on October 23, 1988.

5.   The commemoration of Lithuania's Independence Day, Febru-
     ary 16, 1989, in Gediminas Square, Vilnius. Courtesy of Kęstu-
     tis Jankauskas.

6. The commemoration of Lithuania's Independence Day, February 16, 1989, by unveiling a plaque near the house in which the Act of Lithuanian Independence was signed in Vilnius on February 16, 1918. Photo A. Žižiūnas. *Courtesy of the Lithuanian National State Archyve.*

7. Mass celebrating the return of the remains of St. Casimir to the Cathedral Basilica of Vilnius on March 4, 1989. Photo J. Kazlauskas. Courtesy of Dalia Kazlauskienė.

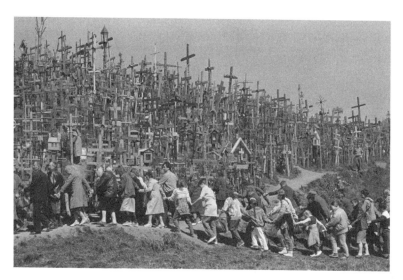

8. The Hill of Crosses, May 2, 1989. Photo Romualdas Požerskis. *Courtesy of Romualdas Požerskis.*

9. The flag of Lithuania being raised, and the Soviet symbol covered in the Lithuanian Parliament, March 11, 1990. Photo J. Kazlauskas. Courtesy of Dalia Kazlauskienė.

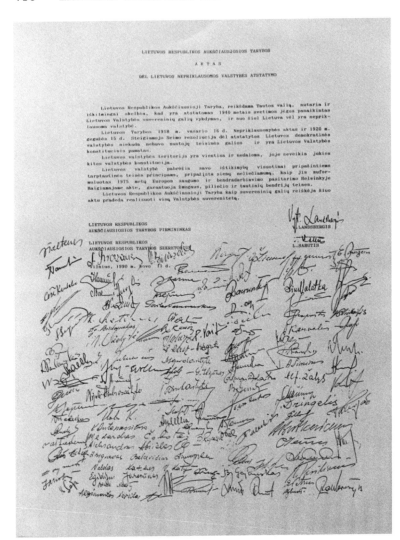

10. The Act of Restoration of Lithuania's Independence, March 11,
1990. *Courtesy of the Lithuanian State New Archive.*

11. "Goodbye Party Comrades". The dismantling of the Lenin
monument in Vilnius, August 23, 1990. Courtesy of Antanas
Sutkus.

To Angela Nelsas
With best wishes,   *Geo Bush*

12. Angela Nelsas, Chairwoman of the Lithuanian American Community and President of the Baltic American Freedom League, organizing a meeting for the Baltic Leaders with President George H. W. Bush, inviting the United States to recognize the re-establishment of Lithuanian independence. *Courtesy of Mrs. Angela Nelsas.*

13. The storming of the Television Tower in Vilnius, January 13, 1991. Photo Zenonas Nekrošius. *Courtesy of Zenonas Nekrošius.*

14. At a dinner hosted by the Speaker of the House in the U.S. Capitol: Congressman Christopher Cox (sponsor of the resolution HCR 51 on the demilitarization of the Königsberg-Kaliningrad region), Angelė K. Nelsas, President of the Baltic American Freedom League and Congressman John Shimkus. Inscribed on the photo: "to Angela – our leader! Thanks for all you do from your adopted Lithuanian – Chris". "Angela, thank you for all you do for the United States and Lithuania. Sincerely, John Shimkus". *Courtesy of Angela Nelsas.*

15. Mrs. Angela Nelsas, President of the Baltic American Freedom
League, meeting with Professor Condoleezza Rice, National Security Advisor to George W. Bush, on October 21, 2000, and
succeeding in obtaining a written statement that the United
States support NATO enlargement and the Baltic NATO membership. *Courtesy of Mrs Angela Nelsas.*

16. Saulius Kuprys, President of the American Lithuanian Council,
    Senator Richard Lugar and the author, Dr. Darius Furmo-
    navičius, discussing the problem of the militarization of the oc-
    cupied Königsberg-Kaliningrad region during the 7th JBANC
    conference "Oil and Blood: Baltic Energy and the Legacy of
    Communism" in Washington, D.C. on February 10, 2007. *From
    the author's archive.*

17. Lithuanian President Gitanas Nausėda and the author, Dr. Darius Furmonavičius, Prayer Breakfast in the Lithuanian Embassy London on May 7, 2023. *From the author's archive.*

18. Lithuanian President Vytautas Landsbergis and the author, Dr. Darius Furmonavičius, Discussing NATO enlargement before Vilnius' NATO summit on June 20, 2023. *From the author's archive.*

19. Former Lithuanian President Dalia Grybauskaite and the author Dr Darius Furmonavicius in King's College, University of Cambridge on 6 January, 2024.

Cartoons

1. Playing "Freedom March' (from "Dagbladet", 1990). Reprinted from "Pasaulis apie Vytautą Landsbergį" Tėvynės Sąjungos Leidinys. Tekstai ir politinės karikatūros. Leidinį sudarė A. Vaišnoras, redaktorius A. Vidžiūnas, meninis redaktorius A. Šimkus (Vilnius: Tėvynės Sąjunga, 1997), p. 10.

2. Fraternity in Lithuania (from "Welt", 1990). Reprinted from "Pasaulis apie Vytautą Landsbergį" Tėvynės Sąjungos Leidinys. Tekstai ir politinės karikatūros. Leidinį sudarė A. Vaišnoras, redaktorius A. Vidžiūnas, meninis redaktorius A. Šimkus (Vilnius: Tėvynės Sąjunga, 1997), p. 10.

Maps

Maximum extent of the Baltic culture during the Bronze Age

1. The Bronze and the Early Iron Age of the Maritime Balts. From
    Marija Gimbutas, *The Balts* (London: Thames and Hudson,
    1963), p. 63. *Reprinted courtesy of the estate of Prof. Marija Gimbu-
    tas.*

2. Lithuania Under Vytautas the Great. From Constantine R. Jurgėla, *Lithuania and the United States: the Establishment of State Relations* (Chicago: Lithuanian Historical Society, 1985), p. 258. *Courtesy of the Lithuanian Research Centre/Lithuanian Historical Society. The author is very grateful to Dr Robert Vitas, Chairman of the Board of the Lithuanian Research Centre in Chicago, for the permission to publish this map and all important discussions and insights.*

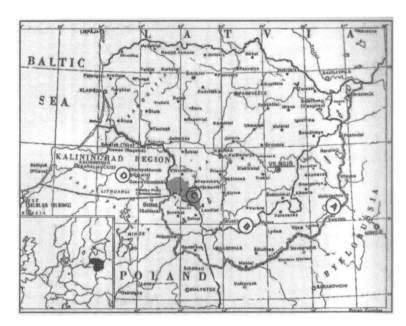

3. Lithuania's border 1920 and 1945. From Adolfas Damušis, *Lithuania against Soviet and Nazi aggression* (Chicago: the American Foundation for Lithuanian Research, 1998), p. 7. *Courtesy of Ambassador Gintė Damušis. The author is grateful to daughter of Prof. Dr. Adolfas Damušis, Ambassador Gintė Damušis, for all important discussions and insights.*

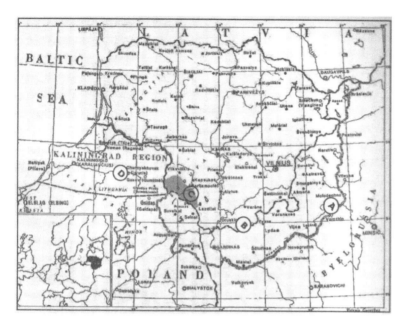

4. The Hitler - Stalin Pact of 1939. From Adolfas Damušis, *Lithuania against Soviet and Nazi aggression* (Chicago: the American Foundation for Lithuanian Research, 1998), p. 20. *Courtesy of Ambassador Gintė Damušis. The author is grateful to daughter of Prof. Dr. Adolfas Damušis, Ambassador Gintė Damušis, for all important discussions and insights.*

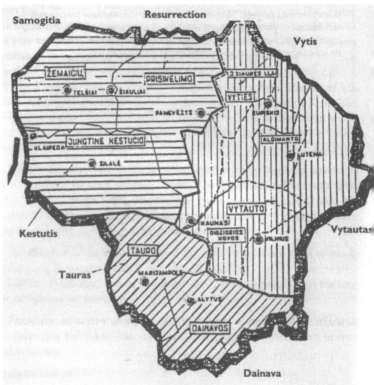

5.   Locations of Lithuanian Partisan Districts. From Adolfas Da-
    mušis, *Lithuania against Soviet and Nazi aggression* (Chicago: The
    American Foundation for Lithuanian Research, 1998), p. 256.
    *Courtesy of Ambassador Gintė Damušis. The author is grateful to
    daughter of Prof. Dr. Adolfas Damušis, Ambassador Gintė Damušis,
    for all important discussions and insights.*

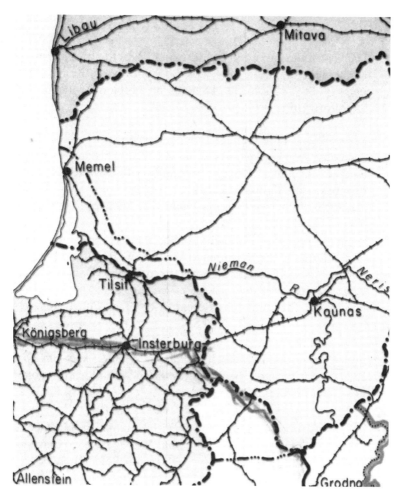

6. The Red Line drawn by Stalin himself at the Teheran confer-
    ence of 1943 which is not yet erased from the map of Europe
    (the line drawn with the red pencil across Konigsberg, Inster-
    burg, down along the border of Lithuania). From *Foreign Rela-
    tions of the United States. Diplomatic Papers. The Conferences at
    Cairo and Teheran. 1943* (Washington, D.C.: United States Gov-
    ernment Printing Office, 1961), grayscale extract from the color
    map facing p. 601.

Tables

1. Dates of the recognition of Lithuania de facto and de jure, by the sovereign states of the world. (From Kaslas, Bronis J. Papers, IV Box, p. 138-139. Archives of the Hoover Institution, Standford University).

2. Recognition of Lithuanian Independence during 1991. (from Arvydas Anušauskas, Juozapas R. Bagušauskas, Česlovas Bauža, Danutė Blažytė, Vitalija Ilgevičiūtė, Vanda Kašauskienė, Algimantas Liekis, *Lietuvos Suvereniteto Atkūrimas 1988-1991 metais* (Vilnius: Diemedis, 2000), pp. 470-472).

3. Population Loss of Lithuania during the First Soviet Occupation. Summary of Exterminated Victims of Lithuania's Population by Soviet Occupation Forces (from Adolfas Damušis, *Lithuania against Soviet and Nazi aggression* (Chicago: The American Foundation for Lithuanian Research, 1998), p. 270).

4. Victims of the Nazi Occupation among the Lithuanian population. (from Adolfas Damušis, *Lithuania against Soviet and Nazi aggression* (Chicago: The American Foundation for Lithuanian Research, 1998), p. 208).

5. Jewish Victims of the Holocaust in Lithuania. (from Adolfas Damušis, *Lithuania against Soviet and Nazi aggression* (Chicago: The American Foundation for Lithuanian Research, 1998), p. 208).

6. Total Population Losses in Lithuania during the Nazi occupation of 1941-1944. (From Adolfas Damušis, *Lithuania against Soviet and Nazi aggression* (Chicago: The American Foundation for Lithuanian Research, 1998), p. 208).

Table 1

Dates of the recognition of Lithuania de facto and de jure, by the sovereign states of the world.[772]

August 22, 1919	Norway, *de facto*
November 8, 1919	Latvia, *de facto*
November 17, 1919	Finland, *de facto*
May 11, 1920	France, *de facto*
July 4, 1920	Poland, *de facto*
March 10, 1921	Estonia, *de facto*
March 14, 1921	Argentina, *de jure*
May 5, 1921	Mexico, *de facto*
August 19, 1921	Switzerland, *de facto*
September 4, 1921	Norway, *de jure*
September 22, 1921	Lithuania admitted to the League of Nations
September 28, 1921	Sweden, *de jure*
September 30, 1921	Denmark, *de jure*
October 6, 1921	The Nertherlands, *de jure*
October 14, 1921	Finland, *de jure*
December 9, 1921	Brazil, *de jure*

---

772   Data of the recognition of Lithuania, de facto and de jure, by the sovereign states of the world. Kaslas, Bronis J. Papers, IV box, p. 138-139. Archives of the Hoover Institution, Sandford University. Prof. Bronis Kaslas commented that there were no recognitions of Lithuania either *de facto* or *de jure* between July 4, 1920 and March 10, 1921, and in fact only two states, Norway and Argentina, had recognized Lithuania *de jure* until the admission of Lithuania to the League of Nations in late September 1921, 'although the country had been independent for more than two years. Lithuania's recognition problems stemmed mainly from her chronic conflict with Poland. Poland still had ambitions of reacting the Lublin Union of 1569 and of presiding over a power bloc from the Baltic to the Black Sea. More importantly, in October 1920, Poland had seized and incorporated Vilnius and the Vilnius region, i.e., Lithuania's capital and 33,000 square kilometers of her territory. The result was the complete breakdown of relations between Poland and Lithuania for eighteen years. At the time, (1920), Poland enjoyed great popularity among the Western Powers, especially France, which hoped that a Great Poland would be the bulwark both of the "cordon sanitaire" against the USSR, and of the French two front encirclement of Germany – thus Polish opposition seriously hampered Lithuania's attempts to gain recognition." Kaslas, Bronis J. Papers, IV box, p. 138.

January 5, 1922	Czechoslovakia, *de jure*
May 9, 1922	Venezuela, *de jure*
May 23, 1922	Greece, *de jure*
May 29, 1922	Chile, *de jure*
June 14, 1922	Bolivia, *de jure*
July 13, 1922	The Conference of Ambassadors (England, France, Italy, Japan), de jure
July 27, 1922	Spain, *de jure*
July 28, 1922	United States of America, *de jure*
November 1, 1922	Iceland, *de jure*
November 10, 1922	The Holy See, *de jure*
December 27, 1922	Belgium, *de jure*
December 28, 1922	Panama, *de jure*
January 5, 1923	Costa Rica, *de jure*
January 30, 1923	Siam, *de jure*
February 5, 1923	Peru, *de jure*
February 9, 1923	Paraguay, *de jure*
February 12, 1923	China, *de jure*
February 13, 1923	Liberia, *de jure*
February 26, 1923	Guatamala, *de jure*
May 11, 1923	Cuba, *de jure*
August 11, 1923	Persia, *de jure*
November 6, 1923	Equador, *de jure*
February 7, 1924	Austria, *de jure*
August 21, 1924	Roumania, *de jure*
November 3, 1924	Bulgaria, *de jure*

Table 2

Recognition of Lithuanian Independence during 1991[773]

February 11, 1991	Iceland
March 17, 1991	Zimbabwe
May 31, 1991	Moldova
August 3, 1991	Croatia
August 24, 1991	Denmark
	Norway
	Hungary
August 25, 1991	Argentina
	France
August 26, 1991	Austria
	Bulgaria
	Italy
	Canada
	Poland
	Malta
	Portugal
	Romania
	San Marin
	Ukraine
August 27, 1991	Ireland
	Albania
	Australia
	Belgium
	United Kingdom
	Spain
	Sweden
	Germany

---

773   Lietuvos Valstybės Tarptautinis Pripažinimas 1991 m. In Arvydas Anušauskas, Juozapas R. Bagušauskas, Česlovas Bauža, Danutė Blažytė, Vitalija Ilgevičiūtė, Vanda Kašauskienė, Algimantas Liekis, *Lietuvos Suvereniteto Atkūrimas 1988-1991 metais* (Vilnius: Diemedis, 2000), pp. 470-472.

	Georgia
August 28, 1991	Chile
	South Africa
	Finland
	Switzerland
	Uruguay
August 29, 1991	Czechoslovakia
August 30, 1991	The Holy See
August 31, 1991	Kyrgyzstan
September 2, 1991	Ecquador
	Nyderlands
	USA
September 3, 1991	Greece
	Nicaragua
	Slovenia
	Turkey
September 4, 1991	Brasil
	Tunisia
	Israel
September 5, 1991	South Korea
	Mexico
September 6, 1991	Egypt
	Guinea
	Japan
	Columbia
	North Korea
	Soviet Union of Socialist Republics
	Singapore
September 7, 1991	Afganistan
	Peru
	Senegal
September 8, 1991	Pakistan
September 9, 1991	Bolivia
	India
	Cuba

	Thailand
	Vietnam
	Syria
September 10, 1991	Azerbaijan
	Iran
	Nepal
September 11, 1991	Madagascar
	Malaysia
September 12, 1991	Armenia
	Cyprus
September 13, 1991	Yemen
September 15, 1991	Bahrain
	Jordan
	Kuwait
September 16, 1991	Philippines
	Saudi Arabia
September 17, 1991	Indonesia
	Namibia
September 19, 1991	United Arab Emirates
September 20, 1991	Laos
September 24, 1991	Turkmenistan
September 25, 1991	Panama
September 30, 1991	Uzbekistan
October 22, 1991	Mauritius
November 2, 1991	Sri Lanka
December 23, 1991	Gana
	Kazakhstan
December 24, 1991	Mozambique
December 25, 1991	Tajikistan
December 27, 1991	Algeria
	Belarus
December 30, 1991	Lebanon

Table 3

Population Loss in Lithuania during the First Soviet Occupation[774]

	Victims	Number
1.	Leading political, cultural, social personalities arrested and deported to the Gulag on July 11-19, 1940	2,000
2.	Military personnel, officers and regulars, arrested and incarcerated in Gulag concentration camps	6,500
3.	Political prisoners, Liquidated during the first Soviet occupation in 1940-1941	9,500
4.	Members of families in first mass deportation to Gulag camps June 14-17, 1941	34,260
5.	Lithuanian activists liquidated shortly before the outbreak of World War II June 18-22, 1941	1,600
6.	Lithuanian insurgents killed during the uprising of June 22-25, 1941	2,000
7.	Members of the Jewish community retreated to Soviet Union	15,000
8.	Lithuanian military and some civilians forced to retreat with Red Army deep into Soviet Union	5,000
9.	Lithuanian citizens of real or assumed German descent repatriated to Germany	60,000
	Total loss of population during first Soviet occupation	135,860

---

[774] Damušis, *Lithuania against Soviet and Nazi aggression*, p. 51. *Courtesy of Ambassador Ginté Damušis.* The author is grateful to daughter of Prof. Dr. Adolfas Damušis, Ambassador Ginté Damušis, for all important discussions and insights.

Table 4

Summary of Exterminated Victims of Lithuania's Population by Soviet Occupation Forces[775]

Victims	Number
Eleven mass deportations of families to the Gulag system during two occupational periods: June 15, 1940 - June 29, 1941 and 1944 - 1953	442,060
Individually arrested and deported to Gulag concentration camps	92,600
Lithuanian officers and soldiers forced To retreat to the Soviet Union June 22 - 29, 1941	5,000
Jews who retreated with the Red Army to the Soviet Union June 23 - 29, 1941	15,000
Lithuanian insurgents killed during the Uprising June 22 - 25, 1941	2,000
Lithuanian fighters for freedom and their Enemies *stribs*, killed in battles	36,000
Total number of victims	592,660
Approximate number who Returned alive to Lithuania	119,475
Victims of genocide, annihilated by Soviet occupational forces	473,185

---

775   Damušis, *Lithuania against Soviet and Nazi aggression*, p. 270. *Courtesy of Ambassador Gintė Damušis.* The author is grateful to daughter of Prof. Dr. Adolfas Damušis, Ambassador Gintė Damušis, for all important discussions and insights.

Table 5

Victims of the Nazi Occupation among the Lithuanian population[776]

Individuals deported as forced labor, incarcerated,
and perished in concentration camps..17,000

Farmers annihilated for non-delivery of requisitioned food quotas.......11,000

Transport and security forces who deserted, were caught, imprisoned
and killed on the front lines or in the concentration camps.................13,000

Citizens exterminated at locations Alytus, Pirciupis, etc. 4,000

Total victims of Nazi annihilation..45,000

---

[776] Damušis, *Lithuania against Soviet and Nazi aggression*, p. 208. *Courtesy of Ambassador Gintė Damušis.* The author is grateful to daughter of Prof. Dr. Adolfas Damušis, Ambassador Gintė Damušis, for all important discussions and insights.

Table 6

Jewish Victims of the Holocaust in Lithuania[777]

Total population of Jews in Lithuania in July
1940..234,021

Individuals deported or survived

> Jews, factory or business owners, Zionists deported to the Gulag Concentration camps in Siberia...7,000
>
> Émigrés abroad from Lithuania in 1939-1940................................6,000
>
> Persons who retreated to Soviet Russia with Red Army, June 1941....15,000
>
> Jews deported to Estonia during the Nazi occupation....................13,000
>
> Survivors of the Holocaust...28,000
>
> Subtotal...69,000

A.   Total Holocaust victims in Lithuania..165,021

---

[777]   Damušis, *Lithuania against Soviet and Nazi aggression*, p. 208. *Courtesy of Ambassador Gintė Damušis.* The author is grateful to daughter of Prof. Dr. Adolfas Damušis, Ambassador Gintė Damušis, for all important discussions and insights.

Table 7

Total Population Losses in Lithuania during the Nazi occupation of 1941-1944[778]

Lithuanian victims of annihilation (Table 2) 45,000

Jewish Lithuanian victims of Holocaust in Lithuania (Table 3).........165,021

Émigrés to Western democracies and to Germany........................120,000

TOTAL...330,021

---

778   Damušis, *Lithuania against Soviet and Nazi aggression,* p. 208. *Courtesy of Ambassador Gintė Damušis.* The author is grateful to daughter of Prof. Dr. Adolfas Damušis, Ambassador Gintė Damušis, for all important discussions and insights.

Index

Adamkus, Valdas 315, 316, 321,
    322, 327, 329, 359, 361, 374
  Königsberg 17, 18, 23, 35, 50,
      261, 296, 335, 336, 337, 338,
      339, 341, 343, 344, 345, 348,
      349, 354, 358, 360, 361, 362,
      363, 364, 365, 370, 371, 373,
      374, 376, 391, 392, 393, 407,
      422, 424
  meetings with Pres. Bill Clinton
      286, 306, 318, 319, 320, 321
  meetings with Pres. George W.
      Bush 15, 32, 184, 186, 187,
      188, 189, 190, 192, 194, 195,
      196, 197, 200, 210, 213, 214,
      219, 221, 223, 229, 230, 234,
      237, 245, 246, 247, 251, 255,
      256, 257, 293, 314, 316, 317,
      320, 325, 328, 331, 350, 367,
      375, 386, 397, 420, 423
  meetings with Prime Minister
      Tony Blair 327
  meetings with Vladimir Putin
      17, 94, 259, 322, 323, 324,
      347, 350, 357, 360, 361, 371,
      374, 378
  NATO membership 9, 15, 16, 21,
      23, 27, 33, 34, 128, 255, 261,
      265, 266, 285, 286, 287, 298,
      299, 300, 301, 302, 304, 305,
      306, 307, 308, 309, 310, 311,
      312, 313, 314, 315, 316, 317,
      318, 319, 320, 321, 322, 323,
      325, 326, 327, 328, 329, 330,
      331, 332, 333, 335, 336, 347,
      350, 358, 360, 367, 368, 369,
      370, 371, 372, 373, 374, 375,
      376, 377, 378, 385, 390, 392,
      393, 395, 398, 399, 403, 404,
      407, 408, 423, 426
  Northern European pipeline 360

  President of Lithuania 91, 256,
      319, 382, 386
Adolphus, Gustavus 45
Adomaitis, Regimantas 134
Albright, Madeleine 318, 319
Algirdas, Grand Duke 11, 37
Aliulis, Vaclovas 141, 226, 390,
    397
Ambrazevičius, Juozas *see*
    Brazaitis 68, 70, 73, 76, 77,
    79, 80, 81, 102, 397, 404, 405
Ancram, Michael 347, 348
Antanaitis, Vaidotas 143
Antanavičius, Kazimieras 130
Anušauskas, Arvydas 375, 436,
    439
Ash, Timothy Garton 121, 399
Asmus, Ronald D
    Baltic American communities 9,
        116, 225, 226, 317, 330, 376,
        412, 420, 422, 424
    NATO enlargement 301, 302,
        306, 313, 315, 316, 318, 319,
        323, 325, 326, 327, 330, 367,
        368, 369, 404, 408, 423, 426
Asmus, Ronald D. 301, 316, 317,
    318, 319, 320, 399, 404
    Baltic American communities
        34
    strategy towards the Baltic States
        301
Astakhov, Georgi 60
Atkočiūnas, Edmundas 147
Attlee, Clement 342
Augustus II, King 45
Austin, Lloyd James III 375, 376

Aves, Jonathan 20, 178, 401

Aybet, Gülnur 265

Aznar, Jose Maria 357

Ažubalis, Audrius 181, 185, 391

Bakatin, Vadim V. 201

Baker III, James A. 22, 32, 179,
    184, 188, 189, 190, 195, 199,
    200, 206, 210, 212, 213, 214,
    215, 216, 219, 220, 221, 223,
    229, 243, 246, 248, 251, 257,
    277, 279, 336, 397
  disintegration of the Soviet Union
    219
  Elements of a Final Settlement
    336
  January 13, 1991 in Lithuania
    405
  private papers 22
  *Soviet economic blockade of
    Lithuania* 32, 207
  visit to Lithuania 174, 185, 326,
    375

Balakauskas, Osvaldas 391

Baltin, Edmundas 143

Baltrukonytė, Lina 244

Balutis, Bronius 27, 59, 273, 389

Baranauskas, Boleslovas 72, 237

Basanavičius, Jonas 49

Bator, Stefan 44, 45

Batūra, Romas 31, 153, 154, 168,
    399

Bauža, Česlovas 436, 439

Beddin, John S. 345, 389

Bering, Helle 324, 325

Beriozovas, Vladimiras 157

Berlusconi, Silvio 357

Beschloss, Michael R. 187, 189,
    192, 195, 196, 197, 200, 210,
    211, 213, 214, 216, 219, 220,
    397

Besmertnykh, Aleksandr 221

Bičkauskas, Egidijus 218, 221

Bildt, Carl 291, 301, 404

Blair, Tony 327

Blažytė, Danutė 130, 134, 141,
    399, 409, 436, 439

Bobelis, Kazys 281, 282

Bolen, Charles E. 338

Bondevik, Kjell Magne 279

Boruta, Jonas 399

Bower, Tom 399

Bradley, Nicolas 399

Brandišauskas, Valentinas 72,
    399

Brazaitis, Juozas see
    Ambrazevičius 399
  partisan war 399
  Prime Minister 12, 51, 64, 70,
    73, 76, 148, 156, 184, 191,
    196, 199, 204, 206, 207, 208,
    209, 212, 213, 215, 217, 233,
    234, 235, 236, 244, 254, 255,
    256, 270, 282, 291, 301, 313,
    315, 327, 339, 340, 342, 343,
    357, 359, 363, 364, 365, 369,
    376, 377, 378
  Provisional Government 28, 67,
    70, 72, 73, 74, 75, 76, 78, 79,
    80, 82, 85, 87, 90, 94
  Soviet occupation 20, 24, 26, 30,
    31, 32, 37, 54, 62, 63, 69, 85,
    97, 98, 102, 113, 118, 128,
    129, 146, 153, 154, 159, 162,
    163, 225, 226, 263, 272, 288,
    307, 367, 369, 393, 442, 443
  the Uprising of 1941 72

Brazauskas, Algirdas 138, 144,
    157, 161, 162, 166, 169, 170,
    171, 174, 175, 180, 208, 209,
    319, 359, 372, 374, 397
  economic blockade 32, 158, 181,
    205, 206, 207, 210, 220, 221,
    222, 245, 278, 359

leadership of the Communist
  Party in Lithuania 136, 137,
  216, 217, 238
Lithuanian flag 113
meetings with Gorbachev 20, 21,
  31, 32, 33, 38, 88, 121, 122,
  123, 124, 125, 127, 136, 138,
  145, 154, 156, 159, 166, 169,
  171, 172, 173, 174, 175, 178,
  180, 181, 182, 184, 185, 186,
  187, 188, 190, 192, 195, 196,
  197, 198, 199, 200, 201, 202,
  203, 204, 205, 207, 208, 209,
  213, 215, 216, 218, 219, 220,
  221, 228, 229, 230, 232, 233,
  235, 236, 239, 242, 245, 246,
  248, 249, 250, 251, 252, 264,
  274, 275, 281, 282, 383, 384,
  385, 386, 389, 398, 403, 412
meetings with President Bill
  Clinton 286, 287, 306, 316,
  318, 319, 320, 321, 397
relationship with the Kremlin 208
social problems 372

Brenner, Michael J. 266

Brezhnev, Leonid 110, 114, 160,
  252, 268

Brodsky, Josef 248

Bronstein, Mikhail 135

Brzezinski, Zbigniew 266, 303,
  305, 397, 405

Bubnys, Vytautas 134, 136, 139,
  143

Bučelis, Balys 218, 383

Budreckis, Algirdas 69, 400

Bulavas, Juozas 134

Bulvyčius, Vytautas 73

Bumblauskas, Alfredas 38, 394,
  405

Buračas, Antanas 130, 134, 139,
  143, 147
Lithuanian flag 113

Burokevičius, Mykolas 202

Bush, George H. W.
  disintegration of the Soviet Union
    219
  meetings with Pres. Landsbergis
    18, 24, 26, 31, 32, 33, 38, 76,
    79, 88, 105, 127, 128, 129,
    130, 133, 134, 135, 139, 141,
    142, 145, 146, 147, 149, 158,
    159, 173, 174, 176, 177, 179,
    180, 181, 182, 183, 184, 185,
    186, 187, 190, 191, 192, 193,
    194, 195, 196, 197, 198, 199,
    200, 201, 204,205, 207, 208,
    209, 210, 211, 212, 213, 214,
    215, 217, 219, 220, 221, 222,
    225, 227, 228, 229, 230, 232,
    233, 234, 235, 236, 238, 239,
    241, 242, 248, 249, 252, 255,
    256, 258, 263, 272, 274, 284,
    286, 287, 288, 289, 290, 293,
    300, 301, 304, 305, 306, 307,
    318, 332, 348, 349, 353, 354,
    355, 356, 357, 358, 374, 378,
    384, 385, 386, 387, 393, 394,
    395, 397, 398, 407, 408, 426
  Münich 210, 211, 213
  Secretary James Baker 22, 32,
    179, 184, 188, 189, 190, 195,
    199, 200, 206, 210, 212, 213,
    214, 215, 216, 219, 220, 221,
    223, 229, 243, 246, 248, 251,
    257, 277, 279, 336, 397
  withdrawal of Russian troops
    261, 267, 276, 286, 289, 312,
    335, 369, 373, 375

Bush, George W.
  Baltic NATO membership 301,
    305, 325, 326, 333, 423
  meetings with Gerhard Schröder
    325, 361
  meetings with Pres. Valdas
    Adamkus 299, 315, 316, 321,
    327, 328, 329, 359, 361, 374
  speech at Warsaw University
    314, 329
  vision of Europe 307, 315, 316,
    332, 368, 369

Būtėnas, Julius 72

Byrnes, James Francis 183, 337

Čekuolis, Algimantas 134, 136

Čepaitis, Virgilijus 134

Čiudiškis, Bronius 91

Čiurlionis, Mikalojus
    Konstantinas 130

Clark, Terry D. 341

Clemens, Walter C 25, 31, 32,
    178, 179, 273, 400, 405
    independence movements 31, 166,
        178
    Soviet collapse 31, 122, 241, 272,
        274
    the US non-recognition policy
        14, 22, 24, 26, 27, 31, 71, 123,
        142, 188, 225, 270, 296, 337,
        346, 367, 404

Clinton, William 286, 287, 306,
    316, 318, 319, 320, 321, 397
    meeting with Pres. Valdas
        Adamkus 299, 315, 316, 321,
        322, 327, 328, 329, 359, 361,
        374, 382, 397
    new Europe 184, 306
    vision of Europe 307, 315, 316,
        332, 368, 369
    withdrawal of Soviet troops from
        Lithuania and the Baltic states
        257, 258

Columbus 37

Cox, Michael 273, 274

Crowe, William 191

Cuellar, Xavier Peres 241

Curzon, Lord George Nathaniel
    337, 338

Damušis, Adolfas 28, 67, 69, 70,
    71, 74, 76, 79, 80, 81, 82, 83,
    84, 87, 89, 90, 91, 92, 93, 94,
    95, 117, 309, 311, 312, 333,
    400, 405, 432, 433, 434, 436,
    442, 443, 444, 445, 446
    anti-Nazi resistance 105, 117
    Ateitis, 30, 106, 271, 272, 398,
        409
    Catholic youth organisation 271
    Lithuania against Soviet and Nazi
        aggression 28, 81, 400, 432,
        433, 434, 436, 442, 443, 444,
        445, 446
    Lithuanian Constitution 227,
        228, 386
    Nazi occupation of Lithuania 96
    Soviet-Nazi pact 25, 142, 150,
        173, 180, 271, 345
    strategy and tactics of resistance
        against Nazi occupation 85

Damušytė, Gintė
    compatibility with NATO 9, 15,
        16, 21, 23, 27, 33, 34, 128,
        255, 261, 265, 266, 285, 286,
        287, 298, 299, 300, 301, 302,
        304, 305, 306, 307, 308, 309,
        310, 311, 312, 313, 314, 315,
        316, 317, 318, 319, 320, 321,
        322, 323, 325, 326, 327, 328,
        329, 330, 331, 332, 333, 335,
        336, 347, 350, 358, 360, 367,
        368, 369, 370, 371, 372, 373,
        374, 375, 376, 377, 378, 385,
        390, 392, 393, 395, 398, 399,
        403, 404, 407, 408, 423, 426
    cooperation with Georgia 19,
        33, 185, 312, 323, 363, 440
    membership action plan (MAP)
        328, 333

Daumantas, Juozas see Lukša
    14, 29, 71, 101, 102, 387, 397

Daunoras, Vaclovas 134

Davy, Richard 274, 400

DeConcini, Dennis 281

Dekanozov, Vladimir 64

Deksnys, J. see Prapuolenis 74,
    76

Demm, Eberhard 368, 400, 408

Dempsey, Judy 357

Deutsch, Karl 266, 303, 400

Dimanis, Sergei 292

Dubinin, Soviet Ambassador
    192

Dumas, Roland 253, 396

Duncan, Peter J. S. 20, 178, 401

Eden, Anthony Robert 327, 337

Ehrlinger, Erich 95

Eidintas, Alfonsas 88, 91, 384,
    400

Eisenhower, Dwight D. 197

Eismuntas, Eduardas 142, 143

Elizabeth of Habsburg 43

Elleman-Jensen, Uffe 236, 279

Evans, John 279

Falin, Valentin 201

Finkelstein, Eithan 114

Fischer, Joschka 325

Fisher, Jane 279

Fitzwater, Marlin 197, 237

Ford, Gerald 114, 270, 367

Freedman, Laurence 274, 401

Fried, Daniel 329

Fry, John 267, 400

Fuerth, Leon 324

Furmonavicius, Darius 18, 349,
    356, 392, 394, 405, 425, 426
    Japanese Northern territories 23
    Königsberg region 17, 18, 23,
        335, 338, 344, 345, 348, 349,
        358, 360, 362, 363, 364, 365,
        371, 373, 374, 391, 392, 393
    NATO enlargement 301, 302,
        306, 313, 315, 316, 318, 319,
        323, 325, 326, 327, 330, 367,
        368, 369, 404, 408, 423, 426
    *Northern European Security
        Community* 21, 24, 286, 405
    President Jacques Chirac 326,
        361, 382

Soviet terror 32, 74, 104
    Ukraine 17, 18, 33, 40, 180, 183,
        312, 313, 323, 353, 363, 377,
        378, 379, 407, 439

Gaigalaitė, Aldona 72

Gajauskas, Balys 150, 271

Ganušauskas, Edmundas 209

Garuckas, Karolis 114, 271

Gaškaitė, Nijolė 71, 98, 401

Geda, Sigitas 134, 143, 148

Gediminas, Grand Duke 11, 29,
    41, 43, 144, 147, 173, 244,
    254, 255, 256, 286, 414
    *Gediminas street in Vilnius
        (former headquarters of KGB)*
        29

Genzelis, Bronius 130, 132, 133,
    134, 135, 136, 138, 143, 159,
    397
    *resignation of Rimgaudas
        Songaila* 134, 138, 143, 157,
        159

Germanas-Meškauskas, Pranas
    86

Gerner, Kristian 21, 401

Gerutis, Albertas 401

Gimbutas, Marija 39, 401, 430

Gintas, Danielius 91

Girenko, Andrei N. 201

Girnius, Juozas 75

Girnius, Kęstutis 29, 71, 98, 103
    *partisan war during the Soviet
        occupation* 28, 29, 70, 71, 72,
        80, 98, 99, 102, 105, 106, 107,
        118, 367

Gladkov, Fyodor 74

Goble, Paul 324, 394

Godmanis, Ivars 255

Gorbachev, Mikhail 20, 21, 31, 32, 33, 38, 88, 121, 122, 123, 124, 125, 127, 136, 138, 145, 154, 156, 159, 166, 169, 171, 172, 173, 174, 175, 178, 180, 181, 182, 184, 185, 186, 187, 188, 190, 192, 195, 196, 197, 198, 199, 200, 201, 202, 203, 204, 205, 207, 208, 209, 213, 215, 216, 218, 219, 220, 221, 228, 229, 230, 232, 233, 235, 236, 239, 242, 245, 246, 248, 249, 250, 251, 252, 264, 274, 275, 281, 282, 383, 384, 385, 386, 389, 398, 403, 412

   communist coup d'état 15, 32, 55, 95, 181, 231, 283

   election of candidates to the Communist Party conference 136, 159

   Empire mentality 156

   failure in Lithuania 9, 11, 12, 13, 14, 15, 17, 18, 19, 20, 21, 22, 23, 24, 25, 26, 27, 28, 29, 30, 31, 32, 33, 34, 37, 38, 39, 40, 41, 42, 43, 44, 45, 46, 47, 48, 49, 50, 51, 52, 53, 54, 55, 56, 57, 58, 59, 60, 61, 62, 63, 65, 67, 68, 69, 70, 71, 72, 73, 74, 75, 76, 77, 78, 79, 80, 81, 82, 83, 84, 85, 86, 87, 88, 89, 90, 91, 92, 93, 94, 95, 96, 97, 98, 99, 100, 101, 102, 103, 104, 105, 106, 107, 108, 110, 111, 112, 113, 115, 117, 118, 119, 121, 122, 123, 124, 125, 126, 127, 128, 129, 130, 132, 133, 134, 135, 136, 137, 138, 139, 140, 141, 142, 143, 144, 145, 146, 147, 148, 150, 151, 153, 154, 155, 157, 158, 159, 160, 161, 162, 164, 165, 166, 168, 169, 170, 171, 172, 173, 174, 175, 176, 177, 178, 179, 180, 181, 183, 184, 185, 186, 187, 188, 189, 190, 191, 192, 193, 194, 195, 196, 197, 198, 199, 200, 201, 202, 203, 204, 205, 207, 208, 209, 210, 212, 214, 215, 216, 217, 218, 219, 221, 222, 225, 226, 227, 228, 229, 230, 231, 233, 234, 235, 237, 238, 239, 240, 241, 242, 243, 244, 245, 246, 247, 248, 249, 250, 251, 252, 253, 254, 255, 256, 257, 258, 260, 261, 263, 264, 267, 269, 270, 271, 272, 273, 274, 275, 276, 277, 278, 280, 281, 283, 284, 285, 286, 287, 288, 289, 290, 292, 293, 294, 295, 296, 297, 298, 299, 300, 301, 302, 303, 304, 305, 306, 307, 308, 309, 310, 311, 312, 313, 315, 316, 317, 318, 319, 320, 321, 322, 326, 327, 328, 329, 330, 331, 332, 333, 335, 336, 339, 340, 341, 342, 343, 345, 346, 347, 348, 349, 353, 355, 356, 357, 358, 359, 361, 362, 363, 365, 367, 368, 369, 370, 372, 373, 374, 375, 376, 377, 379, 381, 382, 383, 384, 385, 386, 387, 388, 389, 390, 392, 393, 395, 396, 398, 399, 400, 401, 402, 403, 404, 405, 406, 407, 408, 409, 414, 415, 417, 418, 422, 429, 431, 432, 433, 434, 436, 437, 442, 443, 444, 445, 446

   final phase of the Soviet Union 13, 14, 15, 17, 18, 20, 21, 22, 23, 25, 26, 27, 28, 31, 32, 34, 38, 55, 56, 57, 58, 60, 62, 63, 65, 67, 68, 71, 73, 77, 78, 88, 97, 102, 103, 108, 110, 113, 115, 116, 117, 123, 126, 127, 133, 138, 141, 142, 143, 146, 148, 150, 153, 154, 155, 158, 160, 161, 162, 163, 164, 165, 166, 167, 168, 169, 170, 172, 173, 174, 176, 177, 178, 179, 181, 182, 183, 186, 189, 190, 191, 194, 196, 198, 202, 205,

206, 207, 208, 209, 210, 212,
213, 214, 216, 218, 219, 220,
221, 222, 225, 227, 231, 233,
236, 237, 238, 240, 241, 242,
243, 244, 245, 246, 247, 249,
250, 253, 255, 257, 258, 259,
260, 261, 268, 270, 273, 275,
276, 278, 280, 281, 282, 285,
293, 296, 297, 304, 305, 327,
331, 335, 336, 337, 339, 340,
341, 342, 343, 344, 345, 346,
354, 361, 367, 368, 369, 371,
375, 379, 401, 402, 403, 404,
405, 407, 440, 442, 443
Lithuanian independence 29, 51,
70, 74, 106, 110, 133, 154,
176, 189, 194, 211, 368, 369,
408
meeting with Algirdas Brazauskas
138, 144, 157, 161, 162, 166,
169, 170, 171, 174, 175, 180,
208, 209, 319, 359, 372, 374,
397
military actions 241, 243, 247,
249
*non-interference in Eastern
Europe* 41, 96, 121, 157, 171,
172, 180, 252, 265, 266, 274,
281, 282, 295, 307, 315, 343,
353, 363, 381, 385, 403, 405
perestroika 128, 156, 404
*separation of the Lithuanian
Communist Party from the
Soviet Communist party* 341
Soviet collapse 31, 122, 241,
272, 274
visit to Lithuania 174, 185, 326,
375
Gordon, Philip H. 266
Gore, All 318, 324
Göring, Hermann 82
Grand Duke Mindaugas see
Mindaugas 11, 40
Grava, Uldis 269
Gražulis, Petras 123, 124, 147

Great Duchy of Lithuania 12,
44, 45, 46, 47, 48
Greffe, Heinz 75
Grigas, Robertas 244
Grinius, Juozas 55
Grinius, Kazys 55
Grose, Peter 101, 401
Gudaitis, Romas 136, 218
Gudavičius, Edvardas 401
Gureckas, Algimantas P. 355,
356, 407
Gurevičius, A. 88
Hainsworth, Paul 274, 405
Hamann, Guenther 89, 92, 93
Hannibalsson, Jon Baldvin 247,
279
Harriman, Averell W. 345
Harrison, Ernest J. 37, 401
Havel, Vaclav 191, 333, 384, 387
Hedlund, Stefan 21, 401
Helms, Jesse 194, 330, 331, 384
Henri of Valois, see also King
Henry III 44
Hiden, John 401
Baltic states 37, 68, 99, 101, 104,
163, 240, 278, 286, 301, 302,
317, 318, 319, 320, 326, 331,
346, 371, 375, 376, 402, 404,
408
Grand Duke Mindaugas 11, 40
Klaipėda region 13, 55, 56, 58,
61, 89, 111, 118, 140, 203,
235, 368
Hill, Christopher 265, 417
Himmler, Heinrich 89, 90, 97
Hint, Maati 168

Hitler, Adolf 63, 67, 69, 81, 87,
    88, 89, 96, 97, 98, 115, 118,
    123, 133, 150, 160, 167, 182,
    183, 184, 189, 198, 210, 375,
    401, 403, 413, 433
    Lithuanian Activist Front 73,
        75, 76, 79, 80, 84, 88, 93, 184
    Nazi occupation of Lithuania 96
    Soviet-Nazi (Moscow) pact 25,
        142, 150, 173, 180, 271, 333,
        345, 357

Hogg, Douglas 255

Hoon, Geoffrey 327

Hoover, Herbert 23, 24, 28, 270,
    381, 382, 390, 436, 437

Hosking, Geoffrey A. 20, 178,
    401

Hough, William J.H. 142

Hoyer, Steny 280, 281

Huisman, Sander 364

Hull, Cordell 384

Hunter, Robert 266

Husein, Sadam 334

Iešmantas, Gintautas 109, 150

Inhofe, James 330

Ivanauskas, Gintautas –
    Vytautas 72

Ivanauskas, Vytautas Gintautas
    72

Ivinskis, Zenonas 80, 81, 82, 85,
    86, 87, 401, 407

Jaeger, Karl 89, 92, 93

Jancar, Barbara W. 113, 407

Jarvis, Erick 323

Jazov, Dmitri T. 123

Jensen, Uffe Elleman 236, 279

Jermalavičius, Juozas 238

Jockus, Arvydas 394

John Paul II, Pope 112

Johnson, Garry 304

Juozaitis, Arvydas 130, 134,
    135, 143, 147, 172, 179, 180,
    385, 394
    Soviet military force 9, 64, 136,
        181, 185, 187, 203, 208, 233,
        235, 241, 242, 243, 244, 246,
        249, 266, 360
    speech on August 23, 1988 146,
        159, 180, 394

Jurevičius, Mečislovas 271

Jurgėla, Constantine 431

Jurgutis, Vladas 86

Jurkans, Janis 278

Juzeliūnas, Julius 134, 143, 149,
    175

Kalanta, Romas 112, 113

Kalinin, Mikhail Ivanovich 336,
    354

Kalugin, Oleg 209

Kampelman, Max 279, 280, 281

Kant, Immanuel 354, 361, 365

Kaplan, Morton 273, 403

Kapočius, Feliksas 102

Kašauskas, Raimundas 171

Kašauskienė, Vanda 130, 399,
    409, 436, 439

Kasayanov, Mikhail 357

Kašėta, Algis 71, 401

Kaslas, Bronis J. 59, 64, 345, 381,
    401, 436, 437
    Baltic Alliance (Baltic Entente)
        13, 57, 58
    recognition of Lithuania 188, 205,
        222, 252, 255, 258, 261, 282,
        296, 436, 437
    Soviet occupation of Lithuania
        20, 24, 26, 30, 31, 32, 37, 54,
        62, 63, 69, 85, 97, 98, 102,
        113, 118, 128, 129, 146, 153,
        154, 159, 162, 163, 225, 226,

263, 272, 288, 307, 367, 369, 393, 442, 443

Katilius-Boydstun, Dalia 407

Kaušpėdas, Algirdas 134, 136

Kelam, Tunne 361

Kempton, Daniel 341

Kershaw, Ian 401

Kersten, Charles J. 80

Kęstutis, Grand Duke 11, 29, 41, 71, 98, 103, 398, 401

Kiaupa, Zigmantas 401

Kisielius, Petras 94

Kissinger, Henry 241

Kizas, Virginijus 257

Klaiber, Klaus-Peter 299

Klein, Jean 266, 345

Klimas, Petras 27, 28, 381

Kohl, Helmut 211, 212, 214, 247, 256, 386

Kojelis, Juozas 116, 226, 273, 274, 385

Kojelis, Linas 116, 226, 273, 274, 385

Kontrimaitė, M. 143

Kovoliov, Sergej 111

Kowalewski, David 108, 109, 407

Kozyrev, Andrei 258, 259, 294

Kramer, Mark 371

Krausnick, Helmut 89, 90, 91, 407

Krickus, Richard 20, 157, 177, 232, 271, 273, 337, 402
    Kriegsheim, Lieutenant Colonel 87
    Petkevičius 128, 134, 136, 143, 157
    Soviet collapse 31, 122, 241, 272, 274

Viktoras Petkus, see Petkus 114, 150, 271

Kriuchkov, Vladimir 161, 201

Krivickas, Domas 407

Kronkaitis, Jonas 299, 308, 385

Krushchev, Nikita 110

Kšanavičius, Arvydas 78

Kubilius, Andrius 309, 363, 402, 407

Kudaba, Česlovas 131, 134, 143

Kudirka, Simas 49, 108, 150, 383

Kudirka, Vincas 49, 108, 150, 383

Kukk, Juri 115

Kuodytė, Dalia 71, 401

Kupčikas, Dainius 238

Kūris, Pranas 212

Kuzmickas, Bronius 134, 261, 394

Kuzmin, Fiodor 236

Kviklys, Bronius 82, 402

Landsbergis, Gabrielius 378

Landsbergis, Vytautas 18, 24, 26, 31, 32, 38, 76, 79, 88, 105, 127, 128, 129, 133, 134, 135, 139, 141, 142, 145, 146, 147, 159, 173, 174, 175, 176, 177, 179, 180, 182, 191, 193, 195, 197, 198, 199, 204, 207, 211, 214, 220, 222, 225, 227, 229, 230, 232, 233, 234, 235, 236, 237, 238, 239, 242, 248, 249, 255, 256, 258, 263, 272, 274, 284, 286, 287, 289, 290, 293, 300, 301, 304, 305, 306, 307, 318, 332, 348, 353, 354, 355, 356, 357, 358, 374, 384, 386, 387, 393, 426

Boris Yeltsin, see Yeltsin 34, 111,
  177, 208, 242, 254, 258, 260,
  264, 291, 321
Čiurlionis, see Čiurlionis 130
collapse of the Soviet Union 31,
  78, 177, 178, 223, 258, 273,
  304, 368, 369, 375
creeping occupation 186
CSCE, Helsinki summit 9, 21, 34,
  190, 247, 259, 264, 268, 269,
  272, 276, 277, 278, 279, 280,
  281, 282, 283, 284, 286, 289,
  290, 292, 295, 390, 407
economic blockade 32, 158, 181,
  205, 206, 207, 210, 220, 221,
  222, 245, 278, 359
European security 19, 23, 33, 34,
  35, 265, 279, 295, 300, 301,
  303, 306, 313, 326, 392, 393
Helsinki Final Act 194, 268, 278,
  283, 295, 386
January 13, 1991 in Lithuania
  405
Juozas Urbšys, see Urbšys 27, 59,
  61, 62, 63, 64, 147, 217, 398
Königsberg region 17, 18, 23, 33,
  35, 50, 215, 261, 296, 300,
  322, 335, 336, 337, 338, 339,
  341, 343, 344, 345, 347, 348,
  349, 350, 351, 352, 354, 355,
  356, 357, 358, 359, 360, 361,
  362, 363, 364, 365, 370, 371,
  373, 374, 376, 385, 391, 392,
  393, 405, 407, 422, 424
legal continuity of the Lithuanian
  state 225, 272
Liberation of Lithuania from
  Soviet occupation 27, 102,
  226, 272, 281
memoirs 21, 73, 178, 183, 184,
  190, 195, 207, 274, 286, 338,
  397, 398
Münich 210, 211, 213
NATO membership 34, 301, 304,
  305, 308, 312, 313, 317, 319,
  325, 326, 327, 328, 329, 332,
  333, 369, 378, 423

new Ribbentrop-Molotov pact
  357
non-violent response 32
partisan war 28, 29, 70, 71, 72,
  80, 98, 99, 102, 105, 106, 107,
  118, 367
peaceful liberation 22, 25, 133,
  367, 369
President of the Supreme Council
  of the Republic of Lithuania
  175
proposal for negotiations with the
  Kremlin 228
restoration of Lithuania's
  independence 135, 150, 176,
  179, 216
Sąjūdis 14, 20, 26, 30, 31, 32, 38,
  77, 78, 79, 80, 87, 99, 100,
  101, 105, 106, 122, 126, 127,
  128, 129, 130, 131, 132, 133,
  134, 135, 136, 137, 138, 140,
  141, 142, 143, 144, 145, 147,
  150, 153, 154, 155, 156, 157,
  158, 159, 160, 161, 162, 163,
  164, 165, 166, 168, 170, 171,
  172, 173, 174, 175, 177, 178,
  179, 180, 182, 203, 207, 209,
  227, 272, 276, 372, 384, 385,
  387, 396, 397, 398, 399, 405,
  409, 414
Sąjūdis Founding Group 144,
  146, 154
Soviet occupation of Lithuania
  146, 162
the second Münich 213
welcome to international
  community of nations 17, 20,
  78, 122, 167, 188, 276, 283,
  298, 368, 369
Landsbergis-Žemkalnis,
  Vytautas 76, 129
Lane, Thomas 97, 98, 402, 403
Lange, Falk 269
Laurinavičius, Bronius 271
Laurinkus, Mečys 143
Lautenberg, Frank 281

Lazauskas, Stanislovas 106

Lazauskienė, Ona 110, 411

Lenin, Vladimir 125, 156, 163, 172, 193, 203, 357, 419

Leonavičius, Bronius 134

Leszczynski, Stanislaw 46

Lethi, Marko 365

Lieven, Anatol 21, 286, 408

Ligachev, Yegor 171, 172, 174, 175, 191

Lipmaa, Endel 280

Liulevičius, Vėjas Gabriel 301, 402

Lobjakas, Ahto 357

Lohan, Gerhard 353

Lopata, Raimundas 322, 402

Lord Halifax, Viscount Halifax see Wood, Edward Frederick Lindley 59, 382, 389

Lozoraitis, Stasys, Jr. 125
collapse of the Soviet Union 31, 78, 177, 178, 223, 258, 273, 304, 368, 369, 375
continuity of state 20, 229, 256
liberation of Lithuania from Soviet occupation 154

Lukauskaitė-Poškienė, Ona 114

Lukša, Juozas see Daumantas 14, 71, 101

Lukšienė, Meilė 134

Mačiulis, Jonas 49, 402

Mackevičius, Mečislovas 76, 77, 86, 408

Maironis see Mačiulis, Jonas 49

Major, John 101, 255, 327, 356

Makashov, General 157

Maldonis, Alfonsas 134

Marcinkevičius, Justinas 127, 134, 146, 395

Masliukov, Arkadi 201

Mastny, Vojtech 274, 402

Matlock, Jack 21, 178, 197, 237, 398

Matulionis, Jonas 76

Mažvydas, Martynas 345

Medalinskas, Alvydas 134, 143

Medvedev, Nikolai 169, 218

Medvedev, Vadim A. 169, 218

Meri, Lennart 278, 287, 306, 319

Meškauskas, Juozas 80

Mickevičius, Adomas 14, 113, 123, 129, 148, 413

Mickevičius, Vincas Krėvė 14, 113, 123, 129, 148, 413

Mikučiauskas, Vladislovas 148

Milosz, Czeslaw 240, 248, 395

Mindaugas, King 11, 40

Minkevičius, Jokūbas 134, 136

Misiūnas, Romualdas 29, 68, 99, 402
partisan war 28, 29, 70, 71, 72, 80, 98, 99, 102, 105, 106, 107, 118, 367

Mitkin, Nikolai 157

Mitterand, Fracois 211

Molotov, Vyacheslav
Königsberg and adjacent areas 341
new Ribbentrop-Molotov pact 357
Potsdam conference 335, 338, 339, 341, 342, 346, 381, 382
Soviet-Nazi pact 13, 25, 31, 35, 67, 100, 115, 116, 123, 129, 133, 142, 146, 150, 153, 159, 162, 163, 173, 180, 199, 205, 258, 271, 276, 326, 333, 343, 345, 357, 359, 413

spheres of influence 35, 60, 61, 306

Mulroney, Brian 213

Narutis, Pilypas 73, 184

Nasevičius, N. 76

Nasvytis, Algimantas 134

Natkevičius, Ladas 62

Nelsas, Angelė 412, 420, 422, 423

Noël, Roger 368, 400

Novak, Michael 268, 274, 402

Novickis, Antanas 76

Nurick, Robert 301, 404

Ohman, Jonas 398

Oldberg, Ingmar 341

Oliker, Olga 353

Orban, Viktor 365

Ozolas, Romualdas 134, 143, 156, 233, 234, 395

Packer, Anthony 24, 31, 177, 179, 408

Pajaujis, Juozas 76, 402

Pakalnis, Romas 134

Paksas, Rolandas 370, 406

Paleckis, Justas 65, 68

Panic, Milan 290

Patten, Chris 354

Pavlov 229, 345

Pečeliūnas, Povilas 109, 271

Pečiulis, Saulius 134, 143

Peter the Great, Tsar 46

Petersen, Roger D. 96, 403

Petkevičius, Vytautas 128, 134, 136, 143, 157

Petkus, Viktoras 114, 150, 271

Petrovski, Vladimir 278

Pijus XII 29

Plechavičius, Povilas 86

Pohl, General von 87

Poniatowski, Stanislaw August 46

Porat, Dina 90

Povilionis, Vidmantas 243

Powell, Colin 314

Požėla, Juras 136

Prapuolenis see Deksnys 74, 76

Prapuolenis, Leonas 74, 76

Preston, Thomas H. 59, 382

Prodi, Romano 364

Prunskienė, Kazimira 130, 134, 139, 143, 191, 196, 197, 199, 204, 207, 212, 213, 214, 215, 216, 217, 234, 235, 244

Prunskis, Juozas 93, 403

Pugevičius, Casimir 117, 405

Pugo, Boris 249

Puodžius, Stasys 86

Putin, Vladimir 17, 94, 259, 322, 323, 324, 347, 350, 357, 360, 361, 371, 374, 378
  campaign against NATO
    enlargement 9, 15, 16, 21, 23, 27, 33, 34, 128, 255, 261, 265, 266, 285, 286, 287, 298, 299, 300, 301, 302, 304, 305, 306, 307, 308, 309, 310, 311, 312, 313, 314, 315, 316, 317, 318, 319, 320, 321, 322, 323, 325, 326, 327, 328, 329, 330, 331, 332, 333, 335, 336, 347, 350, 358, 360, 367, 368, 369, 370, 371, 372, 373, 374, 375, 376, 377, 378, 385, 390, 392, 393, 395, 398, 399, 403, 404, 407, 408, 423, 426
  East Germany 274, 405
  Kaliningrad region 23, 33, 215, 261, 300, 322, 335, 336, 338, 347, 349, 355, 359, 360, 361,

364, 370, 371, 374, 376, 407, 424

Russian propaganda 94, 292

War in Ukraine 17, 18, 33, 40, 180, 183, 312, 313, 323, 353, 363, 377, 378, 379, 407, 439

Radžvilas, Vytautas 134, 403

Raig, Ivar 135

Rajackas, Raimundas 134

Ralston, Joseph 324

Raštikis, Stasys 62, 64, 75, 76, 77, 87, 398, 408

Rauca, Sergeant 89

Rauch, George von 53, 403

Reagan, Ronald 225, 273, 297, 325, 367, 385, 412

Remeikis, Thomas 90, 103, 106, 107, 117, 271, 388, 403, 408

Remnick, David 129, 396

Renteln, Adrian von 75, 86

Reshetov, Yuri 278

Ribbentrop, Joachim von 13, 31, 35, 58, 60, 61, 62, 67, 100, 115, 116, 123, 129, 133, 146, 153, 159, 162, 163, 199, 205, 258, 263, 272, 276, 326, 333, 337, 343, 345, 357, 359, 375, 407, 408, 413
  requiring the cession of the territory of Klaipėda 13, 55, 56, 58, 61, 89, 111, 118, 140, 203, 235, 368
  Soviet-Nazi pact 25, 142, 150, 173, 180, 271, 345
  zones of influence 133

Rifkind, Malcolm 327

Rimas, Algis 330

Robertson, Lord of Port Ellen 313, 323

Roosevelt, Franklin D. 9, 14, 27, 345

Ross, Dennis 199, 214

Rubenstein, Joshua 109, 403

Rudis, Gediminas 147

Rupšytė, Angonita 136, 385, 396

Rüütel, Arnold 220, 230, 236, 329

Ryzhkov, Nikolai 204, 221, 389

Sadūnaitė, Nijolė 112, 272, 398

Safire, William 192

Saja, Kazys 150

Sakalauskas, Artūras 149

Sakalauskas, Vaclovas 210

Sakalauskas, Vytautas 184

Sakharov, Andrei 111, 115, 271

Salmon, Patrick 121, 270, 327, 401

Šaltenis, Arvydas 134

Saudargas, Algirdas 225, 254, 278, 283, 284, 286, 313, 393, 396, 408

Savisaar, Edgar 255

Schlager, Erika B. 284

Schröder, Gerhard 325, 361

Schulenburg, Friedrich Werner von der 60, 63

Scowcroft, Brent 192, 251, 397

Sedaitis, Judith 70, 219, 390, 404

Senn, Alfred Erich 20, 33, 178, 274, 275, 368, 369, 400, 403, 408
  collapse of the Soviet Union 31, 78, 177, 178, 223, 258, 273, 304, 368, 369, 375
  liberation of Lithuania from Soviet occupation 154

Šepetys, Lionginas 147

Šerkšnys, Gediminas 286

Sforza, Bona 43

Shevardnadze, Eduard 178, 195, 199, 206, 212, 213, 214, 220, 237, 336

Shultz, George 240

Sigismund Augustus, Grand Duke 43, 44

Sigismund I, Holy Roman Emperor 45

Sigismund III Vasa, King 45

Sigismund the Elder, Grand Duke 43

Simitis, Constantin 357

Šimutis, Leonardas 24, 27, 226, 398

Skabeikis, M. 117, 405

Skipaitis, Rapolas 76

Škirpa, Kazys 62, 70, 73, 76, 79, 94, 398, 404
  Lietuvių Aktyvistų Frontas (Lithuanian Activist Front) 73, 75, 76, 79, 80, 84, 88, 93, 184

Skučas, Artūras 128, 134, 143

Skuodis, Vytautas 109

Sladkevičius, Vincentas Cardinal 272

Slavin, Alexander 87

Šlepetys 76

Šleževičius, Mykolas 51

Smetona, Antanas 13, 27, 51, 54, 64
  President 10, 13, 14, 15, 18, 22, 24, 26, 27, 32, 38, 51, 54, 64, 68, 88, 91, 97, 105, 114, 128, 129, 172, 175, 176, 182, 184, 187, 188, 191, 192, 194, 195, 196, 197, 199, 200, 202, 204, 210, 211, 213, 214, 215, 217, 219, 220, 223, 225, 228, 233, 234, 237, 239, 242, 245, 246, 247, 249, 255, 256, 257, 258, 261, 267, 270, 286, 287, 292, 293, 299, 300, 304, 306, 314, 315, 316, 317, 318, 319, 321, 322, 323, 324, 325, 326, 327, 328, 329, 332, 333, 336, 340, 342, 343, 344, 345, 346, 347, 348, 349, 350, 353, 354, 355, 356, 357, 359, 360, 361, 364, 367, 369, 372, 374, 375, 379, 382, 384, 385, 386, 389, 393, 396, 406, 412, 420, 422, 423, 424, 425, 426
  the State Council 228

Smith, David 365, 402, 403, 407

Sniečkus, Antanas 65, 114, 149, 238

Socor, Vladimir 370, 372

Solana, Javier 321

Solomon, Gerald B. H. 310, 330, 403

Songaila, Gintaras 134

Songaila, Rimgaudas 157

Stahelin, Jen 257

Stahlecker, Franz W. 89, 91, 92, 93

Stalin 17, 18, 23, 53, 55, 62, 63, 64, 65, 68, 74, 90, 94, 97, 98, 107, 115, 123, 125, 133, 148, 149, 150, 160, 167, 175, 183, 186, 189, 198, 271, 297, 322, 335, 337, 338, 339, 340, 341, 342, 343, 345, 371, 375, 407, 413, 433, 435
  division of Europe 35, 146, 268
  East Prussia 17, 46, 48, 50, 56, 183, 336, 337, 339, 340, 342, 356, 365, 376
  occupation of the Baltic states 37
  Potsdam conference 335, 338, 339, 341, 342, 346, 381, 382
  Soviet occupation of Lithuania 146, 162
  Soviet terror 32, 74, 104

Soviet-Nazi pact 25, 142, 150, 173, 180, 271, 345
    Teheran conference of 1943 435
Stanislaus II 46
Stankevičius, Česlovas 390, 396, 408
    BALTBAT 9, 312
    Meeting with Gorbachev 20, 21, 31, 32, 33, 38, 88, 121, 122, 123, 124, 125, 127, 136, 138, 145, 154, 156, 159, 166, 169, 171, 172, 173, 174, 175, 178, 180, 181, 182, 184, 185, 186, 187, 188, 190, 192, 195, 196, 197, 198, 199, 200, 201, 202, 203, 204, 205, 207, 208, 209, 213, 215, 216, 218, 219, 220, 221, 228, 229, 230, 232, 233, 235, 236, 239, 242, 245, 246, 248, 249, 250, 251, 252, 264, 274, 275, 281, 282, 383, 384, 385, 386, 389, 398, 403, 412
    membership in the CSCE 9, 21, 34, 190, 247, 259, 264, 268, 269, 272, 276, 277, 278, 279, 280, 281, 282, 283, 284, 286, 289, 290, 292, 295, 390, 407
    NATO membership 9, 15, 16, 21, 23, 27, 33, 34, 128, 255, 261, 265, 266, 285, 286, 287, 298, 299, 300, 301, 302, 304, 305, 306, 307, 308, 309, 310, 311, 312, 313, 314, 315, 316, 317, 318, 319, 320, 321, 322, 323, 325, 326, 327, 328, 329, 330, 331, 332, 333, 335, 336, 347, 350, 358, 360, 367, 368, 369, 370, 371, 372, 373, 374, 375, 376, 377, 378, 385, 390, 392, 393, 395, 398, 399, 403, 404, 407, 408, 423, 426
    total and unconditional defense 308
Štaras, Povilas 72
Starovoitova, Galina 258
Statkus, V. 76

Stein, George H. 96, 403
Stetten, Wolfgang von 326
Stimson, Henry L. 14, 24, 404
Stoltenberg, Thorvald 253
Štromas, Aleksandras 107, 273, 404
Suessmuth, Rita von 256
Suraska, Wisla 20, 178, 404
Sužiedėlis, Saulius 97, 111, 345, 404, 408
Svarinskas, Alfonsas 112, 147
Talbot, Strobe 197, 210, 213, 216, 320
Tamkevičius, Sigitas 112, 147, 150
Tarasenko, Sergei 199, 214
Tauras, K.V. see Daumantas 100, 102, 398
Teivens, Aina 269
Terleckas, Antanas 115, 124, 141
Terleckas, Vladas 176
Thatcher, Margaret 197, 214, 270, 282, 283, 327, 364, 390
    European Union 9, 10, 27, 261, 265, 292, 307, 316, 331, 332, 335, 336, 348, 357, 359, 364
Thom, François 59, 90, 97, 98, 103, 106, 107, 117, 271, 282, 388, 400, 402, 403, 408
Tokes, Rudolf L. 113, 407
Tomkus, Vytautas 134, 139
Trapans, Jan A. 121, 165, 404, 409
Trilupaitienė 345
Truman, Harry 340, 342, 343, 344, 345, 346, 347, 381, 382
    Iron Curtain 14, 71, 101, 401

Königsberg 17, 18, 23, 35, 50,
    261, 296, 335, 336, 337, 338,
    339, 341, 343, 344, 345, 348,
    349, 354, 358, 360, 361, 362,
    363, 364, 365, 370, 371, 373,
    374, 376, 391, 392, 393, 407,
    422, 424
  Potsdam conference 335, 338,
    339, 341, 342, 346, 381, 382

Truscott, Peter 259, 260, 404

Truska, Liudas 148

Ulevičius, Bonifacas 71, 401

Urban, William 368, 400, 408

Urbšys, Juozas 27, 59, 61, 62, 63,
    64, 147, 217, 398
  Soviet-Nazi pact 25, 142, 150,
    173, 180, 271, 345

Uspaskych, Victor 373

Vagnorius, Gediminas 244, 254,
    255, 256

Vainauskas, Pranas 76

Vaišvila, Zigmas 134, 143

Valdemaras, Augustinas 12, 51

Valionis, Antanas 362

Valiūnas, Joseph 269

Valiušaitis, Vidmantas 143

Valteris, Normundas 310

Vardys, Vytautas S. 30, 70, 81,
    98, 99, 103, 106, 107, 108,
    109, 111, 112, 115, 117, 121,
    122, 127, 144, 145, 146, 150,
    151, 165, 219, 245, 247, 248,
    249, 250, 251, 271, 272, 390,
    396, 404, 407, 408, 409
  Chronicle of the Catholic
    Church of Lithuania 14,
    109, 111, 117
  dissident movement 30, 108, 109,
    323
  Nazi occupation of Lithuania 96
  perestroika 128, 156, 404

Sąjūdis 14, 20, 26, 30, 31, 32, 38,
    77, 78, 79, 80, 87, 99, 100,
    101, 105, 106, 122, 126, 127,
    128, 129, 130, 131, 132, 133,
    134, 135, 136, 137, 138, 140,
    141, 142, 143, 144, 145, 147,
    150, 153, 154, 155, 156, 157,
    158, 159, 160, 161, 162, 163,
    164, 165, 166, 168, 170, 171,
    172, 173, 174, 175, 177, 178,
    179, 180, 182, 203, 207, 209,
    227, 272, 276, 372, 384, 385,
    387, 396, 397, 398, 399, 405,
    409, 414

Varenikov, Valentin 182, 185

Vasili I 42

Venclova, Tomas 114, 271

Vilkas, Eduardas 130, 134, 136,
    409

Vitalone, Claudio 254

Vitas, A. Robert 24, 134, 404

Vytautas Magnus, Grand Duke
    38, 41, 53, 54, 73, 124, 178

Waldheim, Kurt 110, 116

Warner, John 330

Wilhelm, Hans-Heinridn 89,
    407

Wörner, Manfred 304

Yakovlev, Alexander 144, 145,
    155, 156, 157, 201, 404

Yazov, Dimitry 191, 199, 236,
    249, 384

Yeltsin, Boris 34, 111, 177, 208,
    241, 242, 254, 258, 259, 260,
    261, 264, 288, 291, 293, 295,
    321, 360
  NATO enlargement 301, 302,
    306, 313, 315, 316, 318, 319,
    323, 325, 326, 327, 330, 367,
    368, 369, 404, 408, 423, 426
  President Clinton 319

Soviet collapse 31, 122, 241, 272, 274

Žalys, Vytautas 400

Zdebskis, Juozas 112

Žebriūnas, Arūnas 134, 139, 143

Zelenskyy, Volodymyr 379

Zeligowski, Lucjan 52

Žemaitis, Juozas 72

Zhirinovski, Vladimir 259

Zhitnikov, General 184, 185

Zubov, Andrei 97

Žumbakis, Povilas 227, 228, 229

SOVIET AND POST-SOVIET POLITICS AND SOCIETY

Edited by Dr. Andreas Umland | ISSN 1614-3515

1   *Андреас Умланд (ред.)* | Воплощение Европейской конвенции по правам человека в России. Философские, юридические и эмпирические исследования | ISBN 3-89821-387-0

2   *Christian Wipperfürth* | Russland – ein vertrauenswürdiger Partner? Grundlagen, Hintergründe und Praxis gegenwärtiger russischer Außenpolitik | Mit einem Vorwort von Heinz Timmermann | ISBN 3-89821-401-X

3   *Manja Hussner* | Die Übernahme internationalen Rechts in die russische und deutsche Rechtsordnung. Eine vergleichende Analyse zur Völkerrechtsfreundlichkeit der Verfassungen der Russländischen Föderation und der Bundesrepublik Deutschland | Mit einem Vorwort von Rainer Arnold | ISBN 3-89821-438-9

4   *Matthew Tejada* | Bulgaria's Democratic Consolidation and the Kozloduy Nuclear Power Plant (KNPP). The Unattainability of Closure | With a foreword by Richard J. Crampton | ISBN 3-89821-439-7

5   *Марк Григорьевич Меерович* | Квадратные метры, определяющие сознание. Государственная жилищная политика в СССР. 1921 – 1941 гг | ISBN 3-89821-474-5

6   *Andrei P. Tsygankov, Pavel A.Tsygankov (Eds.)* | New Directions in Russian International Studies | ISBN 3-89821-422-2

7   *Марк Григорьевич Меерович* | Как власть народ к труду приучала. Жилище в СССР – средство управления людьми. 1917 – 1941 гг. | С предисловием Елены Осокиной | ISBN 3-89821-495-8

8   *David J. Galbreath* | Nation-Building and Minority Politics in Post-Socialist States. Interests, Influence and Identities in Estonia and Latvia | With a foreword by David J. Smith | ISBN 3-89821-467-2

9   *Алексей Юрьевич Безугольный* | Народы Кавказа в Вооруженных силах СССР в годы Великой Отечественной войны 1941-1945 гг. | С предисловием Николая Бугая | ISBN 3-89821-475-3

10 *Вячеслав Лихачев и Владимир Прибыловский (ред.)* | Русское Национальное Единство, 1990-2000. В 2-х томах | ISBN 3-89821-523-7

11 *Николай Бугай (ред.)* | Народы стран Балтии в условиях сталинизма (1940-е – 1950-е годы). Документированная история | ISBN 3-89821-525-3

12 *Ingmar Bredies (Hrsg.)* | Zur Anatomie der Orange Revolution in der Ukraine. Wechsel des Elitenregimes oder Triumph des Parlamentarismus? | ISBN 3-89821-524-5

13 *Anastasia V. Mitrofanova* | The Politicization of Russian Orthodoxy. Actors and Ideas | With a foreword by William C. Gay | ISBN 3-89821-481-8

14 *Nathan D. Larson* | Alexander Solzhenitsyn and the Russo-Jewish Question | ISBN 3-89821-483-4

15 *Guido Houben* | Kulturpolitik und Ethnizität. Staatliche Kunstförderung im Russland der neunziger Jahre | Mit einem Vorwort von Gert Weisskirchen | ISBN 3-89821-542-3

16 *Leonid Luks* | Der russische „Sonderweg"? Aufsätze zur neuesten Geschichte Russlands im europäischen Kontext | ISBN 3-89821-496-6

17 *Евгений Мороз* | История «Мёртвой воды» – от страшной сказки к большой политике. Политическое неоязычество в постсоветской России | ISBN 3-89821-551-2

18 *Александр Верховский и Галина Кожевникова (ред.)* | Этническая и религиозная интолерантность в российских СМИ. Результаты мониторинга 2001-2004 гг. | ISBN 3-89821-569-5

19 *Christian Ganzer* | Sowjetisches Erbe und ukrainische Nation. Das Museum der Geschichte des Zaporoger Kosakentums auf der Insel Chortycja | Mit einem Vorwort von Frank Golczewski | ISBN 3-89821-504-0

20 *Эльза-Баир Гучинова* | Помнить нельзя забыть. Антропология депортационной травмы калмыков | С предисловием Кэролайн Хамфри | ISBN 3-89821-506-7

21 *Юлия Лидерман* | Мотивы «проверки» и «испытания» в постсоветской культуре. Советское прошлое в российском кинематографе 1990-х годов | С предисловием Евгения Марголита | ISBN 3-89821-511-3

22 *Tanya Lokshina, Ray Thomas, Mary Mayer (Eds.)* | The Imposition of a Fake Political Settlement in the Northern Caucasus. The 2003 Chechen Presidential Election | ISBN 3-89821-436-2

23 *Timothy McCajor Hall, Rosie Read (Eds.)* | Changes in the Heart of Europe. Recent Ethnographies of Czechs, Slovaks, Roma, and Sorbs | With an afterword by Zdeněk Salzmann | ISBN 3-89821-606-3

24 *Christian Autengruber* | Die politischen Parteien in Bulgarien und Rumänien. Eine vergleichende Analyse seit Beginn der 90er Jahre | Mit einem Vorwort von Dorothée de Nève | ISBN 3-89821-476-1

25 *Annette Freyberg-Inan with Radu Cristescu* | The Ghosts in Our Classrooms, or: John Dewey Meets Ceauşescu. The Promise and the Failures of Civic Education in Romania | ISBN 3-89821-416-8

26 *John B. Dunlop* | The 2002 Dubrovka and 2004 Beslan Hostage Crises. A Critique of Russian Counter-Terrorism | With a foreword by Donald N. Jensen | ISBN 3-89821-608-X

27 *Peter Koller* | Das touristische Potenzial von Kam''janec'–Podil's'kyj. Eine fremdenverkehrsgeographische Untersuchung der Zukunftsperspektiven und Maßnahmenplanung zur Destinationsentwicklung des „ukrainischen Rothenburg" | Mit einem Vorwort von Kristiane Klemm | ISBN 3-89821-640-3

28 *Françoise Daucé, Elisabeth Sieca-Kozlowski (Eds.)* | Dedovshchina in the Post-Soviet Military. Hazing of Russian Army Conscripts in a Comparative Perspective | With a foreword by Dale Herspring | ISBN 3-89821-616-0

29 *Florian Strasser* | Zivilgesellschaftliche Einflüsse auf die Orange Revolution. Die gewaltlose Massenbewegung und die ukrainische Wahlkrise 2004 | Mit einem Vorwort von Egbert Jahn | ISBN 3-89821-648-9

30 *Rebecca S. Katz* | The Georgian Regime Crisis of 2003-2004. A Case Study in Post-Soviet Media Representation of Politics, Crime and Corruption | ISBN 3-89821-413-3

31 *Vladimir Kantor* | Willkür oder Freiheit. Beiträge zur russischen Geschichtsphilosophie | Ediert von Dagmar Herrmann sowie mit einem Vorwort versehen von Leonid Luks | ISBN 3-89821-589-X

32 *Laura A. Victoir* | The Russian Land Estate Today. A Case Study of Cultural Politics in Post-Soviet Russia | With a foreword by Priscilla Roosevelt | ISBN 3-89821-426-5

33 *Ivan Katchanovski* | Cleft Countries. Regional Political Divisions and Cultures in Post-Soviet Ukraine and Moldova | With a foreword by Francis Fukuyama | ISBN 3-89821-558-X

34 *Florian Mühlfried* | Postsowjetische Feiern. Das Georgische Bankett im Wandel | Mit einem Vorwort von Kevin Tuite | ISBN 3-89821-601-2

35 *Roger Griffin, Werner Loh, Andreas Umland (Eds.)* | Fascism Past and Present, West and East. An International Debate on Concepts and Cases in the Comparative Study of the Extreme Right | With an afterword by Walter Laqueur | ISBN 3-89821-674-8

36 *Sebastian Schlegel* | Der „Weiße Archipel". Sowjetische Atomstädte 1945-1991 | Mit einem Geleitwort von Thomas Bohn | ISBN 3-89821-679-9

37 *Vyacheslav Likhachev* | Political Anti-Semitism in Post-Soviet Russia. Actors and Ideas in 1991-2003 | Edited and translated from Russian by Eugene Veklerov | ISBN 3-89821-529-6

38 *Josette Baer (Ed.)* | Preparing Liberty in Central Europe. Political Texts from the Spring of Nations 1848 to the Spring of Prague 1968 | With a foreword by Zdeněk V. David | ISBN 3-89821-546-6

39 *Михаил Лукьянов* | Российский консерватизм и реформа, 1907-1914 | С предисловием Марка Д. Стейнберга | ISBN 3-89821-503-2

40 *Nicola Melloni* | Market Without Economy. The 1998 Russian Financial Crisis | With a foreword by Eiji Furukawa | ISBN 3-89821-407-9

41 *Dmitrij Chmelnizki* | Die Architektur Stalins | Bd. 1: Studien zu Ideologie und Stil | Bd. 2: Bilddokumentation | Mit einem Vorwort von Bruno Flierl | ISBN 3-89821-515-6

42 *Katja Yafimava* | Post-Soviet Russian-Belarussian Relationships. The Role of Gas Transit Pipelines | With a foreword by Jonathan P. Stern | ISBN 3-89821-655-1

43 *Boris Chavkin* | Verflechtungen der deutschen und russischen Zeitgeschichte. Aufsätze und Archivfunde zu den Beziehungen Deutschlands und der Sowjetunion von 1917 bis 1991 | Ediert von Markus Edlinger sowie mit einem Vorwort versehen von Leonid Luks | ISBN 3-89821-756-6

44 *Anastasija Grynenko in Zusammenarbeit mit Claudia Dathe* | Die Terminologie des Gerichtswesens der Ukraine und Deutschlands im Vergleich. Eine übersetzungswissenschaftliche Analyse juristischer Fachbegriffe im Deutschen, Ukrainischen und Russischen | Mit einem Vorwort von Ulrich Hartmann | ISBN 3-89821-691-8

45 *Anton Burkov* | The Impact of the European Convention on Human Rights on Russian Law. Legislation and Application in 1996-2006 | With a foreword by Françoise Hampson | ISBN 978-3-89821-639-5

46 *Stina Torjesen, Indra Overland (Eds.)* | International Election Observers in Post-Soviet Azerbaijan. Geopolitical Pawns or Agents of Change? | ISBN 978-3-89821-743-9

47 *Taras Kuzio* | Ukraine – Crimea – Russia. Triangle of Conflict | ISBN 978-3-89821-761-3

48 *Claudia Šabić* | „Ich erinnere mich nicht, aber L'viv!" Zur Funktion kultureller Faktoren für die Institutionalisierung und Entwicklung einer ukrainischen Region | Mit einem Vorwort von Melanie Tatur | ISBN 978-3-89821-752-1

49 *Marlies Bilz* | Tatarstan in der Transformation. Nationaler Diskurs und Politische Praxis 1988-1994 | Mit einem Vorwort von Frank Golczewski | ISBN 978-3-89821-722-4

50 *Марлен Ларюэль (ред.)* | Современные интерпретации русского национализма | ISBN 978-3-89821-795-8

51 *Sonja Schüler* | Die ethnische Dimension der Armut. Roma im postsozialistischen Rumänien | Mit einem Vorwort von Anton Sterbling | ISBN 978-3-89821-776-7

52 *Галина Кожевникова* | Радикальный национализм в России и противодействие ему. Сборник докладов Центра «Сова» за 2004-2007 гг. | С предисловием Александра Верховского | ISBN 978-3-89821-721-7

53 *Галина Кожевникова и Владимир Прибыловский* | Российская власть в биографиях I. Высшие должностные лица РФ в 2004 г. | ISBN 978-3-89821-796-5

54 *Галина Кожевникова и Владимир Прибыловский* | Российская власть в биографиях II. Члены Правительства РФ в 2004 г. | ISBN 978-3-89821-797-2

55 *Галина Кожевникова и Владимир Прибыловский* | Российская власть в биографиях III. Руководители федеральных служб и агентств РФ в 2004 г.| ISBN 978-3-89821-798-9

56 *Ileana Petroniu* | Privatisierung in Transformationsökonomien. Determinanten der Restrukturierungs-Bereitschaft am Beispiel Polens, Rumäniens und der Ukraine | Mit einem Vorwort von Rainer W. Schäfer | ISBN 978-3-89821-790-3

57 *Christian Wipperfürth* | Russland und seine GUS-Nachbarn. Hintergründe, aktuelle Entwicklungen und Konflikte in einer ressourcenreichen Region| ISBN 978-3-89821-801-6

58 *Togzhan Kassenova* | From Antagonism to Partnership. The Uneasy Path of the U.S.-Russian Cooperative Threat Reduction | With a foreword by Christoph Bluth | ISBN 978-3-89821-707-1

59 *Alexander Höllwerth* | Das sakrale eurasische Imperium des Aleksandr Dugin. Eine Diskursanalyse zum postsowjetischen russischen Rechtsextremismus | Mit einem Vorwort von Dirk Uffelmann | ISBN 978-3-89821-813-9

60 *Олег Рябов* | «Россия-Матушка». Национализм, гендер и война в России XX века | С предисловием Елены Гощило | ISBN 978-3-89821-487-2

61 *Ivan Maistrenko* | Borot'bism. A Chapter in the History of the Ukrainian Revolution | With a new Introduction by Chris Ford | Translated by George S. N. Luckyj with the assistance of Ivan L. Rudnytsky | Second, Revised and Expanded Edition ISBN 978-3-8382-1107-7

62 *Maryna Romanets* | Anamorphosic Texts and Reconfigured Visions. Improvised Traditions in Contemporary Ukrainian and Irish Literature | ISBN 978-3-89821-576-3

63 *Paul D'Anieri and Taras Kuzio (Eds.)* | Aspects of the Orange Revolution I. Democratization and Elections in Post-Communist Ukraine | ISBN 978-3-89821-698-2

64 *Bohdan Harasymiw in collaboration with Oleh S. Ilnytzkyj (Eds.)* | Aspects of the Orange Revolution II. Information and Manipulation Strategies in the 2004 Ukrainian Presidential Elections | ISBN 978-3-89821-699-9

65 *Ingmar Bredies, Andreas Umland and Valentin Yakushik (Eds.)* | Aspects of the Orange Revolution III. The Context and Dynamics of the 2004 Ukrainian Presidential Elections | ISBN 978-3-89821-803-0

66 *Ingmar Bredies, Andreas Umland and Valentin Yakushik (Eds.)* | Aspects of the Orange Revolution IV. Foreign Assistance and Civic Action in the 2004 Ukrainian Presidential Elections | ISBN 978-3-89821-808-5

67 *Ingmar Bredies, Andreas Umland and Valentin Yakushik (Eds.)* | Aspects of the Orange Revolution V. Institutional Observation Reports on the 2004 Ukrainian Presidential Elections | ISBN 978-3-89821-809-2

68 *Taras Kuzio (Ed.)* | Aspects of the Orange Revolution VI. Post-Communist Democratic Revolutions in Comparative Perspective | ISBN 978-3-89821-820-7

69 *Tim Bohse* | Autoritarismus statt Selbstverwaltung. Die Transformation der kommunalen Politik in der Stadt Kaliningrad 1990-2005 | Mit einem Geleitwort von Stefan Troebst | ISBN 978-3-89821-782-8

70 *David Rupp* | Die Rußländische Föderation und die russischsprachige Minderheit in Lettland. Eine Fallstudie zur Anwaltspolitik Moskaus gegenüber den russophonen Minderheiten im „Nahen Ausland" von 1991 bis 2002 | Mit einem Vorwort von Helmut Wagner | ISBN 978-3-89821-778-1

71 *Taras Kuzio* | Theoretical and Comparative Perspectives on Nationalism. New Directions in Cross-Cultural and Post-Communist Studies | With a foreword by Paul Robert Magocsi | ISBN 978-3-89821-815-3

72 *Christine Teichmann* | Die Hochschultransformation im heutigen Osteuropa. Kontinuität und Wandel bei der Entwicklung des postkommunistischen Universitätswesens | Mit einem Vorwort von Oskar Anweiler | ISBN 978-3-89821-842-9

73   *Julia Kusznir* | Der politische Einfluss von Wirtschaftseliten in russischen Regionen. Eine Analyse am Beispiel der Erdöl- und Erdgasindustrie, 1992-2005 | Mit einem Vorwort von Wolfgang Eichwede | ISBN 978-3-89821-821-4

74   *Alena Vysotskaya* | Russland, Belarus und die EU-Osterweiterung. Zur Minderheitenfrage und zum Problem der Freizügigkeit des Personenverkehrs | Mit einem Vorwort von Katlijn Malfliet | ISBN 978-3-89821-822-1

75   *Heiko Pleines (Hrsg.)* | Corporate Governance in post-sozialistischen Volkswirtschaften | ISBN 978-3-89821-766-8

76   *Stefan Ihrig* | Wer sind die Moldawier? Rumänismus versus Moldowanismus in Historiographie und Schulbüchern der Republik Moldova, 1991-2006 | Mit einem Vorwort von Holm Sundhaussen | ISBN 978-3-89821-466-7

77   *Galina Kozhevnikova in collaboration with Alexander Verkhovsky and Eugene Veklerov* | Ultra-Nationalism and Hate Crimes in Contemporary Russia. The 2004-2006 Annual Reports of Moscow's SOVA Center | With a foreword by Stephen D. Shenfield | ISBN 978-3-89821-868-9

78   *Florian Küchler* | The Role of the European Union in Moldova's Transnistria Conflict | With a foreword by Christopher Hill | ISBN 978-3-89821-850-4

79   *Bernd Rechel* | The Long Way Back to Europe. Minority Protection in Bulgaria | With a foreword by Richard Crampton | ISBN 978-3-89821-863-4

80   *Peter W. Rodgers* | Nation, Region and History in Post-Communist Transitions. Identity Politics in Ukraine, 1991-2006 | With a foreword by Vera Tolz | ISBN 978-3-89821-903-7

81   *Stephanie Solywoda* | The Life and Work of Semen L. Frank. A Study of Russian Religious Philosophy | With a foreword by Philip Walters | ISBN 978-3-89821-457-5

82   *Vera Sokolova* | Cultural Politics of Ethnicity. Discourses on Roma in Communist Czechoslovakia | ISBN 978-3-89821-864-1

83   *Natalya Shevchik Ketenci* | Kazakhstani Enterprises in Transition. The Role of Historical Regional Development in Kazakhstan's Post-Soviet Economic Transformation | ISBN 978-3-89821-831-3

84   *Martin Malek, Anna Schor-Tschudnowskaja (Hgg.)* | Europa im Tschetschenienkrieg. Zwischen politischer Ohnmacht und Gleichgültigkeit | Mit einem Vorwort von Lipchan Basajewa | ISBN 978-3-89821-676-0

85   *Stefan Meister* | Das postsowjetische Universitätswesen zwischen nationalem und internationalem Wandel. Die Entwicklung der regionalen Hochschule in Russland als Gradmesser der Systemtransformation | Mit einem Vorwort von Joan DeBardeleben | ISBN 978-3-89821-891-7

86   *Konstantin Sheiko in collaboration with Stephen Brown* | Nationalist Imaginings of the Russian Past. Anatolii Fomenko and the Rise of Alternative History in Post-Communist Russia | With a foreword by Donald Ostrowski | ISBN 978-3-89821-915-0

87   *Sabine Jenni* | Wie stark ist das „Einige Russland"? Zur Parteibindung der Eliten und zum Wahlerfolg der Machtpartei im Dezember 2007 | Mit einem Vorwort von Klaus Armingeon | ISBN 978-3-89821-961-7

88   *Thomas Borén* | Meeting-Places of Transformation. Urban Identity, Spatial Representations and Local Politics in Post-Soviet St Petersburg | ISBN 978-3-89821-739-2

89   *Aygul Ashirova* | Stalinismus und Stalin-Kult in Zentralasien. Turkmenistan 1924-1953 | Mit einem Vorwort von Leonid Luks | ISBN 978-3-89821-987-7

90   *Leonid Luks* | Freiheit oder imperiale Größe? Essays zu einem russischen Dilemma | ISBN 978-3-8382-0011-8

91   *Christopher Gilley* | The 'Change of Signposts' in the Ukrainian Emigration. A Contribution to the History of Sovietophilism in the 1920s | With a foreword by Frank Golczewski | ISBN 978-3-89821-965-5

92   *Philipp Casula, Jeronim Perovic (Eds.)* | Identities and Politics During the Putin Presidency. The Discursive Foundations of Russia's Stability | With a foreword by Heiko Haumann | ISBN 978-3-8382-0015-6

93   *Marcel Viëtor* | Europa und die Frage nach seinen Grenzen im Osten. Zur Konstruktion ‚europäischer Identität' in Geschichte und Gegenwart | Mit einem Vorwort von Albrecht Lehmann | ISBN 978-3-8382-0045-3

94   *Ben Hellman, Andrei Rogachevskii* | Filming the Unfilmable. Casper Wrede's 'One Day in the Life of Ivan Denisovich' | Second, Revised and Expanded Edition | ISBN 978-3-8382-0044-6

95   *Eva Fuchslocher* | Vaterland, Sprache, Glaube. Orthodoxie und Nationenbildung am Beispiel Georgiens | Mit einem Vorwort von Christina von Braun | ISBN 978-3-89821-884-9

96   *Vladimir Kantor* | Das Westlertum und der Weg Russlands. Zur Entwicklung der russischen Literatur und Philosophie | Ediert von Dagmar Herrmann | Mit einem Beitrag von Nikolaus Lobkowicz | ISBN 978-3-8382-0102-3

97   *Kamran Musayev* | Die postsowjetische Transformation im Baltikum und Südkaukasus. Eine vergleichende Untersuchung der politischen Entwicklung Lettlands und Aserbaidschans 1985-2009 | Mit einem Vorwort von Leonid Luks | Ediert von Sandro Henschel | ISBN 978-3-8382-0103-0

98 *Tatiana Zhurzhenko* | Borderlands into Bordered Lands. Geopolitics of Identity in Post-Soviet Ukraine | With a foreword by Dieter Segert | ISBN 978-3-8382-0042-2

99 *Кирилл Галушко, Лидия Смола (ред.)* | Пределы падения – варианты украинского будущего. Аналитико-прогностические исследования | ISBN 978-3-8382-0148-1

100 *Michael Minkenberg (Ed.)* | Historical Legacies and the Radical Right in Post-Cold War Central and Eastern Europe | With an afterword by Sabrina P. Ramet | ISBN 978-3-8382-0124-5

101 *David-Emil Wickström* | Rocking St. Petersburg. Transcultural Flows and Identity Politics in the St. Petersburg Popular Music Scene | With a foreword by Yngvar B. Steinholt | Second, Revised and Expanded Edition | ISBN 978-3-8382-0100-9

102 *Eva Zabka* | Eine neue „Zeit der Wirren"? Der spät- und postsowjetische Systemwandel 1985-2000 im Spiegel russischer gesellschaftspolitischer Diskurse | Mit einem Vorwort von Margareta Mommsen | ISBN 978-3-8382-0161-0

103 *Ulrike Ziemer* | Ethnic Belonging, Gender and Cultural Practices. Youth Identitites in Contemporary Russia | With a foreword by Anoop Nayak | ISBN 978-3-8382-0152-8

104 *Ksenia Chepikova* | ‚Einiges Russland' - eine zweite KPdSU? Aspekte der Identitätskonstruktion einer postsowjetischen „Partei der Macht" | Mit einem Vorwort von Torsten Oppelland | ISBN 978-3-8382-0311-9

105 *Леонид Люкс* | Западничество или евразийство? Демократия или идеократия? Сборник статей об исторических дилеммах России | С предисловием Владимира Кантора | ISBN 978-3-8382-0211-2

106 *Anna Dost* | Das russische Verfassungsrecht auf dem Weg zum Föderalismus und zurück. Zum Konflikt von Rechtsnormen und -wirklichkeit in der Russländischen Föderation von 1991 bis 2009 | Mit einem Vorwort von Alexander Blankenagel | ISBN 978-3-8382-0292-1

107 *Philipp Herzog* | Sozialistische Völkerfreundschaft, nationaler Widerstand oder harmloser Zeitvertreib? Zur politischen Funktion der Volkskunst im sowjetischen Estland | Mit einem Vorwort von Andreas Kappeler | ISBN 978-3-8382-0216-7

108 *Marlène Laruelle (Ed.)* | Russian Nationalism, Foreign Policy, and Identity Debates in Putin's Russia. New Ideological Patterns after the Orange Revolution | ISBN 978-3-8382-0325-6

109 *Michail Logvinov* | Russlands Kampf gegen den internationalen Terrorismus. Eine kritische Bestandsaufnahme des Bekämpfungsansatzes | Mit einem Geleitwort von Hans-Henning Schröder und einem Vorwort von Eckhard Jesse | ISBN 978-3-8382-0329-4

110 *John B. Dunlop* | The Moscow Bombings of September 1999. Examinations of Russian Terrorist Attacks at the Onset of Vladimir Putin's Rule | Second, Revised and Expanded Edition | ISBN 978-3-8382-0388-1

111 *Андрей А. Ковалёв* | Свидетельство из-за кулис российской политики I. Можно ли делать добро из зла? (Воспоминания и размышления о последних советских и первых послесоветских годах) | With a foreword by Peter Reddaway | ISBN 978-3-8382-0302-7

112 *Андрей А. Ковалёв* | Свидетельство из-за кулис российской политики II. Угроза для себя и окружающих (Наблюдения и предостережения относительно происходящего после 2000 г.) | ISBN 978-3-8382-0303-4

113 *Bernd Kappenberg* | Zeichen setzen für Europa. Der Gebrauch europäischer lateinischer Sonderzeichen in der deutschen Öffentlichkeit | Mit einem Vorwort von Peter Schlobinski | ISBN 978-3-89821-749-1

114 *Ivo Mijnssen* | The Quest for an Ideal Youth in Putin's Russia I. Back to Our Future! History, Modernity, and Patriotism according to Nashi, 2005-2013 | With a foreword by Jeronim Perović | Second, Revised and Expanded Edition | ISBN 978-3-8382-0368-3

115 *Jussi Lassila* | The Quest for an Ideal Youth in Putin's Russia II. The Search for Distinctive Conformism in the Political Communication of Nashi, 2005-2009 | With a foreword by Kirill Postoutenko | Second, Revised and Expanded Edition | ISBN 978-3-8382-0415-4

116 *Valerio Trabandt* | Neue Nachbarn, gute Nachbarschaft? Die EU als internationaler Akteur am Beispiel ihrer Demokratieförderung in Belarus und der Ukraine 2004-2009 | Mit einem Vorwort von Jutta Joachim | ISBN 978-3-8382-0437-6

117 *Fabian Pfeiffer* | Estlands Außen- und Sicherheitspolitik I. Der estnische Atlantizismus nach der wiedererlangten Unabhängigkeit 1991-2004 | Mit einem Vorwort von Helmut Hubel | ISBN 978-3-8382-0127-6

118 *Jana Podßuweit* | Estlands Außen- und Sicherheitspolitik II. Handlungsoptionen eines Kleinstaates im Rahmen seiner EU-Mitgliedschaft (2004-2008) | Mit einem Vorwort von Helmut Hubel | ISBN 978-3-8382-0440-6

119 *Karin Pointner* | Estlands Außen- und Sicherheitspolitik III. Eine gedächtnispolitische Analyse estnischer Entwicklungskooperation 2006-2010 | Mit einem Vorwort von Karin Liebhart | ISBN 978-3-8382-0435-2

120 *Ruslana Vovk* | Die Offenheit der ukrainischen Verfassung für das Völkerrecht und die europäische Integration | Mit einem Vorwort von Alexander Blankenagel | ISBN 978-3-8382-0481-9

121 *Mykhaylo Banakh* | Die Relevanz der Zivilgesellschaft bei den postkommunistischen Transformationsprozessen in mittel- und osteuropäischen Ländern. Das Beispiel der spät- und postsowjetischen Ukraine 1986-2009 | Mit einem Vorwort von Gerhard Simon | ISBN 978-3-8382-0499-4

122 *Michael Moser* | Language Policy and the Discourse on Languages in Ukraine under President Viktor Yanukovych (25 February 2010–28 October 2012) | ISBN 978-3-8382-0497-0 (Paperback edition) | ISBN 978-3-8382-0507-6 (Hardcover edition)

123 *Nicole Krome* | Russischer Netzwerkkapitalismus Restrukturierungsprozesse in der Russischen Föderation am Beispiel des Luftfahrtunternehmens „Aviastar" | Mit einem Vorwort von Petra Stykow | ISBN 978-3-8382-0534-2

124 *David R. Marples* | 'Our Glorious Past'. Lukashenka's Belarus and the Great Patriotic War | ISBN 978-3-8382-0574-8 (Paperback edition) | ISBN 978-3-8382-0675-2 (Hardcover edition)

125 *Ulf Walther* | Russlands „neuer Adel". Die Macht des Geheimdienstes von Gorbatschow bis Putin | Mit einem Vorwort von Hans-Georg Wieck | ISBN 978-3-8382-0584-7

126 *Simon Geissbühler (Hrsg.)* | Kiew – Revolution 3.0. Der Euromaidan 2013/14 und die Zukunftsperspektiven der Ukraine | ISBN 978-3-8382-0581-6 (Paperback edition) | ISBN 978-3-8382-0681-3 (Hardcover edition)

127 *Andrey Makarychev* | Russia and the EU in a Multipolar World. Discourses, Identities, Norms | With a foreword by Klaus Segbers | ISBN 978-3-8382-0629-5

128 *Roland Scharff* | Kasachstan als postsowjetischer Wohlfahrtsstaat. Die Transformation des sozialen Schutzsystems | Mit einem Vorwort von Joachim Ahrens | ISBN 978-3-8382-0622-6

129 *Katja Grupp* | Bild Lücke Deutschland. Kaliningrader Studierende sprechen über Deutschland | Mit einem Vorwort von Martin Schulz | ISBN 978-3-8382-0552-6

130 *Konstantin Sheiko, Stephen Brown* | History as Therapy. Alternative History and Nationalist Imaginings in Russia, 1991-2014 | ISBN 978-3-8382-0665-3

131 *Elisa Kriza* | Alexander Solzhenitsyn: Cold War Icon, Gulag Author, Russian Nationalist? A Study of the Western Reception of his Literary Writings, Historical Interpretations, and Political Ideas | With a foreword by Andrei Rogatchevski | ISBN 978-3-8382-0589-2 (Paperback edition) | ISBN 978-3-8382-0690-5 (Hardcover edition)

132 *Serghei Golunov* | The Elephant in the Room. Corruption and Cheating in Russian Universities | ISBN 978-3-8382-0570-0

133 *Manja Hussner, Rainer Arnold (Hgg.)* | Verfassungsgerichtsbarkeit in Zentralasien I. Sammlung von Verfassungstexten | ISBN 978-3-8382-0595-3

134 *Nikolay Mitrokhin* | Die „Russische Partei". Die Bewegung der russischen Nationalisten in der UdSSR 1953-1985 | Aus dem Russischen übertragen von einem Übersetzerteam unter der Leitung von Larisa Schippel | ISBN 978-3-8382-0024-8

135 *Manja Hussner, Rainer Arnold (Hgg.)* | Verfassungsgerichtsbarkeit in Zentralasien II. Sammlung von Verfassungstexten | ISBN 978-3-8382-0597-7

136 *Manfred Zeller* | Das sowjetische Fieber. Fußballfans im poststalinistischen Vielvölkerreich | Mit einem Vorwort von Nikolaus Katzer | ISBN 978-3-8382-0757-5

137 *Kristin Schreiter* | Stellung und Entwicklungspotential zivilgesellschaftlicher Gruppen in Russland. Menschenrechtsorganisationen im Vergleich | ISBN 978-3-8382-0673-8

138 *David R. Marples, Frederick V. Mills (Eds.)* | Ukraine's Euromaidan. Analyses of a Civil Revolution | ISBN 978-3-8382-0660-8

139 *Bernd Kappenberg* | Setting Signs for Europe. Why Diacritics Matter for European Integration | With a foreword by Peter Schlobinski | ISBN 978-3-8382-0663-9

140 *René Lenz* | Internationalisierung, Kooperation und Transfer. Externe bildungspolitische Akteure in der Russischen Föderation | Mit einem Vorwort von Frank Ettrich | ISBN 978-3-8382-0751-3

141 *Juri Plusnin, Yana Zausaeva, Natalia Zhidkevich, Artemy Pozanenko* | Wandering Workers. Mores, Behavior, Way of Life, and Political Status of Domestic Russian Labor Migrants | Translated by Julia Kazantseva | ISBN 978-3-8382-0653-0

142 *David J. Smith (Eds.)* | Latvia – A Work in Progress? 100 Years of State- and Nation-Building | ISBN 978-3-8382-0648-6

143 *Инна Чувычкина (ред.)* | Экспортные нефте- и газопроводы на постсоветском пространстве. Анализ трубопроводной политики в свете теории международных отношений | ISBN 978-3-8382-0822-0

144 *Johann Zajaczkowski* | Russland – eine pragmatische Großmacht? Eine rollentheoretische Untersuchung russischer Außenpolitik am Beispiel der Zusammenarbeit mit den USA nach 9/11 und des Georgienkrieges von 2008 | Mit einem Vorwort von Siegfried Schieder | ISBN 978-3-8382-0837-4

145 *Boris Popivanov* | Changing Images of the Left in Bulgaria. The Challenge of Post-Communism in the Early 21st Century | ISBN 978-3-8382-0667-7

146 *Lenka Krátká* | A History of the Czechoslovak Ocean Shipping Company 1948-1989. How a Small, Landlocked Country Ran Maritime Business During the Cold War | ISBN 978-3-8382-0666-0

147 *Alexander Sergunin* | Explaining Russian Foreign Policy Behavior. Theory and Practice | ISBN 978-3-8382-0752-0

148 *Darya Malyutina* | Migrant Friendships in a Super-Diverse City. Russian-Speakers and their Social Relationships in London in the 21st Century | With a foreword by Claire Dwyer | ISBN 978-3-8382-0652-3

149 *Alexander Sergunin, Valery Konyshev* | Russia in the Arctic. Hard or Soft Power? | ISBN 978-3-8382-0753-7

150 *John J. Maresca* | Helsinki Revisited. A Key U.S. Negotiator's Memoirs on the Development of the CSCE into the OSCE | With a foreword by Hafiz Pashayev | ISBN 978-3-8382-0852-7

151 *Jardar Østbø* | The New Third Rome. Readings of a Russian Nationalist Myth | With a foreword by Pål Kolstø | ISBN 978-3-8382-0870-1

152 *Simon Kordonsky* | Socio-Economic Foundations of the Russian Post-Soviet Regime. The Resource-Based Economy and Estate-Based Social Structure of Contemporary Russia | With a foreword by Svetlana Barsukova | ISBN 978-3-8382-0775-9

153 *Duncan Leitch* | Assisting Reform in Post-Communist Ukraine 2000–2012. The Illusions of Donors and the Disillusion of Beneficiaries | With a foreword by Kataryna Wolczuk | ISBN 978-3-8382-0844-2

154 *Abel Polese* | Limits of a Post-Soviet State. How Informality Replaces, Renegotiates, and Reshapes Governance in Contemporary Ukraine | With a foreword by Colin Williams | ISBN 978-3-8382-0845-9

155 *Mikhail Suslov (Ed.)* | Digital Orthodoxy in the Post-Soviet World. The Russian Orthodox Church and Web 2.0 | With a foreword by Father Cyril Hovorun | ISBN 978-3-8382-0871-8

156 *Leonid Luks* | Zwei „Sonderwege"? Russisch-deutsche Parallelen und Kontraste (1917-2014). Vergleichende Essays | ISBN 978-3-8382-0823-7

157 *Vladimir V. Karacharovskiy, Ovsey I. Shkaratan, Gordey A. Yastrebov* | Towards a New Russian Work Culture. Can Western Companies and Expatriates Change Russian Society? | With a foreword by Elena N. Danilova | Translated by Julia Kazantseva | ISBN 978-3-8382-0902-9

158 *Edmund Griffiths* | Aleksandr Prokhanov and Post-Soviet Esotericism | ISBN 978-3-8382-0963-0

159 *Timm Beichelt, Susann Worschech (Eds.)* | Transnational Ukraine? Networks and Ties that Influence(d) Contemporary Ukraine | ISBN 978-3-8382-0944-9

160 *Mieste Hotopp-Riecke* | Die Tataren der Krim zwischen Assimilation und Selbstbehauptung. Der Aufbau des krimtatarischen Bildungswesens nach Deportation und Heimkehr (1990-2005) | Mit einem Vorwort von Swetlana Czerwonnaja | ISBN 978-3-89821-940-2

161 *Olga Bertelsen (Ed.)* | Revolution and War in Contemporary Ukraine. The Challenge of Change | ISBN 978-3-8382-1016-2

162 *Natalya Ryabinska* | Ukraine's Post-Communist Mass Media. Between Capture and Commercialization | With a foreword by Marta Dyczok | ISBN 978-3-8382-1011-7

163 *Alexandra Cotofana, James M. Nyce (Eds.)* | Religion and Magic in Socialist and Post-Socialist Contexts. Historic and Ethnographic Case Studies of Orthodoxy, Heterodoxy, and Alternative Spirituality | With a foreword by Patrick L. Michelson | ISBN 978-3-8382-0989-0

164 *Nozima Akhrarkhodjaeva* | The Instrumentalisation of Mass Media in Electoral Authoritarian Regimes. Evidence from Russia's Presidential Election Campaigns of 2000 and 2008 | ISBN 978-3-8382-1013-1

165 *Yulia Krasheninnikova* | Informal Healthcare in Contemporary Russia. Sociographic Essays on the Post-Soviet Infrastructure for Alternative Healing Practices | ISBN 978-3-8382-0970-8

166 *Peter Kaiser* | Das Schachbrett der Macht. Die Handlungsspielräume eines sowjetischen Funktionärs unter Stalin am Beispiel des Generalsekretärs des Komsomol Aleksandr Kosarev (1929-1938) | Mit einem Vorwort von Dietmar Neutatz | ISBN 978-3-8382-1052-0

167 *Oksana Kim* | The Effects and Implications of Kazakhstan's Adoption of International Financial Reporting Standards. A Resource Dependence Perspective | With a foreword by Svetlana Vlady | ISBN 978-3-8382-0987-6

168 *Anna Sanina* | Patriotic Education in Contemporary Russia. Sociological Studies in the Making of the Post-Soviet Citizen | With a foreword by Anna Oldfield | ISBN 978-3-8382-0993-7

169 *Rudolf Wolters* | Spezialist in Sibirien Faksimile der 1933 erschienenen ersten Ausgabe | Mit einem Vorwort von Dmitrij Chmelnizki | ISBN 978-3-8382-0515-1

170 *Michal Vít, Magdalena M. Baran (Eds.)* | Transregional versus National Perspectives on Contemporary Central European History. Studies on the Building of Nation-States and Their Cooperation in the 20th and 21st Century | With a foreword by Petr Vágner | ISBN 978-3-8382-1015-5

171 *Philip Gamaghelyan* | Conflict Resolution Beyond the International Relations Paradigm. Evolving Designs as a Transformative Practice in Nagorno-Karabakh and Syria | With a foreword by Susan Allen | ISBN 978-3-8382-1057-5

172 *Maria Shagina* | Joining a Prestigious Club. Cooperation with Europarties and Its Impact on Party Development in Georgia, Moldova, and Ukraine 2004–2015 | With a foreword by Kataryna Wolczuk | ISBN 978-3-8382-1084-1

173 *Alexandra Cotofana, James M. Nyce (Eds.)* | Religion and Magic in Socialist and Post-Socialist Contexts II. Baltic, Eastern European, and Post-USSR Case Studies | With a foreword by Anita Stasulane | ISBN 978-3-8382-0990-6

174 *Barbara Kunz* | Kind Words, Cruise Missiles, and Everything in Between. The Use of Power Resources in U.S. Policies towards Poland, Ukraine, and Belarus 1989–2008 | With a foreword by William Hill | ISBN 978-3-8382-1065-0

175 *Eduard Klein* | Bildungskorruption in Russland und der Ukraine. Eine komparative Analyse der Performanz staatlicher Antikorruptionsmaßnahmen im Hochschulsektor am Beispiel universitärer Aufnahmeprüfungen | Mit einem Vorwort von Heiko Pleines | ISBN 978-3-8382-0995-1

176 *Markus Soldner* | Politischer Kapitalismus im postsowjetischen Russland. Die politische, wirtschaftliche und mediale Transformation in den 1990er Jahren | Mit einem Vorwort von Wolfgang Ismayr | ISBN 978-3-8382-1222-7

177 *Anton Oleinik* | Building Ukraine from Within. A Sociological, Institutional, and Economic Analysis of a Nation-State in the Making | ISBN 978-3-8382-1150-3

178 *Peter Rollberg, Marlene Laruelle (Eds.)* | Mass Media in the Post-Soviet World. Market Forces, State Actors, and Political Manipulation in the Informational Environment after Communism | ISBN 978-3-8382-1116-9

179 *Mikhail Minakov* | Development and Dystopia. Studies in Post-Soviet Ukraine and Eastern Europe | With a foreword by Alexander Etkind | ISBN 978-3-8382-1112-1

180 *Aijan Sharshenova* | The European Union's Democracy Promotion in Central Asia. A Study of Political Interests, Influence, and Development in Kazakhstan and Kyrgyzstan in 2007–2013 | With a foreword by Gordon Crawford | ISBN 978-3-8382-1151-0

181 *Andrey Makarychev, Alexandra Yatsyk (Eds.)* | Boris Nemtsov and Russian Politics. Power and Resistance | With a foreword by Zhanna Nemtsova | ISBN 978-3-8382-1122-0

182 *Sophie Falsini* | The Euromaidan's Effect on Civil Society. Why and How Ukrainian Social Capital Increased after the Revolution of Dignity | With a foreword by Susann Worschech | ISBN 978-3-8382-1131-2

183 *Valentyna Romanova, Andreas Umland (Eds.)* | Ukraine's Decentralization. Challenges and Implications of the Local Governance Reform after the Euromaidan Revolution | ISBN 978-3-8382-1162-6

184 *Leonid Luks* | A Fateful Triangle. Essays on Contemporary Russian, German and Polish History | ISBN 978-3-8382-1143-5

185 *John B. Dunlop* | The February 2015 Assassination of Boris Nemtsov and the Flawed Trial of his Alleged Killers. An Exploration of Russia's "Crime of the 21st Century" | ISBN 978-3-8382-1188-6

186 *Vasile Rotaru* | Russia, the EU, and the Eastern Partnership. Building Bridges or Digging Trenches? | ISBN 978-3-8382-1134-3

187 *Marina Lebedeva* | Russian Studies of International Relations. From the Soviet Past to the Post-Cold-War Present | With a foreword by Andrei P. Tsygankov | ISBN 978-3-8382-0851-0

188 *Tomasz Stępniewski, George Soroka (Eds.)* | Ukraine after Maidan. Revisiting Domestic and Regional Security | ISBN 978-3-8382-1075-9

189 *Petar Cholakov* | Ethnic Entrepreneurs Unmasked. Political Institutions and Ethnic Conflicts in Contemporary Bulgaria | ISBN 978-3-8382-1189-3

190 *A. Salem, G. Hazeldine, D. Morgan (Eds.)* | Higher Education in Post-Communist States. Comparative and Sociological Perspectives | ISBN 978-3-8382-1183-1

191 *Igor Torbakov* | After Empire. Nationalist Imagination and Symbolic Politics in Russia and Eurasia in the Twentieth and Twenty-First Century | With a foreword by Serhii Plokhy | ISBN 978-3-8382-1217-3

192 *Aleksandr Burakovskiy* | Jewish-Ukrainian Relations in Late and Post-Soviet Ukraine. Articles, Lectures and Essays from 1986 to 2016 | ISBN 978-3-8382-1210-4

193 *Natalia Shapovalova, Olga Burlyuk (Eds.)* | Civil Society in Post-Euromaidan Ukraine. From Revolution to Consolidation | With a foreword by Richard Youngs | ISBN 978-3-8382-1216-6

194 *Franz Preissler* | Positionsverteidigung, Imperialismus oder Irredentismus? Russland und die „Russischsprachigen", 1991–2015 | ISBN 978-3-8382-1262-3

195 *Marian Madeła* | Der Reformprozess in der Ukraine 2014-2017. Eine Fallstudie zur Reform der öffentlichen Verwaltung | Mit einem Vorwort von Martin Malek | ISBN 978-3-8382-1266-1

196 *Anke Giesen* | „Wie kann denn der Sieger ein Verbrecher sein?" Eine diskursanalytische Untersuchung der russlandweiten Debatte über Konzept und Verstaatlichungsprozess der Lagergedenkstätte „Perm'-36" im Ural | ISBN 978-3-8382-1284-5

197 *Victoria Leukavets* | The Integration Policies of Belarus and Ukraine vis-à-vis the EU and Russia. A Comparative Analysis Through the Prism of a Two-Level Game Approach | ISBN 978-3-8382-1247-0

198 *Oksana Kim* | The Development and Challenges of Russian Corporate Governance I. The Roles and Functions of Boards of Directors | With a foreword by Sheila M. Puffer | ISBN 978-3-8382-1287-6

199 *Thomas D. Grant* | International Law and the Post-Soviet Space I. Essays on Chechnya and the Baltic States | With a foreword by Stephen M. Schwebel | ISBN 978-3-8382-1279-1

200 *Thomas D. Grant* | International Law and the Post-Soviet Space II. Essays on Ukraine, Intervention, and Non-Proliferation | ISBN 978-3-8382-1280-7

201 *Slavomír Michálek, Michal Štefansky* | The Age of Fear. The Cold War and Its Influence on Czechoslovakia 1945–1968 | ISBN 978-3-8382-1285-2

202 *Iulia-Sabina Joja* | Romania's Strategic Culture 1990–2014. Continuity and Change in a Post-Communist Country's Evolution of National Interests and Security Policies | With a foreword by Heiko Biehl | ISBN 978-3-8382-1286-9

203 *Andrei Rogatchevski, Yngvar B. Steinholt, Arve Hansen, David-Emil Wickström* | War of Songs. Popular Music and Recent Russia-Ukraine Relations | With a foreword by Artemy Troitsky | ISBN 978-3-8382-1173-2

204 *Maria Lipman (Ed.)* | Russian Voices on Post-Crimea Russia. An Almanac of Counterpoint Essays from 2015–2018 | ISBN 978-3-8382-1251-7

205 *Ksenia Maksimovtsova* | Language Conflicts in Contemporary Estonia, Latvia, and Ukraine. A Comparative Exploration of Discourses in Post-Soviet Russian-Language Digital Media | With a foreword by Ammon Cheskin | ISBN 978-3-8382-1282-1

206 *Michal Vít* | The EU's Impact on Identity Formation in East-Central Europe between 2004 and 2013. Perceptions of the Nation and Europe in Political Parties of the Czech Republic, Poland, and Slovakia | With a foreword by Andrea Petö | ISBN 978-3-8382-1275-3

207 *Per A. Rudling* | Tarnished Heroes. The Organization of Ukrainian Nationalists in the Memory Politics of Post-Soviet Ukraine | ISBN 978-3-8382-0999-9

208 *Kaja Gadowska, Peter Solomon (Eds.)* | Legal Change in Post-Communist States. Progress, Reversions, Explanations | ISBN 978-3-8382-1312-5

209 *Pawel Kowal, Georges Mink, Iwona Reichardt (Eds.)* | Three Revolutions: Mobilization and Change in Contemporary Ukraine I. Theoretical Aspects and Analyses on Religion, Memory, and Identity | ISBN 978-3-8382-1321-7

210 *Pawel Kowal, Georges Mink, Adam Reichardt, Iwona Reichardt (Eds.)* | Three Revolutions: Mobilization and Change in Contemporary Ukraine II. An Oral History of the Revolution on Granite, Orange Revolution, and Revolution of Dignity | ISBN 978-3-8382-1323-1

211 *Li Bennich-Björkman, Sergiy Kurbatov (Eds.)* | When the Future Came. The Collapse of the USSR and the Emergence of National Memory in Post-Soviet History Textbooks | ISBN 978-3-8382-1335-4

212 *Olga R. Gulina* | Migration as a (Geo-)Political Challenge in the Post-Soviet Space. Border Regimes, Policy Choices, Visa Agendas | With a foreword by Nils Muižnieks | ISBN 978-3-8382-1338-5

213 *Sanna Turoma, Kaarina Aitamurto, Slobodanka Vladiv-Glover (Eds.)* | Religion, Expression, and Patriotism in Russia. Essays on Post-Soviet Society and the State. ISBN 978-3-8382-1346-0

214 *Vasif Huseynov* | Geopolitical Rivalries in the "Common Neighborhood". Russia's Conflict with the West, Soft Power, and Neoclassical Realism | With a foreword by Nicholas Ross Smith | ISBN 978-3-8382-1277-7

215 *Mikhail Suslov* | Geopolitical Imagination. Ideology and Utopia in Post-Soviet Russia | With a foreword by Mark Bassin | ISBN 978-3-8382-1361-3

216 *Alexander Etkind, Mikhail Minakov (Eds.)* | Ideology after Union. Political Doctrines, Discourses, and Debates in Post-Soviet Societies | ISBN 978-3-8382-1388-0

217 *Jakob Mischke, Oleksandr Zabirko (Hgg.)* | Protestbewegungen im langen Schatten des Kreml. Aufbruch und Resignation in Russland und der Ukraine | ISBN 978-3-8382-0926-5

218 *Oksana Huss* | How Corruption and Anti-Corruption Policies Sustain Hybrid Regimes. Strategies of Political Domination under Ukraine's Presidents in 1994-2014 | With a foreword by Tobias Debiel and Andrea Gawrich | ISBN 978-3-8382-1430-6

219 *Dmitry Travin, Vladimir Gel'man, Otar Marganiya* | The Russian Path. Ideas, Interests, Institutions, Illusions | With a foreword by Vladimir Ryzhkov | ISBN 978-3-8382-1421-4

220 *Gergana Dimova* | Political Uncertainty. A Comparative Exploration | With a foreword by Todor Yalamov and Rumena Filipova | ISBN 978-3-8382-1385-9

221 *Torben Waschke* | Russland in Transition. Geopolitik zwischen Raum, Identität und Machtinteressen | Mit einem Vorwort von Andreas Dittmann | ISBN 978-3-8382-1480-1

222 *Steven Jobbitt, Zsolt Bottlik, Marton Berki (Eds.)* | Power and Identity in the Post-Soviet Realm. Geographies of Ethnicity and Nationality after 1991 | ISBN 978-3-8382-1399-6

223 *Daria Buteiko* | Erinnerungsort. Ort des Gedenkens, der Erholung oder der Einkehr? Kommunismus-Erinnerung am Beispiel der Gedenkstätte Berliner Mauer sowie des Soloveckij-Klosters und -Museumsparks | ISBN 978-3-8382-1367-5

224 *Olga Bertelsen (Ed.)* | Russian Active Measures. Yesterday, Today, Tomorrow | With a foreword by Jan Goldman | ISBN 978-3-8382-1529-7

225 *David Mandel* | "Optimizing" Higher Education in Russia. University Teachers and their Union "Universitetskaya solidarnost'" | ISBN 978-3-8382-1519-8

226 *Mikhail Minakov, Gwendolyn Sasse, Daria Isachenko (Eds.)* | Post-Soviet Secessionism. Nation-Building and State-Failure after Communism | ISBN 978-3-8382-1538-9

227 *Jakob Hauter (Ed.)* | Civil War? Interstate War? Hybrid War? Dimensions and Interpretations of the Donbas Conflict in 2014–2020 | With a foreword by Andrew Wilson | ISBN 978-3-8382-1383-5

228 *Tima T. Moldogaziev, Gene A. Brewer, J. Edward Kellough (Eds.)* | Public Policy and Politics in Georgia. Lessons from Post-Soviet Transition | With a foreword by Dan Durning | ISBN 978-3-8382-1535-8

229 *Oxana Schmies (Ed.)* | NATO's Enlargement and Russia. A Strategic Challenge in the Past and Future | With a foreword by Vladimir Kara-Murza | ISBN 978-3-8382-1478-8

230 *Christopher Ford* | Ukapisme – Une Gauche perdue. Le marxisme anti-colonial dans la révolution ukrainienne 1917-1925 | Avec une préface de Vincent Présumey | ISBN 978-3-8382-0899-2

231 *Anna Kutkina* | Between Lenin and Bandera. Decommunization and Multivocality in Post-Euromaidan Ukraine | With a foreword by Juri Mykkänen | ISBN 978-3-8382-1506-8

232 *Lincoln E. Flake* | Defending the Faith. The Russian Orthodox Church and the Demise of Religious Pluralism | With a foreword by Peter Martland | ISBN 978-3-8382-1378-1

233 *Nikoloz Samkharadze* | Russia's Recognition of the Independence of Abkhazia and South Ossetia. Analysis of a Deviant Case in Moscow's Foreign Policy | With a foreword by Neil MacFarlane | ISBN 978-3-8382-1414-6

234 *Arve Hansen* | Urban Protest. A Spatial Perspective on Kyiv, Minsk, and Moscow | With a foreword by Julie Wilhelmsen | ISBN 978-3-8382-1495-5

235 *Eleonora Narvselius, Julie Fedor (Eds.)* | Diversity in the East-Central European Borderlands. Memories, Cityscapes, People | ISBN 978-3-8382-1523-5

236 *Regina Elsner* | The Russian Orthodox Church and Modernity. A Historical and Theological Investigation into Eastern Christianity between Unity and Plurality | With a foreword by Mikhail Suslov | ISBN 978-3-8382-1568-6

237 *Bo Petersson* | The Putin Predicament. Problems of Legitimacy and Succession in Russia | With a foreword by J. Paul Goode | ISBN 978-3-8382-1050-6

238 *Jonathan Otto Pohl* | The Years of Great Silence. The Deportation, Special Settlement, and Mobilization into the Labor Army of Ethnic Germans in the USSR, 1941–1955 | ISBN 978-3-8382-1630-0

239 *Mikhail Minakov (Ed.)* | Inventing Majorities. Ideological Creativity in Post-Soviet Societies | ISBN 978-3-8382-1641-6

240 *Robert M. Cutler* | Soviet and Post-Soviet Foreign Policies I. East-South Relations and the Political Economy of the Communist Bloc, 1971–1991 | With a foreword by Roger E. Kanet | ISBN 978-3-8382-1654-6

241 *Izabella Agardi* | On the Verge of History. Life Stories of Rural Women from Serbia, Romania, and Hungary, 1920–2020 | With a foreword by Andrea Pető | ISBN 978-3-8382-1602-7

242 *Sebastian Schäffer (Ed.)* | Ukraine in Central and Eastern Europe. Kyiv's Foreign Affairs and the International Relations of the Post-Communist Region | With a foreword by Pavlo Klimkin and Andreas Umland| ISBN 978-3-8382-1615-7

243 *Volodymyr Dubrovskyi, Kalman Mizsei, Mychailo Wynnyckyj (Eds.)* | Eight Years after the Revolution of Dignity. What Has Changed in Ukraine during 2013–2021? | With a foreword by Yaroslav Hrytsak | ISBN 978-3-8382-1560-0

244 *Rumena Filipova* | Constructing the Limits of Europe Identity and Foreign Policy in Poland, Bulgaria, and Russia since 1989 | With forewords by Harald Wydra and Gergana Yankova-Dimova | ISBN 978-3-8382-1649-2

245 *Oleksandra Keudel* | How Patronal Networks Shape Opportunities for Local Citizen Participation in a Hybrid Regime A Comparative Analysis of Five Cities in Ukraine | With a foreword by Sabine Kropp | ISBN 978-3-8382-1671-3

246 *Jan Claas Behrends, Thomas Lindenberger, Pavel Kolar (Eds.)* | Violence after Stalin Institutions, Practices, and Everyday Life in the Soviet Bloc 1953–1989 | ISBN 978-3-8382-1637-9

247 *Leonid Luks* | Macht und Ohnmacht der Utopien Essays zur Geschichte Russlands im 20. und 21. Jahrhundert | ISBN 978-3-8382-1677-5

248 *Iuliia Barshadska* | Brüssel zwischen Kyjiw und Moskau Das auswärtige Handeln der Europäischen Union im ukrainisch-russischen Konflikt 2014-2019 | Mit einem Vorwort von Olaf Leiße | ISBN 978-3-8382-1667-6

249 *Valentyna Romanova* | Decentralisation and Multilevel Elections in Ukraine Reform Dynamics and Party Politics in 2010–2021 | With a foreword by Kimitaka Matsuzato | ISBN 978-3-8382-1700-0

250 *Alexander Motyl* | National Questions. Theoretical Reflections on Nations and Nationalism in Eastern Europe | ISBN 978-3-8382-1675-1

251 *Marc Dietrich* | A Cosmopolitan Model for Peacebuilding. The Ukrainian Cases of Crimea and the Donbas | With a foreword by Rémi Baudouï | ISBN 978-3-8382-1687-4

252 *Eduard Baidaus* | An Unsettled Nation. Moldova in the Geopolitics of Russia, Romania, and Ukraine | With forewords by John-Paul Himka and David R. Marples | ISBN 978-3-8382-1582-2

253 *Igor Okunev, Petr Oskolkov (Eds.)* | Transforming the Administrative Matryoshka. The Reform of Autonomous Okrugs in the Russian Federation, 2003–2008 | With a foreword by Vladimir Zorin | ISBN 978-3-8382-1721-5

254 *Winfried Schneider-Deters* | Ukraine's Fateful Years 2013–2019. Vol. I: The Popular Uprising in Winter 2013/2014 | ISBN 978-3-8382-1725-3

255 *Winfried Schneider-Deters* | Ukraine's Fateful Years 2013–2019. Vol. II: The Annexation of Crimea and the War in Donbas | ISBN 978-3-8382-1726-0

256 *Robert M. Cutler* | Soviet and Post-Soviet Russian Foreign Policies II. East-West Relations in Europe and the Political Economy of the Communist Bloc, 1971–1991 | With a foreword by Roger E. Kanet | ISBN 978-3-8382-1727-7

257 *Robert M. Cutler* | Soviet and Post-Soviet Russian Foreign Policies III. East-West Relations in Europe and Eurasia in the Post-Cold War Transition, 1991–2001 | With a foreword by Roger E. Kanet | ISBN 978-3-8382-1728-4

258 *Paweł Kowal, Iwona Reichardt, Kateryna Pryshchepa (Eds.)* | Three Revolutions: Mobilization and Change in Contemporary Ukraine III. Archival Records and Historical Sources on the 1990 Revolution on Granite | ISBN 978-3-8382-1376-7

259 *Mikhail Minakov (Ed.)* | Philosophy Unchained. Developments in Post-Soviet Philosophical Thought. | With a foreword by Christopher Donohue | ISBN 978-3-8382-1768-0

260 *David Dalton* | The Ukrainian Oligarchy After the Euromaidan. How Ukraine's Political Economy Regime Survived the Crisis | With a foreword by Andrew Wilson | ISBN 978-3-8382-1740-6

261 *Andreas Heinemann-Grüder (Ed.)* | Who Are the Fighters? Irregular Armed Groups in the Russian-Ukrainian War in 2014–2015 | ISBN 978-3-8382-1777-2

262 *Taras Kuzio (Ed.)* | Russian Disinformation and Western Scholarship. Bias and Prejudice in Journalistic, Expert, and Academic Analyses of East European, Russian and Eurasian Affairs | ISBN 978-3-8382-1685-0

263 *Darius Furmonavicius* | LithuaniaTransforms the West. Lithuania's Liberation from Soviet Occupation and the Enlargement of NATO (1988–2022) | With a foreword by Vytautas Landsbergis | ISBN 978-3-8382-1779-6

264 *Dirk Dalberg* | Politisches Denken im tschechoslowakischen Dissens. Egon Bondy, Miroslav Kusý, Milan Šimečka und Petr Uhl (1968-1989) | ISBN 978-3-8382-1318-7

265 *Леонид Люкс* | К столетию «философского парохода». Мыслители «первой» русской эмиграции о русской революции и о тоталитарных соблазнах XX века | ISBN 978-3-8382-1775-8

266 *Daviti Mtchedlishvili* | The EU and the South Caucasus. European Neighborhood Policies between Eclecticism and Pragmatism, 1991-2021 | With a foreword by Nicholas Ross Smith | ISBN 978-3-8382-1735-2

267 *Bohdan Harasymiw* | Post-Euromaidan Ukraine. Domestic Power Struggles and War of National Survival in 2014–2022 | ISBN 978-3-8382-1798-7

268 *Nadiia Koval, Denys Tereshchenko (Eds.)* | Russian Cultural Diplomacy under Putin. Rossotrudnichestvo, the "Russkiy Mir" Foundation, and the Gorchakov Fund in 2007–2022 | ISBN 978-3-8382-1801-4

269 *Izabela Kazejak* | Jews in Post-War Wrocław and L'viv. Official Policies and Local Responses in Comparative Perspective, 1945-1970s | ISBN 978-3-8382-1802-1

270 *Jakob Hauter* | Russia's Overlooked Invasion. The Causes of the 2014 Outbreak of War in Ukraine's Donbas | With a foreword by Hiroaki Kuromiya | ISBN 978-3-8382-1803-8

271 *Anton Shekhovtsov* | Russian Political Warfare. Essays on Kremlin Propaganda in Europe and the Neighbourhood, 2020-2023 | With a foreword by Nathalie Loiseau | ISBN 978-3-8382-1821-2

272 *Андреа Пето* | Насилие и Молчание. Красная армия в Венгрии во Второй Мировой войне | ISBN 978-3-8382-1636-2

273 *Winfried Schneider-Deters* | Russia's War in Ukraine. Debates on Peace, Fascism, and War Crimes, 2022–2023 | With a foreword by Klaus Gestwa | ISBN 978-3-8382-1876-2